BIOGRAPHICAL DIRECTORY
OF THE
UNITED STATES
EXECUTIVE BRANCH,
1774–1989

Biographical Directory
of the
United States
Executive Branch,
1774–1989

Robert Sobel,
EDITOR-IN-CHIEF

GREENWOOD PRESS
New York • Westport, Connecticut • London

Library of Congress Cataloging-in-Publication Data

Biographical directory of the United States executive branch,
    1774–1989 / Robert Sobel, editor-in-chief.
        p.   cm.
    ISBN 0–313–26593–3 (lib. bdg. : alk. paper)
    1. Statesmen—United States—Biography—Dictionaries. 2. United
States—Officials and employees—Biography—Dictionaries.
3. Cabinet officers—United States—Biography—Dictionaries.
4. Presidents—United States—Biography—Dictionaries. 5. Vice-
Presidents—United States—Biography—Dictionaries. I. Sobel,
Robert, 1931 Feb. 19–
E176.B578   1990
353.04′092′2—dc20
    [B]   89–25779

British Library Cataloguing in Publication Data is available.

Library of Congress Catalog Card Number: 89–25779
ISBN: 0–313–26593–3

First published in 1990

Greenwood Press, 88 Post Road West, Westport, CT 06881
An imprint of Greenwood Publishing Group, Inc.

Printed in the United States of America

The paper used in this book complies with the
Permanent Paper Standard issued by the National
Information Standards Organization (Z39.48–1984).

10 9 8 7 6 5 4 3 2 1

To David Christman

Contents

Preface

More than 650 men and women have served in the cabinets of American presidents. Researchers in American political history who have an adequate library at their disposal may discover basic information about most of them without too much difficulty. A few, however, prove elusive, having served in minor posts for short periods of time during which little that was eventful occurred. Others, the most prominent and famous cabinet members, are the subjects of lengthy studies and articles, through which the researcher may have to wade before he uncovers an important date or event that he needs in his work. For those who wish to make a study of a particular department or administration, the effort may be tedious and time-consuming. It is for individuals such as these, as well as for the general student of political history, that this volume has been compiled and written.

The *Biographical Directory of the United States Executive Branch, 1774–1989* contains career biographies of all cabinet heads, as well as of presidents, vice-presidents, and presidents of the Continental Congress. Only those individuals confirmed in office by the Senate have been included; acting cabinet officials—of whom there were many, especially in the nineteenth century—have been omitted since almost all served for very short periods of time. Each biography includes the most significant dates in the subject's life, family and other personal information, religious affiliation where available, service prior to and after cabinet duty, and place of death and interment. In addition, each biography contains a short bibliographic reference to important primary and secondary works to be consulted for additional information. Indexes, consisting of tables to enable the researcher to more easily relate the individual to his times and place and service, are included.

The need for a single-volume work of this nature is obvious to anyone who has worked in the field of political history. Indeed, it was just such a need that prompted us to undertake the first edition of the work in 1971, and then the update in 1977. Since then there has been a rapid changeover in personnel and even the elimination of some cabinet offices and the addition of others. There was the complete change of the cabinet that occurred in 1977 when Ronald Reagan succeeded Jimmy Carter, and the somewhat less thorough housecleaning when George Bush succeeded Reagan in 1989. In fact, there are more than 20 percent more biographies in this work than in the first edition. In addition to the new entries, older ones have been updated where appropriate.

The writing of individual biographies was done by a team of historical researchers. The pre–1971 essays were undertaken by Karen Bragg, Tapper Bragg, Janice Daar, Aaron Hause, Arthur Kurzweil, Richard Mark, Karen Mitura, Connie Panzarino, Mark Rosenblatt, Joseph Sconzo, and Dennis Steigerwald. The writers for the period from 1971 through 1977 were Kenny Franks, Margaret Karafian, Michael Kass, Stephan Manzi, William Maynard, Patricia Page, Steven Rosman, Barbara Simpson, Roy Sudlow, Helene Vecchione, Harry Weber, and Carolynn Weinstock. The post–1977 biographies were written by Jay Goodale, David Sarnoff, Jocelyn Nuttall, Denise Holton, Miriam Delphin, Angela Malacari, Golda Blum, Lynn Poppe, and Andrew Myers.

ROBERT SOBEL

New College,
Hofstra University

BIOGRAPHICAL DIRECTORY
OF THE
UNITED STATES
EXECUTIVE BRANCH,
1774–1989

Biographies

Biography

A

ACHESON, Dean Gooderham. Born in Middletown, Conn., April 11, 1893; son of Edward Campion and Eleanor Gertrude (Gooderham) Acheson; Episcopalian; married Alice Stanley on May 5, 1917; father of Jane, David Campion, and Mary Eleanor; attended Groton School, Groton, Mass.; received B.A. from Yale in 1915; earned LL.B. from Harvard in 1918; was ensign in U.S. Navy for six months; became private secretary to Louis D. Brandeis, associate justice of Supreme Court; joined law firm of Covington, Burling and Rublee, 1921; became a partner in 1926, and remained member of the firm, renamed Burling, Rublee, Acheson, and Short, until 1946; appointed first under-secretary of the treasury by Franklin D. Roosevelt in May 1933 and served until November 1933, acting as secretary during the illness of Woodin; appointed chairman of the committee to investigate administrative procedure in the Executive Branch, February 1939; served as assistant secretary of state, 1941–1945; headed Atlantic City meeting which organized United Nations Relief and Rehabilitation Administration, 1943, and was chairman of council for two years; delegate to United Nations Monetary and Financial Conference in 1944, and helped establish International Bank for Reconstruction and Development and International Monetary Fund; appointed undersecretary of state on August 16, 1945, and served until June 1947, often acting as secretary of state; formulated Acheson-Lilienthal report; made member of Commission on Organization of the Executive Branch of Government by Herbert Hoover, and served as its vice-president until May 1949; member and chairman of the American section of United States-Canadian Permanent Joint Defense Board, 1947–1948; appointed SECRETARY OF STATE in the cabinet of President Truman on January 19, 1949, and served until January 19, 1953; most important contributions were formulation of North Atlantic Treaty, establishment of the North Atlantic Treaty Organization (NATO), of which he was chairman 1949–1950, implementation of the President's Point-Four Program to aid underdeveloped areas of the world, formulation of seven-point program for peace with Soviet Union, engineering of United Nations intervention on behalf of South Korea and declaration of Communist China as aggressor; granted honorary LL.D. degrees from Wesleyan University in 1947 and from Harvard in 1950; received Freedom House Award in 1950; advisor to Presidents Kennedy and Johnson on foreign policy matters; published *A Democrat Looks at His Party* (1955), *A Citizen Looks at Congress* (1957), *Power and Diplomacy* (1958), *Sketches of Men I Have Known* (1965), *Morning and Noon* (1965), and *Present at the Creation* (1969); member of American Bar Association; died on October 12, 1971. Dean G. Acheson, *Morning and Noon* (1965); Howard Ferer, ed., *Harry S. Truman, 1884– : Chronology, Documents, Bibliographical Aids* (1969).

ADAMS, Brockman. Born in Atlanta, Ga., January 13, 1927; son of Vera Eleanor (Beemer) and Charles Leslie Adams; Episcopalian; graduated from public high school in 1944 and enlisted in the navy; spent the first part of his tour at the University of Washington in an officer training program; after the war returned to the university and majored in economics while minoring in nuclear physics; ranked number one in his class, was president of the student body, and graduated summa cum laude in 1949; graduated from Harvard Law School in 1952; in that same year was admitted to the Washington State Bar and was juris doctor for the Harvard Law School; married Mary Elizabeth Scott of Jacksonville, Fla., on August 16, 1952; father of Scott Leslie, Lewis Dean, Katherine Elizabeth, and Aleen Mundy; after graduation from Harvard joined law firm of Little, Lesourd, Palmer, Scott, and Slemmons, and eventually became a partner; in 1960 became a partner of LeSourd, Patten, and Adams; was chairman of the 1960 John F. Kennedy presidential campaign in western Washington; appointed attorney for the western district of Washington by Kennedy in 1961; elected to the Eighty-Ninth Congress on November 3, 1964; subsequently elected to the Ninetieth, Ninety-First, Ninety-Second, Ninety-Third, and Ninety-Fourth congresses; representative of the seventh district of Washington; has served on the House Interstate and Foreign Commerce Committee and the District of Columbia Committee; former vestryman of the Epiphany Episcopal Church; former trustee of the University of Washington Alumni Association and the Civic Unity Committee of Seattle; former president of the Neighborhood Settlement House member of the Puget Sound Association (president from 1962 to 1963); instructor for the American Institute of Banking from 1954 to 1960; received the Distinguished Service Award from the Seattle Junior Chamber of Commerce in 1960; became chairman, in 1974, of the House Budget Committee, where he helped create legislation that reorganized the bankrupt eastern rail system; executive director of the Washington district Jimmy Carter for president campaign; considered the leading expert on transportation in the House; on January 20, 1977, was sworn in as the SECRETARY OF TRANSPORTATION in the first cabinet of

President Jimmy Carter, and served until July 20, 1979; partner in the firm of Garvey, Schubert, Adams, and Barer from 1979 to 1986; elected U.S. senator for the state of Washington in 1987; member of the American Bar Association, Washington Bar Association, and Seattle-King County Bar Association. *Congressional Dictionary 1976*, 94th Congress, 2nd session; *Newsweek* (December 27, 1976); *New York Times* (December 15, 1976, and July 21, 1979); *Time* (December 20 and 27, 1976); *Who's Who in America, 1976*, Bicentennial edition; *U.S. News and World Report* (July 30, 1979); *Who's Who In America, 1988–1989*.

ADAMS, Charles Francis. Born in Quincy, Mass., August 2, 1866; son of John Quincy Adams, Jr. and Fanny (Crowninshield) Adams; great-grandson of John Quincy Adams and great-great-grandson of John Adams; Unitarian; married Frances Lovering, daughter of Mass. representative William C. Lovering; father of Charles Francis, Jr. and Catherine; graduated Harvard in 1892; toured Europe for one year; was admitted to the bar in 1893; became councilman in Quincy; mayor of Quincy in 1896 and 1897; practiced law in Boston; became businessman; treasurer of the Corporation of Harvard College, 1898–1929; won International Yacht races, 1920–1929; appointed SECRETARY OF THE NAVY in the cabinet of President Hoover, and served from March 5, 1929 to March 3, 1933; most important contribution was success of London Naval Conference of 1930 in formulation of naval treaty; president of Harvard board of overseers, 1930–1943; chairman of the board of New York, New Haven and Hartford Railroad in 1951; chairman of Community Mobilization for Human Rights; died in Boston, June 10, 1954; interment in Mount Wollaston Cemetery. Eugene Lyons, *Herbert Hoover: A Biography* (1964).

ADAMS, John. Born in Braintree (now Quincy), Mass., October 30, 1735; son of John and Susanna (Boylston) Adams; Unitarian; married Abigail Smith on October 25, 1764; father of John Quincy (sixth President of the United States), Abigail Amelia, Susanna, Charles, and Thomas Boylston; graduated Harvard in 1755; taught school at Worcester, Mass., studied law, and was admitted to the bar in 1758; opened legal practice in Suffolk County; joined the Sons of Liberty and appeared before Governor Hutchinson to argue against the Stamp Act; elected to represent Boston in the General Court (a legislative body), in 1768; elected delegate to the 1st Continental Congress on September 5, 1774; elected delegate to the 2d Continental Congress on May 10, 1775; was signer of the Declaration of Independence; proposed George Washington to become general of the American Army; became head of the War Department but resigned and was appointed commissioner to the court of France in 1778; in 1780, was appointed minister plenipotentiary to Holland, where he successfully negotiated a loan in 1782, and also negotiated a treaty of amity and commerce; was the first minister to England, serving from 1785 to 1788; elected the first VICE-PRESIDENT on the Federalist ticket headed by George Washington in 1788; reelected in 1792, he served until

March 3, 1797; elected PRESIDENT of the U.S., also on the Federalist ticket, serving from March 4, 1979 to March 3, 1801; served as a delegate to the Constitutional Convention of Massachusetts in 1820; authored *Essay on Canon And Federalist Law* (1768), *Thoughts On Government* (1776), and *A Defence Of The Constitutions of Government Of The United States Of America* (1787); died in Quincy, Mass., July 4, 1826; interment in the First Unitarian Church Cemetery, Quincy. Catherine Drinker Bowen, *John Adams and the American Revolution* (1950); David Hawke, *A Transaction of Free Men: The Birth and Course of the Declaration of Independence* (1964).

ADAMS, John Quincy. Born in Braintree (now Quincy), Mass., July 11, 1767; son of John Adams, second President of the United States, and Abigail (Smith) Adams; Unitarian; married Louisa Catherine Johnson on July 26, 1797; father of George Washington, John, Jr., and Louisa Catherine; graduated from Harvard in 1787; admitted to the bar in 1790; practiced law in Newburyport, Mass.; attracted the notice of Washington because of his views on neutrality and was appointed minister to the Netherlands in 1794; appointed to the mission in Berlin, where he negotiated a treaty; returned to the U.S. in 1801 and resumed law practice in Boston; elected to the U.S. Senate in 1803; opposed the acquisition of the Louisiana Territory; regarded as an apostate by the Federalists, he was forced to resign from the Senate in 1808; subsequently appointed minister to Russia by President Monroe, he saw the U.S. declare war against Great Britain in 1812 and later was instrumental, along with Gallatin, in drawing up a peace treaty in 1814; appointed SECRETARY OF STATE by President Monroe on March 5, 1817, and served until March 3, 1825; conducted very delicate and important negotiations, resulting in the treaty for the cession of the Floridas by Spain; opposed to slavery, he nevertheless approved of the Missouri Compromise, feeling that it was a calamitous issue which could well lead to the dissolution of the Union; credited, along with the President, for the declaration of the Monroe Doctrine which, in effect, stated that any further colonization by any European power in this hemisphere would be regarded as a "manifestation of an unfriendly disposition toward the United States"; elected as a Democrat-Republican, he became the sixth PRESIDENT of the U.S., serving one term, 1825–1829; elected to the U.S. House of Representatives in 1831, he served in that body until his death seventeen years later; died in Washington, D.C. on February 23, 1848; interment in the First Unitarian Church, Quincy, Mass. Robert Abraham East, *John Quincy Adams: The Critical Years, 1785–1794* (1962); Leonard Falkner, *The President Who Wouldn't Retire* (1967).

AGNEW, Spiro Theodore. Born in Baltimore, Md., November 9, 1918; son of Theodore S. Agnew, restaurateur, and Margarate (Akers) Agnew; Episcopalian; married Elinor Isobel Judefind on May 27, 1942; father of James Rand, Paula Lee, Susan Scott, and Elinor Kimberly; attended the public schools; attended Johns Hopkins University, 1937–1940; entered the Baltimore Law School,

1940, while working as a clerk at the Maryland Casualty Co. and later as a supermarket manager and claims adjuster for the Lumberman's Mutual Casualty Co.; during World War II, won a Bronze Star while serving as company combat commander in France and Germany with the 10th Armored Division of the U.S. Army; returned to law studies at Baltimore Law School, receiving his LL.B. in 1947; admitted to the bar in 1949 and began practice in the Baltimore suburb of Towson after serving an apprenticeship with the firm of Karl F. Steinmann; formerly a Democrat, but became a member of the Republican party; appointed to the Zoning Board of Appeals of Baltimore County in 1961 and served from 1962 to 1967; elected governor of Maryland in 1966; nominated as the Republican vice-presidential candidate on August 8, 1968; elected VICE-PRESIDENT under Richard M. Nixon on November 5, 1968, and took the oath of office on January 20, 1969; sworn into office for a second term on January 20, 1973; obliged to resign the vice-presidency on October 10, 1973, under fear of impeachment or indictment on criminal charges; an active spokesman for Nixon administration policies; international trade consultant with Pathlite Inc., 1974– ; publications include *The Canfield Decision* (1976), *Go Quietly . . . or Else* (1980). Ann Pinchot et al., *Where He Stands: The Life and Convictions of Spiro T. Agnew* (1968); Earl Mazo and Stephen Hess, *Nixon: A Political Portrait* (1969); *New York Times* (January 21, 1973); *Time* (April 27, 1981); *International Who's Who, 1988.*

AKERMAN, Amos Tappan. Born in Portsmouth, N.H., February 23, 1821; son of Benjamin Akerman, land surveyor, and Olive (Meloon) Akerman; married Martha Rebecca Galloway about 1850; attended common schools; studied at Phillips Exeter Academy; graduated from Dartmouth College in 1842; moved to Georgia and began teaching in Augusta; became tutor for Berrien children and studied law under Berrien; admitted to the bar in 1844; moved to Elberton, Ga., and practiced law in partnership with Robert Heston; served in Confederate army in General Robert Toombs' brigade, and later in quartermaster's department; member of state constitutional convention of 1868; made U.S. district attorney in 1869; appointed ATTORNEY GENERAL in the cabinet of President Grant on June 23, 1870, and served from August 8, 1870 to December 13, 1871; most important contribution was rejection of railroad claims to certain government lands, a decision which caused the President, under pressure from the railroads, to ask for his resignation; unsuccessful Republican candidate for U.S. Senate in 1873; retired to private law practice; died in Centersville, Ga., December 21, 1880. L. L. Knight, *Georgia and Georgians* (1917); Phillip R. Moran, *Ulysses S. Grant, 1822–1885: Chronology, Documents, Bibliographical Aids* (1968).

ALEXANDER, Joshua Willis. Born in Cincinnati, Ohio, January 22, 1852; son of Thomas W. and Jane (Robinson) Alexander; married to Roe Ann Richardson on February 3, 1876; father of Samuel, Walter, Julia, Frances, George, Roena, Preston, and Lawrence; moved to Missouri with his mother in 1863 and lived in Canton, Davies County; attended public, private, and high schools; was graduated from Christian University (now Culver-Stockton College), Canton, Mo. in 1872; moved to Gallatin, Mo. in 1873 and studied law; admitted to the bar in 1875 and began practice in Gallatin; public administrator of Davies County from 1877 until 1881; served as secretary and later as president of the Board of Education of Gallatin, 1882–1901; member of the Missouri House of Representatives, 1883–1887, serving as speaker in 1887; mayor of Gallatin, 1891 and 1892; member of the board of managers of the State Hospital, 1893–1896; judge of the 7th Judicial Circuit of Missouri from 1901 until 1907; elected as a Democrat to the 60th Congress (House) and to six succeeding Congresses, serving from March 4, 1907 until December 15, 1919 when he resigned; chairman of the commission of the U.S. to the International Conference on Safety of Life at Sea, which met in London from November 12, 1913 until January 20, 1914, as a result of the sinking of the S.S. *Titanic*; appointed SECRETARY OF COMMERCE in the cabinet of President Wilson on December 11, 1919; resigned with the outgoing administration on March 4, 1921; returned to Gallatin and the practice of law; delegate-at-large to the State Constitutional Convention, 1922; died in Gallatin, Mo. on February 27, 1936; interment in Brown Cemetery. E. David Cronon, ed., *The Cabinet Diaries of Josephus Daniels, 1913–1921* (1963); Arthur S. Link, *Woodrow Wilson: Confusions and Crises* (1964).

ALGER, Russell Alexander. Born in Lafayette, Ohio, February 27, 1836; son of Russell and Caroline (Moulton) Alger; married Annette Henry in 1861; father of nine children; orphaned at age 12, he worked on a farm for seven years to defray expenses at Richfield Academy during winters; admitted to the bar in 1859 and began practice in Cleveland; moved to Michigan and engaged in lumber business January 1, 1860; enlisted in a Michigan cavalry regiment on September 2, 1861, rose from captain to colonel, was distinguished in the Gettysburg campaign and under Sheridan in the Shenandoah Valley, became brigadier general in 1864, and major general of volunteers in 1865; invested in pine lands after Civil War and made a fortune; elected governor of Michigan on the Republican ticket, 1885–1887; was leading candidate for president in the Republican national convention of 1888; was one-term commander-in-chief of Grand Army of the Republic, 1889–1890; appointed SECRETARY OF WAR in the cabinet of President McKinley on March 5, 1897, and served until his resignation at McKinley's request on August 1, 1899; under his secretaryship, department was criticized for unpreparedness and maladministration: posts of command filled with elderly officers near retirement age, bureaus encrusted with routine of an army of 25,000, no general staff, jealousies between officers of the line and bureaus that governed them, no study given to problems arising in event of war, no allotment secured for defense, unpreparedness of U.S. military to meet Spanish American War; Dodge report on conduct of the war plus that of the "embalmed beef" commission resulted in his resignation; published *The Spanish American War* in 1901; appointed U.S. senator from Michigan on September

27, 1902, and elected senator in February 1903; died before end of term in Washington, D.C., January 24, 1905. Arthur M. Alger, *Genealogical History of That Branch of the Alger Family which Springs from Thomas Alger of Taunton and Bridgewater in Massachusetts* (1876); obituary notices in *Boston Transcript* (February 8, 1905) and *Boston Globe* (February 1, 1905).

ANDERSON, Clinton Presba. Born in Centerville, S.D., October 28, 1895; son of Andrew Jay and Hattie Belle (Presba) Anderson; Presbyterian; married Henrietta McCartney on June 22, 1921; father of Sherburne Presba and Nancy; attended the South Dakota schools, Wesleyan University in Mitchell, S.D., 1913–1915, and the University of Michigan at Ann Arbor, 1915–1916; moved to Albuquerque, N.M. in 1917; worked as reporter and editor in Albuquerque, 1918–1922; manager of the insurance department of the New Mexico Loan and Mortgage Co., 1922–1924; appointed treasurer of the State of New Mexico, serving during 1933 and 1934; administrator of the New Mexico Relief Administration in 1935 and 1936; president of the Mountain States Mutual Casualty Co., 1937 until his death; chairman and executive director of the Unemployment Compensation Commission of New Mexico, 1936–1938; managing director of the U.S. Coronado Exposition Commission in 1939 and 1940; elected as a Democrat to the 77th and 78th Congresses (House), serving in all from January 3, 1941 until his resignation on June 30, 1945; joined the Truman cabinet as SECRETARY OF AGRICULTURE on June 2, 1945, serving from June 30, 1945 until his resignation on May 10, 1948; during his incumbency, he met the record world food requirements outlined by President Truman's Nine Point Famine Relief Program by issuing regulations conserving wheat, diminishing the consumption of grain by livestock, and assembling grains and other essential foods for export; resigned from the cabinet to enter the Democratic primary for U.S. Senator from New Mexico; was elected in 1948 and reelected in 1954, 1960, and 1966; chairman of the Joint Committee on Atomic Energy; died on November 11, 1975. Cabell B. H. Phillips, *The Truman Presidency: The History of a Triumphant Succession* (1966); Alfred Steinberg, *The Man from Missouri: The Life and Times of Harry S. Truman* (1962).

ANDERSON, Robert Bernard. Born in Burleson, Johnson County, Tex., June 4, 1910; son of Robert Lee Anderson, mayor of Burleson, and Lizzie Ethel (Haskew) Anderson; Methodist; married Ollie May Rawlings on April 10, 1935; father of James Richard and Gerald Lee; attended public schools of Godley, Tex.; graduated Weatherford College of Southwestern University in 1927; studied at University of Texas; taught Spanish, history, and mathematics and coached football at Burleson High School in 1929; began University of Texas Law School in 1929, received LL.B. in 1932, and was admitted to the bar in 1932; began practice in Fort Worth, Tex.; made assistant attorney general of Texas, 1933; adjunct professor of law at University of Texas; appointed state tax commissioner in 1934 and ex-officio member of State Racing Commission, 1938; on executive committee of Texas Research Council; chairman of State Board of Education, 1949; president of Texas Mid-Continent Oil and Gas Association, 1947–1951; chosen aide to secretary of the army, 1952; appointed secretary of the navy by President Dwight D. Eisenhower, 1953–1954; was deputy secretary of defense from 1954 to 1955; became president of Ventures, Ltd.; appointed SECRETARY OF TREASURY in the cabinet of President Eisenhower; served from July 29, 1957, to January 20, 1961; practiced law in partnership with Carl M. Loeb, Rhoades, and Company, 1961–1973; president of Robert B. Anderson & Co.; affiliated with Southwestern Bell Telephone Company and Times Publishing Company; vice-president of Associated Refiners, Inc.; member of National Advisory Heart Council, Texas Economy Commission, and National Manpower Commission; on National Executive Board of Boy Scouts of America; partner in law firm of Anderson, Pendelton, 1973–1989; in 1987 was sentenced to a prison term of five months after having been found guilty of income tax evasion in 1983 and 1984 and of operating an illegal offshore bank; disbarred by Appellate Division of New York State Supreme Court in 1989; died on August 14, 1989 in New York, N.Y. Dean Albertson, ed., *Eisenhower as President* (1963); David A. Frier, *Conflict of Interest in the Eisenhower Administration* (1969); *New York Times Biographical Service* (March 1987); *New York Times* (August 16, 1989).

ANDRUS, Cecil D. Born in Hood River, Oreg., August 25, 1931; son of Hal Stephen and Dorothy (Johnson) Andrus; married Carol Mea May on August 27, 1949; father of Tanna Lee, Tracy Sue, and Kelly Kay; attended Oregon State University in Corvallis, Oreg., 1948–1949; served in the U.S. Naval Reserve, 1951–1955; member of the Veterans of Foreign Wars; elected Man of the Year in 1959; member of the Idaho Senate, 1961–1966 and 1969–1970; director of the Idaho Taxpayers Association, 1964–1966; Idaho general manager of the Paul Revere Life Insurance Company, 1969–1970; elected governor of Idaho, 1970, and reelected in 1974; member of the Executive Committee of the National Governor's Conference, 1971–1972; chairman of the Federation of Rocky Mountain States, 1971–1972; on December 12, 1976, was nominated by President-Elect Jimmy Carter to be the SECRETARY OF THE INTERIOR; served until January 23, 1981; awarded the Collier County Conservancy medal in 1979; named the Conservationalist of the Year by the National Wildlife Foundation, 1980; recipient of the Distinguished Citizen's Award from Oregon State University, 1980; director of Albertson Incorporated, 1985–1987; chairman of the board of trustees of the College of Idaho, 1985– ; director, Beker Industries Corporation, 1981– ; elected governor of Idaho, January 1987; Democrat. *Who's Who in America, 1974–1975; Congressional Quarterly, Weekly Report*, Vol. 34 (December 26, 1976); *Time* (December 27, 1976); *U.S. News and World Report* (January 10, 1977); *International Who's Who, 1988; Who's Who in America, 1988–1989.*

ARMSTRONG, John. Born in Carlisle, Pa., November 25, 1758; son of John Armstrong, Irish immigrant who became member of Congress, and Rebecca (Lyon) Armstrong; Catholic; brother of James Armstrong, member of Congress; married Alida Livingston in 1789; father of William Goforth; entered Princeton College in 1773, and left in 1775 to enter colonial army, and served on staffs of Mercer and Gates; made adjutant general of southern army, 1780; wrote Newbury letters; served as secretary of Pennsylvania, 1783–1787; became member of Congress in 1787; moved to Red Hook, N.Y., 1789, and pursued agricultural interests; chosen U.S. senator in January 1800, to fill unexpired term of John Lawrence, was reelected and sat, November 6, 1800–February 5, 1802; appointed to fill vacancy of Senator DeWitt Clinton, and served from November 10, 1803 to June 30, 1804; appointed minister to France, June 30, 1804–September 14, 1810, and was acting minister to Spain, 1806; appointed brigadier-general on July 6, 1812, and given command of district of New York; appointed SECRETARY OF WAR in the cabinet of President Madison on January 13, 1813, and served from February 5, 1813 to August 29, 1814; although he improved general condition of the army, failure of expedition against Canada and destruction of Washington by British caused Madison to ask for his resignation; retired to Red Hook, N.Y. to pursue agricultural interests and writing; published *Notices of the War of 1812* in 1836, wrote *A Treatise on Argus and Library of American Biographies*; died in Red Hook, N.Y., April 1, 1843; interment in Rhinebeck Cemetery, Rhinebeck, N.Y. E. D. Ingraham, *A Sketch of Events which Preceded The Capture of Washington by the British on the 24th of August, 1814* (1849); Ian Elliot, *James Madison, 1751–1836: Chronology, Documents, Bibliographical Aids* (1969).

ARTHUR, Chester Alan. Born in Fairfield, Vt., October 5, 1830; son of William Arthur, clergyman, and Malvina (Stone) Arthur; Episcopalian; married Ellen Lewis Herndon on October 25, 1859; father of William Lewis Herndon, Chester Alan, and Ellen Herndon; attended public schools; taught penmanship at Pownal, Vt., graduated Union College in July 1848, taught school and studied law, 1846–1853; became principal of academy in North Pownal, Vt., 1851; admitted to the bar in 1854 and began practice in New York City; made judge advocate of 2d Brigade, New York State Militia in 1857; became engineer-in-chief on Governor Morgan's staff with rank of brigadier general in 1860; quartermaster general, July 10–December 31, 1862; resumed practice of law in New York City in 1863; collector of Port of New York from November 24, 1871 to July 11, 1878; resumed practice of law, 1878; delegate from New York to Republican national convention in Chicago in 1880; nominated VICE-PRESIDENT on ticket with James Garfield on November 5, 1880, elected and served from March 4, 1881 to September 19, 1881; became PRESIDENT on the death of Garfield, and served from September 20, 1881 to March 3, 1885; most important contributions were organization of Civil Service Commission, securing of right to establish repair and coaling station at Pearl Harbor, Hawaii, establishment of territorial government in Alaska; unsuccessful candidate for presidential nomination in 1884; returned to law practice; died in New York City, November 18, 1886; interment in Rural Cemetery, Albany, N.Y. Peter R. Levin, *Seven By Chance* (1948).

B

BACON, Robert. Born in Jamaica Plain, Mass., July 5, 1860; son of William Benjamin and Emily Crosby (Low) Bacon; Presbyterian; married Martha Waldron Cowdin on October 10, 1883; father of Robert Law, Gasper Griswold, Elliot Cowdin, and Martha; attended Hopkinson's School; graduated from Harvard, 1880; started business career with Lee, Higginson and Co., 1881–1883; became partner in E. Rollins Morse and Brother, 1883–1894; accepted partnership in J. P. Morgan and Co., 1894–1903; helped the government in the panic of 1895; involved in the formation of the United States Steel Corp., 1901; involved in negotiations resulting in formation of Northern Securities Corp.; assistant secretary of state to Elihu Root, 1905, and acting secretary of state in summer of 1906 during Root's absence; appointed SECRETARY OF STATE in the cabinet of President Theodore Roosevelt on January 27, 1909, serving until March 5, 1909, when Taft became President; major contribution was his competent service; appointed ambassador to France by President Taft in December 1909, resigning in January 1912; became Fellow of Harvard, 1912; requested by Carnegie Endowment to make a trip to South America in 1913, and published his impressions in *For Better Relations with Our Latin American Neighbors: A Journey to South America* (1915); drove ambulance in France during World War I, 1914; returned to the U.S. and entered military training camp at Plattsburg, N.Y. as a private, 1915; candidate for U.S. Senate on platform of support for the Allies and preparedness, 1916; commissioned major in quartermaster corps of Army and sailed for France with General Pershing in May 1917; chief of the American Military Mission at British General Headquarters; promoted to lieutenant colonel of infantry shortly before Armistice; left Paris for the U.S. in March 1919, and died in New York City, May 29, 1919; interment in New York City. James Brown Scott, *Robert Bacon, Life and Letters* (1923); MS Archives of the State

Department, *Foreign Relations of the United States (1906–12)*, James F. Rhodes, *McKinley and Roosevelt Administrations, 1879–1909* in *History of the United States*, vol. 9 (1922); George E. Mowry, *Era of Theodore Roosevelt, 1900–1912* (1958).

BADGER, George Edmund. Born in New Bern, N.C., April 17, 1795; son of Thomas Badger, lawyer, and Lydia (Cogdell) Badger; married Rebecca Turner, later married Mary Polk, and later married Delia (Haywood) Williams; father of several children; attended local academies in New Bern; attended Yale, 1810–1811; studied law in New Bern, was admitted to the bar in 1811, and was appointed solicitor for the district; made aide-de-camp with rank of major in militia, 1814; elected to the House of Commons from New Bern, 1816; moved to Hillsboro to take over law practice of Thomas Ruffin, and later moved to Warrenton; elected judge of superior court in 1820, and served until his resignation in 1825; practiced law in Raleigh; supported Jackson in 1828; became Whig, 1836; appointed SECRETARY OF THE NAVY in the cabinet of President William H. Harrison and continued under Tyler, serving from March 5, 1841 to September 11, 1841; most important contributions were recommendation of home squadron to patrol Caribbean and Gulf and securing of authority for construction of two steam vessels; elected U.S. senator, 1846, to complete an unexpired term, was reelected in 1848 for a full term, and served until 1855; continued practice of law; regent of Smithsonian Institute; chairman of county court of Wake; active in organization of Constitutional Union Party, 1860–1861, and candidate of same party; elected to convention calling for secession; died in Raleigh, N.C., May 11, 1866; interment in Oakwood Cemetery. William A. Graham, *Discourse in Memory of the Life and Character of the Honorable George E. Badger* (1866); Freeman Cleaves, *Old Tippecanoe* (1939); Robert Seager, *And Tyler Too* (1963).

BAKER, James Addison, III. Born in Houston, Tex., April 28, 1930; son of James A. Baker, a well-to-do attorney, and Bonner (Means) Baker; Protestant; married to the late Mary McHenry in 1953, and remarried to Susan Garrett Winson on August 6, 1973; father of James A. IVth, Stewart M., John C., and Douglas B. by his first wife, as well as two sons and a daughter from Susan Baker's first marriage; Baker's youngest daughter, Mary Bonner, was born in 1977 from his second marriage; attended the Hill School, a college preparatory school in Pottstown, Pa.; received a B.A. from Princeton University in 1952; enlisted in the U.S. Marine Corps 1952–1954; studied law at the University of Texas; earned J. D. and honorary LL. D in 1957; admitted to Texas Bar in 1957; joined Houston corporate law firm of Andrews, Kurth, Campbell, and Jones, 1957, and later was a partner until 1981; Republican; named state Republican finance chairman under President Richard M. Nixon in 1972; chosen undersecretary of commerce in Gerald R. Ford's administration, 1975–1976; succeeded Rogers C. B. Morton as deputy chairman for delegate operations of the President

Ford Committee on August 25, 1976; appointed chief delegate hunter for the Ford campaign at the Republican National Convention in Kansas City, Missouri, in 1976; announced candidacy for the office of state attorney general of Texas, 1978; became campaign chairman of George Bush's bid for the GOP presidential nomination, 1980; made member of President Elect Ronald Reagan's Transition Team, 1980–1981; chosen as senior advisor and debate coordinator for Ronald Reagan's campaign, 1980–1981; commissioned as White House Chief of Staff and Assistant to President Reagan on November 14, 1980, serving until 1985; head of Reagan's reelection campaign in 1984; appointed SECRETARY OF THE TREASURY in the Reagan Administration on January 29, 1985, and resigned on August 5, 1988; took over as chairman of George Bush's presidential campaign on August 17, 1988; confirmed as SECRETARY OF STATE on January 25, 1989; major contributions included: made an effort in negotiating an unsuccessful deal that was supposed to include $300 billion in spending cuts, 1980; refused a proposal that would have curbed benefits for early retirees, instead opting for a bipartisan commission that recommended a sizable increase in the payroll tax, 1981; helped to obtain passage of landmark tax reform legislation, 1986; drove down the value of the dollar in concert with the other industrial democracies; continued U.S. support of Contra rebels fighting the government of Nicaragua and the UNITA rebels in Angola; advocated a review of U.S. policy toward South Africa; honorary Treasurer of the American Red Cross; served a five-year term on the board of trustees of the Woodrow Wilson International Center for Scholars in the Smithsonian Institution; chairman of the Library of Congress; member of the National Security Council, the American, Texas, and Houston Bar Associations, the Advisory Council on Historic Preservation, the American Judicature Society, the Foreign-Trade Zone Board, the Pension Benefit Guaranty Corporation, the executive branch of the President's Export Council, and Phi Delta Phi honorary legal fraternity; active in many civic endeavors including Texas Children's Hospital and M.D. Anderson Hospital and Tumor Institute. *Current Biography, 1982; 1987 Federal Staff Directory; Who's Who, 1987; Congressional Directory 100th Congress, 1987–1988; The New Republic* (Oct. 17, 1988); *Facts on File, 1989.*

BAKER, Newton Diehl. Born in Martinsburg, W. Va., December 3, 1871; son of Newton Diehl Baker, physician and soldier in the Confederate Army, and Mary (Dukehart) Baker; Episcopalian; married Elizabeth Leopold, July 5, 1902; father of Elizabeth, Newton, and Margaret; entered Johns Hopkins University in 1888, graduating in 1892; obtained law degree from Washington and Lee University in 1894; admitted to the bar in 1895 and began practice in Martinsburg; from 1896 to 1897 served as private secretary to Postmaster General William L. Wilson; moved to Cleveland, Ohio to join a law firm there; appointed assistant director of Cleveland law department in 1902; in January 1903 became city solicitor, and was reelected to that position four times, serving until 1912; elected mayor of Cleveland in 1912 and served two terms; delegate to the 1912 Democratic national convention; appointed SECRETARY OF WAR on March 6, 1916 in the cabinet of President Wilson to fill the vacancy left by the resignation of Lindley M. Garrison; most important contributions were ordering troops to pursue Pancho Villa's raiders who had crossed the border into New Mexico, administering wartime conscription act, and reorganizing administrative structure of War Department; served until March 4, 1921, when he returned to Cleveland and the practice of law; appointed by President Coolidge as member of the Permanent Court of Arbitration at The Hague in 1928 and reappointed by President Roosevelt in 1935; Protestant co-chairman of National Conference of Christians and Jews from 1928 to 1937; member in 1929 of the National Commission on Law Enforcement and Observance, created by President Hoover; president (1928–1931) Woodrow Wilson Foundation; president American Judicature Society, 1930–1937; director Cleveland Trust Company, B&O Railroad Company, Railroad Corporation of America, and Goodyear Tire and Rubber Company; died in Cleveland on December 25, 1937; buried in Lake View Cemetery, Cleveland, Ohio. Frederick Palmer, *Newton D. Baker—America at War* (1931); Clarence H. Cramer, *Newton D. Baker: A Biography* (1961); Daniel R. Beaver, *Newton D. Baker and the American War Effort, 1917–1919* (1966).

BALDRIDGE, (Howard) Malcolm. Born in Omaha, Nebr., October 4, 1922; son of Howard Malcolm Baldridge, lawyer, and Regina (Conell) Baldridge; married Margaret Trowbridge Murray on March 31, 1951; father of Megan Brewster and Mary Trowbridge; studied at Hotchkiss School in Connecticut; graduated from Yale University in 1944 with a B.A. in English; joined the army in 1943 as a private and later served in the field artillery brigade of the 27th infantry division in the Pacific theatre; discharged as a captain in 1946; worked for Eastern Malleable Iron Company in Naugatuck, Conn., beginning as foundry foreman in 1947, and made managing director of its Frazer and Jones division in 1951; vice-president of Eastern Malleable Iron Company in 1957 and president in 1960; joined Scovill Manufacturing Company in Waterbury, Conn., as executive vice-president, 1962; president and chief executive officer of Scovill 1963, and chairman of the board, 1969; while reorganizing Scovill, held directorships in AMF, Inc., White Plains, N.Y.; Connecticut Mutual Life Insurance Company of Hartford; Bendix Corporation; IBM, Inc.; Eastern Company; and Uniroyal, Inc.; trustee for the Swiss Reinsurance Company; member of the Business Council and the Council on Foreign Relations, Inc.; involved in incorporating the Easter Seal Society; director and chairman of the Red Cross fund drive, 1968; trustee of the Waterbury Hospital; helped to found the Waterbury Non-Profit Development Corporation, promoting low-income housing and developing employment and recreational facilities for blacks; chairman of the Waterbury Mayor's Citizens Advisory Committee; member of the Connecticut Governor's Committee on the Status of Women and the Connecticut Citizens Commission on the State Legislature, and delegate to the Connecticut-Constitutional Convention, 1965; member of the Connecticut State Republican budget committee and the finance committee and chairman from 1969 to 1972; member of the Republican platform committee; delegate to every Republican National Convention since 1964; Connecticut cochairman of the United Citizens for Nixon-Agnew; cochairman of the Connecticut Reagan-Bush for President Committee and national vice-chairman of the Business for Reagan-Bush Committee; member of the national Republican finance committee; nominated SECRETARY OF COMMERCE by President Reagan on December 11, 1980, and confirmed by Congress on January 22, 1981; sat on the Council on Commerce and Trade, as chairman; also on the Council on Economic Affairs and the Council on Natural Resources; led the move to convince Japan to accept voluntary restraints on its exports; in his private life became a professional steer roper in 1960; competed in ten rodeos a year; won the Professional Rodeo Cowboys Association's Man of the Year award; had holdings in the Southwest Grazing and Macron farms, a cattle raising partnership; died on July 25, 1987, in a Walnut Creek, Calif., after falling from a horse while practicing for a rodeo competition. *Look* (December 15, 1970); *Congressional Quarterly Weekly Report* (December 20, 1980); *New York Times* (December 27, 1981); *Current Biography, 1982*; *Collier's Encyclopedia*, 1988 Yearbook.

BALLINGER, Richard Achilles. Born in Boonesboro, Iowa, July 9, 1858; son of Richard H. and Mary E. (Norton) Ballinger; married Julia A. Bradley on August 26, 1886; father of Edward B. and Richard T.; attended local schools, the state university at Lawrence, and Washburn College at Topeka, Kans., graduating from Williams College, Williamstown, Mass. in 1884; admitted to the bar at Springfield, Ill. in 1886; became city attorney of Kankakee, Ill., 1888; elected judge of the Superior Court in Port Townsend, Wash., 1894–1897; elected mayor of Seattle on the Republican ticket, serving 1904–1906; appointed commissioner of the General Land Office by Secretary of the Interior Garfield in March 1907; resumed law practice in 1908; a delegate to the Republican national convention of 1908 which nominated Taft for president, he subsequently became active in the national campaign; became SECRETARY OF THE INTERIOR in the cabinet of President Taft on March, 5, 1909 and served until March 6, 1911; became the center of the insurgent fight for the maintenance of former President Theodore Roosevelt's conservation policies; when, over the protests of Gifford Pinchot, chief of the Department of Agriculture's Bureau of Forestry, Ballinger opened a tract of valuable coal land in Alaska for private sale—land which Roosevelt had previously withdrawn from the market—advocates of conservation called for his dismissal; despite an exposé by Brandeis, attorney for the conservationists, Ballinger was sustained by a close vote of the investigating congressional committee; public criticism forced his resignation from the cabinet a year later, hastening the rift between Taft and Roosevelt which led to Roosevelt's formation of the Progressive party in 1912; compiled *Community Property* (1890), a volume relating to the property rights of husband and wife, and also compiled the Codes of Washington, known as *Ballinger's Annotated Codes and*

Statutes (1897); died June 6, 1922. James L. Penick, Jr., *Progressive Politics and Conservation* (1968); Norman M. Wilensky, *Conservatives in the Progressive Era: The Taft Republicans of 1912* (1965).

BANCROFT, George. Born in Worcester, Mass., October 3, 1800; son of Rev. Aron and Lucretia (Chandler) Bancroft; Congregationalist; married Sarah H. Dwight in 1827, and after her death married Mrs. Elizabeth (Davis) Bliss in 1838; father of George, Jr., John, and two daughters; after a common school education, attended Phillips Exeter Academy; entered Harvard in 1813, graduating in 1817, having devoted himself to metaphysics and moral philosophy and the study of Greek and Greek literature; pursued his education at the University of Gottingen in Germany; returned to America in 1822, accepting a tutorship in Greek at Harvard; published a volume of poems in 1823 and a translation of Heeren's *Politics of Ancient Greece* in 1824; one of the founders of the Round Hill School for boys at Northampton, Mass., he sold his interest in 1831; appointed collector of the port of Boston by President Van Buren, 1832–1834; published the first of his scholarly 10–volume *History of the United States* in 1834, a work which he was finally to complete forty years later; became a delegate to the Democratic national convention of 1844 and that same year was defeated in his own campaign for the governorship of Massachusetts; appointed SECRETARY OF THE NAVY by President Polk on March 10, 1845, and served until September 8, 1846; made his secretaryship memorable by establishing the Naval Academy at Annapolis, Md.; issued the order to the Navy to take possession of California, an order which was subsequently carried out; as acting secretary of war in May 1845, he signed the order causing General Zachary Taylor to cross the Texas frontier with his troops, an action directly leading to the Mexican War; appointed U.S. minister to Great Britain, 1846–1849, by President Polk; devoted himself to the completion of his *History of the United States*, published in 1874; conferred the honorary degree of Doctor of Civil Law by Oxford in 1849; published also *A History of the Formation of the Constitution*, 2 vols. (1882); died in Washington, D.C., January 17, 1891; interment in Worcester, Mass. Charles Allan McCoy, *Polk and the Presidency* (1960); Charles Grier Sellers, *James Knox Polk* (1957).

BARBOUR, James. Born at "Frascati," near Gordonsville, Va., June 10, 1775; son of Col. Thomas and Mary (Thomas) Barbour; Presbyterian; married to Lucy Johnson in 1792; father of five children; attended the common schools; studied law; admitted to the bar at Orange County Court House in 1794; elected to the Virginia House of Delegates in 1798, retaining that position until 1812; elected speaker of the House of Delegates in 1809; elected governor of Virginia in 1812; elected to the U.S. Senate in 1815; during the first session of the 16th Congress in 1819, he was elected president *pro tempore*, and during his term, he served as chairman of the Military Affairs and Foreign Relations Committees; appointed SECRETARY OF WAR by President John Quincy Adams on March 7, 1825 and remained loyal to Adams throughout that administration, thereby incurring the wrath of his fellow Virginians; staunchly defended national policy against criticisms from his native state; never a fanatic on the slavery question, he approved of the Panama Congress, which aroused the fears of many southerners; manifested a spirit of benevolence toward the Indians, for whom he finally recommended a territorial government west of the Mississippi; resigned his secretaryship on May 25, 1828 to accept the appointment of minister to Great Britain; recalled from his post by President Jackson in 1829; died at his home in Barboursville, Va., June 8, 1842; interment in the family cemetery. Robert Abraham East, *John Quincy Adams: The Critical Years, 1785–1794* (1962); W. La Feber, ed., *John Quincy Adams and the American Continental Empire* (1965).

BARKLEY, Alben William. Born near Lowes, Graves County, Ky., November 24, 1877; son of John W. Barkely, a former tenant farmer and railroad section hand, and Electra A. (Smith) Barkley; Methodist; married Dorothy Brower on June 23, 1903; father of Laura Louise, Francis, and David; later married Jane (Mrs. Carleton S.) Hadley on November 18, 1949; worked on father's farm and attended public schools; received B.A. from Marvin College in Clinton, Ky., 1897; studied law one year at Emory University in Oxford, Ga. and at University of Virginia Law School in Charlottesville; was admitted to the bar in 1901, and began practice in Paducah, Ky.; was prosecuting attorney for McCracken County Court, 1905–1909; sat as judge of McCracken County Court from 1909–1913; became member of U.S. House of Representatives from Kentucky, and served from March 4, 1913 to March 3, 1927; chairman of Democratic state conventions of 1919 and 1924; delegate to all Democratic national conventions from 1920 to 1940; elected U.S. senator from Kentucky, and served from March 4, 1927 to January 19, 1949, being Democratic majority leader, 1937–1947, and Democratic minority leader, 1947–1948; chief of U.S. delegation to Interparliamentary Union conference in Rome, 1948; elected VICE-PRESIDENT in the administration of President Truman, and served from January 20, 1949 to January 20, 1953; elected member of U.S. Senate from Kentucky and served from January 3, 1955 to death; died in Lexington, Va., April 30, 1956; interment in Paducah, Ky. Jane R. Barkley and F. S. Leighton, *I Married the Veep* (n.d.); Barton J. Bernstein and A. F. Matusow, *Truman Administration: A Documentary History* (1966).

BARR, Joseph Walker. Born in Vicennes, Ind., January 17, 1918; son of Oscar Lynn and Stella Florence (Walker) Barr; married Beth Ann Williston, September 3, 1939; father of Bonnie (Mrs. Michael Gilliom), Cherry (Mrs. Donald N. Briggs), Joseph Williston, Elizabeth Eugenia (Mrs. Andrew LoSasso), and Lynn Hamilton (Mrs. Keith Feinberg); Episcopalian; graduated with A.B. in economics from Depauw University, Greencastle, Ind., 1939; received an M.A. in theoretical economics, Harvard University, 1941; obtained an LL.D. from Vincennes University, 1966; served as lieutenant commander in World War II, 1942–1945;

won a Bronze Star for sinking a German ship at Anzio; helped manage the family business in grain elevators, farm equipment financing, and real estate in succeeding years; treasurer, O.L. Barr Grain Company, 1946– ; Democratic member of the Eighty-Sixth Congress for the 11th Independent District, Indiana, January 3, 1959, to January 20, 1961; assistant to secretary of treasurer in liaison work with Congress, 1961–1964; chairman of the Federal Deposit Insurance Corporation, 1964–1965; undersecretary of the treasury, 1965–1968; replaced Henry H. Fowler as SECRETARY OF TREASURY in the cabinet of president Lyndon B. Johnson; served from December 23, 1968, to January 20, 1969; president of the American Security and Trust Company, Washington, D.C., 1969–1972, and chairman of the board, 1972–1974; partner J&J Company, 1976– ; director of the Minnseota Mining and Manufacturing Co., Commercial Credit Company, Burlington Industries, and Washington Gas Light Co.; member of the advisory committee of the Export Import Bank of the United States; trustee of Depauw University; on the board of directors of the Student Loan Marketing Association; on the board of regents, Georgetown University; member of Phi Beta Kappa; Democrat. *Current Biography Yearbook, 1968*; *New York Times* (December 24, 1968); *Who's Who in America, 1975–1976, International Who's Who, 1988*; *Who's Who in America, 1988–1989.*

BARRY, William Taylor. Born near Lunenburg, Va., February 5, 1785; son of John and Susannah (Dozier) Barry; married to Lucy Overton in 1824, and after her death, to Catherine Mason; family early moved to Kentucky, settling in Fayette County; attended the common schools, Pisgah Academy, and the Kentucky Academy in Woodford County, Ky.; entered William and Mary College at Williamsburg, Va., graduating in 1803; received his legal training at Transylvania College; passed bar in 1805 and commenced the practice of law in Lexington, Ky.; elected to the Kentucky House of Representatives as a Democrat in 1809; enlisted in the War of 1812, serving as secretary and aide-de-camp to General Shelby; reelected to the Kentucky legislature in 1814; won election to the U.S. Senate in 1815, resigning in 1816 to accept appointment as judge of the Circuit Court for the 11th district of Kentucky, 1816–1817; elected to the State Senate in 1817; elected lieutenant governor of Kentucky in 1820; became leader of the "Relief Party" in 1821; professor of law and politics at Transylvania College in 1822; appointed secretary of state of Kentucky in 1824; appointed chief justice of the state Court of Appeals on January 10, 1825; ran for governor in 1828, but was defeated; allied his statewide forces with the presidential candidacy of Andrew Jackson, who appointed him POSTMASTER GENERAL on March 9, 1829, elevating the office to cabinet level as a special mark of gratitude; charged with malfeasance in office, Barry successfully refuted the charges, but resigned on April 8, 1835; appointed by President Jackson to be envoy extraordinary and minister plenipotentiary to Spain on May 1, 1835; died en route to his new mission on May 1, 1835, in Liverpool, England; interment in England, and reinterment in the State Cemetery at Frankfort, Ky., in 1864, with a marker placed on the grave by the Kentucky legislature in 1865. Edwin Charles Rozwenc, *The Meaning of Jacksonian Democracy* (1963); Harold Coffin Syrett, *Andrew Jackson: His Contributions to the American Tradition* (1953).

BATES, Edward. Born in Belmont, Va., September 4, 1793; son of Thomas Fleming and Caroline Matilda (Woodson) Bates; brother of Missouri congressman James Woodson Bates; Quaker; married Julia Davenport Coalter on May 29, 1823; father of seventeen children; attended Charlotte Hall Academy in St. Mary's County, Md.; acted as sergeant in a volunteer brigade in the War of 1812; moved to St. Louis, Mo. in 1814; studied law and was admitted to the bar in 1817, commencing his legal practice in St. Louis; elected circuit prosecuting attorney in 1818; member of the state constitutional convention in 1820; designated state's attorney in 1820; elected to the Missouri House of Representatives in 1822; served as U.S. district attorney from 1821 to 1826; elected as an Adams Anti-Democrat to the 20th Congress (House), serving from March 4, 1827 to March 3, 1829; unsuccessful candidate for reelection in 1828 to the 21st Congress; resumed the practice of law; elected to the Missouri Senate in 1830 and to the Missouri House of Representatives in 1834; declined appointment as secretary of war in 1850 under President Fillmore; designated judge of the St. Louis Land Court, 1853–1856; joined the cabinet of President Lincoln as AT-TORNEY GENERAL on March 5, 1861, serving until his resignation on November 24, 1864; he disagreed with many of Lincoln's war policies, feeling that constitutional rights were giving way before the encroachments of the military authorities; died in St. Louis, Mo., March 25, 1869; interment in Bellefontaine Cemetery, St. Louis. Courtlandt Canby, ed., *Lincoln and the Civil War: A Profile and a History* (1960); Jesse Burton Hendrick, *Lincoln's War Cabinet* (1946).

BAYARD, Thomas Francis. Born in Wilmington, Del., October 29, 1828; son of James Asheton Bayard, U.S. senator, and Ann (Francis) Bayard; French Huguenot ancestry; married Louise Lee in October 1856, and after her death, married Mary W. Clymer on November 7, 1889; father of five children; attended private school in Flushing, N.Y.; worked in counting houses in New York, Philadelphia, and the West Indies; did not attend college, but studied law and was admitted to the Delaware bar in 1851; served as U.S. district attorney for Delaware, 1853–1854; moved to Philadelphia in 1855, but returned to practice law in Delaware in 1856 and became a permanent resident of Wilmington in 1858; favored states' rights, but was influential in getting Delaware to remain in the Union; elected to the U.S. Senate as a Democrat in 1869 and served until 1885; became a leader of the Democrats in that body, and served on the committees of finance, public lands, and revision of laws; served on the electoral commission of 1876 which resolved the disputed Hayes-Tilden presidential election; was president *pro tem* of the Senate in 1881; as contender for the presidential nomination at the Democratic national conventions of 1876, 1880, and 1884, he advocated sound currency, low tariffs, civil service reform, and limitation of power and activity of the federal government; resigned from the Senate to become SECRETARY OF STATE in the first administration of President Cleveland on March 6, 1885, and served in that post throughout the administration; as Secretary, he introduced civil service reform to the State Department, opposed and nullified the Frelinghuysen-Zavala Treaty under which the U.S. was to build a canal in Nicaragua, attempted to settle the North Atlantic fisheries dispute by negotiating the Bayard-Chamberlain Treaty of February 15, 1888 with Great Britain; charging that the treaty surrendered rights of the U.S., the Republican-controlled Senate rejected it, but the dispute was resolved by a modus vivendi; lent good offices of the U.S. to settle the boundary dispute between Venezuela and Great Britain regarding one of the latter's South American colonies; left office on March 5, 1889, at conclusion of Cleveland's first term; appointed U.S. ambassador to Great Britain during Cleveland's second administration, in 1893; first U.S. diplomatic minister to hold ambassadorial rank; resigned in 1897 because of ill health, and returned to the U.S. to live in retirement; died in Dedham, Mass., September 28, 1898; interment in Swedes Cemetery, Wilmington, Del. Edward Spence, *An Outline of the Public Life and Services of Thomas F. Bayard* (1880); R. M. McElroy, *Grover Cleveland* (1923); Allan Nevins, *Grover Cleveland: A Study in Courage* (1938).

BELKNAP, William Worth. Born in Newburgh, N.Y., September 22, 1829; son of General William Goldsmith Belknap, prominent in the Mexican War, and Ann (Clark) Belknap; married Cora LeRoy; later married Carrie Tomlinson, and after her death married her widowed sister, Mrs. John Bower; entered Princeton in 1848 and received his B.A. in 1852; studied law in Georgetown, D.C. under Hugh Caperton, and was admitted to the bar in 1851; practiced in Keokuk, Iowa with R. P. Lowe; member of Iowa legislature, 1857–1858; made brigadier general in command of the 4th Division of the 17th Corps on July 3, 1864; mustered out on July 27, 1865; became collector of internal revenue in Iowa; appointed SECRETARY OF WAR in the cabinet of President Grant on October 25, 1869, and took office on November 1, 1869; impeached by the House, though not by the Senate, for taking bribes, he resigned on March 1, 1876; moved to Philadelphia; returned to Washington, D.C. and practiced law; died in Washington D.C. on October 13, 1890. Jesse R. Grant, *In the Days of My Father General Grant* (1925); Ulysses S. Grant, III, *Ulysses S. Grant, Warrior and Statesman* (1969).

BELL, Griffin B. Born in Americus, Ga., October 31, 1918; son of A. C. and Thelma (Pitcher) Bell; Baptist; married to Mary Foy Powell, February 20, 1943; father of Griffin B.; attended Georgia Southwestern College, Americus; LL.D. degree, cum laude, Mercer University, 1967; admitted to the Georgia bar, 1948; served in the U.S. Army, 1941–1946; attained the rank of major; private law practice in Savannah, Ga., and Rome, Ga., 1947–1953; partner, King and Spalding Law Firm, Atlanta, Ga., 1953–1959; managing partner, King and Spalding Law Firm, 1959–1961; Georgia campaign manager for John F. Kennedy, 1960; appointed by President John F. Kennedy as United States Judge, Fifth Circuit Court of Appeals, 1961; served in that position until 1976; chairman, Atlanta Commission on Crime and Delinquency, 1965–1966; member, visiting Committee, Vanderbilt University Law School, Nashville, Tenn.; trustee, Institute on Continuing Legal Education in Georgia, American Law Institute; member, Board of Directors of the Federal Judicial Center, 1974–1976; on December 20, 1976, nominated by President-Elect Jimmy Carter to be ATTORNEY GENERAL, and confirmed on January 23, 1977; served until July 19, 1979; chairman of the American Delinquency Confederation on Security and Co-operation in Europe, Madrid, 1980; president of the American College of Trial Lawyers, 1985–1986; member of the Secretary of State's Advisory Committee on South America, 1986; member of the American Bar Association; currently senior partner in King and Spalding Law Firm, Atlanta, Ga. *Who's Who in America, 1974–1975; Congressional Quarterly, Weekly Report*, Vol. 34 (December 26, 1976); *Time* (January 3, 1977); *U.S. News and World Report* (January 10, 1977); *New York Times* (July 20, 1979); *International Who's Who, 1988.*

BELL, John. Born on a farm near Nashville, Tenn., February 15, 1797; son of Samuel and Margaret (Edmiston) Bell; married first to Sally Dickinson, and after her death to Mrs. Jane (Ervin) Yeatman; after attending the common schools, he entered Cumberland College (now the University of Nashville) and graduated in 1814 at the age of 17; admitted to the bar in 1817, before he was 21, he began practicing law in Franklin, Tenn.; served one session (1817) as a state senator, also before he reached his majority; moved to Nashville, devoting himself exclusively to the practice of law; in 1827, he began the first of fourteen successive years in the U.S. House of Representatives, serving until 1841; initially a staunch supporter of Jackson in Congress, he ultimately broke with him and became one of the founders of the Whig party in Tennessee; in 1834, he won the speakership of the House of Representatives; appointed SECRETARY OF WAR in the cabinet of President William H. Harrison on March 5, 1841, and resigned on September 11, 1841 when President Tyler rejected the legislative program of the Whigs; remained in retirement until 1847, when he was elected to the U.S. Senate, continuing in that office until 1859; though a slaveowner, he was basically a moderate, having no sympathy with either Northern or Southern extremists; nominated for the presidency in 1860, under the Constitutional Union party banner, but was defeated by Lincoln; an opponent of secession, his influence kept Tennessee in the Union for a time; he recommended an armed neutrality, but was against federal "coercion" of secessionist states, and when Tennessee was invaded by federal troops, he threw his support to the secessionists; fled to the lower South, and returned to Tennessee when the war was over; died at his home near Cumberland Furnace, Tenn., September 10, 1869; interment in Mount Olivet Cemetery, near Nashville. James A. Green, *William*

Henry Harrison, His Life and Times (1941); Oscar Doane Lambert, *Presidential Politics in the United States, 1840–1844* (1936).

BELL, Terrel Howard. Born at Lava Hot Springs, Idaho, November 11, 1921; son of Willard Dewain and Alta (Martin) Bell; married Betty Ruth Fitzgerald in 1957; father of four sons; attended Southern Idaho College of Education and Utah University; served with the U.S. Marine Corps; worked as a high school teacher of chemistry and physics in Eden, Ohio, 1946–1947; Superintendent of Schools, Rockland Valley Schools (Idaho), 1947–1954, Star Valley School District (Afton, Wyoming), 1955–1957, Weber City School District (Utah), 1957–1962; professor of school administration at Utah State University, 1962–1963; superintendent of public instruction for the state of Utah, 1963–1970; associate commissioner, Regional Office Coordination, U.S. Office of Education, Department of Health, Education and Welfare, and Acting Commissioner of Education, 1970; deputy commissioner of school systems, 1971; commissioner of education, 1974–1976; superintendent of Granite School System (Utah), 1971–1974; commissioner of education for the State of Utah, 1976–1980; named to the position of SECRETARY OF EDUCATION in the cabinet of President Ronald Reagan, January 7, 1981; confirmed and approved on January 22, 1981; first official major act was to revoke bilingualism rules that had required public schools to teach non–English speaking students in their native language; named in August 1981 to a commission to study school standards in the United States; announced resignation on November 8, 1984, effective December 31, 1984; professor at Utah University, 1985– ; chairman of the Utah Textbook Committee and the Utah Course Study Committee; executive officer of the Utah Board of Education; member of the American Association of School Administrators, Council of Chief State School Officer; author of *The Prodigal Pedagogue* (1956); *Effective Teaching: How to Recognize and Reward Competence* (1962); *A Philosophy of Education for the Space Age* (1963); *Your Child's Intellect—A Guide to Home-Based Pre-School Education* (1972); *A Performance Accountability System for School Administrators* (1974); and *Active Parent Concern* (1976). *Facts on File* (1981 and 1984); *International Yearbook and Statesmen's Who's Who, 1985; International Who's Who, 1988–1989.*

BENNETT, William John. Born in Brooklyn, N.Y., July 3, 1943; Roman Catholic; married Mary Elayne Glover on May 29, 1982; father of John, born in 1984; attended Williams College, graduated with a B.A. in 1965, and received an honorary LL.D. in 1983; received Ph.D. from the University of Texas in 1970; received J.D. from Harvard University in 1971; worked as an assistant to the president of Boston University from 1972 to 1976; executive director of the National Humanities Center, Research Triangle Park, North Carolina, 1976–1979, and president and director, 1979–1981; associate professor at North Carolina State University, 1979–1981; president and chairman of the National Endowment for Humanities (NEH) in Washington, D.C., 1981–1985; nominated on January 10, 1985, for the position of SECRETARY OF EDUCATION in the cabinet of President Ronald Reagan and was sworn in on February 6, 1985; served as Secretary of Education from 1985 to 1988; well-known for being a controversial, outspoken figure; advocated cuts in financial assistance for higher education and a restructuring of the government assistance programs; announced his resignation on May 9, 1988, effective in September 1988, because of his belief that the November presidential election would preclude any serious accomplishments until the installation of the next administration; named as the first director of the Office of National Drug Control Policy, January 12, 1989; confirmed as "drug czar" on March 9, 1989; received honorary Litt.D. from Gonzaga University, 1982; received honorary Hh.D. from Franklin College, 1982, University of North Carolina, 1984, George Washington University, 1985, Gaullaudet College, 1985, and The Citadel, 1986; received honorary Lh.D. from University of New Hampshire, 1982, Manhattan College, 1983, Elon College, 1984, Loyola College, 1983, and the University of Notre Dame, 1984; a former Democrat, who joined the Republican Party in 1986; partner in Dunnels, Duvall, Bennett, and Porter, Washington, 1988–1989; director of the office of National Drug Control Policy in the administration of President George Bush; has contributed articles to *Newsweek, Commentary, The Public Interest,* and *Change*; coauthor of *Country by Race: Equality from the Founding Fathers to Bakke and Weber*; author of *Our Children and Our Country: Improving America's Schools and Affirming the Common Culture,* and of *American Education: Making It Work. International Yearbook and Statesmen's Who's Who; Who's Who in the World; Directory of American Scholars, 1982; Current Biography, 1985; Facts on File* (1988 and 1989); *International Who's Who, 1988–1989; The New York Times* (March 2, 1989).

BENSON, Ezra Taft. Born on a farm at Whitney, Idaho, August 4, 1899; son of George Taft and Sara S. (Dunkley) Benson; Mormon; married Flora Smith Amussen on September 10, 1926; father of Reed, Mark, Barbara, Beverly, Bonnie, and Flora Beth; worked on family farm; attended elementary school at Whitney; studied at Oneida State Academy in Preston, Idaho, 1914–1918; took correspondence course, and then attended Utah State Agricultural College, 1918–1921; president of the Newcastle District of the Church of Jesus Christ Latter-day Saints, 1921–1923; went on two-year proselytizing mission for the Mormons to Great Britain and Europe; operated own farm, 1923–1929; received B.S. from Brigham Young University, 1926, and M.S. in agricultural economics from Iowa State College, 1927; became county agricultural agent for extension service of University of Idaho in Preston, 1929; employed as extension economist and marketing specialist by University of Idaho Cooperative Council, 1930, and was secretary there from 1933 to 1938; appointed executive secretary of National Council of Farmer Cooperatives, 1939–1944; member of National Farm Credit Committee and served on National Agricultural Advisory Commission, 1940–1941; became member of executive committee of board of trustees of American

Institute of Cooperation in 1942, and was chairman of the board in 1952; member of the Region Twelve Executive Committee, 1945; U.S. delegate to first International Conference of Farm Organizations, 1946; director of Farms Foundation, 1946–1950; appointed SECRETARY OF AGRICULTURE in the cabinet of President Dwight D. Eisenhower on November 24, 1952; toured the United States to prepare, and took office on January 21, 1953; served until January 20, 1961; most important contribution was his proposal that farmers wanted no government help and felt no need for price supports at more than 90 percent of parity; wrote articles on agriculture and religion; member of the national executive board of the Boy Scouts Of America, 1948–1966; president of the Church of Jesus Christ Latter-day Saints in Salt Lake City, 1985– ; board of trustees, Brigham Young University, American Marketing Association, Farm Economics Association, and Delta Nu, Alpha Zeta. Dean Albertson, ed., *Eisenhower as President* (1963); David A. Frier, *Conflict of Interest in the Eisenhower Administration* (1969); *Who's Who in America, 1988–1989*.

BERGLAND, Bob Selmer. Born in Roseau, Minn., July 22, 1928; son of Selmer Bennett and Mabel (Evans) Bergland; Lutheran; married to Helen Elaine Gromm, June 24, 1950; father of Dianne, Linda, Stevan, Jon, Allan, Billy, and Franklyn; studied agriculture for two years at the University of Minnesota, Minneapolis; field representative, Minnesota Farmers Union, 1948–1950; purchased his own farm in 1950; worked in Florida as a construction laborer and carpenter; secretary, Roseau County, Minn., Democratic Farmer-Labor Party, 1951–1952; chairman, Minnesota State Agricultural Stabilization and Conservation Service Committee, U.S. Department of Agriculture, 1963–1968; unsuccessful candidate for U.S. House of Representatives, 1968; elected to the Ninety-Third Congress of the United States, from the seventh district of Minnesota, 1970; reelected in 1976; Minnesota Farmers Union; Mason; Lion; Minnesota Democratic Farmer-Labor party; on December 20, 1976, nominated by President-Elect Jimmy Carter to be SECRETARY OF AGRICULTURE; served until January 23, 1981; contributions included push for bills to guarantee loans and price support boosts for farmers during the Soviet grain embargo; member of the Minnesota Farmers Union, National Farmer's Organization. *Who's Who in America, 1974–1975; Congressional Quarterly, Weekly Report*, Vol. 34 (December 26, 1976); *Time* (January 3, 1977); *U.S. News and World Report* (January 10, 1977); *Newsweek* (January 28, 1980); *International Who's Who, 1988*.

BERRIEN, John MacPherson. Born at Rocky Hill, near Princeton, N.J., August 23, 1781; son of Major John and Margaret (MacPherson) Berrien; French Calvinist; moved with his family to Savannah, Georgia in 1782; after preparatory schooling in New York, he matriculated at Princeton and was graduated in 1796; returned to Savannah; studied law and was admitted to the bar in 1799; commenced his practice in Louisville, Ky. and then in Augusta, Ga.; elected solicitor of the Eastern Circuit in 1809, a position he held until 1821; captain of the

Georgia Hussars, a Savannah volunteer company, in the war of 1812; served one term in the state Senate from 1822 to 1823; elected as a Democrat to the U.S. Senate in 1824, resigning in 1829; invited to join the cabinet of President Jackson as ATTORNEY GENERAL on March 9, 1829, a position he held until June 22, 1831, when he became estranged from the President on account of the Eaton affair; resumed private life and his law practice for the next ten years, until 1841, when he was elected to the U.S. Senate as a Whig, serving until May 18, 1845, when he resigned to accept an appointment to the Supreme Court of Georgia; delegate to the Whig Convention at Baltimore in 1844; issued *An Address To The People Of The United States* (February 1849), in which he pleaded for a compromise of the slavery question; withdrew from the Whig Party in 1850; rejected secession but believed that resistance within the Union was a necessity; re-elected to U.S. Senate Nov. 14, 1845–Mar. 3, 1847, Nov. 13, 1847–May 28, 1852; joined the American or Know-Nothing Party; presided over the Know-Nothing Party convention held in the District of Columbia in December 1855; died in Savannah, Ga., on January 1, 1856; interment in Laurel Grove Cemetery, Savannah, Ga. Harold Coffin Syrett, *Andrew Jackson: His Contributions To The American Tradition* (1953); John William Ward, *Andrew Jackson—Symbol For An Age* (1955).

BIBB, George Mortimer. Born in Prince Edward County, Va., October 30, 1776; son of Richard and Lucy (Booker) Bibb; twice married and the father of seventeen children; graduated from Hampden-Sidney and William and Mary College in 1792; studied law and was admitted to the bar in 1798, commencing his legal practice in Virginia; moved to Lexington, Ky.; appointed to the bench of the Court of Appeals in 1808, the highest court in the state, and, in 1809, was elevated to the chief justiceship, resigning in 1810; elected to the U.S. Senate as a "War Hawk" in 1811; took a prominent part in forcing war against Great Britain and in loyally upholding President Madison in carrying it out; resigned his Senate seat in 1814, taking up residence in Frankfort, Ky., resuming his law practice there; elected to the lower house of the Kentucky legislature in 1817; appointed chief justice of the Court of Appeals again in 1828; resigned his judicial post in 1828, returning to the U.S. Senate, serving the full six year term; an early admirer of President Jackson, he broke with him on the bank question; became chancellor of the Louisville Court of Chancery, 1835–1844; appointed SECRETARY OF THE TREASURY on June 15, 1844, serving until the close of the Tyler administration on March 4, 1845; authored: *Reports Of Cases At Common Law And In Chancery In The Kentucky Court of Appeals* (1811); died in Georgetown, District of Columbia, on April 14, 1859; interment in the State Cemetery, Frankfort, Ky. Robert J. Morgan, *A Whig Embattled, The Presidency Under John Tyler* (1954); Oliver Perry Chitwood, *John Tyler, Champion Of The Old South* (1964).

BIDDLE, Francis Beverley. Born in Paris, France, May 9, 1886; son of Algernon Sydney and Frances (Robinson) Biddle; married Katherine Garrison on April 27, 1918; father of Edmund Randolph and Garrison Chapin; after attending the Haverford Academy in Haverford, Pa., 1895–1899, and the Groton Academy in Groton, Mass., 1899–1905, he entered Harvard, graduating in 1909; received his law degree in 1911; secretary to Justice Oliver Wendell Holmes of the U.S. Supreme Court, 1911–1912; was admitted to the Pennsylvania bar in 1912; member of the Philadelphia law firm of Barnes, Biddle and Meyer, 1917–1939; served as special assistant to the U.S. attorney from the eastern district of Pennsylvania; chairman of the National Labor Relations Board in Washington, D.C. during 1934 and 1935; chief counsel to investigate the Tennessee Valley Authority in 1938 and 1939; appointed judge of the U.S. Circuit Court of Appeals, 1939–1940; appointed solicitor general of the U.S. by President Franklin D. Roosevelt in 1940; joined the Roosevelt cabinet as ATTORNEY GENERAL on September 5, 1941, was continued in office by President Truman, and served until June 30, 1945; during his secretaryship, he appointed the Interdepartmental Committee on Investigations, which made the first attempt to suggest procedures for loyalty investigations, and he submitted to it a list compiled by the Federal Bureau of Investigation containing the names of alleged subversive organizations; during 1945 and 1946, he served as a member of the International Military Tribunal sitting in Nuremberg, Germany, to determine the war guilt of Nazi leaders; delegate at large to the Democratic national conventions in 1944 and 1952; elected chairman of Americans for Democratic Action on June 4, 1951; appointed a member of the Permanent Court of Arbitration at The Hague; authored *Mr. Justice Holmes* (1942), *Democratic Thinking and the War* (1944), *World's Best Hope* (1949), *The Fear of Freedom* (1951), and *Natural Law and the Supreme Court* (1961); died at Cape Cod, Mass., October 4, 1968. Paul K. Conkin, *The New Deal* (1967); Cabell B. H. Phillips, *The Truman Presidency: The History of a Triumphant Succession* (1966).

BISSELL, Wilson Shannon. Born in New London, N.Y., December 31, 1847; son of John and Isabella Jeannette (Hally) Bissell; married Louisa Fowler in 1889; no children; moved to Buffalo, 1851; attended local schools of Buffalo until 1863; sent to Hopkins grammar school, New Haven, Conn.; graduated Yale, 1869; studied law in office of Messrs. Laning, Cleveland and Folsom; admitted to the bar, 1871; received LL.D. from Yale, 1893; went into partnership with Honorable Lyman K. Bass in 1872; joined by Cleveland, firm became Cleveland and Bissell, 1875, and reorganized to become Bissell, Carey and Cooke, 1894; took prominent part in Cleveland's campaign for governor, 1882, and campaigns for president, 1884 and 1892; president of Buffalo Club, 1888; elected delegate to the national convention at the state convention in New York City in May 1888, but resigned to accept the nomination for presidential elector-at-large; appointed POSTMASTER GENERAL in the cabinet of President Cleveland on March 3, 1893, and served until his resignation on April 4, 1895; shortened time of transcontinental mail transmission by fourteen hours, eliminated steamboat subsidies on slow ships, and transferred contracts for printing stamps from private parties to Bureau of Engraving and Printing at Washington; resumed legal practice in Buffalo, N.Y.; president, trustee and real estate commissioner of Buffalo library; active member of Buffalo Historical Society; chancellor of Buffalo University, 1902; died October 6, 1903. *Sixth Biographical Record, Class of Sixty-Nine, Yale College* (1895); H. W. Hill, *Municipality of Buffalo* (1923); Robert L. Vexter, ed., *Grover Cleveland; 1837–1908: Chronology, Documents, Bibliographical Aids* (1968).

BLACK, Jeremiah Sullivan. Born at Glades, near Stony Creek, Pa., January 10, 1810; son of Henry and Mary (Sullivan) Black; Campbellite (religious sect); married Mary Forward in 1836; father of Chauncey F. and Mary F.; educated locally at Staystown, Berlin, and Somerset schools, completing his education at the academy in Bridgeport, Pa.; studied law in 1827 and was admitted to the bar on December 3, 1830; appointed deputy attorney general for Somerset County, 1831; president judge of the Court of Common Pleas for the 16th Judicial District in 1842; elected in 1851 to the Supreme Court of Pennsylvania and reelected in 1854, serving the first three years as chief justice; invited to join the Buchanan cabinet as ATTORNEY GENERAL on March 6, 1857; successfully handled many of the problems involved in land claims in California, uncovering many that were fraudulent; attacked squatter sovereignty, basing his arguments on the ground that territorial legislatures could not make laws violating the Fifth Amendment; appointed SECRETARY OF STATE by President Buchanan on December 17, 1860; when South Carolina seceded from the Union, he urged the President to send supplies to aid Major Anderson in Charleston Harbor against insurgency; sent a circular letter to our foreign ministers, urging them to do what they could to prevent any recognition of the Confederacy by foreign powers; retired from political life after Lincoln's inauguration on March 4, 1861; appointed to the U.S. Supreme Court on February 5, 1861, his nomination being rejected by disgruntled Republicans and Southern sympathizers; U.S. Supreme Court reporter, 1861–1864, he prepared *Black's Reports*, Volumes 1 and 2; aided and advised President Andrew Johnson and was to be one of his counsels before the Impeachment Court but withdrew in a fit of pique; met with a serious accident in 1869 which deprived him of the use of his right arm; helped revise the Pennsylvania constitution of 1873; was counsel for Samuel Tilden before the electoral commission in 1877; died in York, Pa., on August 19, 1883. Philip Shriver Klein, *President James Buchanan, A Biography* (1962); David Mayer Silver, *Lincoln's Supreme Court* (1956).

BLAINE, James Gillespie. Born at West Brownsville, Pa., January 31, 1830; son of Ephraim Lyon and Maria Louise (Gillespie) Blaine; Congregationalist; married Harriet Stonwood on June 30, 1850; father of seven children; educated at the local schools; attended Washington College, Washington, Pa., graduating in 1847; taught at the Western Military Institute, Blue Lick Springs, Ky.; returned to Pennsylvania, teaching at the Pennsylvania Institute for the Blind in Philadelphia, where he commenced the study of law; after marriage, moved to Augusta, Me.; elected chairman of the Republican state committee in 1859, retaining this post until 1881; elected to the state legislature, 1859–1862, holding the position of speaker of the House of Representatives in 1861 and 1862; commenced his career of public speaker in 1860; elected to the U.S. House of Representatives, 1863–1876; served in the U.S. Senate, 1876–1881; became a candidate for president in 1876 and 1880, losing to Hayes and Garfield respectively; appointed SECRETARY OF STATE on March 5, 1881, by President Garfield; resigned his position upon Garfield's assassination, but was asked to remain until December 12, 1881, by President Arthur; renominated for the presidency at the Republican national convention of 1884, he lost to Grover Cleveland; appointed SECRETARY OF STATE by President Benjamin Harrison on March 5, 1889 and served until June 3, 1892; organized and presided over the first Pan American Congress, promoted the theory of reciprocal tariffs, secured treaty concerning Pacific seal-hunting with Great Britain, pursued policy of America for the Americans; authored *Twenty Years of Congress*, 2 vols. (1884); died in Washington, D.C., January 27, 1893; interment in Oak Hill Cemetery and reinterred, at the request of the state of Maine, in the Blaine Memorial Park, Augusta, Me., June 1920; David Saville Muzzey, *James G. Blaine: A Political Idol of Other Days* (1963); Alice Felt Tyler, *The Foreign Policy of James G. Blaine* (1965).

BLAIR, Montgomery. Born in Franklin County, Ky., May 10, 1813; son of Francis Preston Blair, journalist and politician, and Eliza (Gist) Blair; religious, but anti-ritualistic; married Caroline Buckner; after her death, married Mary Elizabeth Woodbury; attended local schools; appointed to West Point by President Jackson in 1831; graduated in 1835 to become a lieutenant in the army; served in the Seminole War; resigned in 1836 to study law at Transylvania University, Lexington, Ky.; became protégé of Thomas Hart Benton, 1837, and settled in St. Louis; was admitted to the bar in 1839; appointed U.S. district attorney for Missouri in 1839, but was removed by Tyler for political reasons; was mayor of St. Louis, 1842–1843; served as judge of court of common pleas from 1843 until his resignation in 1849; resumed practice of law; moved to Maryland in 1853 and practiced law; made first solicitor in U.S. court of claims by President Buchanan in 1855; became counsel for Dred Scott; delegate to Democratic national conventions of 1844, 1848 and 1852; presided over state Republican convention at Baltimore in 1860, and was delegate from Maryland to Chicago national convention; appointed POSTMASTER GENERAL in the cabinet of President Lincoln, serving from March 9, 1861 to September 23, 1864; most important contributions were organization of postal system for the army, introduction of compulsory payment of postage and free delivery in cities, improvement of registry system, establishment of railway post office, organization of postal draft plan, stopping franking privileges of postmasters, and helping to bring about Postal Union Convention at Paris in 1863; supported Seymour in 1868, Greeley in 1872 and Tilden in 1876; established the *Union*, a Washington paper, with financial support of W. W. Corcoran; member of Maryland House of Representatives, 1878; unsuccessful candidate for Congress in 1882; began writing the life of Andrew Jackson; died in Silver Spring, Md., July 27, 1883. Dorothy Canfield, *The Cabinet Politician: The Postmaster General 1829–1900* (1943).

BLISS, Cornelius Newton. Born in Fall River, Mass., January 26, 1833; son of Asahel Newton and Irene Borden (Luther) Bliss; married Elizabeth Mary Plummer on March 30, 1859; father of one son and one daughter; attended public schools of Fall River and Fishers Academy; in 1847, became clerk in dry goods store of Edward S. Keep, stepfather, in New Orleans; took beginner's place in M. Beebe and Company of Boston, and rose to member of firm; became New York partner of J. S. and E. Wright of Boston, 1866; upon death of Wrights, company took name of Bliss, Falyan and Company, and Bliss remained at its head until death; supported Chester A. Arthur for presidency in 1884; chairman of Republican state committee, 1887; treasurer of Republican national committee in 1892; offered Treasury portfolio, 1896; appointed SECRETARY OF THE INTERIOR in the Cabinet of President McKinley on March 5, 1897, and served until his resignation on February 20, 1899; most important contributions were acceptance of secretaryship politically for McKinley and competent administration of his office; declined nomination for vice-president, 1900; repeatedly declined candidacy for state and municipal offices, but gave of his services as a member of civic and political committees; advocate of high protective tariff and president of Protective Tariff League; official in many large financial and industrial organizations; president of Fourth National Bank; president of New York Hospital; died October 9, 1911. J. H. Bliss, *Genealogy of the Bliss Family in America* (1881); *New York Times* (October 10, 1911); Robert Dallek, *McKinley's Decision, War on Spain* (1970); Margaret K. Leech, *In the Days of McKinley* (1959); H. Wayne Morgan, *William McKinley and his America* (1963).

BLOCK, John Rusling. Born in Galesburg, Ill., February 15, 1935, son of Julius (Judd) and Madeline (Maddy) Block; Protestant; married Susan (Sue) Rathjo; father of Hans, Cynthia, and Kristi; attended Knoxville High School, studied vocational agriculture and took part in varsity sports; entered the U.S. Military Academy at West Point and was active in many intramural sports; after graduation in 1957 served for three years as a platoon leader in the crack 101st Airborne Division of paratroopers at Fort Benning, Ga.; returned to the family farm in 1960 and established a partnership with his father; on their 300–acre tract they raised corn and soybeans and bred hogs, sending 200 to market a year; over the next two decades the farm expanded into a 3,000–acre, multimillion-dollar agribusiness with a sophisticated indoor hog operation that produced 6,000 swine per year; won the American Jaycees Outstanding Farmer Award in 1969; in 1977 James R. Thompson, Jr., the Republican governor of Illinois, appointed Block director of the State's Department of Agriculture; in an effort to increase exports of corn and soybeans, he traveled to the Soviet Union, Europe, Japan, China, and Taiwan: for his efforts, Governor Thompson bestowed on him the Outstanding Achievement Award; President-Elect Ronald Reagan nominated Block for the post of SECRETARY OF AGRICULTURE on December 23, 1980; at his confirmation hearing, Block pledged to promote farm exports aggressively and expressed his opposition to the grain embargo against the Soviet Union; confirmed by the Senate on January 22, 1981; with the lifting of the grain embargo against the Soviet Union on April 25, 1981, Block scored an early victory within the Reagan administration; he also lobbied in Congress on behalf of the administration's four-year farm bill, which was finally passed by Congress in December 1981; resigned February 14, 1986; president of the National-American Wholesale Grocers Association. *New York Times* (December 23, 1980); *Current Biography Yearbook 1982.*

BLOUNT, Winton Malcolm. Born in Union Springs, Ala., February 1, 1921; son of Winton M. Blount, owner of a shortline railroad and construction materials business, and Clara Bella (Chalker) Blount; Presbyterian; married Mary Katherine Archibald on September 2, 1942; father of Winton M. III, Thomas A., S. Roberts, Katherine Blount Miles, Joseph W.; attended the public schools of Union Springs and Staunton Military Academy, Va.; studied at the University of Alabama, 1939–1941, where he graduated with a B.A.; served as a lieutenant in U.S. Army Air Corps., 1942–1945; founded Blount Brothers Corp., general contractors, in 1946 and served as president and chairman of the board until December 1968; chairman of the board, Benjamin F. Shaw Company, piping contractors of Wilmington, Del., until December 1968; past director, Gulf American Fire and Casualty Company, the First National Bank of Montgomery, Ala., Kershaw Manufacturing Company, and Jackson-Atlantic, Inc.; president, Alabama State Chamber of Commerce; director, Southern States Industrial Council, Southern Research Institute, and National Association of Manufacturers; director, chairman of the executive committee, and treasurer of Young President's Organization; elected president of the U.S. Chamber of Commerce, 1968; appointed POSTMASTER GENERAL in the cabinet of President Richard M. Nixon on December 11, 1968; was confirmed by the Senate on January 20, 1969, and took the oath of office on January 22, 1969; served until October 29, 1971; most important contributions were filling postmaster vacancies by a merit system to end patronage, emphasizing management techniques at a regional level, and helping to initiate negotiations during the nation's first strike by postal workers in March 1970; chairman of the board and chief executive officer of Blount, Inc., Montgomery, Ala., 1974– ; trustee, University of Ala., Rhodes College; named Man of the Year, Montgomery, 1961; recipient of citation for distinguished service to City of Montgomery, 1966; National Brothers Award, National Council of

Christians and Jews, 1970; Silver Plate Award of American Business Press, 1971; nonmember award for Outstanding Achievement in Construction, The Moles, 1980. *Newsweek*, vol. 72 (December 23, 1968); *New York Times* (October 30, 1971); *International Who's Who, 1988; Who's Who in America, 1988–1989.*

BLUMENTHAL, Werner Michael. Born in Oranienburg, Germany, January 3, 1926; son of Ewald and Rose Valerie Blumenthal; Jewish ancestry; moved to San Francisco in 1947; became a naturalized citizen in 1952; obtained a B.A. degree in international economics from the University of California at Berkeley in 1951; elected to Phi Beta Kappa; obtained an M.A. in economics and an M.P.A. in public affairs from Princeton University in 1953; received his Ph.D. from Princeton in 1956; was a fellow of the Social Research Council, 1953–1954; taught economics and was a research associate at Princeton, 1954–1957; labor arbitrator of the State of New Jersey, 1955–1957; vice-president, member of the board of directors of Crown Cork International Corporation, 1957–1961; served as deputy assistant secretary of state under President John F. Kennedy., 1961–1963; served as President Lyndon B. Johnson's deputy special representative for trade negotiations with the rank of ambassador, 1963–1967; president of the New York City branch of Bendix International, 1967–1970; member of Board of Directors of Bendix, 1967–1977; named vice-chairman of the parent, Bendix Corporation, in Southfield, Mich., 1970; advanced to president and chief operating officer in 1971, and president and chief executive officer, 1972–1977; appointed SECRETARY OF THE TREASURY in the cabinet of President Jimmy Carter, and served from January 23, 1977, to July 19, 1979; member of the board of directors of the UNISYS Corporation (formerly Burroughs Corporation), 1979– ; vice-chairman and chief executive officer of UNISYS Corporation, 1980–1981; advanced to chairman and chief executive officer in 1981 and currently holds this position; member of the board of directors of Tenneco, Inc., Pillsbury Company, Chemical New York Corporation, Detroit Renaissance, New Detroit, Detroit Symphony Orchestra; vice-president and member, board of directors, of the Detroit Area Council Boy Scouts of America; Board of Directors and member of the executive committee of the United Foundation of Detroit; member of the Business Council and Business Roundtable; American Economics Association; Trustee of the Rockefeller Foundation. *Current Biography, 1977; New York Times* (July 21 and 28, 1979); *Business Week* (October 29, 1979); *International Who's Who, 1988; Who's Who in America, 1988–1989.*

BONAPARTE, Charles Joseph. Born in Baltimore, Md., June 9, 1851; son of Jerome Napoleon and Susan May (Williams) Bonaparte; grandson of Napoleon's brother Jerome; Catholic; married Ellen Channing Day on September 1, 1875; no children; graduated from Harvard Law School in 1874; began practice of law; champion of civil service reform; chairman of Civil Service Reform League until 1905; president and promoter of National Municipal League; member of executive committee of National Civic Federation; member of Board of

Indian Commissioners, 1902–1904; awarded Laetare medal by Notre Dame University; appointed SECRETARY OF THE NAVY in the cabinet of President Theodore Roosevelt on July 1, 1905 and served until December 16, 1906; most important contributions were investigation to compare U.S. naval administration with that of foreign navies, and the proposal of a bill to rectify the faults in the department; appointed ATTORNEY GENERAL by President Roosevelt on December 17, 1906 and served until March 4, 1909; most important contributions were rendering of 135 opinions and organization of a detective force of special agents; resumed practice of law in Baltimore; overseer of Harvard University; trustee of Catholic University of America at Washington, D.C.; followed Roosevelt and the Progressive party, 1912; labored to prevent rupture in the Republican party in 1916; died at "Bella Vista" near Baltimore, Md., June 28, 1921. J. B. Bishop, *Charles Joseph Bonaparte, His Life and Public Services* (1922); obituary, *Baltimore Sun* (June 29, 1921); James F. Rhodes, *McKinley and Roosevelt Administrations, 1897–1909* in *History of the United States*, vol. 9 (1922); George E. Mowry, *Era of Theodore Roosevelt, 1900–1912* (1958).

BORIE, Adolph Edward. Born in Philadelphia, Pa., November 25, 1809; son of John Joseph and Sophia (Beauveau) Borie; married Elizabeth Dundas McKean in 1839; no children; after completing the common schools, he entered the University of Pennsylvania, graduating in 1825, at the age of 16; furthered his education in Paris, France; returned to the U.S. in 1828 and entered his father's mercantile business which dealt with the silk and tea trade with Mexico, the West Indies and the Far East; upon his father's death, he inherited the business; became consul to Belgium, 1843–1848; elected president of the Bank of Commerce of Philadelphia in 1848, a position he held until his death; although a champion of Whig policies, he supported President Lincoln in 1860 and upon the outbreak of the Civil War, became an ardent Unionist; one of the founders and first president of the Union League in Philadelphia, 1862; invited to join the cabinet of President Grant as SECRETARY OF THE NAVY on March 5, 1869, entering upon his duties on March 9, 1869; finding that his business affairs needed his personal attention, he resigned on June 25, 1869; accompanied former President Grant in his tour around the world in 1877; died in Philadelphia on February 5, 1880. William Best Hesseltine, *Ulysses S. Grant, Politician* (1957); Louis Arthur Coolidge, *Ulysses S. Grant* (1917).

BOUDINOT, Elias. Born in Philadelphia, Pa., May 2, 1740; son of Elias Boudinot III, postmaster and silversmith, and Catherine (Williams) Boudinot; Episcopalian; married to Hannah Stockton, sister of Richard Stockton, a signer of the Declaration of Independence, on April 21, 1762; father of Susan Vergereau; received a classical education; studied law; admitted to the bar in 1760 and began practice in Elizabethtown, N.J.; member of the board of trustees of Princeton College 1772–1821; became member of the Committee of Correspondence for Essex County, N.J. on June 11, 1774; member of the New Jersey Provincial

Congress, 1775; member of the Committee of Safety, 1775; member of the Continental Congress in 1777, 1778, and 1781–1784; appointed by Congress on June 6, 1777 as commissary general of prisoners in the Revolutionary Army and served until 1779; elected PRESIDENT OF THE CONTINENTAL CONGRESS on November 4, 1782 and thus served until November 2, 1783; secretary of foreign affairs in the Congress, 1783–1784; signed the treaty of peace with England; resumed law practice; elected to the 1st, 2d, and 3d Congresses of the U.S., serving from March 4, 1789 to March 3, 1795, but was not a candidate for renomination in 1794; was the first counsellor named by the U.S. Supreme Court, February 5, 1790; Director of the Mint from October 1795 to July 1, 1805, when he resigned; elected first president of the American Bible Society in 1816; author of *The Age of Revelation* (1801), *Memoirs of the Life of the Reverend William Tennet* (1807), *The Second Advent* (1815), and *A Star in the West* (1816); died on October 24, 1821 in Burlington, N.J.; interment in St. Mary's Protestant Episcopal Church Cemetery. Jane J. Boudinot, *The Life, Public Services, Addresses, and Letters of Elias Boudinot* (1896); E. C. Burnett, *The Continental Congress* (1964).

BOUTWELL, George Sewall. Born in Brookline, Mass., January 28, 1818; son of Sewall and Rebecca (Marshall) Boutwell; married Sarah Adelia Thayer in 1841; attended the public schools; taught school in Shirley, Mass.; appointed postmaster of Groton in 1841; studied law sporadically, and was eventually admitted to the bar in January 1862, but never actually practiced; an active Democrat, he represented Groton in the lower house of the state legislature from 1842 to 1850; state bank commissioner, 1849–1851; elected governor of Massachusetts in 1851 and 1852 by the legislature; organizer of the state Republican party in 1855, representing its radical wing; member of the Washington, D.C. peace convention held in 1861 in an effort to prevent the impending war; first commissioner of internal revenue in 1862 and 1863; elected to the U.S. House of Representatives, 1863–1869, during which time he served on the Joint Committee on Reconstruction; helped in the framing of the Fourteenth Amendment and was a staunch advocate of the Fifteenth Amendment; one of the seven chosen to conduct the impeachment proceedings against President Andrew Johnson; appointed SECRETARY OF THE TREASURY by President Grant on March 11, 1869, and served until March 17, 1873; worked to improve the organization of the department and to reduce the national debt; on September 24, 1869, an attempt to corner the gold market was broken by his release of Treasury gold, causing the day to be called "Black Friday" by ruined speculators; served as U.S. senator from Massachusetts, 1873–1877; appointed by President Grant to codify and edit the Statutes at Large in March 1877; served as U.S. Consul to Haiti in 1885, to Hawaii in 1886, and to Chile, 1893–1894; president of the Anti-Imperialist League, 1895–1905; author of *The Constitution of the United States at the End of the First Century* (1895) and *The Crisis of the Republic* (1901); died in Groton, Mass., February 27, 1905; interment in Groton Cemetery. John Y. Simon, ed.,

The Papers of Ulysses S. Grant (1967); Louis Arthur Coolidge, *Ulysses S. Grant* (1917).

BOWEN, Otis Ray. Born in Fulton County, near Rochester, Ind., February 26, 1918; son of Vernie and Pearl (Wright) Bowen; Lutheran; married Elizabeth A. Steinmann on February 25, 1939 (deceased, January 1981); father of Richard, Judith (McGrew), Timothy, and Robert; married Rose May Hockstetler on September 26, 1981; attended Indiana University and graduated with an A.B. in chemistry in 1939; graduated with an M.D. in 1942; worked as an intern at Memorial Hospital, South Bend, Ind., 1942–1943; served up to the rank of captain in the U.S. Army Medical Corps, 1942–1946; practiced general medicine in Bremen, Ind., 1946–1972; past staff member of Bremen Community Hospital, Parkview Hospital in Plymouth, Ind., Memorial Hospital in South Bend, Ind., St. Joseph's Hospital in Mishawaka, Ind.; clinical professor of family medicine at the Indiana University School of Medicine, 1976–1985; coroner, Marshall City, Ind., 1952–1956; member of the Republican Party; member, Indiana House of Representatives, 1956–1958, 1960–1972, and minority leader, 1965–1967; speaker, 1967–1972; director of Health Services, Marshall County Civil Defense, 1959–1962; chairman, Public Health Commission, 1961–1965; chairman of special legislative commission investigation of Aid for Dependent Children program, 1963–1964; vice-chairman of legislative council of Indiana General Assembly, 1967–1968; vice-chairman of the legislative council of Indiana (General Assembly), 1967–1968, and chairman, 1970–1972; elected governor of Indiana, 1973–1981; member, Council of State Governments, 1973–1981; member of executive committee, Education Commission of States, 1973–1981, chairman-elect, 1976–1977, and chairman, 1977–1978; member, Midwest Governors Conference, 1973–1981, vice-chairman, 1977–1978, and chairman, 1978; member, Republican Governors Conference, 1973–1981, and chairman, 1978; member, National Governors Conference, 1973–1981, and chairman, 1979; past chairman of the Committee on Crime Reduction and Public Safety; past member of the President's Commission on Federal Paperwork, President's Commission on Science and Technology; member, President's Commission on Federalism, 1981–1982; member of the staff of the department of family medicine at Long Hospital in Indianapolis, 1981–1985; named to the position of SECRETARY OF HEALTH AND HUMAN SERVICES in the cabinet of President Ronald Reagan, November 7, 1985; confirmed on December 12, 1985; was critical of plans to cut back on Medicaid and other funding; was asked by President Reagan to resign along with other cabinet members, on November 10, 1988, to clear the way for the appointees of the next administration; past chairman, Interstate Mining Commission; past medical services director Marshall County Civil Defense; member, Midwest Governors Great Lakes Conference; former member, advisory commission on curricula at Vincennes University; honorary director, Center for Public Services at Anderson College; chairman, Advisory Council on Social Security, 1982; chairman, advisory council of BACCHUS, 1979–1985; contributor of numerous articles to various medical journals; past trustee, Ancilla College; trustee, Valparaiso University, 1978–1985; past member of the advisory council of the United Student Aid Fund; member, advisory board of the Indianapolis chapter of the Fellowship of Christian Athletes; member and past chairman of Lutheran School Board, Bremen; past vice-president of the congregation and past financial board chairman of St. Paul's Lutheran Church, Bremen; board of governors, Riley Memorial Association, 1981–1985; board of directors, Greater Indianapolis Council on Alcoholism, 1982–1985; Lilly Endowment Foundation; received Merit Award from Indiana Public Health Association, 1971, Presidential Citation from New York University, and Maynard K. Hine award from the Indiana Dental Association; named Alumni of the Year by Indiana University Medical School, 1971; received Distinguished Service Award from the Future Farmers of America, 1976, Public Service award from the Indiana Society of Public Administration, and George F. Hixson award from Kiwanis International, 1987; member, AMA (Dr. Benjamin Rush Award, 1973); Indiana Medical Association (legislative commission, 1958–1971, 13th District councilor, 1965–1971); 13th District Medical Association (past president); Marshall County Medical Association (past president); American General Practice Association; Indiana General Practice Association; 13th District General Practice Association; Farm Bureau; Marshall County Tb Society (past vice-president); Bremen Chamber of Commerce; American Legion; Veterans of Foreign Wars; Alpha Omega Alpha; Phi Beta Pi; Delta Chi (Delta Chi of the Year, 1987); Kiwanis. *Facts on File* (1985 and 1988); *International Who's Who, 1989.*

BOYD, Alan Stephenson. Born in Jacksonville, Fla., July 20, 1922; son of Clarence and Elizabeth (Stephenson) Boyd; married Flavil Juanita Townsend on April 3, 1943; father of Mark; attended local schools of Jacksonville; studied at University of Florida, 1939–1941; became pilot with troop transport command of U.S. Army, served 1942–1945, and was discharged with the rank of major; admitted to Virginia bar in 1947; received LL.B. from University of Virginia in 1948; admitted to Florida bar; began practice of law, and continued until 1957; made chairman of civil committee for development of aviation in Florida in 1954; chosen general counsel for Florida State Turnpike Authority in 1955; member of Florida Railroad and Public Utilities Commission in Tallahassee, and served as chairman of the board, 1957–1958; appointed member of Civil Aeronautics Board on November 11, 1959, and reappointed in 1961; chosen undersecretary of commerce in charge of transportation, 1965–1967; appointed SECRETARY OF TRANSPORTATION in the cabinet of President Lyndon B. Johnson, and served from January 16, 1967, to January 20, 1969; most important contributions were oil pollution study, proposal of highway safety rules, and urge for railroad strike bill action; became president and chief executive officer of Illinois Central Railroad and Dade County Bar Association, 1969–1976; president and chief executive officer of Amtrak, Washington, 1978–1982; chairman, Airbus Industries North America, 1982– ; also president and chief executive officer, 1986– ; trustee, Analytic Services, Inc., Arlington, Va., 1969– ; National Association of Railroad and Utilities Commissioners; Kiwanis; Florida and Dade County Bar Association; Democrat; Episcopalian. R. C. Sizemore, "Alan S. Boyd, Transportation Chief," *Electronics* (May 15, 1967); Hugh Sidney, *A Very Personal Presidency: Lyndon Johnson in the White House* (1968); *International Who's Who, 1980; Who's Who in America, 1988–1989.*

BRADFORD, William. Born in Philadelphia, Pa., September 14, 1755; son of Colonel William Bradford, printer and Revolutionary soldier, and Rachael (Budd) Bradford; Presbyterian; married Susan Vergereau Boudinot, daughter of Elias Boudinot; placed in care of clergy in Philadelphia; attended Princeton College 1769–1772; continued study for an additional year, studying theology under Dr. Witherspoon and law under Edward Shippen; wrote prose and verse modeled on Shenstone and Addison; volunteered as private in 1776, made major in brigade of General Roberdeau in 1776, later accepted a company under Colonel Hampton's command in a regiment of regulars; commissioned lieutenant colonel and made deputy quartermaster general; served two years, resigning because of poor health; April 10, 1777, elected by Congress as deputy muster-master general, ranked as colonel in the Continental Army; studied law and was admitted to bar of the Supreme Court in September 1779; appointed attorney general of Pennsylvania in August 1780, serving eleven years; served as judge of Supreme Court of Pennsylvania, 1791–1794; influenced revision of Pennsylvania criminal jurisprudence, publishing "An Inquiry into How Far the Punishment of Death is Necessary in Pennsylvania" in 1793; appointed ATTORNEY GENERAL in the cabinet of President Washington on January 28, 1794, serving until death; died August 23, 1795; interment in the Second Presbyterian Church in Philadelphia. Horace Binney Wallace, sketch in *American Law Journal* (April 1852); R. W. Griswald, *The Republican Court* (1856).

BRADY, Nicholas Frederick. Born in New York City, April 11, 1930; son of James C. Brady, a financier, and Eliot (Chase) Brady; raised in Far Hills, N.J.; married Katherine Douglas on September 5, 1952; father of Nicholas, Christopher, Anthony, and Katherine; Republican; attended St. Mark's School in Southboro, Mass.; obtained B.A. degree from Yale in 1952; received M.B.A. from Harvard in 1954; upon graduation joined Dillon, Read, and Co., an investment banking firm; appointed president of the firm in 1971; joined the family-controlled Purolator Courier Corp. in 1961 and served as chairman from 1971 until 1987; served on board of NCR Corporation; was chairman of the Jockey Club, and an official of the Augusta National Golf Club; enjoyed tennis and golf; served as chairman of the finance committee for Raymond H. Bateman's campaigns for governor of New Jersey in 1969 and 1977; cochaired the New Jersey presidential campaign of George Bush in 1980; was a Bush delegate to the Republican National Convention in Detroit in 1980; appointed to the U.S. Senate by Governor Thomas Kean of New Jersey in April 1982; resigned from the Senate in December 1982; appointed by President Ronald Reagan to the

National Bipartisan Committee on Central America in July 1983; served as chairman of the Commission on Executive, Legislative, and Judicial Salaries in 1985; chaired the commission to study the causes and impact of the stock market crash (The Brady Commission) in 1987–1988, through which he recommended reforms to curb market volatility and restore investor confidence; appointed SECRETARY OF THE TREASURY in the cabinet of President Reagan on September 15, 1988, and reappointed by President George Bush; most important contributions were opposition to higher interest rates and attempts to rectify the federal budget deficit; called for higher salaries for government officials; suggested depositor fees to assist in the bailout of the savings and loans. *The Almanac of American Politics*, 1984, 1988; *Current Biography Yearbook; Who's Who, 1988; Business Week*, (November 14, 1988).

BRANCH, John. Born in Halifax, N.C., November 4, 1782; son of Colonel John and Mary (Bradford) Branch; married first to Elizabeth Foort and upon her death, to Mrs. Eliza (Jordan) Bond; after a common education at the local schools, he entered the University of North Carolina and graduated in 1801; studied law and was admitted to the bar, but never actually engaged in a legal practice; appointed judge for the Western District of Florida by President Monroe, 1822; elected North Carolina state senator, 1811, 1813–1817, 1822, and 1834; speaker of the State Senate from 1815 to 1817; elected governor, 1817–1820; elected U.S. senator from North Carolina in 1822 and took his seat in 1823, holding same until 1829; appointed SECRETARY OF THE NAVY on March 9, 1829, joining the cabinet of President Jackson and holding office until 1831; during his secretaryship, he sought revision of the law respecting the Marine Corps, and equalization of pay; with the "reorganization" of the cabinet, due to the Eaton affair, he was forced to resign; as a mark of public confidence, he was unanimously elected to the House of Representatives in 1831 and served until 1833; a Democrat, he bolted the party in 1836 to oppose Van Buren; appointed governor of the Florida Territories by President Tyler on June 21, 1844, serving until 1845 when Florida was admitted into the Union and a governor was duly elected; died at Enfield, N.C. on January 4, 1863; interment in the family plot. James Parton, *The Presidency of Andrew Jackson* (1967); Robert V. Remini, *Andrew Jackson* (1966).

BRANNAN, Charles Franklin. Born in Denver, Colo., August 23, 1903; son of John Brannan, electrical engineer, and Ella Louise (Street) Brannan; Quaker; married Eda V. Seltzer on June 29, 1932; no children; attended public schools; graduated West High School in 1921; studied at Regis College; received LL.B. from University of Denver in 1929, was admitted to the bar, and practiced in Denver, 1929–1935; appointed assistant regional attorney of U.S. Department of Agriculture's Resettlement Administration in Denver, 1935; became regional attorney in department's office of solicitor in Denver in 1937; half-owner of cattle ranch, 1940–1948; made regional director of Farm Security Administration for Colorado, Wyoming and Montana, 1941–1944; chosen assistant secretary of agriculture under Claude R. Wickard and then Clinton P. Anderson, 1944–1948; was agricultural advisor to American delegation to United Nations Conference for International Organization in San Francisco; vice-chairman of board of directors of Commodity Credit Corporation; appointed SECRETARY OF AGRICULTURE in the cabinet of President Truman on May 29, 1948, and served from June 2, 1948 to January 20, 1953; most important contributions were introduction of price support recommendations called Brannan Plan, grain storage program, and ratification of International Wheat Agreement; advisor to Economic and Social Council of United Nations; chairman of U.S. delegation to Inter-American Conference on Agriculture, December 1950; president of University of Denver Alumni Association; member of Soil Conservation Society, Colorado Society, Sigma Alpha Epsilon, Phi Alpha Delta, and Denver, Civitan and Athletic clubs of Denver; practiced law in Denver, 1953– ; general counsel of National Farmers Union, 1953– ; president of the board of Water Commissioners, Denver, Colo., 1976; member of the board of directors of the Central Bank of Denver (Colorado), 1976; resides in Denver. Barton J. Bernstein and A. J. Matusow, *The Truman Administration: A Documentary History* (1966); *Who's Who in American Politics, 1977; Who's Who, 1989.*

BRECKINRIDGE, John. Born near Staunton, Va., December 2, 1760; son of Robert and Letitia (Preston) Breckinridge; Presbyterian; married Mary Hopkins Cabell in 1785; father of nine children; grandfather of John Cabell Breckinridge, Vice-President under Buchanan; educated at Augusta Academy (now Washington and Lee University), Lexington, Va., and at William and Mary College, Williamsburg, Va.; while still a student, he was elected to represent Botetourt County in the state legislature in 1780, but because of his youth was not permitted to take his seat; studied law and was admitted to the bar in 1785; elected to the U.S. House of Representatives in 1792, but resigned and moved to Lexington, Ky., where he developed an estate called "Cabell's Dale"; appointed state attorney general in 1795, following his defeat for U.S. Senate; elected to represent Fayette County in the lower house of the state legislature in 1798, and was reelected until 1801, acting as speaker for the last two years; elected to the U.S. Senate in 1801, resigning in 1805; invited to join the cabinet of President Jefferson as ATTORNEY GENERAL on August 7, 1805, and held that position until his death; believing that the national government was making little effort to open the Mississippi River, he looked with favor on George Rogers Clark's efforts to open navigation there, and promised a money subscription to the undertaking; died at "Cabell's Dale," near Lexington, Ky., December 14, 1806; interment in Lexington Cemetery. Stuart Gerry Brown, *Thomas Jefferson* (1963); John Dos Passos, *The Head and Heart of Thomas Jefferson* (1954).

BRECKINRIDGE, John Cabell. Born at "Cabell's Dale," near Lexington, Ky., January 21, 1821; son of Joseph Cabell and Mary Clay (Smith) Breckinridge; grandson of John Breckinridge, U.S. Attorney General under Jefferson;

Presbyterian; married Mary C. Burch in December 1843; father of five children; attended Pisgah Academy, Woodford County, Ky., continuing at Centre College, Danville, Ky., from which he graduated in 1839; studied law at the College of New Jersey (now Princeton) and at Transylvania College in Lexington, Ky., in 1840 and 1841; admitted to the bar in 1841, commencing his practice in Frankfort, Ky.; moved to Burlington, Iowa, and pursued the practice of law; returned to Kentucky, settling in Lexington in 1845; commissioned a major, he led the 3d Kentucky Volunteers into Mexico during the Mexican War; elected to the state legislature to represent Fayette County in 1849; a Democrat, he opposed the Emancipationists; elected to the U.S. House of Representatives in 1851 and served until 1855; delivered the funeral oration for Henry Clay; elected VICE-PRESIDENT under James Buchanan on March 4, 1857, and served until March 3, 1861; unsuccessful candidate for president on the Southern Democratic ticket; elected to the U.S. Senate eighteen months before his term as vice-president was to expire; an ardent Southerner, he opposed President Lincoln's entire war policy; expelled from the U.S. Senate by a resolution of that body in April 1861; when, in September 1861, Kentucky abandoned her neutrality in favor of the Union cause, he fled the state to avoid arrest; indicted for treason on November 6, 1861 in the federal district court at Frankfort, and declared a traitor by the U.S. Senate on December 2, 1861; served as brigadier general in the Confederate Army at Bowling Green, and was later made major general; fought in the battles of Vicksburg, Murfreesboro, and Jackson, Miss., in 1862 and 1863; appointed secretary of war in the cabinet of the Confederate states by Jefferson Davis in April 1865; after the Confederate surrender, he fled to Cuba and then to Europe, where he remained until 1868, when he went to Toronto, Canada; in March 1869 he was given permission by the federal government to return to Lexington, Ky., where he resumed his law practice; died in Lexington on May 17, 1875; interment in Lexington Cemetery. Philip Shriver Klein, *President James Buchanan, A Biography* (1962); Morton Garfinkle, ed., *Lincoln and the Coming of the Civil War* (1959).

BRENNAN, Peter Joseph. Born in New York City, N.Y., on May 24, 1918; son of John H. and Agnes (Moore) Brennan; Catholic; married to Josephine Brinkley; father of Peter J., Jr., Joan, and Peggy; educated in public schools; attended the College of the City of New York; enlisted in the U.S. Naval Reserve in 1944, and served on submarines in the Pacific Theatre of Operations; rose to the rank of Petty Officer, Second Class; painter; member, Local 1456, Painters, Decorators, and Paperhangers of America; business agent, Local 1456, 1947; maintenance chairman, Building and Construction Trades Council of Greater New York, 1951; president, Building and Construction Trades Council of Greater New York, 1957; vice-president, New York State AFL-CIO; member, National Advisory Committee on the Education of Disadvantaged Children; member, New York State Job Development Advisory Committee; member, Safety Advisory Committee to the New York State Labor Department; New York State Work-

men's Compensation Advisory Committee; member, Advisory Board for Prevailing Wages for Public Works in New York State; on November 29, 1972,
nominated by President Richard M. Nixon to be SECRETARY OF LABOR of the
United States, and on January 31, 1973, appointment was confirmed by the
United States Senate; was the first labor leader to be named Secretary of Labor
in twenty years; one of first acts was to force a temporary halt to the Long Island
Railroad strike that had paralyzed New York City; while Secretary of Labor,
lost much labor support because President Nixon vetoed the Minimum Wage
Bill; named to the Wage and Price Council and Economic Policy Board by
President Gerald R. Ford; in December 1974 declined an offer to become United
States Ambassador to Ireland, and on February 6, 1975, resigned as Secretary
of Labor; after leaving office, returned to New York City, and renewed his
association with the Building and Construction Trades Council of Greater New
York; president of N.Y.C. Building and Construction Trades Council, 1975;
awards from Police Athletic League, United Service Appeal, Greater New York
Fund, Veterans of Foreign Wars, John F. Kennedy Library, and Congressional
Medal of Honor Society. Henry H. Schulte, Jr., ed., *Facts on File Yearbook,
1973* (1974); Henry H. Schulte, Jr., ed., *Facts on File Yearbook, 1974*; Charles
Monaghan, ed., *Facts on File Yearbook, 1975*; Charles Moritz, ed., *Current
Biography Yearbook*, (1973); *Who's Who in American Politics, 1979–1980*.

BREWSTER, Benjamin Harris. Born in Salem County, N.J., October 13,
1816; son of Francis Enoch and Maria (Hampton) Brewster, both of colonial
stock; married Elizabeth von Myerbach de Reinfeldts in 1857; later married Mary
Walker, daughter of Robert H. Walker who was Secretary of the Treasury under
Polk, in 1870; father of one son; studied under Eli K. Price of Philadelphia;
graduated Princeton College in 1834; was admitted to the Philadelphia bar in
1838, and became a leading member; commissioner to adjudicate claims against
U.S. by Cherokee Indians, 1846; became attorney general of Pennsylvania in
1867 and 1868; was special counsel for government in Star Route Prosecution
with George Bliss, September 1881; appointed ATTORNEY GENERAL in the cabinet
of President Arthur, on December 19, 1881, and served from January 3, 1882
to March 5, 1885; was chief prosecutor in Star Route frauds of post office
department; retired to private life, 1885; died in Philadelphia, April 4, 1888.
Eugene C. Savidge, *Life of Benjamin Brewster, With Discourses and Addresses*
(1891); George F. Howe, *Chester A. Arthur: A Quarter Century of Machine
Politics* (1957).

BRINEGAR, Claude Stout. Born on December 16, 1926, in Rockport, Calif.;
son of Claude Leroy Brinegar and Lyle (Rawles) Stout Brinegar; served with
the United States Air Force, 1945–1947; attended Stanford University and received B.A. in economics, 1950, M.S. in mathematical statistics, 1951, and
Ph.D. in economics, 1954; employed as a research assistant at the Food Research
Institute in Stanford, Calif., and as an economic consultant at Emporium-Capwell

Corp. in San Francisco from 1950 to 1953; worked from 1953 to 1973 for the Union Oil Co. in California, becoming manager of economics and corporate planning in 1962 and vice-president of economics and corporate planning in 1965; between 1965 and 1968, also served as president of the Pure Oil Co. division of Union Oil Co.; subsequently served terms as president of Pure Transportation Co. (from 1966 to 1972), and of the Union 76 division in Los Angeles from 1968 to 1973, also acting as Senior Vice-President and Member of the Executive Committee of Union Oil Co.; owning twenty-five percent of the Daytona Speedway in Florida, Brinegar acted as a director of the International Speedway Corp. in Daytona Beach; also taught as an extension instructor at UCLA between 1955 and 1960 at Whittier College in 1956, and at California Institute of Technology in 1957; served on the board of directors of the Los Angeles County Mental Health Association from 1964 to 1965 and the American Petroleum Institute from 1970 to 1973; selected by President Richard M. Nixon to be his second-term SECRETARY OF TRANSPORTATION on December 1, 1972; appointment was confirmed by the Senate on January 19, 1973, amid opposition from several environmental groups because of his involvement with the oil industry; he was sworn into his position on February 2, 1973, by President Nixon. As Secretary of Transportation, he dealt directly with the increasing fuel shortages in the United States; began probes of price gouging and other fuel-related problems, and studied their effects on industry; met with trucking representatives on several occasions to urge their cooperation with such fuel-saving plans as the fifty-five-mile-per-hour speed limit; proposed a railroad reorganization program by which Congress could create a federally charted private corporation to deal with the northeastern rail crisis; signed an agreement with Soviet Civil Aviation Minister Bugayev to expand commercial air service between the United States and the Soviet Union, and flew, in April 1974, on the inaugural flight between the two nations; also dealt extensively with controversial legislation that would provide for federal funding for urban mass transit; due largely to the change from the Nixon to the Ford Administration, submitted his resignation on December 18, 1974, effective February 1, 1975; returned to the Union Oil Co., where he was elected senior vice-president and a member of the Executive Committee. *Who's Who in America*, 1976–1977; *New York Times Biographical Edition* (December 1972); *The New York Times Index*, 1972, 1973, 1974, 1975; *Newsweek* (December 18, 1972).

BRISTOW, Benjamin Helm. Born in Elkton, Ky., June 20, 1832; son of Francis M. Bristow, lawyer, politician, and member of Congress, 1854–1855 and 1858–1861, and Emily E. (Helm) Bristow; married Abbie S. Briscoe on November 21, 1854; graduated Jefferson College of Pennsylvania, 1851; studied law with father, was admitted to the bar in 1853, and went into practice with father; moved to Hopkinsville, Ky. in 1858 to practice law; helped recruit 25th Kentucky Infantry; entered military service as lieutenant colonel on September 20, 1861, fought at Fort Donelson, Fort Henry and Pittsburgh Landing; was wounded at Shiloh; rose to major general; elected state senator from Christian County in 1863, and served until his resignation in 1865; removed to Louisville and was appointed assistant U.S. attorney; became U.S. attorney for district of Kentucky on May 4, 1866, and continued in this position until his resignation, effective January 1, 1870; appointed solicitor general by President Grant in 1870, and served until his resignation on November 12, 1872; became counsel for Texas & Pacific Railroad; practiced law; appointed SECRETARY OF THE TREASURY in the cabinet of President Grant on June 2, 1874, and served from June 4, 1874 to June 20, 1876; most important contributions were abolition of office of supervising architect, dismissal of second comptroller and leading subordinates for inefficiency, pressure brought on detective force, break-up of Whiskey Ring, consolidation of many collection districts in customs and internal revenue services, and argument for resumption of specie payments; leading candidate for presidential nomination at Republican national convention in Cincinnati, Ohio in 1876; moved to New York, 1878; formed law partnership with Peet, Burnett and Opdyke in October 1878; elected second president of the American Bar Association, 1879; vice-president of Civil Service Reform Association; member of Metropolitan Union and Union League organizations; died in New York City, June 22, 1896. *Some Facts about the Life and Public Services of Benjamin H. Bristow* (1876); Ross A. Webb, *Border State Dilemma: Benjamin Helm Bristow and Kentucky Politics* (1969).

BROCK, William Emerson, III. Born in Chattanooga, Tenn., November 23, 1930; son of William Emerson, Jr., and Myra (Kruesi) Brock; Presbyterian; married Laura Handley ("Muffet") on January 1, 1957; father of William Emerson IV, Oscar Handley, John Kruesi, and Laura Hutcheson; widowed in 1985; married Sandra Schubert Mitchell on December 5, 1986; attended McCallied School (preparatory); received a B.S. in commerce from Washington and Lee University in 1953; joined the navy as an ensign in 1953; attached to the Seventh Fleet in the Far East; discharged as lieutenant (J.G.) in 1956; since 1961 has been in the Naval Reserve; joined family business in 1956, starting as assistant in the production control department; director of the company and vice-president in charge of marketing, 1961; member of the Steering Committee of the Chatanooga Area Literacy Movement, 1960–1962; director and chairman of the education committee of the Tennessee Junior Chamber of Commerce, 1961–1962; occupied a seat representing the Third Congressional Tennessee District for three terms, 1963–1971; first Republican in more than forty years to serve as representative of the third district; assigned to the Banking and Currency Committee, 1963; named to the Republican Congressional Campaign Committee for Republican candidates seeking election to the House of Representatives, 1963; U.S. Senate, 1970–1977; chairman, Republican National Committee, 1977–1981; U.S. Trade Representative, 1981–1985; named SECRETARY OF LABOR by President Ronald Reagan on March 15, 1985, and served until November 1, 1987; initiated a movement toward integration and other civic betterment organizations; favored appropriation bill for military construction; named by President Richard Nixon to speak for him on major issues; organized teams to learn the cause of student unrest in the colleges, resulting in the appointment of the Scranton Commission; approved an increase in retirement benefits for railroad workers and pay for civil service employees; chairman of the Dole for President Committee, 1987; recipient of Distinguished Service Award, Jaycees Chattanooga; decorated with the Korean Battle and United Nations Service ribbons; mediated the dispute between Texas Air and the unions; rebuilt the Republican party from top to bottom and shifted the party's financial base from big donors to small contributors. *Current Biography, 1971; Collier's Encyclopedia* (Yearbook 1985 and 1987); *International Yearbook and Statesmen's Who's Who, 1988*; Hedrick Smith, *The Power Game* (1988).

BROWN, Aaron Venable. Born in Brunswick County, Va., August 15, 1795; son of Rev. Aaron Brown, minister and justice, and Elizabeth (Melton) Brown; Methodist; married first to Sarah Burruss; father of four children; remarried to Mrs. Cynthia (Pillow) Saunders in 1845; father of one son; attended schools of North Carolina and went to Westrayville Academy in Nash County in 1810; entered the University of North Carolina in 1812, graduating in 1814; moved to Tennessee and studied law with Judge Trimble in Nashville; was admitted to the bar in 1816 and began practice in Nashville; took over law practice of Alfred M. Harris in Pulaski; went into partnership with James K. Polk in Maury County; elected to Tennessee State Senate from Lincoln and Giles counties, and served 1821–1825 and 1826–1827; chosen to represent Giles County in lower house of state legislature, 1831; elected as Democrat to the 26th, 27th and 28th Congresses (House), and served from March 4, 1839 to March 3, 1845; elected governor of Tennessee in 1845 but was denied reelection in 1847; was a member of Nashville convention of 1840 and wrote Tennessee platform; member of Democratic convention in 1852; received votes for vice-president in Cincinnati convention of 1856; appointed POSTMASTER GENERAL in the cabinet of President Buchanan, and served from March 6, 1857 to March 8, 1859; most important contributions were establishment of a shorter mail route to California via the Isthmus of Tehuantepec, overland route from Memphis to St. Louis and San Francisco, and route across continent by way of Salt Lake City; died in Washington, D.C., March 8, 1859; interment in Mount Olivet Cemetery, Nashville, Tenn. Dorothy Canfield, *The Cabinet Politician: The Postmasters General, 1829–1900* (1943); Irving Sloan, ed., *James Buchanan, 1791–1868: Chronology, Documents, Bibliographical Aids* (1968).

BROWN, Harold. Born in New York City, N.Y., on September 19, 1927; son of A. H. and Gertrude (Cohen) Brown; married to Colene Dunning McDowell, October 29, 1953; father of Deborah Ruth and Ellen Dunning; received A.B. degree from Columbia University, New York City, 1945; M.A. degree, Columbia University, 1946; Lydig Fellow, Columbia University, 1948–1949; received

Ph.D. in physics, Columbia University, 1949; doctorate in engineering, Stevens Institute of Technology, Hoboken, N.J., 1964; received LL.D. and L.I.U. degrees from Gettysburg College, Gettysburg, Pa., 1966, Occidental College, Los Angeles, Calif., 1969, and the University of California, Berkeley, 1969; research scientist, Columbia University, 1945–1950; lecturer in physics, Columbia University, 1947–1948; lecturer in physics, Stevens Institute of Technology, 1949–1950; research scientist, Radiation Laboratory, University of California, Berkeley, 1950–1952; lecturer in physics, University of California, Berkeley, 1951–1952; group leader to director, Livermore Radiation Laboratory, 1952–1961; member of board of directors for Schroders Ltd., IBM, and Times-Mirror Corporation; member, Polaris Steering Committee, 1956–1958; member, Air Force Science Advisory Board, 1956–1961; member, President's Science Advisory Committee, 1958–1961; senior science advisor, Conference on Discontinuance of Nuclear Test, 1958–1959; director, Defense Research and Engineering, United States Department of Defense, 1961–1965; United States Secretary of the Air Force, 1965–1969; National Academy of Engineering; American Physics Society; American Academy of Arts and Sciences; Phi Beta Kappa; Sigma Xi; on December 21, 1976, nominated by President-Elect Jimmy Carter, to be SECRETARY OF DEFENSE of the United States; president of California Institute of Technology, Pasadena, 1969–1977; delegate to the Strategic Arms Limitation Talks, 1969–1977; member of the executive committee, Trilateral Commission, 1973–1976; chairman, technical assessment advisory council to U.S. Congress, 1974–1977; member of the National Academy of Sciences, 1977; served as Secretary of Defense, January 23, 1977–January 20, 1981; during his term in office, a mechanical error placed U.S. forces on a false nuclear war alert for six minutes on November 9, 1979; Ph.D. chairman at the Johns Hopkins Foreign Policy Institute, School of Advanced International Studies, since 1984 (visiting professor, 1981–1984); named to study panel of mx missiles on January 3, 1982, and resigned from panel on January 21, 1982; honorary Doctorate of Science: University of Rochester, 1975; Brown University, 1977; Union of the Pacific (San Francisco), 1978; University of South Carolina, 1979; Franklin and Marshall College, 1982; Chung Ang University (Seoul, Korea), 1983; Joseph C. Wilson Award, 1976; presidential Medal of Freedom, 1981; distinguished contributions to higher education, Stony Brook Foundation, 1979; consultant and corporate director: self-employed, 1987– ; author of *Thinking about National Security: Defense and Foreign Policy in a Dangerous World* (1983). *Facts on File*, (1978 and 1982); *Who's Who in Frontiers of Science and Technology, 1985*; *Who's Who in American Politics, 1987–1988*; *Who's Who in Engineering, 1988*; *Who's Who, 1989*; *Who's Who in America, 1974–1975*; Congressional Quarterly, *Weekly Report*, Vol. 34 (December 25, 1976); Henry H. Schulte, Jr., ed., *Facts on File Yearbook 1976* (1976); *U.S. News & World Report* (January 10, 1977).

BROWN, Walter Folger. Born in Massillon, Ohio, May 31, 1869; son of James Marshal and Lavinia (Folger) Brown; married Katharin Hafer on September 10, 1903; after completing his preliminary education, he entered Harvard, graduating with an A.B.; entered Harvard Law School, graduating in 1894; began law practice in Toledo, Ohio, working for his father's law firm, 1894–1905; became a leader of the Ohio state Republican party; appointed chairman of the Congressional Joint Committee on Reorganization and special representative of President Harding to study the machinery of the federal government, 1921–1924; appointed assistant secretary of commerce by President Coolidge, serving from November 2, 1927 to March 4, 1929; joined the cabinet of President Hoover as POSTMASTER GENERAL on March 5, 1929, entering upon his duties the following day and serving until March 3, 1933; during his incumbency, he gave stimulus to the growth and modernization of commercial aviation in the U.S. by awarding long-term air-mail contracts to the most efficient airlines; upon his political retirement, he resumed the practice of law in Toledo; director of National Can Co. and Toledo Trust Co.; president of the Toledo Humane Society; chairman of the trustees of the Lucas County Child Welfare Board; died in Toledo, Ohio, January 26, 1961. Eugene Lyons, *The Herbert Hoover Story* (1959); Ray Lyman Wilbur, *The Hoover Policies* (1937).

BROWNELL, Herbert, Jr. Born in Peru, Neb., February 20, 1904; son of Herbert Brownell, college professor, and May Adeline (Miller) Brownell; Methodist; married Doris A. McCarter on June 16, 1934; father of Joan, Ann, Thomas McCarter, and James Barker; attended public schools in Lincoln, Neb.; went to Lincoln High School, graduating in 1920; received B.A. from University of Nebraska, 1924; taught journalism at Done College in 1924; received LL.B. from Yale, 1927, and was admitted to New York bar in 1928; practiced law with Root, Clark, Buckner, and Ballantine of New York City, 1927–1929; associated with Lord, Day, & Lord of New York City, 1929–1932; unsuccessful candidate for State Assembly in 1931; elected New York state assemblyman for 10th District of Manhattan in 1932, was reelected five times and served from 1933 to 1937; managed Dewey's campaign for governor in 1942 and his presidential campaigns in 1944 and 1948; national chairman of Republican party, 1944–1946; played prominent part in 1952 campaign; appointed ATTORNEY GENERAL in the cabinet of President Eisenhower, serving from January 21, 1953 to January 26, 1958; most important contributions were practice of recommendation of judicial appointments after candidates passed by American Bar Association, establishment of civil rights division run by assistant attorney general, Internal Security Division, abolition of salaried witnesses; after leaving the cabinet, returned to the practice of law; member of American Bar Association, American Law Institute, New York State Bar Association, Association of the Bar of the City of New York; chairman of the Commission on International Rules of Judicial Procedure, 1958–1959; president of the Association of the Bar of the City of New York, 1962–1964; president of the American Judicature Society, 1966–1968; president of the Study of the Colorado River, 1973– ; attorney at Lord, Day, and Lord, 1957–1977, legal counsel, 1976– . David A. Frier, *Conflict of Interest in the Eisenhower Administration* (1959); Dean Albertson, ed., *Eisen-*

hower as President (1963); *International Who's Who, 1982–1983; Who's Who in American Politics, 1987–1988; Who's Who in America, 1988–1989.*

BROWNING, Orville Hickman. Born in Cynthiana, Ky., February 10, 1806; son of Micaijah and Sally (Brown) Browning; married Eliza Caldwell in 1836; attended Augusta College; studied law in Cynthiana; was admitted to the bar in 1831, settled in Quincy, Ill. and began practice; served in Illinois Volunteers in Black Hawk War of 1832; elected to state senate as a Whig in 1836, and served until 1843; elected to the lower house in the General Assembly, 1842; ran for Congress in 1843, 1850 and 1852 and was defeated; delegate to anti-Nebraska convention at Bloomington, Ill. to help form Republican party and write platform, May 29, 1856; member of state delegation to Republican convention of 1860; appointed Republican senator to fill unexpired term of Stephen A. Douglas, and served from June 26, 1861 to January 12, 1863; returned to Washington to establish law practice with Thomas Ewing, ex-Senator Cowan and Britton Hill in 1863; supported Andrew Johnson; became Johnson's advisor on Illinois patronage in May of 1866; was active in Philadelphia Convention; appointed SEC-RETARY OF THE INTERIOR in the cabinet of President Johnson on July 27, 1866, and served from September 1, 1866 to March 3, 1869; served as ATTORNEY GENERAL *ad interim*, March 13, 1868 to July 14, 1868 under Johnson; stood with Johnson through impeachment trials; elected on Democratic ticket to state constitutional convention, 1869–1870; became one of special attorneys for Chicago, Burlington and Quincy; returned to law; died in Quincy, Ill., on August 10, 1881. *Chicago Daily Tribune* (August 12, 1881); Lately Thomas, *First President Johnson* (1968).

BRYAN, William Jennings. Born in Salem, Ill., March 19, 1860; son of Silas Lillard Bryan, judge of circuit court, and Mary Elizabeth (Jennings) Bryan; Presbyterian; married Mary Baird on October 1, 1884; father of William Jennings, Jr., Ruth, and Grace; attended local schools and Whipple Academy in Jacksonville, Ill.; graduated from Illinois College in 1881; graduated from Union College of Law in Chicago, 1883; practiced law in Jacksonville, 1883–1887; moved to Lincoln, Neb., 1887; elected to the 52d Congress (House) on the Democratic ticket in 1891, and served two consecutive terms; defeated as a candidate for senator in 1894; retired temporarily from politics to become editor of the *Omaha World-Herald*; returned to politics as a delegate to the Democratic national convention of 1896, and there spoke out strongly for bimetallism in his famous "Cross of Gold" speech; was subsequently nominated to run for president against McKinley; in May 1898, he raised the 3d Regiment of the Nebraska Volunteer Infantry for the Spanish-American War, becoming its colonel; nominated for president in 1900 by the Democratic, Populist, and Silver Republican parties, campaigning on a platform of anti-imperialism, but was defeated again by McKinley; returned to journalism, establishing in Lincoln, Neb., a political newspaper expressing his views, called *The Commoner*; nominated in 1908 for the presidency at the Democratic national convention in Denver, and ran on a platform of political reforms and measures for governmental regulation of business, but was defeated by Taft; appointed SECRETARY OF STATE in the cabinet of President Wilson on March 5, 1913; most important contributions were the negotiation of thirty treaties with foreign governments to attempt peaceful solutions to any disputes, improvement of relations with Latin America by repudiating "dollar diplomacy," signing a treaty with Colombia in April 1914 to end the Panama dispute, and opposing the preferential treatment of American commerce through the Panama Canal; opposed anything except strict neutrality in European affairs, and thus resigned from office on June 8, 1915 to protest the firm stand against Germany taken by Wilson in the second "*Lusitania* note''; became active in prohibition and women's suffrage efforts; president of the National Dry Federation in 1918; in 1924, drafted the text of a resolution passed by the Florida legislature declaring it subversive to teach Darwinism; enlisted as counsel for Tennessee in the Scopes "Monkey Trial"; died on July 26, 1925 at Winchester, Tenn., near Dayton, the scene of the trial. *National Cyclopedia of American Biography*, vol. 19 (1926); Joseph Fuller, "William Jennings Bryan," in S. F. Bemis, *The American Secretaries of State*, vol. 10 (1928); *Dictionary of American Biography*, vol. 2 (1929); M. R. Werner, *Bryan* (1929); *Who Was Who in America*, vol. 1 (1943).

BUCHANAN, James. Born at Cove Gap, near Mercersburg, Pa., April 23, 1791; son of James and Elizabeth (Speer) Buchanan; bachelor; moved to Mercersburg with his family in 1799; was privately tutored and then attended the village academy; entered Dickinson College, Carlisle, Pa., graduating in 1809; studied law and was admitted to the bar in 1812, commencing his practice in Lancaster, Pa.; one of the first volunteers in the War of 1812, serving in a company of dragoons; elected a member of the Pennsylvania House of Representatives as a Federalist in 1814 and 1815; unsuccessful candidate for election in 1818 to the 16th Congress; elected to the 17th Congress (House) and to the four succeeding Congresses, serving from March 4, 1821 to March 3, 1831; one of the managers appointed by the House of Representatives to conduct the impeachment proceedings against James H. Peck, judge of the U.S. District Court of Missouri; minister to Russia from June 1832 to August 1834; elected as a Democrat to the U.S. Senate in 1835 and reelected in 1837 and 1843, resigning on March 5, 1845 to accept a cabinet portfolio; appointed SECRETARY OF STATE by President Polk on March 6, 1845, serving until March 7, 1849; while secretary, he sent a note to Mexico which held that the annexation of Texas must be considered as an accomplished fact, following up the note by sending troops to Texas and a minister (John Slidell) to Mexico who was instructed to refuse negotiations of the Texas boundary; prompted President Polk to restate the Monroe Doctrine, intended to discourage British designs in California and British acquisitions in Yucatan; envoy extraordinary and minister plenipotentiary to Great Britain from 1853 to 1856; elected PRESIDENT of the

U.S. in November 1856 on the Democratic ticket, serving from March 4, 1857 to March 3, 1861; arrayed himself on the side of the pro-slavery advocates, opposing the Wilmot Proviso and the anti-slavery movements generally; died in Wheatland, near Lancaster, Pa., on June 1, 1868; interment in Woodward Hill Cemetery, Lancaster, Pa. Philip Shriver Klein, *President James Buchanan, A Biography* (1962); Charles Allan McCoy, *Polk and the Presidency* (1960).

BURLESON, Albert Sidney. Born in San Marcos, Tex., June 7, 1863; son of Edward Burleson, veteran of the Mexican War and major in the Confederate army, and Emma (Kyle) Burleson; married Adele Steiner on December 22, 1889; father of Laura, Lucy, and Adele; attended public schools and the Coronal Institute of San Marcos; attended the Texas Agricultural and Mechanical College, College Station, Tex.; graduated Baylor University at Waco in 1881; graduated the University of Texas with law degree in 1884; admitted to the bar in 1885 and began practice in Austin, Tex.; assistant city attorney, 1885–1890; district attorney for 26th judicial district of Texas, 1891–1898; elected as a Democrat to the 56th and to seven succeeding Congresses (House) retaining his seat for fourteen years, 1899–1913, and serving on the appropriations, agriculture, foreign affairs, and census committees; resigned to accept the appointment of POST-MASTER GENERAL on March 4, 1913 in the cabinet of President Wilson; most important contributions were expansion of postal savings system, rural mail service, and parcel post system, bringing the department out of deficit, adjusting railway mail rates, initiation of air mail service, motorizing many postal operations, urging public ownership of telephone and telegraph, and banning from the mail publications critical of the administration, under authority of wartime statutes; left office with the outgoing administration on March 4, 1921 and retired from public life; chairman of the U.S. Telegraph and Telephone Administration in 1918; chairman of the U.S. Commission to the International Wire Communication Conference in 1920; returned to Austin, Texas and engaged in banking; also interested in agriculture pursuits and the raising of livestock; died in Austin on November 24, 1937; interment in Oakwood Cemetery. Zechariah Chafee, Jr., *Free Speech in the U.S.* (1941); Arthur S. Link, *Woodrow Wilson: The New Freedom* (1956), *Woodrow Wilson: The Struggle for Neutrality, 1914–1915* (1960), and *Woodrow Wilson: Confusions and Crises, 1915–1916* (1964).

BURNLEY, James Horace, IV. Born in High Point, N.C., July 30, 1948; son of James Horace III and Dorothy Mary (Rockwell) Burnley; Baptist, married to Jane Nady; father of Jay and Anne; B.A., magna cum laude, Yale University, 1970; J.D., Harvard University, 1973; Associate with Brooks, Pierce, Mc-Lendon, Humphrey, and Leonard, 1973–1975; partner with Turner, Enochs, Foster, Sparrow, and Burnley, 1975–1981; director, VISTA, 1981–1982; associate deputy attorney general, Department of Justice, 1982–1983; general counsel, Department of Transportation, 1983; deputy secretary, Department of Transportation, 1983–1987; nominated by President Ronald Reagan to be SEC-

RETARY OF TRANSPORTATION on October 8, 1987; confirmed on November 30, 1987; sworn in on December 3, 1987; as secretary, he was a strong advocate of the deregulation policies of the administration; also worked to improve air safety conditions by imposing random drug testing on transportation workers in the private sector; intensified regulations regarding airline security procedures; worked to reform the Federal Aviation Administration; served until the completion of Reagan's second term; resigned on January 20, 1989. *New York Times* (October 9, October 10, and November 27, 1987); *Facts on File Yearbook* (1987 and 1988); *Who's Who in America: 1988–1989*.

BURR, Aaron. Born on February 6, 1756 in Newark, N.J.; son of Aaron Burr, a scholar, theologian and second president of the College of New Jersey, and Esther (Edwards) Burr, daughter of Jonathan Edwards, the famous New England theologian; Presbyterian; married Mrs. Theodosia (Bartow) Prevost in 1872; father of Theodosia; second marriage in July 1833 to Mrs. Eliza Jumel; received early education by private tutors; entered the sophomore class of the College of New Jersey (now Princeton) at age 13 in 1769 and graduated in 1772; studied theology for a short while but turned quickly to law in 1774; entered the Continental Army in 1775; fought in battles at Quebec, Monmouth and New Haven; resigned from the army on March 10, 1779; in ill health, he studied law at Raritan, New Jersey in 1780; obtained license as attorney and counselor-at-law on April 17, 1782; moved to New York in 1783; appointed member of the New York state legislature in 1784; appointed attorney general of New York state by Governor George Clinton in 1789 and 1790; elected to the U.S. Senate and served from March 4, 1791 to March 3, 1797; not reelected to the Senate in 1797; presided at state constitutional convention in 1801; elected VICE-PRESIDENT under Jefferson and served from March 4, 1801 to March 3, 1805; challenged and killed Alexander Hamilton in a duel at Weehauken, N.J., July 7, 1804, as a result of a lasting enmity that existed in contests for the Senate, presidency, and governorships; fled to South Carolina when accused of murder; returned to Washington and completed his term as vice-president; accused of treason in August 1807 for trying to begin and head a republic in the Southwest; was acquitted and went abroad in 1808, returning in 1812; continued his law practice in New York City in 1812; died in Port Richmond, Staten Island, N.Y., September 14, 1836; interment in the President's lot, Princeton Cemetery, Princeton, N.J. Matthew L. Davis, ed., *Memoirs of Aaron Burr* (1836–37); S. H. Wandell and Meade Minnegerode, *Aaron Burr* (1925); Thomas P. Abernethy, *The Burr Conspiracy* (1954).

BUSH, George Herbert Walker. Born in Milton, Mass., June 12, 1924; son of Prescott Sheldon Bush, banker and senator, and Dorothy (Walker) Bush; Episcopalian; married Barbara Pierce on January 6, 1945; father of George W., John E., Neil M., Marvin P., and Dorothy W.; received his preliminary education at the Greenwich Country Day School (Conn.) and Phillips Academy, Andover,

Mass.; graduated with a B.A. in economics from Yale University in 1948; belonged to Phi Beta Kappa and Delta Kappa Epsilon; received numerous honorary degrees from U.S. colleges and universities: Adelphi University, Austin College, Allegheny College, and Beaver College; enlisted as ensign in the naval reserves during World War II in 1942, released as lieutenant in 1945, the youngest commissioned pilot in the navy at that time; supply salesman, Dresser Industries, Midland, Tex., 1948–1950; cofounder of the Bush-Overby Development Co., Houston, Tex., 1951–1953; cofounder and director of Zapata Petroleum Corporation, 1953–1959; founder and president of Zapata Off-Shore Co., Houston, Tex., 1954–1964; chairman of the board of Zapata Off-Shore Co., 1964–1966; chairman, Republican party, Harris County, Tex.; 1963–1964; defeated in Texas Senate race by Ralph W. Yarborough on November 4, 1964; delegate to the Republican national convention, 1964 and 1968; elected to House of Representatives, from Seventh District in Houston, Tex., on November 8, 1966, and reelected 1968; representative from Texas, ninetieth and ninety-first congresses, January 3, 1967–January 3, 1971; defeated in Texas Senate race by Lloyd M. Bentsen, Jr., 1970; appointed U.S. ambassador to the United Nations on December 11, 1970, and served 1971–1973; chairman of the Republican National Committee, 1973–1974; U.S. Liaison Officer for the People's Republic of China, 1974–1975; director of the U.S. Central Intelligence Agency, 1976–1977; chairman of the executive committee, First International Bank, Houston, Tex., 1977–1979; director of Eli Lilly Co., Texasgulf Inc., Purolator Inc., and First International Bancshares, Dallas, Tex., 1977–1979; adjunct professor at Rice University, 1977–1980; candidate for the Republican nomination for president in 1979 and withdrew from the race in May 1980; nominated for Vice-President at the Republican national convention on July 17, 1980; sworn in as the forty-third VICE-PRESIDENT OF THE UNITED STATES on January 20, 1981; became chairman of the Presidential Task Force on Regulatory Relief in 1981; named chairman of the administration's Special Situation Group, March 1981; became chairman of the task force to study problems dealing with immigration, crime, and drug smuggling in January 1982; won reelection as VICE-PRESIDENT on November 6, 1984; inaugurated on January 20, 1985; for a few hours during President Reagan's cancer surgery became the first stand-in president under the twenty-fifth Amendment on July 13, 1985; during his vice-presidency he traveled to seventy-three foreign countries, of which his Soviet Union trips in 1982 and February 1984 were most important; the first trip was made on the occasion of Leonid Brezhnev's death and the second trip on the death of his successor, Yuri Andropov; the most crucial event that George Bush had to face was the Iran-Contra scandal which did not prevent him from entering the presidential race; became a candidate for the Republican nomination for president in 1988, running against Michael Dukakis; the Bush campaign emphasized the need for peace and prosperity, and, most important, continuing friendly relations with the Soviet Union; elected PRESIDENT OF THE UNITED STATES on November 8, 1988; inaugurated as the forty-first president of the United States on January 20, 1989;

wants to be known as the education president; member of Trilateral Commission; received numerous awards, including Award of Distinguished Flying Cross, three Air Medals, National Security Medal, and the National Intelligence Service Medal; author of *Looking Forward* (1987). Joseph Nathan Kane, *Facts about the Presidents* (1981); *Current Biography, 1983*; *Business Week* (August 22, 1988); *Federal Staff Directory, 1988; Who's Who, 1989*.

BUTLER, Benjamin Franklin. Born in Kinderhook Landing (Stuyvesant), N.Y., Dec. 17, 1795; son of Medad Butler, mechanic and merchant, and Hannah (Tylee) Butler; descendant of Oliver Cromwell; Presbyterian; married Harriet Allen in 1818; father of Blanche; attended district school and Hudson Academy; studied law, was admitted to the Albany, N.Y. bar in 1817, and began practice in partnership with Martin Van Buren in Albany; became district attorney of Albany, 1821–1824; was associated with John Duer and John C. Spenser on commission for revision of New York state statutes, in 1825; member of state legislature, 1827–1833; declined appointment to state Supreme Court; appointed ATTORNEY GENERAL in the cabinet of President Jackson on November 15, 1833, continued under Van Buren, and served from November 18, 1833 to August 31, 1838; served as SECRETARY OF WAR in the cabinet of President Jackson in the interim of October 6, 1836 to March 3, 1837; U.S. attorney for southern district of New York, 1838–1841 and 1845–1848; toured Europe, 1858; died in Paris, France, on November 8, 1858; interment in New York City. L.B. Proctor, *Bench and Bar of New York* (1870); Ronald Shaw, *Andrew Jackson, 1767–1845: Chronology, Documents, Bibliographical Aids* (1969).

BUTZ, Earl Lauer. Born in Albion, Ind., July 3, 1909; son of Herman Lee, a farmer, and Ada Tillie (Lower) Butz; two brothers, Verlo R. and Dale E., and two sisters, Mrs. Ruth E. Buffenbarger and Mrs. Marie M. Howard; Lutheran; married Mary Emma Powell, December 22, 1937; two children, William Powell and Thomas Earl; grew up on his family's farm and later studied animal husbandry and agricultural economics at Purdue; while in graduate school he was a research fellow with the Federal Land Bank of Louisville, Ky., which extends credit to farmers for the purchase of land, and he wrote his doctoral dissertation on the Federal land bank system; between 1942 and 1951 did research for the Brookings Institution in Washington, D.C., and during that period published the books *The Production Credit System for Farmers* (1944) and *Price Fixings for Food Stuffs* (1952) and the pamphlets *Seasonal Variation of Food Farm Prices* (1942) and *Veal Calf Prices in Indiana* (1944); B.S.A. degree, Purdue, 1932; Ph.D., 1937; assistant professor, Purdue, 1937–1939; associate professor, 1939–1943; professor, 1943–1946; dean of the School of Agriculture, 1946–1954 and 1957–1967; Assistant Secretary of Agriculture, 1954–1957; unsuccessful bid for Republican gubernatorial nomination in Indiana, 1968; dean of School of Continuing Education and vice-president of Purdue Research Foundation, 1968–1971; director of Standard Life Insurance, 1951–1971; Ralston Purina Co., 1958–

1971; International Minerals and Chemical, 1960–1971; Stokely-Van Camp Co., 1969–1971; member of White House Task Force for Foreign Economic Development, 1969–1970; American Farm Economics Association (vice-president, 1948, secretary, 1953–1954); various other farm and agricultural societies; SECRETARY OF AGRICULTURE, December 8, 1971, to October 4, 1976; resigned Cabinet post after receiving criticism and a presidential reprimand for a remark he made in reference to Negroes. Chairman, U.S. delegation to the Food and Agriculture Organization, Rome, Italy, 1972–1976; delegate to the World Food Conference, 1974; professor, Purdue Research Foundation, 1976– ; delegate, Republican national convention, 1976; pleaded guilty to tax evasion on May 22, 1981, and sentenced and fined on June 19, 1981; counsellor to the president for natural resources, January 1983–May 1983. *Current Biography, 1972; Who's Who in America, 1976; Facts on File* (October 9, 1976); *New York Times* (October 5, 1976); *Facts on File, 1981; International Who's Who, 1982–1983; Who's Who in American Politics, 1987–1988.*

BYRNES, James Francis. Born in Charleston, S.C., May 2, 1879; posthumous son of James F. Byrnes, planter, and Elizabeth E. (McSweeney) Byrnes; Episcopalian; married Maud (Busch) Perkins on May 2, 1906; attended St. Patrick's Parochial School in Charleston; became clerk in law firm of Mordecai and Gadsden at the age of 14; studied under Judge Benjamin H. Rutledge; became court stenographer in 2d Circuit Court of South Carolina; moved to Aiken, and studied law in his spare time; was admitted to South Carolina bar in 1903; began practice of law; bought Aiken *Journal and Review*, and was editor from 1903 to 1907; elected solicitor of South Carolina 2d Judicial Court, 1908; chosen member of U.S. House of Representatives, was reelected six times, and served from 1911 to 1925; was unsuccessful candidate for U.S. Senate in 1924; practiced law with Nichols, Wyche, and Byrnes in Spartanburg; elected member of the U.S. Senate in 1930 and reelected in 1936; made associate justice of Supreme Court, 1941, and served until 1942; became director of economic stabilization in October 1942; headed War Mobilization Board from May 28, 1943 to April 1945; contender for vice-presidency, 1944; accompanied President Franklin D. Roosevelt to Yalta Big Three Conference, 1945; appointed SECRETARY OF STATE in the cabinet of President Truman on July 2, 1945, and served from July 3, 1945 to January 7, 1947; most important contributions were formulation of peace plans, formulation of United Nations Atomic Energy Commission, and Stuttgart speech urging self-sufficient, democratic German state; wrote *Speaking Frankly* in 1947; practiced law with Hogan and Hartson in Washington, D.C.; elected governor of South Carolina, 1950–1955; member of Masons, Shriners and Knights of Pythias; died on April 9, 1972. Deane and David Heller, *Paths of Diplomacy* (1967).

C

CALHOUN, John C. Born in Abbeville District, S.C., March 18, 1782; son of Patrick and Martha (Caldwell) Calhoun; Presbyterian; married Floride Bonneau Calhoun, a cousin, in January 1811; father of nine children; schooled under his brother-in-law, Moses Waddel, in Columbia County, Ga. until 1796; entered Yale in 1802, graduating September 12, 1804; studied law in Abbeville, S.C. and in Litchfield, Conn. at Tapping Reeves' School, 1805–1806; apprenticed in the offices of Henry W. De Saussure in Charleston, S.C.; admitted to the bar in 1807, opening an office in Abbeville, S.C.; elected to the South Carolina legislature in 1808; elected to the U.S. Congress (House), 1811–1817, presenting a report on June 3, 1812 recommending war with England; although Monroe was the author, Calhoun gained the credit; backed the Treaty of Ghent, but in a January 31, 1816 speech, advocated build-up of arms; advocated a national bank and a protective tariff for internal improvement; appointed SECRETARY OF WAR in the cabinet of President Monroe, October 8, 1817, entering duties December 10, 1817, serving until March 7, 1825; as Secretary, he was concerned with reforming the department, with the West, with Indian affairs, and with building national roads; elected VICE-PRESIDENT under John Q. Adams in 1824, reelected in 1828 on Andrew Jackson's ticket; defeated the Woolens Bill by his vote in 1827, which marked his switch towards opposing protective tariffs; in August 1831 he published a letter to Governor Hamilton stating the nullification doctrine, whereby a state convention had the power to declare a Congressional act null within the state; this prompted South Carolina to nullify the 1828 and 1832 tariff acts; resigned the vice-presidency on December 28, 1832, to voice the nullification doctrine from the Senate floor, being seated January 4, 1833; appointed SECRETARY OF STATE in the cabinet of President Tyler on March 6, 1844, and served until March 6, 1845; in office he praised slavery and stated that abolition in Texas would affect other states; anti-slavery votes defeated the treaty these sentiments were aimed at; signed the April 12, 1844 Treaty of Annexation which proposed that the Republic of Texas become a U.S. territory and was defeated by more than a two-thirds vote on June 8, 1844, having been opposed by Clay and Van Buren in the "Hammett letter"; attempted and failed in negotiations with Mexico under Santa Anna to assure recognition of Texas; opposed English interests in Texas abolition; began negotiations with Britain over boundary rights to the Columbian basin and Oregon concluded under James Buchanan; retired from the cabinet in 1845, becoming involved in railroad affairs; replaced D. F. Huger in the U.S. Senate, 1845–1850; died in Washington D.C. on March 31, 1850; his last words were, "the South, the poor South"; carried in state to Charleston; interment in Saint Philips Churchyard, Charleston, S.C. Samuel Flagg Bemis, *The American Secretaries of State and Their Diplomacy* (1958); Gerald Mortimer Capers, *John C. Calhoun, Opportunist: A Reappraisal* (1960); Richard Nelson Current, *John C. Calhoun* (1963).

CALIFANO, Joseph Anthony, Jr. Born in Brooklyn, N.Y., May 15, 1931; son of Joseph Anthony and Katherine (Gill); married to Gertrude Zawacki, July 4, 1955; father of Mark Gerard, Joseph Anthony, III, and Claudia Francis; received A.B. degree, Holy Cross College, Worcester, Mass., 1952; LL.D. degree, Harvard University, Cambridge, Mass., 1955; admitted to the New York bar, 1955; served in the United States Naval Reserve, 1955–1958, attaining the rank of lieutenant; employed with Dewey, Ballantine, Busby, Palmer and Wood Law Firm, New York City, 1958–1961; special assistant to General Counsel, United States Department of Defense, 1961–1962; special assistant to the Secretary of the Army, 1963–1964; special assistant to the Secretary of Defense and Deputy Secretary of Defense, 1964–1965; special assistant to the President, 1965–1969; member, Arnold and Porter law firm, Washington, D.C., 1969–1971; general counsel, Democratic National Committee, 1970–1972; became partner in Williams, Connolly, and Califano Law Firm, Washington, D.C., 1971; Distinguished Civilian Service Award, Department of the Army, 1964; Man of the Year Award, Justinian Society of Lawyers, 1966; one of Ten Outstanding Young Men of America, 1966; American Federation, District of Columbia, Bar Associations; American Judicature Society; author of *The Student Revolution: A Global Confrontation* (1969); Democrat; on December 23, 1976, was nominated by President-Elect Jimmy Carter to be SECRETARY OF HEALTH, EDUCATION, AND WELFARE of the United States; partner at Williams, Connolly, and Califano, Washington, 1971–1976 (law practice); sworn in as Secretary of Health, Education, and Welfare on January 25, 1977 and fired on July 19, 1979; separated from wife Trudy Califano on January 19, 1979; partner at Califano, Ross, and Heineman, Washington, 1980–1982 (law practice); named to serve on House Ethics Committee on July 26, 1982; partner at Dewey, Ballantine, Bushby, Palmer, and Wood, 1983– (law practice); author of *A Presidential Nation* (with H. Simons, 1975); *Media and the Law* (with H. Simons, 1976); *The Media and*

Business (1978); *Governing America: An Insider's Report from the White House and the Cabinet* (1982); *Report on Drug Abuse and Alcoholism* (1982); *America's Health Care Revolution: Who Lives? Who Dies? Who Pays?* (1986). *Who's Who in America, 1974–1975*; Congressional Quarterly, *Weekly Report*, Vol. 34 (December 26, 1976); *Time* (December 27, 1976); *U.S. News & World Report* (January 10, 1977); *Facts on File, 1979*; *Who's Who in American Politics, 1987–1988*; *Who's Who in America, 1988–1989*; *The Writer's Directory, 1988–1989*.

CAMERON, James Donald. Born in Middletown, Pa., March 14, 1833; son of Simon Cameron, Secretary of War under Lincoln, and Margaret (Brua) Cameron; Catholic; married Mary McCormick; later married Elizabeth Sherman in 1878; graduated Princeton in 1852; returned to native town and began business career; became clerk in father's Bank of Middletown and was soon promoted through the ranks to become president; active in forwarding Union troops over "Cameron Road"; was president of Northern Central Railroad Company, 1863–1874; appointed SECRETARY OF WAR in the cabinet of President Grant on May 22, 1876, and served from June 1, 1876 to March 12, 1877; criticized for using office to political ends by putting federal troops at the disposal of Republican politicians of Florida and Louisiana to enhance Hayes' chances of winning electoral votes; elected as Republican member of U.S. Senate to fill unexpired term of father on March 5, 1877; was reelected in 1879, 1885 and 1891, and served in all from March 20, 1877 to March 3, 1897; chairman of Republican national committee, 1879; retired; died in Lancaster County, Pa., on August 30, 1918; interment in Harrisburg Cemetery, Harrisburg, Pa. Alexander K. McClure, *Old Time Notes of Pennsylvania* (1905); Charles R. Williams, *Life of Rutherford B. Hayes* (1914); Allan Nevins, *Hamilton Fish: The Inner History of the Grant Administration* (n.d.).

CAMERON, Simon. Born in Maytown, Pa., March 8, 1799; son of Charles and Martha (Pfoutz) Cameron; married Margaret Brua; father of James Donald Cameron, Secretary of War under Grant, and four other children; became apprentice for a printing firm in Harrisburg at the age of 10; edited *Bucks County Messenger* in Doylestown, Pa. in 1821, and when paper merged with *Doylestown Democrat* to become *Bucks County Democrat*, returned to Harrisburg; became management partner in the *Pennsylvania Intelligence* with Charles Mowry, 1821; went to Washington to study national political movements, 1822, and worked in printing house of Gales and Seaton printing Congressional debates; returned to Harrisburg and the *Republican*, 1824; was made adjutant general of the state in 1826; became contractor for construction of canals and began what was later to become the Northern Central Railroad; supported Jackson in 1830; aided Van Buren in 1832; set up Bank of Middletown in 1832; entered the iron business; appointed commissioner to settle claims of Winnebago Indians in 1838; elected as a Whig, Native American, and Protectionist Democrat member of U.S. Senate to fill vacancy caused by resignation of James Buchanan, acted with Democratic party, and served from March 13, 1845 to March 3, 1849; defeated in senatorial reelections of 1849 and 1855; supported Republican Fremont in 1856; reelected to U.S. Senate, and served from March 4, 1857 to March 4, 1861, when he resigned to become SECRETARY OF WAR; was candidate for presidential nomination at Republican national convention of 1860, and lost vice-presidential nomination; appointed SECRETARY OF WAR in the cabinet of President Lincoln on March 5, 1861, and served from March 11, 1861 to January 14, 1862; most important aspects were criticisms for mismanagement of the department which bred much corruption and advocation of freeing and arming slaves; organized Union forces for field duty; served as minister to Russia from January 1862 to November 8, 1863; unsuccessful candidate for Senate, 1863; was delegate to Republican national convention of 1864 in Baltimore; delegate to Loyalists' convention at Philadelphia in 1866; chosen U.S. senator in 1867, was reelected in 1873, and served from March 4, 1867 until resignation on March 12, 1877; retired to farm in Donegal Springs, 1877; traveled through Europe and the West Indies; died near Maytown, Pa., on June 26, 1889; interment in Harrisburg Cemetery, Harrisburg, Pennsylvania. Erwin Bradley, *Simon Cameron: Lincoln's Secretary of War* (1965).

CAMPBELL, George Washington. Born in the Parish of Tongue in the Shire of Sutherland, Scotland on February 8, 1768; son of Archibald Campbell, physician, and Elizabeth (Mackay) Campbell; in 1812, married Harriet Stoddert, daughter of Benjamin Stoddert; father of four children; family migrated to Mecklenburg County, N.C.; graduated Princeton with high honors 1794; studied law and began practice in Knoxville, Tenn.; elected to Congress (House) in 1803, serving until 1809, during which period, acted as chairman of the Ways and Means Committee, supported Jefferson's administration; dueled with B. Gardenier, who claimed the House of Representatives was under French influence; served on Tennessee Supreme Court of Errors and Appeals, 1809–1811; elected to U.S. Senate as an advocate of war with England, serving 1811–1814; introduced Secretary Armstrong's letter proposing military alternatives such as increasing the bounty, and suggesting a conscripted militia; appointed SECRETARY OF THE TREASURY in the cabinet of President Madison on February 9, 1814, serving until his resignation on September 4, 1814 due to ill health; as secretary he arranged to borrow funds in Europe through Astor, believed along with Monroe and Rush that the proposed treaty with Great Britain should not omit the issue of impressment, but felt it should not be made an ultimatum; reelected to the Senate (1815–1818), serving as chairman of the Finance Committee; supported charter of the Second Bank of the United States; appointed minister to Russia in April 1818, serving until 1820 when he was granted permission to resign after three of his children died of typhus in St. Petersburg; under Secretary Adams' direction, on way to his post in Russia, Campbell adjusted Denmark's claims for U.S. privateers disrupting commerce during the War of 1812; appointed judge of the U.S. District Court of Tennessee; named a member of the commission to study French war claims in 1831 by Secretary Livingston; died in Nashville, Tenn., on February 17, 1848. Irving Brant, *James Madison* (1956); Gaillard Hunt, *The Life of James Madison* (1968).

CAMPBELL, James. Born in Southwark, Pa., September 1, 1812; son of Anthony and Catherine (McGarvey or Doran) Campbell; Roman Catholic; married Emilie S. Chapron on October 28, 1845; father of two sons; studied law in the office of Edward D. Ingraham; admitted to the bar on September 14, 1833; appointed by Governor Porter to Pennsylvania Court of Common Pleas, 1842–1852; nominated for associate justice of the Supreme Court in 1851, but defeated by strong anti-Catholic sentiment; appointed attorney general of Pennsylvania by Governor Bigler in 1852; appointed POSTMASTER GENERAL by President Pierce in return for political support rendered, serving from March 7, 1853 to March 6, 1857; accomplishments include the abolition of franking privileges, establishment of registry system, some success lowering postage rates with foreign countries; retired in 1857 to his law practice and the directorship of Girard College and Jefferson Medical College; died in late January 1893 in Philadelphia; interment in St. Mary's Church. John M. Campbell, American Catholic Historical Society, *Records*, vol. 5 (1894); J. Herman Schauinger, *Profiles in Action* (1966).

CARLISLE, John Griffin. Born in Campbell (now Kenton) County, Ky., September 5, 1835; son of L. H. Carlisle, farmer, and Mary A. (Reynolds) Carlisle; married Mary Jane Goodson on January 15, 1857; father of William Kinkead and Libbon Logan; attended public schools of Campbell County; farmed during day, and read and studied at night; at age 17, taught in county school and read law; moved to Covington where he taught while studying law with J. W. Stevenson and W. B. Kinkead; admitted to the bar in 1858; began practice of law; elected to Kentucky House of Representatives, and served two terms, 1859–1861; nominated for presidential elector on Democratic ticket in 1864, but chose not to run; ran for State Senate, 1865; elected to State Senate, 1867; was delegate-at-large from state of Kentucky to Democratic national convention at New York City in 1868; reelected to State Senate, 1869; elected lieutenant governor of Kentucky, and served 1871–1875; chosen alternate presidential elector of state at large, 1876; nominated and elected to the 45th Congress (House), taking seat in March, 1877; reelected to Congress six times, serving until May, 1890; was elected speaker of the House in 1883, 1885, and 1887; was U.S. senator from Kentucky, May, 1890–Feb. 1893; had presidential prospects in 1892; appointed SECRETARY OF THE TREASURY in the cabinet of President Cleveland on March 4, 1893 and served until March 4, 1897; confronted with fast disappearing gold reserve, announced that there would be no more gold certificates made, but resorted to various bond issues to help maintain gold reserve; practiced law in New York; was vice-president of Anti-Imperialist League; died in New York City, July 31, 1910; interment in Linden Grove Cemetery, Covington, Ky. Henry J. Ford, *The*

Cleveland Era (1921); Robert L. Vexter, ed., *Grover Cleveland, 1837–1908: Chronology, Documents, Bibliographical Aids* (1968); James A. Barnes, *John Carlisle, Financial Statesman* (1967); Margaret K. Leech, *In the Days of McKinley* (1959).

CARLUCCI, Frank Charles, III. Born in Scranton, Pa., October 18, 1930; son of Frank Charles Carlucci, Jr., insurance broker, and Roxanne (Baron) Carlucci; married to Jean Anthony in 1954; father of Karen and Frank; married Marcia Myers on April 15, 1976; attended Wyoming Seminary College Preparatory School at Kingston, Pa.; obtained A.B. from Princeton in 1952; worked briefly as a rental agent and salesman; served in the U.S. Navy as a gunnery officer on the USS *Rombach* from 1952 to 1954; entered the Harvard Graduate School of Business Administration in 1955; business executive; joined Jantzen Swimwear, Inc., firm in 1955, in Portland, Oreg., as a management trainee; joined the U.S. Foreign Service in July 1956; assigned to be vice-consul and economic officer at the U.S. embassy in Johannesburg, South Africa, in 1957; appointed vice-consul and then second secretary and political officer in the U.S. embassy at Leopoldville (former Belgian Congo) in March 1960; commissioned to the Congo desk at the State Department, 1962; became consul general in Zanzibar, 1964; held administrative posts at the U.S. embassy in Rio de Janeiro, Brazil, from 1965 to 1969; made director for operations of the antipoverty agency, 1969; confirmed as director of the Office of Economic Opportunity, March 1971; appointed by President Richard Nixon as associate director of the Office of Management and Budget, September 1, 1971; promoted to deputy director, July 1972; assigned as ambassador to Portugal from 1974 to 1977; selected as undersecretary of health, education, and welfare, 1977–1978; obtained the post of CIA deputy director, January 1978–1981; deputy secretary of defense, February 4, 1981, to December 16, 1982; became president of Sears World Trade, Inc., 1984–1986; chairman and chief executive officer, 1984– ; appointed SECRETARY OF DEFENSE under the Ronald Reagan administration on November 20, 1987, and served until December 16, 1988; on January 5, 1989, joined the Carlyle Group, a merchant bank; Republican; most important contributions were coordination of the federal relief effort for flood victims of tropical storm Agnes, in Wilkes-Barre area of Pennsylvania, August 12, 1972; commandeered contractors for electric, heating, and plumbing repairs so that flood victims could return home before winter; provided free legal services, health assistance, services to the elderly, and wrote literature explaining how those services could be obtained; urged the imposition of increased payroll taxes for catastrophic illness insurance, August 1974; kept Portugal allied with the West by resisting Secretary of State Henry Kissinger's inclination to write off that nation, 1976; opposed the S.1721, Oversight Intelligence Act of 1988; honoraries received include the State Department's superior service award for his work in the Congo and its highest foreign service citation, 1962; the State Department's superior honor award, for his service in Brazil, 1969; honorary degrees from Wilkes College and Kings College, 1973;

Health, Education and Welfare Distinguishing Civilian award, 1975; Defense Department Distinguishing Civilian Award, 1977; Distinguishing Intelligence Medal, 1981; Presidential Citizens award, 1983. *New York Times* (March 13, 1976); *Current Biography, 1981; Who's Who in America, 1981; Facts on File* (1982 and 1989); *Congressional Digest, 1988.*

CARTER, Jimmy (James Earl, Jr.). Born in Plains, Ga., on October 1, 1924; son of James Earl Carter, Sr., a merchant and warehouseman, and Lillian (Gordy) Carter; Baptist; married Rosalynn Smith on July 7, 1946; father of John William, James Earl 3d, Jeffrey, and Amy; graduated from Plains High School, 1941; attended Georgia Southwestern College, 1941–1942, Georgia Institute of Technology, 1942–1943; appointed to the U.S. Naval Academy, 1943; graduated in 1946 with B.S.; commissioned ensign; advanced to lieutenant commander; served on battleships for two years and submarines for five; began work on nuclear submarine program under Admiral Hyman Rickover, 1951; postgraduate studies in nuclear physics at Union College, 1952; after his father's death in 1953, he resigned from the Navy and returned to Plains to run the family peanut farm and warehouses; served as chairman of the Sumter County School Board, 1955–1962; Democrat; elected State Senator in 1962 after challenging opponent's narrow victory which proved to be fraudulent; served two terms as Senator, 1962–1966; defeated in primaries for Democratic gubernatorial nomination, 1966; returned to business and began organizing campaign for 1970 gubernatorial election; elected governor on November 3, 1970; achievements as governor included successful government reorganization, introduction of zero-based budgeting, prison reform, improved mental health services and environmental controls; added to the state's budget surplus without any significant increase in taxes and appointed blacks to all levels of state government; designated chairman of the National Democratic Party 1974 Campaign Committee; upon expiration of his term as governor in 1974, he began an active campaign for the 1976 Democratic presidential nomination; won seventeen out of the twenty-six primaries he entered and was nominated for president by the Democratic Party on July 14, 1976, at Madison Square Garden, New York City; unemployment was his main campaign issue; elected PRESIDENT on November 2, 1976; inaugurated on January 22, 1977; hostage crisis began on November 4, 1979, when militants stormed the U.S. embassy in Teheran, Iran, holding 66 people hostage; announced grain embargo and other sanctions against the Soviet Union, January 4, 1980; issued letter to U.S. Olympic Committee urging withdrawal from the Moscow games, January 20, 1980, which the United States did on February 20, 1980; broke diplomatic relations with Iran on April 7, 1980; hostage rescue attempt failed, April 24, 1980; on July 2, 1980, signed a bill that required young men to register for a possible draft; renominated for president at the Democratic national convention in New York City on August 14, 1980; lost the 1980 presidential election to Ronald Reagan, who won by a landslide, on November 4, 1980; professor, Emory University, Atlanta, 1982– ; founder, Carter Center,

Emory University, 1982; member of the board of directors, Habitat for Humanity, 1984–1987; chairman, Board of Trustees of the Carter Center, Inc., 1986– , Carter Human Rights Foundation, 1986 and Global 2000, Inc., 1986– ; Honorary degrees: LL.D. from Notre Dame, 1977, Emory University, 1979, New York Law School and Bates College, 1985; Hon. D.E. Georgia Institute of Technology, 1979; Hon. Ph.D. Weizmann Institute of Science, 1980; awards include Gold Medal, International Institute for Human Rights, 1979; Harry S. Truman Public Service Award, 1981; Albert Schweitzer prize for Humanitarianism, 1987; member of Lions, American Legion, Baptist Brotherhood Commission; author of *Why Not the Best?* (1976); *A Government as Good as Its People* (1977); *Keeping Faith: Memoirs of a President* (1982); *The Blood of Abraham: Insights into the Middle East* (1985); and *Everything to Gain: Making the Most of the Rest of Your Life* (1987). *Time* (January 3, 1977); David Kucharsky, *The Man from Plains; the Mind and Spirit of Jimmy Carter* (1976); Leslie Wheeler, *Jimmy Who?* (1976). *Facts on File, 1980; Who's Who in American Politics, 1987–1988*; Charles Jones, *The Trusteeship Presidency* (1988); *The Writers Directory, 1988–1989*.

CASS, Lewis. Born in Exeter, N.H., October 9, 1782; son of Jonathan and Mary (Gilman) Cass; married Elizabeth Spencer in 1806; no children; attended Exeter Academy; moved in 1799 to Wilmington, Del. where he taught school; moved again at the end of 1799 to Marietta, Ohio; studied law in Marietta under R. J. Meigs who was later to become governor of Ohio; admitted to bar in 1802; elected to the state House of Representatives in 1806; served as U.S. Marshall for the district of Ohio from 1807 until his resignation in 1812; joined American forces in May 1812 as a colonel in the 27th Regiment, U.S. Infantry; promoted to brigadier general March 20, 1813; accomplishments during War of 1812 include vital contributions to General Harrison's victory over British forces under Proctor and the Indians under Tecumseh; appointed military and civil governor of Michigan Territory, October 29, 1813, served until 1831; resigned from Army May 1, 1814; appointed SECRETARY OF WAR by President Jackson, August 1, 1831, served until October 5, 1836; most important contribution was his instrumental part in moving the Creek and Seminole Indians west of the Mississippi; resigned cabinet position when appointed envoy extraordinary and minister plenipotentiary to France, served from October 24, 1836 until November 12, 1842; elected from Michigan on Democratic ticket to U.S. Senate where he served from March 4, 1845 until May 29, 1848; resigned from Senate to seek the presidency on the Democratic ticket in 1848; reelected to Senate January 20, 1849 to fill vacancy caused by his own resignation after unsuccessful presidential bid; elected to second term in Senate and served March 4, 1849 until March 3, 1857; elected president *pro tem* of Senate December 4, 1854, and served until December 5, 1854; most important contributions were his leadership of 54–40 faction of Senate, introduction and defense of the principle of popular sovereignty in the territories, co-championed the Compromise of 1850 with Henry Clay; appointed SECRETARY OF STATE by President Buchanan on March 6, 1857, served until his resignation on December 14, 1860; most important contributions were his instrumental part in ending the rights of visitation and search of vessels at sea, famous dispatch of June 27, 1859 regarding the neutral policy of the U.S. in reference to the Italian War, condemned doctrine of secession and advocated force to avoid it; retired to Detroit, Mich. to literary pursuits; died in Detroit, on June 17, 1866; interment in Elmwood Cemetery. Andrew C. McLaughlin, *Lewis Cass* (1919); Irving Stone, *They Also Ran* (1966).

CAVAZOS, Lauro Fred. Born at King Ranch, Tex., January 4, 1927; son of Lauro Fred and Tomasa (Quintanilla) Cavazos; Roman Catholic; married Peggy Ann Murdock on December 28, 1954; father of Lauro, Sarita, Ricardo, Alicia, Victoria, Roberto, Rachel, Veronica, Tomas, and Daniel; served with U.S. Army, 1945–1946; graduated Texas Tech University, B.A., 1949, and M.A., 1951; received Ph.D., Iowa State University, 1954; worked as a teaching assistant at Texas Tech University, 1949–1951, and president of their health sciences center, 1980– ; instructor of anatomy at Medical College of Virginia, assistant professor of anatomy, 1956–1960, and associate professor, 1960–1964; professor of anatomy at Tufts University School of Medicine, 1964–1980, chairman of department, 1964–1972, associate dean, 1972–1973, acting dean, 1973–1975, and dean, 1975–1980; science staff, New England Medical Center Hospital, Boston, 1974–1980; member of advisory committee fellows program, National Board of Medical Examiners, 1978; project site visitor, National Library of Medicine, 1978; member of biomedical library review committee, 1981–1985; consultant, council of medical education, Texas Medical Association, 1980– ; active on Pan American Health Organization board of regents, Uniformed Services University Health Sciences, 1980–1985; member, board of directors, Diamond Shamrock R&M, Inc., 1987– ; member, editorial boards of *Anatomical Record*, 1970–1973, *Medical College of Virginia Quarterly*, 1964– , *Tufts Health Sciences Review*, 1972– , and *Journal of Medical Education*, 1980– 1985; contributor of articles to professional journals and chapters to books; board of directors and campaign chairman, Texas Tech University United Way, 1980; member, Texas Governor's Task Force on Higher Education, 1980–1982; member, Texas Governor's Higher Education Management Effectiveness Council, 1980–1982, and chairman from 1981 to 1982; trustee, Southwest Research Institute, 1982– ; chairman, Lubbock Boy Scout Campaign, 1981; Southwest Athletic Conference Council President, 1987– ; named as SECRETARY OF EDUCATION in the cabinet of President Ronald Reagan on August 9, 1988; confirmed and sworn in, September 20, 1988; asked to retain his position in the cabinet by President George Bush, on November 21, 1988; elected as a Distinguished Graduate of Texas Tech University, 1977; received education and teaching awards from his graduating medical class, five years; recipient of Alumni Achievement awards from Iowa State University, 1979; honored with the Lauro F. Cavazos Award from Texas Tech University, 1987; named to the Hispanic Hall of Fame by *Hispanic Business* magazine, 1987; member of the American

Association of Anatomists, Endocrine Society, Histochemical Society, American Association for the Advancement of Science (AAAS), Association of American Medical Colleges, Pan American Association of Anatomy (founding councilor from United States., representative of American Association of Anatomy, 1974–); Philosophical Society of Texas, Texas Science and Technical Council (chairman, education committee, 1984–1985); Lubbock Chamber of Commerce (board of directors); Tufts Medical Alumni Association (honorary); and Sigma Xi. *Facts on File, 1988; Who's Who in the World, 1989.*

CELEBREZZE, Anthony Joseph. Born in Anzi, Italy, September 4, 1910; son of Rocco Celebrezze, railroad laborer, and Dorothy (Marcoguiseppe) Celebrezze; Roman Catholic; married Anne Marco on May 7, 1938; father of Anthony Joseph, Jean Anne, and Susan Marie; attended public schools of Cleveland, Ohio; studied at John Carroll University, 1930–1931; received LL.B. from Ohio Northern University in 1936; was admitted to the Ohio bar in 1938, and began work in legal department of Ohio State Bureau of Unemployment, 1938–1939; practiced law in Cleveland from 1939 to 1952, with the exception of time spent serving as seaman in the U.S. Navy during World War II; elected to Ohio State Senate in 1950, and was reelected in 1952; elected mayor of Cleveland in 1953, and was reelected in 1955, 1957, and 1959 and 1961; appointed member of Advisory Commission of Intergovernmental Relations in 1959, and reappointed in 1962; made president of U.S. Conference of Mayors in 1962; appointed SECRETARY OF HEALTH, EDUCATION AND WELFARE in the cabinet of President Kennedy, continued under Lyndon Johnson, and served from July 31, 1962 to August 17, 1965; most important contributions were endorsement of Medicare for the aged and refusal of aid to parochial schools as unconstitutional; chosen member of 6th Circuit Court of Appeals, 1965– was president of American Municipal Association from 1948 to 1959. New York Times, *The Kennedy Years* (1964); Hugh Sidey, *A Very Personal Presidency: Lyndon Johnson in the White House* (1968).

CHANDLER, William Eaton. Born in Concord, N.H., December 28, 1835; son of Nathan S. and Mary Ann (Tucker) Chandler; Catholic; married Ann Caroline Gilmore, daughter of Joseph A. Gilmore, governor of New Hampshire, in 1859; remarried to Lucy Lambert Hale in 1874; no children; attended local schools of Pembroke, N.H.; studied at academies in Thetford, Vt.; graduated Harvard Law School in 1854; was admitted to the bar in 1855, and began practice in Concord, N.H.; became reporter for New Hampshire Supreme Court, 1859; became journalist; active in politics; elected to the state legislature in 1863, and was reelected twice, serving as speaker of New Hampshire assembly; chairman of Republican state committee; was solicitor and judge advocate general of U.S. Navy Department, 1865; appointed first assistant secretary of treasury, and remained in this position from June 6, 1865 to November 30, 1867; practiced law; was national committeeman from New Hampshire, and participated in four presidential campaigns of 1868, 1872, 1876 and 1880; counsel for Hayes electors before Florida board of electors, 1876; reelected member of state House of Representatives in 1881; nominated solicitor general by Garfield, but nomination never confirmed by Senate; appointed SECRETARY OF THE NAVY in the cabinet of President Arthur on April 12, 1882, and served from April 17, 1882 to March 5, 1885; most important contribution was modernization of navy by obtaining congressional authorization to build steel ships; continued activity with newspaper, 1885; elected to U.S. Senate on June 14, 1887 to fill unexpired term of Austin F. Pike, reelected for full term beginning March 4, 1889, and served until March 3, 1901: published *New Hampshire, A Slave State*; reelected to U.S. Senate in 1895, and sat from June 18, 1895 to March 3, 1901, being defeated as candidate in 1901; chairman of Spanish Treaty Claims Commission, 1901–1908: practiced law in Concord, N.H. and Washington, D.C.; died in Concord, N.H., November 2, 1917; interment in Blossom Hill Cemetery. *Daily Patriot*, November 30, 1917; George F. Howe, *Chester A. Arthur: A Quarter Century of Machine Politics* (1957).

CHANDLER, Zachariah. Born in Bedford, N.H., December 10, 1813; son of Samuel and Margaret (Orr) Chandler; married Letitia Grace Douglass, December 10, 1844; no children; attended the common schools; moved to Detroit, 1833, and opened general store; made fortune by pursuing trade, banking and land speculation; made campaign speeches for Taylor, 1848; was mayor of Detroit, 1851–1852; defeated as Whig candidate for governor in 1852; delegate to Republican national convention in Pittsburgh, 1856; chosen U.S. senator to succeed Lewis Cass in 1857, and sat until March 3, 1875; raised and equipped first regiment of Michigan volunteers; member of Joint Committee on Conduct of the War; active member of Republican Congressional Committee, and chairman of campaigns of 1868 and 1876; defeated in reelection to Senate, 1874; appointed SECRETARY OF THE INTERIOR in the cabinet of President Grant, and served from October 19, 1875 to March 11, 1877; most important contributions were dismissals for dishonesty or incompetence; reelected to U.S. Senate to fill vacancy caused by resignation of Isaac P. Christiancy in February 1879, and served until death; died in Chicago, Ill., November 1, 1879; interment in Elmwood Cemetery, Detroit, Mich. Wilmer C. Harris, *Public Life of Zachariah Chandler, 1851–1875* (1917); Mary George, *Zachariah Chandler: A Political Biography* (1969).

CHAPIN, Roy Dikeman. Born in Lansing, Mich., February 23, 1880; son of Edward Cornelius and Ella Rose (King) Chapin; married Inez Tiedeman on November 4, 1914; father of Roy Dikeman, Joan King, John Carsten, Sara Ann, Daniel, and Marian; attended Lansing High School; entered University of Michigan, but left in 1901 to take position with Olds Motor Works in Detroit; made general sales manager of Olds Motor Works, 1904–1906; started E. R. Thomas–Detroit Company with Edwin R. Thomas, and became treasurer and general manager, 1906–1908; made secretary of Hudson Motor Car Company in 1909, president from 1909–1923, and chairman of board of directors in 1923; delegate to National Good Roads Association convention; chairman of highways transport committee of Council of National Defense during World War I; appointed interim secretary of commerce on August 8, 1932; appointed SECRETARY OF COMMERCE in the cabinet of President Hoover on December 14, 1932, and served until March 3, 1933; returned to Hudson Motor Car Company as chairman of the board, and again became president in 1934; died in Detroit, Mich. on February 16, 1936. John C. Long, *Roy D. Chapin* (1945); Joseph Brandes, *Herbert Hoover and Economic Diplomacy: Department of Commerce Policy* (1962).

CHAPMAN, Oscar Littleton. Born in Omega, Va., October 22, 1896: son of James Jackson Chapman, farmer, and Rosa Archer (Blunt) Chapman; Methodist: married to Olga Pauline Edholm on December 21, 1920; after death of first wife remarried to Ann Kendrick on February 24, 1940; father of James Raleigh; attended Randolph Macon Academy, Bedford, Va.; served as a pharmacist's mate in the U.S. Navy during the World War I; attended the University of Denver, 1922–1924, and the University of New Mexico, 1927–1928; studied law at the Westminster Law School, Denver, Colo., and graduated in 1929; assistant and then chief probation officer of the Juvenile Court of Denver, 1921–1929; admitted to the bar, 1929, and practiced in Denver, 1929–1933; appointed assistant secretary of the interior in the cabinet of President Franklin Roosevelt in May, 1933; appointed by President Roosevelt to the interdepartmental committee to coordinate health and welfare services of the government, 1935, to the Committee on Vocational Education, 1936, and to the committee to review charges of subversive activity against federal employees, 1931–1942; member of the U.S. delegation to the Inter-American Indian Congress in Mexico, 1940; appointed undersecretary of the interior in the cabinet of President Truman in March, 1946; vice-chairman of the Inter-American Conference on Conservation of Renewable Natural Resources, 1948; deputy chairman of U.S. participants to the United Nations Scientific Conference on Conservation and Utilization of Resources, 1949; appointed SECRETARY OF THE INTERIOR in the cabinet of President Truman on January 19, 1950, having previously served *ad interim*, 1949–1950, and served until his resignation on January 20, 1953; member of the National Issues Committee, 1953; campaign aide to Lyndon B. Johnson in the 1960 presidential race; died in Washington, D.C., on February 8, 1978; interment in Arlington National Cemetery. Barton J. Bernstein and A. J. Matusow, *The Truman Administration: A Documentary History* (1966); Cabell B. H. Phillips, *The Truman Presidency* (1966); *New York Times Biographical Service* (1978); *Who Was Who, 1971–1980.*

CHASE, Salmon Portland. Born in Cornish, N.H., January 13, 1808; son of Ithamar Chase, a farmer who held various state and local political offices as Federalist, and Janette (Ralston) Chase; married Katherine Jane Garmiss on March 4, 1834; married Eliza Ann Smith on September 26, 1839; remarried to

Sarah Bella Dunlap Ludlow, November 6, 1846; father of Katherine, Janette, and four other daughters; moved with family to Keene, N.H.; attended district schools of Keene; went to private school of Mr. Dunham at Windsor, Vt.; put under care of uncle Philander Chase, bishop of Ohio, after father's death; entered church school of uncle in Worthington, near Columbus, Ohio; attended Cincinnati College, 1821–1822; spent short time in preparatory study, entered Dartmouth College as a junior, and graduated in 1826; sought government clerkship through his uncle, Senator Dudley Chase, but was refused; conducted school for boys in Washington; was admitted to the bar on December 14, 1829; settled in Cincinnati, assisted in the organization of the Cincinnati Lyceum; wrote *The Life and Character of Henry Brougham* and compiled *Statutes of Ohio*; defended escaping slaves; joined Liberty party after nomination of Birney, 1840; wrote most of resolutions of Buffalo convention of August, 1843; played major role in South and West Liberty Convention at Cincinnati, 1845; active in Free Soil movement of 1848; elected to U.S. Senate on February 22, 1849, and served from March 4, 1849 to March 3, 1855; joined Republican party; elected governor of Ohio in 1855 as Free Soil Democrat, and was reelected in 1857 as a Republican; was aspirant for presidential nomination, 1856, and again in 1860; chosen U.S. senator again in 1860, took seat on March 4, 1861, but resigned on March 6, 1861 to accept appointment as SECRETARY OF THE TREASURY in the cabinet of President Lincoln, and served from March 7, 1861 to June 3, 1864; most important contributions were aid in establishing national banking system, confiscation of rebel property, approval of admission of West Virginia to the Union, and work with congressional committees to draw up remedial legislation to ease deranged currency; served as Ohio commissioner at Peace Convention at Washington in February 1861; appointed chief justice of Supreme Court on December 6, 1864; member of National Peace Convention, 1868; presided at impeachment trial of President Andrew Johnson, 1868; died in New York City, May 7, 1873; interment in Oak Hill Cemetery, Washington, D.C.; reinterment in Spring Grove Cemetery, Cincinnati, Ohio. Robert B. Warden, *Account of the Private Life and Public Services of Salmon Portland Chase* (1874); Albert Hart, *Salmon Portland Chase* (1899); Salmon Portland Chase, *Inside Lincoln's Cabinet: The Civil War Diaries of Salmon P. Chase*, David Donald, ed. (1960).

CHENEY, Richard Bruce. Born in Lincoln, Nebr., January 30, 1941; Methodist; married Lynne Ann Vincent, 1964; father of Elizabeth and Mary; attended elementary and high school in Casper, Wyo.; graduated Natrona County High School, Casper, Wyo., 1959; attended Yale University, New Haven, Conn.; and Casper College, Casper, Wyo.; received B.A. from University of Wyoming in 1965; earned M.A. from University of Wisconsin in 1968; Republican; Ph.D candidate, University of Wisconsin, Madison, Wis., 1968; financial consultant; vice-president of Bradley, Woods, and Co. from 1973 to 1974 and 1976 to 1978; congressional fellow, 1968–1969; named as special assistant to the director of the Office of Economic Opportunity, 1969–1970; appointed White House staff assistant, 1971; assistant director, Cost of Living Staff, from 1971 to 1973; served as deputy assistant to the president, 1974–1975; appointed White House chief of staff in 1975 and served until 1976; elected to House of Representatives in 1978; chairman of the Republican Policy Committee; served a term on the House Ethics Committee; served on the Water and Power Resources Subcommittee; permanently assigned to the House Interior Committee; major contributions were support of Ronald Reagan's economic program, passed amendment that the board not be authorized to alter any law regulating state water rights, lobbied for the 1982 Reagan-oriented tax increase, supported the Reagan policies in Lebanon, introduced legislation in the ninety-eighth Congress banning oil and gas leasing in Wyoming wilderness areas and added 651,049 additional wilderness acres, proposed a historic preservation bill that offered federal money to include new buildings in the National Register of Historic Places, which later became a law; appointed SECRETARY OF DEFENSE on March 18, 1989, in the cabinet of George Bush; member of University of Wyoming Alumni Association and United Methodist Church; in 1976, awarded one of ten Outstanding Young Men in the Nation awards by the U.S. Jaycees; chairman, Republican Policy Committee, ninety-seventh through one hundredth Congresses; Select Committee to Investigate Covert Arms Deals with Iran. *Congressional Quarterly, 1979; Politics in America* (1982 and 1986); *People Weekly* (June 27, 1983); *The Almanac of American Politics, 1984; New York Times* (March 18, 1989).

CIVILETTI, Benjamin Richard. Born in Peekskill, N.Y., July 17, 1935; married to Gaile L. Lundgren; father of Benjamin H., Andrew W., and Lynne T.; received B.A. from Johns Hopkins University in 1957; obtained LL.B. degree from the University of Maryland, 1961; served as clerk to the U.S. district court judge for Maryland; became assistant U.S. district court judge for Maryland; became assistant U.S. attorney in Baltimore, September 1962; joined Venable, Baetjer, and Howard law firm as an associate, October 1964; became a partner in the firm in 1969; chosen to head the criminal division of the Justice Department, February 16, 1977; made deputy attorney general in the cabinet of President Jimmy Carter on January 26, 1978; appointed ATTORNEY GENERAL on August 16, 1979, and served until January 1981; resumed private practice in Baltimore; most important contributions were direction of the efforts of a group of inspectors general to conduct a coordinated interagency campaign against white-collar crime; improved the administration of the Justice Department's Office of Management and Finance; increased the coordination of law enforcement among agencies of his proceedings against illegal Iranian immigrants, 1979; went to The Hague to present to the International Court of Justice the U.S. case for the release of the American hostages in Teheran; member of the Court of Appeals of Maryland from 1970 to 1976; the Mayor's Commission to Investigate Baltimore City Jails, 1972–1973; the judiciary committee of the Bar Association of Baltimore, 1972 to 1975; and the Maryland State Legislature's Task Force on Crime, 1975–1976; member of Omicron Delta Kappa, Phi Alpha Delta, and the

American Judicative Society; elected a fellow in the American College of Trial Lawyers; appointed amicus curiae by the United States district court and chief Justice Warren E. Burger for the Supreme Court, 1977. *Time* (July 30, 1979); *New York Times* (October 17, 1979); *U.S. News and World Report* (December 10, 1979); *Current Biography, 1980; Who's Who in America, 1986.*

CLARK, Tom Campbell. Born in Dallas, Tex., September 23, 1899; son of William H. Clark, lawyer who was active in public affairs and the Democratic party, and Virginia Maxey (Falls) Clark; Presbyterian; married Mary Jane Ramsey on November 8, 1924; father of William Ramsey (U.S. Attorney General under Lyndon Johnson), Mildred, and Thomas Campbell; attended public schools; went to Bryan High School, and edited the school paper; studied at the Virginia Military Institute, 1917–1918; served in World War I as sergeant in 153rd Infantry; received B.A. from University of Texas in 1921, and LL.B. in 1922; was admitted to the Texas bar in 1922; became civil district attorney of Dallas County, 1927–1932; resumed private practice of law in partnership with William McGraw; campaigned for the election of McGraw for attorney general of Texas, 1934; practiced law alone, 1935; employed by Texas Petroleum Council in January 1935; appointed to Department of Justice as special assistant to Attorney General Homer Cummings, 1943; appointed first assistant to Assistant Attorney General Thurman Arnold; became assistant attorney general in March 1943; appointed ATTORNEY GENERAL in the cabinet of President Truman on June 15, 1945, and served from July 1, 1945 to August 23, 1949; most important contributions were reorganization of Justice Department by consolidation of some of its seven divisions, campaign against black markets, and demobilization and general reconversion after the war; appointed associate justice of Supreme Court, taking oath of office on August 24, 1949, and served until 1967; president of Institute of Judicial Administration, 1966–1967; chairman, National Collegiate State Trial Judges; engaged in antitrust action and prosecution of alleged Communists; after retirement from Supreme Court, served on various circuits of U.S. Court of Appeals; died June 13, 1977, in New York City. Howard Furer, ed., *Harry S. Truman, 1884–   : Chronology, Documents, Bibliographical Aids* (1969); Barton J. Bernstein and A. J. Matusow, *The Truman Administration: A Documentary History* (1966); *Current Biography; 1977; New York Times* (June 14 and 17, 1977).

CLARK, William Patrick. Born in Oxnard, Calif., October 23, 1931; son of William Petit Clark and Bernice (Gregory) Clark; Roman Catholic; married Joan M. Brauer in Switzerland on May 5, 1955; father of Monica, Peter, Nina, Colin, and Paul; attended Stanford University, 1949–1951; attended Loyola University Law School in Los Angeles, 1952; drafted into the U.S. Army, 1953; served as a counterintelligence agent in Germany; returned to Loyola University Law School in 1955; admitted to the California bar in 1958; senior partner in the law firm Clark, Cole, and Fairfield, Oxnard, Calif., 1958–1966; chief of staff to

Governor Ronald Reagan, California, 1966–1969; judge, California Superior Court, San Luis Obispo, 1969–1971; justice of the California Court of Appeals, Los Angeles, 1971–1973; California Supreme Court Justice, San Francisco, 1973–1981; deputy secretary of state under President Ronald Reagan, sworn into office on March 6, 1981; contributions included defending U.S. "tight money" policy at Organization for Economic Cooperation and Development meeting in Paris, headed delegation to South Africa for talks on independence for Nambia, talks with Japan resulted in the lifting of threatened Japanese ban on imports of California produce; appointed assistant to the president for National Security on January 4, 1982, replacing Richard V. Allen; most important contribution was initiation of an extended analysis of U.S. military objectives and capabilities on a global scale; appointed SECRETARY OF THE INTERIOR on October 12, 1983, replacing James Watt; served until March 4, 1985; counsellor in law firm of Roger's and Well's, Washington and Los Angeles, 1985– ; president; Clark Company, Paso Robles, Calif.; chairman, the President's Task Force on Nuclear Weapons Program Management, 1985; member of the President's Task Force on Defense Management, 1985–1986; member of the President's General Advisement Committee on Arms Control, 1986–1989; treasurer of the Ronald Reagan Presidential Foundation. *Current Biography, 1982; Science News* (October 22, 1983); *Time* (October 23, 1983); *Who's Who in The World*, 1988.

CLARK, William Ramsey. Born in Dallas, Tex., December 18, 1927; son of Tom C. Clark, U.S. Attorney General under President Truman and Associate Justice of the U.S. Supreme Court, 1949–1967, and Mary Jane (Ramsey) Clark; Presbyterian; married Georgia Welch on April 16, 1949; father of Ronda Kathleen and Tom C.; attended public schools of Dallas and Los Angeles; graduated Woodrow Wilson High School in Washington, D.C. in 1945; enlisted in the U.S. Marine Corps and was discharged as a corporal in 1946; received B.A. from University of Texas in June 1949; earned M.A. in American history and J.D. from University of Chicago in December 1950; admitted to Texas bar; joined law firm of Clark, Coon, Holt and Tish, and later became partner in firm, renamed Clark, West, Keller, Clark and Ginsberg; admitted to practice before the U.S. Supreme Court in 1956; supported Adlai Stevenson in presidential campaign of 1956, and John Kennedy in 1960; chosen assistant attorney general in charge of litigation of federal lands, February 16, 1961–February 13, 1965; headed federal civilian forces in University of Mississippi riots, 1962; served in Birmingham, Ala., 1963; made director of American Judicature Society in 1963; president of American Bar Association and Southwest Legal Foundation, 1964–1965; became acting attorney general on October 13, 1966; received honorary LL.D. from Loyola University, 1967; appointed ATTORNEY GENERAL in the cabinet of President Lyndon B. Johnson on March 10, 1967, and served until January 20, 1969; most important contributions were action against segregation in Southern schools, support of bill outlawing wiretapping in cases not affecting national security, support of Supreme Court ruling in *Miranda* vs. *Arizona*, and opposition to capital punishment; resumed private practice of law; member of Federal, American, and Dallas bar associations; adjunct professor of law at Howard University, 1969–1972; Brooklyn Law School, 1973– ; defeated for U.S. Senate in 1974; adjunct professor at Brooklyn Law School until 1981; author of *Crime in America*. "Watch on the Attorney General," *Harper's*, vol. 235 (November 1967); Hugh Sidey, *A Very Personal Presidency: Lyndon Johnson in the White House* (1968); *Who's Who, 1989*.

CLAY, Henry. Born in the district known as "The Slashes," Hanover County, Va., April 12, 1777; son of Rev. John and Elizabeth (Hudson) Clay; Baptist; married to Lucretia Hart in 1799; father of six daughters and five sons, including Thomas H., minister to Guatemala under President Lincoln, and James B., *chargé d'affaires* in Lisbon, Portugal, under President Taylor; attended the public schools; family moved to Richmond, Va., where he worked as a clerk in a law office; studied law in 1796; admitted to the bar in 1797; moved to Kentucky and commenced his practice in Lexington in 1797; became a member of the Kentucky House of Representatives in 1803; elected to the U.S. Senate to fill an unexpired term, from November 19, 1806 to March 3, 1807, which service was rendered in contravention of the Constitution's age requirement of 30 years; elected to the Kentucky House of Representatives again in 1808 and 1809, serving as speaker in 1809; elected to the U.S. Senate again on January 4, 1810, to fill a vacancy until March 3, 1811; elected to the U.S. House of Representatives as a "War Hawk," serving in the 12th and 13th Congresses from March 4, 1811 to January 19, 1814, when he resigned: elected speaker of the House on November 4, 1811 and served until he resigned; appointed by President Madison to be one of the Commissioners to negotiate the peace treaty with Great Britain in 1814 (Treaty of Ghent); reelected to the 14th, 15th, and 16th Congresses (March 4, 1815–March 3, 1821) and elected speaker of the House again on December 4, 1815, serving in that office until October 28, 1820; developed an American system of protective tariffs, securing the passage of the highest protective tariff enacted up to that time (1824); unsuccessful candidate for the presidency in 1824; reelected to the 18th and 19th Congresses, serving from March 3, 1823 to March 6, 1825; served as speaker of House from Dec. 1, 1823 until the close of the 18th Congress; invited to join the cabinet as SECRETARY OF STATE by President John Quincy Adams on March 7, 1825, serving until March 3, 1829; during his incumbency, he concluded a number of treaties with Great Britain, chiefly concerning commerce and trade; sought to establish between the U.S. and foreign countries fair reciprocity as to trade and navigation; elected to the U.S. Senate on November 10, 1831 and reelected in 1836, serving until March 31, 1842, when he resigned; unsuccessful candidate for the presidency in 1832 and again in 1844 on the Whig ticket; again elected to the U.S. Senate on March 4, 1849, serving until his death; died in Washington, D.C., on June 29, 1852; interment in Lexington Cemetery, Lexington, Ky. Clement

Eaton, *Henry Clay and the Art of American Politics* (1957); Katherine E. Wilkie, *The Man Who Wouldn't Give In* (1961).

CLAYTON, John Middleton. Born in Dagsborough, Del., July 24, 1796; son of James and Sara (Middleton) Clayton; Quaker; married Sarah Ann Fisher in 1822; father of several sons; graduated from Yale in 1815; studied law at Litchfield Law School; admitted to the bar in November 1819; opened law practice in Dover, Del.; member of Delaware House of Representatives in 1824; secretary of state for Delaware from 1826 until 1828; elected to U.S. Senate as a National Republican in 1829, served from March 4, 1829 until his resignation on December 29, 1836; accomplishments include research resulting in the reorganization of the Post Office, aided Henry Clay in drafting the tariff of 1833; elected chief justice of Delaware in 1837, served until 1839; reelected to Senate in 1845 as a Whig, served from March 4, 1845 until his resignation on February 23, 1849; appointed SECRETARY OF STATE by President Zachary Taylor in February 1849, served March 7, 1849 until July 22, 1850; accomplishments include negotiation of the Clayton-Bulwer Treaty with Sir Henry Bulwer-Lytton of Britain, drafting of a program for opening relations with the Orient later to be used by Perry in Japan; reelected to the Senate as a Whig, served March 4, 1853 until his death on November 9, 1856 in Dover, Del.; interment in Dover Presbyterian Church. Mary M. Williams, "John M. Clayton," in *American Secretaries of State and Their Diplomacy*, vol. 2 (1928).

CLEVELAND, Grover. Born in Caldwell, N.J., March 18, 1837, with the given name of Stephen Grover; son of Richard Falley and Anne (Neal) Cleveland; Presbyterian; married Frances Folsom in the White House on June 2, 1886; he was the first president to marry in the White House and the first president to have a child born in the White House; father of Ruth, Esther, Marion, Richard Folsom, and Francis Grover; moved with his family to Fayetteville, N.Y., in 1840; attended the village schools and clerked in the local grocery store in Clinton, N.Y.; became assistant teacher at the New York Institution for the Blind in 1853; clerk and copyist for a Buffalo law firm, at which time he studied law; admitted to the New York bar in 1859; edited *American Shorthorn Herd Book* (1861); elected ward supervisor in Buffalo in November 1862; appointed assistant district attorney of Erie County, N.Y., 1863–1865; unsuccessful candidate for district attorney in 1865; elected sheriff of Erie County, 1871–1873; elected mayor of Buffalo in 1882; elected governor of New York, serving from January 1, 1883 to January 6, 1885; elected PRESIDENT on the Democratic ticket, serving from March 4, 1885 to March 3, 1889; nominated for a second term in 1888 but was defeated by Benjamin Harrison, whereupon he resumed his private law practice; elected PRESIDENT again in 1892, becoming the only president to serve two nonconsecutive terms; inaugurated March 4, 1893 and served until March 3, 1897; trustee of Princeton University in 1901; first Democratic chief executive elected after the Civil War; author of *Principles and Purposes of Our Form of*

Government (1892); *Self Made Man in America* (1897); *Independence of the Executive* (1900); *Presidential Problems* (1904); died in Princeton, N.J.; July 24, 1908; interment in Princeton, N.J. Horace Samuel Merrill, *Bourbon Leader: Grover Cleveland and the Democratic Party* (1957); Allan Nevins, *Grover Cleveland, A Study in Courage* (1932).

CLIFFORD, Clark McAdams. Born in Fort Scott, Kan., December 25, 1906; son of Frank Andrew Clifford, Missouri Pacific Railway official, and Georgia (McAdams) Clifford; married Margery Pepperell Kimball on October 3, 1931; father of Margery Pepperell, Joyce Carter, and Randall; moved to St. Louis with family; attended public schools of St. Louis; graduated Soldan High School in 1922; received LL.B. from Washington University in St. Louis, 1928; admitted to St. Louis Bar in 1928 and became member of the law firm of Holland, Lashly and Donnell, 1928–1933; was partner in Lashly and Lashly, 1933–1937, and later with Lashly, Lashly, Miller and Clifford, 1938; taught trial psychology at Washington University; commissioned lieutenant in the U.S. Naval Reserve in 1944, serving in Pacific Naval Supply Offices in San Francisco; made assistant to director of logistics division; appointed lieutenant commander in July 1945 and went to Washington as assistant to President's naval aide; promoted to captain, and made President's naval aide, 1946; special counsel to President Truman, 1946–1950, and aided in formulation of Truman Doctrine; returned to private practice of corporation law with Clifford and Miller in Washington, D.C., February 1950; active in Kennedy's campaign; chosen member of Committee on the Defense Establishment by President Kennedy in 1960; made member of Kennedy's Foreign Advisory Board on May 16, 1961; sent to New York City to settle steel industry question, 1962; appointed chairman of Foreign Intelligence Advisory Board on April 23, 1963, and served as such until 1968; became advisor to President Lyndon Johnson; sent on fact-finding mission to Asia, 1965; made member of committee to study Middle East crisis in June 1967; appointed SECRETARY OF DEFENSE in the cabinet of President Johnson on January 18, 1968 and served from March 1, 1968 to January 20, 1969; most important contributions were limitation of bombing of North Vietnam, continuation of peace negotiations without South Vietnamese representatives, efforts to secure release of *Pueblo* and crew from North Korea, and elimination of racial discrimination in military housing; director of National Bank of Washington, Sheraton Corp., and General Aniline and Film Corp.; trustee of Washington University; senior partner, Clifford and Warnke, 1969– ; special counsel and special envoy of the president of the United States; director of Knight-Ridder Newspapers; chairman of board of First American Bankshares, Inc.; Medal of Freedom with Distinction, U.S.A., 1969; enjoys golfing. Patrick Anderson, *Presidents' Men* (1968); D. Horowitz and D. Welsh, "Clark Clifford, Attorney at Law," *Ramparts*, vol. 7 (August 24, 1968); *Who's Who, 1986; Standard and Poor's Register of Corporate Directors and Executives, 1987; Who's Who in the World, 1987; Who's Who, 1989.*

CLIFFORD, Nathan. Born in Rumney, N.H., August 18, 1803; son of Deacon Nathaniel Clifford, small farmer, and Lydia (Simpson) Clifford; married Hannah Ayer about 1827; attended village schools; entered Haverhill Academy at 14; taught district school, and gave singing lessons; studied for one year at the Literary Institution at New Hampton, N.H.; studied law in Rumney in the office of Josiah Quincy, was admitted to the bar, and began practice in Newfield, Me., 1824; Democratic member of lower house of Maine legislature, 1830–1834, was reelected three times to the Assembly, and served as speaker during the last two terms; delegate to Democratic national convention in Baltimore, 1832; and made attorney general of state, 1834–1838; elected member of U.S. House of Representatives in 1838, was reelected twice, and served from March 4, 1839 to March 3, 1843; retired to Newfield, and practiced law; appointed ATTORNEY GENERAL in the cabinet of President Polk, and served from October 17, 1846 to June 20, 1848, resigning March 18, 1848; most important contribution was action as intermediary between President Polk and Secretary of State Buchanan over Mexican War issues; sent on diplomatic mission to Mexico; became envoy extraordinary and minister plenipotentiary to Mexico, March 18, 1848 to September 6, 1849; practiced in Portland, Me.; unsuccessful candidate for U.S. Senate, 1850 and 1853; appointed associate justice of U.S. Supreme Court, and took seat on January 28, 1858; presided over Supreme Court as senior associate justice *ad interim*, March 7, 1873 to March 3, 1874; president of electorial commission convened in 1877; died in Cornish, Me., July 25, 1881; interment in Evergreen Cemetery, Portland, Me. Philip Q. Clifford, *Nathan Clifford, Democrat* (1922); Allan Nevins, ed., *James K. Polk: The Diary of a President* (1968); Charles Sellers, *James K. Polk*, 2 vols., (1957 and 1966).

CLINTON, George. Born in Little Britain, Ulster (now Orange) County, N.Y., July 26, 1739; son of Charles and Elizabeth Denniston Clinton; Presbyterian; married Cornelia Tappen on February 7, 1770; father of one son and five daughters; ran away in 1755 and shipped on the *Defiance*, a privateer heading to fight the French; returned and entered his father's regiment and accompanied the expedition against Fort Frontenac led by Colonel John Bradstreet; studied law with Chief Justice William Smith in New York City; returned to Ulster County to practice law, sometime between 1758 and 1768; elected a member of the New York Provincial Assembly in 1768; elected as delegate to the 2d Continental Congress in 1775; became brigadier general of militia in December 1775; in June 1777, elected as first governor of New York state; presided at state convention in 1778 to ratify Federal constitution which he himself opposed; provided for the public defense and security as governor during the Revolutionary War; reelected governor in 1780 and served until 1795; after war, devoted attention to education and internal improvements, especially open interior navigation and communication which culminated in construction of the Erie Canal under the direction of his nephew, DeWitt Clinton; headed New York militia to assist Massachusetts in overcoming Shays' Rebellion in 1787; elected VICE-PRESIDENT under Jefferson and served from March 4, 1805 to March 3, 1809; noted for great impartiality and promptness in his decisions; elected VICE-PRESIDENT under James Madison and served from March 4, 1809 to April 20, 1812; voted against the bill to recharter the Bank of the United States; died in office on April 20, 1812 in Washington, D.C.; interment, in Kingston, N.Y. E. Wilder Spaulding, *His Excellency, George Clinton, Critic of the Constitution* (1938); E. Wilder Spaulding, *New York in the Critical Period 1783–1789* (1932).

COBB, Howell. Born at "Cherry Hill," Jefferson County, Ga., September 7, 1815; son of John A. Cobb, planter and member of state legislature, and Sarah (Rootes) Cobb; married Mary Ann Lamar, 1834; moved to Athens, Ga.; graduated Franklin College (part of University of Georgia) in 1834; studied law, was admitted to the bar in 1836, and began practice in Athens; presidential elector on Van Buren–Johnson ticket, 1836; served as solicitor-general of western circuit, 1837–1841; elected as Democrat to 28th Congress, 1842, was reelected three times, and served from March 4, 1843 to March 3, 1851; speaker of the House of Representatives in the 31st Congress; governor of Georgia, 1851–1853; elected to 34th Congress, and served from March 4, 1855 to March 3, 1857; appointed SECRETARY OF THE TREAS-URY in the cabinet of President Buchanan, and served from March 6, 1857 to December 10, 1860; most important contributions were purchase of bonds with surplus, and a decrease in public debt; appointed brigadier general of Confederate Army on February 13, 1862, and was promoted to rank of major general on September 9, 1863; advocated succession, and was chairman of convention of delegates of southern states which met in Montgomery, Ala., February 24, 1864, to plan Confederate form of government; surrendered to General Wilson at Macon, April 20, 1864; opposed congressional reconstruction; died in New York City, October 9, 1868; interment in Oconee Cemetery, Athens, Ga. J. Sloan, ed., *James Buchanan, 1791–1868: Chronology, Documents, Bibliographical Aids* (1968).

COHEN, Wilbur Joseph. Born in Milwaukee, Wis., on June 10, 1913; son of Aaron Cohen, store-owner, and Bessie (Rubenstein) Cohen; Jewish; married Eloise Bittel on April 8, 1938; father of Christopher, Bruce, and Stuart; graduated Lincoln High School in 1930; received Ph.B. from the University of Wisconsin in 1934; helped draft Social Security Act, 1935; was technical advisor to chairman Altmeyer of Social Security Board from 1936 to 1952; directed bureau of research and statistics in Social Security Administration, 1953–1956; held chair as professor of public welfare administration at the University of Michigan, 1956; consultant on aging in Senate Committee on Labor and Public Welfare, 1956–1957 and 1959; consultant to United Nations from 1956 to 1957; visiting professor at University of California, Los Angeles, 1957; chairman of advisory council for Retirement Advisors, Inc., 1958–1960; member of Public Assistance Advisory Council in 1959; consultant to White House Conference on Aging from 1959 to 1960; counsel to Senator John F. Kennedy in 1960; became assistant secretary of health, education and welfare for legislation, 1961–1965; chosen undersecretary of health, education and welfare, 1965–1967; was acting secretary of health, education and welfare from March 1, 1968 to March 22, 1968; appointed SECRETARY OF HEALTH, EDUCATION AND WELFARE in the Cabinet of President Lyndon B. Johnson, and served from March 22, 1968 to January 20, 1969; most important contributions were increase in medical research of National Institutes of Health, establishment of community health programs, programs to train teachers and administrators to teach skills to uneducated adults; became consultant to Ford Foundation; made Dean of School of Education at University of Michigan; wrote essays, articles, *Retirement Policies Under Social Security* (1957), parts of *Social Security Programs, Problems, and Policies* (1960) and *Income and Welfare in the United States* (1962); taught at the universities of Michigan and Texas; headed American Public Welfare Association; founded Save Our Security (SOS), a coalition that blocked many proposed cuts in welfare programs; died on May 18, 1987, in Seoul, South Korea, where he was to speak at a conference on welfare for the aging. Hugh Sidey, *A Very Personal Presidency: Lyndon Johnson in the White House* (1968); Rowland Evans and Robert Novak, *Lyndon B. Johnson: The Exercise of Power* (1966); *Current Biography, 1987; New York Times* (May 19, 1987).

COLBY, Bainbridge. Born in St. Louis, Mo., December 22, 1869; son of John Peck Colby, lawyer and officer in the Civil War, and Frances (Bainbridge) Colby; Episcopalian; married to Nathalie Sedgwick on June 22, 1895, divorced in 1929; married Anne (Ahlstrand) Ely on November 1, 1929; father by first wife of Katharine, Nathalie, and Frances; graduated from Williams College in Mass., 1890; attended Columbia University in New York City from 1890 to 1891, and received an LL.B. degree at the New York Law School in 1892; admitted to the bar in 1892 and began his practice in New York; represented Samuel Clemens (Mark Twain) in 1894 in settlement of affairs of that writer's publishing house; elected to the New York state assembly in 1901; broke from Republican party in 1912 to support Theodore Roosevelt and the Progressive party, and was in charge of the contests to seat delegates pledged to Roosevelt at the Republican national convention in Chicago; delegate to the first Progressive national convention in Chicago, 1912; candidate for governor of New York in Progressive state convention, September 1912; Progressive party nominee for U.S. senator in 1914 and again in 1916; in a nationwide speaking tour, supported Woodrow Wilson for reelection in 1916, and formed a committee of Progressives which cooperated with the Democratic national committee; appointed as counsel for a joint committee of the New York state legislature in its investigation of public service commissions and public utilities in 1916; in 1917, appointed as special assistant to the U.S. attorney general in proceedings for the enforcement of the Sherman Anti-Trust Act; appointed by Wilson commissioner of U.S. Shipping Board, and served as vice-president of the U.S. Shipping Board Emergency Fleet from 1917–1919; was member of the American Mission to the Inter-Allied Conference at Paris, November 1917; appointed SECRETARY OF STATE in the cabinet of President Wilson on March 22, 1920, serving until March 4, 1921; most important contributions were the development of a U.S. position toward communist Russia through a declaration in August 1920 supporting the autonomy of Poland, appointing commissioners to help ease tensions between the U.S. and Mexico, sending "Mesopotamia note" to Britain in November 1920 declaring the right of the U.S. to have voice in affairs concerning mandates, and improving relations with Latin America through official visits to several nations; after his retirement, entered into law partnership with Wilson; in 1934 received an honorable mention in the Pulitzer Prize competition for his editorial, "Freedom of the Press"; died in Bemus Point, N.Y., on April 11, 1950. *National Cyclopedia of American Biography*, vol. 48 (1926); John Spargo, "Bainbridge Colby," in S. F. Bemis, *The American Secretaries of State*, vol. 10 (1928); *Who Was Who in America*, vol. 3 (1957); *Encyclopedia Americana*, vol. 7 (1968).

COLEMAN, William Thaddeus, Jr. Born July 7, 1920, in Germantown district of Philadelphia, Penn.; son of William Thaddeus and Laura Beatrice (Mason) Coleman; father a director of Germantown boys club for forty years; younger brother Robert V. Coleman, and older sister, Mrs. Wilburn Dooley; married Lovida Hardin on February 10, 1945, a graduate of Boston University; father of William T. 3d, Lovida H., Jr., and Hardin L.; Republican; upon graduation from Germantown High School went to the University of Pennsylvania from which he received his B.A. degree summa cum laude in 1941; Harvard Law School until 1943, when he left to enlist in the United States Army Air Corps; returned to Harvard after the war; became member of the board of editors of the *Harvard Law Review*; awarded the Joseph E. Beale Prize and graduated first in his class; received his LL.B. degree magna cum laude in 1946; admitted to the Pennsylvania bar in 1947; became law clerk to Associate Justice Felix Frankfurter of the United States Supreme Court; in 1949 joined the New York law firm of Paul, Weiss, Rifkind, Wharton & Garrison; in 1952 joined the Philadelphia firm of Richardson Dilworth; became a partner in 1956; specialized in corporate and antitrust legislation; represented Philadelphia, Cincinnati and other cities in mass transit and labor matters; became a director of Pan American World Airways, the Penn Mutual Life Insurance Co., the First Pennsylvania Banking and Trust Co., the Rand Corp. and other corporations; became a member of the board of governors of the American Stock Exchange; interested himself in civil rights law and coauthored the brief presented to the United States Supreme Court in the *Brown vs. Board of Education* case; defended civil rights activists during the 1950s and 1960s; served in President Eisenhower's administration from 1959 to 1961 on the President's Commission on Employment Policy; was consultant from 1963 to 1975 to the United States Arms Control and Disarmament Agency; appointed senior consultant and assistant counsel to the Warren Commission in 1964 which investigated the assassination of President John F. Kennedy; served as co-chairman for the White House Conference to Fulfill These Rights (1965–1966); served as member of the United States delegation to the twenty-fourth

session of the United Nations General Assembly (1969); served as member of
the legal advisory committee of the Council on Environmental Quality (1970);
became a member of President Richard M. Nixon's Phase II Price Commission
and National Commission on Productivity (1971–1972); served from 1963 to
1965 on the governor of Pennsylvania's Commission on Constitutional Revision
and from 1967 to 1975 as commissioner of Philadelphia's Fairmount Park Commission; appointed by President Gerald Ford and sworn into office as SECRETARY
OF TRANSPORTATION on March 7, 1975; sent to Congress in September of 1975
"A Statement of National Transportation Policy," a comprehensive outline of
national transportation priorities; approved on February 4, 1976, the landing in
New York and Washington, D.C., of the supersonic jet Concorde on a sixteen-
month trial basis; returned to law practice on January 21, 1977; became a partner
of the Dillworth firm. Lives in Mount Airy, a residential neighborhood of Philadelphia. *Newsweek* (February 16, 1976); *Current Biography*, (March 1976);
National Review (March 5, 1976); *Aviation Week and Space Technology* (April
12, 1976); *In Black and White, 1985; Who's Who in America, 1986.*

COLFAX, Schuyler. Born in New York, N.Y., March 23, 1823; posthumous
son of Schuyler Colfax and Hannah Stryker Colfax; grandson of William Colfax,
commander of Washington's bodyguard during Revolutionary War; married Evelyn Clark of New York on October 10, 1844; married Ellen W. Wade on
November 18, 1868; one son; attended public schools of New York; became
clerk in store; moved with family to Indiana after mother remarried, 1836;
appointed deputy auditor of St. Joseph County, Ind., to aid auditor George
Matthews, his stepfather; was assistant enrolling clerk of state senate, 1842–
1844; bought interest in South Bend *Free Press* and changed its name to *St.
Joseph Valley Register*, 1845; was secretary of Chicago Rivers and Harbors
Convention of 1847; delegate to Whig national convention in 1848; member of
Indiana state constitutional convention of 1850; unsuccessful Whig candidate
for Congress in 1850; delegate to Whig national convention, 1852; served as
member of U.S. House of Representatives from Indiana from March 4, 1855 to
March 3, 1869; was speaker of the House of Representatives from December
7, 1863 to March 3, 1869; inaugurated VICE-PRESIDENT in the administration of
President Grant, and served from March 4, 1869 to March 3, 1873; unsuccessful
candidate for vice-presidential nomination in 1872; charged with corruption in
Credit Mobilier scandal, but was exonerated; lectured; died in Mankato, Minn.
on January 13, 1885. O. J. Hollister, *Life of Schuyler Colfax* (1886); Allan
Nevins, *Hamilton Fish: The Inner History of the Grant Administration* (n.d.).

COLLAMER, Jacob. Born in Troy, N.Y., January 8, 1791; son of Samuel
and Elizabeth (Van Ormun) Collamer; married Mary N. Stone on July 15, 1817;
father of Harriet, Mary, Edward, Ellen, Frances, and William; moved with father
to Burlington, Vt.; worked on farm and attended common schools; graduated
University of Vermont in 1810; studied law at St. Alban's with Benjamin Swift;

served as lieutenant of artillery in state militia during War of 1812; was admitted to the bar in 1813, and began practice in Woodstock and Royalton, Vt., in partnership with Judge James Barrett; member of State Assembly, 1821–1822, was reelected in 1827, and served until 1828; state attorney for Windsor County, 1822–1824; elected associate justice of Supreme Court of Vermont in 1833, and served until 1842; member of constitutional convention of 1836; elected to 28th, 29th, and 30th Congresses (House) as Whig, and served from March 4, 1843 to March 3, 1849; received LL.D. from University of Vermont, 1849; appointed POSTMASTER GENERAL in the cabinet of President Taylor, continued under President Fillmore, and served from March 8, 1849 to July 22, 1850; returned to practice of law in Vermont; elected judge of circuit court, and served from November 8, 1850 to October 3, 1854; elected Republican member of U.S. Senate in 1855, and was reelected in 1861, serving from March 4, 1855 until death; received LL.D. from Dartmouth College, 1860; was professor of medical jurisprudence at Vermont Medical College; died in Woodstock, Vt., November 9, 1865; interment in River Street Cemetery. Dorothy Canfield, *The Cabinet Politician: The Postmasters General 1829–1900* (1943); Robert J. Rayback, *Millard Fillmore* (1959); Holman Hamilton, *Soldier in the White House* (1966).

COLMAN, Norman Jay. Born near Richfield Springs, N.Y., May 16, 1827; son of Hamilton and Nancy (Sprague) Colman; married to Clara Porter in 1851, and after her death, to Catherine Wright in 1866; attended the common schools; taught school in Louisville, Ky.; studied law, and received LL.B. from University of Louisville in 1851; moved to New Albany, Ind., and began practice of law; elected district attorney, 1852; moved to St. Louis; served as Unionist lieutenant colonel in 85th Missouri Militia during Civil War; began publishing agricultural paper, *Colman's Rural World*, 1865; elected to Missouri state legislature in 1865; member of Missouri state board of agriculture, 1865–1911; appointed U.S. commissioner of agriculture by President Cleveland in 1885; when department was elevated to the executive level on February 11, 1889, was appointed SECRETARY OF AGRICULTURE in the cabinet of President Cleveland, and served from February 13, 1889 to March 4, 1889; most important contribution was authorship of Hatchet Bill; devoted self to editorial management of journal; elected president of National Editorial Association and Missouri Press Association; died in St. Louis, Mo., on November 3, 1911. Robert L. Vexter, ed., *Grover Cleveland, 1837–1908: Chronology, Documents, Bibliographical Aids* (1968).

CONNALLY, John Bowden. Born in Floresville, Tex., February 27, 1917; son of John Bowden and Lea (Wright) Connally; married Ida Nell Brill on December 21, 1940; father of John Bowden III, Sharon, and Mark; attended public schools in San Antonio and Floresville from September 1923 until June 1933; entered University of Texas in 1933 and graduated in 1941 with a degree in law; was admitted to the bar in September 1941; entered the Naval Reserve as an ensign on June 11, 1941 and was released from active duty in January,

1946; in 1946 helped found radio station KVET and served as its president and manager for three years; selected to serve as a special assistant to Senator Lyndon B. Johnson during Johnson's 1949 senatorial campaign; worked as an attorney in the Austin firm of Powell, Wirtz, and Rauhut, 1950–1952; in 1952, joined the Ft. Worth firm of Richardson and Bass; on January 25, 1961 he succeeded William F. Franke as secretary of the navy; elected governor of Texas on November 3, 1962, and served until 1969; served as partner in the Houston law firm of Vinson, Elkins, Searles, and Connally from 1969 until December 1970; on December 9, 1970, was appointed to the cabinet post of SECRETARY OF THE TREASURY by Richard M. Nixon; helped reformulate American international financial policies, and led in the creation of the Smithsonian Agreements; resigned on May 16, 1972, and named as counselor to the president, while practicing law in Texas; charged by the Watergate grand jury with having accepted ten thousand dollars from milk producers in return for urging increased price supports but was found innocent; served on the president's Foreign Intelligence Advisory Board, 1972–1974 and 1976–1977; partner in the law firm of Vinson, Elkins, Searles, and Connally from 1972 to 1985; joined Barnes and Connally in 1985 and is currently a partner; declared bankruptcy in 1986. *Dictionary of American Biographies; Time* (January 6, 1961); *New York Times* (December 7–11, 1970); *Who's Who in American Politics; Time* (April 27 and September 10, 1979); *The Almanac of American Politics, 1984.*

CONNOR, John Thomas. Born in Syracuse, N.Y., November 3, 1914; son of Michael J. and Mary V. (Sullivan) Connor; married Mary O'Boyle on June 22, 1940; father of John Thomas, Jr., Geoffrey, and Lisa Forrestal; received B.A. from Syracuse University in 1936; earned LL.B. from Harvard Law School, 1939; was admitted to the New York bar and became an associate in New York City office of Cravath, de Gersdorff, Swaine and Wood; went to Washington as general counsel for Office of Scientific Research and Development in 1942; commissioned second lieutenant in Marine Corps, 1944, served in the Pacific as air combat intelligence officer, and was recalled to Washington to advise the War Department, 1943, and to take over Office of Scientific Research and Development, 1942–1944; served briefly as counsel of Office of Naval Research, 1946; appointed special assistant to the secretary of the navy, 1945–1947; became general attorney for Merck and Co., 1947, became secretary and counsel, chosen vice-president in 1950, and served as president in 1955 and 1956; appointed SECRETARY OF COMMERCE in the cabinet of President Lyndon B. Johnson, and served from January 18, 1965 to January 18, 1967; most important contribution was suggestion for merger of departments of labor and commerce; made president of Allied Chemical Corp.; was chairman and director of Manufacturing Chemists Association, director of Pharmaceutical Manufacturer's Association; made trustee of Committee for Economic Development; member of American Management Association's advisory committee for management training of government executives; chairman of New Jersey Committee for Improving Science and

Math in Secondary Schools; member of New Jersey State Water Resources Advisory Committee; trustee of Thomas Alva Edison Foundation; took active role in fund-raising campaigns for New Jersey Association for Mental Health and Seton Hall College of Medicine and Dentistry; captain in Marine Corps Reserve; president of Allied Chemical Corp. from 1967 to 1968, director from 1967 to 1980, chief executive officer from 1968 to 1979, became chairman of the board in 1969 until 1979; chairman on the board of Shroders, Inc., N.Y.C.; director of the J. Henry Shroders Ltd. and Merck and Co., Inc.; member of the Business Council and the Council of Foreign Relations; trustee of Syracuse University; recipient of presidential certificate of merit, 1948; N.J. Brotherhood Award NCCJ, 1959; Jefferson medal of the N.J. Patent Law Association, 1962; Harvard Business Club award, 1965; named N.J. Business Statesman of the Year, 1964; Public Services Award; Phi Beta Kappa. Rowland Evans and Robert Novak, *Lyndon B. Johnson: The Exercise of Power* (1966); Hugh Sidey, *A Very Personal Presidency: Lyndon Johnson in the White House* (1968); *Who's Who in America, 1986; Who's Who, 1989.*

CONRAD, Charles Mynn. Born in Winchester, Va., December 24, 1804; son of Frederick and Frances (Thurston) Conrad; married M.W. Angela Lewis, granddaughter of Fielding Lewis and Elizabeth, George Washington's sister; moved with family first to Mississippi, and later to Teche County, La., near New Iberia; attended school of Dr. Huld in New Orleans; studied law in the office of Abner L. Duncan, was admitted to the bar in 1828, and began practice; elected to the state legislature (House), 1830–1842; member of U.S. Senate to fill vacant seat caused by the resignation of Alexander Mouton, took seat on April 14, 1842, and served until March 3, 1843; practiced law in New Orleans, 1843–1848; delegate to Louisiana state constitutional convention, 1844; elected to U.S. House of Representatives in 1848, and served from March 4, 1849 to August 17, 1850; appointed SECRETARY OF WAR in the cabinet of President Fillmore, continued into the Pierce administration, and served from August 15, 1850 to March 6, 1853; appointed SECRETARY OF STATE *ad interim* in the cabinet of President Fillmore, October 25, 1852 to November 6, 1852; returned to Louisiana to practice of law; attended Provisional Confederate Congress at Montgomery, Alabama as member from Louisiana, 1861; member of two confederate congresses; entered army, and rose to rank of brigadier general; resumed practice of law; died in New Orleans, La., February 11, 1878; interment in Girod Street Cemetery. Alcee Fortier, *Louisiana* (1914); Robert J. Rayback, *Millard Fillmore* (1959); Irving J. Sloan, ed., *Franklin Pierce, 1804–1869: Chronology, Documents, Bibliographical Aids* (1968).

COOLIDGE, Calvin. Born at Plymouth Notch, Vt., July 4, 1872; son of John Calvin and Victoria Josephine (Moor) Coolidge; Congregationalist; married Grace Anna Goodhue on October 4, 1905; father of John and Calvin, Jr.; after attending the public schools, Black River Academy, Ludlow, Vt., and St. Johnsbury Academy, he entered Amherst College in Massachusetts, graduating in 1895; studied law, was admitted to the bar in 1897, and began law practice in Northampton, Mass.; elected to the city council in 1899; city solicitor in 1900 and 1901; clerk of the courts in 1904; elected to the Vermont House of Representatives in 1907 and 1908; resumed the practice of law in Northampton; elected mayor of Northampton in 1910 and 1911; elected state senator from 1912 to 1915, serving as president of that body in 1914 and 1915; elected lieutenant governor of Massachusetts from 1916 to 1918, ascending to the governorship in 1919; as governor, he sent out the militia to stop the strike of Boston's policemen in 1919; president of the Nonotuck Savings Bank in 1918; elected VICE-PRESIDENT on the Republican ticket headed by Warren G. Harding in November, 1920; inaugurated on March 4, 1921, he served until August 3, 1923, when, upon the death of President Harding, he automatically became PRESIDENT: elected PRESIDENT in his own right in November 1924, he served until March 3, 1929; served as chairman of the Non-Partisan Railroad Commission and as honorary president of the Foundation of the Blind; president of the American Antiquarian Society from 1930 to 1932; conducted a syndicated newspaper column upon leaving the White House; authored *The Autobiography of Calvin Coolidge* (1929); died at "The Beeches," Northampton, Mass., on January 5, 1933; interment in the family burial ground in Plymouth Cemetery, Plymouth Notch, Vt. Edward Connery Lathem, ed., *Meet Calvin Coolidge: The Man Behind The Myth* (1960); Harold Underwood Faulkner, *From Versailles to the New Deal: A Chronicle of the Harding, Coolidge, Hoover Era* (1950).

CORTELYOU, George Bruce. Born in New York, N.Y., July 26, 1862; son of Peter Crolins and Rose (Seary) Cortelyou; married Lily Morris Hinds in 1888; father of five children; graduated Hempstead Institute on Long Island in 1879; graduated State Normal School of Westfield, Mass., 1882; studied law; studied music at New England Conservatory in Boston while teaching in Cambridge; took course in clinics at New York Hospital while studying shorthand to take and transcribe testimony in medical cases; received LL.B from Georgetown University Law School, 1895; received LL.M from George Washington University, 1896; honorary degrees of LL.D from Georgetown University, University of Illinois, and Kentucky Wesleyan University; general law and verbatim reporter with James E. Munson, 1883–1885; entered customs office as stenographer and typist in 1889; transferred to Washington as clerk in postmaster general's office, 1891; on recommendation of Postmaster General Bissell, became stenographer to President Cleveland, 1895; Cleveland commended him to his successor, President McKinley, who made him assistant secretary in March 1897; in April 1900, became secretary to the President; continued as secretary under Roosevelt; appointed SECRETARY OF COMMERCE AND LABOR in the cabinet of President Theodore Roosevelt on February 16, 1903, and served until June 30, 1904; elected chairman of Republican national committee to manage campaign for Roosevelt; appointed POSTMASTER GENERAL in the cabinet of President

Roosevelt on March 4, 1905, and served until March 3, 1907; most important contributions were establishment of tenure during good behavior for fourth class postmasters within same classification as far as law permitted, perfection of rural free delivery system, tightening of regulations intended to prevent use of mails for immoral and fraudulent purposes, postal deficit reduced to lowest point in years, and extension of parcel post agreements with foreign countries; appointed SECRETARY OF THE TREASURY in the cabinet of President Roosevelt on March 4, 1907, and served until his resignation on March 3, 1909; most important contributions were easing of markets before onset of panic by making weekly deposits of cash in banks in areas where currency seemed scarcest and urging Congress to act to provide a more elastic currency; retired to New York to become head of Consolidated Gas Company; died in New York City, October 23, 1940. James F. Rhodes, *McKinley and Roosevelt Administrations, 1897–1909* in *History of the United States*, vol. 9 (1922); George E. Mowry, *Era of Theodore Roosevelt, 1900–1912* (1958).

CORWIN, Thomas. Born in Bourbon County, Ky., July 29, 1794; son of Matthew Corwin, speaker of state assembly, and Patience (Halleck) Corwin; not a church member; married Sarah Ross in 1822; moved with family to Lebanon, Warren County, Ohio, 1798; self-educated; read law; admitted to the bar in 1817, and began practice in Lebanon, Ohio; became prosecuting attorney for Warren County, and served from 1818–1828; member of the General Assembly of Ohio in 1821, 1822, and 1829; elected as Whig to U.S. House of Representatives, and served from March 4, 1831 to May 30, 1840; became governor in 1840, was defeated in reelection of 1842, and refused nomination in 1844; presidential elector in Ohio Whig convention of 1844; member of U.S. Senate from March 4, 1845 to July 20, 1850; appointed SECRETARY OF THE TREASURY in the cabinet of President Fillmore, continued under President Pierce and served from July 23, 1850 to March 6, 1853; elected member of U.S. House of Representatives in 1858, and served from March 4, 1859 to March 12, 1861; was minister to Mexico from March 22, 1861 to September 1, 1864; opened law office in Washington, D.C., and practiced there until his death on December 18, 1865; interment in Lebanon Cemetery, Lebanon, Ohio. Addison Peale Russell, *Thomas Corwin, A Sketch* (1882); Robert J. Rayback, *Millard Fillmore* (1959); Irving J. Sloan, *Franklin Pierce, 1804–1869: Chronology, Documents, Bibliographical Aids* (1968).

COX, Jacob Dolson, Jr. Born in Montreal, Canada, on October 27, 1828; son of Jacob Dolson Cox, building contractor, and Thedia R. (Kenyon) Cox; married Helen Finney in 1849; father of five sons and two daughters; returned with family to New York City; entered seven-year apprenticeship as clerk in law office, 1842; went into office of banker and broker, 1844; studied mathematics and classical languages; entered preparatory department of Oberlin College, and graduated in 1851; served as superintendent of schools and principal of the high school at

Warren, Ohio, 1851–1853; read law, and began practice in 1853; was delegate to convention at Columbus, 1855; elected to State Senate in 1858; part of radical anti-slavery group with James Garfield, Governor-elect Dennison, and Governor Salmon P. Chase; made brigadier general of volunteers, 1861, and participated in Kanawha Valley campaign and battles of South Mountain and Antietam; advanced to rank of major general on October 6, 1862, reduced to former rank in April, and recommissioned in December of 1864; elected governor of Ohio, 1866, served until 1868; appointed SECRETARY OF THE INTERIOR in the Cabinet of President Grant, and served from March 5, 1869 to November 1, 1870; most important contributions were putting merit system into operation and advocating new civil service reform movement; resumed law practice in Cincinnati; moved to Toledo to become president of Wabash Railway, 1873; became dean of Cincinnati Law School in 1881; was president of University of Cincinnati from 1885 to 1889; declined post of railroad commissioner in New York City; declined offer to the Spanish mission, 1897; presented his library to Oberlin, and retired to write; published *The Battle of Franklin, Tennessee, November 30, 1864* in 1897 and *Military Reminiscences of Civil War* in 1900; died in Magnolia, near Gloucester, Mass., August 4, 1900; interment in Spring Grove Cemetery, Cincinnati, Ohio. J. R. Ewing, *Public Services of Jacob Dolson Cox* (1902); Jacob Dolson Cox, *Military Reminiscences of Civil War* (1900); Allan Nevins, *Hamilton Fish: The Inner History of the Grant Administration* (1970).

CRAWFORD, George Washington. Born near Augusta, Ga., December 22, 1798; son of Peter and Mary Crawford; unmarried; graduated College of New Jersey (now Princeton) in 1820; studied law with Henry Wilde; admitted to the bar in 1822; began practice of law in Augusta; attorney general of Georgia, 1827–1831; member of state legislature from 1837 to 1842; elected to U.S. House of Representatives to fill unexpired term of R. W. Habersham, and served from January 7, 1843 to March 4, 1843; chosen governor of Georgia as Whig in 1843 and 1845, serving until 1847; appointed SECRETARY OF WAR in the cabinet of President Taylor on March 8, 1849, and served from March 14, 1849 to July 22, 1850; retired; member of southern commercial convention at Montgomery, Ala. in 1858; chairman of state secession convention, 1861; toured Europe; died in Belair, Ga., on July 22, 1872; interment in Summerville Cemetery. Richard H. Shryock, *Georgia and the Union in 1850* (1926); Brainerd Dyer, *Zachary Taylor* (1967).

CRAWFORD, William Harris. Born in Nelson County, Va., February 24, 1772; son of Joel and Fannie (Harris) Crawford; married Susanna Girardin in 1804; father of eight children; moved with his family to Edgefield District, S.C., in 1779, and later, to Columbia County, Ga., in 1783; pursued classical studies in a private school and in Richmond Academy, Augusta, Ga.; studied law and was admitted to the bar in 1799, commencing the practice of his profession in Lexington, Ga.; appointed to prepare a digest of the laws of Georgia in 1799;

elected to the Georgia House of Representatives from 1803 to 1807; elected to the U.S. Senate to fill a vacancy, served from November 7, 1807 to March 23, 1813; elected president *pro tempore* of the Senate upon the death of Vice President Clinton on March 24, 1812; declined the portfolio of Secretary of War tendered to him by President James Madison in 1813; designated minister to France, serving that mission from April 3, 1813 to April 22, 1815; invited to join the cabinet of President Madison as SECRETARY OF WAR on August 1, 1815, but was subsequently appointed SECRETARY OF THE TREASURY on October 22, 1816; continued in that office by President James Monroe, serving until March 7, 1825; unsuccessful candidate for president in 1824; because of illness, he declined the tender of President John Quincy Adams that he continue as Secretary of the Treasury; during his incumbency, his administration was criticized and subsequently made the subject of a Congressional investigation, but the committee unanimously declared the charges unfounded; returned to Georgia and was appointed judge of the Northern Circuit Court in 1827, which position he held until his death; died in Oglethorpe County, Ga., on September 15, 1834; interment on his estate, "Woodlawn", near Crawford, Oglethorpe County, Ga. Gaillard Hunt, *The Life of James Madison*, (1968); Arthur Styron, *The Last of the Cocked Hats; James Monroe and the Virginia Dynasty* (1945).

CRESWELL, John Angel James. Born in Port Deposit, Md., November 18, 1828; son of John G. and Rebecca E. (Webb) Creswell; Catholic; married Hannah J. Richardson sometime after 1850; no children; graduated Dickinson College in 1848; studied law, was admitted to the bar of Maryland in 1850, and went into practice; was loyalist member of Maryland House of Delegates in 1861 and 1862; became assistant adjutant general; member of U.S. House of Representatives from March 4, 1863 to March 3, 1865; elected to U.S. Senate to fill unexpired term of Thomas H. Hicks, and served from March 9, 1865 to March 3, 1867; appointed POSTMASTER GENERAL in the cabinet of President Grant, and served from March 5, 1869 to July 6, 1870; most important contributions were reduction of cost of ocean transportation to foreign countries, increase in speed of mail by giving mail carriage to best and quickest steamers (four of which were to sail each week) and advertising in advance the vessels chosen, and introduction of 1¢ post cards; one of U.S. counsel before court of commissioners on *Alabama* until 1876; became vice-president of National Bank of Elkton; practiced law in Elkton, Md.; died near Elkton, December 23, 1891; interment in Elkton Presbyterian Cemetery. Allan Nevins, *Hamilton Fish: The Inner History of the Grant Administration* (1970); Dorothy Canfield, *The Cabinet Politician: The Postmasters General 1829–1900* (1943).

CRITTENDEN, John Jordan. Born near Versailles, Ky., September 9, 1787; son of John and Judith (Harris) Crittenden; married three times: to Sally O. Lee, in 1811, to Mrs. Maria K. Todd, in 1826, and to Mrs. Elizabeth Ashley, in 1853; father of five sons and four daughters; attended Pisgah Academy and then a school in Jessamine County to be prepared for college; entered Washington College (now Washington and Lee University), Lexington, Va., completing his studies at William and Mary College, from which he graduated in 1806; returned to Kentucky; studied law; admitted to the bar in 1807, commenced his law practice in Russellville, Ky.; appointed attorney general for the Illinois Territory in 1809 and 1810; served in the War of 1812 as aide de camp to General Sam Hopkins and to Governor Shelby; resumed the practice of law in Russellville; elected to the Kentucky House of Representatives from 1811 to 1817, serving as speaker during the last term in office; elected to the U.S. Senate, serving from March 4, 1817, to March 3, 1819; again elected to the state legislature in 1825 and 1829; appointed U.S. district attorney by President John Quincy Adams in 1827 but was removed by President Jackson in 1829; nominated by President Adams as an associate justice of the U.S. Supreme Court but was not confirmed by the Senate; again elected to the U.S. Senate, serving from March 4, 1835 to March 3, 1841; appointed ATTORNEY GENERAL by President William H. Harrison, serving from March 5, 1841, to September 13, 1841, having been continued in office by President Tyler, following the death of President Harrison; resigned his cabinet post on September 13, 1841; appointed to the U.S. Senate on March 31, 1842; elected to the U.S. Senate for a full term beginning March 4, 1843, serving until his resignation on June 12, 1848; elected governor of Kentucky in 1848, serving until his resignation on July 22, 1850; appointed ATTORNEY GENERAL again, this time by President Fillmore, serving from July 22, 1850 to March 7, 1853; reelected to the U.S. Senate, serving from March 4, 1855 to March 3, 1861; elected as a Unionist to the 37th Congress, serving from March 4, 1861 to March 3, 1863, and was a candidate for reelection at the time of his death; died in Frankfort, Ky., on July 26, 1863; interment in State Cemetery in Frankfort. James A. Green, *William Henry Harrison, His Life and Times* (1941); Robert J. Rayback, *Millard Fillmore: Biography of a President* (1959).

CROWNINSHIELD, Benjamin Williams. Born in Boston, Mass., December 27, 1772; son of George Crowninshield, merchant and sea captain, and Mary (Derby) Crowninshield; married Mary Boardman on January 1, 1804; no children; sent to sea as a cabin-boy, eventually gaining a command; leading merchant in Salem, Mass. and partner in George Crowninshield and Sons; president of the Salem Merchant's Bank, organized in 1811 in opposition to the Federalist banks; succeeded Jacob Crowninshield to the Massachusetts House of Representatives in 1811, and was a member of the Massachusetts State Senate in 1812; appointed SECRETARY OF THE NAVY in the cabinet of President Madison on December 19, 1814 and took office January 16, 1815, continuing under Monroe until resigning October 1, 1818; presidential elector in 1820 on the ticket of Monroe and Tompkins; elected Massachusetts state senator, 1822; entered Congress as the Democratic representative of Salem District on March 4, 1823, continuing until March 3, 1831; supported John Quincy Adams; member of the

Massachusetts House in 1833; retired to Boston; died in Boston on February 3, 1851; interment in Mount Auburn Cemetery, Cambridge, Mass. Theodore Roosevelt, *The Naval War of 1812* (1882); George Morgan, *The Life of James Monroe* (1921).

CUMMINGS, Homer Stille. Born in Chicago, Ill., April 30, 1870; son of Uriah and Audie (Schuyler Stille) Cummings; married Cecilia Waterbury in 1929; married Julia Alter in 1942; received Ph.B. from Yale University in 1891, and LL.B. in 1893; was admitted to the Connecticut bar in 1893, and began practice in Stamford, Conn.; became active in the Democratic party; was thrice elected mayor of Stamford, and served in that capacity from 1900 to 1902 and from 1904 to 1906; president of Mayors' Association of Connecticut, 1902–1903; corporate counsel, 1908–1912; elected vice-chairman of Democratic national committee in 1913; was state attorney for Fairfield County from July 1, 1914 to November 1, 1924; unsuccessful candidate for U.S. Senate, 1916; member of State Council of Defense in 1917; chairman of Democratic national committee, 1919–1920, and member for 25 years; pursued business interests while privately practicing law; became chairman of the Commission on State Prison Conditions; declined offer of governor-generalship of Philippines; appointed ATTORNEY GENERAL in the cabinet of President Franklin D. Roosevelt, and served from March 4, 1933 to January 1, 1939; most important contributions were defense of constitutionality of Securities and Exchange Commission, Tennessee Valley Authority, rejection of gold clause from federal contract, Agricultural Adjustment Administration, National Recovery Administration, and other New Deal measures, extension of powers of Federal Bureau of Investigation to cover such crimes as bank robbery, kidnapping and others, and establishment of Alcatraz island prison in San Francisco Bay, 1934; went into private practice; published *Liberty under Law and Administration* in 1934, and *We Can Prevent Crime* in 1937; member of American Judicature Society; died in Washington, D.C., September 10, 1956. H. F. Bremer, ed., *Franklin D. Roosevelt, 1882–1945: Chronology, Documents, Bibliographical Aids* (1969); Paul K. Conklin, *The New Deal* (1967).

CURTIS, Charles. Born in North Topeka, Kans., January 25, 1860; son of Oren A. and Ellen (Papan) Curtis; Episcopalian; married Anna E. Baird on November 27, 1884; father of Permelia, Harry King and Leona; received a common school education in the North Topeka schools and rode as a jockey during the summer horseracing seasons; studied law in Topeka and was admitted to the bar in 1881, commencing his legal practice there; prosecuting attorney of Shawnee County from 1885 to 1889; elected as a Republican to the U.S. House of Representatives, serving in the 53rd and six succeeding Congresses, from March 4, 1893 until January 28, 1907, when he resigned, having been elected to the U.S. Senate to fill a vacancy; reelected to a full six-year Senate seat, serving in all from March 4, 1907 until March 3, 1913; unsuccessful candidate for reelection in 1912; president *pro tempore* of the Senate from December 4 to

December 12, 1911; chairman of the Kansas delegation to the Republican national convention in Chicago in 1908; delegate to several Republican state conventions; again elected to the U.S. Senate for the term commencing March 4, 1915, and reelected in 1920 and 1926, serving continuously until his resignation on March 3, 1929; elected Republican whip of the Senate in 1915, serving in that capacity until 1924; elected majority leader of the Senate in 1924, serving until his resignation; elected VICE-PRESIDENT with President Hoover at the head of the Republican ticket, serving from March 4, 1929 to March 3, 1933; unsuccessful vice-presidential candidate for reelection in 1932; resumed the practice of law in Washington, D.C., and died there on February 8, 1936; interment in Topeka Cemetery, Topeka, Kans. Eugene Lyons, *Our Unknown Ex-President, A Portrait of Herbert Hoover* (1948); Dorothy Horton McGee, *Herbert Hoover: Engineer, Humanitarian, Statesman* (1965).

CUSHING, Caleb. Born Salisbury, Essex County, Mass., January 17, 1800; son of John Newmarch Cushing, merchant and ship-owner, and Lydia (Dow) Cushing; married Caroline Wilde on November 23, 1824; childless; entered Harvard at the age of 13, and graduated 1817; studied law at Harvard; appointed tutor of mathematics and natural philosophy at Harvard, 1820–1821; studied in law office of Ebenezer Mosely at Newburyport; was admitted to the bar in 1822; prominent leader of Essex County bar with Rufus Choate; representative in state legislature from Newburyport, 1825; elected senator from Essex County in 1826; returned to practice of law in 1829; studied literature, law, statistics and institutions of countries while traveling in Europe, 1829–1831; served in U.S. House of Representatives from March 4, 1835 to March 3, 1843, failing to win reelection; appointed secretary of the treasury, but appointment never confirmed by Senate; appointed commissioner and then envoy extraordinary and minister plenipotentiary to China, and served from May 8, 1843 to March 4, 1845; member of state legislature, 1845 and 1846; was colonel of volunteers of Massachusetts regiment during Mexican War, and appointed brigadier general on April 14, 1847; unsuccessful Democratic candidate for governor, 1847 and 1848; member of state legislature, 1850; declined offer of attorney generalship of Massachusetts, 1851; was mayor of Newburyport, 1851–1852; appointed ATTORNEY GENERAL in the cabinet of President Pierce, continued under President Buchanan, and served from March 7, 1853 to March 5, 1857; most important contribution was Cushing's Ukase, favoring Kansas-Nebraska Act; president of Democratic national conventions in Charleston, S.C. in 1860, and at Baltimore, Md.: member of commission to revise and codify laws of Congress, 1866–1870; sent to Bogota on diplomatic mission to negotiate treaty for building ship canal across Isthmus; one of U.S. counsel at Geneva to settle *Alabama* claims, 1872–1874; nominated chief justice of Supreme Court, 1874, but nomination never confirmed; served as minister to Spain from January 6, 1874 to April 9, 1877; published *History of Newburyport* (1826), *The Practical Principles of Politics* (1826); *The Life of*

William H. Harrison (1840), and other books; died in Newburyport, Mass., January 2, 1879; interment in Highland Cemetery. Claude M. Fuess, *Life of Caleb Cushing* (1923); Irving J. Sloan, *Franklin Pierce, 1804–1869; Chronology, Documents, Bibliographical Aids* (1968).

D

DALLAS, Alexander James. Born on the island of Jamaica, British West Indies, June 21, 1759; son of Dr. Robert C. and Sarah Kormack (Hewett) Dallas; Presbyterian; married Arabella Maria Smith on September 4, 1780; father of George Mifflin Dallas, vice-president of the United States under Polk; read law at Edinburgh and Westminster; migrated to the U.S. in 1783; admitted to practice in Pennsylvania State Supreme Court in 1785; editor of the *Columbian Magazine*; held office of Pennsylvania secretary of state from 1791–1801 by three consecutive appointments; appointed secretary of the Commonwealth of Pennsylvania by Governor Thomas Mifflin on January 19, 1791; founded Pennsylvania Democratic Society in 1793; in 1794, appointed aide-de-camp and postmaster general to Governor Mifflin during the Whiskey Rebellion; published "Features of Jay's Treaty," which he opposed in 1795, and a four-volume edition of *Reports of Cases* in the United States and Pennsylvania before and following the Revolution; appointed recorder of Philadelphia by Governor McKean in 1801; appointed U.S. attorney for the eastern district of Pennsylvania by President Jefferson, serving 1801–1814, and handled the Olmstead Case; appointed SECRETARY OF THE TREASURY in the cabinet of President Madison on October 6, 1814, serving until October 20, 1816; on entering office Dallas was faced with the need for an effective system of taxation, a national bank to collect and distribute revenue, and an end to parsimony in appropriations for war operations; under his term in 1815 the proposed national bank was postponed, leaving a budget deficit of $16 million; his bank plan was redesigned by Webster and Calhoun, removing features meant to aid the Treasury, because of which Madison vetoed the bill; succeeded in chartering the United States Bank, which was failing, for twenty-one years with a capital of $35 million and twenty-five directors; from March 14 to August 8, 1815 Dallas discharged the duties of SECRETARY OF WAR as well as his Treasury duties, and in this office, he completed Madison's "war exposé" and criticized Andrew Jackson in the false belief that he continued martial law in New Orleans after hostilities ceased; aided in establishing the Constitutional Republican party in March 1805; resigned both cabinet positions on October 20, 1816; died in Trenton, N.J., January 16, 1817. Irving Brant, *James Madison* (1956); Gaillard Hunt, *The Life of James Madison* (1968).

DALLAS, George Mifflin. Born in Philadelphia, Pa., July 10, 1792; son of Alexander James Dallas, Secretary of the Treasury under Madison, and Arabella Maria (Smith) Dallas; Presbyterian; married Sophia Chew (or Nicklin) on May 23, 1816; father of eight children; graduated Princeton in 1810; admitted to bar in 1813; served as secretary to Albert Gallatin, minister to Russia, from 1813 until October 1814; upon his return from Russia served as a clerk for his father; served as consul for the Second Bank of the United States from 1815 until 1817; appointed deputy attorney general of Philadelphia in 1817; elected mayor of Philadelphia in 1829; served as U.S. district attorney for the eastern district of Pennsylvania from 1829 until 1831; elected as a Democrat to the U.S. Senate to fill the vacancy caused by the resignation of Isaac D. Barnard, serving from December 13, 1831 until March 3, 1833; appointed attorney general of Pennsylvania by Governor Wolf in 1833, served until 1835; appointed envoy extraordinary and minister plenipotentiary to Russia by President Van Buren, served from March 7, 1837 until July 29, 1839; elected VICE-PRESIDENT on the Democratic ticket with James K. Polk, and served from March 4, 1845 until March 3, 1849; accomplishments include his tie-breaking vote which passed the Walker Bill, this vote being cast according to administration policy and despite his personal objections; appointed envoy extraordinary and minister plenipotentiary to Great Britain by President Pierce, and served from February 4, 1856 until May 16, 1861; died in Philadelphia, Pa., on December 31, 1864; interment in St. Peter's Churchyard. Klyde H. Young and L. Middleton, *Heirs Apparent* (1948); Donald Drew Egbert and D. M. Lee, *Princeton Portraits* (1947).

DANIELS, Josephus. Born in Washington, N.C., May 18, 1862; son of Josephus Daniels, ship's carpenter, and Mary Cleaves (Seabrook) Daniels; Methodist; married Addie Worth Bagley on May 2, 1888; father of Adelaide, Josephus, Worth, Jonathan, Frank, and Addie; attended Wilson Collegiate Institute; at the age of 18 became editor of the Wilson Advance, a weekly newspaper which he later purchased; in 1882, established with his brother the *Kinston* (N.C.) *Free Press* and also became part owner of the *Rocky Mount Reporter*; studied law at the University of North Carolina, 1884–1885; admitted to the bar, 1885, but never practiced; state printer for North Carolina, 1893–1895; chief clerk of the U.S. Department of the Interior, 1893–1895; purchased the *News and Observer* of Raleigh, N.C., and remained its owner, editor, and publisher, voicing Democratic opinion; from 1896 to 1916 represented North Carolina on the Democratic national committee and served as publicity director for the Bryan and Wilson campaigns; appointed SECRETARY OF THE NAVY on March 5, 1913 in the Cabinet of President Wilson, remaining in office the full eight years of that administration; most important contributions were establishing schools on warships and in navy yards, directing the seizure of the port of Vera Cruz, Mexico during 1914 incident there, inaugurating the first continuing program for building up the Navy, and organizing in 1915 the Naval Consulting Board headed by Thomas A. Edison to help develop new naval inventions; retired when Wilson left office and returned to his newspaper in Raleigh; appointed U.S. ambassador to Mexico by President Franklin Roosevelt in 1933 and helped to solve disputes over oil interests and religious issues, serving in that capacity until his resignation in 1941; author of *The Navy and the Nation* (1919), *Our Navy At War* (1922), *Life of Woodrow Wilson* (1924), and a five-volume autobiography; died in Raleigh, N.C., on January 15, 1948. Josephus Daniels, *Tar Heel Editor* (1924), *Editor in Politics* (1940), *The Wilson Era: Years of Peace* (1944), *The Wilson Era: Years of War and After* (1945), and *Shirt Sleeve Diplomat* (1947); Joseph L. Morrison, *Josephus Daniels* (1966); Leon H. Canfield, *The Presidency of Woodrow Wilson* (1966).

DAUGHERTY, Harry Micajah. Born in Washington Court House, Ohio, January 26, 1860; son of John Harry and Jane Amelia (Draper) Daugherty; Methodist; married on September 3, 1884 to Lucy Matilda Walker; father of Emily Belle and Draper Mallie; graduated from the University of Michigan with a law degree in 1881 and began practice at Washington Court House; elected town clerk, 1882; member of the city council; member of the Ohio House of Representatives from Fayette County for two terms, 1890–1894; moved to Columbus, Ohio in 1893; member of the law firm of Daugherty, Todd, and Rarey, 1902–1921; defeated in contests for nominations for attorney general of Ohio in 1895, congressman in 1896, governor in 1897, and U.S. senator in 1902, 1908, and 1916; chairman of the state executive committee in 1912; appointed AT-TORNEY GENERAL on March 5, 1921 in the cabinet of President Harding and continued in this post under President Coolidge; most important contributions were establishment of new division in Department of Justice to investigate fraud in war contracts, establishment of first federal prison for persons not previously convicted of crimes, enforcement of Prohibition, and the use of injunction to end the railroad shopmen's strike of 1922; object of Congressional impeachment resolution of September 11, 1922, but exonerated of charges the following month; asked to resign by President Coolidge on March 24, 1924 during a Senate investigation of his official conduct; resigned from office on March 28, 1924; resumed law practice in Columbus, Ohio; acquitted of charges of conspiracy to defraud the U.S. government, 1927; retired from law practice in 1932; author, with Thomas Dixon, of *The Inside Story of the Harding Tragedy* (1932); died on October 12, 1941 in Columbus, Ohio. Samuel Hopkins Adams, *The Incredible Era* (1939); Andrew Sinclair, *The Available Man* (1965).

DAVIS, Dwight Filley. Born in St. Louis, Mo., July 5, 1879; son of John Tildon Davis, merchant, and Maria Jeanette (Filley) Davis; Baptist; married Helen Brooks on November 15, 1904; father of Dwight Filley, Alice Brooks, Cynthia, and Helen Brooks; later married Pauline (Morton) Sabin on May 8, 1936; attended Smith Academy in St. Louis; graduated Harvard in 1900; received law degree from Washington University in 1903; member of Public Baths Commission of St. Louis; on the board of Public Library, 1904–1907; vice-president of St. Louis Playground Association; was public recreation commissioner, 1906–1907; member of control board of Museum of Fine Arts, 1906–1907; representative to House of Delegates, 1907–1909; on executive committee of National Municipal League, 1908–1910; member of Board of Freeholders, 1909–1911; park commissioner, 1911–1915; chairman of City Planning Commission, 1911–1916; member of board of public improvements, 1911–1915; served on board of overseers of Harvard University, 1915–1921 and 1926–1932; trained in first Plattsburg Military Training Camp, 1915; visited Norway, Denmark, Sweden and England for Rockefeller War Relief Commission, 1916–1917; enlisted as private in World War I received commission in August 1917, and rose to major and chief of staff in 35th Division; promoted to lieutenant colonel, and was twice cited for bravery; received Distinguished Service Cross, and was admitted to French Legion of Honor, 1932; became colonel of Officers' Reserve Corps; unsuccessful candidate for Republican nomination as U.S. senator from Missouri in 1920; appointed member of War Finance Corporation, 1921; chosen assistant secretary of war in 1923, and was acting secretary of war in 1925; appointed SECRETARY OF WAR in the cabinet of President Coolidge on October 13, 1925, and served from October 14, 1925 to March 5, 1929; chosen governor general of the Philippine Islands in 1929, and served until 1932; member of board of directors of Lehman Corporation, 1941–1942; director general of Army Specialist Corps from June 1942 to November 1942, when became advisor with rank of major general; director of Security Building Company, State National Bank, Mortgage Trust Company, Mortgage Guarantee Company, St. Louis Tenement House Association, and St. Louis Association for the Prevention of Tuberculosis; chairman of board of trustees of Brookings Institution, 1939; was president of Davis Estate; died in Washington, D.C., November 28, 1945. Donald R. McCoy, *Calvin Coolidge* (1967).

DAVIS, James John. Born in Thedegar, South Wales, October 27, 1873; son of David James and Esther Ford (Nichols) Davis; Baptist; married to Jean Rodenbaugh on November 26, 1914; father of James, Jane, Jean, Joan, and Jewell; emigrated with his parents to the U.S. in 1881; lived first in Pittsburgh, Pa., later moving to Sharon, Pa.; attended the public schools and Sharon Business College; apprenticed as a puddler in the steel industry at age 11, and worked in Sharon, Pittsburgh, and in Birmingham, Ala.; moved to Elwood, Ind. in 1893 and worked in steel and tin-plate mills; president of the Amalgamated Association of Iron, Steel, and Tin Workers of America; elected city clerk of Elwood in

1898, and served until 1902; recorder of Madison County, Ind., 1903–1907; moved to Pittsburgh in 1907; general director of the Loyal Order of Moose, 1907; chairman of the Loyal Order of Moose War Relief Commission in 1918 and visited camps in the U.S., Canada, and Europe; appointed SECRETARY OF LABOR in the cabinet of President Harding on March 5, 1921; most important contributions were increasing public works construction to provide employment, settling of labor disputes, providing low-cost housing for tenant workers, providing machinery for securing restrictions on immigration in accordance with the 1921 quota law, creating an Immigration Board of Review, and initiating studies of mothers' pension laws, child dependency, and juvenile delinquency laws; reappointed SECRETARY OF LABOR by President Coolidge in 1925 and by President Hoover in 1929; resigned from office on December 9, 1930, following his election to the U.S. Senate as a Republican from Pennsylvania to fill the vacancy caused by the refusal of the Senate to seat William S. Vare; reelected in 1933 and again in 1939, serving in all from December 2, 1930 to January 3, 1945; unsuccessful candidate for reelection in 1944; appointed by Vice-President John N. Garner to serve on a special Senate committee investigating the Tennessee Valley Authority; author of an autobiography, *The Iron Puddler* (1922), *Selective Immigration* (1926), and *You and Your Job*, with John C. Wright, (1927); died in Tacoma Park, Md., on November 22, 1947; interment in Uniondale Cemetery, Pittsburgh, Pa. James John Davis, *The Iron Puddler* (1922); Andrew Sinclair, *The Available Man* (1965); Francis Russell, *The Shadow of Blooming Grove: Warren G. Harding and His Times* (1968).

DAVIS, Jefferson. Born in Christian (now Todd) County, Ky., June 3, 1808; son of Samuel Davis, a commander in the Revolutionary War, and Jane (Cook) Davis; Baptist; married Sarah Knox Taylor, daughter of President Zachary Taylor, in July, 1825; later married Varina Howell on Feb. 26, 1845; no children; enrolled in Roman Catholic Seminary, St. Thomas's College, Washington County, Ky., 1815–1817; attended local schools until 1821; attended Transylvania University, 1821–1824; attended West Point, 1824–1828; graduated as a second lieutenant in the U.S. Army; military apprenticeship of almost seven years spent in Wisconsin and Illinois; took part in Black Hawk Indian War of 1832; stationed in Fort Crawford, Wis. under Commander Zachary Taylor in 1833; resigned from the army on June 30, 1835; spent 1835–1845 as a planter in Mississippi; elected to U.S. House of Representatives as a Democrat from Mississippi in 1845; resigned to command regiment in Mexican War in June 1846; won reputation as a soldier at battle of Buena Vista in 1846; resigned from army again in 1846; elected to U.S. Senate from Mississippi in 1847; supported President Polk in 1848; opposed the admission of California to the Union; resigned from Senate in 1851; became SECRETARY OF WAR in the cabinet of President Pierce on March 7, 1853 and served until March 2, 1857; most important contributions were his inducement of Pierce to acquire the region now known as the Gadsden Purchase and, hoping for Southern expansion to the Pacific, he promoted a southern route for the proposed transcontinental railroad; U.S. Senator from Mississippi, 1857–1861; elected President of the Confederate States of America on February 18, 1861; imprisoned at Fortress Monroe, Virginia in 1865; indicted for treason, released on bond on May 14, 1867; retired to private life at Beauvoir, his home in Biloxi, Miss.; devoted years 1878–1881 to writing *The Rise And Fall Of The Confederate Government*; died in New Orleans, December 6, 1889; interment in Hollywood Cemetery, Richmond, Va. William E. Dodd, *Jefferson Davis* (1907); Dunbar Rowland, *Jefferson Davis, Constitutionalist, His Letters, Papers, and Speeches* (1923); Eric Langhein, *Jefferson Davis, Patriot: A Biography* (1962).

DAWES, Charles Gates. Born in Marietta, Ohio, on August 27, 1865; son of Rufus R. and Mary Beman (Gates) Dawes; Congregationalist; married Caro D. Blymer on January 24, 1889; father of Rufus Fearing, Carolyn, Dana Mc-Crutcheon, and Virginia; attended Marietta Academy; graduated Marietta College in 1884; received LL.B. from Cincinnati Law School in 1886, was admitted to the bar, and began practice of his profession in Lincoln, Neb., 1887, as member of firm of Dawes, Coffroth, and Cunningham; published *The Banking System of the United States*; became president of the La Crosse Gas and Light Company, 1894; in charge of Illinois Republican campaign in 1896; was U.S. comptroller of the currency, 1898–1901; organized Central Trust Company in 1902, served as president, 1902–1921, and was chairman of the board, 1921–1925; wrote *Essays and Speeches* (1915); commissioned major of 17th Engineers, U.S. Army on June 11, 1917; commissioned lieutenant colonel on July 16, 1917; chief of supply procurement on staff of commander-in-chief of American Expeditionary Forces; commissioned brigadier general on October 15, 1918; member of Liquidation Commission, 1918; resigned from the army on August 31, 1919; unsuccessful candidate for Republican presidential nomination, June 1920; became director of U.S. Bureau of the Budget in 1921; wrote *A Journal of the Great War* (1921); published *The First Year of the Budget of the United States* (1923); was brigadier general of Officers' Reserve Corps, 1921–1926; president of reparations committee which worked out "Dawes Plan," 1923; received Nobel Peace Prize with Sir Austen Chamberlain in 1925; elected VICE-PRESIDENT in the administration of President Coolidge in November 1924, and served from March 4, 1925 to March 3, 1929; received four votes for Republican presidential nomination in June 1928; was ambassador to Great Britain from 1929 to 1932; delegate to London Naval Conference, 1930; president of Reconstruction Finance Corporation from February 1932 to June 1932; published *Notes as Vice-President* (1935), *How Long Prosperity?* (1937), *Journal as Ambassador to Great Britain and A Journal of Reparations* (1939), and *A Journal of the McKinley Years* (1951); president of Home for Destitute Crippled Children; treasurer of Chicago Bureau of Charities; died in Evanston, Ill. on April 23, 1951; interment in Chicago. Charles G. Dawes, *Notes as Vice-President* (1935); Donald R. McCoy, *Calvin Coolidge* (1967).

DAY, James Edward. Born in Jacksonville, Ill., October 11, 1914; son of James Allmond and Frances (Wilmot) Day; Methodist; married Mary Louise Burgess on July 2, 1941; father of Geraldine, Mary Louise, and James Edward; attended public schools of Springfield, Ill.; received B.A. from University of Chicago in 1935; treasurer of Lincoln's Inn Society, 1936–1937; legislative editor of *Harvard Law Review*; earned LL.B. from Harvard in 1938, and was admitted to the Illinois bar; became law clerk for firm of Sidney, Austin, Burgess and Harper, 1939; trained as officer in Naval Reserve, 1940–1941; was called into active duty as an ensign in 1942 and discharged as lieutenant in 1945; resumed practice of law with Sidney, Austin, Burgess and Harper, 1945–1949; wrote *Bartholf St.* (1947); legal and legislative assistant to Governor Adlai E. Stevenson, 1949; member and secretary of Illinois Commission on Intergovernmental Cooperation from 1949 to 1953; appointed insurance commissioner by Governor Stevenson, 1950–1953; made associate general solicitor of Prudential Insurance Company of America in 1953, chosen associate general counsel in 1956, and moved to Los Angeles, Cal. branch to become senior vice-president of western operations, 1957; member of Democratic State Finance Committee in California and Chairman's Advisory Committee of the Los Angeles County Democratic Central Committee, 1958–1966; was vice-chairman of Governor's Commission on Metropolitan Area Problems from 1959 to 1961; wrote *Descendants of Christopher Day of Bucks County, Pennsylvania* (1959); appointed POSTMASTER GENERAL in the cabinet of President Kennedy on December 17, 1960, and served from January 21, 1961 to September 29, 1963; most important contributions were stabilization of postal deficit through rates increase; affiliated with Peoples Life Insurance Company; treasurer of Stride Water Development Committee; vice-president of Y.M.C.A.; member of board of fellows of Claremont College; organizer and chairman of Democratic Associates, Incorporated; president of National Civil Service League, 1964–1966; member of American Bar Association; received honorary LL.D. from Illinois College and University of Nevada, 1962; member of Phi Kappa Psi; partner in charge of Washington, D.C., office of the Chicago law firm Sidney and Austin from 1963 to 1973; partner in the firm of Cox, Langford, and Brown, 1973– ; partner in the firm of Squire, Sanders, Dempsey, Cleveland, and Washington, 1973– ; director and member of the executive committee of four companies in the Zurich Insurance Group; director and member of the executive committee of People's Life Insurance Co., Washington; director of Medical Mutual Liability Society, Md.; voting trustee of common stock, Conrail; special counsel of the consumer electronics group the Electronics Industries Assistant; vice-chairman of the Governor's Committee on Metropolitan Area Problems, Calif., 1959–1961; member of the advisory board of the U.S. Customs Bureau from 1966 to 1968; member of the California Governor's Business Advisory Council, 1959–1961; belonged to the National Civil Service League, Citizens Conference on State Legislatures, and Methodist clubs; Democrat; National Press; International Lawyers; Touchdown; Union; author of *Humor in Public Speaking* (1965). New York Times, *The Kennedy*

Years (1964); James MacGregor Burns, *John Kennedy: A Political Profile* (1959); *International Who's Who, 1984; Who's Who in America, 1986.*

DAY, William Rufus. Born in Ravenna, Ohio, April 17, 1849; son of Luther Day, judge of Ohio Supreme Court, and Emily Spalding; grandson of Rufus Spalding, also judge in Ohio Supreme Court; graduated from the University of Michigan in 1870; read law at Ravenna, and spent another year at the University of Michigan; admitted to Ohio bar in 1872 and began practice at Canton; elected judge of court of common pleas in 1886; appointed by President Benjamin Harrison U.S. district judge for northern district of Ohio in 1889, but resigned because of ill health before taking office; appointed SECRETARY OF STATE in the cabinet of President McKinley on April 26, 1898, and served until September 16, 1898; most important contributions were negotiations with Spain over Cuba, securing recall of Spanish General Weyler and the promise of reforms, and securing neutrality and good will of western Europe during war; chairman of U.S. peace commission at Paris to make peace with Spain; judge of federal circuit court of appeals, 6th circuit, 1899–1903; appointed associate justice of U.S. Supreme Court in 1903, and served until his resignation in 1922; became umpire in Mixed Claims Commission, 1922, and served until pneumonia forced him to resign in May 1923; retired to Mackinac Island, Mich., where he died on July 9, 1923. *Outlook* (July 18, 1923); *World's Work* (September, 1923); *New York Times* (July 10, 1923).

DEARBORN, Henry. Born in North Hampton, N.H., February 23, 1751; son of Simon and Sarah (Martson) Dearborn; married Mary Bartlett in 1771; married Dorcas (Osgood) Marble in 1780; father of Henry Alexander Scammell Dearborn, politician and author; married Sarah Bowdain in 1813; attended local schools; studied medicine under Dr. Hall Jackson; began practice in Nottingham Square, 1772; joined militia, and became captain; fought in Bunker Hill, marched into Quebec with Benedict Arnold in 1775, made major of 3d New Hampshire Regiment on March 19, 1777, served at Valley Forge, 1777–1778, and was discharged from the army in June 1783; pursued agriculture in Kennebec County, Me.; chosen brigadier general, and then major general of militia; made U.S. marshall for District of Maine in 1790; member of 3d and 4th Congresses, 1793–1797; appointed SECRETARY OF WAR in the Cabinet of President Jefferson, and served from March 5, 1801 to February 16, 1809; most important contribution was plan for removal of Indians from beyond Mississippi; became collector for Port of Boston in March 1809; made senior major general of U.S. army, 1812–1813; given command of New York City in 1813; discharged on June 15, 1815; appointed minister to Portugal, 1822–1824; retired to Roxbury, Mass., where he died on June 6, 1829; interment in Forest Hills Cemetery, Boston. Justin H. Smith, *Arnold's March from Cambridge to Quebec* (1903); Henry Graff, *Thomas Jefferson* (1968).

DELANO, Columbus. Born in Shoreham, Vermont, on June 5, 1809; son of James and Lucinda (Bateman) Delano; married Elizabeth Leavenworth on July 13, 1834; father of Elizabeth and John Delano; moved with mother to Mount Vernon, Ohio, 1817; educated in frontier village manner; worked in woolen mill; read law; admitted to the bar, 1831; elected prosecuting attorney of Knox County in 1832; elected to Congress in 1844, and served from 1845–1847; was Whig candidate for governor in 1846, and was defeated by two votes; member of banking firm of Delano, Dunlevy and Company, 1850–1855; turned to agriculture and sheep farming; delegate to Republican national conventions of 1860 and 1864; commissary general of Ohio; member of state House of Representatives for one term in 1863; member of U.S. House of Representatives, 1865–1869; appointed commissioner of Internal Revenue, 1869; appointed SECRETARY OF THE INTERIOR in the cabinet of President Grant, and served from November 1, 1870 to September 30, 1875; most important contribution was the investigation of charges of fraudulence in Bureau of Indian Affairs; was president of National Wool Growers Association; trustee of Kenyon College; died in Mount Vernon, Ohio, October 23, 1893; interment in Mount View Cemetery; Phillip R. Morgan, ed., *Ulysses S. Grant, 1822–1885: Chronology, Documents, Bibliographical Aids* (1968); Allan Nevins, *Hamilton Fish: The Inner History of the Grant Administration* (1970).

DENBY, Edwin. Born in Evansville, Ind., February 18, 1870; son of Charles Denby, lawyer and U.S. minister to China, and Martha (Fitche) Denby; Episcopalian; married March 18, 1911 to Marion Thurber; father of Edwin, Jr. and Marion; attended the public schools; went to China upon father's appointment there in 1885 and worked in Chinese customs service, 1887–1894; returned to the U.S. in 1894 to study at the University of Michigan; received law degree in 1896; admitted to the bar, 1896, and began practice in Detroit; during the Spanish-American War, served as gunner's mate, third class, U.S. Navy on the *Yosemite*; member of the Michigan House of Representatives, 1903; elected as a Republican to the 59th, 60th and 61st Congresses, serving from March 4, 1905 until March 3, 1911; chairman of the House Naval Affairs Committee; unsuccessful candidate for reelection in 1910; president of the Detroit Charter Commission, 1913 and 1914; president, Detroit Board of Commerce, 1916 and 1917; during the World War I, enlisted as a private in the Marine Corps, 1917; retired as major in the Marine Corps Reserve in 1919; appointed chief probation officer in recorder's court of Detroit, and in the circuit court of Wayne County in 1920; appointed SECRETARY OF THE NAVY in the cabinet of President Harding on March 4, 1921, serving also under President Coolidge; implicated in the "Teapot Dome Scandal" concerning the handling of naval oil reserves, and subsequently submitted his resignation effective March 10, 1924; later exonerated of charges by the U.S. Supreme Court in 1927; returned to Detroit and law practice; also engaged in banking and various business enterprises; died in Detroit on February 8, 1929; interment in Elmwood Cemetery, Detroit. Samuel Hopkins Adams, *The Incred-*

ible Era (1939); Burl Noggle, *Teapot Dome: Oil and Politics in the 1920's* (1962); Francis Russell, *The Shadow of Blooming Grove: Warren G. Harding and His Times* (1968).

DENNISON, William. Born in Cincinnati, Ohio, November 23, 1815; son of William Dennison, businessman, and Mary (Carter) Dennison; married a Miss Neil, daughter of William Neil; graduated Miami University of Ohio in 1835; read law with George H. Pendleton; was admitted to the bar in 1840; went into practice of law; elected to State Senate as Whig, 1848; president of Exchange Bank; member of city council; organized Franklin County Agricultural Society; became Republican, 1852; attended convention at Pittsburgh in February, 1856; acting chairman of Ohio delegation in Philadelphia Convention of June 1856; governor of Ohio, 1859–1861; chairman of Republican national convention, 1864; appointed POSTMASTER GENERAL in the cabinet of President Lincoln on September 24, 1864, took office on October 1, 1864, continued under Andrew Johnson, and served until July 16, 1866; mentioned for vice-presidential nomination; nomination for U.S. Senate defeated, 1880; was chairman of Sherman Committee in Ohio, 1880; established Columbus Rolling Mills company; benefactor of Dennison University; died in Granville, Ohio, June 15, 1882. D. V. Ryan, *History of Ohio* (1912); J. G. Randall, ed., *Lincoln the President* (1970); Claude G. Bowers, *Tragic Era: The Revolution after Lincoln* (1929).

DENT, Frederick Baily. Born in Cape May, N.J., August 17, 1922; son of Magruder and Edith (Baily) Dent; Episcopalian; married Mildred Carrington Harrison on March 11, 1944; father of Frederick Baily, Mildred Hutcheson, Pauline Harrison, Diana Gwynn, and Magruder Harrison; was graduated from St. Paul's, in Concord, N.H., 1940; BA, Yale, 1943; U.S. Naval Reserve until 1946; in 1946 joined textile sales concern of Joshua L. Baily and Company, Inc. (founded by maternal great grandfather); joined Mayfair Mills in 1947 (family-owned since 1930s); became president of Mayfair Mills in 1958; became chairman of Spartanburg, S.C., County Planning and Development Commission in 1960; became president of the American Textile Manufacturers Institute in 1967; member of the Commission of an All-Volunteer Armed Force (Gates Commission), 1969–1970; received the New York Board of Trade's Textile Award in 1971; appointed SECRETARY OF COMMERCE by President Richard Nixon on December 6, 1972; appointed member of the Council of Wage and Price Stability by President Gerald Ford in August 1974; one of most vociferous defenders, among Cabinet members, of President Nixon during Watergate Affair; credited with introducing energy conservation program for industry; urged United States to negotiate agreements with foreign countries to limit the volume of textile imports; named by President Ford to post of President's Special Representative for Trade Negotiations on February 27, 1975; returned to family business on January 21, 1977; past director, General Electric Co., Crompton Co., Scott Paper Co., S.C. Johnson and Son, Inc., Joshua L. Baily and Co., S.C.

National Corp., S.C. National Bank; chairman of Spartanburg County Planning and Development Commission, 1960–1972; Business Council; Trustee Institute of Textile Technology; Spartanburg Day School; mem.corp. Yale University served with U.S. Naval Reserves, 1943–1946. *Nation's Business* (September 1973); *Commerce Today* (February 19, 1973); Robert Vexler, *Vice-Presidents & Cabinet Members*, Vol. 2, (1975); *The New York Times* (December 7, 1972); *The New York Times* (February 19 and 28, 1975); *The New York Times* (March 16, 1975); *Who's Who in America, 1986.*

DERN, George Henry. Born in Hooper, Neb., September 8, 1872; son of John and Elizabeth Dern; Congregationalist; married Lottie Brown on June 7, 1899; father of seven children; graduated Freemont Normal College in 1888; attended the University of Nebraska from 1893 until 1894; moved to Utah in December 1894 to enter the mining profession; chosen manager of Consolidated Mercury Gold Mines in 1901; cooperated with Theodore P. Holt in the invention of the Holt-Dern Ore Roaster for the treatment of low-grade silver, and was instrumental in the development of the vacuum slime filtration process for the separation of good ore from impurities; chosen grand master of the Masonic Order in Utah in 1913; elected to the Utah State Senate in 1914, served until 1923; elected governor of Utah in 1924 and 1928, served from 1924 until 1932; chairman of National Governor's Conference in 1930; appointed SECRETARY OF WAR on March 4, 1933 by President Franklin D. Roosevelt, and served until his death in Washington, D.C., on August 27, 1936; accomplishments include administration of the New Deal's Civilian Conservation Corps, and initiation of projects for dredging the Mississippi and Missouri river systems; interment in Mount Olivet Cemetery, Salt Lake City. V. E. Thurman, *Who's Who in the New Deal* (1936).

DERWINSKI, Edward Joseph. Born in Chicago, September 15, 1926; son of Casimir Ignatius and Sophia (Zmijewski) Derwinski; Roman Catholic; married Patricia Van Der Giessen; father of Maureen Sue and Michael Stephen; graduated from Loyola University in 1951 with a B.Sc. in History; served with U.S. Army Infantry, 1945–1946; member, Republican party; president and director of Pullman Savings and Loan Association, 1946– ; member of Illinois House of Representatives, 1957–1958; named one of ten outstanding young men of Chicago, 1959 and 1961; member of the eighty-sixth through the ninety-fifth congresses, from the fourth Illinois district; appointed counsellor to the State Department, 1983, and later became undersecretary for security assistance, science, and technology; member, Foreign Affairs Committee, Africa Subcommittee, State Department Organization and Foreign Operations Subcommittee, International Organizations and Movements Subcommittee, Post Office and Civil Service Subcommittee, Census and Statistics Subcommittee, Manpower and Civil Service Subcommittee, Postal Operations Subcommittee; nominated on December 22, 1988, by President George Bush for the position of head of the Veterans Administration, and then became SECRETARY OF VETERANS AFFAIRS when the

Veterans Administration became a cabinet department on March 15, 1989; confirmed by the Senate on March 2, 1989; national director, Polish Highlanders; past state vice-commander, Polish Legion of American Veterans; vice-president executive committee, InterParliamentary Union; member, Veterans of Foreign Wars, Catholic War Veterans, Polish Alma Mater, American Legion, Amvets, Polish Roman Catholic Union, Polish National Alliance, Moose, Knights of Columbus, Kiwanis. *Who's Who in Government, 1988*; *Facts on File* (1988 and 1989).

DEVENS, Charles. Born in Charlestown, Mass., April 4, 1820; son of Charles and Mary (Lithgow) Devens; never married; prepared at Boston Latin School; graduated Harvard in 1838; studied at Harvard Law School; was admitted to the bar in 1840, began practice of law in Northfield, and later Greenfield, Mass.; was Massachusetts state senator for two terms, 1848–1849; became U.S. marshal for district of Massachusetts, 1849–1853; resumed practice of law in Worcester in partnership with George F. Hoar and J. Henry Hill, 1854; served as city solicitor, 1856–1858; promoted steadily in state militia to become brigadier general; became major of 3d Battalion of Massachusetts Rifles, 1861; appointed colonel 15th Massachusetts Regiment; made brigadier general of volunteers of Couch's Division of IV Corps on April 15, 1862; nominated governor, 1862, and defeated; led advance on Richmond, brevetted major general, April 3, 1865, and mustered out in June 1866; appointed justice of the superior court in 1867; named judge of supreme court of Massachusetts, 1873; received LL.D. from Harvard, 1877; appointed ATTORNEY GENERAL in the cabinet of President Hayes on March 10, 1877, and continued under Garfield, serving from March 12, 1877 to March 4, 1881; was re-appointed judge of state supreme court, and served until death; president of Harvard Alumni Association, 1886; died in Boston, January 7, 1891. Interred at Trinity Church with military honors. W. G. Adams, *Genealogical and Personal Memoirs* (1910); Arthur Bishop, *Rutherford B. Hayes, 1822–1893: Chronology, Documents, Bibliographical Aids* (1969); Theodore C. Smith, *Life and Letters of James Abram Garfield* (1968).

DEXTER, Samuel. Born in Boston, Mass., May 14, 1761; son of Samuel Dexter, merchant, scholar, and philanthropist, and Hannah (Sigourney) Dexter; in 1786, married Catherine Gordon, sister of William Gordon, legislator, congressman, and attorney general of New Haven; father of Franklin; studied under Reverend Aaron Putnam; attended Harvard 1777–1781, graduating with highest honors; studied law with Levi Lincoln at Worcester, Mass.; admitted to Worcester County bar in 1784; began law practice at Lunenberg in 1786; served as Massachusetts state representative, 1788–1790; Massachusetts congressional representative, 1793–1795; elected U.S. senator, serving from March 4, 1799 until May 30, 1800 when he resigned to accept an appointment as SECRETARY OF WAR in the cabinet of President John Adams, entering upon duties June 12, 1800 and serving until December 31, 1800, when he began serving in that position *ad* *interim* until March 5, 1801; appointed *ad interim* SECRETARY OF THE TREASURY by President Adams on January 1, 1801, serving until March 6, 1801; returned to law practice, and argued before the Supreme Court; changed from Federalist to Republican in 1812 in support of President Madison's war program; lost election for governor of Massachusetts when he turned against Republican party policy following his 1816 nomination; opposed the Hartford Convention; declined President Adams' offer of a mission to Spain in 1815; president of the first temperance society in Massachusetts; conferred LL.D. by Harvard in 1813; died in Athens, N.Y. on May 3, 1816. Zoltan Haraszti, *John Adams and the Prophets of Progress* (1952); Manning J. Dauer, *The Adams Federalists* (1953); Stephen G. Kurtz, *The Presidency of John Adams* (1957).

DICKERSON, Mahlon. Born at Hanover Neck (now Morris Plains), N.J., April 17, 1770; son of Jonathan and Mary (Coe) Dickerson; bachelor; educated by private tutors and then entered Princeton, graduating in 1789; studied law and was admitted to the bar in 1793; served as private in the 2d Regiment Cavalry, a New Jersey Detached Militia, during the Whiskey Rebellion; moved to Philadelphia, Pa., and was admitted to practice in the Pennsylvania courts in 1797; state commissioner of bankruptcy in 1802; adjutant general, 1805–1808; city recorder, 1808–1810; returned to Morris County, N.J., in 1810; elected to the New Jersey General Assembly from 1811 to 1813; law reporter for the New Jersey Supreme Court from 1813 to 1815; elected governor of New Jersey from 1815 to 1817; elected as a Democrat to the U.S. Senate and was reelected in 1823, serving in all from March 4, 1817 to January 30, 1829, when he resigned; reelected to fill a Senate vacancy from January 30, 1829 to March 3, 1833; member of the New Jersey Council, serving as its vice-president in 1833; declined appointment as minister to Russia in 1834; joined the cabinet of President Van Buren as SECRETARY OF THE NAVY, serving from June 30, 1834, to June 25, 1838, when ill health forced his resignation; U.S. district judge of New Jersey in 1840; delegate to the State Constitutional Convention of 1844; retired to his estate ''Ferromonte''; died in Succasunno, Morris County, N.J., on October 5, 1853; interment in the Presbyterian Cemetery. Robert Remini, *Martin Van Buren and the Making of the Democratic Party* (1919); Edwin Palmer Hoyt, *Martin Van Buren* (1964).

DICKINSON, Donald McDonald. Born in Port Ontario, N.Y., January 17, 1846; son of Col. Asa C. and Minerva (Holmes) Dickinson; married Frances Platt on June 15, 1869; two children; family moved to St. Clair County, Mich. in 1848, and then to Detroit in 1852; attended Detroit public schools and also had private tutors; graduated from University of Michigan Law School in Ann Arbor in 1867; admitted to Michigan bar in 1867; became a leading lawyer in the midwest, and argued cases before the U.S. Supreme Court; became secretary of Democratic state central committee in 1872 and chairman of that body in 1876; chairman of Michigan delegation to Democratic national convention in

1880; member of Democratic national committee, 1880–1885; became early supporter of the presidential candidacy of Grover Cleveland; became titular head of Democratic party in Michigan and consultant to President Cleveland on all Michigan appointments; nominated by Cleveland as POSTMASTER GENERAL on December 6, 1887; confirmed by Senate on January 16, 1888, served until March 4, 1889, at the conclusion of first Cleveland administration; Michigan legislature named new county in his honor in 1891; architect of second successful Cleveland presidential campaign in 1892; declined posts of secretary of state and minister to Great Britain in second Cleveland administration; served as senior counsel for the U.S. before the Joint High Commission on Bering Sea Claims in 1896; member of Court of Arbitration to settle controversy between the U.S. and the Republic of El Salvador in 1902; opposed nomination of William Jennings Bryan in 1896 and 1900; supported reelection of President McKinley in 1900; supported Theodore Roosevelt's third party campaign in 1912, feeling that both major parties had become reactionary; died at his home in Trenton, Mich. on October 15, 1917. John Fitzgibbon, "Don M. Dickinson, One of the State's Two Great Democrats," *Detroit News*, (October 17, 1917); Allan Nevins, *Grover Cleveland: A Study in Courage* (1938).

DICKINSON, Jacob McGavock. Born in Columbus, Miss., January 30, 1851; son of Henry and Anna (McGavock) Dickinson; married Martha Overton on April 20, 1876; father of three sons; moved to Nashville, Tenn. after the Civil War; graduated from the University of Nashville in 1872; studied law at Columbia College; finished his law studies in Leipzig and Paris; admitted to Tennessee bar in 1874; accepted temporary appointments to the Tennessee Supreme Court in 1891, 1892, and 1893; served as U.S. assistant attorney general, 1895–1897; served as a consul for the U.S. before the Alaskan Boundary Tribunal in 1903; helped organize the American Society of International Law in 1906; served as president of the American Bar Association, 1907–1908; served on the Executive Council of the American Society of International Law from 1907 until 1910, and as its vice president from 1910 on; appointed SECRETARY OF WAR by President Taft on March 5, 1909, served until May 1911; served as U.S. special assistant attorney general in the prosecution of United States Steel Corporation in 1913, and again in connection with the labor cases in 1922; served as president of Izaak Walton League from 1927 to 1928; died in Washington, D.C., December 13, 1928; interment in Nashville, Tenn. Blewett Lee, "Jacob McGavock Dickinson: 1851–1928," *Journal of the American Bar Association* (February, 1929): 69–71.

DILLON, Clarence Douglas. Born in Geneva, Switzerland, April 21, 1909; son of Clarence Dillon, investment banker, and Ann McEldin (Douglas) Dillon; Episcopalian; married Phyllis Chess Ellsworth on March 10, 1931; father of Phyllis Ellsworth and Joan Douglas; attended Groton School; received B.A. from Harvard in 1931; worked for Dillon, Read and Company of New York City, and was member of New York Stock Exchange, 1931–1936; elected vice-president and director of Dillon, Read and Company, 1938; called to Washington to aid in statistical control center for U.S. Naval Department in 1940; commissioned ensign in U.S. Naval Reserve in October 1940, was called to active duty in 1941, rose from ensign to lieutenant commander, and discharged in 1945; chairman of board of directors of Dillon, Read and Company, 1946–1953; president of United States and Foreign Securities Corporation, 1937–1946, and director from 1946–1953; president of United States International Securities Corporation; director of Amerada Petroleum Corporation from 1947 to 1953; member of board of overseers of Harvard, 1952–1958; U.S. ambassador extraordinary and plenipotentiary to France, 1953–1957; made deputy undersecretary of state, 1957–1958; became undersecretary of state for economic affairs, 1958–1959; chosen undersecretary of state, 1959–1960; appointed SECRETARY OF THE TREASURY in the cabinet of President Kennedy and continued under President Lyndon B. Johnson, serving from January 21, 1961 to March 31, 1965; most important contributions were formulation of new tax policy and aid in founding Alliance for Progress; member of boards of governors of Metropolitan Museum of Art and New York Hospital; trustee of Groton School; member of Society of the Cincinnati, Society of Colonial Wars, Century Association, and Knickerbocker Club; chairman of U.S. and Foreign Securities Corp. 1967 to 1984; director of Council on Foreign Relations, 1965 to 1978, and vice-chairman of the council, 1977 to 1978; appointed president of the Board of Overseers, Harvard College, 1968 to 1972; chairman of Rockefeller Foundation, 1971 to 1975; chairman of Brookings Institution, 1971 to 1975; managing director of Dillon, Read, and Co., Inc., 1971 to 1983; trustee emeritus, Metropolitan Museum of Art (president from 1970 to 1977, chairman 1977 to 1983); honorary degree of laws: New York University, 1956; Lafayette College, 1957; University of Hartford, Conn., 1958; Columbia University, 1959; Harvard University, 1959; Williams College, 1960; Rutgers University, 1961; Princeton University, 1961; University of Pennsylvania, 1962; Bradley University, 1964; Middlebury College, 1965; Tufts University, 1982; Marymount Manhattan College, 1984; collects art; raises Guernsey cattle on farm in Somerset County, N.J. Jim F. Heath, *J.F.K. and the Business Community* (1969); Hobart Rowan, *Free Enterprises: Kennedy, Johnson and the Business Establishment* (1964); *Who's Who in America, 1986; Who's Who, 1989.*

DIX, John Adams. Born in Boscawen, N.H., July 24, 1798; son of Colonel Timothy Dix, merchant and local leader of Boscawen, and Abigail (Wilkins) Dix; Episcopalian; married Catherine Morgan in 1826; father of seven children; studied at school of Salisbury and Phillips Exeter Academy; entered College of Montreal, and was recalled after fifteen months for War of 1812; appointed cadet in 1812; became an ensign in 1813; was second lieutenant of 21st infantry of New Hampshire, 1814, and was promoted to major; continued in service after war and appointed aide-de-camp; studied law under direction of General William

Wert; was admitted to Washington bar in 1824; practiced in Washington, 1826; was special messenger to Copenhagen, 1826–1828; practiced law in Coopers-town, N.Y. for two years; moved to Albany, and was appointed adjunct-general of state, 1830; appointed N.Y. secretary of state and superintendent of common schools, 1833–1839; became part of "Albany Regency" ruling Democratic party; established and edited *Northern Light*, 1841–1843; member of assembly, 1841; went abroad in 1842; member of U.S. Senate as a Democrat, 1845–1849; nom-inated governor of New York by Free Soil party, 1848, but was defeated; appointed assistant treasurer at New York by President Pierce; was president of Mississippi and Missouri Railroad Company, 1853; supported Buchanan, 1856; appointed postmaster of New York in 1860; appointed SECRETARY OF THE TREAS-URY in the cabinet of President Buchanan on January 11, 1861, and served until March 4, 1861; most important contributions were obtaining of five millions at an average rate of slightly more than 10 percent, dispatching, on January 29, 1861, a message to treasurer's official at New Orleans containing orders to take over a revenue cutter even at risk of violence, and reorganization of department; was first president of Union Defense Committee, and presided at Union Square meeting of April 24, 1861; commissioned major general of volunteers in June, and commanded department of Maryland; commanded Fortress Monroe, 1862; commanded department of East with headquarters at New York, 1863; translated *Dies Irae* (1863); was president of Union Pacific Railroad Company, 1863–1868; appointed naval officer of port of New York, 1866; served as minister to France, 1866–1869; became governor of New York in 1872; vestryman of Trinity Church Corporation, he became comptroller in 1872; delegate to convention of New York diocese, and deputy to general convention of church; acted as president of Erie Railroad Company, 1872; renominated for governor, 1874, but defeated; wrote *A Winter in Madeira and a Summer in Spain and Florence*; published *Speeches and Occasional Addresses* (1864) and *Stabat Mater* (1868); original trustee of Astor Library; retired to New York City; died in New York City, April 21, 1879; interment in Trinity Cemetery. Morgan Dix, *Memoirs of John Adams Dix* (1st ed., 1883; 2d ed., 1969); D. S. Alexander, *Political History of the State of New York* (1906); Philip G. Auchampaugh, *James Buchanan and his Cabinet on the Eve of Secession* (1965).

DOAK, William Nuckles. Born near Rural Retreat, Va., December 12, 1882; son of Canaro Drayton and Elizabeth (Dutton) Doak; married Emma Maria Cricher in 1908; attended public schools of the area; studied at a business college at Bristol, Va.; worked for Norfolk and Western railroad at Bluefield, W. Va., 1900; elected member of Brotherhood of Railroad Trainmen in 1904; was sec-retary-treasurer of southern association of general committees of Order of Rail-road Conductors and Brotherhood of Railroad Trainmen, 1909–1916; general chairman for Norfolk and Western systems, 1912–1916; elected a vice-president of the Brotherhood in 1916, and became national legislative representative in Washington, D.C.; became member of Railway Board of Adjustment Number

One, 1918; in charge of national wage movement, 1919–1920; served on train service board of adjustment for southern and eastern territories from 1921 to 1928; elected first vice-president of the Brotherhood, 1922; active role in territorial wage movement, 1923–1924; unsuccessful candidate for U.S. Senator in 1924; served on committees to decide wages, 1926–1927; chosen assistant president of the Brotherhood, 1927; elected managing editor of *The Railroad Trainmen* and national legislative representative in 1928; appointed SECRETARY OF LABOR in the Cabinet of President Hoover on December 8, 1930, and served from December 9, 1930 to March 3, 1933; most important contributions were fight to restrict immigration as a protective measure for American labor, enforcement of immigration laws, fingerprinting of all aliens to determine those guilty of illegal entry into the U.S., increase in number of aliens leaving the country to exceed those entering, proposal of five-day work week with six-hour day, and securement of congressional approval to increase federal employment services; granted D.H.L. from Lincoln Memorial University, 1931; retired to gardening; died in McLean, Va., October 23, 1933. Eugene Lyons, *Herbert Hoover: A Biography* (1964).

DOBBIN, James Cochran. Born in Fayetteville, N.C., January 17, 1814; son of John Moore and Anness (Cochran) Dobbin; married Louisa Holmes, who died in 1848; attended schools in Fayetteville and the Bingham School in Hillsboro; entered the University of North Carolina in 1828, and was graduated in 1832; studied law for three years and was admitted to the North Carolina bar in 1835; opened a law office in Fayetteville; elected to Congress in 1846 and served one term; elected to the North Carolina House of Commons 1848, 1850, 1852; was the speaker of that body in 1850; headed North Carolina delegation to Democratic national convention in Baltimore in 1852, where he made the speech which started a stampede to Franklin Pierce of N.H., resulting in the latter's nomination as the Democratic presidential candidate; nominated by North Carolina Democrats for U.S. senator, but, because of a legislative deadlock, no candidate was elected; appointed SECRETARY OF THE NAVY by President Franklin Pierce in March 1853; confirmed by the Senate on March 7, 1853, and took office on March 8, 1853; recommended such reforms as the building of six steam frigates and five steam sloops, giving half pay to retired officers, creation of an effective system of punishment to replace flogging, the establishment of a naval apprentice system, the enlistment of seamen for definite term of years; declined offer of seat in U.S. Senate to remain in cabinet until the close of Pierce administration; retired from cabinet on March 4, 1857, and returned to Fayetteville where he died on August 4, 1857. S. A. Ashe, *Biographical History of North Carolina*, vol. 6 (1907); Roy Franklin Nichols, *Franklin Pierce, Young Hickory of the Granite Hills* (1969).

DOLE, Elizabeth Hanford. Born in Salisbury, N.C., July 20, 1936; daughter of John Van Hanford and Mary Ella (Cathey); Methodist; married Robert J. Dole, U.S. Senator from Kansas, on December 6, 1975; attended Duke University and received Master's degree in education and government at Harvard; received law degree from Harvard Law School; admitted to the bar in 1966; appointed deputy special assistant to president; staff assistant to assistant secretary of health, education and welfare; executive director, Presidential Committee on Consumer Interest, 1969–1971; deputy director, Office of Consumer Affairs, 1971; member, Federal Trade Commission, 1973; chairman, Voters for Ronald Reagan/George Bush 1980; director, Human Services Group for Office of Executive Branch Management, Office of President-Elect; former member, Board of Directors, American Council on Young Political Leaders; currently member, Board of Directors, National Council on Aging; currently member, National Advisory Council, National Federation of Republican Women; formerly assistant to President Reagan for public liaison. Appointed by President Reagan on January 5, 1983, and confirmed by the Senate on February 1, 1983, as SECRETARY OF TRANSPORTATION, succeeding Drew Lewis. While serving in that post, she dealt with an air traffic controllers' strike and a truckers strike. Resigned office October 1, 1987, to campaign with her husband in his unsuccessful bid for president in 1988. Appointed by President Bush and confirmed by the Senate to serve as SECRETARY OF LABOR on January 31, 1989. Recipient of many degrees and awards; Phi Beta Kappa, Phi Lambda Theta, Pi Sigma Alpha; Arthur S. Fleming Award for Outstanding Government Service, 1972; one of America's Two Hundred Faces for the Future, *Time*, 1974; member, Harvard Law School Association Council; formerly member, Washington Opera Board; currently member, Board of Advisors, Duke Business School; currently member, Board of Overseers, JFK School of Government, Harvard University. *N.Y. Times Biographical Services* (1980); *Who's Who in America*, 1982–1983; *Current Biography*, 1983; *100th Congressional Directory, 1987–1988*; *Who's Who in American Politics*, 1987–1988.

DONALDSON, Jesse Monroe. Born on a farm near Shelbyville, Ill., August 17, 1885; son of Moses Martin Donaldson, merchant and local postmaster, and Amanda Saletha (Little) Donaldson; Methodist; married Nell Graybill on August 14, 1911; father of three children; attended public schools of Oconee, Ill. and the Shelbyville Normal School; studied at Teacher's Normal College and Sparks Business College in Shelbyville; taught in the public schools of Shelby, Montgomery, and Christian counties in Illinois, 1903–1908; gave up teaching when, on May 15, 1908, he became one of the first three letter-carriers in Shelbyville; left post office in 1910 to become a clerk in U.S. War Department; returned to the postal service on July 1, 1911, becoming post office clerk and supervisor at Muskogee, Okla.; assigned as postal inspector in the Kansas City, Mo. division on May 11, 1915; appointed postal inspector in charge of the Chattanooga, Tenn. division on August 1, 1932; transferred to Washington, D.C., where he became deputy second assistant postmaster general on June 12, 1933; promoted to deputy first assistant postmaster general on April 1, 1936; appointed chief post office inspector on March 1, 1945, and first assistant postmaster general on July 5,

1946; chief spokesman for the department before Congress; nominated POST-MASTER GENERAL in November 1947 by President Truman and confirmed by the U.S. Senate on December 16, 1947, becoming the first letter-carrier in the history of the department to rise through the ranks to this office; established highway post office service, expanded railway postal transportation, reduced home mail deliveries from two to one a day; resigned from the cabinet on January 20, 1953, at the end of the Truman administration, and retired; died in Kansas City, Mo., March 25, 1970. Jonathan Daniels, *The Man of Independence* (1950); *Newsweek* (December 8, 1947).

DONOVAN, Raymond James. Born in Bayonne, N.J., August 31, 1930; married Catherine Sblendorio in 1957; father of Kenneth, Mary Ellen and Keith; Roman Catholic; graduated from St. Andrew's parochial school; became minor seminarian with the Missionary Servants of the Most Holy Trinity in Cottontown, Ala.; went on to Notre Dame Seminary in New Orleans, La., working summers as a unionized laborer; received his bachelor's degree in philosophy in 1952; gave up his studies for the priesthood and returned to New Jersey; worked for the American Insurance Company; joined Schiavone Construction Company in Secaucus, N.J., as major shareholder and vice-president in charge of labor relations, finance, bonding, insurance, and real estate, 1959; became executive vice-president, 1971; originally a Democrat, he gravitated to conservative Republicans; President Ronald Reagan nominated him as SECRETARY OF LABOR on December 16, 1980, and was confirmed by Congress on February 3, 1981, after charges of alleged payoffs could not be corroborated by the FBI; the reforms brought about by his department under his tutelage were heavily criticized; he was considered a tough negotiator with the labor unions; resigned from his post, March 24, 1985; was acquitted of all charges after a nine-month trial in June 1987. *Current Biography, 1982; Newsweek* (October 15, 1984); *U.S. News and World Report* (January 21 and March 25, 1985); *Time* (June 8, 1987).

DUANE, William John. Born in Clonmel, Tipperary County, Ireland, May 9, 1780; son of William Duane, editor of the *Aurora*, and Catherine (Corcoran) Duane; married Deborah Bache; no children; tutored by mother; attended private school for fifteen months; learned printing; came to Philadelphia in 1796; worked in composing room of *True American*; employed by *Aurora*; went into partnership with William Levis, paper merchant, in 1806; member of Pennsylvania House of Representatives, 1809; published *The Law of Nations Investigated* in 1809; defeated in reelection for state House of Representatives, 1810; published *Letters on International Improvements*, 1811; studied law, 1812, and admitted to the Philadelphia bar on June 13, 1815; unsuccessful candidate for U.S. Congress in 1816; unsuccessful candidate for state legislature, 1817; reelected to state House of Representatives in 1819; became prosecuting attorney for mayor's court, 1820; refused Congressional nomination in 1824; member of Democratic Committee of Correspondence for Philadelphia, 1828; became member of Select Council of Philadelphia in 1829; made commissioner under treaty with Denmark, 1831; appointed SECRETARY OF THE TREASURY in the Cabinet of President Jackson on May 29, 1833, and served from June 11, 1833 to September 22, 1833; most important contribution was refusal to remove money from U.S. Bank at Jackson's request; practiced law; published *Narrative and Correspondence Concerning the Removal of The Deposits*; was director of Girard College; died in Philadelphia on September 27, 1865. *Biographical Memoir of William J. Duane* (1868); Ronald Shaw, *Andrew Jackson, 1767–1845: Chronology, Documents, Bibliographical Aids* (1969).

DULLES, John Foster. Born in Washington, D.C., February 25, 1888; son of Allen Macy and Edith (Foster) Dulles; Presbyterian; married Janet Pomeroy Avery on June 26, 1912; father of John Watson and Lillian Pomeroy Avery; after attending the public schools of Watertown, N.Y., he entered Princeton University, graduating in 1900; attended the Sorbonne, Paris, France, in 1908 and 1909; graduated from the Law School of George Washington University, Washington, D.C., in 1911; admitted to the bar in 1911; served as special agent for the Department of State in Central America in 1917; served as a captain and major during World War I; served in U.S. Army Intelligence in 1917 and 1918; assistant to the chairman of the War Trade Board in 1918; counsel to the American Committee to Negotiate Peace in 1918 and 1919; member of the Reparations Committee and Supreme Economic Council in 1919; legal advisor to the Polish Plan of Financial Stability in 1927; American representative to the Berlin Debt Conference in 1933; member of the U.S. delegation to the San Francisco Conference on World Organization in 1945; advisor to the Secretary of State at the Council of Foreign Ministers in London, in 1945, Moscow and London, in 1947, and Paris, in 1949; representative to the General Assembly of the United Nations, 1946–1950 and chairman of the U.S. delegation in Paris in 1948; trustee of the Rockefeller Foundation; chairman of the Board of the Carnegie Endowment for International Peace; member of the New York State Banking Board, 1946–1949; appointed as a Republican to the U.S. Senate to fill a vacancy caused by the resignation of Senator Robert F. Wagner, serving from July 7, 1949 to November 8, 1949; consultant to the Secretary of State in 1951 and 1952; invited to join the Federal cabinet as SECRETARY OF STATE by appointment of President Eisenhower on January 20, 1953, serving until his resignation due to illness on April 15, 1959; as special representative of the President with the rank of Ambassador, he negotiated the Japanese Peace Treaty in 1951, and the Australian, New Zealand, Philippine, and Japanese Security Treaties in 1950 and 1951; authored *War, Peace And Change* (1939); died in Washington, D.C., on May 24, 1959; interment in Arlington National Cemetery. Roscoe Drummond, *Duel at the Brink: John Foster Dulles' Command of American Power* (1960); John Robinson Beal, *John Foster Dulles: A Biography* (1957).

DUNCAN, Charles William, Jr. Born in Houston, Tex., September 9, 1926; son of Charles William and Mary Lillian (House) Duncan; Methodist; married Thetis Anne Smith, June 10, 1957; father of Charles William III and Mary Anne; served in U.S. Army Air Force 1944–1946; received B.S. degree in chemical engineering from Rice University in 1947; roustabout and chemical engineer for Humble Oil and Refining Co., 1947; graduate work in management at the University of Texas, 1948–1949; started work for Duncan Foods Co., Houston, Tex., 1948; administrative vice-president, Duncan Foods Co., 1957–1958; president and chairman of the advisory board, Duncan Foods Co., 1958–1964; president, Coca-Cola Co., Food Division, Houston, Tex., 1964–1967; chairman, Coca-Cola Europe, 1967–1970; executive vice-president, Coca-Cola Co., Atlanta, Ga., 1970–1971; president, Coca-Cola Co., 1971–1974; chairman, Board of Directors, Rotan Mosle Finance Corporation, Houston, Tex., 1974–1977; deputy secretary, Department of Defense, 1977–1979; nominated for SECRETARY OF ENERGY by President Jimmy Carter on July 20, 1979, to replace James R. Schlesinger; confirmed on July 31, 1979; sworn in on August 24, 1979; involved in delicate negotiations with various OPEC nations to continue the U.S. stockpiling of petroleum reserves for strategic purposes; worked to provide poor and middle-income families with government aid to help them meet the cost of rising fuel bills; served until January 20, 1981; serves on the board of directors of many companies, universities, and institutes, including Coca-Cola Texas, American Express, Texas, and United Technologies Corp.; member of the Council on Foreign Relations; in 1988 became chairman, Board of Directors, of Duncan, Cook and Co., a Houston, Tex.; investing firm. *New York Times* (July 21, 1976, and August 25, 1979); *Facts on File Yearbook* (1979 and 1980); *Who's Who in America, 1988–1989*.

DUNLOP, John Thomas. Born in Placerville, Calif., July 5, 1914; son of John W. and Antonia D. (Forni) Dunlop; married Dorothy Webb, July 6, 1937; father of John Barrett, Beverly Claire, and Thomas Frederick; received A.B. degree from the University of California in 1935; received Ph.D. in 1939; received LL.D. from the University of Chicago in 1968; acting instructor, Stanford University, 1936–1937; instructor, Harvard University, 1938–1945; vice chairman, Boston Regional War Labor Board, 1944–1945; associate professor of economics, 1945–1950; chairman, National Joint Board for Settlement of Jurisdictional Disputes in Building and Construction, 1945–1947; member, National Labor Relations Board, 1948–1952; member, Atomic Energy Labor Panel, 1948–1953; member, Board of Inquiry, Bituminous Coal Industry, 1950; appointed professor of economics, 1950; arbitrator, Emergency Board, 1954–1955, 1960 and 1966; member, Presidential Railroad Commission, 1960–1962; member, Missile Sites Labor Commission, 1961–1967; member, Presidential Committee on Equal Employment Opportunity, 1964–1965; dean, Faculty Arts and Sciences, 1970–1973; director, Cost of Living Council, 1973–1974; American Academy of Arts and Sciences; American Philosophical Society; author of *Wage Determination and*

Trade Unions (1944), *Collective Bargaining—Principles and Cases* (1949), *Industrial Relations System* (1958); co-author, *Labor and the American Community* (1970); Republican; nominated by President Gerald Ford on February 8, 1975, for the office of SECRETARY OF LABOR, and on March 6 the U.S. Senate confirmed his appointment; during his administration the labor unions boycotted the loading of grain sold to the Soviet Union, and the possible deficits in the financing of the Social Security Administration came to light; having taken an active role in the drafting of federal legislation dealing with construction picketing, Dunlop resigned January 14, 1976, shortly after President Ford vetoed the act; left office on February 1, 1976, and returned to Harvard. Recipient of Murray, Meany, Green award, AFL-CIO, 1987; Author of *Business and Public Policy* (1980) and *Dispute Resolution: Negotiation and Consensus Building* (1984). *Saturday World News Digest* (February 15, 1975, and January 17, 1976); National Journal, *Ford's Presidency* (1976); Henry H. Schulte, Jr., ed., *Facts on File Yearbook*, 1975; *Who's Who, 1989.*

DURKIN, Martin Patrick. Born in Chicago, Ill., March 18, 1894; son of James J. Durkin, stationary engineer, and Mary Catherine (Higgins) Durkin; Roman Catholic; married Anna H. McNicholas on August 29, 1921; father of Martin P., William J., and John F.; attended parochial schools; took courses in heating and ventilation engineering; worked in packing house; became steamfitter's helper in 1911, and after six years made journeyman in the union; served as private in U.S. Army in France during World War I; elected assistant business agent of Steamfitters Local 597, United Association of Journeymen and Apprentices of the Plumbing and Pipe Fitting Industry of the U.S. and Canada, 1921–1933; was vice-president of Chicago Building Trades Council, 1927–1933; made state director of labor for Illinois, 1933–1941; president of International Association of Governmental Labor Officials, 1933–1955; was national secretary-treasurer of United Association of Plumbers and Steamfitters, AFL, in 1941, and was elected president in 1943; appointed SECRETARY OF LABOR in the cabinet of President Eisenhower, and served from January 21, 1953 to October 8, 1953, resigning after disagreement over Taft-Hartley Act; most important contribution was legislation setting up unemployment compensation, state employment service, and state conciliation and mediation service; member of Defense Mobilization Board, National Security Resources Board, and National War Labor Board in 1953; director of Union Labor Life Insurance Company and National Safety Council; received Rerum Novarum Award from St. Peter's College of New Jersey, 1953; vice-president of Catholic Conference on Industrial Problems; belonged to Knights of Columbus and Holy Name Society; died in Washington, D.C. on November 13, 1955. Dean Albertson, ed., *Eisenhower as President* (1963); David A. Frier, *Conflict of Interest in the Eisenhower Administration* (1969).

E

EATON, John Henry. Born near Scotland Neck, Halifax County, N.C., June 18, 1790; son of John Eaton, maker of chaises, county coroner, and assemblyman, and Elizabeth Eaton; married Myra Lewis sometime before 1816; remarried to Margaret O'Neill in 1829; attended the common schools; went to University of North Carolina, Chapel Hill, from 1803 to 1804; studied law, was admitted to the bar, and began practice in Franklin, Tenn., 1808; became a private soldier in 1812; elected to state House of Representatives in 1815 and 1816; published *The Life of Andrew Jackson, Major General in the Service of the United States* in 1817; pursued land speculation, 1817; appointed member of U.S. Senate to fill unexpired term of George W. Campbell, and served from September 5, 1818 to March 3, 1821; elected to U.S. Senate in September, 1821, reelected in 1826, and served from September 27, 1821 to March 9, 1829; appointed SECRETARY OF WAR in the cabinet of President Jackson, and served from March 9, 1829 until his resignation on June 19, 1831 over the scandal concerning his second wife; was territorial governor of Florida, 1834–1836; made envoy extraordinary and minister plenipotentiary to Spain, 1836–1840; died in Washington, D.C., on November 17, 1856; interment in Oak Hill Cemetery. William Terrell Lewis, *Genealogy of the Lewis Family* (1983); Ronald Shaw, *Andrew Jackson, 1767–1845: Chronology, Documents, Bibliographical Aids* (1969).

EDISON, Charles. Born in Llewellyn Park, West Orange, N.J., August 3, 1890; son of Thomas Alva Edison, inventor, and Mina (Miller) Edison; married to Carolyn Hawkinson on March 27, 1918; no children; attended the Dearborn-Morgan school, the Cartaret Academy, Orange, N.J., and the Hotchkiss School, Lakeville, Conn.; attended the Massachusetts Institute of Technology, 1909–1913, and was graduated as an engineer; worked in the Edison Illuminating

Company, Boston, 1914; returned to Orange, 1915, and worked in Edison Industries; chairman of several directing boards of Edison Industries and assistant to his father, 1916; president and director of Thomas A. Edison, Inc., 1926; also president of City View Storage Company, Metropolitan Cement Company, Pohatcong Railroad Company, and the E.K. Medicinal Gas Laboratories, Inc.; appointed to the New Jersey state recovery board, and member of the Regional Labor Board, 1933; compliance director for the National Recovery Administration; state director of the New Jersey National Emergency Council; regional director of the Federal Housing Administration, 1934; member of the National Recovery Board by appointment of President Franklin D. Roosevelt, 1935; appointed assistant secretary of the navy by President Roosevelt on November 17, 1936; served as acting secretary during the illness and after the death on July 7, 1939 of Claude A. Swanson; appointed SECRETARY OF THE NAVY in the Cabinet of President Roosevelt on December 30, 1939; most important contributions were opposing the scrapping of World War I destroyers, a move which helped make them available for Britain early in World War II, and supervising the Navy's intensive shipbuilding program; resigned his post on July 10, 1940 upon receiving the Democratic nomination for governor of New Jersey; elected governor of New Jersey in November 1940 and served until 1944; chairman of the board of the McGraw-Edison Company, 1957–1961; served on the executive committee of the New York Conservative Party and enrolled as a party member in 1963, after having been affiliated first with the Republican and then with the Democratic parties; author of a book of poetry, *Flotsam and Jetsam* (1967), written under the pen name of "Tom Sleeper"; died in New York City on July 31, 1969. T. R. Fehrenbach, *F.D.R.'s Undeclared War: 1939–1941* (1967); A. J. Wann, *President as Chief Administrator: A Study of Franklin D. Roosevelt* (1968).

EDWARDS, James. Born in Hawthorne, Fla., June 24, 1927; son of Morton Edwards and Bertie Hieronymus; Presbyterian; married Ann Norris Darlington on March 22, 1951; father of James Jr. and Catherine; entered as seaman, U.S. Maritime Service, 1944; released as deck officer, 1947; received B.S. from Charleston College, Charleston, S.C. 1950; deck officer, Alcoa Steamship Co., 1950–1951; earned D.M.D. from the University of Louisville School of Dentistry, 1955; recalled as dental officer, U.S. Navy, 1955–1957; Lt. Commander, Naval Reserve, 1957–1967; studied at University of Pennsylvania Graduate Medical School, 1957–1958; oral surgery residency at Henry Ford Hospital in Detroit, 1958–1960; assisted in fund raising for the Barry Goldwater Campaign, Charleston County, South Carolina, 1964; chairman of the Charleston County Republican Committee, 1964–1969; delegate to the Republican national convention in the years 1968, 1972, 1976, 1980, and 1984; dental representative on South Carolina Governor's Statewide Committee for Comprehensive Health Care Planning, 1968–1972; presidential appointee to the Federal Hospital Council, 1969–1973; chairman of the South Carolina First Congressional District Republican

Committee, 1970–1971; unsuccessful candidate for the U.S. House of Representatives, 1971; member of the South Carolina Statewide Steering Committee for the Republican Party, 1972–1974; chairman of the Charleston County Republican Steering Committee, 1972–1974; elected to the South Carolina State Senate and served from 1972 to 1974; elected governor of South Carolina and served from 1975 to 1978; appointed SECRETARY OF ENERGY by President Ronald Reagan and served from January 15, 1981, to November 6, 1982; working to scale back and eventually abolish the Department of Energy, Edwards moved to deregulate the energy industries, removing price controls on oil and gasoline, but continued to push for government research into nuclear power and synthetic fuels, including the building of demonstration plants; presently a professor of dentistry at the College of Dental Medicine of the Medical University of South Carolina. *New York Times* (January 8 and 13, 1981; November 6, 1982); *Who's Who in American Politics, 1987–1988*.

EISENHOWER, Dwight David. Born in Denison, Tex., October 14, 1890; son of David Jacob and Ida Elizabeth (Stover) Eisenhower; Presbyterian; married Mary [Mamie] Geneva Doud of Boone, Iowa, on July 1, 1916; father of David Dwight and John Sheldon Doud; moved to Abilene, Kans. with his family in 1892; attended the grade and high schools of Abilene; entered West Point on June 14, 1911, graduating on June 12, 1915, 61st in a class of 164, and was commissioned a second lieutenant of infantry and assigned to the 19th Infantry Division, San Antonio, Tex.; appointed commander of the 301st Tank Battalion in January 1921; executive officer of Camp Gaillard, Panama Canal Zone, from 1922 to 1924; attended the Command and General Staff School, Fort Leavenworth, Kans., graduating in 1926; attended Army War College in Washington, D.C., graduating in 1928; appointed assistant executive in the office of the assistant secretary of war, serving from 1929 to 1933; appointed special assistant to the Army chief of staff, General Douglas MacArthur, in February 1933, with the rank of major, accompanying him to the Philippine Islands in 1935, and remaining in that post until 1939; following the outbreak of World War II, he returned to the U.S., joining the 15th Infantry Division at Fort Ord, Cal., as executive officer; appointed chief of the War Plans Division of the War Department General Staff in February 1942; appointed major general in April 1942; appointed commanding general of the European Theater of Operations on June 25, 1942; appointed lieutenant general in July 1942; appointed commander in chief of Allied Forces in North Africa on November 8, 1942; appointed full general in February 1943; directed the invasion of Sicily and Italy from July to December 1943; appointed supreme commander of the Allied Expeditionary Force on December 24, 1943; led the D-Day invasion of Normandy, France, on June 6, 1944; appointed general of the army on December 20, 1944; commander of the U.S. occupation forces in Europe from May to November 1945; appointed chief of staff of the U.S. Army from November 19, 1945, until his retirement from the Army on February 7, 1948; appointed president of Columbia University on June 7, 1948; declined to seek U.S. presidency in July 1948; granted an indefinite leave of absence from Columbia University in 1951 to serve as commander of the North Atlantic Treaty Organization (NATO) forces in Europe; resigned from the Army in June 1952; received the Republican nomination for the presidency in July 1952; elected PRESIDENT on November 4, 1952; inaugurated on January 20, 1953, and reelected for a second term on November 6, 1956, serving until January 20, 1961; upon leaving the White House, he returned to his Gettysburg, Pa., estate; his five-star rank was restored by Congress on March 4, 1961; he was the first president to serve with three Congresses in which both chambers were controlled by an opposing political party; he was the oldest president to leave office; authored *Crusade In Europe* (1957); *The White House Years*, 2 vols. (1963–1965); *At Ease—Stories I Tell To Friends* (1967); died in Washington, D.C., on March 28, 1969; interment in Abilene, Kans. Arthur Larson, *Eisenhower: The President Nobody Knew* (1968).

ELKINS, Stephen Benton. Born on a farm near New Lexington, Ohio, September 26, 1841; son of Colonel Philip Duncan and Sarah Pickett (Withers) Elkins; married Sarah Jacobs on June 10, 1866; father of two daughters; married Hallie Davis on April 14, 1875; father of Davis Elkins, U.S. Senator, and five other children; attended public schools; moved with family to farm on Missouri River, Westport, Mo.; received B.A. from University of Missouri at Columbia in 1860, and M.A. in 1868; taught county school at Cass County, Mo., in 1861; became Union army captain in 77th Missouri Infantry; went to law school; was admitted to the Missouri bar in 1864; moved to Messilia, N.M., and practiced law; studied Spanish; elected to territorial legislature in 1864, and reelected in 1865; made territorial district attorney in 1866, and served until January 14, 1867; served as attorney general of the territory from January 1867 to March 1867; chosen U.S. district attorney, 1867–1870; elected Republican territorial delegate to 43d Congress in 1872, was reelected in 1874, and served from March 4, 1873 to March 3, 1877; invested in Colorado mines; practiced law, 1876; president of Santa Fe First National Bank; became political lieutenant and advisor to James G. Blaine in 1884; member of Republican national committee; moved to Elkins, W.Va., in 1890; appointed SECRETARY OF WAR in the cabinet of President Benjamin Harrison on December 22, 1891, and served from December 24, 1891 to March 5, 1895; elected to U.S. Senate in 1895, reelected in 1901 and 1907, and served from March 4, 1895 until death; bought Morgantown and Kingwood Railroad, 1902; bought interest with Henry G. Davis in Coal and Coke Railway; died in Washington, D.C., on January 4, 1911; interment in Maplewood Cemetery, Elkins, W.Va. Charles M. Pepper, *Life and Times of Henry Gassaway Davis* (1920); H. J. Sievers, ed., *Benjamin Harrison, 1833–1901: Chronology, Documents, Bibliographical Aids* (1969).

ENDICOTT, William Crowninshield. Born in Salem, Mass., November 19, 1826; baptized William Gardner, but changed name by a legal act on April 19, 1837; son of William Putnam and Mary (Crowninshield) Endicott; descendant of John Endicott, colonial governor of Massachusetts; grandson of Jacob Crown-inshield, member of Congress; married Ellen Peabody, his cousin, on December 13, 1859; father of William and Mary; attended Salem Latin School; graduated Harvard College, 1847; studied law in office of Nathaniel J. Lord in Salem; went to Harvard Law School, 1849–1850; admitted to Essex county bar in 1850; granted LL.D. from Harvard, 1882; was co-partner with Jairus Ware Perry in firm of Perry and Endicott; lectured; member of common council of Salem for three years, and president of it in 1857; elected city solicitor of Salem, 1858–1863; president of Salem Bank, 1858–1864; president of Salem National Bank; trustee of Salem Savings Bank until death; Whig, but turned Democrat; unsuc-cessful candidate for state attorney general in 1866, 1867, and 1868; was defeated running for Congress in 1870; appointed associate justice of Massachusetts Su-preme Court in 1873, and served until resignation in 1882; traveled; nominated governor by Democrats, 1884, and lost; appointed SECRETARY OF WAR in the cabinet of President Cleveland on March 6, 1885, and served until March 4, 1889; most important contributions were introduction of reforms such as Endicott Board of Fortifications, surrender of Apache Indians under Geronimo in 1886, approval of proposal to return captured Confederate flags to Southern states to which they belonged; was president of Peabody Education Fund; original trustee of Groton Society; first president of University of Boston; member of Saturday Club of Boston, Colonial Society of Massachusetts, and American History As-sociation; died in Boston, Mass., May 6, 1900; interment in Harmony Grove Cemetery, Salem. Henry J. Ford, *Cleveland Era* (1921); Robert L. Vexter, ed., *Grover Cleveland, 1837–1908: Chronology, Documents, Bibliographical Aids* (1968); H. J. Sievers, ed., *Benjamin Harrison, 1833–1901: Chronology, Doc-uments, Bibliographical Aids* (1969).

EUSTIS, William. Born in Cambridge, Mass., June 10, 1753; son of Benjamin Eustis, doctor, and Elizabeth (Hill) Eustis; married Caroline Langdon on Sep-tember 24, 1810; childless; attended public schools; went to Boston Latin School; graduated Harvard in 1772; studied medicine under Dr. Joseph Warren, 1772; began practice in Boston; served as physician in Revolutionary army, and cared for wounded of Bunker Hill; resumed practice of medicine in Boston; was surgeon on march against Shays, 1786–1787; made vice-president of the Society of the Cincinnati, 1786–1810 and 1820; member of Massachusetts General Court (leg-islature) from 1788 to 1794; elected to U.S. House of Representatives in 1800, and served from March 4 1801 to March 3, 1805; appointed SECRETARY OF WAR in the cabinet of President Jefferson on February 17, 1809, reappointed under Madison on March 7, 1809, and served from April 8, 1809 to December 31, 1812; most important contributions were defense of Embargo and Non-Intercourse Acts, reorganization and expansion of army, and role in debate against Harrison Gray Otis and Samuel Dexter; made minister to Holland in 1814; chosen member of U.S. Congress, and served from August 1, 1820 to March 3, 1823; unsuccessful candidate for governor of Massachusetts in 1820,

1821, and 1822; elected governor in 1823 and 1824; died in Boston, Mass., February 6, 1825; interment in Granary Burying Ground. S. E. Morison, *The Life and Letters of Harrison Gray Otis, Federalist, 1765–1848* (1913); Ian Elliot, *James Madison, 1751–1836: Chronology, Documents, Bibliographical Aids* (1969).

EVARTS, William Maxwell. Born in Boston, Mass., February 6, 1818; son of Jeremiah Evarts, lawyer and author of *Panoplist*, and Mehitabel (Sherman) Barnes Evarts; married Helen Minerva Wardner on August 30, 1843; father of twelve children; attended Boston public schools; studied at Boston Latin School; entered Yale in 1833, received B.A. in 1837, and M.A. in 1840; founder of *Yale Literary Magazine*; studied law in office of Horace Everett at Windsor, Vt.; went to Dane Law School of Harvard College; studied law under Daniel Lord of New York City in 1839; admitted to New York bar on July 16, 1841; opened practice in New York City in October 1841; went into partnership with Charles E. Butler, 1842; chosen assistant U.S. attorney for southern district of New York, 1849–1853; opposed slavery; made chairman of New York delegation to Republican national convention in May 1860; unsuccessful candidate for U.S. Senate, 1861; helped form Union Defense Committee in New York; sent on mission to Great Britain, April–July 1863 and December 1863–June 1864; trustee of Peabody Educational Fund from 1867 to death; delegate to N.Y. state constitutional convention of 1867; appointed ATTORNEY GENERAL in the cabinet of President Andrew Johnson, and served from July 15, 1868 to March 3, 1869; president of Association of the Bar of the City of New York, 1870–1880; member of Yale College Corporation from 1872 to 1891; appointed SECRETARY OF STATE in the cabinet of President Hayes, and served from March 12, 1877 to March 4, 1881; most important contributions were raising standard of consular services and idea of series consular reports; U.S. delegate to international monetary conference in Paris, 1881; elected to U.S. Senate as Republican on January 20, 1885, and served from March 4, 1885 to May 3, 1891; founder and vice-president of Association of Bar of New York; died in New York City on February 28, 1901; interment in Ascutney Cemetery, Windsor, Vt. Sherman Evarts, *Arguments and Speeches of William Maxwell Evarts*, 3 vols. (1919); Brainerd Dyer, *Public Career of William M. Evarts* (1933, 1969).

EVERETT, Edward. Born in Dorchester, Mass., April 11, 1794; son of Rev. Oliver Everett, pastor of New South Church of Boston, 1782–1792, and Lucy (Hill) Everett; Unitarian; married Charlotte Gray Brooks in 1822; father of six children; attended public schools in Boston; graduated Harvard University in 1811; was tutor at Harvard from 1812 to 1814; studied theology, and was ordained pastor of Brattle Street Unitarian Church in Boston, February 9, 1814; traveled; was professor of Greek literature at Harvard, 1815–1820; was Eliot professor of Greek literature, 1820–1826; served as overseer of Harvard, 1827–1847, 1849–1854, and 1862–1865; elected as a Republican to 19th U.S. Congress, was reelected four times, serving from March 4, 1825 to March 3, 1835, and declined candidacy for renomination in 1834; governor of Massachusetts, 1836–1840; appointed U.S. envoy extraordinary and minister plenipotentiary to Great Britain, and served from September 13, 1841 to August 8, 1845; declined offer of diplomatic representative to China, 1843; elected president of Harvard University, and served, 1846–1849; wrote Hulsemann letter, 1850, stating U.S. had a right to interfere and aid any other nation struggling for popular government; appointed SECRETARY OF STATE in the cabinet of President Fillmore to fill the vacancy caused by the death of Daniel Webster and served from November 6, 1852 to March 3, 1853; most important contribution was rejection of proposal of U.S. unification with England and France in an alliance guaranteeing Cuba to Spain; member of U.S. Senate from March 4, 1853 to June 1, 1854; was unsuccessful candidate for the vice-presidency on Constitutional-Union ticket with Bell, 1860; gave address of dedication of national cemetery at Gettysburg, Pa., on November 19, 1863; presidential elector on Republican ticket of Lincoln, 1864; died in Boston, Mass., January 15, 1865; interment in Mount Auburn Cemetery, Cambridge, Mass. P. R. Frothingham, *Edward Everett, Orator and Statesman* (1925); Robert J. Rayback, *Millard Fillmore* (1959).

EWING, Thomas. Born near West Liberty, Va., December 28, 1789; son of George and Rachel (Harris) Ewing; Catholic; married Maria Willis Boyle on January 7, 1820; father of Hugh Boyle, Thomas Jr. (congressman), and four other children; adopted William T. Sherman, 1829, and appointed him to West Point in 1836; moved with family to Waterford, Va., 1793, and then to Ames Township, Athens County, Ohio in 1798; educated by elder sister; worked in Kanawha salt works to earn money for college; received B.A. from Ohio University in 1815; studied law in office of General Philemon Beecher in Lancaster, Ohio; was admitted to the bar in August 1816 and began practice of his profession; defeated as candidate for state legislature, 1823; became U.S. senator, serving from 1831 to 1837; was defeated in reelection of 1836, and resumed law practice in Lancaster; appointed SECRETARY OF THE TREASURY in the cabinet of President William H. Harrison and continued under Tyler, serving from March 5, 1841 to September 13, 1841; most important contribution was help in drafting bills for re-charter of national bank; resigned when bills were vetoed two times, and returned to practice of law; appointed SECRETARY OF THE INTERIOR in the cabinet of President Taylor, and continued under Fillmore, serving from March 8, 1849 to July 22, 1850; most important contributions were recommendations for erection of a mint near the California gold mines and building of a railroad to the Pacific; appointed to fill unexpired term of Corwin in the Senate, 1850; retired from public life in 1851; appointed delegate to Peace Convention in 1861; recommended for Secretary of War by President Johnson in 1868 but Senate never acted upon the recommendation; died in Lancaster, Ohio, October 26, 1871; interment in St. Mary's Cemetery. Ellen Ewing Sherman, *Memorial of Thomas Ewing of Ohio* (1873); Freeman Cleares, *Old Tippecanoe* (1939); Robert J. Rayback, *Millard Fillmore* (1959).

F

FAIRBANKS, Charles Warren. Born in Unionville Center, Ohio, May 11, 1852; son of Loriston Monroe Fairbanks, a New England pioneer of Puritan stock, and Mary Adelaide (Smith) Fairbanks; Methodist; married Cornelia Cole on October 6, 1874; father of six children; attended local schools; graduated Ohio Wesleyan University, Delaware, Ohio, in 1872; became agent of Associated Press in Pittsburgh, Pa., and Cleveland, Ohio; studied law, was admitted to the Ohio bar in 1874, and moved to Indianapolis, Ind., to begin practice; trustee of Ohio Wesleyan University, 1885; managed political campaign of Walter Gresham in 1888; was unsuccessful candidate for U.S. Senate from Ohio, 1892; chairman of Indiana Republican state conventions of 1892 and 1898; chosen delegate at large to Republican national conventions of 1896, 1900, and 1904; elected to U.S. Senate in 1896, and served from March 4, 1897 to March 3, 1905; appointed member of U.S. and British Joint High Commission in Quebec, 1898, to deal with Canadian issues; elected VICE-PRESIDENT in the administration of President Theodore Roosevelt, and served from March 4, 1905 to March 3, 1909; chairman of the platform committee which nominated Taft, 1912; unsuccessful Republican candidate for vice-president on ticket with Charles E. Hughes in 1916; resumed practice of law; died in Indianapolis, Ind., June 4, 1918; interment in Crown Hill Cemetery. F. E. Leupp, "Charles Warren Fairbanks," *Independent* (July 7, 1904); James F. Rhodes, *McKinley and Roosevelt Administrations, 1897–1909* (1922); George E. Mowry, *Era of Theodore Roosevelt, 1900–1912* (1958).

FAIRCHILD, Charles Stebbins. Born in Cazenovia, N.Y., April 30, 1842; son of Sidney Thompson Fairchild, attorney for New York Central Railroad, and Helen (Childs) Fairchild; married Helen Linklaen on June 1, 1871; attended Oneida Conference Seminary in Cazenovia; graduated from Harvard College in

1863; graduated from Harvard Law School in 1865; admitted to the bar in 1866, and joined his father's law firm in Albany, N.Y.; became active in New York state Democratic party as protégé of Horatio Seymour and Samuel Tilden; appointed deputy attorney general of New York State in 1874; in that post, he won conviction of New York City police commissioners Gardner and Charlick and handled fraud prosecutions of the Canal Ring; nominated as attorney general in Democratic state convention in 1875; elected to office in November 1875; as attorney general, he was also commissioner of land office, commissioner of canal fund, member of canal board, member of board of state charities, trustee of state capital and state hall; under pressure of Canal Ring and Tammany Hall, he was denied renomination as attorney general in 1877 and left office in 1878; spent two years in Europe, returning in 1880 to practice law in New York City; appointed assistant secretary of the treasury by President Cleveland in 1885; in that post, he headed a study to reorganize department; became acting secretary of the treasury when Secretary Daniel Manning fell ill on March 23, 1886; appointed SECRETARY OF THE TREASURY by Cleveland on April 1, 1887, following Manning's resignation because of ill health; as Secretary, he invested $28 million of sinking fund in Government bonds and sought to maintain standard of currency; left office on March 5, 1889, at conclusion of Cleveland's first administration; became a businessman and philanthropist; served as president of New York Security and Trust Company until 1905 and later as the president of the Atlanta and Charlotte Air Line Rail Road; was president of New York Reform Club; member of Monetary Commission and of Indianapolis Monetary Conference in 1897; in politics, he opposed the pledging of New York delegation to David Hill for presidential nomination at Democratic national convention in Chicago in 1892; as permanent chairman of state convention, he fought presidential nomination of William Jennings Bryan at the Democratic national convention in Indianapolis in 1896; sought to have Supreme Court delay enforcement of women's suffrage amendment to Constitution in 1920; died at Cazenovia on November 24, 1924. C. C. Jackson and A. S. Pier, "Charles Stebbins Fairchild," in *Harvard Grads' Magazine* (June 1925); Allan Nevins, *Grover Cleveland: A Study in Courage* (1938).

FALL, Albert Bacon. Born near Frankfort, Ky., November 26, 1861; son of William R. and Edmonia (Taylor) Fall; Quaker; married Emma Garland Morgan on May 7, 1883; father of four children; attended the public schools in Nashville, Tenn., but principally self-taught; began work in a cotton factory in Nashville at age 11; taught school; studied law and was admitted to the bar in 1891; began practice at Las Cruces, N.M.; made a specialty of Mexican law; engaged in mining, lumber, real estate, railroads, farming, and stock-raising enterprises in New Mexico and Mexico; member of the territorial House of Representatives in 1891 and 1892; appointed judge of the 3d judicial district, 1893; appointed associate justice of the New Mexico Supreme Court, 1893; territorial attorney general in 1897 and again in 1897 and again in 1907; member of the Territorial

Council in 1897; during Spanish-American War, served as captain in the 1st
Territorial Infantry; changed party affiliation from Democratic to Republican
about 1900; member of 1911 convention which framed New Mexico constitution
prior to its admission to statehood the following year; elected in 1912 as one of
the first two senators from New Mexico; reelected in 1918, serving until his
resignation on March 4, 1921; spokesman for rights of Americans in Mexico
and advocate of U.S. entry into the League of Nations; appointed SECRETARY
OF THE INTERIOR on March 4, 1921 in the cabinet of President Harding, and
served until his resignation on March 4, 1923; central figure in the "Teapot
Dome Scandal" of April 1922, concerning the leasing of government oil reserves
under control of the Department of the Interior to private companies; charged
by the Senate with fraud and corruption in execution of leases and contracts with
the private companies, 1924; indicted June 1924 and convicted of accepting a
$100,000 bribe, October 1929; fined the amount of the bribe and sentenced to
one year in prison, 1931–1932, in the New Mexico penitentiary at Santa Fe;
first cabinet member to be convicted of a felony; after serving his sentence,
returned to his ranch at Three Rivers, N.M.; hospitalized from 1942 until 1944;
died in El Paso, Tex. on November 30, 1944; interment in Evergreen Cemetery.
Morris Robert Werner and John Starr, *Teapot Dome* (1959); Burl Noggle, *Teapot
Dome: Oil and Politics in the 1920's* (1962); Albert Bacon Fall, *The Memoirs
of Albert B. Fall* (1966).

FARLEY, James Aloysius. Born in Grassy Point, N.Y., May 30, 1888; son
of James Farley, brick manufacturer, and Ellen (Goldrick) Farley; Roman Catholic; married Elizabeth Finnegan on April 28, 1920; father of Elizabeth, Ann,
and James A.; attended public schools, ran errands, and sold papers to help
support family after father's death; helped run family's small grocery store and
saloon; worked in Morrissey's brickyard; graduated Stony Point High School in
1905; studied bookkeeping at Packard Commercial School in New York City;
worked for Merlin, Kerlholtz Paper Company as bookkeeper; became sales
manager for Universal Gypsum Company, 1906, moving up to correspondent
and salesman, and remaining until 1926; elected clerk of Stony Point; delegate
to Democratic state convention of 1913; appointed a port warden for New York
City, 1918; chairman of Rockland County Democratic committee until 1929;
supervisor of Rockland County, 1920–1923; helped renominate Alfred Smith as
governor of New York, 1922; organized James A. Farley and Company in 1926;
organized General Building Supply Corporation in 1929, and served as president
until 1933; chairman of state Democratic committee, 1930–1944; published *Behind the Ballots* in 1938; supported Franklin D. Roosevelt; appointed POSTMASTER
GENERAL in the cabinet of President Roosevelt, and served from March 4, 1933
to September 9, 1940; chairman of the Board of the Coca-Cola Export Company;
reelected president of General Builders Supply Corporation, 1949; trustee of the
Commission of Economic Development, Cordell Hull Foundation; director of
Empire State Foundation; member of Commission on Organization of Executive

Branch of Government, 1953; member of New York State Banking Board, 1955; member of Elks, Redmen, Eagles, Knights of Columbus; died on June 9, 1976. James A. Farley, *Jim Farley's Story* (1948); H. F. Bremer, ed., *Franklin D. Roosevelt, 1882–1945: Chronology, Documents, Bibliographical Aids*, (1969); Paul K. Conklin, *New Deal* (1967).

FESSENDEN, William Pitt. Born at Boscawen, N.H., October 16, 1806; son of Samuel and Ruth (Greene) Fessenden; married Ellen Maria Deering on April 23, 1832; spent his early youth at Fryeburg, Me.; entered Bowdoin College, Brunswick, Me., graduating in 1823; studied law and was admitted to the bar in 1823, establishing his legal practice in Bridgeton, Bangor and, finally, Portland; elected to the state legislature on an anti-Jackson ticket in 1831; became active in the Whig Party and in 1837, accompanied Daniel Webster on a tour of the western states; reelected to the Maine legislature in 1839; elected as a Whig to the U.S. House of Representatives, serving from 1841 to 1843; delegate to the Whig conventions of 1840, 1848, and 1852; served two terms in the state legislature, 1845–1846 and 1853–1854; was several times an unsuccessful candidate for U.S. Senate and House of Representatives; on January 4, 1854, an anti-slavery combination in the state legislature elected him to the U.S. Senate where, in 1857, he became a member of the Finance Committee; elected to the U.S. Senate for a full six-year term in 1859, resigning in 1864, upon being tendered a Cabinet portfolio by President Lincoln; appointed SECRETARY OF THE TREASURY on July 1, 1864, entering upon his duties on July 5, 1864, and serving until March 3, 1865; during his incumbency, he stood firm against further inflation and when the war was over, assumed the offensive against greenback heresies; author of the plan for issuing government bonds; he also raised the interest rates on government bonds; reelected to a third term as U.S. senator on January 5, 1865; chairman of the Joint Committee on Reconstruction; insisted that reconstruction was a function of Congress and not of the president; though he disapproved of many of President Andrew Johnson's policies, he refused to vote for conviction during the impeachment proceedings; died in Portland, Me. on September 8, 1869; interment in Evergreen Cemetery in Portland. Philip Gerald Auchampaugh, *James Buchanan and his Cabinet on the Eve of Secession* (1926); William Best Hesseltine, *Lincoln's Plan of Reconstruction* (1963).

FILLMORE, Millard. Born in Locke Township (now Summerhill), N.Y., January 7, 1800; son of Nathaniel and Phoebe (Millard) Fillmore; married Abigail Powers on February 5, 1826, and upon her death married Mrs. Caroline (Carmichael) McIntosh on February 10, 1858; father of Millard Powers and Mary Abigail; reared on a farm; attended the local rural schools but was largely self-instructed; taught school at Scott, N.Y. while studying law; admitted to the bar in 1823, and began practice in East Aurora, N.Y.; moved to Buffalo, N.Y. in 1830; served in the State Assembly from 1829 to 1831; elected as a Whig to the 23d Congress, serving from March 4, 1833 to March 3, 1835; elected to the

25th, 26th, and 27th Congresses, serving from March 4, 1837 to March 3, 1843; declined to be a candidate for renomination in 1842; unsuccessful Whig candidate for governor in 1844; elected state comptroller in 1847, serving until his resignation on February 20, 1849; elected VICE-PRESIDENT on the Whig ticket headed by Zachary Taylor in 1848, inaugurated on March 4, 1849, and served until July 9, 1850; upon the death in office of President Taylor, he became PRESIDENT, his administration commencing on July 9, 1850 and terminating on March 3, 1853; unsuccessful Whig candidate for President in 1852; unsuccessful National American (Know-Nothing Party) candidate for president in 1856; president of the Buffalo Historical Society; commanded a corps of home guards during the Civil War; first chancellor of the University of Buffalo; he was the second vice-president to succeed to the presidency as a result of the death of the president; died in Buffalo, N.Y. on March 8, 1871; interment in Forest Hills Cemetery, Buffalo. Robert J. Rayback, *Millard Fillmore: Biography of a President* (1959); Silas Bent McKinley, *Old Rough and Ready, The Life and Times of Zachary Taylor* (1946).

FINCH, Robert H. Born in Tempe, Ariz., October 9, 1925; son of Robert L. Finch, member of the state legislature, and Gladys (Hutchinson) Finch; Presbyterian; married to Carol Crother on February 14, 1946; father of Maureen, Kevin, Priscilla, and Cathleen; moved as a boy to Inglewood, Calif., where he attended the public schools; served as a first lieutenant in the Marine Corps during World War II; attended Occidental College in Los Angeles, and was graduated in 1947; went to Washington as an administrative aide to Representative Poulson; editor of the National Young Republican Federation newspaper, 1948; studied law at the University of Southern California and obtained his degree in 1951; first lieutenant during Korean War, 1951–1953; admitted to the bar and began practice with the firm which eventually became Finch, Bell, Duitsman, and Margulis; unsuccessful Republican candidate for Congress, 1952 and 1954; chairman of the Republican central committee of Los Angeles County, 1956–1958; administrative assistant to Richard Nixon's campaign director in the presidential race of 1960; campaign manager for George Murphy in the California senatorial race of 1964; elected lieutenant governor of California on November 8, 1966; appointed SECRETARY OF HEALTH, EDUCATION, AND WELFARE in the cabinet of President Nixon on December 11, 1968, and took the oath of office on January 23, 1969; most important contributions were cutting off of funds to three segregated Southern school districts, and setting more stringent standards to control automobile pollution; resigned on June 5, 1970; appointed counselor on domestic affairs to President Nixon; resumed law practice in Los Angeles in 1972; lost Republican primary for U.S. Senate seat in 1976; partner, Fleming, Anderson, McClung, and Finch, 1977– ; special counsel, Karr, Tuttle, Koch, Campbell, Mawer, Morrow, and Sax, 1986– ; chairman, Corporate Health Committee, United Way Planning Council, 1978–1982; received U.S. Department of Health Services commendation for leadership against Acquired Immune Deficiency Syndrome (AIDS), 1987. *Time*, vol. 92 (December 13, 1968); *Life*, vol. 66 (January 24, (1969); Earl Mazo and Stephan Hess, *Nixon: A Political Portrait* (1969).

FISH, Hamilton. Born in New York, N.Y., August 3, 1808; son of Nicholas and Elizabeth (Stuyvesant) Fish; Episcopalian; married Julia Kean on December 15, 1836; father of three daughters, and of Nicholas (a diplomat), Hamilton, (member of the 61st Congress), and three other sons; attended private school of M. Bancel; graduated Columbia College in 1827; studied law in office of Peter A. Jay for three years, was admitted to the bar in 1830, and began practice of law in partnership with William B. Lawrence; was candidate for State Assembly in 1834; member of Congress, 1843–1845; defeated for lieutenant governorship of state in 1846, but was elected in 1847; elected governor, 1848; served as U. S. senator, 1851–1857; spent two years in Europe; served on Union defense committee of State of New York and on commission of federal government for relief of Civil War prisoners, 1867–1869; appointed SECRETARY OF STATE in the cabinet of President Grant on March 11, 1869, and served from March 17, 1869 to March 11, 1877; most important contributions were settlement of controversy with Great Britain over damage borne by Northern commerce during the Civil War because of British policy of neutrality, negotiation with Spain over Cuba, treaty of commercial reciprocity with Hawaii; was trustee of Columbia College; served as president-general of Society of the Cincinnati; was president of Union League Club and New York Historical Society; died in Garrison, N.Y., September 7, 1893; interment in St. Philip's Cemetery. A. E. Corning, *Hamilton Fish* (1918); Allan Nevins, *Hamilton Fish: The Inner History of the Grant Administration* (1957).

FISHER, Walter Lowrie. Born in Wheeling, W. Va., July 4, 1862; son of Daniel Webster Fisher, Presbyterian clergyman and president of Hanover College, and Amanda D. (Kouns) Fisher; married Mabel Taylor on April 22, 1891; father of Walter, Arthur, Thomas, Frederick, Margaret, Howard, and Ruth; attended Marietta College, Ohio in 1879; entered Hanover College, Hanover, Ind. in 1880 and was graduated in 1883; studied law; admitted to the bar in 1888 and practiced in Chicago with the firm of Matz, Fisher, and Boyden until 1911; special assessment attorney of Chicago, 1889; appointed secretary of the Municipal Voters League of Chicago in 1901 and served until 1906 when he was appointed president; appointed special transportation counsel for Chicago, 1907; elected president of the Conservation League of America, 1908; helped organize the National Conservation Association, 1909, and became its vice-president, 1910; member of the Federal Railroad Securities Commission by appointment of President Taft, 1910–1911; appointed SECRETARY OF THE IN-TERIOR in the cabinet of President Taft on March 7, 1911 to fill the vacancy caused by the retirement of Richard A. Ballinger; most important contribution was encouragement of Alaskan development, conservation programs, and the development of national parks; served until the end of the Taft administration, March 3, 1913; returned to Chicago and resumed law practice; special advisor to Judge H. Wilkerson, 1930–1932; appointed by a federal court to guide the merger of transit lines in Chicago, 1933; author of *Alaskan Coal Problems* (1911), and several published articles and addresses; died in Winnetka, Ill. on November 9, 1935. Henry F. Pringle, *Life and Times of William Howard Taft: A Biography* (1939); Norman M. Wilensky, *Conservatives in the Progressive Era* (1965).

FLEMMING, Arthur Sherwood. Born in Kingston, N.Y., June 12, 1905; son of Harvey Hardwick Flemming, judge of surrogate court, and Harriet (Sherwood) Flemming; Methodist; married Bernice Virginia Moler on December 14, 1934; father of Elizabeth Ann, Susan Harriet, Harry Sherwood, Arthur Henry, and Thomas Madison; graduated Kingston High School; worked as newspaper reporter, 1922; received B.A. from Ohio Wesleyan University, in 1922; instructor in government and debate coach at American University, 1927–1930; received M.A. in political science from American University, 1928; member of editorial staff of *United States Daily*, 1930–1934; editor of *Uncle Sam's Diary*, 1932–1935; granted LL.B. from Washington University; became director of American University School of Public Affairs, 1934–1938; appointed executive officer of the university in 1938; made Republican member of U.S. Civil Service Commission by Franklin D. Roosevelt in July 1939, and remained as such until August 1948; received LL.D. from Ohio Wesleyan University in 1941; became chief of labor supply with Office of Product Management, 1941–1942; earned LL.D. from American University, 1942; member of War Manpower Commission, 1942–1945; trustee of Ohio Wesleyan University; chosen one of four members of Hoover Commission on July 17, 1947; elected president of Ohio Wesleyan University in June 1948, taking office on July 31, 1948; made chairman of personnel advisory board of Atomic Energy Commission in September 1948; became vice-president of National Council of Churches of Christ in America, 1950–1954 and 1964–1966, and was made president in 1967; chosen assistant to Director of Defense Mobilization and chairman of manpower policy committee of Office of Defense Mobilization, February 1951, and was acting head in January 1953; member of President's Advisory Committee on Government Organization in 1953; became director of Office of Defense Mobilization, June 1953; member of National Security Council beginning in 1953; appointed SECRETARY OF HEALTH, EDUCATION AND WELFARE in the cabinet of President Eisenhower, and served from August 1, 1958 to January 19, 1961; became president of University of Oregon, 1961– ; member of national advisory commission of Peace Corps, 1961–; Dean Albertson, ed., *Eisenhower as President* (1963); David A. Frier, *Conflict of Interest in the Eisenhower Administration* (1969).

FLOYD, John Buchanan. Born in Smithfield, Va., June 1, 1806; son of John Floyd, governor of Virginia, and Letitia (Preston) Floyd; married cousin, Shelly Buchanan Preston, in 1830; father of one adopted daughter; received education from mother with aid of father's library; graduated South Carolina College in 1829; studied law and was admitted to the bar in 1835; began practice of law in Wytheville, Va.; led by Arkansas cotton boom to take up large-scale cotton planting and law, lost health and fortune; began practice in Abingdon Va.; elected delegate from county to General Assembly in 1847, and reelected in 1848; elected governor for three terms beginning January 1, 1849 and serving until 1852; appointed SECRETARY OF WAR in the cabinet of President Buchanan, and served from March 6, 1857 to January 18, 1861; most important contributions were appointment of quartermaster general Joseph E. Johnston, report on sending of arms to Southern states with view to approaching war, and Major Anderson's occupation of Fort Sumter; returned to Virginia; made brigadier general in 1861; made major general by General Assembly of Confederate Army, 1863; died near Abingdon, Va., August 26, 1863. N. J. Floyd, *Biographical Genealogy of the Virginia Kentucky Floyd Families* (1912); Irving J. Sloan, ed., *James Buchanan, 1791–1868: Chronology, Documents, Bibliographical Aids* (1968).

FOLGER, Charles James. Born on the island of Nantucket, Mass., April 16, 1818; son of Thomas Folger; married Susan Rebecca Worth on June 17, 1844; no children; moved to Geneva, N.Y. at age 12; graduated Geneva (later Hobart) College in 1836; studied law under Sibley and Worden in Canandaigua; was admitted to the bar of Albany, N.Y. in 1839; began law practice in Lyons; returned to Geneva in 1840 and practiced law; appointed justice of the peace, 1841; appointed judge of court of common pleas of Ontario County, 1844; made master and examiner in chancery and served, 1845–1846; was county judge, 1851–1855; elected state senator in 1861, was reelected three times, acting for four years as president *pro tempore*, and served until 1869; chairman of judiciary committee in state convention of 1867; candidate for U.S. Senate, 1867; active in Republican national convention at Chicago, 1868; appointed by Grant U.S. assistant treasurer in New York City, 1869; elected associate judge of state court of appeals in 1870; appointed by Governor Cornell to fill unexpired term of Chief Justice Church; appointed SECRETARY OF THE TREASURY in the cabinet of President Arthur on October 27, 1881, and served from November 14, 1881 to September 4, 1884; most important contribution was classification of offices in departments under Civil Service rules; nominated for governor, 1882; died in Geneva, N.Y., September 4, 1884. Charles Andrews, *An Address Commemorative of the Life of the Late Hon. Charles J. Folger* (1885); George F. Howe, *Chester A. Arthur: A Quarter Century of Machine Politics.*

FOLSOM, Marion Bayard. Born in McRae, Ga., November 23, 1893; son of William Bryant and Margaret Jane (McRae) Folsom; Presbyterian; married Mary Davenport on November 16, 1918; father of Jane McRae, Marion Bayard, and Frances; after receiving his elementary and secondary education at the local schools, he entered the University of Georgia, graduating in 1912, and then attended the Graduate School of Business Administration at Harvard, receiving an M.B.A. Degree in 1914; joined the Eastman Kodak Company, Rochester, N.Y. in 1914, becoming assistant to the president of the company in 1921, assistant to the chairman of the board in 1925, assistant treasurer in 1930 and, finally, treasurer in 1935, remaining in that office until 1953; served in the U.S. Army during World War I with the rank of captain in the quartermaster corps; member of the Federal Advisory Council on Social Security during 1937 and 1938; member of the regional War Manpower Committee from 1942 to 1945; appointed employer delegate of the U.S. to the International Labor Conference in Geneva, Switzerland, in 1936; member of Department of Commerce Business Advisory Council, 1936–1948; president of the Eastman Savings and Loan Association of Rochester, N.Y., from 1947 to 1952; vice-chairman of the president's Advisory Committee on the Merchant Marine during 1947 and 1948; director of the Lincoln Rochester Trust Company from 1929 to 1949; trustee of the Rochester Savings Bank from 1931 to 1939; director of the Federal Reserve Bank of New York from 1949 to 1953; invited to join the Eisenhower cabinet as SECRETARY OF HEALTH, EDUCATION AND WELFARE on July 20, 1955, entering upon his duties on August 1, 1955, serving until August 1, 1958; during his secretaryship, medical research activities were expanded greatly and important new health legislation was enacted including programs for construction of research facilities; he also broadened efforts to control air and water pollution; upon his retirement, was reelected to the board of directors of the Eastman Kodak Company in August 1958; reelected trustee of the Rochester Savings Bank; director of the U.S. Chamber of Commerce from 1942 to 1948; member of the Board of Overseers of Harvard College; trustee of the University of Rochester; member of the Board of Governors of the American Red Cross from 1953 to 1958; trustee of the Allendale School, Rochester, New York; director of the Rochester General Hospital; continues to be engaged in activities with the Eastman Kodak Company. Arthur Larson, *Eisenhower: The President Nobody Knew* (1968); Robert J. Donovan, *Eisenhower: The Inside Story* (1956).

FORD, Gerald Rudolph, Jr. Born in Omaha, Neb., July 14, 1913; son of Gerald R. and Dorothy (Gardner) Ford; Episcopalian; married Elizabeth Bloomer, October 15, 1948; father of Michael, John, Steven, and Susan. Received A.B. degree, University of Michigan, Ann Arbor, 1935; LL.B. degree, Yale, 1941; numerous honorary degrees; admitted to the Michigan bar, 1941; served in the U.S. Navy, 1942–1946; attained the rank of lieutenant commander; practiced law in Grand Rapids, Mich., 1941–1949; member, Buchen and Ford Law Firm; member, United States House of Representatives, 1949–1973; delegate, Interparliamentary Union, 1959 and 1961; minority leader, United States House of Representatives, 1965–1973; Distinguished Service Award, one of ten outstanding young men in the United States, Junior Chamber of Commerce, 1950; Silver Anniversary All-American, *Sports Illustrated*, 1959; Distinguished Congressional Service Award, American Political Science Association, 1961; Delta Kappa Epsilon; Phi Delta Phi; Mason; Republican; after the resignation of Vice-President Spiro T. Agnew on October 10, 1973, Ford was nominated by President Richard M. Nixon, on October 12, to be VICE-PRESIDENT of the United States; nomination was confirmed by the U.S. Senate on November 27, 1973, and by the U.S. House of Representatives on December 6; on that same day Ford resigned from the House of Representatives, and was inaugurated as Vice-President; on August 8, 1974, Nixon announced decision to resign as President because of Watergate scandal; when Nixon left office on August 9, 1974, Ford was sworn in as PRESIDENT of the United States; the first President to assume office without being chosen by the electorate, he granted Nixon a full pardon for his participation in the Watergate controversy on September 8, 1974; during his administration, he was faced with the problem of reviving the American economy, and by the end of 1976 it was again on the upswing; in addition, he implemented a limited form of pardon for those who violated the conscription laws or deserted the military in opposition to the Vietnam War; in an attempt to check inflation, placed an embargo on foreign wheat sales, which was a crippling blow to the nation's wheat farmers; on November 2, 1976, he was defeated in the presidential election by Jimmy Carter, and left office on January 20, 1977. U.S. Government, *Biographical Directory of the American Congress, 1774–1971* (1971); *Who's Who in America, 1974–1975*; National Journal, *Ford's Presidency* (1976); Henry H. Schulte, Jr., ed., *Facts on File Year Book 1975*.

FORRESTAL, James Vincent. Born in Matteawan, N.Y., February 15, 1892; son of James Forrestal, builder and postmaster, and Mary A. (Foohey) Forrestal; Catholic; married Josephine Ogden on October 12, 1926; father of Michael and Peter; attended local schools; graduated Matteawan High School in 1908; became reporter for *Journal*; later worked for *Mount Vernon Argus* and *Poughkeepsie News Press*; entered Dartmouth College in 1911; transferred to Princeton University, 1912–1915; was chairman of *The Daily Princetonian*; worked in purchasing department of New Jersey Zinc Company; was cigar salesman for Tobacco Products Corp.; became bond salesman for New York investment banking house of William A. Read and Company in January 1916; enlisted as seaman second-class in U.S. Navy, assigned to aviation section, sent to Canada to train with Canadian Flying Corps, and was discharged as lieutenant in 1919; commissioned lieutenant in Naval Reserves; headed bond sales department of Dillon, Read and Company, became vice-president in 1923, and was made president in January 1938; chosen administrative assistant to President Franklin D. Roosevelt in 1940; named undersecretary of the Navy in August 1940; became acting secretary of the Navy on May 10, 1944; appointed SECRETARY OF THE NAVY in the cabinet of President Franklin D. Roosevelt, continued under Truman, and served from May 18, 1944 to September 17, 1947; most important contributions were advocation of naval supremacy and aid in reorganization of armed forces; appointed first SECRETARY OF DEFENSE in the cabinet of President Truman on July 26, 1947, and served from September 17, 1947 to March 22, 1949; most important contribution was solving of problems of consolidation; died in Bethesda, Md., on May 22, 1949. Walter Millis, ed., *The Forrestal Diaries* (1951); Robert G. Albion and Robert H. Connery, *Forrestal and the Navy* (1962).

FORSYTH, John. Born in Fredericksburg, Va., October 22, 1780; son of Robert Forsyth, major in Revolutionary War and first marshal of Georgia, and Fanny (Johnson) Forsyth; married Clara Meigs; father of John and Julia; graduated from Princeton in 1799; studied law under Mr. Noel, and was admitted to the Augusta, Ga. bar in 1802; appointed attorney general of Virginia in 1808; served as representative to Congress, 1813–1818; served as U.S. senator, 1818–1819 and 1823–1827; appointed minister to Spain in 1819, serving until 1823; served as governor of Georgia, 1827–1829; delegate to antitariff convention at Milledgeville, Ga. in 1832; appointed SECRETARY OF STATE in the cabinet of President Jackson on June 27, 1834, and served from July 1, 1834, continuing in the Van Buren administration until March 3, 1841; most important contributions were negotiation of agreement with France over treaty of 1831 and opposition to admission of Texas to Union; died in Washington, D.C., October 21, 1841; interment in Congressional Cemetery. Jennie Forsythe Jeffries, *A History of the Forsythe Family* (1920); Alvin Duckett, *John Forsythe: Political Tactician* (1962); Ronald Shaw, *Andrew Jackson, 1767–1845: Chronology, Documents, Bibliographical Aids* (1969); Irving J. Sloan, ed., *Martin Van Buren, 1782–1862: Chronology, Documents, Bibliographical Aids* (1969).

FORWARD, Walter. Born in Old Granby (now East Granby), Conn., January 24, 1786; son of Samuel and Susannah (Holcombe) Forward; Methodist; married Henrietta Barclay on January 31, 1808; no children; attended common schools; moved with family to Aurora, Ohio; worked on father's farm; settled in Pittsburgh, and studied law in office of Henry Baldwin; edited *Tree of Liberty* for Baldwin; admitted to the bar in 1806; became prominent trial lawyer; chosen member of 17th Congress to fill vacant seat of Henry Baldwin, elected to 18th Congress, and served from October 8, 1822 to March 3, 1825; unsuccessful candidate for reelection to Congress, 1824; declined presidential nomination in 1824; delegate to general convention of National Republicans at Baltimore, 1830; prominent in formation of Whig party, 1834; member of Pennsylvania constitutional convention, 1837–1838; declined appointment of district attorney for western district of New York; became first comptroller of Pennsylvania currency, April 6, 1841 to September 13, 1841; appointed SECRETARY OF THE TREASURY in the cabinet of President Tyler, and served from September 13, 1841 to March 1, 1843; resumed practice of law; made chargé d'affaires to Denmark on November 8, 1849, serving until 1851; became presiding judge of district court of Allegheny County; worked for temperance; founded Pittsburgh Philosophical and Philological Society; died in Pittsburgh, Pa. on November 24, 1852; interment in Allegheny Cemetery. J. N. Boucher, *A Century and a Half of Pittsburgh and Her People* (1908); Robert Seager, *And Tyler Too* (1963).

FOSTER, Charles. Born in Fostoria, Ohio, April 12, 1828; son of Charles W. Foster, owner of general store, and Laura (Crocker) Foster; married Ann M. Olmstead in 1853; father of two daughters; attended public schools; entered academy at Norwalk at age 12 and remained there two years; worked in family general store; pursued banking, gas, and oil ventures; recruited for Civil War, and supported Union cause financially; elected to U.S Congress in 1870, reelected in 1872, 1874, and 1876, and served from March 4, 1871 to March 3, 1879; unsuccessful candidate for reelection to Congress in 1878; elected governor by Republicans as sound money candidate in 1879; delegate-at-large to Republican national convention, 1880; appointed SECRETARY OF THE TREASURY in the cabinet of President Benjamin Harrison, and served from February 24, 1891 to March 5, 1893; most important contributions were favoring international bimetallism over domestic free coinage, policy of Sherman Silver Purchase Act; followed business pursuits; died in Springfield, Ohio, on January 9, 1904; interment in Fountain Cemetery, Fostoria, Ohio. Nevin O. Winter, A *History of Northwest Ohio* (1917); H. J. Sievers, ed., *Benjamin Harrison, 1833–1901: Chronology, Documents, Bibliographical Aids* (1969).

FOSTER, John Watson. Born in Pike County, Ind., March 2, 1836; son of Matthew Watson, farmer, and Eleanor (Johnson) Watson; married Mary Parke McFerson in 1859; attended public schools; graduated from Indiana State University in 1855; studied law at Harvard and later in a law office; admitted to the bar in 1857 and began practice at Evansville with Conrad Baker; anti-slavery; volunteered for Union service at outbreak of Civil War; appointed major of 25th Indiana Volunteers, rose to colonel, and brevetted brigadier general; edited *Evansville Daily Journal*; postmaster of Evansville, 1869; chairman of state Republican convention of Indiana, 1872; appointed minister to Mexico by Grant, 1873; minister to Russia, 1880–1881; became minister to Spain in 1883; resumed practice of law; became special agent of state department to assist in negotiation of reciprocity treaties in Madrid in November 1890; was agent for U.S. in Bering Sea arbitration; appointed SECRETARY OF STATE in the cabinet of President Benjamin Harrison on June 29, 1892, and served until February 23, 1893; most important contributions were negotiation of treaty of annexation with Republic of Hawaii and settlement of *Baltimore* incident; invited to join Chinese commissioners in negotiation of peace with Japan, 1894; was agent in charge of preparing case for U.S. in Alaskan–Canadian boundary dispute with Great Britain, 1903; represented China at Second Hague Conference in 1907; published A *Century of American Diplomacy, 1776–1876* (1900), *American Diplomacy in the Orient* (1903), *Arbitration and the Hague Court* (1904), *The Practice of Diplomacy* (1906), *War Stories for my Grandchildren* (1918); died November 15, 1917. Jose L. Suarez, *Mr. John W. Foster* (1918); William R. Castle, Jr., *American Secretaries of State and their Diplomacy* (1928); H. J. Sievers, ed., *Benjamin Harrison, 1833–1901: Chronology, Documents, Bibliographical Aids* (1969).

FOWLER, Henry Hamill. Born in Roanoke, Va., September 5, 1908; son of Mack Johnson and Bertha (Browning) Fowler; Episcopalian; married Trudye Pamela Hathcote on October 19, 1938; father of Mary, Susan, and Henry Hamill; received B.A. from Roanoke College in 1929; earned LL.B. from Yale University in 1932, J.S.D. in 1933, and LL.D. in 1962; admitted to the Virginia bar in 1933; became counsel for Tennessee Valley Authority, 1934–1938, and was made assistant general counsel in 1939; was special assistant to attorney general as chief counsel of subcommittee of Senate Committee on Education and Labor, 1939–1940; chosen special counsel for Federal Power Commission in 1941; made assistant general counsel for Office of Production Management, 1941; member of War Production Board from 1942 to 1944; became economic advisor to U.S. Mission of Economic Affairs in London, 1944; was special assistant to administrator of Foreign Economic Administration in 1945; formed law firm of Fowler, Leva, Hawes and Symington, 1946 to 1951; made deputy administrator of National Production Authority in 1951, and became administrator in 1952; was administrator of Defense Production Administration from 1952 to 1953; practiced law with firm, 1953–1961; delegate to Democratic national convention, 1956; under-secretary of the treasury, 1961–1964; returned to practice of law, 1964–1965; appointed SECRETARY OF THE TREASURY in the cabinet of President Lyndon B. Johnson, and served from April 1, 1965 to January 20, 1969; most important contribution was reduction of silver content in coins to conserve national silver reserves; accepted partnership in Goldman Sachs & Co. in 1969; member of Intergovernmental Relations Advisory Committee; was U.S. representative on International Monetary Fund, World Bank, and International American Development Bank; trustee of Roanoke College; member of the national committee on money and credit; partner in Goldman Sachs and Co., New York City, 1969–1981, chairman, Goldman Sachs International Corp., New York City, 1969–1984; cochairman, Citizens Network for Foreign Affairs, 1987– ; trustee, Lyndon B. Johnson Foundation. Rowland Evans and Robert Novak, *Lyndon B. Johnson: The Exercise of Power* (1966); Hugh Sidey, *A Very Personal Presidency: Lyndon Johnson in the White House* (1968); *Who's Who, 1989.*

FRANCIS, David Rowland. Born in Richmond, Ky., October 1, 1850; son of John B. and Eliza Caldwell (Rowland) Francis; married Jane Perry on January 20, 1876; father of John D. Perry, David Rowland Jr., Charles Broaddus, Talton Turner, Thomas, and Sidney R.; attended the Rev. Robert Breck's Richmond Academy for Girls as companion to Breck's son; received B.A. from Washington University in St. Louis, 1870, and numerous honorary degrees; became shipping clerk for wholesale grocery firm of Shryock and Rowland in St. Louis; with brother Sidney, organized commission house in 1877 called D. R. Francis and Brother, later called Francis, Brother and Co., and was president until death; elected president of St. Louis Merchants' Exchange, 1884; elected mayor of St. Louis on Democratic ticket, 1885; served as governor of Missouri, 1888–1892;

appointed SECRETARY OF THE INTERIOR in the cabinet of President Cleveland to succeed Hoke Smith on September 1, 1896, and continued under McKinley until March 4, 1897; most important contributions were addition of one million acres to the forest reserves of the nation and institution of reforms in the department which were ratified and continued by the McKinley administration; published *A Tour of Europe in Nineteen Days* (1903); one of originators of the movement to commemorate the anniversary of the Louisiana Purchase by an exposition in St. Louis; chief executive of the Louisiana Purchase Exposition held April 30 to December 1, 1904; published *Universal Exposition of 1904* (1913); appointed U.S. ambassador to Russia by President Wilson in 1916; recognized by Soviet regime of November 1917, remained at post even though U.S. government did not recognize new government, and served until his resignation due to ill health; attended peace conference at Paris; benefactor of Washington University and Missouri University; vice-president of Merchants' LacLede National Bank; president of Madison Ferry Co., director of Mississippi Life Insurance Co.; owner of St. Louis *Republic*, which he sold to St. Louis *Globe Democrat*; president of board of curators of University of Missouri, Hospital Saturday and Sunday Association, and Missouri Historical Society; director of St. Louis art museum; decorated by numerous foreign governments; died in St. Louis, Mo., January 15, 1927. Walter B. Stevens, *David R. Francis, Ambassador Extraordinary and Plenipotentiary* (1919); Harry B. Hawes, "David Rowland Francis," in Missouri Historical Society Collections (October 1927); Robert L. Vexter, ed., *Grover Cleveland, 1837–1908: Chronology, Documents, Bibliographical Aids* (1968); Margaret K. Leech, *In the Days of McKinley* (1959).

FREEMAN, Orville Lothrop. Born in Minneapolis, Minn., May 9, 1918; son of Orville Freeman, merchant, and Frances (Schroeder) Freeman; Lutheran; married Jane Charlotte Shields on May 2, 1942; father of Constance Jane and Michael Orville; attended public schools of Minnesota; received B.A. from University of Minnesota in 1940; called to active duty in 1941, commissioned second lieutenant in Marine Corps Reserve, and was discharged with rank of major in 1945; received LL.B. from University of Minnesota in 1946; became member of Democratic Farm-Labor party's central committee for Hennepin county, and was secretary of state central committee, 1946–1949; director of Minneapolis Family and Children Service; admitted to the Minnesota bar in 1947, and went into private practice as member of Larson, Loevinger, Lindquist and Freeman, 1947–1955; chosen state chairman of Democratic Farm-Labor party in 1948, and managed Hubert H. Humphrey's campaign for senator; unsuccessful candidate for state attorney general, 1950; was president of Minnesota Association of Claimants Compensation Attorney's Cooperation Services Incorporated in 1950; unsuccessful candidate for governor in 1952; elected governor in 1954, and was reelected in 1956 and 1958; appointed SECRETARY OF AGRICULTURE in the cabinet of President Kennedy, continued under Lyndon B. Johnson, and served from January 21, 1961 to January 21, 1969; most important contributions were feed-grain reduction program, reduction of wheat grown, extension of Agricultural Trade Development and Assistance Act, and research on foodstuffs for survival after nuclear attack; president EDP Technology International, 1969–1970 and Business International, 1970– ; former deacon of Ebenezer Lutheran Church; member of American Judicature Society, American Civil Liberties Union, Minnesota Bar Association, American Veterans Committee, Veterans of Foreign Wars, American Legion, Disabled Veterans of America, Marine Corps League. New York Times, *The Kennedy Years* (1964); James MacGregor Burns, *John Kennedy: A Political Profile* (1959).

FRELINGHUYSEN, Frederick Theodore. Born in Millstone, N.J., August 4, 1817; son of Frederick Frelinghuysen, lawyer, and Mary (Dumont) Frelinghuysen; orphaned at the age of three, and was adopted by uncle Theodore Frelinghuysen; married Matilde E. Griswold on January 25, 1842; father of Matilde Griswold, Frederick, Charlotte Louise, George Griswold, Sarah Helen, and Theodore; studied at Somerville and Newark academies; graduated Rutgers College in 1836; studied law in uncle's office in Newark; admitted to New Jersey bar, 1839; succeeded to uncle's practice, and became counsel for Central Railroad of New Jersey and Morris Canal and Banking Company; was city attorney of Newark, 1849; elected to city council; represented New Jersey at Peace Congress in Washington, 1861; attorney general of New Jersey, 1861–1866; appointed U.S. senator in 1866, elected in 1867, and served until 1869; appointed minister to Great Britain by President Grant in July 1870, but declined; reelected to senate in 1871, and served until 1877; resumed practice of law; appointed SECRETARY OF STATE in the cabinet of President Arthur on December 12, 1881, and served from December 19, 1881, to March 5, 1885; most important contributions were reversal of mediation of U.S. in dispute between Chile and Peru over Tacna and Arica, action in regard to American rights in controversy with Great Britain concerning plan for construction of interoceanic canal across Nicaragua, favoring closer commercial relations with countries of Latin America on basis of reciprocity, support of American commercial interests in Germany and France, negotiation for a naval base at Pearl Harbor in Hawaii, opening up treaty relations with Korea, and authorization for participation of U.S. in Berlin Conference of 1884; president of American Bible Society, 1884–1885; trustee of Rutgers College for 35 years; returned to Newark; died in Newark, N.J., May 20, 1885; interment in Mt. Pleasant Cemetery. P. M. Brown, *The American Secretaries of State and their Diplomacy* (1928); W. E. Sackett, *Modern Battles of Trenton* (1895); George F. Howe, *Chester A. Arthur: A Quarter Century of Machine Politics* (1957).

G

GAGE, Lyman Judson. Born in DeRuyter, N.Y., June 28, 1836; son of Eli A. and Mary (Judson) Gage; Methodist; married Sarah Etheridge in 1864, Mrs. Cornelia (Washburne) Gage, his brother's widow, on June 7, 1887, and Mrs. Frances Ada Ballou of San Diego on November 25, 1909; no children; attended the common schools in Madison County; moved to Rome, N.Y. and attended Rome Academy; received LL.D. from Beloit in 1897, from New York University in 1903; at age 14, became mail agent on Rome and Watertown Railroad; entered Oneida Central Bank of Rome as office boy and junior clerk in 1853; left Rome for Chicago, 1855; became clerk in lumber yard; became bookkeeper for Merchants' Savings, Loan, and Trust Company in 1858; became cashier, 1861; received similar position with First National Bank of Chicago; 1868; organizer and treasurer of The Honest Money League of the North West against irredeemable paper money, 1870s; vice-president of American Bankers Association, 1882; elected president of American Bankers Association, 1883; president of Chicago board of directors of World's Columbia Exposition and earned national prominence, 1890–1891; elected president of First National Bank; offered position as secretary of treasury by President Cleveland, but refused, 1892; defended gold standard in campaign of 1896; appointed SECRETARY OF TREASURY in cabinet of President McKinley in 1897, reappointed by President Theodore Roosevelt on March 5, 1901 and served until January 31, 1902; most important contributions were the popularizing of government bond sale at 3% interest in 1898 and influence in passing act of March 14, 1900 which established the gold standard; president of United States Trust Company of New York, 1902–1906; retired and moved to Point Loma, Cal., in 1907; died in San Diego, Cal., January 26, 1927. Moses P. Handy, "Lyman J. Gage," in *Revolution of Revolutions* (1897); A. T. Andreas, *History of Chicago* (1886); James F. Rhodes, *The McKinley and Roo-*

sevelt Administrations, 1897–1909 in *History of the United States*, vol. 9 (1922); Robert Dallek, *McKinley's Decision, War on Spain* (1970); Margaret K. Leech, *In the Days of McKinley* (1959); H. Wayne Morgan, *William McKinley and his America* (1963).

GALLATIN, Albert. Born in Geneva, Switzerland on January 29, 1761; son of Jean and Sophie Albertine (Rolaz) Gallatin, and member of an aristocratic family prominent in the history of the Duchy of Savoy in Geneva in the 14th century; Huguenot; orphaned at age 9 and lived with Catherine Pictet, a close family friend; married Sophie Allegre in May 1789; no children; second marriage on November 11, 1793 to Hannah Nicholson; father of Frances; attended boarding school, 1773–1775; attended the Academy at Geneva in 1775 and graduated in 1779; refused a commission of lieutenant colonel in a Hessian regiment which was to fight in the colonies; left Geneva in 1780 for France; left on May 27, 1780 for America; arrived at Cape Ann, Mass., on July 14, 1780; settled in Boston in 1781 and taught French at Harvard College; in July 1782 he bought land on the low banks between the Monongahela and the Kanawha rivers and settled in Fayette County, Pa., in 1784; received considerable sums in 1786 from his family inheritance which made him a prominent figure in western Pennsylvania; became member of a conference held at Harrisburg in 1788 to consider means for revising the U.S. Constitution; member of a convention to revise the Pennsylvania constitution in 1790; elected to the state legislature as a representative of Fayette County in October, 1790; elected again to the same post in 1791 and 1792; worked on the reform of the penal code, establishing statewide education, removal of antiquated survivals from the statute law, and the abolition of slavery; elected to U.S. Senate on February 28, 1793; his eligibility was challenged on the grounds that he had not been a citizen for nine years and his election was canceled on February 28, 1794; returned in 1794 to Fayette County and literally saved Pennsylvania from civil war in the Whiskey Rebellion through his eloquent oratory and courage; elected to U.S. House of Representatives and served for three terms, 1795–1801; worked in public finance and on the creation of the ways and means committee to ensure the accountability of the Treasury to the Congress; became SECRETARY OF THE TREASURY under Jefferson, May 14, 1801, and continued under Madison until February 9, 1814 with a year in Europe from April 12, 1813 to February 9, 1814; most important contributions included reducing the public debt from more than $86 million to less than $46 million, attempting to deal successfully with the War of 1812 by reviving the internal taxes and obtaining a loan of $16 million from Pennsylvania and New York to help the increase in the public debt due to the War of 1812; failed in his mission to have the Bank of the United States rechartered in 1811; left on May 9, 1813 for diplomatic service abroad; went to St. Petersburg to obtain Russia's mediation between England and the United States; successful in work on Treaty of Ghent in 1814; appointed minister to France and remained abroad until 1823; president of the National Bank of New York, 1831–1839; became president of the New York Historical Society in 1843; founded American Ethnological Society in 1842; died in Astoria, Long Island, N.Y., on August 12, 1849. Henry Adams, *The Life of Albert Gallatin* (1879); Raymond Walters, *Albert Gallatin, Jeffersonian Financier* (1957).

GARDNER, John William. Born in Los Angeles, Calif., October 8, 1912; son of William Frederick and Marie (Flora) Gardner; married Aida Marroquin on August 13, 1934; father of Stephanie and Francesca; received B.A. from Stanford University in 1935, and M.A. in 1936; became assistant professor of psychology at University of California; earned Ph.D. from University of California in 1938; was made professor of psychology at Connecticut College for Women in New London, 1938; chosen assistant professor of psychology at Mount Holyoke College, South Hadley, Mass., 1940; head of Latin American section of Foreign Broadcast Intelligence Service of the Federal Communications Commission, 1942; enlisted in U.S. Marine Corps in 1943, served in Office of Strategic Services in Europe, and was discharged as captain; became consultant to U.S. Air Force and Department of Defense; made executive associate of Carnegie Corporation in 1946, became vice-president in 1949, and president, 1955–1965; vice-chairman of board of trustees of New York School of Social Work, 1949–1955; member of Council on Foreign Relations, Ford Foundation's advisory committee on international training and research, and Sigma Xi; was chairman of social science panel of Science Advisory Board of U.S. Air Force, 1951–1955; became trustee of Metropolitan Museum of Art, 1957–1965; member of advisory committee on social sciences of National Science Foundation, 1959–1962; director of Woodrow Wilson Foundation, 1960–1963; wrote *Excellence: Can We Be Equal and Excellent Too?* (1961); was chairman of U.S. Advisory Commission on International Educational and Cultural Affairs, 1962–1964; made chairman of White House Conference on Education in 1965; appointed SECRETARY OF HEALTH, EDUCATION AND WELFARE in the cabinet of President Lyndon B. Johnson, and served from August 18, 1965 to January 20, 1969; most important contribution was enforcement of civil rights in the department and welfare programs; directed special study of urban problems for Carnegie Corporation of New York; made chairman of Urban Coalition Action Council; senior fellow, Aspen Institute for Humanistic Studies, 1981–1984; trustee, Stanford University, 1968–1982; author of *No Easy Victories* (1968), *The Recovery of Confidence* (1970), *In Common Cause* (1972), *Know or Listen to Those Who Know* (1975), *Morale* (1978), and *Quotations of Wit and Wisdom* (1980). "Mr. Gardner Joins the Coalition," *Time* (February 23, 1968); "Matter of Priority," *Newsweek* (February 26, 1968); Hugh Sidey, *A Very Personal Presidency: Lyndon Johnson in the White House* (1968); *Who's Who, 1989*.

GARFIELD, James Abram. Born in Orange, Ohio, November 19, 1831; son of Abram and Eliza (Ballou) Garfield; attended Disciples of Christ Church; married Lucretia Rudolph on November 11, 1858; father of Eliza Arabelle, Harry

Augustus, James Rudoph (Secretary of the Interior under Theodore Roosevelt), Mary, Irvin McDowell, Abram and Edward; spent his boyhood working on a farm, aiding in the support of his widowed mother; attended the district schools about three months each winter; driver and helmsman on the Ohio Canal, at age 17; attended Geauga Seminary in Chester, Ohio, in March 1849; taught in a district school in the fall of 1849; attended the Eclectic Institute, Hiram, Ohio, from 1851 to 1854; entered Williams College, Williamstown, Mass., graduating in 1858; professor of ancient languages and literature at Hiram College, Hiram, Ohio; president of Hiram College from 1859 to 1861; elected to the Ohio State Senate in 1859, serving until 1861; studied law and was admitted to the Ohio bar in 1860, commencing practice in Hiram; entered the Union Army during the Civil War and was commissioned lieutenant colonel; commanded 42d Regiment, Ohio Volunteer Infantry, in 1861; was subsequently promoted to major general; resigned from the U.S. Army on November 8, 1870; appointed a member of the electoral commission, created by an Act of Congress and approved on January 29, 1877, to decide the election contests in various states in the presidential election of 1876; elected to the U.S. Senate on January 13, 1880, for the term commencing March 4, 1881, but declined to accept his seat on December 23, 1880, having also been elected PRESIDENT, to which office he had been nominated on June 8, 1880, at the Republican national convention held in Chicago; inaugurated on March 4, 1881, serving until his death in office on September 19, 1881 from an assassin's bullets; died in Elberon, N.J., where he had been removed for the purpose of convalescing; interment in Lake View Cemetery, Cleveland, Ohio; he was the fourth president to die in office, the second to be assassinated; authored *Works of James A. Garfield*, 2 vols. (1882–1883). Bill Severn, *Teacher, Soldier, President: The Life of James A. Garfield* (1964); Theodore C. Smith, ed., *Life and Letters of James A. Garfield*, 2 vols. (1925).

GARFIELD, James Rudolph. Born in Hiram, Ohio, October 17, 1865; son of James Abram Garfield, President of the United States, and Lucretia (Rudolph) Garfield; married Helen Newell on December 30, 1890; father of four sons; attended local schools of Washington, D.C.; went to St. Paul's School, Concord, N.H.; graduated Williams College in 1885; began legal studies at Columbia University, and continued in office of Bangs and Stetson in New York City; admitted to Ohio bar, 1888; went into practice in partnership with elder brother; member of state senate, 1896–1899; appointed on U.S. Civil Service Commission, 1902–1903; became commissioner of corporations of the department of commerce and labor in February 1903; appointed SECRETARY OF THE INTERIOR in the cabinet of President Theodore Roosevelt on March 4, 1907, and served until the end of Roosevelt's administration on March 4, 1909; most important contributions were reorganization of department abolishing divisions of Indian affairs, Indian territories, patents and miscellaneous, and lands and railroads, consolidation of department files, labors of secretary's office brought up to date, inauguration of system of inspection and reports, and insuring regular cabinet meetings; died March 25, 1950. James F. Rhodes, *The McKinley and Roosevelt Administrations, 1897–1909* in *History of the United States*, vol. 9 (1922); George E. Mowry, *Era of Theodore Roosevelt 1900–1912* (1958).

GARLAND, Augustus Hill. Born in Covington, Tenn., June 11, 1832; son of Rufus K. and Barbara (Hill) Garland; married Virginia Sanders in 1853; attended private school in Washington; studied at St. Mary's College in Lebanon, Ky.; graduated St. Joseph's College in Bardstown, Ky., 1849; taught school in Sevier County; studied law with Thomas Hubbard, stepfather; admitted to bar in 1853; began practice in Washington, Ark.; removed to Little Rock, Ark. three years later; went into practice with Ebenezer Cummins; admitted to practice in U.S. Supreme Court, 1860; was elector on Bell-Everett ticket; delegate from Pulaski County to convention of 1861; one of five delegates elected by convention to Provisional Congress; served as representative of 3d (southern) district in first Congress of the Confederacy, 1861–1864; was member of Senate at Richmond, 1864–1865; secured pardon from President Johnson, July 15, 1865, and applied for reinstatement of license to practice before Supreme Court; elected to U.S. Senate, 1866, but not permitted to take seat; was acting secretary of state for Arkansas, 1874; elected governor of Arkansas in latter part of 1874; elected U.S. senator, 1876, took seat on March 4, 1877, and served two terms, until 1885; appointed ATTORNEY GENERAL in the cabinet of President Cleveland on March 6, 1885 and served until March 4, 1889; wrote *Experiences in the Supreme Court of the United States* (1898); practiced law in Washington, D.C.; died in Washington, D.C.; January 26, 1899; interment in Mount Holly Cemetery. Josiah Shinn, *Pioneers and Makers of Arkansas* (1908); Farrar Newberry, *A Life of Mr. Garland of Arkansas* (1908); Henry J. Ford, *Cleveland Era* (1921); Robert L. Vexter, ed., *Grover Cleveland, 1837–1908: Chronology, Documents, Bibliographical Aids* (1968); H. J. Sievers, ed., *Benjamin Harrison, 1833–1901: Chronology, Documents, Bibliographical Aids* (1969).

GARNER, John Nance. Born near Detroit, Tex., November 22, 1868; son of John Nance Garner, Confederate cavalry trooper; married Ettie Rheiner in 1895; attended public schools; entered Vanderbilt University at Nashville; studied law in Clarksville, Tex.; was admitted to the bar in 1890, and began practice in Uvalde County, Tex., joining firm which later became Clark, Fuller and Garner; acquired *The Uvalde Leader*; sat as judge of Uvalde County, 1893–1896; chosen member of the Texas House of Representatives and served from 1898 to 1902; delegate to Democratic national conventions of 1900, 1916 and 1924; elected to U.S. House of Representatives for the 58th through 72d Congresses, and served from March 4, 1903 to March 3, 1933; was chosen House minority leader in 1928; elected speaker of the House on December 7, 1931; was reelected to Congress, and elected VICE-PRESIDENT in the administration of President Franklin D. Roosevelt on November 8, 1832, serving in the latter position from March 4, 1933 to January 19, 1941, never taking his congressional seat; most important contributions were opposition to administration on spending, attempt to "pack" Supreme Court, and New Deal measures and inducement of legislation through Congress; opposed Roosevelt in 1940; retired to private life, pursuing ranch, real estate and banking interests; donated $1 million to Southwest Texas Junior College, 1961; died in Uvalde, Tex., November 7, 1967. H. F. Bermer, ed., *Franklin D. Roosevelt, 1882–1945: Chronology, Documents, Bibliographical Aids* (1969); Paul K. Conklin, *The New Deal* (1967).

GARRISON, Lindley Miller. Born in Camden, N.J., November 28, 1864; son of Joseph Fithian Garrison, physician, minister, and author of *The American Prayer Book* (1887), and Elizabeth Vanarsdale (Grant) Garrison; Episcopalian; married Margaret Hildeburn on June 30, 1900; no children; attended the public schools and the Protestant Episcopal Academy of Philadelphia, Pa.; attended Phillips Exeter Academy, 1884–1885; spent a year at Harvard University as a special student; graduated from the University of Pennsylvania Law School in 1886 and admitted to the bar that same year; began practice in Philadelphia in the offices of Redding, Jones, and Carson; in 1888 moved his practice to Camden, N.J.; from 1898 to 1904 was a partner in a Jersey City law firm; appointed to the bench as vice-chancellor of New Jersey on June 15, 1904 and served until 1913; appointed SECRETARY OF WAR on March 5, 1913 in the cabinet of President Wilson; most important contributions were formulating a program for the development of the country's military strength, inaugurating system of military training camps for college students, writing of bill granting practical autonomy to the Philippines, sending a large contingent of the army to patrol the Mexican border; resigned along with Assistant Secretary Breckinridge on February 11, 1916, when his plans for military expansion were rejected by Congress and the President; returned to law practice as a member of Hornblower, Miller, Garrison, and Potter of New York City; on December 31, 1918 took over receivership of the Brooklyn Rapid Transit Company; died in Seabright, N.J. on October 19, 1932. David F. Houston, *Eight Years With Wilson's Cabinet* (1926); Arthur S. Link, *Woodrow Wilson: The Struggle for Neutrality, 1914–1915* (1960), and *Woodrow Wilson: Confusions and Crises, 1915–1916* (1964); Leon H. Canfield, *The Presidency of Woodrow Wilson* (1966).

GARY, James Albert. Born in Uncasville, Conn., October 22, 1833; son of James Sullivan and Pamelia (Forrist) Gary; married Lavina W. Corrie in 1856; father of Stanley and seven daughters; attended Rockhill Institute of Maryland; received B.A. from Allegheny College in 1854; from age 13, worked six months a year at his father's business, Alberton Manufacturing Company; nominated unsuccessfully by Whigs for Connecticut State Senate, 1858; president of Citizens National Bank; president of Merchants and Manufacturers Association; vice-president of Consolidated Gas Company; director of several financial institutions; chairman of board of trustees of Brown Memorial Presbyterian Church; chairman of board of trustees of Enoch Pratt Free Library; entered partnership with father in 1861, and business became James S. Gary and Son; after death of father, took over entire firm, 1870; defeated as Republican candidate for representative in Congress for 5th district of Maryland, 1870 and 1872; influential in Republican state and national conventions, 1872–1896; elected chairman of state delegation over the opposition of J.A.J. Creswell, state boss, 1872; Republican candidate for governor, 1879; elected national committeeman in 1880; supported Sherman for president, and then swung to Garfield; chairman of state central committee, 1883; withdrew as national committeeman, and made member of finance committee, 1896; appointed POSTMASTER GENERAL in the cabinet of President McKinley on March 5, 1897, and served until his resignation due to poor health on April 20, 1898; most important contribution was his argument on behalf of postal savings; went back to businesses; died in Baltimore, Md. on October 31, 1920. J. T. Scharf, *History of Baltimore City and County* (1881), and *A History of the City of Baltimore: Its Men and Institutions* (1902); Dorothy G. Fowler, *The Cabinet Politician: The Postmasters General, 1829–1900* (1943); Margaret K. Leech, *In the Days of McKinley* (1959); H. Wayne Morgan, *William McKinley and his America* (1963).

GATES, Thomas Sovereign, Jr. Born in Philadelphia, Pa., April 10, 1906; son of Thomas Sovereign Gates, lawyer, banker and president of University of Pennsylvania, and Marie (Rogers) Gates; married Millicent Anne Brengle on September 29, 1928; father of Millicent Anne, Patricia S., Thomas S., and Katharine Curtin; attended Chestnut Hill Academy; received B.A. from University of Pennsylvania in 1928; associated with Drexel and Company, 1928; joined U.S. Naval Reserve in 1935; made partner of Drexel and Company in 1940; graduated Quonset Point Air Intelligence School, assigned to staff of commander-in-chief of Atlantic Theatre; served on U.S.S. *Monterey* in Pacific, 1943; participated in invasion of France, 1944; sent back to Pacific; made commander of U.S. Naval Reserve in 1945; chosen director of Beaver Cool Corp. in 1946, and became vice-president in 1948; appointed undersecretary of the Navy, 1955–1957, and served as secretary of the navy, 1957–1959; chosen deputy secretary of defense, 1959–1960; appointed SECRETARY OF DEFENSE in the cabinet of President Eisenhower on December 2, 1959, resigned on January 7, 1961, and served until January 20, 1961; was president and director of Morgan Guaranty Trust Company from 1961 to 1965 when he became chairman of the board; trustee of Foxcroft School and life trustee of University of Pennsylvania; member of Academy of Political Science, Council of Foreign Relations, and Phi Beta Kappa; vice-president of Navy League of United States. Dean Albertson, *Eisenhower as President* (1963).

GERRY, Elbridge. Born in Marblehead, Mass., July 17, 1744; son of Thomas Gerry, merchant and commander of local fort, and Elizabeth (Greenleaf) Gerry; married Ann Thompson on January 12, 1786; father of three sons and two daughters; pursued classical studies; graduated Harvard, 1762; entered counting house of father; served in colonial house of representatives, 1772–1775 and became member of the assembly of Massachusetts Bay (general court) in 1773; elected to Essex County convention, 1774; appointed by provincial congress on committee on public safety and supplies, 1775; elected to Continental Congress in January, 1776, served until 1781, was reelected, and served, 1782–1785; signed Declaration of Independence on September 3, 1776; delegate to New Haven price-fixing convention, 1778; member of Massachusetts House of Representatives, 1786; member of U.S. constitutional convention held in Philadelphia, 1787; pursued merchant trade; elected as Anti-Federalist to 1st and 2d Congresses, serving from March 4, 1789 to March 3, 1793; was official representative to France in 1797; unsuccessful candidate for governor of Massachusetts, 1801 and 1812; elected governor in 1810 and 1811; inaugurated VICE-PRESIDENT in the administration of President Madison on March 4, 1813, and served until his death on November 23, 1814 in Washington, D.C.; interment in Congressional Cemetery. J. T. Austin, *The Life of Elbridge Gerry* (1828; 2d ed., 1969); Irving Brant, *James Madison* (1956); Ian Elliot, ed., *James Madison, 1751–1836: Chronology, Documents, Bibliographical Aids* (1969).

GILMER, Thomas Walker. Born in Gilmerton, Va., April 6, 1802; son of George and Elizabeth (Hudson) Gilmer; married Anne Baker in 1826; no children; received early education from Dr. Frank Carr, a classical scholar; studied under John Robertson; studied law under his uncle Pendy R. Gilmer at Liberty, Va.; aided in studies by correspondence with Francis W. Gilmer, another uncle; admitted to bar in Albemarle County, 1828; was delegate to Staunton convention; edited *The Virginia Advocate*; represented Albemarle County in house of delegates, 1829–1836; appointed by Governor Floyd commissioner of the state to prosecute revolutionary claims of Virginia; supported Jackson, 1832, until, following Jackson's proclamation against South Carolina in 1833, he joined Whigs; was agent for Virginia capitalists in Texas, 1837; member of the legislature again in 1838 and 1839, at which time he served as speaker of the House of Delegates; elected governor of Virginia on February 14, 1840, and served from March 31, 1840 to March 1, 1841; elected to U.S. House of Representatives and took seat on May 31, 1841; aided Tyler in movement to annex Texas; defeated for reelection in 1843; appointed SECRETARY OF THE NAVY in the Cabinet of President Tyler on February 15, 1844, and served from February 19, 1844 to February 28, 1844 when he was killed in the catastrophic explosion on the steamer *Princeton*; interment in Mt. Air. J. H. Speed, *The Gilmers in America* (1897); Robert Seager, *And Tyler Too* (1963); Hugh P. Fraser, *Democracy in the Making: The Jackson-Tyler Era* (1938).

GILPIN, Henry Dilworth. Born in Lancaster, England, April 14, 1801; son of Joshua Gilpin, Philadelphia merchant, and Mary (Dilworth) Gilpin; married Eliza (Sibley) Johnston on September 3, 1834; no children; attended school of Dr. Hamilton at Hemel-Hempstead, England; graduated University of Pennsylvania, 1819; read law in office of Joseph R. Ingersoll; admitted to the Pennsylvania bar in 1822; secretary of Chesapeake and Delaware Canal Company; began practice of law; editor of *Atlantic Souvenir*, 1825; brought out second edition of Jobb Sanderson's *Biography of the Signers to the Declaration of Independence* in 1828; contributed to *American Quarterly Review* and *Democratic Review*; wrote pamphlet called *A Memorial of Sundry Citizens of Pennsylvania relative to the Treatment and Removal of the Indians*; became attorney for eastern district of Pennsylvania on December 30, 1831; appointed government director of Bank of the United States, 1833; published *Reports of Cases Adjudged in the District Court of the United States for the Eastern District of Pennsylvania 1828–36*, 1837; appointed solicitor of Treasury, 1837; appointed ATTORNEY GENERAL in the Cabinet of President Van Buren, and served from January 11, 1840 to March 4, 1841; most important contributions were argument in Amistad Case against John Quincy Adams and participation in cases arising under Florida Treaty; settled in Philadelphia to life of literary ease; toured Europe in 1850s; president of Pennsylvania Academy of the Fine Arts; vice-president of Historical Society of Pennsylvania, 1852–1858; director of Girard College; trustee of University of Pennsylvania; died in Philadelphia, January 29, 1860. Jacob Painter, *The Gilpin Family* (1870); Irving I. Sloan, ed., *Martin Van Buren, 1782–1862; Chronology, Documents and Bibliographical Aids* (1969).

GLASS, Carter. Born in Lynchburg, Va., January 4, 1858; son of Robert Henry Glass, newspaper editor and postmaster at Lynchburg, and Augusta (Christian) Glass; Methodist; married on January 12, 1886 to Aurelia McDearmon; father of Paulus, Mary, Carter, and Augusta; after death of first wife in 1937, married Mary (Scott) Meade on June 22, 1940; attended public and private schools until the age of 14, when he became a printer's apprentice in the office of the *Lynchburg Daily Republican*; worked for three years as a clerk in the office of the auditor of the Atlantic, Mississippi, and Ohio Railroad; in 1880 became a reporter and editorial writer for the *Lynchburg News*, later purchasing that newspaper and two others; served as clerk of the Lynchburg city council from 1881 to 1901; elected as state senator in 1899 and reelected in 1901; was a delegate to the state constitutional convention, 1901–1902, and took an active part in suffrage revision; elected to the 57th through 66th Congresses, serving from 1902 until his resignation in 1918; as chairman of the Committee on Banking and Currency, he was patron and floor manager of the Federal Reserve Bank Act in the House, and he became known as the "father" of the Federal Reserve System; served as chairman of the Joint Congressional Committee reporting on the Federal Farm Loan Act of 1916; appointed SECRETARY OF THE TREASURY on December 16, 1918 in the cabinet of President Wilson to fill the vacancy caused by the resignation of William G. McAdoo; most important contributions were helping to organize post-war financing for the government, setting up a fund to help pay off the country's war debt; resigned on February 2, 1920 to accept U.S. senatorship by appointment of the governor of Virginia following the death of Thomas S. Martin; elected to that position in 1924 and reelected in 1930, 1936, and 1942; served as president *pro tempore* of the Senate, 1941–1945, also as chairman of the Appropriations Committee and member of the Foreign Relations Committee; delegate to the Democratic national convention, 1916–1928; twice unanimously endorsed by Virginia Democratic convention for presidential nominee, 1920 and 1924; in 1933, offered, but declined, the post of secretary of the treasury in the Cabinet of President Franklin Roosevelt; died in Washington, D.C. on May 28, 1946; interment in Spring Hill Cemetery, Lynchburg, Virginia. Rixey Smith and Norman Beasley, *Carter Glass: A Biography* (1939); Arthur S. Link, *Woodrow Wilson and The Progressive Era, 1910–1917* (1954) and *Woodrow Wilson: The New Freedom* (1956); Leon H. Canfield, *The Presidency of Woodrow Wilson* (1966).

GOFF, Nathan, Jr. Born in Clarksburg, Va. (later W.Va.), February 9, 1843; son of Waldo Porter Goff, merchant, prominent man in local affairs and state senator, and Harriet Louise (Moore) Goff; Episcopalian; married Laura Ellen Despard on November 7, 1865; father of Waldo Perry and Guy Despard (U.S. Senator from West Virginia); remarried to Katherine Penny on August 28, 1919; attended Northwestern Academy at Clarksburg; studied at Georgetown University; went to New York University law school, received LL.B. in 1866, was admitted to the bar of West Virginia, and began practice in Clarksburg; at outbreak of Civil War was put in 3d regiment of Virginia volunteer infantry, became lieutenant of company G, adjutant of G and major of 4th regiment of Virginia volunteer cavalry; was a prisoner for four months in Libby prison, 1864; elected to the state legislature, 1867; appointed U.S. attorney for district of West Virginia in 1868, and served until his resignation on January 6, 1881; unsuccessful Republican candidate for Congress, 1870; delegate to Republican national conventions of 1872, 1876 and 1880; unsuccessful candidate for governor in 1876 and 1888; appointed SECRETARY OF THE NAVY in the cabinet of President Hayes, and served from January 6, 1881 to March 5, 1881; reappointed U.S. district attorney of West Virginia, 1881; elected to 48th Congress in 1882, and reelected in 1884 and 1886; appointed judge of 4th circuit by President Benjamin Harrison in 1892; elected U.S. senator by West Virginia legislature on February 24, 1913, took seat on April 1, 1913, and served until March 3, 1919; held oil, gas, coal, and real estate interests; died in Clarksburg, W. Va., April 24, 1920; interment in Odd Fellows Cemetery. Arthur Bishop, *Rutherford B. Hayes, 1822–1893; Chronology, Documents, Bibliographical Aids* (1969); Harry Barnard, *Rutherford B. Hayes and His America* (1954).

GOLDBERG, Arthur Joseph. Born in Chicago, Ill., August 8, 1908; son of Joseph and Rebecca (Perlstein) Goldberg; Jewish; married Dorothy Kurgans on July 18, 1931; father of Barbara and Robert Michael; attended public schools of Chicago; employed as delivery boy for Chicago shoe factory; studied at Crane Junior College of City College of Chicago, 1924–1926; labored with construction

gangs; received B.S.L. from Northwestern University in 1929, was admitted to
the Illinois bar, and became associate lawyer with firm of Kamfner, Horowitz,
Halligan and Daniels, 1929–1931; earned J.D. from Northwestern University,
1930; associate lawyer with Pritzker and Pritzker of Chicago, 1931–1933; practiced independently from 1933 to 1945; commissioned as special assistant with
Office of Strategic Services in 1942, and was discharged with rank of major in
1945; became partner in law office of Goldberg and Devoe, 1945–1947; made
professor of law at John Marshal Law School, 1945–1948; lectured at Chicago
School of Industrial Relations; director of Amalgamated Trust and Savings Bank,
and Amalgamated Life Insurance Company, 1946–1959; became senior member
of Goldberg, Devoe, Shadur and Mikva in 1947; made general counsel for
Congress of Industrial Organizations and United Steelworkers of America in
1948; opened second law office under Goldberg, Feller and Bredhoff, 1948;
special counsel for AFL-CIO; appointed SECRETARY OF LABOR in the cabinet of
President Kennedy, and served from January 21, 1961 to September 24, 1962;
most important contributions were fight against unemployment, creation of Area
Redevelopment Act of 1961, increase in minimum wage, pilot program to train
and place youth in Newark, N.J., reorganization of Office of Manpower Administration, suggestion for White House Conference on National Economic Issues,
negotiations on harbor strike, formulation of President's Advisory Committee
on Labor-Management Policies, and work to eliminate racial discrimination in
employment; director of National Legal Aid Association; trustee and director of
Carnegie Endowment for Peace; member of executive committee of American
Committee for a United Europe; associate justice of U.S. Supreme Court, 1962–
1965; served as U.S. representative to the United Nations, 1965–1968; returned
to private practice; unsuccessful Democratic candidate for governor of New York,
1970; Charles Evans Hughes Professor, Woodrow Wilson School of Diplomacy,
Princeton University, 1968–1969; distinguished professor, School of International Relations, Colombia University, 1969–1970; University Professor of Law
and Diplomacy, American University, 1971–1973; distinguished professor, Hastings College of the Law, University of California at San Francisco, 1974;
recipient of numerous awards including Presidential Medal of Freedom, 1978;
wrote *AFL-CIO: Labor United* (1956); *Defenses of Freedom* (1966); *Equal Justice: The Warren Era of the Supreme Court* (1972); published articles in numerous
magazines; member of American, Illinois, Chicago, and Washington, D.C., bar
associations. Hugh Sidey, *John F. Kennedy, President* (1963); New York Times,
The Kennedy Years (1964); *Who's Who in America, 1984.*

GOLDSCHMIDT, Neil Edward. Born in Eugene, Oreg., June 16, 1940; son
of Lester and Annette (Levin) Goldschmidt; Jewish; married Margaret Wood in
1965; father of Rebecca M. and Joshua E.; attended South Eugene High School,
graduating in 1958; received a bachelor of arts degree in political science from
University of Oregon in 1963, served as president of the student body, 1962–
1963; interned in Washington, D.C., as a congressional staff fellow, 1963–1964;

Civil Rights Worker in Mississippi, 1964; received his LL.B. from the University of California at Berkeley in 1967 and was admitted to the bar that same year; director of Portland Legal Aid Society, 1967; commissioner of the City of Portland, 1967–1970; mayor of Portland, 1973–1979; youngest mayor in Portland's history; contributions as mayor included the improvement of Portland's economy with a twenty-two block downtown transit mall, the development of a fourteen-mile railroad system connecting Portland and the suburb of Gresham, and revitalization of central city neighborhoods; chairman of the U.S. Confederation of Mayors Standing Committee on Transportation; named SECRETARY OF TRANSPORTATION in the second cabinet of president Jimmy Carter on July 27, 1979, replacing Brock Adams; served until January 23, 1981; chairman of the Standing Committee in Housing and Community Development, 1976–1979; Energy Task Force of the National League of Cities, 1977–1979; vice president of international marketing, Nike Incorporated, 1981– ; governor of Oregon, 1987– ; honors include Junior First Citizen, Portland Jaycees, 1972; one of Nation's Ten Outstanding Men of The Year, Jaycees, 1972; *Time* Magazine's 200 Faces for the Future, 1974. *New York Times* (July 28, 1979, and November 6, 1986); *Time* (August 6, 1979); *Current Biography, 1980; United States Congressional Staff Directory, 1988; International Who's Who, 1988; Who's Who in American Politics, 1988–1989.*

GOOD, James William. Born in Cedar Rapids, Iowa, September 24, 1866; son of Henry and Margaret (Coombs) Good; Presbyterian; married Lucy Deacon on October 4, 1894; father of James William and Robert Edmund; attended common schools; received B.S. from Coe College of Iowa in 1892; earned LL.B. from University of Michigan Law School in 1893; admitted to bar, 1893; began practice with Oliver H. Carson in firm of Carson and Good in Indianapolis, Ind.; formed partnership with Charles J. Deacon in Cedar Rapids; city attorney for Cedar Rapids, 1906–1908; practiced with Deacon, Good, Sargent and Spangler, 1908–1921; elected to 61st Congress in 1908, reelected three times, and served from March 4, 1909 to June 15, 1921, when resigned; returned to practice in Evanston, Ill. under Good, Childs, Bobb and Westcott; western manager for President Coolidge, 1924; appointed SECRETARY OF WAR in the cabinet of President Hoover on March 5, 1929, and served from March 6, 1929 until his death; trustee of Coe College; member of American, Illinois, Iowa, and Chicago bar associations; died in Washington, D.C., on November 18, 1929; interment in Oak Hill Cemetery. W. F. Wiloughby, *The National Budget System* (1927); Harris G. Warren, *Herbert Hoover and the Great Depression* (1959).

GORE, Howard Mason. Born in Harrison County, W. Va., October 12, 1877; son of Solomon Deminion Gore, farmer, and Marietta Payne (Rogers) Gore; Baptist; married to Roxalene Corder on September 30, 1906; attended the public schools; was graduated from West Virginia University in 1900; partner in farming, merchandising, livestock breeding, and hotel ownership with the firm of

H. M. Gore & Brothers; president of the West Virginia Livestock Association, 1912–1916; appointed assistant food administrator for West Virginia, and later assistant to the U.S. Food Administrator during World War I; member of the state board of education, 1920–1925; appointed Chief of Trade Practices in the division of packers and stockyard administration, Department of Agriculture, 1921; appointed assistant secretary of agriculture by President Coolidge, 1923; elected Republican governor of West Virginia, 1924; appointed SECRETARY OF AGRICULTURE in the cabinet of President Coolidge on November 21, 1924 to fill the vacancy caused by the death of Henry C. Wallace; resigned the cabinet post on March 4, 1925 to assume the governorship, and thus served until 1929; unsuccessful candidate for U.S. Senator, 1928; appointed West Virginia Commissioner of Agriculture, 1931, and served until 1933; helped establish and manage livestock auction markets beginning in 1933; appointed a member of the West Virginia Public Service Commission, 1941; also member of the first board of directors of the National Producers' Livestock Cooperative Association and the West Virginia Farm to Market Roads Administration; died in West Virginia on June 20, 1947. William A. White, *A Puritan in Babylon: The Story of Calvin Coolidge* (1938); Donald R. McCoy, *Calvin Coolidge* (1967); Jules Abels, *In the Time of Silent Cal* (1969).

GORHAM, Nathaniel. Born in Charlestown, Mass., May 21, 1738; son of Nathaniel and Mary (Soley) Gorham; married to Rebecca Call in 1763 and father of nine children, among them Benjamin Gorham, member of Congress; attended the public schools; served as a merchant's apprentice until 1759; engaged in business pursuits; member of the colonial legislature, 1771–1775; delegate to the Provincial Congress in 1774 and 1775; member of the Board of War, 1778–1781; delegate to the state constitutional convention, 1779–1780; member of the State Senate, 1780 and 1781; member of the State House of Representatives, 1781–1787, serving as speaker in 1781, 1782, and 1785; member of the Continental Congress in 1782, and 1783 and 1785–1787; appointed judge of the Middlesex court of common pleas, July 1, 1785 and served until his resignation in 1796; PRESIDENT OF THE CONTINENTAL CONGRESS from June 6, 1786 to February 2, 1787; delegate to the federal Constitutional Convention at Philadelphia in 1787; delegate to the state constitutional convention which ratified the Federal Constitution in 1788; member of the Council, 1788–1789; engaged in real estate pursuits in the Genesee Valley, N.Y.; died in Charlestown, Mass. on June 11, 1796; interment in Phipps Street Cemetery. E. C. Burnett, *Letters of Members of the Continental Congress* (1921–1931); E. C. Burnett, *The Continental Congress* (1964).

GRAHAM, William Alexander. Born near Vesuvius Furnace in Lincoln County, N.C., September 5, 1804; son of Joseph and Isabella (Davidson) Graham; married Susannah Sarah Washington on June 8, 1836; ten children; attended local public schools, the Classical Academy at Statesville, and Hillsboro Academy; entered University of North Carolina in 1820, and graduated in 1824; studied law under Chief Justice Thomas Ruffin and was admitted to North Carolina bar in 1826; settled in Hillsboro to practice law; served as a member of the North Carolina House of Commons, 1833–1840, and was selected twice as speaker of that body; elected by state legislature to the U.S. Senate on November 24, 1840, and took his seat on December 10, 1840; retired from the Senate on March 4, 1843; nominated for governor of North Carolina by Whig state convention in Raleigh on December 7, 1843, and elected in August 1844; reelected in 1846; declined nomination for third term, and retired from office in January 1849; offered the post of minister to either Spain or Russia, but declined both; appointed SECRETARY OF THE NAVY by President Fillmore in July 1850; in that post, he organized reforms in the Navy, organized the expedition of the Amazon River, and sent Commodore M. C. Perry on his expedition to Japan which opened that nation to the West; resigned from cabinet in June 1852 when he was nominated as vice-president on the losing Whig presidential ticket headed by General Winfield Scott; returned to private life in North Carolina; served in North Carolina state legislature in 1854; ceased to be a Union supporter when North Carolina passed the ordinance of secession on April 20, 1861; elected to the Senate of the Confederacy, and took his seat in 1864; elected to the U.S. Senate, after the war, in 1866, by the General Assembly of North Carolina, but was not permitted to take his seat; remained active in North Carolina affairs in an advisory capacity; became one of the original trustees of the Peabody Fund in 1866; died in Saratoga Springs, N.Y. on August 11, 1875, while trying to arbitrate boundary dispute between Maryland and Virginia. Montford Mc-Gehee, *Life and Character of the Hon. Wm. A. Graham* (1877); Robert J. Rayback, *Millard Fillmore: Biography of a President* (1959).

GRANGER, Francis. Born in Suffield, Conn., December 1, 1792; son of Gideon Granger, who served in the administrations of Presidents Jefferson and Madison, and Mindwell (Pease) Granger; married Cornelia Rutson Van Rensselaer in 1816; graduated from Yale College in 1811; moved to Canandaigua, N.Y. in 1814; elected to New York State Assembly in 1825; reelected in 1826, and served until 1828; unsuccessful candidate of National Republicans for lieutenant governor of New York in 1828; served a second term on New York State Assembly from 1830 until 1832; unsuccessful candidate of National Republicans and Anti-Masons for governor of New York in 1830 and again in 1832; elected as Whig to U.S. House of Representatives in 1834, served March 4, 1835 until March 3, 1837; unsuccessful Whig and Anti-Masonic candidate for U.S. vice-president in 1836; again elected as Whig to U.S. House of Representatives, served March 4, 1839 until his resignation on March 5, 1841; appointed POST-MASTER GENERAL by President William H. Harrison, served March 6, 1841 until September 18, 1841; elected to U.S. House of Representatives, served November 27, 1841 until March 3, 1843; chairman of Whig convention of 1850; member of peace convention of 1861 at Washington, D.C.; died in Canandaigua, N.Y. on August 31, 1868; interment in Woodlawn Cemetery. F. B. Dexter, *Biographical Sketches of Graduates of Yale College*, vol. 6 (1912).

GRANGER, Gideon. Born in Suffield, Conn., September 19, 1767; son of Gideon and Tryphosa (Kent) Granger; married Mindwell Pease in 1790; father of three sons, one of whom, Francis, was U.S. Postmaster General under President William H. Harrison; prepared for college by his pastor, he entered Yale, graduating in 1787; studied law and was admitted to the bar in 1787, commencing his law practice in Suffield; elected to the state legislature in 1792 and with the exception of two sessions, represented Suffield in that body until 1801; took a prominent part in the adoption of the Common School Law of 1795, the authorship of which is generally attributed to him; allied himself with the Republican party in 1798 and was the unsuccessful candidate for Congress that year; supported Jefferson for president in 1796; appointed to the cabinet of President Jefferson at POSTMASTER GENERAL on November 28, 1801, a post he held until March 17, 1814, having been continued in office during the first administration of President Madison; resumed the practice of law and moved to Whitestown (now Whitesboro), N.Y.; in 1816, he settled at Canandaigua, N.Y., establishing his permanent residence there; served in the New York state senate from 1820 to 1821; authored *A Vindication of the Measures of the Present Administration* (1803) and *An Address to the People of New England* (1808); died on December 31, 1822, at Canandaigua, N.Y. Henry Graff, *Thomas Jefferson* (1968).

GRANT, Ulysses Simpson. Born Hiram Ulysses Grant in Point Pleasant, Ohio, April 27, 1822; son of Jesse Root Grant, leather tanner and factory manager, and Hanna (Simpson) Grant; Methodist; married Julia Boggs Dent on October 22, 1848; father of Frederick Dent, Ulysses Simpson, Ellen (Nellie) Wrenshall, and Jesse Root; attended local schools; worked on father's farm, 1829–1839; appointed to U.S. military academy at West Point, on July 1, 1839, and graduated July 1, 1843, being brevetted second lieutenant of 4th Infantry; served in Mexican War, 1846; brevetted first lieutenant for conduct in Battle of Molino on September 8, 1847; brevetted captain for service in Battle of Chapultepec on September 13, 1847; commissioned first lieutenant on September 16, 1847; commissioned captain on August 5, 1853; resigned from Army on July 31, 1854; went into farming and real estate business in St. Louis, Mo.; worked in father's warehouse and leather store in Galena, Ill., 1860; drilled volunteers during Civil War, 1861; made brigadier general of volunteers on May 17, 1861; commissioned colonel of 21st Illinois Infantry Regiment on June 17, 1861; became major general of volunteers on February 16, 1862, captured Vicksburg, and became major general of U.S. Army on July 4, 1863; participated in the Battle of Chattanooga; made lieutenant general of U.S. Army on March 9, 1864; accepted General Lee's surrender at Appomattox, Va., on April 9, 1865; commissioned general of Army by Congress on July 25, 1866; appointed SECRETARY OF WAR in the cabinet of

President Andrew Johnson in the interim of August 12, 1867 to January 12, 1868; elected PRESIDENT for two terms, serving from March 8, 1869 to March 3, 1877; toured the world from 1877 to 1879; visited the South, Cuba, and Mexico in 1880; unsuccessful candidate for presidential nomination on the Republican ticket in 1880; failure of Grant and Ward of New York left him financially unstable, 1884; wrote *Memoirs* in 1885; was baptized Methodist on April 2, 1885; died on July 23, 1885, in Mt. McGregor, N.Y.; interment in Grant's Tomb, New York City. Ulysses Grant, *Personal Memories of Ulysses S. Grant*, 2 vols. (1885–1886).

GREGORY, Thomas Watt. Born in Crawfordsville, Miss., November 6, 1861; son of Francis Robert Gregory, physician and captain in the Confederate Army, and Mary C. (Watt) Gregory; Presbyterian; married on February 22, 1893 to Julia Nalle; father of Jane, Thomas, Nalle, and Cornelia; graduated Southwestern Presbyterian University in Clarkesville, Tenn. in 1883; studied law at the University of Virginia and graduated from the University of Texas with a law degree in 1885; assistant city attorney of Austin, 1891–1894; delegate to the Democratic national conventions of 1904 and 1912; appointed special assistant to U.S. Attorney General James C. McReynolds by President Wilson to represent the government against the New York, New Haven and Hartford Railroad Company; appointed ATTORNEY GENERAL on August 29, 1914 in the cabinet of President Wilson, succeeding McReynolds and serving until his resignation on March 4, 1919; most important contributions were prosecuting violators of American neutrality before World War I and, after the outbreak of the war, enforcing espionage, sedition, sabotage, and trading-with-the-enemy acts, administering the Selective Service, enlarging the government's investigating agencies, organizing the American Protective League as a volunteer secret service, starting several anti-trust suits, and securing reforms in federal prison administration; offered the post of Supreme Court justice in 1916 by President Wilson, but declined because of a hearing impairment; adviser to the Versailles Peace Conference; member of Wilson's second industrial conference, 1919–1920; practiced law in Washington after 1920 as a member of the firm of Gregory and Todd; moved his practice to Houston, Tex. in 1923; regent of the University of Texas; died in New York City on February 26, 1933. Charles Seymour, *The Intimate Papers of Colonel House*, 4 vols. (1926–1928); W. A. White, *Woodrow Wilson: The Man, His Times, and His Task* (1924); Arthur S. Link, *Woodrow Wilson and the Progressive Era, 1910–1917* (1954), and *Woodrow Wilson: Confusions and Crises, 1915–1916* (1964).

GRESHAM, Walter Quintin. Born near Lanesville, Ind., March 7, 1832; son of William Gresham, cabinet-maker, colonel in state militia, and sheriff of Harrison County, and Sarah (Davis) Gresham; Methodist; married Matilda McGrain on February 11, 1858; father of Kate and Otto; taught at log schoolhouse in Gresham Woods; attended Corydon Seminary, Corydon, Ind., for two years;

employed as clerk in office of Harrison County auditor in 1849; went to Indiana University at Bloomington, 1851–1852; studied law for two years in office of Judge William A. Porter of Corydon; admitted to the bar on April 1, 1854; went into partnership with Thomas C. Slaughter; joined Republican party, 1856; practiced law alone, 1858; elected to state legislature, 1860, and served as chairman of house military committee; enlisted as private during Civil War, subsequently commissioned lieutenant colonel of 38th and colonel of 53rd infantries, and brevetted major general in March 1865; resumed practice of law with John Butler, and thereafter practiced alone; member of committee on resolutions at Indiana state Republican convention; unsuccessful candidate for Congress, 1866; financial agent for Indiana, 1867–1869; was U.S. district judge for Indiana, 1869–1882; acted as federal judge in Indiana railroad strike, 1877; appointed POST-MASTER GENERAL in the cabinet of President Arthur on April 3, 1883, and served until September 24, 1884; most important contributions were campaign to suppress Louisiana lottery, reduction of letter postage rate from 3¢ to 2¢, increment of allowable weight from one-half ounce to one full ounce, improvement of foreign postal service, reestablishment of fast mails, and reduction of letter postage to Canada; appointed SECRETARY OF THE TREASURY in the cabinet of President Arthur on September 25, 1884, and served until October 28, 1884; appointed U.S. judge for the 7th circuit, 1884; supported the Democratic candidate, Grover Cleveland, 1892; appointed SECRETARY OF STATE in the cabinet of President Cleveland on March 6, 1893, and served until his death on May 28, 1895; most important contributions were refusal to repeal sections 19 and 20 of the federal criminal code of the civil rights act, prominent part in Bering Sea arbitration, acquisition of Hawaiian Islands, settlement of Brazil insurrection, withdrawal of British troops from Corinto in Nicaraguan controversy, prominent part in boundary dispute between British Guiana and Venezuela, and receipt of apology from Spanish government over Allianca incident: assailed immorality of slavery and demanded equal protection for Negroes, but opposed unlimited Negro suffrage: died in Washington, D.C., May 28, 1895; interment in Arlington National Cemetery one year after funeral in Chicago. Matilda Gresham, *Life of Walter Quintin Gresham, 1832–1895* (1919); George F. Howe, *Chester A. Arthur: A Quarter Century of Machine Politics* (1957); Henry J. Ford, *The Cleveland Era* (1921); Robert L. Vexter, ed., *Grover Cleveland, 1837–1908: Chronology, Documents, Bibliographical Aids* (1968).

GRIFFIN, Cyrus. Born in Farnham Parish, Richmond County, Va., July 16, 1748; son of Colonel LeRoy and Mary Ann (Bertrand) Griffin; married to Lady Christina Stuart in 1770; educated in England; studied law at Edinburgh University and the Middle Temple, London; returned to Virginia in 1774 and began law practice; active in pre-Revolutionary movements; addressed the Plan of Reconciliation between Great Britain and the colonies to the Earl of Dartmouth, 1775; member of the colonial House of Burgesses in 1777, 1778, 1786, and 1787; elected a member of the Continental Congress and served, 1778–1781,

1787, and 1788; appointed by Congress as judge of the Court of Appeals in Cases of Capture on April 28, 1780 and thus served until 1787; last PRESIDENT OF THE CONTINENTAL CONGRESS, serving from January 22, 1788 until the dissolution of that body; president of the Supreme Court of the Admiralty; appointed by President Washington as commissioner to the Creek Nation in 1789; elected by the Virginia legislature as a member of the Privy Council; appointed by President Washington a judge of the U.S. District Court of Virginia and served from December 1789 until his death; helped preside over the trials of James T. Callender for libel, and of Aaron Burr for treason; died in Yorktown, Va. on December 14, 1810; interment in Bruton Churchyard, Williamsburg, Va. Daniel Grinnan, "Cyrus Griffin," *Virginia Law Register* (January 1928); E. C. Burnett *The Continental Congress* (1964).

GRIGGS, John William. Born on a farm near Newton, N.J., July 10, 1849; son of Daniel and Emeline (Johnson) Griggs; descendant of ancestors who founded Griggstown, New Jersey in 1773; married Carolyn Webster in 1874; married Laura Elizabeth Price in 1893; father of two sons and five daughters; attended Collegiate Institute at Newton, N.J.; went to Lafayette College, 1865–1868, began study of law under former Congressman Robert Hamilton at Newton, and finished with Socrates Tuttle in 1871; admitted to bar, 1871, and formed partnership with Tuttle; elected to General Assembly, 1876, and was chairman of the committee on the revision of the laws; reelected in 1877; defeated in 1878, and appointed counsel to Board of Chosen Freeholders of Passaic County; opened own office, 1879; served as city counsel of Paterson, 1879–1882; elected to State Senate in 1882, was reelected, and served as president until 1886; delegate at large to Republican national convention of 1888; considered by President Benjamin Harrison for Supreme Court; declined a judgeship on highest court of New Jersey tendered by Democratic Governor Werts; nominated and elected governor in 1895; appointed ATTORNEY GENERAL in the cabinet of President McKinley on January 25, 1898, and served until March 30, 1901; major contribution was his able advocacy in the Insular Cases; resumed practice of law; appointed to the Permanent Court of Arbitration at The Hague, and served, 1901–1902; aspirant for U.S. Senate, 1902; president of Marconi Wireless Telegraph Company; general counsel and director of the Radio Corporation of America and other corporations at time of death; died on November 28, 1927. William Nelson and C. A. Shriver, *History of Paterson and Its Environs* (1920); Robert Dallek, *McKinley's Decision, War on Spain* (1970); Margaret K. Leech, *In the Days of McKinley* (1959).

GRONOUSKI, John A. Born in Dunbar, Wisc., October 26, 1919; son of John Austin and Mary (Riley) Gronouski; Roman Catholic; married Mary Louise Metz on January 24, 1948; father of Stacey and Julie; attended St. Peter's School in Oshkosh, Wisc.; studied at Oshkosh Teachers College; received B.A. from University of Wisconsin in January 1942; entered Army Air Corps as private in

April 1942, served as navigator with 8th Air Force; discharged as first lieutenant in October 1945; earned M.A. from University of Wisconsin, 1947; lectured on public finance and banking at University of Maine from 1948 to 1950; moved to Chicago to become research associate for Federation of Tax Administrators, November 1952 to August 1956; taught statistics at Roosevelt College Evening School, 1953; received Ph.D. from University of Wisconsin in 1955; became research associate for University of Wisconsin; was professor of finance at Wayne State University in Detroit in 1957; appointed research director of Wisconsin Department of Taxation, 1959; chosen executive director of Revenue Survey Commission in 1959; made state commissioner of taxation, 1960; appointed POSTMASTER GENERAL in the cabinet of President Kennedy on September 9, 1963, continued under Lyndon Johnson, and served from September 30, 1963 to November 2, 1965; most important contributions were use of zip code, vertical improved mail system of delivery, proposal to do away with airmail postage and move first class mail under priority class; appointed ambassador to Poland, 1965–1968; trustee of John F. Kennedy Library; member of editorial advisory board of *National Tax Journal*; member of American Economic Association and National Tax Association; on board of directors of Pulaski Foundation; honorary co-chairman of committee for endowed chair in Polish studies at University of Chicago; member of Polish Institute of Arts and Sciences; granted honorary Ph.D. from Alliance College; New York Times, *The Kennedy Years* (1964); James MacGregor Burns, *John Kennedy: A Political Profile* (1959).

GRUNDY, Felix. Born in Berkeley County, Va., September 11, 1777; son of George Grundy; married Anne P. Rodgers; moved to Kentucky with his parents in 1780; received early schooling at Bardstown Academy; studied law under George Nicholas; admitted to the Kentucky bar in 1797; served on committee to remodel Kentucky state constitution in 1799; member of Kentucky House of Representatives, 1800–1805; appointed associated justice of Kentucky Supreme Court of Errors and Appeals in 1806; appointed chief justice of Kentucky Supreme Court in 1807, only to resign his position that same year and move to Nashville, Tenn. to practice law; elected as a War Democrat to the U.S. House of Representatives, serving from March 4, 1811 until his resignation in 1814; member of Tennessee House of Representatives, 1819–1825; aided Judge W. L. Brown in adjusting Tennessee-Kentucky state line in 1820; selected to fill U.S. Senate vacancy caused by transferral of John H. Eaton from Senate to the position of Secretary of War by President Jackson, and served in the Senate from October 19, 1829 until his resignation on July 4, 1838; appointed ATTORNEY GENERAL July 5, 1838 by President Van Buren; resigned his cabinet position on December 1, 1839, having been elected to Senate on November 19, 1839; following questions which arose concerning his eligibility for election to the Senate while holding a cabinet position, he resigned from the Senate and was reelected the same day, serving from December 14, 1839 until his death in Nashville, Tenn., on December 19, 1840; interment in Mount Olivet Cemetery, Nashville. J. W.

Caldwell, *Sketches of the Bench and Bar of Tennessee* (1898); J. M. Bright, *An Oration on the Life, Character, and Services of the Honorable Felix Grundy* (1859).

GUTHRIE, James. Born in Bardstown, Ky., December 5, 1792; son of Adam and Hannah (Polk) Guthrie; married Eliza C. Prather on May 13, 1821; father of three daughters; attended McAllister's Academy in Bardstown; engaged in transporting merchandise to New Orleans in 1812; studied law; was admitted to the bar in 1817 and commenced practicing law in Bardstown; appointed commonwealth attorney in 1820, moving to Louisville; elected member of the Kentucky House of Representatives from 1827 to 1829; served in the State Senate, 1831–1840; unsuccessful candidate for election to U.S. Senate in 1835; delegate to and president of the Kentucky Constitutional Convention in 1849; one of the founders of and first president of the University of Louisville; joined the cabinet of President Pierce as SECRETARY OF THE TREASURY on March 7, 1853, serving until March 5, 1857; his incumbency was marked by the overhauling of the Treasury regulations, the reduction of the postal debt, and the weeding out of incompetence; attracted particular attention to himself by his removal of the Collector of the Port of New York for using his office for political purposes; vice-president and then president of the Louisville and Nashville Railroad Company and president of the Louisville and Portland Canal Company; member of the Peace Convention of 1861, held in Washington, D.C., to devise means to prevent the impending war between the North and the South; delegate to the Democratic national convention at Chicago in 1864; elected as a Democrat to the U.S. Senate and served from March 4, 1865 to February 7, 1868, when he resigned because of failing health; died in Louisville, Ky. on March 13, 1869; interment in Cave Hill Cemetery, Louisville. Roy Franklin Nichols, *Franklin Pierce: Young Hickory of the Granite Hills* (1969); Philip Shriver Klein, *President James Buchanan, A Biography* (1962).

H

HABERSHAM, Joseph. Born in Savannah, Ga., July 28, 1751; son of James Habersham, English evangelist, teacher, and merchant, and Mary Bolton Habersham; married Isabella Rae in 1776; father of ten children; educated in New Jersey; sent to England, 1768–1770, where he became a merchant; returned to Georgia where he began a business with his brother, James, and with Joseph Clay, a relative; member of first committee appointed by the Friends of Liberty in Georgia, July 1774; despite his father's Loyalist leanings, took part in the June 11, 1775 siege of Savannah arsenal; made a member of the Georgia Committee of Safety; appointed major of the 1st Georgia battery, February 4, 1776, defending Savannah from naval attack in March 1776; ranked lieutenant colonel at end of war; member of Georgia delegation to the Continental Congress, 1785–1786; speaker of the Georgia Assembly, 1785 and 1790; appointed POSTMASTER GENERAL on February 25, 1795 in the cabinet of President Washington, continuing under Presidents John Adams and Jefferson until November 28, 1801, when he resigned to become president of the United States Branch Bank at Savannah, serving until his death; died in Savannah on November 17, 1815. C. C. Jones, *History of Georgia* (1883); Otis Ashmore, in W. J. Northen, ed., *Men of Mark in Georgia* (1907).

HAIG, Alexander Meigs, Jr. Born in Bala-Cynwyd, Pa., a Philadelphia suburb, on December 2, 1924; son of Alexander Meigs Haig, a lawyer, and Regina Anne (Murphy) Haig; Roman Catholic; married Patricia Antoinette Fox on May 24, 1950; father of Alexander P., Brian F., and Barbara E.; graduated from Lower Merion High School in Pennsylvania, 1942; attended University of Notre Dame, 1943; graduated from U.S. Military Academy with B.S. in 1947; second lieutenant, 1947; served in the military in the following areas: Far East and

Korea, 1948–1951; Europe, 1956–1959; and Vietnam, 1966–1967; military awards: DSC Silver Star with oak leaf cluster; Bronze Star with oak leaf cluster; Air Medal with 23 oak leaf clusters; and Purple Heart; received his M.A. from Georgetown University, 1961; graduated from the Naval War College at Newport, R.I., 1960; attended Army War College, 1966; was assigned as military assistant to secretary of the army, 1964; served as deputy special assistant to secretary of the army and deputy secretary of defense, 1964–1965; became deputy commander at West Point, 1967–1969; military assistant to the assistant of the president for National Security Affairs, 1969–1970; deputy assistant to the president for National Security Affairs, Washington, D.C., 1970–1973; vice-chief of staff, U.S. Army, Washington, D.C., 1973; chief of White House Staff, 1973–1974, when recalled to active duty; retired on August 1, 1973, from the military service; resumed his military career on September 16, 1974; commander-in-chief U.S., European Command, 1974–1979; as NATO commander devoted much of his efforts towards modernization of Western military forces to counter the massive Soviet buildup in Eastern Europe; retired from the military, 1979; president and chief operating officer, United Technologies, 1979–1981; appointed SECRETARY OF STATE on January 21, 1981, and served until June 25, 1982; during his tenure, focused attention on international terrorism, engaged in talks with NATO officials and Soviet Foreign Minister (Andre Gromyko), and worked toward normalization of relations with the People's Republic of China; resigned on June 25, 1982; president of Worldwide Associates, Inc., a Washington-based consulting company, 1983– ; formed the Committee for America, 1986; on March 24, 1987, formally announced his candidacy for the 1988 Republican presidential nomination; honorary degrees include: law degree from Niagara University, and LL.D. from University of Utah, Boston College, St. Anselm's College, Western State School Law, Loyola College, Fairfield University, and Ben Gurion University of the Negev, Israel; honors and awards include Charles Evans Hughes Gold Medal Award of the National Conference of Christians and Jews; Dwight D. Eisenhower Distinguished Service Award and Citation of the Veterans of Foreign Wars of the United States; Hap Arnold Award of the U.S. Air Force Association; member of the Society of First Division; author of *Caveat: Realism, Reagan and Foreign Policy* (1984). *Facts on File, 1982; Current Biography, 1987; New York Times Biographical Service* (March and November 1987); *U.S. News and World Report* (April 6, 1987); *Who's Who in American Politics, 1987–1988; Who's Who in America, 1988; Who's Who, 1989.*

HALL, Nathan Kelsey. Born in Marcellus (now Skaneateles), N.Y., March 28, 1810; son of Ira and Katherine (Rose) Hall; married Emily Paine on November 16, 1832; father of five children; moved to Erie County in early youth with his family; attended the district school; worked as a shoemaker; studied law with Millard Fillmore, then a struggling lawyer in Aurora, N.Y.; while studying law, he taught school; admitted to the bar in 1832, and commenced the practice of law in Buffalo, N.Y.; held various local offices from 1831 to 1837, including those of deputy clerk and clerk of the Board of Supervisors; City Attorney, 1833–1834; member of the Board of Aldermen, 1837; appointed master in chancery by Governor Seward in 1839; appointed judge of the Court of Common Pleas in 1841 by Governor Seward; elected to the New York State Assembly in 1846; elected as a Whig to the 13th Congress, serving from March 4, 1847 to March 3, 1849; invited to join the cabinet of President Fillmore as POSTMASTER GENERAL on July 23, 1850, serving in that capacity until August 31, 1852; appointed U.S. district judge for the Western district of New York on August 31, 1852, holding that position until his death in Buffalo, N.Y. on March 2, 1874; interment in Forest Lawn Cemetery, Buffalo. Robert J. Rayback, *Millard Fillmore: Biography of a President* (1959); Roy Franklin Nichols, *Franklin Pierce: Young Hickory of the Granite Hills* (1969).

HAMILTON, Alexander. Born in the British colony of Nevis in the Leeward Islands, West Indies on January 11, 1757; illegitimate son of Alexander Hamilton, Scottish merchant, and Rachael Fawcett; French Huguenot background; married Elizabeth, daughter of General Philip Schuyler, December 14, 1780; father of eight children; educated by Presbyterian clergyman at St. Croix; worked in general store of Nicholas Cruger in Christianstadt; sent to New York and began studies at Francis Barber's grammar school in Elizabethtown, N.J.; entered King's (now Columbia) College in New York, 1773, and attended until 1776; spoke against England in a mass meeting at "the Fields" (now City Hall Park) on July 6, 1774, and started writing for Holt's *New York Journal, or General Advertiser*; contributor to *A Full Vindication of the Measures of Congress from the Calumnies of Their Enemies*, a December 1774 war pamphlet; replied to the rebuttal of Rev. Dr. Samuel Seabury in *The Farmer Refuted; or, a More Comprehensive and Impartial View of the Disputes Between Great Britain and the Colonies*—these pamphlets were attributed to John Jay; applied for and received command of an artillery company under the provincial convention after examination on March 14, 1776; introduced by General Nathanael Greene to George Washington; made Washington's secretary and an aide-de-camp on March 1, 1777, ranked as lieutenant colonel; reported on the reorganization of the army on May 5, 1778; Congress approved his plan for the inspector general's office, February 18, 1779; appointed head of Lafayette's infantry regiment, fighting at Yorktown; returned to Albany after the Revolution and was admitted to the bar after less than five months' study; entered the Continental Congress in November 1782; retired from Congress in 1783, opening a New York office; defended federal authority in *Rutgers* vs. *Waddington*; Federalist; appointed New York representative to the Annapolis general commercial convention, persuading delegates that smooth commercial exchange was impossible without political unity, hoped for new constitution; seated in 1787 in the New York legislature; appointed to the 1787 Constitutional Convention with Anti-Federalists Robert Yates and John Lansing, also opposed by Governor George Clinton; publication of the

"Federalist" series began October 27, 1787, running seven months in the *Independent Journal*; made his Federalist views prevail, aided by Jay and Robert Livingston, in the New York State convention of 1788; appointed SECRETARY OF THE TREASURY in the cabinet of President Washington on September 11, 1789; reported to the House on the nation's finances on January 14, 1790, believed federal government should assume states' war debts, faced with additional domestic and foreign debts; plans for liquor excise, national bank, and establishment of mint accepted; planned tariff system to promote infant industries, strengthen trade and the central government, and balance industry and agriculture; suppressed Whiskey Rebellion in 1794; resigned January 31, 1795 under financial pressure, his office paying $3,500 per year; continued to advise President Washington; influence on Timothy Pickering and Oliver Wolcott prompted President Adams to reorganize his Cabinet; commissioned inspector general on July 25, 1798 for the support of France; founder of *New York Evening Post*; supported Thomas Jefferson against Aaron Burr and later worked against Burr's 1804 campaign for the governorship of New York; when Dr. Charles D. Cooper charged that Hamilton called Burr "dangerous," Burr challenged Hamilton to a duel in Weehawken, N.J.; wounded by the first shot, Hamilton died July 12, 1804 in the home of William Bayard in Weehawken; interment in Trinity Church Yard, N.Y. Henry Cabot Lodge, *Alexander Hamilton* (1884); W. G. Schouler, *Alexander Hamilton* (1901); Allan McLane Hamilton, *The Intimate Life of Alexander Hamilton* (1910); Charles Beard, *An Economic Interpretation of the Constitution of the United States* (1913); Saul K. Padover, *The Mind of Alexander Hamilton* (1959).

HAMILTON, Paul. Born in St. Paul's Parish, S.C., October 16, 1762; son of Archibald and Rebecca (Branford) Hamilton; married Mary Wilkinson on October 10, 1782; attended the common schools but financial considerations compelled him to withdraw from further formal schooling at 16 years of age; joined a militia company, participating in the unsuccessful siege of Savannah and was with Gates' army when he was routed at the Battle of Camden, on August 16, 1779; served as a "guerrilla" in the later part of the Revolution and was with Hardin when he captured Fort Balfour; became collector of taxes for St. Paul's Parish in 1785 and 1786; was justice of the peace in 1786; elected to the lower house of the state legislature, 1787–1789; member of the convention of 1789 which ratified the federal Constitution; served as state senator, 1794 and 1798–1799; comptroller of finance, 1799–1804; governor of South Carolina, 1804–1806; though a slave owner, he protested against legalizing the African slave trade and urged the South Carolina legislature to prohibit the traffic; invited to join the cabinet of President Madison as SECRETARY OF THE NAVY on March 7, 1809; during his secretaryship, he secured the passage of an act establishing naval hospitals on February 28, 1811; he urged the construction of naval vessels, the navy then consisting of only seventeen ships, but Congress was indifferent to preparedness and it was not until the onset of the War of 1812 that it awoke to the necessity of a less niggardly policy; resigned at the request of President Madison on December 31, 1812; died in Beaufort, S.C. on June 30, 1816. Irving Brant, *James Madison and American Nationalism* (1968); Gaillard Hunt, *The Life of James Madison* (1968).

HAMLIN, Hannibal. Born at Paris Hill, Me., August 27, 1809; son of Cyrus and Anna (Livermore) Hamlin; Unitarian; married first to Sarah Jane Emery on December 10, 1833, and upon her death, to her half-sister, Ellen Vesta Emery in 1856; father of seven children; attended the village schools and Hebron Academy; took charge of his home farm until he was of age; employed as a compositor in a printing shop for a year; studied law and was admitted to the bar in 1833, commencing his legal practice in Hampden, Me.; entered law office of Fessenden and Deblois of Portland; a Jacksonian Democrat, he represented Hampden in the state legislature from 1836 to 1841 and again in 1847, serving as speaker of the House for three terms; elected to the U.S. Senate by the anti-slavery wing of the Maine legislature in 1848, and was reelected in 1851 for a full six-year term; chairman of the Committee on Commerce; though a Pierce supporter in 1852, he went over to the Republicans in 1856, renouncing his Democratic allegiance; resigned from the Senate upon being elected Republican governor of Maine in 1856; elected to the U.S. Senate again in 1857, he resigned his seat on January 17, 1861; elected VICE-PRESIDENT with Abraham Lincoln at the head of the Republican ticket on March 4, 1861, serving until March 3, 1865; a strong advocate of emancipation, he became identified with the ''Radicals'' in Congress; enlisted as a private in the Maine State Guards on July 7, 1864, for a period of sixty days; after retiring from the vice-presidency, he served as collector of the Port of Boston in 1865, resigning because of his disapproval of President Andrew Johnson's policies; reelected to the U.S. Senate, serving from March 4, 1869 to March 3, 1881; chosen a regent for the Smithsonian Institution in 1870; an opponent of the third term movement for President Grant in the convention of 1876; appointed minister to Spain by President Arthur during 1881 and 1882; died in Bangor, Me. on July 4, 1891; interment in Mount Hope Cemetery, Bangor. Morton Garfinkle, ed., *Lincoln and the Coming of the Civil War* (1959); Jesse Burton Hendrick, *Lincoln's War Cabinet* (1946).

HANCOCK, John. Born in Quincy, Mass., January 12, 1737; son of the Rev. John Hancock, pastor, and Mary (Hawke) Hancock; Congregationalist; married to Dorothy Quincy on August 28, 1775; father of one son who died in childhood; raised by his uncle, Thomas Hancock, merchant; pursued classical studies at the Boston Latin School; graduated Harvard College in 1754; trained as a shipping merchant with the firm of his uncle and sent to London in 1760; became partner of Thomas Hancock & Company on January 7, 1763; after death of his uncle in 1764, became head of the company; member of the provincial legislature, 1766–1772; elected to the general court, 1769; head of the town committee, 1770; helped publish the Hutchinson Letters; elected president of the Provincial

Congress, 1774, and reelected in 1775; chairman of a Committee of Safety; member of the Continental Congress, 1775–1780, 1785, and 1786; elected PRESIDENT OF THE CONTINENTAL CONGRESS and served from May 24, 1775 to October 29, 1777 when he resigned; first signer of the Declaration of Independence, 1776; served as senior major general of the Massachusetts Militia during the Revolutionary War; member of the Massachusetts constitutional convention, 1780; elected as the first governor of Massachusetts, and served, 1780–1785; again elected president of the Continental Congress on November 23, 1785, but resigned on May 26, 1786 without having served, due to illness; reelected governor of Massachusetts in 1787 and served until his death; president of the convention to ratify the federal Constitution, 1788; died in Quincy, Mass. on October 8, 1793; interment in Old Granary Burying Ground, Boston. Lorenzo Sears, *John Hancock, the Picturesque Patriot* (1912); William T. Baxter, *House of Hancock* (1945).

HANNEGAN, Robert Emmet. Born in St. Louis, Mo., June 30, 1903; son of John Patrick Hannegan, a St. Louis policeman, and Anna (Holden) Hannegan; Catholic; married Irma Protzmann on November 14, 1929; four children; attended public schools in St. Louis; entered St. Louis University in 1921 and received LL.B. from its Law School in 1925; practiced law in St. Louis, 1925–1941; supplemented his income in the early years by coaching football and swimming at St. Louis University and by playing minor league baseball and professional football; became active in Democratic politics in St. Louis as an associate of Mayor Bernard F. Dickmann; served as Democratic committeeman of the 21st Ward in St. Louis and became chairman of the St. Louis City Democratic central committee in 1934; became the legislative representative of St. Louis to the General Assembly of Missouri in 1935; returned to the committee chairmanship in 1936; managed Harry S. Truman's successful reelection campaign to the U.S. Senate from Missouri in 1940; appointed collector of internal revenue for the eastern district of Missouri by President Franklin D. Roosevelt in June 1942; appointed commissioner of internal revenue in October 1943; resigned as commissioner of internal revenue in January 1944; became chairman of the Democratic national committee on January 22, 1944; urged a reluctant Senator Truman to accept the vice-presidential nomination on the Roosevelt ticket; after Roosevelt's death, he was named POSTMASTER GENERAL by President Truman on May 8, 1945; entered office on July 1, 1945; while in cabinet, he supported Fair Deal policies and felt that knowledge of atomic energy should be shared with Great Britain and the Soviet Union; resigned from the Cabinet because of ill health on December 15, 1947; bought major interest in St. Louis Cardinals baseball team but sold it shortly before his death; died in St. Louis on October 6, 1949. Harry S. Truman, *Memoirs*, 2 vols. (1955); William P. Helm, *Harry Truman: A Political Biography* (1947).

HANSON, John. Born at Mulberry Grove, near Port Tobacco, Md., April 3, 1715; son of Samuel Hanson, member of the General Assembly of Maryland and public official, and Elizabeth (Story) Hanson; married to Jane Contee sometime before 1749; father of nine children, among them Alexander Contee Hanson, chancellor of Maryland; pursued an academic course; engaged in agricultural pursuits; member of the State Assembly, and then the State Senate, from 1756 until 1779; removed to Frederick County, 1773; elected a delegate to the General Congress at Annapolis, 1774; treasurer of Frederick County, 1775; member of the Maryland Convention of 1775 and signed the declaration of the Association of the Freemen of Maryland; chairman of the Committee of Observation and was active in raising troops and providing arms and ammunition against the British; elected a delegate to the Continental Congress on December 22, 1779 and served from 1780 to 1783; elected PRESIDENT OF THE CONTINENTAL CONGRESS on November 5, 1781 and served until November 3, 1782; signer of the Articles of Confederation; retired from public life, 1782; died at Oxon Hill, Md. on November 15, 1783, and there was interred. H. F. Powell, *Tercentenary History of Maryland*, vol. 4 (1925); E. C. Burnett, *Letters of Members of the Continental Congress* (1921–1931); E. C. Burnett, *The Continental Congress* (1964).

HARDIN, Clifford Morris. Born in Knightstown, Ind., October 9, 1915; son of James Alvin Hardin, farmer, and Mabel (Macy) Hardin; Quaker; married to Martha Love Wood on June 28, 1939; father of Susan Carol, Clifford Wood, Cynthia Wood, Nancy Ann, and James Alvin; attended the public schools; attended Purdue University, graduating in 1931; graduate assistant at Purdue, 1937–1939 and 1940–1941, obtaining his masters degree in agricultural economics in 1939; attended the University of Chicago, 1939–1940; awarded Ph.D. by Purdue in 1941; instructor at the University of Wisconsin in 1941, becoming assistant professor of agricultural economics in 1942; moved to Michigan State University in 1944 as associate professor and became professor and chairman of the department of agricultural economics in 1946; member of the U.S. delegation to the International Conference of Agriculture Economists, 1947; assistant director of the agricultural experimental station at Michigan State, 1948, and director, 1949–1953; assistant dean of the Agricultural School, 1953–1954; became chancellor of the University of Nebraska in 1954; appointed trustee of the Rockefeller Foundation, 1961; appointed by President Kennedy in December 1962 as member of a committee to review the U.S. foreign aid program; chairman of the Omaha branch of the Federal Reserve Bank of Kansas City, 1962–1966; co-chairman of the Agriculture Department task force to improve federal-state experimental relationships, 1968; appointed SECRETARY OF AGRICULTURE in the cabinet of President Nixon on December 11, 1968, and took the oath of office on January 22, 1969; resigned his post on November 12, 1971; most important contribution had been instituting reforms in the food stamp program. *Science*, vol. 162 (December 20, 1968); Earl Mazo and Stephan Hess, *Nixon: A Political Portrait* (1969).

HARDING, Warren Gamaliel. Born on a farm in Caledonia (now Blooming Grove), Ohio, November 2, 1865; son of Dr. George Tryon and Phoebe Elizabeth (Dickerson) Harding; Baptist; married Florence (Kling) De Wolfe on July 8, 1891; no children; after receiving his preliminary and secondary education at the public schools in and near Caledonia, he attended Central College at Iberia, Ohio; studied law and was admitted to the bar in 1882; taught school in 1882; engaged in the insurance business; became editor and publisher of the *Marion Star* in 1884; county auditor in Marion, Ohio, in 1895; elected to the Ohio State Senate from 1899 to 1903; served as lieutenant governor of Ohio during 1904 and 1905; unsuccessful candidate for governor on the Republican ticket in 1910; elected to the U.S. Senate in November 1914, serving from March 4, 1915, until his resignation effective January 3, 1921, having been elected PRESIDENT on the Republican ticket; inaugurated on March 4, 1921, serving until his death in office; the sixth president to die in office; the first senator in office to be elected president of the United States; the first president to broadcast over the radio (on June 14, 1922); appointed the first cabinet officer (Interior Secretary Albert Fall) ever convicted of a crime; authored *Rededicating America* (1920), *Our Common Country* (1921); died in San Francisco, Cal., while on a presidential tour of the western states and Alaska, on August 2, 1923; interment in Marion Cemetery, Marion, Ohio; reinterment in Harding Memorial Tomb on December 21, 1927. Francis Russell, *The Shadow of Blooming Grove: Warren G. Harding in His Times* (1968).

HARLAN, James. Born in Clark County, Ill., August 26, 1820; son of Silas and Mary (Conley) Harlan, western pioneer farmers; Methodist; married Ann Eliza Peck in 1845; father of Mary (Mrs. Robert Todd Lincoln); moved with family to Parke County, Ind., in 1824; attended log schoolhouse; taught district school; studied at local seminary; worked with father on farm; helped found Indiana Asbury (later DePauw) University in Greencastle, Ind., 1841; taught school in Missouri; received degree from Indiana Asbury University in 1845; became principal of Iowa City College; chosen superintendent of public instruction as Whig, 1847; studied law, admitted to the bar in 1848, and began practice in Iowa City; declined candidacy for U.S. Senate, 1849; declined nomination for governor in 1850; president of Iowa Conference University (now Iowa Wesleyan), 1853–1855; elected member of U.S. Senate in 1855, served from December 31, 1855 to January 12, 1857 when Senate declared the seat vacant, reelected to fill own vacant seat in 1857, chosen member in regular election of 1861, and served from January 29, 1857 to May 15, 1865; delegate to peace convention in Washington, D.C. in 1861; appointed SECRETARY OF THE INTERIOR in the cabinet of President Andrew Johnson, and served from May 15, 1865 to July 26, 1866; was delegate to Philadelphia Loyalist convention, 1866; again reelected to U.S. Senate, and served from March 4, 1867 to March 3, 1873; president of Ohio Wesleyan University, 1869–1870; unsuccessful candidate for senatorial reelection in 1872; member of second court of *Alabama* claims, 1882–

1886; died in Mount Pleasant, Iowa, on October 5, 1899; interment in Forest Home Cemetery. Johnson Brigham, *James Harlan* (1913); Lately Thomas, *First President Johnson* (1968).

HARMON, Judson. Born in Newton, Ohio, February 3, 1846; son of Benjamin Franklin Harmon, teacher and Baptist preacher, and Julia (Bronson) Harmon; Baptist; married Olivia Scobey of Hamilton in June 1870; father of three daughters; received education at home and in the public schools; received B.A. from Dennison University, 1866; rode out with home guards to help repel incursion of Southern cavalry raider, General Morgan, during summer college vacation; taught school one year as principal at Columbia, Ohio; moved to Cincinnati to read law in office of George Hoadly; received LL.B. from Cincinnati Law School, 1869, and was admitted to the bar; spent seven years in practice; became mayor of Wyoming, Ohio, 1875–1876; elected judge of court of common pleas, but ousted by contest in Ohio Senate, 1876–1877; elected to local superior court, and served until retirement in 1887; took place of Governor Hoadly in law firm of Hoadly, Johnson and Colston, 1887; participated in national Liberal Republican convention at Cincinnati, Ohio in June of 1872; became Democrat; appointed ATTORNEY GENERAL in the cabinet of President Cleveland to succeed Richard Olney on June 8, 1895, and served until March 5, 1897; most important contribution was distinguished service through which he acquired national fame as lawyer and director of prosecution of Trans-Missouri Freight Association and Addystone Pipe and Steel Company under Sherman Act; professor of law at University of Cincinnati, 1896; returned to legal practice in Cincinnati; president of Ohio bar association, 1897–1898; made special commission to investigate charges of rebating by Atchison, Topeka and Santa Fe Railroad in 1905; labored successfully as receiver to restore financial stability of Cincinnati, Hamilton and Dayton, and Père Marquette Railroads, 1905–1909; governor of Ohio, 1908–1913; returned to law practice in Cincinnati, where he died on February 22, 1927; E. O. Randall and D. J. Ryan, *History of Ohio: The Rise and Progress of an American State* (1912); J. K. Mercer, *Ohio Legislative History 1909–1913* (1913); Henry J. Ford, *The Cleveland Era*; Robert L. Vexter, *Grover Cleveland, 1837–1908: Chronology, Documents, Bibliographical Aids* (1968).

HARRIMAN, William Averell. Born in New York, N.Y., November 15, 1891; son of Edward Henry Harriman, financier, and Mary W. (Averell) Harriman, philanthropist; married Kitty Lanier Lawrence on September 21, 1915, and was divorced in 1929; father of Mary and Kathleen; married Mary (Norton) Whitney on February 21, 1930; widowed in 1970; married Pamela Digby Hayward; 1971; attended Groton; graduated Yale in 1913; worked as clerk and section hand in Union Pacific Railroad yards in Omaha, Neb. during college vacations; became vice-president in charge of purchase and supplies for Union Pacific, 1915; bought shipyard in Chester, Pa., and became its chairman of the board, 1918–1927; established W. A. Harriman and Company, a private bank, and was chairman of the board, 1920–1930; became partner in Brown Brothers, Harriman and Company, 1931; chairman of executive committee of Illinois Central Railroad, 1931–1942; made chairman of the board of Union Pacific Railway in 1932; made member of Business Advisory Council for Department of Commerce in 1933, and was chairman, 1937–1940; appointed special assistant administrator of NRA in March 1934; became chief of raw materials branch of Office of Production Management, 1941; chosen by President Franklin D. Roosevelt as defense expediter in London Ministry, March 1941; made ambassador to U.S.S.R. on October 1, 1943, and served until February 1946; director of Illinois Central Railroad, 1946; was ambassador to Great Britain from March 1946 to September 1946; appointed SECRETARY OF COMMERCE in the cabinet of President Truman on January 28, 1947, having previously served an interim appointment in that position from September 28, 1946 to January 27, 1947; served until May 5, 1948; most important contributions were plans for revitalization of Business Advisory Board and aid in Rumanian treaty negotiations; made U.S. representative in Europe under the Economic Cooperative Act of 1948; ambassador extraordinary and plenipotentiary, 1948–1950; special assistant to the President, 1950–1951; American representative of NATO Committee to study Western defense plans, 1951; director of Mutual Security Agency, 1951–1953; elected governor of New York, 1955–1958; made ambassador at large in 1961 and 1965; was assistant secretary of state for Far Eastern Affairs from 1961 to 1963; became undersecretary of state for political affairs, 1963–1965; appointed peace talks representative on Vietnam, March 31, 1968 to January 5, 1969; member of Democratic policy council; drafted resolution to urge pullout from Vietnam; remained active in foreign affairs; went to Moscow to confer with Yuri Andropov, 1983; died at Birchgrove in Yorktown Heights, New York, on July 26, 1986. Howard Furer, ed., *Harry S. Truman, 1884– : Chronology, Documents, Bibliographical Aids* (1969); Clarence B. Randell, *Adventures in Friendship* (1965); Deane Heller and David Heller, *Kennedy Cabinet* (1961); *New York Times Biographical Service* (July 1986).

HARRIS, Patricia Roberts. Born in Mattoon, Ill., May 31, 1924; daughter of Bert Fitzgerald and Hildren Brodie (Johnson) Roberts; married to William Beasley Harris, September 1, 1955; received A.B. degree from Howard University, Birmingham, Ala., 1945; postgraduate studies at the University of Chicago, 1945–1947, and American University, Washington, D.C., 1949–1950; J.D. degree with honors, George Washington University, Washington, D.C., 1960; numerous honorary degrees; admitted to the District of Columbia bar, 1960; program director YWCA, Chicago, 1946–1949; assistant director, American Council on Human Rights, 1949–1953; executive director, Delta Sigma Theta, 1953–1959; trial attorney, U.S. Department of Justice, 1960–1961; Associate Dean of Students and Lecturer of Law, Howard University, Birmingham, Ala., 1961–1963; Professor of Law, Howard University, 1963–1969; dean, School of Law, Howard University, 1969; delegate, Democratic National Committee, 1964 and 1972; Presidential elector, 1964; member, United States-Puerto Rico Commission on the Status of Puerto Rico, 1964–1966; United States Ambassador to Luxembourg, 1965–1967; alternate delegate, United States Mission to the United Nations, 1966; became partner in Fried, Frank, Harris, Shriver and Kampelman law firm, Washington, D.C., 1970; director, Chase Manhattan Bank; director, IBM; director, Scott Paper Company; member, American Council on Human Rights, 1953–1958; chairman, Welfare Committee, National Urban League of the District of Columbia, 1961–1965; vice chairman, National Capitol Area Civil Liberties Union, 1962–1965; co-chairman, National Women's Commission on Civil Rights, 1963–1964; member, Executive Board, District of Columbia Chapter of the N.A.A.C.P.; co-chairman, National Women Committee on Civil Rights, 1963–1964; member, Executive Committee of the National Citizens Committee on Community Relations, 1964–1965; member, Home Rule Committee for the District of Columbia, 1965–1966; became a member of the Committee on Admissions and Grievances, U.S. District Court for the District of Columbia; Woman of the Year in Business and Professions, *Ladies Home Journal*, 1974; Council on Foreign Relations; American Federal Bar Associations; Phi Beta Kappa, Delta Sigma Theta, Kappa Beta Phi; Democrat; nominated on December 21, 1976, by President-Elect Jimmy Carter, to be SECRETARY OF HOUSING AND URBAN DEVELOPMENT of the United States until September 12, 1979, when she became SECRETARY OF HEALTH, EDUCATION AND WELFARE; appointed SECRETARY OF HEALTH AND HUMAN SERVICES on May 4, 1980, when the Department of Education came into existence; served until January 21, 1981; ran for mayor of Washington, D.C., but lost, 1982; returned to George Washington National Law Center as a full-time professor; died in Washington, D.C., on March 23, 1985. *Who's Who in America*, 1974–1975; *Congressional Quarterly, Weekly Report*, Vol. 34 (December 26, 1976); *Time* (December 27, 1976); *U.S. News and World Report* (January 10, 1977); *New York Times Biographical Service* (March 1985); *Annual Obituary, 1985*.

HARRISON, Benjamin. Born in North Bend, Ohio, August 20, 1833; son of John Scott and Lucretia Knapp (Johnson) Harrison; grandson of President William H. Harrison; Presbyterian; married first to Caroline Lavinia Scott on October 20, 1853, and after her death in 1892, to Mary Scott Lord Dimmick on April 6, 1896; father of Russell Benjamin, Mary Scott and Elizabeth; after receiving private tutelage at home and attending College Hill, near Cincinnati, Ohio, he entered Miami University, Oxford, Ohio, graduating in 1852; studied law and was admitted to the bar in 1853, commencing the practice of his profession in Cincinnati; moved to Indiana in 1854, practicing law in Indianapolis; became reporter of decisions of the Indiana Supreme Court in 1860; commissioned a second lieutenant of the Indiana Volunteer Infantry on July 14, 1862, advancing to the rank of captain; went with the regiment to Kentucky and was commissioned colonel, serving until June 1865; served as reporter of the Indiana Supreme Court during 1864 and 1865 while still in military service; promoted to brigadier general on January 23, 1865; unsuccessful candidate for governor of Indiana in 1876; chairman of the Indiana delegation to the Republican national convention in 1880; declined a cabinet portfolio tendered by President Garfield in 1881; member of the Mississippi River Commission in 1879; elected to the U.S. Senate, serving from March 4, 1881 until March 3, 1887; elected PRESIDENT in November 1888, serving from March 4, 1889, until March 3, 1893; though the popular vote went to the incumbent President Grover Cleveland, he won the electoral vote; defeated by Cleveland in a second bid for the presidency; resumed the practice of law upon leaving the White House; served as chief attorney for the republic of Venezuela in Paris, France, in the Venezuela-Great Britain Boundary dispute; delegate to the Republican national conventions of 1884 and 1888; was Chief Executive when Congress first appropriated $1 billion; was the only grandson of a president to become president; authored *This Country of Ours* (1897), *Constitution and Administration of the United States of America* (1897), *Views of an Ex-President* (1901); died in Indianapolis, Ind. on March 13, 1901; interment at Crown Hill Cemetery, Indianapolis. Harry Joseph Sievers, *Hoosier Statesman: From the Civil War to the White House* and *Hoosier President: The White House and After*, 2 vols. (1968).

HARRISON, William Henry. Born in Berkeley, Va., February 9, 1773; son of Benjamin and Elizabeth (Bassett) Harrison; Episcopalian; married Anna Tuthill Symmes on November 25, 1795; father of Elizabeth Bassett, John Cleves Symmes, Lucy Singleton, William Henry, John Scott (father of President Benjamin Harrison), Benjamin, Mary Symmes, Carter Bassett, Anna Tuthill and James Findley; educated under private tutelage, pursuing classical studies; attended Hampden-Sidney College in Virginia, 1787–1790; studied medicine briefly; commissioned by President George Washington, given the rank of ensign in the 1st Infantry on August 16, 1791, serving in the Indian wars; promoted to captain in May 1797 and placed in command of Fort Washington; resigned on June 1, 1798, having been appointed secretary of the Northwest Territories during 1798 and 1799; elected as a delegate from the territory northwest of the Ohio river to the 6th Congress, serving from March 4, 1799 until May 4, 1800, when he resigned; designated territorial governor of Indiana which carried with it the commissionership of Indian Affairs, by appointment of President Jefferson, and subsequently redesignated by President Madison, serving from 1801 until 1813; defeated the Indians at Tippecanoe on November 7, 1811; promoted to major general in the U.S. Army during the War of 1812; defeated the British and the Indians in the Battle of the Thames, October 5, 1813; resigned from the Army in 1814; elected as a Whig to the 14th Congress to fill a vacancy and reelected to the 15th Congress, serving in all from October 8, 1816, until March 3, 1819; elected to the Virginia State Senate from 1819 to 1821; elected to the U.S. Senate in November 1824, serving from March 4, 1825 until May 20, 1828, when he resigned, having been tendered a diplomatic post; appointed minister to Colombia on May 24, 1828, serving until September 26, 1829; unsuccessful Whig candidate for the Presidency in 1836; elected PRESIDENT in November 1840, serving from March 4, 1841 until his death one month later, thereby serving the shortest term of any President; the first President to die in office; the only President whose father was one of the signers of the Declaration of Independence; the oldest President to be elected (68 years of age); authored *Discourses on the Aborigines of the Valley of Ohio* (1839); died in Washington, D.C., on April 4, 1841; interment in the Harrison Tomb, opposite Congress Green Cemetery, North Bend, Ohio; Stanley Young, *Tippecanoe and Tyler, Too!* (1957).

HATHAWAY, Stanley K. Born at Osceola, Neb., July 19, 1924; son of Franklin E. and Velam (Holbrook) Hathaway; Episcopalian; married Roberta Harley, November 25, 1948; father of Susan and Sandra; served in the United States Army Air Corps, 1943–1945; received A.B. degree from the University of Nebraska in 1948; LL.B., University of Nebraska, 1950; admitted to the Wyoming bar; prosecuting attorney, Goshen County, Wyo., 1954–1962; National Committeeman, Young Republican Federation, 1958–1960; committeeman, Wyoming Republican Party, 1960–1962; chairman, Wyoming Republican Party, 1962–1964; Governor of Wyoming, 1967–1975; chairman, Interstate Oil Compact Commission; American Legion, V. F. W., Lions, Masons, Elks, Moose; Republican; in April 1975, nominated by President Gerald Ford to the office of SECRETARY OF THE INTERIOR, and on June 11 appointment was confirmed by the United States Senate; during confirmation hearings, his appointment was opposed because of his "regrettable suppliance to the will of big oil," and his disregard for the safeguarding of natural resources; in July 1975, he was hospitalized for physical exhaustion and treatment for "moderate depression"; resigned his post on July 25, 1975, for "reasons of my personal health." Henry H. Schulte, Jr., ed., *Facts on File Year Book,* 1975; National Journal, *Ford's Presidency* (1975).

HATTON, Frank. Born in Cambridge, Ohio, on April 28, 1846; son of Richard Hatton, publisher of *Republican* newspaper, and Sarah (Green) Hatton; married Lizzie Snyder in 1867; father of one son; tutored by mother; learned typesetting and journalism from father; volunteered in Union army as drummer boy, 1862; enlisted in Ohio regiment; made first lieutenant of 184th Ohio Volunteers in 1864; settled in Iowa; published Mount Pleasant *Journal*; moved to Burlington, and became part owner of *Hawk-Eye*; chosen postmaster of Burlington in 1879; made assistant postmaster general of Washington, D.C., 1881; joined staff of *National Republican* of Washington in 1882; became chief editor of *Mail*, 1884; postmaster general *ad interim* in 1883 and 1884; appointed POSTMASTER GENERAL in the cabinet of President Arthur, and served from October 14, 1884, to March 5, 1885; founded New York *Press* in 1888; died in Washington, D.C., on April 30, 1894. A. M. Antrolus, *History of Des Moines County, Iowa and Its People* (1915).

HAY, John Milton. Born in Salem, Ind., October 8, 1838; son of Dr. Charles and Helen (Leonard) Hay; not religious; married Clara L. Stone on January 8, 1874; father of Helen, Adelbert Stone, Alice, and Clarence; attended local schools in Warsaw, Ill.; enrolled in a private academy at Pittsfield, Ill., and later attended college in Springfield, Ill. in 1852; studied at Brown University in Providence, R.I., 1855–1858; entered law office of his uncle, Milton Hay, at Springfield in 1859; became assistant private secretary to President-elect Lincoln; appointed secretary to the American legation in Paris in 1865, serving until 1867; appointed chargé d'affaires at Vienna, 1867; secretary of the U.S. legation in Madrid, 1869; decided to become a journalist in 1870; published *Castilian Days*, 1871; editorial writer and night editor of the *New York Tribune*, 1874; moved to Cleveland to assist Amasa Stone and write, 1875; appointed assistant secretary of state in 1878; brevetted colonel of U.S. volunteers, 1879; editor of *New York Tribune*, 1881; traveled to and from Europe, 1881–1896; appointed ambassador to Great Britain in 1897; appointed SECRETARY OF STATE in the cabinet of President McKinley on September 20, 1898, continued under President Theodore Roosevelt, and served until his death in 1905; most important contributions were his work in the settlement with Spain, formulation of much of the Open Door policy and responsibility for its general acceptance, prevention of dissolution of China in 1900, postponement of Alaskan boundary dispute leading to victory for the United States, and work on treaties concerning the Panama Canal; died in Newburg, N.H., July 1, 1905. Lorenzo Sears, *John Hay, Author and Statesman* (1914); William Roscoe Thayer, *The Life and Letters of John Hay* (1915).

HAYES, Rutherford Birchard. Born in Delaware, Ohio, October 4, 1822; son of Rutherford and Sophia (Birchard) Hayes; Methodist; married Lucy Webb on December 30, 1852; father of Birchard Austin, James Webb Cook, Rutherford Platt, Joseph Thompson, George Crook, Fanny, Scott Russell, and Manning Force; after receiving his preliminary and secondary education at the local schools, he attended the Methodist Academy at Norwalk, Ohio, the Webb Preparatory School and, finally, Kenyon College, Gambier, Ohio, in 1842; graduated Harvard Law School in January 1845; admitted to the bar on May 10, 1945, commencing the practice of his profession in Lower Sandusky (now Fremont), Ohio; moved to Cincinnati in 1849, continuing the practice of law there; elected city solicitor from 1857 to 1859; entered the Union Army during the Civil War, having been commissioned a major; promoted to major general on March 3, 1865, resigned from the Army on June 8, 1865; elected to the U.S. House of Representatives in the 39th and 40th Congresses, serving in all from March 4, 1865 until July 20, 1867, when he resigned, having been elected governor of Ohio, in which office he served from 1868 to 1872; unsuccessful candidate for election to the 43d Congress; declined appointment as U.S. treasurer at Cincinnati, Ohio; again elected governor, serving from January 1876 until March 2, 1877, when he resigned, having been elected PRESIDENT; inaugurated on March 4, 1877, serving until March 3, 1881; refused to contemplate serving a second term; upon his retirement from the White House, he returned to "Spiegel Grove," his mansion, in March 1881; president of the National Prison Association from 1883 until his death; member of the Board of Trustees of the Peabody Education Fund and the Slater Fund; died in Fremont, Ohio on January 17, 1893; interment in Oakwood Cemetery; following the gift of his estate to the state of Ohio, he was reinterred there in 1915. Harry Barnard, *Rutherford B. Hayes and his America* (1954).

HAYS, William Harrison. Born in Sullivan, Ind., November 5, 1879; son of John T. Hays, lawyer; Presbyterian; married Helen Louise Thomas on November 18, 1902 and father of Will H.; after divorce from first wife, married Jessie Herron Stutsman on November 27, 1930; attended Wabash College in Indiana, graduating in 1900 and receiving Master's degree in 1904 from that institution; admitted to the bar in 1900 and began practice in Sullivan in the firm of Hays and Hays; chairman of the Republican committee of Sullivan County, and member of the Republican state advisory committee, 1904–1908; chairman of the speaker's bureau of the Republican state committee, 1906–1908; city attorney for Sullivan County, 1910–1913; district chairman of the Republican state committee, 1910–1914; chairman of the Republican state central committee in Indiana from 1914 until 1918; chairman of the Indiana state council of defense, 1917; chairman of the Republican national committee from February 1918 until June 7, 1921; appointed POSTMASTER GENERAL in the cabinet of President Harding on March 5, 1921; most important contributions were establishment of the Post Office Welfare Department, extension of rural free delivery, restoration of second-class mailing privileges to newspapers, and reduction of departmental expenditures by $15 million; served until March 4, 1922, resigning to become president of the Motion Picture Producers and Distributors of America, Inc.; formulated production code for filmmakers; director of Continental Banking Company and the Chicago & Eastern Illinois Railroad Company; member of the National Council of the Boy Scouts of America; chairman of the coordinating committee of the American Red Cross and Near East Relief by appointment of President Harding in October 1922; died on March 7, 1954 in Sullivan, Ind. William Allen White, *Puritan in Babylon: The Story of Calvin Coolidge* (1938); Andrew Sinclair, *The Available Man* (1965); Francis Russell, *The Shadow of Blooming Grove: Warren G. Harding and His Times* (1968).

HECKLER, Margaret Mary. Born in Flushing, N.Y., June 21, 1931; daughter of John and Bridget (McKeon) O'Shaughnessy; Roman Catholic; married John M. Heckler, Boston stockbroker, in 1954; divorced February 13, 1985; mother of Belinda, Alison, and John; B.A., Albertus Magnus College, 1953; received LL.B. degree, Boston College, 1956; student at University of Leiden, Holland, 1952; admitted to Massachusetts bar in 1956; member, Massachusetts Governor's Council, 1963–1966; ran as Republican candidate for seat in the U.S. House of Representatives in 1966, defeating, in a major upset, the Democratic incumbent,

Joseph Martin, Jr., a former House Speaker; served as representative from the tenth District, Massachusetts, for sixteen years; member of the ninetieth through ninety-seventh Congresses; founder of Congressional Women's Caucus, 1978; and cochairman, 1978–82; defeated in a bid for reelection in November 1982 after her district was redrawn; nominated for SECRETARY OF HEALTH AND HUMAN SERVICES by President Ronald Reagan on January 12, 1983, to replace Richard S. Schweiker; confirmed March 3, 1983; sworn in on March 9, 1983; major contributions as secretary include efforts to improve the child-care support system and the child-care tax credit system; worked hard to change the image of the Department of Health and Human Services from one whose function was to pursue waste, fraud, and abuse in Federal welfare programs to a department that represented compassion and humane treatment for the underprivileged; resigned on October 1, 1985, amid growing criticism that she was a poor manager and unable to handle the responsibilities of her office; also accused of displaying a weak ideological commitment to the policies of the Reagan administration, opposing the president by her continued support for a Federal Equal Rights Amendment and through her efforts to raise Social Security benefits for women; named ambassador to Ireland on October 1, 1985, served until January 20, 1989; possesses numerous honorary degrees; Outstanding Young Woman of America, 1965; Outstanding Mother of the Year in Politics, 1984; Prince Henry the Navigator Award (Portugal), 1984; National Women's Economic Alliance Excellence in Leadership Award, 1985. *New York Times* (January 13, March 4, June 26, and November 10, 1983; February 14 and October 2, 1985); *Who's Who in American Politics, 1987–1988; Who's Who of American Women, 1989–1990.*

HENDRICKS, Thomas Andrews. Born near Zanesville, Ohio, September 7, 1819; son of John and Jane (Thomson) Hendricks; Episcopalian; married Eliza C. Morgan on September 26, 1845; one son who died in childhood; family moved to Madison, Ind. in 1820, and to Shelby County, Ind. in 1822; attended Shelby County Seminary and the Greenburg Academy; graduated from Hanover College, near Madison, in 1841; read law in Shelbyville under Judge Major in 1842; studied law in Chambersburg, Pa. in 1843 under Judge Alexander Thomson; admitted to the bar in Shelbyville in 1843, where he became a successful lawyer; elected as a Democrat to lower house of Indiana Assembly in 1848; served as chairman of banking committee; elected to Indiana state constitutional convention in 1850, and helped revise state constitution; opposed allowing Negroes to come into Indiana, but denied that he favored slavery; elected to the 32d Congress from Indianapolis in 1851; reelected in 1852, but was defeated in 1854; was a Douglas Democrat who supported the Kansas-Nebraska Act; appointed commissioner of the General Land Office by President Pierce in 1855, but resigned over disagreement with President Buchanan in 1859; unsuccessful Democratic candidate for governor of Indiana in 1860; elected to U.S. Senate by Democratic legislature in 1863, and served one term; opposed Thirteenth Amendment on grounds that the time was wrong and that Negroes were inferior;

supported President Andrew Johnson's plan for reconstruction; opposed Freedmen's Bureau Bill, Civil Rights Bill, and new apportionment of representation; opposed Fourteenth and Fifteenth Amendments and impeachment of President Johnson; unsuccessful contender for presidential nomination at Democratic national convention in 1868; as Democratic candidate, lost Indiana gubernatorial election by narrow margin in 1868; retired from Senate in 1869 and returned to law practice in Indianapolis; nominated for governor for third time in 1872, and was elected, serving from 1873 to 1876; received 42 electoral votes for presidency in 1872, after death of Democratic and Liberal Republican candidate Horace Greeley; vice-presidential candidate on unsuccessful Democratic ticket headed by Samuel J. Tilden in 1876 election which was decided by electoral commission; presidential contender at Democratic national convention in 1884; nominated by that convention as vice-presidential candidate on successful Democratic ticket headed by Grover Cleveland in 1884; vigorous campaigner who brought geographic and ideological balance to ticket; favored "soft money" and was acceptable to machine faction of Democratic party; helped carry Indiana for Cleveland; inaugurated as VICE-PRESIDENT under President Cleveland on March 4, 1885; died suddenly at his Indianapolis home on November 25, 1885, after only eight months in office; interment in Crown Hill Cemetery, Indianapolis. J. W. Holcombe and H. M. Skinner, *Life and Public Services of Thomas A. Hendricks* (1886); David Turpie, *Sketches of My Own Times* (1903); Allan Nevins, *Grover Cleveland: A Study in Courage* (1938).

HENSHAW, David. Born in Leicester, Mass., April 2, 1791; son of David Henshaw, revolutionary patriot and magistrate, and Mary (Sargent) Henshaw; never married; attended free schools; studied at Leicester academy; was druggist's apprentice; went into business until 1829; was banker and insurance man; established *Boston Statesman* in 1821; elected to state legislature in 1826, defeated in reelection of 1827, and reelected in 1830; unsuccessful candidate for Congress, 1827; became collector for Port of Boston, 1827–1830; handled project for running railroad through Berkshires to Albany, N.Y., 1828; incorporator of Western Railroad; director of Boston and Worcester Railroad; Democratic leader of Massachusetts; published *Remarks on the Bank of the United States* (1831) and *Remarks upon the Rights and Powers of Corporations* (1837); representative in state House of Representatives, 1839; published *Letters on the Internal Improvements and Commerce of the West* (1839); unsuccessful candidate for Congress, 1843; appointed SECRETARY OF THE NAVY in the cabinet of President Tyler, and served from July 24, 1843 to February 19, 1844 when Senate rejected his appointment; retired to private life; died on November 11, 1852 in Leicester, Mass. A. B. Darling, *Political Changes in Massachusetts, 1824–48* (1925); Robert Seager, *And Tyler Too* (1963).

HERBERT, Hilary Abner. Born in Lawrenceville, S.C., March 12, 1834; son of Thomas Edward Herbert, planter, and Dorothy League (Young) Herbert; married Ella B. Smith on April 23, 1867; father of Leila; attended public schools of Lawrenceville; went to local schools of Greenville, Ala.; attended University of Alabama and University of Virginia; received law degree from University of Alabama, 1857, and adopted legal profession; enlisted in Confederate army and went through the ranks of captain, major, and lieutenant colonel to colonel of the 8th Alabama volunteers; was severely wounded in Battle of the Wilderness on May 6, 1864; returned to Greenville to engage in practice of law as member of Adams and Herbert in March 1872; elected by Democrats as a member of the 45th Congress, 1876, and being reelected, served in the House of Representatives until 1893; published *Why the Solid South?* in 1890; appointed SEC-RETARY OF THE NAVY in the cabinet of President Cleveland on March 4, 1893, and served until March 4, 1897; most important contributions were construction work on battleships and torpedo boats, enlargement of navy, and good service; renewed law practice in Washington, D.C.; member of Academy of Political and Social Sciences in Philadelphia, Pennsylvania; member of Geographical Society in Washington, D.C.; died on March 6, 1919 in Tampa, Fla. T. M. Owen, *History of Alabama and Dictionary of Alabama Biography* (1921); *Memorial Records of Alabama* (1893); B. F. Riley, *Makers and Romance of Alabama History* (1915); Robert L. Vexter, *Grover Cleveland, 1837–1908: Chronology, Documents, Bibliographical Aids* (1968); Margaret K. Leech, *In the Days of McKinley* (1959).

HERRINGTON, John. Born Los Angeles, Calif., May 31, 1939; son of James Herrington and Mary Herrington; Methodist; married Lois Haight, July 8, 1961; father of Lisa Marie and Victoria Jean; A.B. Stanford University, 1961; J.D. and LL.B., University of California School of Law, 1964; private attorney dealing in corporate, real estate, taxation, and business law from 1965–1981; formerly deputy district attorney, Ventura County; deputy assistant to President Ronald Reagan for presidential personnel, 1981–1983; assistant secretary, Manpower and Reserve Affairs, Department of the Navy, 1981–1983; assistant to the chief of staff, White House, 1983; assistant to the president, White House, 1985–1988; appointed SECRETARY OF ENERGY by President Reagan and served from February 6, 1985, to the change in administration on January 20, 1989; while secretary he radically changed the Federal Government's uranium enrichment program by streamlining for efficiency and closing facilities in Ohio and Tennessee; stopped aid to the Great Plains Coal gratification plant, the nation's most ambitious synthetic fuel project; gave a high priority to nuclear dump cleanup; and continued to study the idea of merging the Energy Department with the Interior Department. *Congressional Record* (February 6, 1985); *New York Times* (February 7 and August 26, 1985; January 20, 1989); *Who's Who in American Politics, 1987–1988.*

HERTER, Christian Archibald. Born in Paris, France, March 28, 1895; son of Albert and Adele (McGinnis) Herter, both Americans; Episcopalian; married Mary Caroline Pratt on August 25, 1917; father of Frederick Pratt, Eliot Miles,

Adele, and Christian Archibald, Jr.; attended Ecole Absatienne, Paris; emigrated to the U.S. in 1904, and studied at Browning School in New York until 1911; graduated Harvard in 1915; attended Columbia University School of Architecture, 1916; sent to American Embassy at Berlin, 1916; headed American delegation in Brussels, 1917; made secretary to commission to negotiate prisoner of war agreements with Germany in 1918; was staff member of American commission to make peace with Germany; went to Europe to assist Hoover in direction of American Relief Administration, 1919; served as assistant secretary of commerce to Hoover, 1919–1924; was executive secretary of European Relief Council from 1920 to 1921; moved from Washington to Boston in 1924, and bought interest in *The Independent*, becoming an editor, 1924–1928; purchased holdings in *The Sportsman*, and was an editor from 1927 to 1936; lectured on government at Harvard, 1929–1930; elected member of Massachusetts House of Representatives, serving from 1931 to 1943, and was speaker of the House, 1939–1943; overseer of Harvard University, 1940–1944; elected member of Congress in 1942, was reelected five times, and served until 1953; elected governor of Massachusetts in 1952 and 1954; made undersecretary of state in 1957; appointed SECRETARY OF STATE in the cabinet of President Eisenhower, and served from April 17, 1959 to January 19, 1961; most important contributions were alleviation of Soviet pressure on West Berlin and negotiations over unarmed American U–2 plane downed in Soviet Union; became co-chairman of U.S. Citizens Committee on NATO and chairman of Atlantic Council of the United States Incorporated, 1961–1962; chosen chief planner and negotiator on foreign trade of U.S. in November 1962; member of Commission for Relief of Belgium Educational Foundation; honorary trustee of Johns Hopkins University; member of international commission of YMCA; was president and chairman of the board of trustees of Foreign Service Educational Foundation; trustee of World Peace Foundation and Boston Library Society; died in Washington, D.C., on December 30, 1967. Dean Albertson, ed., *Eisenhower as President* (1963).

HICKEL, Walter J. Born in Ellinwood, Kans., August 18, 1919; son of Robert A. Hickel, farmer, and Emma (Zecha) Hickel; Roman Catholic; married to Janice Cannon on September 22, 1941 and father of Theodore; after death of first wife married Ermalee Strutz on November 22, 1945 and father of Robert, Walter, John, Joseph, and Karl; attended the public schools of Clafin, Kans.; ended formal education at age 16; moved to California and worked as a carpenter; moved to Alaska in 1940; began working as a bartender, an employee of the Alaska Railroad, and as a construction worker; began building homes, and later built, operated, and developed rental units, residential areas, and hotels; founded the Hickel Construction Company of Anchorage, 1947; served two terms as Republican national committeeman of Alaska, 1954–1964; leader in the fight for Alaskan statehood; became the first elected Republican governor of Alaska, taking office on December 5, 1966; appointed SECRETARY OF THE INTERIOR in the cabinet of President Nixon on December 11, 1968; subject of hearings by

176   HILLS, CARLA ANDERSON

the U.S. Senate Committee on Interior and Insular Affairs which finally recommended his confirmation on January 20, 1969; confirmed by the Senate on January 23 and took the oath of office on January 25, 1969; served until the President requested his resignation on November 26, 1970; most important contributions were supporting a bill requiring oil companies to clean up offshore oil spills at their own expense and urging that such legislation include pollution from detergents, vegetable oils, and other chemicals; now employed in managing his real estate interests. *Time*, vol. 94, p. 42 (August 1, 1969).

HILLS, Carla Anderson. Born in Los Angeles, Calif., January 3, 1934; daughter of Carl Herman, head of a multimillion dollar building supply business, and Edith (Hume) Anderson; Episcopalian; married Roderick Maltman Hills (lawyer, chairman of SEC, 1975–1977) on September 27, 1958; mother of Laura Hume, Roderick Maltman, Megan Elizabeth, and Alison Macbeth; student at Oxford University, England, 1954; graduated with A.B. cum laude, Stanford, 1955; LL.B., Yale, 1958; admitted to the California bar, 1959; admitted to the U.S. Supreme Court bar, 1965; assistant U.S. Attorney, Civil Division, Los Angeles, 1959–1961; partner with her husband in the law firm of Munger, Tolles, Hills and Rickerhauser, Los Angeles, 1962–1974, specializing in antitrust law; became the highest-ranking woman in the Justice Dept., when she served as assistant Attorney General, Civil Division of the Justice Dept., Washington, D.C., 1974–1975; sworn in as SECRETARY OF HOUSING AND URBAN DEVELOPMENT in the cabinet of President Gerald Ford on March 10, 1975, and served until January 20, 1977; as HUD secretary she was the third woman to serve as a cabinet member; as secretary of HUD, abolished rent ceilings in federal housing, supported programs that emphasized the rehabilitation of urban areas, put a major thrust behind existing legislation that provided rent subsidies for low- and moderate-income families, and revived a suspended program that provided interest subsidies for low- and moderate-income families to enable them to become home owners; president of the Federal Bar Association, Los Angeles chapter, 1963; president of the National Association of Women Lawyers, 1965; served on committees of the American Bar Association and the Los Angeles County Bar Association; fellow of the American Bar Foundation; member of the corrections task force under the California Council on Criminal Justice, 1969–1971; member of the standing committee on discipline of the United States District Court for California's central district, 1970–1973; member of the council of the Administrative Conference of the United States, 1972–1974; named U.S. Trade Representative, June 25, 1989; trustee of Pomona College, 1974–; coauthor of *Federal Civil Practice*, 1961; coauthor and editor of *Antitrust Adviser*, 1971. *New York Times* (February 14, 1975); Ross, Irwin, "Carla Hills Gives the Woman's Touch a Brand-New Meaning," *Fortune* (December 1975).

HITCHCOCK, Ethan Allen. Born in Mobile, Ala., September 19, 1835; son of Henry Hitchcock, judge, and Anne (Erwin) Hitchcock; Presbyterian; married Margaret D. Collier on March 22, 1869; father of Sarah, Anne Erwin, and Margaret Dwight; attended private schools in Nashville, Tenn.; studied at military academy at New Haven, Conn., 1855; LL.D., University of Missouri, 1902; LL.D., Harvard, 1906; LL.D., Washington University, 1907; joined brother Henry in St. Louis; went to China, 1860, entering commission business of Olyphant and Company at Hong Kong; became partner of Olyphant and Company, 1866; retired, having made fortune, 1872; traveled, 1872–1874; successful man of affairs in St. Louis, 1874–1897; contributed generously to Republican campaign funds; assisted in preparation of glass schedule in framing of Tariff of 1890 at President McKinley's request; appointed minister and first ambassador to Russia by President McKinley in 1897; appointed SECRETARY OF THE INTERIOR in the cabinet of President Theodore Roosevelt, and served until his resignation on March 4, 1907; most important contributions were dismissal of commission of General Land Office in 1903 and institution of investigations which disclosed far-reaching system of fraud in the administration of public land, removal and prosecution of corrupt officials, successful fight to preserve for the Indians of the Five Tribes their inheritance of oil and gas lands and prevent selfish corporate interests from acquiring valuable mineral rights, introduction of administrative improvements in procedure for leases, limiting of timber-cutting and conduct of Indian affairs, and agreement with executive orders to enlarge forest reserves and withdraw mineral lands from exploitation even against opposition; died in Washington, D.C., on April 9, 1909. General E. A. Hitchcock, *Fifty Years in Camp and Field* (1909); M. L. J. Hitchcock, *The Genealogy of the Hitchcock Family* (1894); James F. Rhodes, *McKinley and Roosevelt Administrations, 1897–1909* in *History of the United States*, vol. 9 (1922); Robert Dallek, *McKinley's Decision, War on Spain* (1970); Margaret K. Leech, *In the Days of McKinley* (1959); H. Wayne Morgan, *William McKinley and His America* (1963).

HITCHCOCK, Frank Harris. Born in Amherst, Ohio, October 5, 1867; son of Rev. Henry Chapman and Mary Laurette (Harris) Hitchcock; Congregationalist; never married; attended common schools; prepared at Somerville (Mass.) Latin School; entered Harvard in 1887, and received B.A. in 1891; worked in Treasury Department, Washington, D.C.; became biologist for Department of Agriculture; studied law; earned LL.B. from Columbian (now George Washington) University in 1894, and LL.M. in 1895; admitted to District of Columbia bar in 1894; made chief of division of common markets, 1897; was chief clerk in Department of Commerce and Labor, 1903–1904; drew up Hitchcock resolutions; chosen assistant secretary of Republican national committee in July 1904; member of Keeps commission, 1905–1906; became first assistant postmaster general, 1905–1908; managed William H. Taft's presidential campaign; made chairman of Republican national committee, June 1908; appointed POSTMASTER

GENERAL in the cabinet of President Taft, and served from March 5, 1909 to March 4, 1913; most important contributions were reduction of deficit to point where department had small surplus, put postal savings system into effect, initiated air mail delivery in 1911; practiced law in New York City, 1914; managed pre-convention campaigns of Charles E. Hughes in 1916, Leonard Wood in 1920, and Hiram Johnson in 1924; moved to Tucson, Ariz., 1928, and became owner and publisher of *Daily Citizen*; Republican national committeeman of Arizona, 1932–1933; was colonel in air corps reserve; died in Tucson, Ariz. on August 25, 1935. H. F. Pringle, *The Life and Times of William Howard Taft*, 2 vols. (1939); Norman M. Wilensky, *Conservatives in the Progressive Era* (1965).

HOAR, Ebenezer Rockwood. Born in Concord, Mass., February 21, 1816; son of Samuel Hoar, Whig Representative from Massachusetts in the House of Representatives, and Sarah (Sherman) Hoar; married Caroline Downes Brooks on November 20, 1840; father of seven children including Sherman Hoar, Democratic Representative from Massachusetts; graduated from Harvard College in 1835; studied law in the office of his father; admitted to bar in 1840; served as an Anti-Slavery Whig in the Massachusetts State Senate in 1846; appointed as judge on the Massachusetts Court of Common Appeals in 1849, served until his resignation in 1855; appointed associate justice of the Supreme Judicial Court of Massachusetts in 1859, served from 1859 until 1969; appointed ATTORNEY GENERAL by President Grant on March 5, 1869, served from March 11, 1869 until his resignation on June 23, 1870; accomplishments during this time included acting against the recognition of Cuban insurgents as belligerents, and telling Senate that the nine new circuit judgeships should go to qualified men rather than as payment for patronage; received nomination from President Grant for associate justice of the Supreme Court in 1869, confirmation denied by Senate; member of joint high commission which framed the Treaty of Washington to settle the *Alabama* claims, 1871–1872; elected to the U.S. House of Representatives, served from March 4, 1873 until March 3, 1875; served as delegate to the Republican national convention in 1876; unsuccessful Republican candidate to U.S. House of Representatives in 1876; member of the board of overseers of Harvard University from 1868 until 1882; died in Concord, Mass. on January 31, 1895; interment in Sleepy Hollow Cemetery. Moorfield Storey and E. W. Emerson, *Ebenezer Hoar* (1911).

HOBART, Garret Augustus. Born in Long Branch, N.J., June 3, 1844; son of Addison Willard and Sophia Vanderveer Hobart; Presbyterian; married Jennie Tuttle on July 21, 1869; father of two children; graduated Rutgers College in 1863; studied law in the office of Socrates Tuttle; licensed to practice law on June 7, 1866; admitted to bar in 1869; chosen city counsel of Paterson, N.J. in 1871; elected to State Assembly in 1872 and 1873; chosen speaker for State Assembly in 1874, served until 1876; served in New Jersey State Senate from

1876 until 1882; served as chairman of Republican state committee from 1880 until 1891; unsuccessful Republican candidate for U.S. Senate in 1883; elected to Republican national committee in 1884; elected VICE-PRESIDENT on the Republican ticket headed by McKinley in 1896, served from March 4, 1897 until his death in Paterson, N.J. on November 21, 1899; accomplishments during this time include casting the deciding vote in Senate against the bill to grant independence to the Philippines; interment in Cedar Lawn Cemetery, Paterson. David Magie, *Life of Garret Augustus Hobart, Twenty-fourth Vice President of the United States* (1910).

HOBBY, Oveta Culp. Born in Killeen, Tex., January 19, 1905; daughter of Isaac William and Emma (Hoover) Culp; Episcopalian; married William Pettus Hobby (governor of Texas, 1917–1921, and publisher of Houston *Post*), on February 23, 1931; mother of William and Jessica; attended public schools, and studied under private tutors; read law in father's office; studied at Mary Hardin-Baylor College in Belton, Tex.; attended University of Texas Law School in 1927; became parliamentarian of Texas House of Representatives, 1925–1931 and 1939–1941; made legal clerk of Texas state Banking Department, active in Democratic national convention of 1928; assistant to city attorney of Houston, 1930; unsuccessful candidate for state legislature; was research editor on Houston *Post* in 1931, became book editor, 1933–1936, made assistant editor, 1936–1938, promoted to executive vice-president, 1938, and then full-time manager; president of Texas League of Women Voters; became executive director of radio station KPRC; director of National Bank of Cleburne; member of board of regents of Texas State Teachers College; wrote *Mr. Chairman* in 1937; went to Washington to head women's division of War Department's Bureau of Public Relations in July 1941; became director of Women's Auxiliary Army Corps with rank of major in May 1942, and retired in 1945; member of board of directors of American Society of Newspaper Editors, Texas Newspaper Publishers Association, and Texas Medical Center; consultant for Hoover Commission for Organization of Executive Branch of Government, 1948; elected president of Southern Newspaper Publishers, 1949; co-editor and publisher of Houston *Post* Publishing Company, 1952; supported Eisenhower, 1952; chosen federal security administrator in 1953; appointed SECRETARY OF HEALTH, EDUCATION, AND WELFARE in the cabinet of President Eisenhower, and served from April 11, 1953 to August 1, 1955; most important contribution was advocation of voluntary, nonprofit insurance plans; president of Houston Post Publishing Company, 1955– ; trustee of American Assembly, 1957– ; editor and chairman of the board of the Houston Post Company, 1965– . Dean Albertson, ed., *Eisenhower as President* (1963).

HODEL, Donald Paul. Born in Portland, Oreg., May 23, 1935; Presbyterian; son of Philip E. and Theresia Rose (Brodt) Hodel; married to Barbara Beecher Stockman on December 10, 1956; father of David Hodel; elder son, Philip, died in the mid–1970s; majored in economics at Harvard University; served as treasurer of the Harvard Young Republican Club in 1955–1956 and as its president in the following academic year; awarded B.A. in 1957; returned to Oregon to enter University of Oregon Law School; during his final year there became editor of the Law Review; earned his LL.D. in 1960; joined the Portland law firm of Davies, Biggs, Strayer, Stoel, and Boleg; in 1968 left that firm to become an attorney for Georgia Pacific, the lumber and paper products company; became active in local Republican party politics; in 1966 and 1967 became a member of the state Republican committee; served on the Central Committee; in 1968 served on the Oregon Reagan for President Committee; attended the G.O.P. convention that year as an alternate delegate; in 1969 named deputy administrator of the Bonneville Power Administration, the federal agency that markets electrical power produced by federal dams in the Pacific Northwest; promoted to administrator in 1972; during his tenure several of the authority's transmission towers were blown up, and Hodel received death threats; stepped down in 1977; became president of the National Electric Reliability Council in 1978; in addition to directing the council's activities from 1978 to 1981, Hodel served as president of Hodel Associates, an energy consulting firm founded with his wife; named undersecretary of the interior by incoming President Ronald Reagan in 1981; served until named SECRETARY OF ENERGY on November 7, 1982; served until March 4, 1985, when he became SECRETARY OF THE INTERIOR; as secretary of energy, he closely associated with groups promoting the use of nuclear energy; at the Interior Department, attempted to win a more conservation-minded reputation, reversing the trend created by James Watt, one of his Reagan administration predecessors; refused to permit contaminated water from farms in the San Joaquin Valley to drain into government national parks; served until January 20, 1989, the inauguration of President George Bush. *New York Times* (June 11, 1985); *Who's Who in America, 1986–1987; Current Biography Yearbook, 1987.*

HODGES, Luther Hartwell. Born in Pittsylvania County, Va., March 9, 1898; son of John James Hodges, farmer, and Lovicia (Gammon) Hodges; Methodist; married Martha Elizabeth Blakeney on June 24, 1922; father of Betsy, Nancy, and Luther Hartwell, Jr.; attended public schools of Spray and Leaksville, N.C.; received B.A. from University of North Carolina in 1919; joined Student Army Training Corps, 1918, and entered U.S. Army as a second lieutenant; became secretary to general manager of Marshal Field and Company textile mills in Leaksville, 1919, chosen manager of Marshal Field blanket mill in Spray in 1927, made production manager of Leaksville mills, 1934, promoted to general manager in 1939, chosen general manager of all mills at home and abroad, 1940, and elected vice-president of mills and sales in 1943, and retired in 1950; chairman of post-war committee, 1943–1945; director of government textile pricing program for Office of Price Administration in 1944; Rotary Consultant to United Nations Conference on International Organization in San Francisco, 1945, and to United Nations Security Council; chosen special consultant to U.S. secretary of agriculture, 1945; chairman of Rotary Convention in Rio de Janeiro, Brazil, 1948; made head of industry division of Economic Cooperation Administration in West Germany in 1950; was consultant to U.S. Department of State on International Management Conference, 1951; member of N.C. Vocational Education Board, 1929–1933, and State Highway Commission, 1933–1937; elected lieutenant governor of North Carolina in November 1952; took over governorship on the death of William B. Umstead in November 1954, was elected governor in 1956, and served until 1961; appointed SECRETARY OF COMMERCE in the cabinet of President Kennedy, continued under Lyndon Johnson, and served from January 21, 1961 to January 17, 1965; most important contributions were encouragement of domestic industrial expansion, passage of Area Redevelopment Act, reorganization of U.S. Bureau of Public Roads, and acceleration of program of U.S. Coast and Geodetic Survey; director of Drexel Industries Incorporated, Servomation Corporation, Williams Brothers, Gulf and Western Industries, and Glen Alden Corporation; president of Rotary, 1967–1968; published *Businessman in the State House and The Business Conscience*; died on October 6, 1974. New York Times, *The Kennedy Years* (1964); Hugh Sidey, *John F. Kennedy, President* (1963).

HODGSON, James D. Born on December 3, 1915, in Dawson, Minn.; son of Fred A. Hodgson, lumberyard owner, and Casahara M. (Day) Hodgson; Presbyterian; married to Maria Denand on August 24, 1943, and father of Nancy Ruth (Mrs. Richard J. Nachman) and Frederic Jesse; attended the University of Minnesota and was graduated in 1938; did postgraduate work at the same institution, 1938–1940, and at the University of California at Los Angeles, 1947–1948; employment supervisor in the Minnesota Department of Employment, 1938–1941; employed in various personnel and labor relations positions by Lockheed Aircraft Corporation, 1941–1969, beginning as a personnel clerk and later becoming corporate vice-president for industrial relations; navy intelligence officer in the Pacific during World War II, 1943–1946; taught a class in labor relations at the University of California; also served as consultant on manpower for the state of California, community advisor for the Industrial Relations Institute of the University of California, and member of the Los Angeles Labor-Management Executive Committee, 1962–1969; consultant to the California State Commission on Automation and Manpower, 1965–1967; appointed undersecretary of labor in the cabinet of President Richard M. Nixon, January 1969; appointed SECRETARY OF LABOR in the cabinet of President Nixon on June 10, 1970, to replace George Shultz; served until January 20, 1973; opposed mandatory government guidelines for wages and prices, and was against coerced resolutions of labor-management disputes, but went on record in favor of legislation that would allow the White House to step in to block transportation strikes when necessary; during his years in service, a program was developed to open jobs for blacks and minorities in the building trades by establishing hiring quotas; the equal employment opportunity program was first applied in

Philadelphia in September 1969 and became known as the Philadelphia Plan; together with Marshall H. Brenner, wrote the article, "Successful Experience; Training Hard-Core Unemployed," *Harvard Business Review* (September 1968). *Current Biography, 1970; Time* (June 22, 1970); *Facts on File*, 1973.

HOLT, Joseph. Born in Breckenridge County, Ky., January 6, 1807; son of John Holt, lawyer, and Eleanor (Stephens) Holt; married Mary Harrison; later married Margaret Wickliffe; attended St. Joseph's College and Centre College; studied law with Robert Wickliffe in Lexington and was admitted to the bar in 1831; practiced law in Elizabethtown with Ben Hardin; moved to Louisville, 1832; assistant editor of *Louisville Advertiser*, 1832–1833; was commonwealth attorney from 1833 to 1835; took part in Democratic national convention in 1835; moved to Mississippi, and practiced law; returned to Louisville; toured Europe and the East, 1848–1849 and 1850–1851; made commissioner of patents in 1857; appointed POSTMASTER GENERAL in the cabinet of President Buchanan, and served from March 14, 1859 to December 31, 1861; appointed SECRETARY OF WAR in the Cabinet of President Buchanan in the interim of January 18, 1861 to March 4, 1861; most important contribution was cooperation with General Scott against demonstrations at Lincoln's inauguration; helped sway Kentucky to Union; toured Massachusetts and New York to gain Union support; investigated war contracts; made judge advocate of army on September 3, 1862; headed bureau of military justice, 1864; tried Lincoln's assassins in military court; published *Vindication of Judge Advocate General Holt from the Foul Slanders of Traitors, Confessed Perjurers and Suborners, Acting in the Interest of Jefferson Davis* (1866); died in Washington, D.C., on August 1, 1894. J. G. Nicolay and John Hay, *Abraham Lincoln* (1890); Irving J. Sloan, ed., *James Buchanan, 1791–1868: Chronology, Documents, Bibliographical Aids* (1968).

HOOVER, Herbert Clark. Born in West Branch, Iowa, August 10, 1874; son of Jesse Clark Hoover, blacksmith, and Hulda Randall (Minthorn) Hoover; Quaker; married to Lou Henry on February 10, 1899, and father of Herbert Clark and Allan Henry; after death of parents, moved to Newburg, Oreg. to live with an uncle, Henry John Minthorn; attended a Quaker academy in Newburg; moved to Salem, Oreg. in 1888 and worked as an office boy while attending night school; studied engineering at Stanford University from 1891 until he graduated in 1895; worked in California gold mines and as a mining engineer in Colorado until 1897 when he joined a British mining firm as chief of gold-mining operations in Western Australia; chief engineer of the Chinese Engineering and Mining Company, moving to Peking in 1899; took part in defense of Tientsin during the Boxer Rebellion; junior partner in British mining firm, 1901–1908; organized a firm of consulting engineers; consultant in North America, Europe, Asia, and Africa until 1913; chairman of the American Relief Committee in London, 1914–1915; appointed head of the Commission for Relief in Belgium, serving until 1919; appointed U.S. food administrator by President

Wilson on April 6, 1917, and served until July 1, 1919; chairman of the Supreme Economic Conference in Paris, 1919; member of the War Trade Council; established and served as chairman of the American Relief Administration from 1919 on; chairman of the European Relief Council from 1920 on; vice-chairman of President Wilson's second Industrial Conference, 1920; received complimentary votes for the Republican presidential nomination at the party's convention of 1920; appointed SECRETARY OF COMMERCE in the cabinet of President Harding on March 5, 1921, and was reappointed by President Coolidge, serving until August 21, 1928; most important contributions were reorganization of the department and the expansion of activities dealing with foreign trade; chairman of the President's Conference on Unemployment, September 1921; member of the advisory committee for the Limitations of Armaments Conference, November 1921; chairman of the Mississippi Flood Relief Commission, 1927; nominated for the presidency on June 14, 1928 by the Republican national convention at Kansas City, Mo.; elected PRESIDENT, taking office on March 4, 1929; most important contributions as president were calling Congress into special session to consider farm relief, recommending tariff revision, appointing the National Commission on Law and Enforcement to investigate Prohibition, recommending the establishment of the Reconstruction Finance Corporation to stimulate economic activity after the 1929 stock-market crash, instituting a moratorium on German war debts in 1931, and announcing in 1932 the Stimson doctrine concerning the Japanese invasion of Manchuria; renominated for president by the Republican national convention of 1932, but defeated by Franklin D. Roosevelt; retired to his home in California; at request of President Truman, undertook coordination of world food supplies of 38 countries, from March to June 1946; at the request of President Truman, studied the economic situation in Germany and Austria, 1947; appointed chairman of the Commission on Organization of the Executive Branch of the Government (the Hoover Commission) on September 29, 1947; reappointed as Commission chairman by President Eisenhower on July 10, 1953, serving until June 30, 1955; author of *Principles of Mining* (1909), *American Individualism* (1922), *America's First Crusade* (1942), *The Problems of Lasting Peace* (with Hugh Gibson, 1942), *The Ordeal of Woodrow Wilson* (1958), and *An American Epic*, 3 vols. (1959–1961); died October 20, 1964, in New York City. Herbert C. Hoover, *The Memoirs of Herbert Hoover*, 3 vols. (1951–1952); Joseph Brandes, *Herbert Hoover and Economic Diplomacy: Department of Commerce Policy, 1921–1928* (1962); Eugene Lyons, *Herbert Hoover: A Biography* (1964).

HOPKINS, Harry Lloyd. Born in Sioux City, Iowa, August 17, 1890; son of David Aldona Hopkins, harnessmaker and merchant, and Anna (Pickett) Hopkins; married Ethel Gross on October 21, 1913, divorced in 1931; father of David Jerome, Barbara, Robert and Stephen Peter; married Barbara MacPherson Duncan in 1931; father of Diana; married Louise Hill (Macy) Brown on July 30, 1942; received B.A. from Grinnell College in 1912, and LL.D. in 1935;

social counselor of summer camp in Bound Brook, N.J. run by Christodora House; became an investigator, and later supervisor of casework for Association of Improving the Condition of the Poor in New York City; made executive secretary of Board of Child Welfare, Public Charities Department of New York in January 1914, and continued until 1917; appointed secretary to general manager of Red Cross in Washington, D.C. in January of 1918, remaining until 1922, and serving thereafter as assistant director and director of civilian relief division, association manager of Gulf division, and manager of Southern division; returned to New York City to become assistant director of New York Tuberculosis Association, 1924–1933; appointed deputy chairman of state Temporary Emergency Relief Administration in 1931 by Governor Franklin D. Roosevelt, and became chairman to succeed Jesse Straus in 1932; was made administrator of Federal Emergency Relief Administration in Washington, 1933; was put in charge of Works Progress (later Projects) Administration, 1935–1938; wrote *Spending to Save* in 1936; appointed SECRETARY OF COMMERCE in the cabinet of President Franklin D. Roosevelt on January 23, 1939, having previously served as such in the interim between December 24, 1938 and January 23, 1939, and served until September 15, 1940; was sent to London to represent Roosevelt in December 1940; appointed head of Lend Lease Program; delegate to London in July 1941, and then to Moscow; resigned as Lend Lease administrator in October 1941, and continued as Roosevelt's aide through World War II; made chairman of Munitions Assignment Board; member of Pacific War Council; member of War Production Board, 1942–1944, and War Resources Board, 1942–1945; advisor to Truman; sent on mission to Moscow to discuss proposed Security Council of United Nations with Stalin and Molotov; resigned from government services to become impartial chairman of New York Women's Coat and Suit Industry, July 1945; died in New York City on January 29, 1946. Searle F. Charles, *Minister of Relief: Harry Hopkins and the Depression* (1963).

HOUSTON, David Franklin. Born in Monroe, N.C., February 17, 1866; son of William Henry Houston, horse dealer and grocer, and Pamela Anne (Stevens) Houston; married Helen Beall on December 11, 1895; father of Duval, David, Elizabeth, Helen, and Lawrence; graduated College of South Carolina in 1877; studied political science and economics at Harvard University from 1891 to 1892, and received his M.A. in 1892; taught political science at the University of Texas, 1894–1902, and served as dean of the faculty, 1899–1902; elected president of the Agricultural and Mechanical College of Texas in 1902; returned to Austin, Tex. in 1905 as president of the University of Texas, serving there until 1908; chancellor at Washington and Lee University in Lexington, Va. from 1908 until 1916; appointed SECRETARY OF AGRICULTURE on March 5, 1913 in the cabinet of President Wilson; most important contributions were enlargement and reorganization of the department's administrative structure, establishment of an Office of Information, an Office of Markets, and through the passage of the Smith-Lever Agricultural Extension Act of 1914, setting up a Cooperative Extension Service

to carry agricultural education to farmers; appointed SECRETARY OF THE TREAS-
URY on January 31, 1920, assuming this position in Wilson's cabinet on February
2, 1920 after the resignation of Carter Glass; in this capacity, elected chairman of
the Federal Reserve Board and his policies there were blamed for allegedly causing decline in farm prices during the summer and autumn of 1920, events leading
to controversy over federal fiscal policies; left the cabinet with the outgoing President on March 4, 1921; became president of Bell Telephone Securities Company
in 1921; elected financial vice-president of American Telephone and Telegraph
Company, 1925; president of the Mutual Life Insurance Company of New York,
1927–1940; author of *A Critical Study of Nullification in South Carolina* (1902),
and *Eight Years With Wilson's Cabinet* (1926); died on September 2, 1940, and
buried in Cold Spring Harbor Memorial Cemetery in New York. David Franklin
Houston, *Eight Years With Wilson's Cabinet* (1926); John W. Payne, Jr., *David F.
Houston: A Biography* (1953); Arthur S. Link, *Woodrow Wilson: The Struggle for
Neutrality, 1914–1915* (1960) and *Woodrow Wilson: Confusions and Crises, 1915–
1916* (1964).

HOWE, Timothy Otis. Born in Livermore, Me., February 24, 1816; son of
Dr. Timothy and Betsy (Howard) Howe; married Linda Ann Haynes on December 21, 1841; father of two children; attended the common schools and Maine
Wesleyan Seminary; admitted to bar in 1839; served as a representative to the
Maine House of Representatives in 1845; moved later in 1845 to Green Bay,
Wis.; served on the 4th Circuit and Supreme Courts of Wisconsin from 1850
until his resignation in 1853; elected as a Union Republican to the U.S. Senate
in 1860, 1866, and 1872, serving from March 4, 1861 until March 3, 1879;
during this time he supported the suffrage bill of the District of Columbia, voted
in favor of the impeachment of President Andrew Johnson, supported the Silver
Bill of 1878; declined the chief justiceship of the Supreme Court offered by
President Grant; served as a member of the commission for the purchase of the
Black Hills Territory from the Indians; appointed by President Garfield to serve
as delegate to the International Monetary Conference held at Paris in 1881;
appointed POSTMASTER GENERAL by President Arthur on December 20, 1881,
served January 5, 1882 until his death in Kenosha, Wis. on March 25, 1883;
accomplishments include reduction of postage and issuance of postal notes;
interment in Woodlawn Cemetery, Green Bay, Wis. J. B. Winslow, *The Story
of a Great Court* (1912).

HUBBARD, Samuel Dickinson. Born in Middletown, Conn., August 10, 1799;
Congregationalist; prepared for college; graduated Yale in 1819; studied law,
and was admitted to the bar; practiced law in Middletown from 1823 to 1837;
gave up law and invested in manufacturing; Whig member of 29th and 30th
Congresses, 1845–1849; published *Letter from S. D. Hubbard of Connecticut,
to his Constituents on the Alarming Crisis in the Affairs of the Country* (1846);
appointed POSTMASTER GENERAL in the cabinet of President Fillmore on August

31, 1852, and served until March 7, 1853; returned to Connecticut, and devoted himself to educational and charitable pursuits; was president of Middletown Bible Society; established City High School; was an original trustee of Wesleyan University; died in Middletown, Conn., October 8, 1855; interment in Indian Hill Cemetery, Middletown. Robert J. Rayback, *Millard Fillmore* (1959); Irving J. Sloan, ed., *Franklin Pierce, 1804–1869: Chronology, Documents, Bibliographical Aids* (1968).

HUFSTEDLER, Shirley Mount. Born in Denver, Colo., August 24, 1925; daughter of Earl Stanley and Eva (von Behren) Mount; married Seth Martin Hufstedler on August 16, 1949; mother of Steven M.; received a B.A. in business administration from the University of New Mexico in 1945; worked as a secretary in Hollywood for one year to earn money for law school; entered Stanford University Law School in 1946; member of the *Stanford Law Review* staff, 1947–1949, articles and book review editor, 1948–1949; received her LL.B. from Stanford in 1949, graduating tenth in her class; admitted to the California bar in 1950; member of Beardsley, Hufstedler, and Kemble law firm in Los Angeles, 1951–1961, practicing general civil law; Los Angeles County superior court judge, 1961–1966; justice of the California Court of Appeals for the Second District, 1966–1968; justice of the U.S. Court of Appeals for the Ninth Circuit, 1968–1979 (second woman in history to achieve this rank); appointed SECRETARY OF EDUCATION in the cabinet of President Jimmy Carter; sworn into office on December 6, 1979, and served until January 23, 1981; presently a partner in Hufstedler, Miller, Carlson, and Beardsley law firm in Los Angeles; director, Hewlett-Packard Company, U.S. West Incorporated, and Harman Industries International; trustee of California Institute of Technology and Occidental College, 1972–   ; member of the Aspen Institute for Humanistic Studies and the Colonial Williamsburg Foundation, 1976–   ; member of the Constitutional Rights Foundation, 1979–1980; Natural Resources Defense Council, 1983–1985; Carnegie Endowment for International Peace, 1983–   ; board of directors of the John T. and Catherine MacArthur Foundation, 1983–   ; Woman of the Year, *Ladies Home Journal*, 1976; recipient of the UCLA medal, 1981; member of the American Bar Association, Los Angeles Bar Association, Town Hall, American Bar Foundation, WomansLawyers Association, American Judicature Society, Association of the Bar of the City of New York, Council on Foreign Relations. *Time* (November 12, 1979); *Current Biography*, 1980; *New York Times* (January 23, 1981, and April 30, 1982); Phi Delta Kappan (March 1981); *Newsweek* (January 2, 1984); *International Who's Who, 1988; Who's Who in America, 1988–1989*.

HUGHES, Charles Evans. Born in Glens Falls, N.Y., April 11, 1862; son of David Charles Hughes, clergyman; Baptist; married Antoinette Carter on December 15, 1888; father of Charles, Helen, Catherine, and Elizabeth; studied at home and at public schools in Newark, N.J. and New York City; student at

Madison University (now Colgate University), 1876–1878; graduated Brown University in 1881; taught at Delaware Academy, Delhi, N.Y.; read law at the New York Law Institute in 1882 and then entered Columbia University, receiving his law degree in 1884; admitted to the bar in 1884; prize fellowship, Columbia University, 1884–1887; professor of law at Cornell University, 1891–1893; practiced law in New York with what eventually became the firm of Hughes, Rounds, and Shurman, 1884–1891 and 1893–1906; lecturer at the New York Law School, 1893–1900; counsel for New York state legislature in investigation of the Consolidated Gas Company in 1905 and subsequently helped in formation of the State Commission of Gas and Electricity to regulate public utilities; counsel for New York state legislature in investigation of life insurance companies from 1905 to 1906, exposing many malpractices and advocating reforms; special assistant to U.S. Attorney General's coal investigation, 1906; nominated for mayor of New York by the Republican convention of 1905, but declined; elected governor of New York in 1906, and reelected in 1908, serving until his resignation on October 6, 1910; in this capacity, improved regulation of public utilities, banking, and insurance, promoted legislation beneficial to labor, and inaugurated a natural resources conservation program; appointed associate justice of the U.S. Supreme Court on May 2, 1910, taking his seat on October 10, 1910; resigned on June 10, 1916 upon receiving the Republican nomination for president; ran unsuccessfully against Woodrow Wilson; returned to his law firm in New York City; became president of the New York Legal Aid Society; in 1917 made chairman of the Draft Appeals Board for New York; assigned by President Wilson to investigate aircraft production program, 1918; appointed SECRETARY OF STATE on March 4, 1921 in the cabinet of President Harding, and continued in this post after Harding's death in the cabinet of President Coolidge; most important contributions were serving as chairman of the International Conference for the Limitation of Armaments in 1921 and there negotiating the first successful agreement for limitation of naval forces, working out the Four-Power and Nine-Power treaties to help solve Far Eastern problems, attempting to promote Germany's economic recovery and ease reparation burdens which led to the adoption of the Dawes Plan and the Young Plan, initiating the Foreign Service, and helping to improve relations with Latin America through conferences and treaties; resigned on March 4, 1925; appointed by President Coolidge a member of the Permanent Court of Arbitration at The Hague on September 30, 1926, and served until his resignation in 1930; chairman of the U.S. delegation to the Sixth Pan-American Conference, 1928; elected by the Council and Assembly of the League of Nations as judge of the Permanent Court of International Justice, serving from 1928 until 1930; appointed by President Hoover chief justice of the U.S. Supreme Court, and took office on February 13, 1930; there championed constitutional freedoms, broadened Congress' power to regulate interstate commerce, and declared unconstitutional several New Deal plans; retired on July 1, 1941; author of *Conditions of Progress in Democratic Government* (Yale Lectures, 1909), *The Pathway of Peace and Other Addresses*

(1925), *Pan American Peace Plans* (Yale Lectures, 1929), and other collections of his speeches and lectures; awarded the Roosevelt medal, 1928, for developing interest in international law, and the American Bar Association medal for conspicuous service to jurisprudence; died in Osterville, Mass. on August 28, 1948. Merlo J. Pusey, *Charles Evans Hughes* (1951); Dexter Perkins, *Charles Evans Hughes and American Democratic Statesmanship* (1956); Charles C. Hyde, *Charles Evans Hughes*, in S. F. Bemis, *The American Secretaries of State and Their Diplomacy*, vol. 9 (1958); Betty Glad, *Charles Evans Hughes and the Illusions of Innocence: A Study in American Diplomacy* (1966).

HULL, Cordell. Born at Olympus, Tenn., October 2, 1871; son of William and Elizabeth (Riley) Hull; Baptist; married Rose Francis Whitney, November 24, 1917; no children; received early education in the local schools; graduated in 1891 from the Cumberland University Law School, Lebanon, Tenn. and was admitted to the bar the same year; practiced law in Celina, Tenn.; member of the Tennessee house of representatives, 1893–1897; army captain during the Spanish American War, in the 4th Tennessee Infantry; resumed law practice; appointed judge of the 5th Judicial District of Tennessee, 1903–1907; elected to Congress in 1906, serving until 1921; elected chairman of the Democratic national committee, 1921–1924; reelected to Congress and served, 1923–1931, gaining a national reputation as a tax and tariff expert; elected to the U.S. Senate from Tennessee in 1930, resigning to accept appointment as SECRETARY OF STATE in the cabinet of Franklin D. Roosevelt on March 4, 1933; served in this post until November 29, 1944, resigning because of ill health; fostered and supported the organization of the United Nations; awarded the Nobel Peace Prize in 1945; advocated reciprocal trade agreements between the United States and the other leading nations of the world; the Trade Agreements Act of 1934 was specifically designed to recapture Latin American markets which the U.S. had been losing to Nazi Germany; a persistent advocate of Roosevelt's "Good Neighbor" policy, he was prominent in the Pan-American Conference held in Havana, Cuba, in 1940; favored the League of Nations and believed that rejection of the League by the United States was a major cause of the disintegration of world peace in the 1930s; *Memoirs of Cordell Hull*, an autobiography in two volumes, was published posthumously in 1948; appointed by President Truman delegate to the United Nations Conference on International Organization held in San Francisco, April-June 1945; called the "Father of the United Nations" by Roosevelt; died at Bethesda, Md. July 23, 1955; interment in Washington Cathedral. Nicholas Halasz, *Roosevelt Through Foreign Eyes* (1961); Basil Rauch, *Roosevelt from Munich to Pearl Harbor: A Study in the Creation of a Foreign Policy* (1967).

HUMPHREY, George Magoffin. Born in Cheboygan, Mich., March 8, 1890; son of Watts Sherman and Caroline (Magoffin) Humphrey; Episcopalian; married Pamela Stark on January 15, 1913; father of Cynthia Pamela, Gilbert Watts, and Caroline Helen; after receiving his preliminary and secondary education in the public schools of Saginaw, he entered the University of Michigan, graduating in 1912; studied law and was admitted to the bar in 1912, joining his father's law firm, Humphrey, Grant and Humphrey in Saginaw, continuing there until 1918; assistant general counsel of the M. A. Hanna Company of Cleveland, Ohio, becoming a junior partner in 1922; elected vice-president in 1924 and president of M. A. Hanna Company in 1929, continuing in that office until 1952 when he became chairman of the board; invited to join the Eisenhower cabinet as SECRETARY OF THE TREASURY on January 21, 1953, serving until his resignation in June 1957; upon assuming office, he took steps to place the national debt on a longer term basis in order to ward off further inflation and to counteract the competition of private offerings needed to finance huge capital outlays; he adopted a policy of offering government securities at the going rate of interest rather than at the artificial Federal Reserve System rate, to attract investment by the general public and to reduce the proportion of such securities held by the Federal Reserve Banks; honorary treasurer of the American National Red Cross; chairman of the Library of Congress Trust Fund; member of the Board of Trustees of the Postal Savings System, the Smithsonian Institution, the National Park Trust Fund Board; trustee of the National Gallery of Art; director of the Federal Farm Mortgage Corporation; honorary chairman of the Board of the M.A. Hanna Company; director of the Canada and Dominion Sugar Company, Limited and the National Bank of Cleveland; a trustee of the Eisenhower Exchange Fellowship, Incorporated; member of the Business Advisory Council for the United States Department of Commerce; trustee of the Robert Alfonso Taft Memorial Foundation, Incorporated; died on January 20, 1970. Arthur Larson, *Eisenhower; The President Nobody Knew* (1968); Emmett John Hughes, *The Ordeal of Power: A Political Memoir of the Eisenhower Years* (1963).

HUMPHREY, Hubert Horatio, Jr. Born in Wallace, S.D., May 27, 1911; son of Hubert Horatio and Christine (Sannes) Humphrey; Congregationalist; married Muriel Fay Buck on September 3, 1936; father of Nancy Faye, Hubert Horatio III, Robert Andrew, and Douglas Sannes; attended public schools of Doland; graduated Doland High School in 1929; entered University of Minnesota; worked with father; went to Denver College of Pharmacy, 1932–1933; was pharmacist with Humphrey Drug Company, Huron, S.D., 1933–1937; received B.A. from University of Minnesota in 1939; earned M.A. from University of Louisiana in 1940; did graduate work at University of Minnesota, 1940–1941; granted numerous honorary degrees; assistant professor of political science at University of Louisiana from 1939 to 1940; assistant instructor of political science at University of Minnesota, 1940–1941; member of WPA administrative staff, 1941–1943; made assistant regional director of War Manpower Commission in 1943; visiting professor of political science at Macalester College in Minnesota, 1943–1944; chosen state campaign manager for Roosevelt-Truman campaign, June-November 1944; elected mayor of Minneapolis, 1945–1948; elected U.S. senator from Minnesota in 1948, 1954, and 1960; chosen Senate majority whip in 1961; U.S. delegate to United Nations, 1956–1958; elected VICE-PRESIDENT under Lyndon B. Johnson on November 3, 1964, and served from January 21, 1965 to January 21, 1969; most important contributions were coordination of civil rights in federal agencies, liaison work with mayors, work as honorary chairman of President's Council on Equal Opportunity, and membership in National Security Council; unsuccessful Democratic candidate for President in 1968; returned to teaching; elected U.S. senator from Minnesota on November 3, 1970; deputy president of the Senate since 1977; member of the board, *Encyclopedia Britannica* since 1969; died at his home in Waverly, Minn., on January 14, 1978; author of *The Cause Is Mankind: A Liberal Program For America* (1964); *School Desegregation: Documents and Commentaries* (1964); *War on Poverty* (1964); editor of *Integration vs. Segregation* (1964); *The Political Philosophy of the New Deal* (1970); *The Education of the Public Man* (1977). Winthrop Griffith, *Humphrey* (1965); Robert Sherrill and Harry W. Ernst, *Drugstore Liberal* (1968); *Who Was Who Yearbook, 1971–1980; N.Y. Times* (January 14, 1978).

HUNT, William Henry. Born in Charleston, S.C., June 12, 1823; son of Thomas and Louisa (Gaillard) Hunt; Episcopalian; married Frances Ann Andrews on November 16, 1848; married Elizabeth Augusta Ridgeby on October 12, 1852; father of six children; married Sarah Barker Harrison in 1866; married Mrs. Louise F. Hopkins on June 1, 1871; moved with family to New Haven, Conn.; attended Hopkins Grammar School; went to Yale College; enrolled in Yale Law School, 1842; studied law in brother's office in New Orleans; admitted to Louisiana bar in 1844, and practiced law in New Orleans until 1878; was Whig, 1844–1854; became Know-Nothing; member of Constitutional Union party, 1860; was Southern Unionist, 1860–1865; entered Confederate service at outset of Civil War, and trained troops; elected state attorney general of Louisiana by Republicans on July 3, 1876, but lost office when Democrats regained power in 1877; chosen associate judge of U.S. Court of Claims on May 15, 1878; appointed SECRETARY OF THE NAVY in the cabinet of President Garfield on March 5, 1881, continued under Arthur, and served from March 7, 1881 to April 11, 1882; most important contribution was appointment of first naval advisory board; made U.S. minister to Russia on April 7, 1882; died in St. Petersburg, Russia on February 27, 1884; interment in Oak Hill Cemetery, Washington, D.C. Thomas Hunt, *The Life of William H. Hunt* (1922); Theodore C. Smith, *Life and Letters of James Abram Garfield* (1925; 2d ed., 1968).

HUNTINGTON, Samuel. Born in Windham, Conn., July 3, 1731; son of Nathaniel Huntington, farmer and clothier, and Mehetable (Thurston) Huntington; married to Martha Devotion in 1761; no children; attended the common schools; served as a cooper's apprentice; studied law; admitted to the bar in 1758 and began practice in Norwich, Conn.; executive councilor in 1763; member of the general assembly of the colony of Connecticut, 1764; appointed Crown attorney in 1765; judge of the superior court, 1774–1784 and chief justice in 1784; member of the Continental Congress from 1775 to 1784; a signer of the Declaration of Independence; elected PRESIDENT OF THE CONTINENTAL CONGRESS to succeed John Jay and served from September 28, 1779 to July 6, 1781 when he retired; was returned again to that office for a short period in 1783; lieutenant governor of Connecticut, 1785; elected governor of Connecticut in 1786 and reelected annually until his death; died at Norwich, Conn. on January 5, 1796; interment in Norwichtown Cemetery. S. O. Huntington, "Samuel Huntington," *The Connecticut Magazine* (May-June 1900); E. C. Burnett, *Letters of Members of the Continental Congress* (1921–1931); E. C. Burnett, *The Continental Congress* (1964).

HURLEY, Patrick Jay. Born in Choctaw Indian Territory (now Lehigh), Okla., January 8, 1883; son of Irish immigrants; Roman Catholic; married Ruth Wilson in 1919; father of Patricia, Ruth, and Mary; entered Baptist Indian University (now Bacone Junior College); began training in Indian Territory volunteer cavalry as private in 1902, and rose to captain by 1907; joined Oklahoma National Guard, 1907; received law degree from National University, Washington, D.C., 1908; earned LL.D. from George Washington University in 1912, and was admitted to practice; practiced in Tulsa; was lawyer for Choctaw Nation, 1912–1917; went to France with American Expeditionary Forces at outset of World War I and attained rank of colonel; reopened Tulsa law office; made fortune in oil, banking, and other businesses; financed Hoover's campaign in Oklahoma; participated in many Republican national conventions; made assistant secretary of war, 1928; appointed SECRETARY OF WAR in the cabinet of President Hoover, and served from December 9, 1929 to March 3, 1933; became a corporation lawyer in Washington; returned to active duty at outset of World War II as brigadier general; appointed minister to New Zealand by President Franklin D. Roosevelt in 1942; sent as presidential representative to U.S.S.R.; drafted Teheran Declaration of December 1943 while in Iran; made ambassador to China, 1944–1945; returned to law; pursued banking; was nominee for U.S. Senate from New Mexico; received Special Grand Order of the Chinese National Government and U.S. Distinguished Service Medal; died in Santa Fe, N.M., July 30, 1963. Don Lohbeck, *Patrick J. Hurley* (1956); Eugene Lyons, *Herbert Hoover: A Biography* (1964).

HYDE, Arthur Mastick. Born in Princeton, Mo., July 12, 1877; son of Judge Ira Barnes Hyde, congressman and lawyer, and Caroline Emity (Mastick) Hyde; Methodist; married Hortense Cullers on October 19, 1904; father of Caroline Cullers; attended public schools of Princeton; studied at Oberlin (Ohio) Academy; received B.A. from University of Michigan in 1899; earned LL.B. from University of Iowa in 1900; was admitted to the Missouri bar, and practiced law in the office of his father until 1915; made captain in Missouri National Guard, 1904–1905; served on county and district committees; served as mayor of Princeton, 1908–1912; unsuccessful candidate for state attorney general on Progressive ticket in 1912; moved to Trenton, Mo., and opened own law office, 1915; conducted loans and investments and dealt in insurance; became director of local bank; pursued farm and lumber interests; was distributor for Buick; served as governor of Missouri, 1921–1925; president of Sentinel Life Insurance Company, 1927–1928; appointed SECRETARY OF AGRICULTURE in the cabinet of President Hoover on March 5, 1929, and served from March 6, 1929 to March 4, 1931; most important contributions were research program to control pests, organization of Federal Drought Relief Committee, advocation of unemployment relief; returned to private law practice in Kansas City, Mo., 1933–1934; returned to Trenton to attend to farm holdings in 1934; trustee of Missouri Wesleyan College and Southern Methodist University; organizer and member of Conference of Methodist Laymen, 1935–1936; died in New York City, October 17, 1947. Eugene Lyons, *Herbert Hoover: A Biography* (1964); Walter Miller, *Life Accomplishments of Herbert Hoover* (n.d.).

I

ICKES, Harold Le Clair. Born in Frankstown Township, Blair County, Pa., March 15, 1874; son of Jesse Boone Williams and Martha Ann (McEwen) Ickes; married first to Anna Wilmarth Thompson on August 11, 1911; father of Raymond; later married Jane Dahlman on May 24, 1938; father of Harold McEwen and Elizabeth; attended the common schools; moved to Chicago upon the death of his mother in 1890; worked his way through the University of Chicago, receiving his B.A. in 1897; did newspaper work for several years on the *Chicago Chronicle* and the *Chicago Tribune*; studied law at the University of Chicago, graduating in 1907; practiced law in Chicago for the next 25 years; took an active interest in politics, never for himself, supporting independent and progressive candidates; elected chairman of the Cook County Progressive Committee in 1912 and later, national committeeman and member of the National Executive Committee of the Progressive party; named delegate-at-large to the 1920 Republican national convention, he opposed the nomination of Warren G. Harding for president; organized the Progressive Republican League for Franklin D. Roosevelt in Chicago in 1932, working actively for the Democratic ticket; appointed SECRETARY OF THE INTERIOR by President Franklin D. Roosevelt on March 3, 1933 and served for a record period of time, resigning from the Truman administration on March 17, 1946; under his guidance, the Department of the Interior actively dedicated itself to the conservation of the nation's resources; particularly interested in the development of low-cost electric energy for the benefit of industrial expansion in the Pacific Northwest; Shasta, Friant, Bonneville, and Grand Coulee dams were all constructed during his administration; campaigned militantly against special interest groups, enabling the National Park Service to serve the recreational needs of the country; appointed the first federal administrator of public works in 1933, having under his jurisdiction, in addition to regular department duties, the expenditure of more than $5 billion for federal and non-federal public works projects, including the construction of thousands of public schools, municipal buildings, water sewage systems, highways, and dams; also directed the first federal low-cost housing project in this country, which provided a stimulus for the nation's construction and materials industries and furnished employment to large numbers of men idled by the Depression; authored *The New Democracy* (1934), *Back to Work* (1935), *Autobiography of a Curmudgeon* (1943), and *My Twelve Years with F.D.R.* (1948); died in Washington, D.C., February 3, 1953; interment in Sandy Spring, Md. Paul K. Conkin, *The New Deal* (1967); R. G. Tugwell, *F.D.R., Architect of an Era* (1967).

INGHAM, Samuel Delucenna. Born at Great Spring, near New Hope, Pa., September 16, 1779; son of Dr. Jonathan and Ann (Welding) Ingham; married first to Rebecca Dodd, in 1800; five children born of this union; upon her death, married Deborah Kay Hall in 1822; three children born of this marriage; after a common school education, he pursued classical studies; engaged in the manufacture of paper; built a paper mill at New Hope in 1800; served in the state House of Representatives in 1806, for one term; after the declaration of war in 1812, elected as a Jeffersonian Democrat to the 13th Congress and was continued in that office until his resignation in 1818; secretary of the commonwealth of Pennsylvania, 1819–1820; elected to the 17th Congress in 1822, returned to that office by his constituents until his resignation in 1829; accepted the position of SECRETARY OF THE TREASURY in Jackson's cabinet, on March 6, 1829, serving for two years; resigned his secretaryship on June 21, 1831 on account of the scandal concerning Mrs. Eaton, wife of the Secretary of War; upon retiring from politics, resumed the manufacture of paper; also engaged in the development of anthracite coal fields; died in Trenton, N.J. on June 5, 1860; interment in Solebury Presbyterian Churchyard, Solebury, Pa. James Parton, *The Presidency of Andrew Jackson* (1967); Robert V. Remini, *Andrew Jackson* (1966).

J

JACKSON, Andrew. Born in Waxhaw, S.C., March 15, 1767; son of Andrew and Elizabeth (Hutchinson) Jackson; Presbyterian; married Mrs. Rachel (Donelson) Robards in August 1791 and remarried her on January 17, 1794, when an issue arose regarding the validity of the first marriage; no children; attended the Old Field School and Humphries Academy; he took part in the Battle of Hanging Rock during the American Revolution, was captured by the British and subsequently confined in the stockade at Camden, S.C.; left an orphan at the age of 14, he worked briefly in a saddler's shop; taught school for a short period of time; studied law in Salisbury, N.C., and was admitted to the bar in 1787, commencing practice in McLeanville, N.C.; appointed solicitor of the western district of North Carolina in 1788; moved to Nashville, Tenn. in October 1788; delegate to the convention to frame a constitution for the new state held in Knoxville in January 1796; upon the admission of Tennessee into the Union, he was elected as a Democrat to the U.S. House of Representatives in the 4th Congress, serving from December 5, 1796 until March 3, 1797; elected to the U.S. Senate for the term commencing March 4, 1797, serving until his resignation in April 1798; elected judge of the Supreme Court of Tennessee in 1798, serving until July 24, 1804; moved to Nashville, engaging in planting and mercantile pursuits; commander of the Tennessee militia in 1812; served in the Creek War of 1813; major general of the Tennessee Volunteer Infantry from 1812 to 1814; commissioned brigadier general of the U.S. Army on April 19, 1814; promoted to major general on May 1, 1816; led his army to New Orleans where he defeated the British on January 8, 1815; negotiated the treaty with the Creek Indians on August 9, 1814; captured Pensacola and Fort Michael, Florida, on November 7, 1814; commanded an expedition which captured Florida in 1817; defeated the Seminole Indians in March 1818: governor of Florida from March 10, 1821 to July 18, 1821; declined the diplomatic post of minister to Mexico; again elected to the U.S. Senate from Tennessee, serving from March 4, 1823 until October 14, 1825, when he resigned; unsuccessful candidate for the presidency in 1824, when he won a plurality of the electoral votes but lost to John Quincy Adams who was chosen President by the U.S. House of Representatives; elected PRESIDENT on the Democratic Republican ticket, in November 1828, and re-elected to a second term in November 1832; inaugurated on March 4, 1829, serving until March 3, 1837; upon leaving the White House, he retired to his country estate, "The Hermitage," near Nashville, Tenn., where he died on June 8, 1845; interment in Hermitage Gardens. James Parton, *The Presidency of Andrew Jackson* (1967); Robert V. Remini, *Andrew Jackson* (1966).

JACKSON, Robert Houghwout. Born in Spring Creek, Pa., February 13, 1892; son of William Eldred and Angelina (Houghwout) Jackson; Episcopalian; married Irene Gerhardt on April 24, 1916; educated at local schools; moved to Jamestown, N.Y.; completed a two-year law course in one year at Albany Law School; admitted to the bar in 1913; practiced in Jamestown; became general counsel for local banking and utility interests; active in the 1932 campaign of Franklin D. Roosevelt for the presidency; appointed general counsel for the Bureau of Internal Revenue; appointed special counsel for the newly created Securities and Exchange Commission in 1935; appointed assistant attorney general in charge of the tax division of the Justice Department; became assistant attorney general in charge of the antitrust division in 1937; appointed U.S. Solicitor General in 1938; appointed ATTORNEY GENERAL in the cabinet of Franklin D. Roosevelt on January 18, 1940, and served until September 4, 1941; appointed by Roosevelt to be associate justice of the Supreme Court in 1941; awarded the Medal of Merit by President Truman in 1946; chief American prosecutor at the post-World War II trial of the German leaders at Nuremberg; his final judicial act was his appearance on the bench while ill, to verify the unanimity of the Supreme Court's ruling against racial segregation in the public schools, in 1954; author of *The Nurnberg Case* (1947) and the posthumous *The Supreme Court in the American System of Government* (1955); died in Washington, D.C., October 9, 1954; interment in Frewsburg, N.Y. Leonard Baker, *Back to Back: The Duel Between FDR and the Supreme Court* (1967); Paul K. Conkin, *The New Deal* (1967).

JAMES, Thomas Lemuel. Born in Utica, N.Y., March 29, 1831; son of William and Jane Maria (Price) James; married four times, to Emily Ida Freedburn in 1852, and later to Mrs. E. R. Borden, then to Edith Colborne, and in 1911 to Mrs. Florence (MacDonnell) Gaffney; received no formal education beyond the common schools except for a short term at the Utica Academy: learned the printer's trade in the office of the Utica *Liberty Press*; by 1851, he was an owner of the paper; purchased the *Madison County Journal*, a Whig newspaper of Hamilton, N.Y., in 1851; was collector of canal tolls at Hamilton on the Erie

Canal, 1854–1855; inspector of customs for the port of New York, 1861–1864; from 1864 to 1870, he occupied the office of weigher at the port of New York and from 1870 to 1873, he was its deputy collector; appointed chairman of the civil service board of the collectors and surveyors offices by Chester A. Arthur, then collector of the port of New York; appointed postmaster of New York by President Grant on March 17, 1873, and reappointed to that position by President Hayes four years later; appointed to the cabinet of President Garfield as POST-MASTER GENERAL on March 5, 1881 and he began his duties on March 8, 1881; continued in office by President Arthur who recommissioned him on October 27, 1881; during his incumbency, he put an end to the so-called Star Route, uncovering dishonesty with reference to mail contracts and steamboats; succeeded in eliminating an annual deficit of $2 million and thus made possible the reduction of letter postage from 3¢ to 2¢; resigned his office on January 4, 1882; moved to Tenafly, N.J. in 1885; elected mayor of Tenafly in 1896; chairman of the board of directors of the Lincoln National Bank from 1882 to 1916; died September 11, 1916 in New York City; interment in New York City. Robert Granville Caldwell, *James A. Garfield, Party Chieftain* (1931); Theodore Clarke Smith, *The Life and Letters of James Abram Garfield* (1925).

JARDINE, William Marion. Born in Oneida County, Idaho, January 16, 1879; son of William and Rebecca Jardine; Congregationalist; married Effie Nebeker on September 6, 1905; father of William N., Marian, and Ruth; lived and worked on ranches; made assistant in department of agronomy; received B.S. from Agricultural College of Utah in 1904; became instructor, 1905, at College of Utah, and became professor, 1905–1906; studied at Graduate School of Utah in 1906; earned honorary LL.D. from Agricultural College of Utah in 1925, Lafayette College in 1927, and Kansas State College in 1938; made agronomist in Kansas State Agricultural College Experiment Station in July 1910; lectured in Graduate School of Agriculture, Michigan State Agricultural College, 1912, and from January to April 1913 was acting director of Experiment Station and dean of agriculture; served as president of Kansas State Agricultural College from 1918 to 1928; appointed SECRETARY OF AGRICULTURE in the cabinet of President Coolidge on February 18, 1928, and served from March 5, 1928 to March 4, 1929; envoy extraordinary and minister plenipotentiary to Egypt, 1930–1933; was state treasure for Kansas from 1933 to 1934; became president of Municipal University of Wichita, Kans., 1934–1939; was public interest director of Federal Home Loan Bank of Topeka; member of Federal Savings and Loan Advisory Council; member of board of directors of National Safety Council; chairman of board of Investment Corporation of America, member and chairman of agricultural production committee of Kansas State Council of Defense, 1917; president of International Dry-Farming Congress and Soil Products Expansion, 1915–1916; president of American Society on Agronomy, 1916–1917; member of executive board of National Research Council; on advisory council of Agricultural Commission of American Banker's Association; member of President's

Agricultural Conference and Fellow American Association for Advancement of Science; member of American Forestry Association; vice president of Washington Academy of Science; died in San Antonio, Tex. on January 17, 1955. Donald R. McCoy, *Calvin Coolidge* (1967); Jules Abels, *In the Time of Silent Cal* (1969).

JAY, John. Born in New York, N.Y., December 12, 1745; son of Peter and Hannah (McVickar) Jay, West Indian merchants; Protestant; married Sarah Livingston in 1774, daughter of William Livingston, Governor of New Jersey; father of William Jay, lawyer; attended boarding school of French Huguenot background at New Rochelle, N.Y., and King's (now Columbia) College in New York City, 1760–1764; studied law under Benjamin Kissam; admitted to bar in 1768, one year before legal apprenticeship of five years ended, and began partnership with Robert R. Livingston, later chancellor of New York and U.S. secretary of foreign affairs; Loyalist until British government imposed taxes in 1773; New York delegate to Congress convening September 1774 in Philadelphia; member of 2d Continental Congress, appointed November 1775 as member of secret committee for correspondence; delegate to New York Provincial Congress in January 1776, chairman of secret committee of safety, sharing in exercise of executive powers; drafted state constitution of New York in March 1777 which was adopted with few modifications until revised by a constitutional convention in 1822; chief justice of New York State *pro tempore* in interval between promulgation of the Constitution and its enactment, 1777–1778; appointed New York member to Continental Congress without vacating his seat on the state bench, then resigned from bench to take appointment as PRESIDENT OF THE CONTINENTAL CONGRESS on December 10, 1778; appointed U.S. minister to Spain on September 27, 1779, arrived Cadiz January 22, 1780 and received no official recognition; participant with Benjamin Franklin in negotiations of peace treaty with British in 1782; left Paris in May 1784, arrived New York July 24, 1784; during period of voyage elected SECRETARY OF FOREIGN AFFAIRS (office later known as Secretary of State) by Congress under the Confederation, officially retained post until the Articles of Confederation were suspended by the U.S. Constitution, continued to act at President Washington's request until Thomas Jefferson returned from Europe on March 21, 1790; an originator of the "Federalist"; offered choice of federal offices by President Washington, selected Chief Justiceship of the Supreme Court, held office from 1789 to 1795; while Chief Justice, nominated by Federalists in 1792 to the governorship of New York against George Clinton, lost when votes of Otsego, Tioga, and Clinton Counties were thrown out on a technicality by returning board with a majority of Clintonians; went to Great Britain at President Washington's request in 1794 to negotiate boundary adjustment and commercial treaty in an effort to avert war; criticism in the U.S. for his connection with the treaty may have prevented the Federalists from nominating him to the Presidency in 1797; while in Europe, elected governor of New York in 1795, reelected 1799, serving in all from 1795

to 1801; last public office was president of the American Bible Society; retired
from public life in 1801, declining renomination for New York governorship
and renomination and reconfirmation as Chief Justice; died in Bedford, N.Y.,
May 17, 1829; interment in family burying ground, Rye, N.Y. William Jay,
The Life of John Jay (1833); George Pellew, *John Jay* (1890); H. P. Johnston,
Correspondence and Public Papers of John Jay (1890–1893); Frank Monaghan,
John Jay (1935); Richard Brandon Morris, *John Jay, the Nation and the Court*
(1967); Donald Lewis Smith, *John Jay: Founder of State and Nation* (1968).

JEFFERSON, Thomas. Born in Shadwell, Va., April 2, 1743; son of Peter
Jefferson, justice of the peace, colonel of county militia, and member of the
House of Burgesses, and Jane (Randolph) Jefferson; nondenominational Prot-
estant; married Mrs. Martha (Wayles) Skelton on January 1, 1772; father of
Martha and Mary (Maria); turned to classical writers for religious inspiration
after analyzing the Bible in historical terms; attended "English School," and
studied Latin under Rev. William Douglas; attended College of William and
Mary in Williamsburg, Va., 1760–1762; began studying law under George
Wythe in 1762; admitted to bar in 1767; elected to House of Burgesses in 1769;
withdrew from law practice in 1774, giving his practice to Edmund Randolph;
wrote "A Summary View of the Rights of British America" in 1774, denying
Parliament's authority over the Colonies; appointed John Randolph's alternate
to the Constitutional Congress in 1774 by the Williamsburg Convention, became
active delegate at Philadelphia on June 20, 1775; resumed seat in Congress on
May 13, 1776, after a four-month absence devoted to his estate; appointed with
Benjamin Franklin, John Adams, Roger Sherman, and R. R. Livingston to draft
a declaration of independence; returned to Virginia legislature in October of 1776
and began revisions of statutory law including repealing laws of entail and
primogeniture, state-supported education, disestablishment of the Church of England as the state church, and revision of the state penal code; declined 1778
appointment with Benjamin Franklin and Silas Dean as U.S. commissioner to
Paris due to his wife's ill health; elected governor of Virginia in 1779, reelected
in 1780, held office until 1781, and declined renomination; affected by his wife's
death on September 6, 1782, announced end of his public life, but was revitalized
by appointment as plenipotentiary to negotiate for peace with England, settlement
made before he sailed; elected to Congress under the Articles of Confederation
in 1783, seated in November in Annapolis, Md.; in this office he formulated
program for western territories which limited slavery and supported Virginia's
ceding its northwestern territory to the United States; accepted Congressional
appointment as plenipotentiary to France on May 7, 1784, replacing Benjamin
Franklin; negotiated consular system between France and the United States,
received six months' leave of absence in November 1789; appointed first SEC-
RETARY OF STATE under the Constitution in the cabinet of President Washington
on March 22, 1790, and served until his resignation on January 1, 1794; period
of cabinet service marked by conflicts with Alexander Hamilton; declined Wash-

ington's request to resume office in 1794; Republican candidate for president in 1796; several votes behind John Adams, Jefferson became VICE-PRESIDENT; engaged in research in law and sciences, wrote "Manual of Parliamentary Practice"; Republican presidential candidate in 1800 against Aaron Burr; both received 73 votes, House elected Jefferson PRESIDENT, Burr vice-president; reelected in 1804, held office until he retired from public life on March 4, 1809 when he was succeeded by James Madison; most important contributions were conciliating antagonism of Republicans and Federalists, purchase of Louisiana Territory in 1803, and imposition of the Embargo Act; died at Monticello, Virginia, on July 4, 1826; interred at Monticello. H. S. Randall, *The Life of Thomas Jefferson* (1858); G. Chinard, *Thomas Jefferson: The Apostle of Americanism* (1929); Claude Gernade Bowers, *Jefferson in Power* (1936); autobiography, *Thomas Jefferson* (1959 ed.); Albert Fried, *The Essential Jefferson* (1963).

JEWELL, Marshall. Born in Winchester, N.H., October 20, 1825; son of Pliny and Emily (Alexander) Jewell; married to Esther E. Dickinson on October 6, 1852; father of two daughters; received a common school training; superintendent of the telegraph line between Boston and New York City, in 1849; became partner in his father's leather-belting business in Hartford, Conn.; part owner of the Hartford *Evening Post*; president of the Southern New England Telephone Company; formally entered politics in 1867; unsuccessful Republican candidate for the Connecticut senate; defeated for the governorship of Connecticut in 1868; elected governor in 1869, 1871 and 1872; upon his retirement from state office, President Grant appointed him minister to Russia in 1873; returned to America and was appointed POSTMASTER GENERAL by President Grant on July 3, 1874; investigated the European postal systems before assuming his new duties; during his administration, fast mail service was initiated between New York City and Chicago; resigned on July 12, 1876, in consequence of a disagreement with the President concerning the Whiskey Ring Scandals, actively siding with Secretary Bristow; became chairman of the Republican national committee, 1880–1883; died at Hartford, Conn., February 10, 1883. John Y. Simon, ed., *The Papers of Ulysses S. Grant* (1967); William Best Hesseltine, *Ulysses S. Grant, Politician* (1957).

JOHNSON, Andrew. Born in Raleigh, N.C., December 29, 1808; son of Jacob and Mary (McDonough) Johnson; nondenominational; married Eliza McCardle on May 5, 1827; father of Martha, Charles, Mary, Robert, and Andrew; took part in debates at Greenville College and Tusculum Academy; bound as tailor's apprentice to James J. Selby of Wake County, N.C. in 1822; opened tailor shop in Laurens, S.C. in 1824; tutored by wife to read and write; organized workingmens' party in 1828; elected alderman of Greenville, Tenn., 1828, and reelected in 1829; chosen mayor of Greenville, 1830–1833; became trustee of Rhea Academy in 1833; elected to Tennessee legislature in 1835, defeated in election of 1837, and reelected in 1839; was Democratic candidate for elector-at-large,

1840; nominated for state senator on October 4, 1841; elected to the U.S. House of Representatives, serving from March 4, 1843 to March 3, 1853; elected governor of Tennessee on October 3, 1853 and reelected in 1855; was member of U.S. Senate from October 8, 1857 to March 4, 1862; appointed military governor of Tennessee with rank of brigadier general, March 4, 1862 to March 3, 1865; elected VICE-PRESIDENT in the administration of President Lincoln in 1864 and served from March 4, 1865 to April 15, 1865, when he became PRESIDENT upon Lincoln's assassination, serving until March 3, 1869; most important contributions were disbanding of Federal army and reestablishment of government in confederate states; House passed resolution to impeach him February 24, 1868, but he was acquitted on May 26, 1868; unsuccessful Democratic candidate for president in 1868; unsuccessful candidate for U.S. Senate in 1869 and for U.S. Congress in 1872; elected to U.S. Senate in 1874 and served from March 4, 1875 until his death at Carter's Station, Tenn., on July 31, 1875; interment in Andrew Johnson National Cemetery, Greenville, Tenn. Lately Thomas, *First President Johnson* (1968); Milton Lomask, *Andrew Johnson: President on Trial* (1960).

JOHNSON, Cave. Born near Springfield, Tenn. January 11, 1793; son of Thomas and Mary (Neal) Johnson; Methodist; married Elizabeth (Dortch) Brunson, February 20, 1838; no children; pursued an academic course; attended Cumberland College (now the University of Nashville); admitted to the bar in 1814 and commenced practice in Clarksville, Tenn.; elected prosecuting attorney for Montgomery County in 1817; became circuit judge in 1820 and continued in that position and in the practice of law until 1829; elected a Democratic representative in the 21st Congress and reelected in the three succeeding Congresses from 1829 to 1837; reelected to the 26th through 28th Congresses, serving from 1839 to 1845; a friend and advisor to President Polk, he was invited to join the cabinet as POSTMASTER GENERAL on March 6, 1845 and served until March 5, 1851; during his incumbency, he succeeded in lowering postal rates and his administration was the first to introduce the use of postage stamps in denominations of 5¢ and 10¢; became Judge of the 7th Judicial Circuit Court in 1850 and 1851; accepted the presidency of the State Bank of Tennessee, serving for six years; a Union man in sentiment during the Civil War, he was elected to the Tennessee State Senate as a Unionist but was obliged to decline to serve on account of his advanced age; appointed U.S. commissioner to settle the dispute between the United States and the Paraguay Navigation Company, in 1860; died in Clarksville, Tenn. on November 23, 1866. Charles Allan McCoy, *Polk and the Presidency* (1960); Charles Grier Sellers, *James Knox Polk* (1957).

JOHNSON, Louis Arthur. Born in Roanoke, Va., January 10, 1891; son of Marcellus A. and Katherine Leftwich (Arthur) Johnson; Episcopalian; married Ruth Frances Maxwell on February 7, 1920; father of Lillian Maxwell and Ruth Katherine; after receiving his elementary and secondary education in the Roanoke public schools, he matriculated at the University of Virginia, graduating in 1912 with an LL.B. degree; admitted to the bar in 1912, commenced practice in Clarksburg, W.Va.; served in the West Virginia House of Representatives, 1916–1924; enlisted in the U.S. Army during World War I and was sent to officers' candidate school; served with the American Expeditionary Forces in France and was discharged with the rank of major; resumed the practice of law after the close of hostilities; delegate to the Democratic national convention in 1924; after 1933, became member of the federal advisory council of the U.S. Employment Service under the Department of Labor; aide to the secretary of war in 1933; appointed assistant secretary of war under Secretary Woodring from 1937 to 1940; personal representative of President Franklin D. Roosevelt to India from March 16, 1942 to December 17, 1942; national chairman of the Democratic finance committee from 1936 to 1940; chairman of the Democratic finance committee in 1948; appointed SECRETARY OF DEFENSE by President Truman on March 23, 1949, serving until September 20, 1950; during his incumbency, he directed his attention to the completion of the unification of the Army, Navy, and Air Force under one administrative department and also to reducing expenditures while maintaining the nation's military strength; director of the Union National Bank and Community Savings and Loan, both of Clarksburg, W.Va.; awarded the Medal of Merit by President Truman for his work during the war, in 1947; died in Washington, D.C., on April 24, 1956. Cabell B. H. Phillips, *The Truman Presidency: The History of a Triumphant Succession* (1966); Alfred Steinberg, *The Man from Missouri: The Life and Times of Harry S. Truman* (1962).

JOHNSON, Lyndon Baines. Born on a farm near Stonewall, Tex., August 27, 1908; son of Sam Ealy Johnson, Jr., rancher, schoolteacher, and state legislator, and Rebekah (Baines) Johnson; member, Disciples of Christ; married Claudia Alta [Lady Bird] Taylor on November 17, 1934; father of Lynda Bird and Lucy Baines; moved to Johnson City, Tex. with family in 1913; attended public schools of Johnson City; graduated Johnson City High School in 1924; taught grade school in Cotulla, Tex., 1928–1929; received B.S. from Southwest Texas State College on August 19, 1930; taught public speaking and debate at Sam Houston High School, 1930–1931; was secretary to Representative Richard M. Kleberg, 1932–1935; studied at Georgetown University Law school in 1935; director of National Youth Administration for Texas, 1935–1937; chosen member of U.S. House of Representatives to fill vacancy caused by death of James Paul Buchanan on April 10, 1937, was reelected five times, and served until December 31, 1948; unsuccessful candidate for U.S. Senate in 1941; commissioned lieutenant commander in U.S. Naval Reserve in December 1941; served in active duty, 1941–1942; made commander of U.S. Naval Reserve on June 1, 1948; elected to U.S. Senate on November 2, 1948, chosen Democratic whip on January 2, 1951, made Democratic leader on January 3, 1953, reelected to Senate in 1954 and 1960, and served until January 3, 1961; inaugurated VICE-PRESIDENT in the administration of President Kennedy on January 20, 1961, and served until

Kennedy's assassination on November 22, 1963; most important contributions were visits to Near East, Greece, Italy and the Scandinavian countries as emissary for the President, pledge of support to Senegal, assurance to pro-Western governments of Southeast Asia of continuing policy of protection; sworn in as PRESIDENT on November 22, 1963, was elected President on November 3, 1964; escalated the war in Vietnam using the Gulf of Tonkin Resolution (August 1964) as a blank check for presidential power; his Great Society programs, including passage of the Civil Rights Bill, were reminiscent of Franklin D. Roosevelt's New Deal; bowing to public pressure and a growing antiwar movement, Johnson announced on March 31, 1968, that he would not seek reelection as president; left office January 20, 1969, and retired to his ranch in Texas; member of American Legion and Veterans of Foreign Wars; died on January 22, 1973; authored *The Vantage Point: Perspectives of the Presidency, 1963–1969* (1971). *Current Biography, 1964*; Rowland Evans and Robert Novak, *Lyndon B. Johnson: The Exercise of Power* (1966); Hugh Sidey, *A Very Personal Presidency: Lyndon Johnson in the White House* (1968); *New York Times* (January 22 and 23, 1973); *The Presidency of Lyndon B. Johnson* (1983); *Nemesis: Truman and Johnson in the Coils of War in Asia* (1984); *Stemming the Tide: Arms Control in the Johnson Years* (1987); *Remembering America: A Voice from the Sixties* (1988).

JOHNSON, Reverdy. Born in Annapolis, Md., May 21, 1796; son of John and Deborah (Griselen) Johnson; married Mary Mackall Bowie on November 16, 1819; after a common school education, he attended St. John's College, Annapolis, Md., graduating in 1811; studied law; admitted to the bar in 1815 and commenced the practice of law in Upper Marlboro, Md.; moved to Baltimore in 1817; made deputy attorney general of Maryland, 1816–1817; an ardent Whig during the life of that party, later affiliated with the Democrats; elected state senator from Baltimore and was returned to office in 1826; resigned in 1828 to pursue his extensive law practice; elected to the U.S. Senate in 1845; deserted the Whigs to uphold President Polk in prosecuting the war with Mexico; opposed the annexation of Mexican Territory, fearing it would revive the whole problem of the extension of slavery; resigned his Senate seat to accept his appointment by President Taylor as ATTORNEY GENERAL on March 8, 1849; was under a cloud owing to an opinion he rendered on the Galphin claim in which Secretary of War Crawford had been the attorney for the claimant; resigned his cabinet position on July 22, 1850, shortly after the advent of the Fillmore administration; member of the Peace Conference held in Washington, D.C., in 1861, to devise means to prevent the impending war between the North and the South; during his incumbency, he upheld President Lincoln's suspension of the writ of *habeas corpus*; elected a member of the Maryland House of Delegates in 1861, he worked hard to keep the state from seceding from the Union; reelected to the U.S. Senate as a Democrat in 1862 but did not take his seat until 1863; voted for the Emancipation Proclamation and for the Thirteenth and Fourteenth Amendments; voted against the impeachment of President Andrew Johnson; appointed minister to Great Britain in 1868 by President Johnson, where he negotiated the Johnson-Clarendon Treaty for the settlement of the *Alabama* claims; returned to the United States in 1869 and resumed the practice of law; died in Annapolis, Md., on February 10, 1876; interment in Greenmount Cemetery, Baltimore, Maryland. Silas Bent McKinley, *Old Rough and Ready, The Life and Times of Zachary Taylor* (1946); Holman Hamilton, *Zachary Taylor* (1941).

JOHNSON, Richard Mentor. Born at Beargrass Creek, a frontier settlement on the site of what is now Louisville, Ky., October 17, 1781; son of Robert and Jemima (Suggett) Johnson; Baptist; although never married, he fathered two daughters by Julia Chinn, a mulatto inherited from his father; attended Transylvania University in 1800, where he studied law under George Nicholas and James Brown; admitted to bar in 1802; elected to Kentucky House of Representatives in 1804, served until 1807; elected as a Democrat to the U.S. House of Representatives, served from March 4, 1807 until March 3, 1819; while retaining his seat in Congress he became a colonel in the U.S. armed forces and commanded a regiment under General W. H. Harrison in the War of 1812; during this time he was in the battle of the Thames and is said to have killed the Indian Chief Tecumseh; returned to Congress and served until 1819; elected to the Kentucky House of Representatives in 1819, which then chose him to represent Kentucky in the U.S. Senate, the result of the vacancy caused by the resignation of John J. Crittenden; served December 10, 1819 until March 3, 1829; unsuccessful candidate for Senate in 1829, he was elected to the U.S. House of Representatives, served March 4, 1829 until March 1837; elected VICE-PRESIDENT under President Van Buren by the Senate on February 8, 1837, as no candidate had a majority of electoral votes, and served March 4, 1837 until March 3, 1841; unsuccessful Democratic candidate for vice-president in 1840; served in Kentucky House of Representatives in 1841 and 1842; organized Columbian College (now Georgetown College); elected to Kentucky House of Representatives in November 1850; died in Frankfort, Ky. on November 19, 1850; interment in Kentucky State Cemetery. L. R. Meyer, *The Life and Times of Colonel Richard Mentor Johnson of Kentucky* (1932).

JONES, Jesse Holman. Born in Robertson County, Tenn., April 5, 1874; son of William Hasque and Anne (Holman) Jones; Methodist; married Mary Gibbs on December 15, 1929; childless; his only formal education was at a rural schoolhouse in Adairsville, Ky.; became manager and later general manager of M. T. Jones Lumber Co. of Dallas, Tex., 1895–1905; organized the South Texas Lumber Co. in 1902; organized the Texas Trust Co. of Houston (now Bankers Mortgage Co.) in 1909 and was director and chairman of the board from its inception until his resignation in 1932; vice-president of the Lumberman's National Bank from 1910 to 1918; chairman of the National Bank of Commerce in Houston; editor and publisher of the *Houston Chronicle*; appointed director of the Reconstruction Finance Corp. from 1932 to 1939; chairman of the executive committee of the Export-Import Bank of Washington, D.C., 1936–1943; member of the War Production Board, 1942–1945; named SECRETARY OF COMMERCE by President Franklin D. Roosevelt on September 16, 1940, entering upon his duties on September 19, 1940 and serving until his resignation in February 1945; he led in rebuilding the nation's industry during the Depression and marshaling its might during World War II; in addition to his secretaryship, he headed 39 other federal bureaus; trustee of George Peabody College for Teachers and of the Tuskeegee Institute; treasurer of the Will Rogers Memorial Commission; president and treasurer of the Woodrow Wilson Birthplace Foundation; Chairman of the Texas Commission for the New York World's Fair in 1939, and the U.S. Golden Gate Exposition in San Francisco from 1937 to 1939; director general of the Texas Centennial Celebration, 1926–1934; authored *Fifty Billion Dollars* (1951); died in Houston, Tex., June 1, 1956. Bascom N. Timmons, *Jesse H. Jones: The Man and the Statesman* (1956); Paul K. Conkin, *The New Deal* (1967).

JONES, William. Born in Philadelphia, Pa. in 1760; pursued academic studies; participated in battles of Trenton, December 26, 1776, and Princeton, January 3, 1777; was third lieutenant on Pennsylvania private ship *St. James*, and served under Captain (later Commodore) Truxton; promoted to first lieutenant in 1781; was wounded twice and taken prisoner twice; became merchant marine, 1790–1793, and was stationed in Charleston, S.C.; returned to Philadelphia, and became a shipping merchant in 1793; elected to U.S. Congress, and served from March 4, 1801 to March 3, 1803; elected member of the American philosophical Society on January 18, 1805; appointed SECRETARY OF THE NAVY in the cabinet of President Madison on January 12, 1813, and served from January 19, 1813 to December 1, 1814; administration criticized for mismanagement during War of 1812; served as acting secretary of the treasury in the interim between Secretaries Gallatin and Campbell, serving from January 19, 1813 to December 9, 1814; devoted himself to business; elected first president of the second United States Bank in July 1816, and was asked to leave because of his mismanagement of affairs in January 1819; collector of customs in Philadelphia, 1827–1829; died in Bethlehem, Pa., September 6, 1831; interment in St. Peter's Churchyard, Philadelphia, Pennsylvania. Bray Hammond, *Banks and Politics in America: From the Revolution to the Civil War* (1957).

K

KATZENBACH, Nicholas de Belleville. Born in Philadelphia, Pa., January 17, 1922; son of Edward Lawrence Katzenbach, corporation lawyer who served as attorney-general of New Jersey from 1924 to 1929, and Maria Louise (Hilson) Katzenbach, member of New Jersey state board of education for 44 years; Episcopalian; married Lydia King Phelps Stokes on June 8, 1946; father of Christopher Wolcott, John Strong Minor, Maria Louise, and Anne de Belleville; graduated from Phillips Exeter Academy in 1939 and entered Princeton University; enlisted in U.S. Army Air Force, commissioned second lieutenant, made navigator, taken prisoner in 1943 by Italians, discharged as first lieutenant; received B.A. from Princeton in 1945; editor in charge of *Yale Law Journal*; earned LL.B. from Yale Law School in 1947; went to England on Rhodes Scholarship, and attended Balliol College of Oxford University, 1947–1949; was admitted to New Jersey bar in 1950; became attorney advisor to secretary of the air force in the Pentagon, 1950–1956; made associate professor of law at Yale University, 1952–1956; was full professor at University of Chicago from 1956 to 1960; went to Geneva to work on international law on Ford Foundation fellowship in 1960; chosen assistant attorney general in charge of Office of Legal Council in 1961; made deputy attorney general in April 1962; became acting attorney general in September 1964; appointed ATTORNEY GENERAL in the cabinet of President Lyndon Johnson, and served from February 13, 1965 to October 3, 1966; most important contributions were assistance in passage of Civil Rights Bill, settlement of General Aniline and Film Corp. controversy; undersecretary of state, 1966–1969; IBM Corp., senior vice president and general counsel, 1969–1979, senior vice president for law and external relations, 1984–1986, also serves on board of directors; practices law; partner Riker, Danzig, Scherer, Hyland, and Perretti, Morristown, N.J., 1986– ; awarded the Woodrow Wilson

Award from Princeton University on February 20, 1965; member of state bars of New Jersey and Connecticut, American Judicature Society, and American Bar Association; wrote *The Political Founders of International Law* with Morton A. Kaplan in 1961, and several articles. J. Neary, "Poker Faced Lawman on the Spot," *Life*, vol. 60 (May 6, 1966); *New York Times Magazine* (December 24, 1967); Rowland Evans and Robert Novak, *Lyndon B. Johnson: The Exercise of Power* (1966); *Who's Who; 1987–1988*.

KELLOGG, Frank Billings. Born in Potsdam, N.Y., December 22, 1856; son of Asa Farnsworth and Abigail (Billings) Kellogg; married Clara M. Cook on June 16, 1886; no children; moved with his family to Viola, Minn. in 1856, and to Toelgin, Minn. in 1872; educated at the public and rural schools; worked on a farm until 1875; studied law and was admitted to the bar in 1877, commencing the practice of his profession at Rochester, Minn.; city attorney of Rochester from 1878 to 1881; city attorney for Olmstead County from 1882 to 1887; established connections with railroad titans as a corporation counsel; delegate to the Republican national conventions of 1904, 1908, and 1912; allied himself with President Theodore Roosevelt's trustbusting activities; federal prosecutor in the government's attack on the General Paper Company in 1905; special counsel to the Interstate Commerce Commission in its investigations of Edward H. Harriman's railroad finances, 1906; government counsel against the Standard Oil Trust, gaining a favorable verdict in the U.S. Circuit Court in 1909; government delegate to the United Congress of Lawyers and Jurists at St. Louis in 1904; chosen president of the American Bar Association in 1912 and 1913; abandoned the Republican Party in 1912, to support Theodore Roosevelt on the Progressive ticket; elected to the U.S. Senate as a Republican from Minnesota in November 1916, serving from March 4, 1917 until March 3, 1923; unsuccessful candidate for reelection in 1922; appointed delegate to the 5th International Conference of American States held at Santiago, Chile, in 1923, by President Harding; appointed minister extraordinary and plenipotentiary to Great Britain by President Coolidge on December 11, 1923, and served until his resignation on March 4, 1925; invited to join the cabinet as SECRETARY OF STATE by President Coolidge on February 17, 1925, entering upon his duties on March 5, 1925 and serving until March 3, 1929; co-author of the Kellogg-Briand Peace Pact which renounced war as an instrument of national policy; resumed the practice of law in St. Paul, Minn.; elected associate judge of the Permanent Court for International Justice in 1930, serving until 1935; awarded the Nobel Peace Prize in 1930; died in St. Paul, Minn. on December 21, 1937; interment in the chapel of St. Joseph of Arimathea in the Washington Cathedral, Washington, D.C.; Harold Underwood Faulkner, *From Versailles to the New Deal; A Chronicle of the Harding, Coolidge, Hoover Era* (1950); Edward Connery Lathem, ed., *Meet Calvin Coolidge; The Man Behind the Myth* (1960); Lewis Ethan Ellis, *Frank B. Kellogg and American Foreign Relations, 1925–1929* (1961).

KEMP, Jack. Born in Los Angeles, Calif.; on July 13, 1935; son of Paul R. Kemp; Presbyterian; married Joanne Main; father of Jeffrey, Jennifer, Judith, and James; received B.A. at Occidental College, Calif., 1957; graduate study at Long Beach University, Calif., and Western University in education and political science; served in the U.S. Army on active duty, 1958; U.S. Army Reserve, 1958–1962; played professional football for the Buffalo Bills as quarterback for thirteen years; named Player of the Year, 1965; All AFL-Quarterback two times; cofounder and president, AFL Players Association, 1965–1970; television and radio commentator; Public Relations Officer for Marine Midland Bank of Buffalo; served as special assistant to the Governor of California, 1967; special assistant to chairman, Republican National Committee, 1969; elected to ninety-second Congress, November 6, 1970, and reelected to each succeeding Congress until his resignation on January 2, 1989; served as chairman, House Republican Conference; member, Appropriations Committee; made an unsuccessful bid for presidency in 1988; appointed by President George Bush and confirmed by the Senate on February 6, 1989, as SECRETARY OF HOUSING AND URBAN DEVELOPMENT, replacing Samuel Pierce; also member Chowder and Marching Society; National Association of Broadcasters, Engineers, and Technicians; and Sierra Club; received Outstanding Young Man of the Year Award, Buffalo Junior Chamber of Commerce; Distinguished Service Award, New York Jaycees; Outstanding Citizens Award, Buffalo Evening News, 1965 and 1974; nominated for the Justice Byron "Whizzer" White Award,; authored *How Much Defense Spending Is Enough?* (1976); *An American Renaissance: A Strategy for the 1980's* (1979). *Who's Who in American Politics*, 1987–1988; *1987–1988 Congressional Directory, 100th Congress.*

KENDALL, Amos. Born in Dunstable, Mass., August 16, 1789; son of Zebedee and Molly (Dakin) Kendall; Baptist; married Mary B. Woolfolk in October 1818; upon her death, he married Jane Kyle on January 15, 1826; father of one daughter; educated at the academy at New Ipswich, N.H.; entered Dartmouth College in 1807, graduating in 1811 at the head of his class; studied law at Groton, Mass.; migrated to Lexington, Ky. in 1814, remaining three until 1829; tutor in the family of Henry Clay during the latter's absence to negotiate the Treaty of Ghent in 1815; moved to Franklin, Ky. in 1816, to manage the newspaper entitled *Argus of Western America*; admitted to the bar in Frankfort in 1814; broke with Clay in 1826 and joined the forces of Andrew Jackson; upon election of Jackson in 1832, he moved to Washington, D.C.; appointed fourth auditor of the Treasury, serving from 1832 to 1935; appointed POSTMASTER GENERAL on May 1, 1835 by President Jackson; recommissioned by President Van Buren on March 4, 1837; one of the group of Jackson's closest advisors known as the "Kitchen Cabinet"; corrected flagrant abuses of the Post Office Department; instituted reforms; paid off the debt of the Department; condoned the legal exclusion of Abolitionist propaganda from the mails by Southern postmasters; principal architect of Jackson's messages to Congress, including the July 10, 1832 message vetoing the bill to recharter the Bank of the United States; returned to journalism in 1840; became an agent for the collection of claims against the government in 1843, one on behalf of the Cherokee Indians; established a biweekly called *Kendall's Expositor* in 1841 and the weekly *Union Democrat* in 1842; became business agent of Samuel F. B. Morse, the inventor of the telegraph, mostly involving patent rights; wrote *Letter on Secession* (1861), vigorously denying the right of the South to secede; a philanthropist in later years, he gave the money which made possible the erection of the Calvary Baptist Church in Washington, D.C.; was the leading spirit in the foundation of the Columbia Institution for the Deaf and Dumb (now Gallaudet College); authored *Life of Andrew Jackson* (1843) and *Autobiography of Amos Kendall*, edited by William Stickney (1872); died in Washington, D.C., on November 12, 1869. Arthur Schlesinger, *The Age of Jackson* (1945); Glyndon Garlock Van Deusen, *The Jacksonian Era* (1959).

KENNEDY, David M. Born in Randolph, Utah, July 21, 1905; son of George and Katherine (Johnson) Kennedy; Mormon; married to Lenora Bingham on November 4, 1925; father of Marilyn Ann, Barbara Ann, Carol Joyce, and Patricia Lenore; attended the public schools; was graduated from Weber College, Ogden, Utah in 1928; served as a Mormon missionary in England for two years; received A.M. degree from George Washington University in 1935 and the LL.B. degree from that institution in 1937; was graduated from the Stonier School of Banking at Rutgers University in 1939; member of the staff of the board of governors of the Federal Reserve System from 1930 to 1946, and served successively as technical assistant in division of bank operations, economist in division of research and statistics, and special assistant to the chairman; joined the Continental Illinois National Bank and Trust Company in Chicago in 1946, becoming second vice-president in 1948 and vice-president in 1951; resigned to serve as special assistant to Secretary of the Treasury George M. Humphrey from October 1953 to December 1954; returned to Continental Illinois Company in 1954 as vice-president; elected director and president, 1956, and elected chairman of the Board of Directors and chief executive officer, 1959; member of the body of thirteen citizens which set up the Communications Satellite Corporation in 1962 by appointment of President Kennedy, and elected to the permanent board of directors, 1964; chairman of the commission to study improvement of federal budget drafting methods in 1967 by appointment of President Lyndon Johnson; appointed SECRETARY OF THE TREASURY in the cabinet of President Nixon on December 11, 1968, took the oath of office on January 22, 1969 and served until his resignation on December 14, 1970; most important contributions were advocating a tight budget, restrictive money policy, and temporarily high interest rates to curb inflation while retaining official U.S. price of gold; also United States Governor of the International Monetary Fund, the International Bank for Reconstruction and Development, the Inter-American Development Bank, and the Asian Development Bank. Earl Mazo and Stephan Hess, *Nixon: A Political Portrait* (1969).

KENNEDY, John Fitzgerald. Born in Brookline, Mass., May 29, 1917; son of Joseph Patrick Kennedy, financier, business executive and ambassador to Great Britain, and Rose (Fitzgerald) Kennedy; Roman Catholic; married Jacqueline Lee Bouvier on September 12, 1953; father of Caroline Bouvier and John Fitzgerald, Jr.; attended the Choate School in Wallingford, Conn., the London School of Economics, and Stanford University; entered Harvard University, graduating in 1940; served as a lieutenant in the U.S. Navy during World War II, from September 1941 until April 1945; awarded the Navy and Marine Corps Medal and the Purple Heart; discharged in April 1945; engaged as a correspondent for a news service, covering the San Francisco Conference, the British Elections of 1945, and the Potsdam Conference in 1945; elected as a Democrat to the U.S. House of Representatives in the 80th, 81st and 82d Congresses, serving from January 3, 1947 until January 3, 1953; elected to the U.S. Senate in November 1952, for the term commencing on January 3, 1953, and reelected in November 1958, for the term ending January 3, 1965; defeated by Estes Kefauver of Tennessee in bid for Democratic vice-presidential nomination in 1956; elected PRESIDENT in November 1960; inaugurated on January 20, 1961, serving until his assassination in Dallas, Texas on November 22, 1963; he was the youngest elected President of the United States, the first President of the Roman Catholic faith, the fifth President who was a graduate of Harvard University, the first President born in the twentieth century, the eighth President to die in office, the fourth President to be assassinated; author of *Why England Slept* (1940), *Profiles in Courage* (1956), *The Strategy of Peace* (1960), *To Turn the Tide* (1962), *The Burden and the Glory* (1964); interred at Arlington National Cemetery. Arthur M. Schlesinger, Jr., *A Thousand Days: John F. Kennedy in the White House* (1965).

KENNEDY, John Pendleton. Born in Baltimore, Md., October 25, 1795; son of John and Nancy (Clayton) Kennedy; married Mary Tennant in 1824 and after her death, married Elizabeth Gray in 1829; no children; educated at Sinclair's Academy, Baltimore, and at Baltimore College (now the University of Maryland), graduating in 1812; volunteered and served in the War of 1812 at the battles of Bladensburg and North Point; studied law; admitted to the bar and commenced practice of law in 1816; became provost of the University of Maryland; elected to the Maryland House of Delegates in 1820, serving from 1821 to 1823; elected as a Whig to fill a vacancy in the U.S. House of Representatives in 1838, serving until 1839; reelected in 1840 and 1842; chaired the committee of commerce in Congress; opposed the annexation of Texas to the Union; wrote a manifesto entitled *A Defense of the Whigs*, in 1844; elected to the Maryland House of Delegates in 1846, becoming speaker; appointed SECRETARY OF THE NAVY by President Fillmore on July 22, 1852; organized four important naval expeditions, including the one commanded by Commodore Matthew C. Perry, which opened the Far East to the West; after leaving office on March 6, 1853, he strove, by writing and speaking, to prevent secession; supported the Union cause in the Civil War, voting for Lincoln in 1864; after the conflict, he favored "amnesty and forgiveness to [those] who have erred"; wrote several works of literary distinction, including *Swallow Barn* (1832), *Horse-Shoe Robinson* (1835), and *Rob of the Bowl* (1838); died in Newport, R.I. on August 18, 1870; interment in Greenmount Cemetery, Baltimore, Md. Robert J. Rayback, *Millard Fillmore: Biography of a President* (1959); Norton Garfinkle, ed., *Lincoln and the Coming of the Civil War* (1959).

KENNEDY, Robert Francis. Born in Brookline, Mass., November 20, 1925; son of Joseph Patrick Kennedy, financier, business executive, and ambassador to Great Britain, and Rose (Fitzgerald) Kennedy; brother of John F. Kennedy, President of the United States, and Edward Kennedy, U.S. Senator; Roman Catholic; married Ethel Skakel on June 16, 1950; father of Kathleen Hartington, Joseph Patrick, Robert Francis, Jr., David Anthony, Mary Courtney, Michael le Moyne, Mary Kerry, Christopher George, Douglas, Rory Elizabeth, and Katherine; attended Milton Academy; received B.A. from Harvard University in 1948; was war correspondent for *Boston Post* in summer of 1948; earned LL.B. from University of Virginia in 1951; admitted to the bar, 1951; became attorney with criminal division of U.S. Department of Justice, 1951–1952; managed campaign of brother John F. Kennedy for U.S. Senate, 1952; made assistant counsel on permanent subcommittee on investigations of Senate government operations committee, 1953; chosen chief minority counsel on Senate permanent subcommittee on investigations under Senator Joseph P. McCarthy in January 1953, and resigned on July 31, 1953; chosen assistant counsel with Commission on Organization of Executive Branch of Government; rejoined Senate subcommittee as chief counsel and staff director in January 1955; admitted to practice before Supreme Court; was special assistant to manager of Adlai E. Stevenson's presidential campaign, 1956; appointed chief counsel of Senate committee to investigate labor-management relations, January 1957–September 1959; manager of John F. Kennedy's presidential campaign; appointed ATTORNEY GENERAL in the cabinet of President Kennedy on January 21, 1961, and continued under Lyndon Johnson until February 12, 1965; most important contributions were exposing of racketeer control of labor unions, investigation of New York City garbage collection industry, work for civil rights, protection of Negro right to vote, anti-trust prosecution, and prevention of growth of crime; wrote *The Enemy Within* (1960), and *Just Friends and Brave Enemies* (1962); member of advisory council of University of Notre Dame Law School; elected U.S. Senator from New York in 1965; in 1968 sought Democratic nomination for President, winning major preference primaries in Indiana, Nebraska and California; assassinated on June 5, 1968 in Los Angeles, Calif.; interment in Arlington National Cemetery. Jay Jacobs and Kristi N. Witken, *R.F.K.: His Life and Death* (1968); Henry A. Zeiger, *Robert F. Kennedy: A Biography* (1969).

KEY, David McKendree. Born in Greenville, Tenn., January 27, 1824; son of John Key, clergyman, and Margaret (Armitage) Key; married Elizabeth Lenoir on July 1, 1857; moved with family to Monroe County, and attended local schools; graduated Hiwassee College in 1850; studied law; admitted to bar in Madisonville, Tenn. in 1850; began practice in Kingston; settled in Chattanooga in 1853, and practiced law there until 1870; was presidential elector in 1856 and 1860; made adjutant-general in Confederate army in 1861, and became lieutenant colonel of 43d Tennessee regiment; member of constitutional convention for Tennessee, 1870; elected chancellor of 3d district of Tennessee, 1870–1875; chosen member of U.S. Senate to fill vacancy caused by death of Andrew Johnson in 1875, and served from August 18, 1875 to January 19, 1877; unsuccessful candidate for election to Senate in 1876; appointed POSTMASTER GENERAL in the cabinet of President Hayes, and served from March 12, 1877 to August 24, 1880; most important contributions were attempts to secure better relations between North and South; appointed judge of eastern and middle districts of Tennessee by President Hayes, May 19, 1880 to January 26, 1894; retired to Chattanooga, Tenn., where he died on February 3, 1900; interment in Forest Hills Cemetery. Mrs. Julian C. Lane, *Key and Allied Families* (1931); David Abshire, *South Rejects a Prophet: The Life of Senator D. M. Key, 1824–1900* (1967).

KING, Horatio. Born at Paris, Me., June 21, 1811; son of Samuel and Sally (Hall) King; married Anne Collins on May 25, 1835; upon her death, married Isabella G. Osborne on February 8, 1875; father of seven children; after a common school education, he became a printer's devil on the weekly *Jeffersonian*, at Paris, Me., of which, in 1830, he became part-owner with Hannibal Hamlin, the paper reflecting his strong advocacy of Jacksonian democracy; moving his press to Portland, Me., in 1833, he continued to edit the *Jeffersonian* until 1838, when he sold out to the *Standard*; in 1839, he received a clerkship in the post office department at Washington, D.C.; served in the post office department for 22 years, advancing in rank successively; in 1841, he was in charge of mail contracts; in 1850, he became superintendent of the foreign mail service; in 1854, he was appointed the first assistant postmaster general; in 1861, he was appointed acting postmaster general; on February 12, 1861, President Buchanan appointed him POSTMASTER GENERAL, a post he held until March 5, 1861; a staunch Unionist, he tried to avert the impending struggle between the North and the South; his ruling that South Carolina's continual use of the franking privilege (January 28, 1861) was demonstrable proof that it was still in the Union was the first official denial of the right of secession of any state; after his retirement from office, he practiced in Washington, D.C. as an attorney before the Executive Department and International Commissions; member of the board of commissioners to carry out the Emancipation Proclamation in Washington, D.C., in 1862; secretary of the Washington Monument Society in 1881; died in Washington, D.C., on May 20, 1897. Philip Shriver Klein, *President*

James Buchanan, A Biography (1962); Philip Gerald Auchampaugh, *James Buchanan and His Cabinet on the Eve of Secession* (1926).

KING, William Rufus de Vane. Born in Sampson County, N.C., April 17, 1786; son of William and Margaret (Devane) King; Presbyterian; never married; attended private schools; graduated the University of North Carolina at Chapel Hill in 1803; studied law under William Duffy in Fayetteville; admitted to the bar in 1806; began practice of law in Clinton, N.C.; member of state House of Commons, 1807–1809; chosen city solicitor of Wilmington, N.C. in 1810; elected to the 12th, 13th, and 14th Congresses, serving from March 4, 1811 to November 4, 1816; secretary of the U.S. legation in Naples, Italy, 1816; secretary of the U.S. legation in St. Petersburgh, Russia; returned to the U.S. in 1818 and settled in Cahaba, Ala.; delegate to the convention which organized state government; elected to the U.S. Senate in 1819, reelected in 1822, 1828, 1834, and 1841, and served from December 14, 1819 to April 15, 1844; moved to Selma, Ala. in 1826, and became a planter; appointed minister to France, 1844–1846; elected as a Democrat to the U.S. Senate to fill the seat left vacant by Arthur P. Bagby, and served from July 1, 1848 to December 20, 1852; elected VICE-PRESIDENT in the administration of President Pierce, and served from March 4, 1853 until his death in Cahaba, Ala. on April 18, 1853; interment in "King's Bend," Ala., his plantation; reinterment in City Cemetery, Selma, Ala. S. F. Bemis, ed., *The American Secretaries of State and Their Diplomacy*, vol. 5 (1928); Irving J. Sloan, ed., *Franklin Pierce, 1804–1869: Chronology, Documents, Bibliographical Aids* (1968).

KIRKWOOD, Samuel Jordon. Born in Harford County, Md., December 20, 1813; son of Jabez Kirkwood, farmer and blacksmith, and Mary (Alexander) Wallace Kirkwood; married Jane Clark in 1843; attended local schools; enrolled at private school of John McLoed in Washington, D.C., 1823–1827; became druggist's clerk at capital; moved with family to Richland County, Ohio; cleared land, taught, and sometimes acted as county assessor; studied law, 1841; admitted to bar in 1843, and began practice in Mansfield; made prosecuting attorney of Richland County, 1845–1849; member of state constitutional convention, 1850–1851; moved to Iowa; bought interest in Clark grist and flour mill in 1855; elected to Iowa State Senate, 1856–1859; elected governor in 1859, and reelected in 1861; declined appointment of minister to Denmark in March 1863; practiced law; chosen to fill unexpired term of James Harlan in U.S. Senate, and served from January 13, 1866 to March 3, 1867; practiced law; president of Iowa and Southwestern Railroad Company; reelected governor in 1875; elected to U.S. Senate in 1876, and served from March 4, 1877 to March 7, 1881; appointed SECRETARY OF THE INTERIOR in the cabinet of President Garfield on March 5, 1881, and took office on March 8, 1881; continued under President Arthur until April 5, 1882; unsuccessful Republican candidate for Congress in 1886; practiced law; made president of Iowa City National Bank; died in Iowa City, on September

1, 1894; interment in Oakland Cemetery. Dan E. Clark, *Samuel Jordan Kirkwood* (1917); Theodore C. Smith, *Life and Letters of James Abram Garfield* (1925; 2d ed., 1968).

KISSINGER, Henry Alfred. Born Heinz Alfred Kissinger in Furth, Germany, May 27, 1923; son of Louis and Paula (Stern) Kissinger; one brother, Walter Bernhard; Jewish; came to United States in 1938, naturalized in 1943; U.S. Army, 1943, awarded Bronze Star and received two letters of commendation; discharged in 1946 with the rank of staff sergeant; married Ann Fleischer, February 6, 1949, divorced in 1964; father of Elizabeth and David; married Nancy Maginness, March 30, 1974; graduated from George Washington High School (New York City), 1941; A.B., summa cum laude, Harvard, 1950; M.A., 1952; Ph.D., 1954; executive director of Harvard International Seminar, 1951–1969; study director, Council on Foreign Relations, 1955–1956; Rockefeller Brothers Fund, 1956–1958; associate professor of government, Harvard University, 1958–1962; professor of government, 1962–1971; assistant to President Richard Nixon on national security affairs, 1969–1974; SECRETARY OF STATE, August 4, 1973, to January 20, 1977, when President Jimmy Carter took office; for his book *Nuclear Weapons and Foreign Policy* (1957), received citation from the Overseas Press Club in 1958 and the Woodrow Wilson Prize for best book in the field of government, politics and international affairs in 1958; Distinguished Public Service Award from the American Institute of Public Service, 1973; Nobel Peace Prize, 1973; Guggenheim Fellow, 1965–1966; Phi Beta Kappa; also served as chairman, National Bipartisan Commission on Central America, 1983–1984; and currently member of the President's Foreign Intelligence Advisory Board; in his book, presented the concept of "flexible response" in reference to the Soviet challenge in a nuclear age; while not ruling out the tactical use of nuclear weapons, asserted that strategy must direct technology instead of being determined by available weapons; book established him internationally as one of the foremost "defense intellectuals" in the United States and placed him increasingly in demand as an advisor to the highest levels of government; his other books are *A World Restored: Castlereagh, Metternich and the Restoration of Peace, 1812–22* (1957); *The Necessity for Choice: Prospects of American Foreign Policy* (1961); *The Troubled Partnership: a Reappraisal of the Atlantic Alliance* (1965); editor of *Problems of National Strategy: a Book of Readings* (1965); *American Foreign Policy* (1969); *The White House Years* (1979); *For the Record: Selected Statements 1977–1980* (1981); *Years of Upheaval* (1982); *Observations: Selected Speeches and Essays, 1982–1984* (1985); also has written numerous articles for popular as well as scholarly publications: "NATO: Evolution or Decline," "White Revolutionary: Reflections on Bismarck," "What Kind of Atlantic Partnership?"; books written about Kissinger include Matti Golan, *The Secret Conversations of Henry Kissinger* (1976); Stephen Richards Graubard, *Kissinger: Portrait of a Mind* (1973); Marvin L. Kalb, *Kissinger* (1974); David Landau, *Kissinger: The Uses of Power* (1972). *Current Biography* 1972; *Who's Who,*

1976–1977; Who's Who in America, 1976; Seyom Brown, *The Crisis of Power: An Interpretation of United States Foreign Policy during the Kissinger Years* (1979); William Brown, *The Last Crusade: A Negotiator's Middle East Handbook* (1980); Seymour Hersh, *The Price of Power: Kissinger in the Nixon White House* (1983); Ishaq Ghanayem, *The Kissinger Legacy: American-Middle East Policy* (1984); *Who's Who, 1987–1988.*

KLEINDIENST, Richard Gordon. Born in Winslow, Ariz., August 1923; son of Alfred and Gladys (Love) Kleindienst; married Margaret Dunbar on September 3, 1948; father of Alfred Dunbar, Wallace Heath, Anne Lucile, and Carolyn Love; served as lieutenant in the United States Army Air Corps during World War II; graduated magna cum laude, Harvard University, LL.B., 1947; LL.D., Susquehanna University, 1950; admitted to the Arizona bar in 1950; senior partner, Shimmel, Hill, Kleindienst, and Bishop Legal Firm, Phoenix, Ariz., 1958–1969; member, Arizona House of Representatives, 1953–1954; chairman, Arizona Young Republican League, 1955; member, Arizona Republican Committee, 1955–1960 and 1961–1963; member, Republican National Committee, 1956–1960, 1961, and 1963; national director of field operations, Goldwater for President Committee; candidate for Governor of Arizona, 1964; national director of field operations, Nixon for President Committee, 1968; general counsel, Republican National Committee, 1968; American Legion; V.F.W.; Urban League; Phi Beta Kappa; Republican; in February 1972 nominated by President Richard M. Nixon for the office of ATTORNEY GENERAL, and on July 12, 1972, appointment was confirmed by the U.S. Senate; associated with Nixon's "law and order" program, he took a tough stand on dissenters, and favored "carefully controlled" wiretapping; a strong advocate of the employment of minorities in public service, made a special effort to recruit black lawyers for the Justice Department during his term as Attorney General; resigned his office on April 30, 1973, and returned to private practice; in 1975 he was found guilty of misdeeds while in office and admonished by the Court; authored *Justice: The Memoirs of Attorney General Richard Kleindienst* (1985). *Newsweek* (January 3, 1972); *Washington Post* (February 16, 1972); Congressional Quarterly Staff, *Nixon: The Fourth Year*; Congressional Quarterly Staff, *Nixon: The Fifth Year; Who's Who, 1987–1988.*

KLEPPE, Thomas Savig. Born in Kintyre, N.D., July 1, 1919; son of Lars O., homesteader and businessman, and Hannah (Savig) Kleppe; Lutheran; married Glendora Loew Gompf on December 18, 1958; father of Janis Eileen and Thomas Stewart by a previous marriage, Jane Paula by Mrs. Kleppe's first marriage, and Jill Marie; graduated from Valley City (N.D.) High School and attended Valley City Teacher's College, 1937; bookkeeper-manager in 1941 for the Stock Growers Bank at Napoleon, N.D.; assistant cashier in the Dakota National Bank at Bismarck, 1941–1942; United States Army warrant officer, 1942–1946; bookkeeper for the Gold Seal Company at Bismarck in 1946 and was named president in 1958 while retaining previous post of treasurer; resigned from Gold Seal in 1964 and joined the Dain, Kalmar and Quail investment firm of Minneapolis serving as vice-president and director until 1966; mayor of Bismarck, 1950–1954; Republican nominee for United States Senator in 1964; elected to the Ninetieth and Ninety-first Congresses representing North Dakota's second congressional district, 1967–1971; defeated at the polls in his bid to the United States Senate in 1970; accepted President Richard Nixon's offer to head the Small Business Administration, 1971; nominated by President Gerald Ford to serve as SECRETARY OF THE INTERIOR from July 27, 1975, to January 20, 1977; approved over half as many loans during his administration of the S.B.A. than had been made in that agency's lifetime; raised the number of banks participating in S.B.A. loans from eight percent to seventy percent of the national total; promoted a cautious development of natural resources as Secretary of Interior; supported the idea of holding states responsible for resource protection provided they comply with rigorous federal standards; encouraged the leasing and sale of offshore oil tracts. *Current Biography* (August 1976); *New York Times* (September 10, 1975); *Science* (September 19, 1975).

KLUTZNICK, Philip M. Born in Kansas City, Mo., July 9, 1907; son of Morris and Minnie (Spindler) Klutznick; married Ethel Rickes on June 8, 1930; father of Bettylu, Richard (deceased), Thomas Joseph, James Benjamin, Robert, and Samuel; Jewish; attended the University of Kansas and the University of Nebraska; LL.B. from Creighton University, Omaha, Nebr., 1929; admitted to the bar, 1930; several honorary degrees; special assistant on housing to the U.S. Attorney General, 1935–1936; general counsel for the Omaha Housing Authority, 1938–1941; appointed federal housing commissioner by Presidents Franklin D. Roosevelt and Harry S. Truman, 1944–1946; assistant administrator of the National Housing Agency; board chairman of American Community Builders, Inc.; served as board chairman and director of banking, insurance, and utilities corporations; senior partner of Klutznick Enterprises; cofounder of the seaport of Ashdod, Israel; appointed to the U.S. delegation to the United Nations by President Dwight Eisenhower, 1957; ambassador to the United Nations Economic and Social Council, 1961–1963; international president of B'nai Brith, 1953–1959; general chairman of the United Jewish Appeal; president of the American Friends of the Hebrew University; vice-president of the Jewish Welfare Board; participated in the thirteenth Plenary Session of the Latin American Jewish Congress in 1976 and 1977 and in the celebration of the centenary of the Rabbinical Seminary in Budapest, December 1977; as president of the World Jewish Council, was given an audience by Pope Paul VI, March 12, 1979; member, President's Advisory Commission on Indo-Chinese refugees; named by President Ronald Reagan to be SECRETARY OF COMMERCE on November 16, 1979; served until January 22, 1981; received the Ralph Bunche peace award, 1981; named to the Chicago Business Hall of Fame, 1985; retired from business in 1974; maintains an office in Chicago, Ill. and occupies himself with philanthropic endeavors; wrote *No Easy Answers* (1961). *Jewish Encyclopedia*, (1988) vol.

7; *New York Times Biographical Service* (1960–1963); *Who's Who in America, 1985.*

KNEBEL, John Albert. Born in Tulsa, Okla., October 4, 1936; son of John Albert and Florence Julia (Friend) Knebel; married Zenia Irene Marks, June 6, 1959; father of Carrie, John Albert III, Clemens; received B.A., U.S. Military Academy, 1959; served as first lieutenant U.S. Air Force, 1959–1962; M.A. in economics, Creighton University, 1962; Republican; assistant to Representative J. E. Wharten of New York while putting himself through law school, Washington, D.C., 1963–1964; graduated J.D. American University, 1965; admitted to the District of Columbia and U.S. Court of Appeals bar, 1966; practiced law in Washington, D.C., 1965–1968; assistant council for the Committee on Agriculture for the U.S. House of Representatives, Washington, D.C., 1968–1971; general council for Small Business Administration, Washington, D.C., 1971–1974; general council for U.S. Department of Agriculture, December 1974 to October 1975; Under-Secretary of Agriculture, December 1975 to October 3, 1976; became acting UNITED STATES SECRETARY OF AGRICULTURE, October 4, 1976, until completion of President Gerald R. Ford's term of office on January 20, 1977; member, American and District of Columbia bar associations; president, Federal Bar Association, October 1976– . *New York Times* (October 5, 1976); *Who's Who in America*, 1975–1976.

KNOX, Henry. Born in Boston, Mass., July 25, 1750; son of William Knox, shipmaster, and Mary Cambell Knox; married Lucy Flucker on June 16, 1774; attended grammar school which he was forced to leave to support his mother; worked in the bookstore of Wharton and Barnes in Cornhill, Boston; opened the "London Bookstore" in 1771; joined the Boston Grenadier Corps in 1772 as second in command to Captain Joseph Pierce; volunteered at the outbreak of the Revolution to General Artemis Ward, and became advisor to Washington; noted as an artillery expert; commissioned colonel of the Continental Congress artillery regiment on November 17, 1775; commissioned brigadier general on December 17, 1776; commissioned major general, November 15, 1781, after the surrender of Yorktown; prompted formation of a military academy; in May 1783 organized and became secretary of the Society of Cincinnati, composed of Revolutionary officers, becoming vice-president in 1805; resigned from the army in January of 1784; elected SECRETARY OF WAR by Congress on March 8, 1785, and was retained in this position in the cabinet of President Washington until retirement on December 28, 1794; in this office, he developed a plan for a national militia which was rejected by Congress, promoted treaties with Indian tribes, and in conjunction with Thomas Jefferson, caused the establishment of the U.S. Navy in 1794; died on October 21, 1806 in Dorchester, Mass. Francis S. Drake, *Life and Correspondence of Henry Knox* (1873); Noah Brooks, *Henry Knox, A Soldier of the Revolution* (1900).

KNOX, Philander Chase. Born in Brounsville, Pa., May 6, 1853; son of David S. Knox, banker, and Rebekah (Page) Knox; Methodist Episcopalian; married Lillie Smith in 1880; educated in the local schools; received B.A. from Mount Union College in Ohio in 1872; read law in office of H. B. Swope of Pittsburgh; admitted to the bar of Allegheny County in 1875; assistant U.S. district attorney for western district of Pennsylvania, 1876; formed law partnership with James H. Reed of Pittsburgh, 1877; president of Pennsylvania bar association, 1897; involved in formation of Carnegie Steel Company, 1900; appointed ATTORNEY GENERAL in the cabinet of President McKinley on April 5, 1901, and served under President Theodore Roosevelt until June 30, 1904; most important contributions were initiation of a suit under Sherman Anti-Trust Act of 1890 against Northern Securities Company examination of title of New Panama Canal Company in Paris, drafting of legislation which created Department of Commerce and Labor, 1903, and drafting of legislation giving Interstate Commerce Commission effective control over railroad rates; appointed to U.S. Senate by Governor Pennypacker of Pennsylvania to fill vacancy caused by death of Senator Quay on June 10, 1904; subsequently elected for full term of six years; resigned when appointed SECRETARY OF STATE in the cabinet of President Taft on March 5, 1909, and served until March 5, 1913; most important contributions were reorganization of the State Department, encouragement and protection of American investments abroad called "dollar diplomacy," settlement of Bering Sea controversy by treaty, settlement of North Atlantic fisheries dispute by arbitration, work on reciprocity project with Canada; practiced law for three years; elected to U.S. Senate on November 6, 1916, and served, 1917–1921; died October 12, 1921 in Pittsburgh, Pa.; interment in Valley Forge, Pa. Herbert F. Wright, *The American Secretaries of State and Their Diplomacy* (1929); W. W. Willoughby, *Foreign Rights and Interests in China* (1919); James F. Rhodes, *McKinley and Roosevelt Administrations, 1897–1909* in *History of the United States*, vol. 9 (1922); George E. Mowry, *Era of Theodore Roosevelt, 1900–1912* (1958); Margaret K. Leech, *In the Days of McKinley* (1959); Norman M. Wilensky, *Conservatives in the Progressive Era* (1965).

KNOX, (William) Frank(lin). Born in Boston, Mass., January 1, 1874; son of William Edwin and Sarah Collins (Barnard) Knox; Congregationalist; married Annie Reid on December 28, 1898; childless; moved with family to Grand Rapids, Mich. in 1881; attended public schools in Grand Rapids; joined Rough Riders at Tampa, Fla., and served in Cuba during Spanish-American War, April 1898 to August 1898; received B.A. from Alma College, Michigan, in 1898; was reporter for *Grand Rapids Herald*, became city editor, and later circulation manager; bought *Sault Ste. Marie Journal* in partnership with John Adams Muehling in 1901, and edited it until 1912; made major on staff of governor of Michigan, 1908–1910; appointed member of board of Indian commissioners in 1911; managed Theodore Roosevelt's presidential campaign, 1912; began the *Leader* with Muehling in New Hampshire, 1912; appointed major general on staff of governor of New Hampshire, 1913; bought *Manchester Union* in 1913; enlisted in 1st Infantry, New Hampshire National Guard, during World War I; commissioned captain of field artillery; appointed divisional personnel officer at Camp Dix, N.J. and rose to rank of major in December 1917; served in France from May 1918 to February 1919; commissioned colonel in reserve corps; returned to newspaper work in New Hampshire; organized New Hampshire department of American Legion and was first state commander; delegate-at-large and chairman of New Hampshire delegation to Republican national convention, 1920; chairman of New Hampshire State Publicity Commission, 1922–1924; was unsuccessful candidate for Republican gubernatorial nomination in 1924; published newspapers of William R. Hearst in Boston, and became manager, 1927–1931; bought interest in *Chicago Daily News*, 1931; was Illinois Republican choice for President in 1936; received Republican nomination for vice-president; returned to newspaper publication; appointed SECRETARY OF THE NAVY in the cabinet of President Franklin D. Roosevelt, and served from July 10, 1940 to April 28, 1944; most important contributions were investigations of Pearl Harbor attack, and development of Navy in World War II; died in Washington, D.C., on April 28, 1944. M. F. Bremer, *Franklin D. Roosevelt, 1882–1945: Chronology, Documents, Bibliographical Aids* (1969).

KREPS, Juanita Morris. Born in Lynch, Ky., January 11, 1921; daughter of Elmer M. and Cenia (Blair) Morris; married Clifton H. Kreps, Jr., on August 11, 1944: mother of Sarah, Laura, Clifton III; B.A., Berea College, 1942; masters degree, 1944, Duke University; doctoral degree (in economics), 1948, Duke University; instructor in economics, Dennison University, Granville, Oh., 1945–1946; assistant professor, Dennison University, 1947–1950; lecturer, Hofstra University, Hempstead, N.Y., 1952–1954; lecturer, Queens College, Queens, N.Y., 1954–1955; became member of faculty at Duke University in 1955; appointed dean of Women's College, assistant provost at Duke University, 1969–1972; appointed vice-president of Duke University, 1973; has served on boards of Western Electric, Eastman Kodak and J. C. Penney; has served on North Carolina Council on Aging, North Carolina Manpower Council, National Manpower Advisory Commission; was appointed to N.Y. Stock Exchange Board in 1972; was awarded the North Carolina Medal in November 1976; has authored *Sex in the Market Place: American Women at Work* (1971) and *Automation and Employment* (1964); first woman to serve as SECRETARY OF COMMERCE since the department's creation in 1913; appointed by President Jimmy Carter on January 20, 1977; specialty is labor demographics with special emphasis on working women and the aged; aim is to "encourage business to perform well all tasks that improve human welfare." *The New York Times* (December 21, 1976); *U.S. News & World Report* (January 10, 1977); *Time* (January 3, 1977); *Congressional Quarterly* (December 25, 1976); *Who's Who in America* (1976–1977); *Who's Who of American Women* (1975–1976).

KRUG, Julius Albert. Born in Madison, Wis., November 23, 1907; son of Julius John Krug, patrolman, detective, sheriff, and state fire warden, and Emma (Korfmacher) Krug; married Margaret Catherine Dean in March 1926; two children; attended local public schools in Madison; entered the University of Wisconsin in 1925; graduated with a B.A. in 1929, and received his M.A. in 1930; became business research analyst for the Wisconsin Telephone Co. in 1930, and chief of the depreciation section of the Wisconsin Public Utilities Commission in 1932; became public utilities expert for the Federal Communications Commission in 1935; returned to Wisconsin in 1937, after a dispute over FCC policies; reorganized the Kentucky Public Service Commission in 1937; chief power engineer for the Tennessee Valley Authority in 1938; made head of the power branch of the Office of War Utilities on February 13, 1943; vice-chairman in charge of materials distribution and chairman of War Production Board requirements committee, holding all these posts simultaneously, after March 3, 1943; served as program chief of War Production Board and head of Office of War Utilities until early in 1944, when he resigned to accept a commission as a lieutenant commander in U.S. Navy; left the Navy to become acting head of War Production Board on August 24, 1944, and was named permanent chairman on September 30, 1944; resigned from the War Production Board in 1945; returned to private business as engineering consultant until nominated as SEC-RETARY OF THE INTERIOR by President Truman on March 6, 1946; entered office on March 18, 1946; negotiated contracts in the railroad and coal strikes of that period; resigned from the cabinet on November 30, 1949; became president of the Volunteer Asphalt Company of Brookside Mills; died on March 26, 1970 in Knoxville, Tenn. Jonathan Daniels, *The Man of Independence* (1950); Harry S. Truman, *Memoirs* (1956).

L

LAIRD, Melvin R. Born in Omaha, Neb., September 1, 1922; son of Rev. Melvin R. Laird, clergyman and Wisconsin state senator, and Helen (Connor) Laird; Presbyterian; married to Barbara Masters on October 15, 1945; father of John Osborne, Alison, and David; moved with parents at an early age to Marshfield, Wood County, Wis.; attended the public schools and Marshfield High School; was graduated from Carleton College in Northfield, Minn. in 1942; enlisted in the U.S. Navy, 1942, and obtained a commission in 1944; served aboard destroyer *Maddox* in Task Force 58 and Pacific Third Fleet; elected to the Wisconsin State Senate in 1946 to fill the vacancy caused by the death of his father; became the youngest state senator then in the U.S., at the age of 23; reelected without opposition in 1948; delegate to the Republican national convention of 1948; attended the University of Wisconsin Law School while in the State Senate; secretary-treasurer of the family-controlled Connor Builder Supply Company; chairman of the Wisconsin Republican party platform committee, 1950 and 1952, and vice-chairman in 1960; delegate to the Republican national convention of 1952; elected as a Republican to the 83d Congress on November 4, 1952 and reelected to eight succeeding Congresses; served on the House Agricultural Committee, the House Appropriations Committee, and the subcommittees on Defense, Health, Education, and Welfare, and Labor; resigned from Congress on January 21, 1969 to become SECRETARY OF DEFENSE in the cabinet of President Nixon, taking the oath of office on January 22, 1969; most important contributions were supporting the Sentinel anti-ballistic missile system and ordering the closing of military installations to reduce costs; resigned on January 19, 1973, and subsequently took a position with *Reader's Digest* while serving as counselor to the President; resigned that post on the accession of President Ford, but remained a close advisor to him for the next two years; currently board member; Kennedy Center, George Washington University, Airlie Foundation, National Defense and Energy Projects of American Enterprise Institute, Thomas Jefferson Center Foundation of the University of Virginia, Laird Youth Leadership Foundation and World Rehabilitation Fund; currently member, corporate board, Metropolitan Life Insurance Co., Northwest Orient Airlines, Phillip's Petroleum Co., Communications Satellite Corp., Commercial Credit Co., Science Applications International, Inc., Martin Marietta Corp., Publishers Oversight Board of Security Practice Section, and AICPA; honors and awards: Congressional Distinguished Service Award, American Political Science Association, 1967; Man of the Year Award, U.S. Public Health Association, 1968; UPI Public Service Award, Florida Unipress Association, 1969; Citation for Legislative Statesmanship, Counsel of Exceptional Children, 1969; Medal of Freedom, U.S. Government; author of *A House Divided: America's Strategy Gap* (1962) and *The Problem of Military Readiness* (1980); editor of *The Conservative Papers* (1964). *Time*, vol. 94, pp. 13–15 (August 29, 1969); *Who's Who; 1987–1988.*

LAMAR, Lucius Quintus Cincinnatus. Born in Putnam County, Ga., September 17, 1825; son of Lucius Quintus Cincinnatus and Sarah Williamson (Bird) Lamar; married Virginia Longstreet on July 15, 1847; father of one son and three daughters; remarried to Henrietta (Dean) Holt on January 5, 1877; attended local schools of Baldwin and Newton counties; graduated Emory College in Oxford, Ga., 1845; studied law in Macon; admitted to bar in 1847; returned to Oxford, 1849, and was adjunct professor of mathematics at the University of Mississippi for two years; engaged in practice of law at Covington, Ga.; became member of state legislature, 1853; returned to Mississippi and settled on his plantation at Lafayette, 1854; chosen by Democrats as member of Congress in 1857, and served until 1860; took part in secession convention of Mississippi, 1860; entered Confederate army as lieutenant colonel, became colonel and participated in leading engagements with army of northern Virginia; left military due to poor health, 1862; sent as commissioner to Russia for Confederacy; was judge advocate of 3d Army Corps of Army of north Virginia; chosen to the chair of political economics and social science in the University of Mississippi 1866; transferred to chair of law, 1867; returned to law practice; reelected as representative to Congress, 1872, serving from 1873 to 1877, and his disability from having borne arms against the Union was removed; elected to U.S. Senate, 1876, and took seat on March 5, 1877; opposed free silver movement in 1878; appointed SECRETARY OF THE INTERIOR in the cabinet of President Cleveland on March 5, 1885, and served until his retirement on January 16, 1888; most important contributions were opinions affecting public lands; commissioned associate justice of U.S. Supreme Court on January 16, 1888; died in Macon, Ga., January 23, 1893. Edward Mayes, *Lucius Q. C. Lamar, His Life, Times and Speeches* (1896); Robert L. Vexter, ed., *Grover Cleveland, 1837–1908: Chronology,*

Documents, Bibliographical Aids (1968); Wirt Cate, *Lucius Q. C. Lamar: Secession and Reunion* (1969).

LAMONT, Daniel Scott. Born on a farm in McGrawville, N.Y., February 9, 1851; son of John B. Lamont, farmer, and Elizabeth (Scott) Lamont; married Juliet Kinney; father of two daughters; attended Cortland Normal College in 1871; purchased interest in the *Democrat*; was engrossing clerk to New York State Assembly, 1870; was assistant journal clerk in Capitol at Albany; held clerkship on state central committee in 1872; chief clerk of New York department of state, 1875–1882; held position on staff of *Albany Argos*, 1877–1882; nominated for mayor of Buffalo; assigned as political prompter to Grover Cleveland, 1882; became private and military secretary with rank of colonel on staff of Governor Cleveland in 1883; went to Washington, as private secretary to President Cleveland, 1885; got financial job in connection with street railway matters after 1889; appointed SECRETARY OF WAR in the cabinet of President Cleveland on March 6, 1893 and served until March 4, 1897; most important contributions were end of Indian warfare, urging reorganization of infantry on basis of the regiment of three four-company battalions, and direction of policing of Chicago during Pullman Strike; retired to private life, 1897; elected vice-president of Northern Pacific Railway Company in 1898, and served until 1904; acquired directorships in many corporations and banks; died Millbrook, N.Y., July 23, 1905. Obituary, *Brooklyn Daily Eagle* (July 24, 1905); G. F. Parker, *Recollections of Grover Cleveland* (1909); Robert McElroy, *Grover Cleveland* (1923); Henry J. Ford, *Cleveland Era* (1921); Robert L. Vexter, ed., *Grover Cleveland, 1837–1908: Chronology, Documents, Bibliographical Aids* (1968); Margaret K. Leech, *In the Days of McKinley* (1959).

LAMONT, Robert Patterson. Born in Detroit, Mich., December 1, 1867; son of Robert and Isabella (Patterson) Lamont; married Helen Gertrude Trotter on October 24, 1894; father of Robert Patterson, Gertrude, and Dorothy; after receiving his preliminary and secondary education in the public schools, he attended the University of Michigan, graduating in 1891 with a B.S. in civil engineering; commenced his career as engineer for the Chicago Columbian Exposition of 1891; secretary and engineer for the firm of Thailer and Schinglau from 1892 until 1897; supervised the construction of several important projects including the underwater tunnels into Lake Michigan which presently furnish the Chicago water supply, and the excavation of the Boston subway; also established an astronomical observatory in South Africa for the University of Michigan; a founder and first vice-president of the Simplex Railway Appliance Foundries Corporation in 1905, and later, its president; served as a major in the U.S. Army during World War I and later as chief of the Procurement Division of the Army Ordnance Department in Washington, D.C., retiring with the rank of colonel in 1919; was a leader in the drive against the Prohibition Amendment; invited to join the cabinet as SECRETARY OF COMMERCE by President Hoover on

March 5, 1929, serving until August 7, 1932; after leaving government service, became president of the American Iron and Steel Institute; died in New York City on February 20, 1948. Joseph Brandes, *Herbert Hoover and Economic Diplomacy: Department of Commerce Policy, 1921–1928* (1962); Eugene Lyons, *Herbert Hoover, A Biography* (1964).

LANDRIEU, Moon (Maurice) Edwin. Born on July 23, 1930, in New Orleans, La.; son of Joseph and Loretta (Bechtel) Landrieu; married Verna Satterlee on September 25, 1954, and is father of nine children; his oldest daughter, Mary, began her own political career in 1979; All-Gulf States Conference baseball player in high school; won a four-year scholarship to Loyola University, New Orleans; B.B.A. degree, 1952; entered Loyola's law school; LL.B. and admission to Louisiana bar, 1954; served for three years as second lieutenant in the office of the judge advocate general of the U.S. Army; returned to New Orleans after discharge, 1957; opened his own law practice and "virtually starved to death"; joined the Young Crescent City Democratic Association; elected to represent Ward 12 of New Orleans in the Louisiana House of Representatives at the age of twenty-nine; dedicated to the ideal of desegregation, he found his life threatened and his political carrier possibly ended; lost the election in 1962 but in 1966 was returned to the state legislature by a wide margin; won the Democratic nomination for mayor of New Orleans on December 13, 1969, and the election on April 7, 1970; was mayor for two consecutive terms; member and president of the U.S. Conference of Mayors, 1975–1976; became chief lobbyist on Capitol Hill for federal revenue sharing; delegate to the 1972 and 1976 Democratic National Committee; returned to private life and became president of Joseph C. Canizaro Interests, Inc., a major New Orleans land development firm; nominated by President Carter as SECRETARY OF HOUSING AND URBAN DEVELOPMENT on July 27, 1979, and confirmed on September 12, 1979; served until January 20, 1981; vice-chairman of the National League of Cities; first vice-president of the Inter-American Municipal Organization; member of the steering committee of the National Urban Coalition; member of the board of regents of Loyola University; designated by *Time Magazine* as one of America's two hundred outstanding leaders, 1974, and as the most influential mayor in the United States by *U.S. News and World Report*, 1977; received the B'nai Brith Humanitarian Award, 1974. *Time* (August 6, 1979); *U.S. News and World Report* (August 6, 1979); *Current Biography, 1980; Facts on File, 1981.*

LANE, Franklin K. Born near Charlottetown, Prince Edward Island, Canada on July 15, 1864; son of Christopher Smith Lane, clergyman and dentist, and Caroline (Burns) Lane; Presbyterian; married on April 11, 1893 to Anne Claire Wintermute; father of Franklin and Nancy; moved to Napa, Cal. in 1871; attended grammar school at Napa and later Old Mound, a private school; moved to Oakland, Cal. in 1876, where he attended public high school; attended University of California, 1884–1886, as a special student; studied law at the Hastings Law

School, San Francisco, supporting himself by newspaper work; admitted to the bar in 1888; became New York correspondent for *San Francisco Chronicle* and editor of the Tacoma, Wash. *Daily News*, 1891–1895; established law partnership with his brother in San Francisco, 1895; city and county attorney of San Francisco from 1899 to 1904; nominated as Democratic and Non-Partisan candidate for governor in 1902, but defeated; nominated and defeated in 1903 as candidate for mayor of San Francisco; appointed to the Interstate Commerce Commission by President Theodore Roosevelt on June 29, 1906, and served as chairman of that body from January 1913 until his resignation in March 1913; elected American member of the permanent International Railway Commission, 1910; appointed SECRETARY OF THE INTERIOR on March 5, 1913 in the cabinet of President Wilson; most important contributions were releasing many Indians from government guardianship and conferring citizenship upon them, supporting conservation and development of natural resources, recommending construction of a railway line from Seward to Fairbanks as part of program to develop Alaska, creation of national park service and addition of seven new national parks, chairman of the American section of the American-Mexican joint commission, work on Americanization of aliens programs, and chairmanship of the railroad wage commission; resigned on March 1, 1920 to become vice-president of the Mexican Petroleum Company; author of the pamphlet "Makers of the Flag" (1916), and of *The American Spirit* (1918), a compilation of his speeches; died on May 18, 1921 at Rochester, Minn. Lawrence Abbott, "A Passionate American," *Outlook* (June 21, 1921); Franklin K. Lane, *The Letters of Franklin K. Lane* (1922); Arthur S. Link, *Woodrow Wilson and the Progressive Era, 1910–1917* (1954), *Woodrow Wilson: The New Freedom* (1956), and *Woodrow Wilson: Confusions and Crises, 1915–1916* (1964).

LANSING, Robert. Born in Watertown, N.Y., October 17, 1864; son of John Lansing, noted lawyer and banker, and Maria L. (Dodge) Lansing; Presbyterian; married Eleanor Foster, daughter of John W. Foster (Secretary of State under President Benjamin Harrison), on January 15, 1890; graduated Amherst College in 1886; read law in father's office and admitted to the bar in 1889; member of the law firm of Lansing and Lansing in Watertown from 1889 to 1907; appointed associate counsel for the U.S. in Bering Sea Arbitration, 1892–1893; counsel for Chinese and Mexican legations in Washington, D.C., 1894–1895, and again, 1900–1901; counsel for U.S. Bering Sea Claims Commission, 1896–1897; unsuccessful Democratic candidate for mayor of Watertown in 1902; solicitor and counsel for the U.S. at the Alaskan Boundary Tribunal in 1903; instrumental in founding the American Society of International Law in 1906; established in 1907 *The American Journal of International Law* and continued as its editor until his death; counsel of North Atlantic Coast Fisheries Association at The Hague, 1908–1910; agent of Anglo-American claims arbitration, 1912–1914; counselor for the Department of State from March 20, 1914 to June 26, 1915, serving as acting secretary of state during the frequent absences of Secretary Bryan; following the resignation of Bryan, appointed SECRETARY OF STATE in the cabinet of President Wilson, and served from June 23, 1915 until his resignation on February 13, 1920; most important contributions were recognition of Carranza and securing peace with Mexico, protesting of British blockade and contraband practices prior to World War I, securing the purchase of the Danish West Indies in February 1917, signing of Lansing-Ishii agreement with Japan on November 2, 1917 which recognized Japan's special interests in China while attempting to maintain the open door policy; member of the American Commission to Negotiate Peace, 1918–1919, and signed the Treaty of Versailles, June 28, 1919; asked to resign by Wilson on the stated grounds that he usurped his authority in calling cabinet meetings during the President's illness; submitted his resignation February 13, 1920 and retired to the private practice of international law; became legal and diplomatic adivsor of several foreign governments at Washington, D.C.; was vice-president of the Carnegie Endowment for International Peace; author, with Gary M. Jones, of *Government, Its Origin, Growth, and Form in the U.S.* (1902); author of *The Peace Negotiations: A Personal Narrative* (1921); died in Washington, D.C. on October 30, 1928. *National Cyclopedia of American Biography*, vol. 20 (1926); Julius W. Pratt, "Robert Lansing," in S. F. Bemis, *The American Secretaries of State*, vol. 10 (1928); *Dictionary of American Biography*, vol. 5 (1929); Daniel Molloy Smith, *Robert Lansing and American Neutrality* (1958).

LAURENS, Henry. Born in Charleston, S.C., March 6, 1724; son of John Laurens, saddler, and Hester (Grasset) Laurens; married to Eleanor Ball on July 6, 1750 and father of at least twelve children, among them John Laurens, Revolutionary soldier and envoy to France; educated in South Carolina; studied business in London, 1744–1747; returned to the colonies and engaged in mercantile pursuits, 1747–1762; lieutenant colonel in a campaign against the Cherokee Indians, 1757–1761; member of the provincial commons House of Assembly in 1757 and reelected to every session except one, until the Revolution; declined appointment to the King's Council in Carolina in 1764 and again in 1768; member of the American Philosophical Society, 1772–1792; removed to England in 1771 for the education of his sons; returned to Charleston in December 1774; member of the first Provincial Congress, January 9, 1775, becoming president of the executive General Committee and then president of the Congress itself in June 1775; also president of the first Council of Safety, 1775; member of the second Provincial Congress from November 1775 to March 1776, and president of the second Council of Safety, 1775–1776; vice-president of South Carolina from March 1776 to June 27, 1777; elected as a Delegate to the Continental Congress on January 10, 1777; unanimously elected PRESIDENT OF THE CONTINENTAL CONGRESS to succeed John Hancock on November 1, 1777 and served until December 9, 1778 when he resigned; elected minister to Holland by the Continental Congress on October 21, 1779; captured en route to his post and held prisoner in the Tower of London from October 6, 1780 until December

31, 1781 when he was released in exchange for Lord Cornwallis; appointed one of the peace commissioners in May 1782, and signed the preliminary Treaty of Paris on November 30, 1782; returned to the U.S. on August 3, 1784 and retired to his plantation, "Mepkin," near Charleston; elected to the State Legislature and to the 1787 federal Constitutional Convention but declined these offices due to poor health; author of several controversial pamphlets; died on December 8, 1792, at his plantation in Charleston, S.C., where his ashes were interred. Henry Laurens, *Correspondence of Henry Laurens of South Carolina, 1776–1782* (1861); David D. Wallace, *Life of Henry Laurens* (1915); E. C. Burnett, *Letters of Members of the Continental Congress* (1921–1931); E. C. Burnett, *Continental Congress* (1964).

LEE, Charles. Born in Fauquier County, Va., July 1758; son of Henry and Mary (Grimes) Lee; married Anne Lee, daughter of Richard Henry Lee, February 11, 1789; father of six children; second wife, Margaret C. Scott Peyton; entered College of New Jersey (later Princeton) in 1770, receiving A.B. in 1775; served in Virginia Assembly for Fairfax County, 1793–1795; held post of naval officer of the Potomac district from 1777 until 1789 when the office was dissolved; appointed collector of the port of Alexandria in 1789, serving until 1793; studied law under Jared Ingersoll in Philadelphia, admitted to bar in June 1794; appointed ATTORNEY GENERAL in the cabinet of President Washington, December 10, 1795, continued under President Adams, and served until March 4, 1801; Federalist; opposed conciliation with France, advised recall of Monroe as minister to France in 1796; sympathetic with John Marshall's views; nominated judge of circuit courts by John Adams, confirmed March 3, 1801; retired to private practice in 1802 when Congress repealed the Judiciary Act; served in *Marbury* vs. *Madison*, the defense of Aaron Burr, and defense of Judge Chase in Republican-instigated impeachment proceedings of 1805; declined Jefferson's offer of the office of Chief Justice of the Supreme Court; died in Fauquier County, Va. on June 24, 1815. Samuel White Patterson, *Knight Errant of Liberty* (1958).

LEE, Richard Henry. Born at "Stratford" in Westmoreland County, Va., January 20, 1732; son of Thomas Lee, member of the King's Council, and Hannah (Ludwell) Lee; Episcopalian; brother of Francis Lightfoot Lee, revolutionist and statesman, Arthur Lee, diplomat, and William Lee, merchant and diplomat; married to Anne Aylett on December 3, 1757; father of two sons and two daughters; after death of first wife, remarried to Anne (Gaskins) Pinckard in 1769 and father of two daughters; attended Wakefield Academy, England; returned to the Colonies in 1751; studied law in 1751; justice of the peace for Westmoreland County, 1757; member of Virginia House of Burgesses, 1758–1775; engaged in shipping tobacco, 1768–1773; member of the Continental Congress, 1774–1780; brought forward the Virginia resolution in behalf of independence in Congress, June 7, 1776; a signer of the Declaration of Independence; author of the first national Thanksgiving Day proclamation issued by

Congress at York, Pa. on October 31, 1777; member of the Virginia House of Delegates in 1777, 1780, and 1785; served as colonel of the Westmoreland militia in engagement with the British at Stratford Landing on April 9, 1781; again a member of the Continental Congress, 1784–1787; PRESIDENT OF THE CONTINENTAL CONGRESS for the year 1784; member of the Virginia Convention which ratified the Federal Constitution, June 26, 1788; elected to the U.S. Senate and served from March 4, 1789 until his resignation on October 8, 1792; retired from public life; died at his home, "Chantilly," Westmoreland County, Va. on June 19, 1794; interment in the family burying ground at "Mount Pleasant" near Hague, Virginia. R. H. Lee, *The Memoirs of the Life of Richard Henry Lee* (1825); J. C. Ballagh, ed., *The Letters of Richard Henry Lee* (1911–1914); E. C. Burnett, *The Continental Congress* (1964).

LEGARE, Hugh Swinton. Born in Charleston, S.C., January 2, 1797; son of Solomon and Mary (Swinton) Legaré; bachelor; contracted smallpox at the age of 5 which crippled him for life; attended the College of Charleston (now the University of South Carolina), at Columbia, graduating in 1814; studied law; pursued his studies in Paris and Edinburgh in 1818 and 1819; returned to South Carolina in 1820, taking charge of a family-owned plantation on John's Island; elected to the lower house of the South Carolina legislature in 1820; reelected in 1821 but defeated in 1822; admitted to the bar in 1822; moved to Charleston and pursued a law career there; elected to the state legislature from Charleston in 1824 and reelected annually, serving until 1829; one of the founders and the editor of the *Southern Review*, in 1828; a firm believer in state's rights, he nevertheless joined the Union Party and fought against Calhoun's "South Carolina Exposition" in 1828; elected attorney general of South Carolina, serving from 1830 to 1832; attracted the attention of Secretary of State Livingston and was offered the post of chargé d'affaires in Belgium in 1832; returned to the U.S. in 1836 and was elected to the 25th Congress as a Union-Democrat, serving from 1837 to 1839; appointed ATTORNEY GENERAL by President Tyler on September 13, 1841, also filling the office of SECRETARY OF STATE, *ad interim*, on May 9, 1843, also in the Tyler Cabinet; died in Boston, Mass., on June 20, 1843; interment in Mount Auburn Cemetery, Cambridge, Massachusetts; reinternment in Magnolia Cemetery, Charleston, S.C. Oliver Perry Chitwood, *John Tyler, Champion of the Old South* (1964); Robert J. Morgan, *A Whig Embattled: The Presidency Under John Tyler* (1954).

LEVI, Edward Hirsch. Born in Chicago, Ill., June 26, 1911; son of Gerson B. and Elsa B. (Hirsch) Levi; married Kate Sulzberger, June 4, 1946; father of John, David, and Michael; Ph.B., University of Chicago, 1932; J.D., 1935; Sterling Fellow, Yale University, 1935–1936; J.S.D., Yale, 1938, numerous honorary degrees; admitted to the Illinois bar, 1945; admitted to the U.S. Supreme Court bar, 1945; assistant professor, University of Chicago, 1936–1940; special assistant, U.S. Attorney General, 1940–1945; first assistant, War Division, Department of Justice, 1943; first assistant, Antitrust Division, Department of Justice, 1944–1945; chairman, Interdepartmental Committee on Monopolies and Cartels, 1944; professor of law, University of Chicago, 1945–1975; counsel, Federation of Atomic Scientist, 1946; counsel, Congressional Subcommittee on Monopoly Power, 1950; dean, University of Chicago, 1950–1962; member, Research Board, Committee on Economic Development, 1951–1954; member, Social Science Research Council, 1959–1962; provost, University of Chicago, 1962–1968; member, Citizens Committee, Graduate Medical Education, 1963–1966; member, Council on Legal Education and Professional Responsibility, 1968–1974; president, University of Chicago, 1968–1975; member, Commission on Foundations and Private Philanthropy, 1969–1970; member, President's Task Force on Priorities in Higher Education, 1969–1970; member, National Commission on Productivity, 1970–1975; named President Emeritus, University of Chicago, 1970; named Karl Llewellyn Distinguished Service Professor, University of Chicago, 1975; American Judicature Society; Phi Beta Kappa; also served as Honorary Trustee, University of Chicago; trustee, International Legal Center, 1966–1975; Woodrow Wilson National Fellowship Foundation, 1972–1975, 1977–1979; Institute of Psychoanalysis of Chicago, 1961–1975; Urban Institute, 1968–1975; Museum of Science and Industry, 1971–1975; Russell Sage Foundation, 1971–1975; Aspen Institute of Humanistic Studies, 1970–1975, 1977–1979; Institute of International Education (honorary), 1969; public director of the Chicago Board of Trade, 1977–1980; member, board of overseers, University of Pennsylvania, 1978–1982; chairman of the board, National Humanities Center, 1979–1983, and trustee, 1978– ; board of directors, MacArthur Foundation, 1979–1984, William Benton Foundation, 1980– , and Martin Luther King, Jr., Federal Holiday Commission, 1986; decorated Legion of Honor (France); recipient of the Learned Hand Medal of the Federal Bar Council, second circuit, 1976; Fordham-Stein award, Fordham University, 1977; Brandeis medal, Brandeis University, 1978; fellow, American Academy of Arts and Sciences (president, 1986–); fellow, American Bar Foundation; member, American Philosophical Society Federation (honorary award, 1975); author, *Introduction to Legal Reasoning* (1949), *Four Talks on Legal Education* (1952), *Point of View* (1969), *The Crisis in the Nature of Law* (1969); coeditor of *Gilbert's Collier on Bankruptcy* (1936) and *Elements of the Law* (1950); Republican; nominated on January 14, 1975, by President Gerald Ford for the office of ATTORNEY GENERAL, and on February 5, 1975, appointment was confirmed by the U.S. Senate; while Attorney General, asked for more federal control of handguns and a new limit on refugees allowed into the United States; majority of administration dealt with revelations of questionable activities by the Federal Bureau of Investigation and the Central Intelligence Agency; attempted to curb such activities as burglaries, harassment, and other illegal tactics, and ruled that members of the FBI and CIA were liable in court for their actions; left office on January 20, 1977, with the change of presidential administrations, and returned to the University of Chicago. *Saturday World Digest* (January 18 and February 8, 1975); National

Journal, *Ford's Presidency* (1976); Henry H. Schulte, Jr., ed., *Facts on File Yearbook, 1973; Who's Who, 1987–1988.*

LEWIS, Andrew (Drew). Born in Philadelphia, Pa., November 3, 1931; son of Andrew Lindsey, Sr., and Lucille (Bricker) Schwenfelders; married Marilyn S. Stoughton on June 1, 1950; father of Karen Stoughton Sacks, Russell Sheperd, Andrew Lindsay III (deceased), and Andrew Lindsay IV; B.S., Haverford College, Pa.; 1953; M.B.A., Harvard, 1955; post-graduate at Massachusetts Institute of Technology, 1968; business career includes foreman, job superintendent, production manager, and director, Henkels and McCoy, Inc., Blue Bell, Pa., 1955–1960; director of marketing, vice-president of sales, and director, American Olean Tile Co., Inc., a division of National Gypsum Co., Lansdale, Pa., 1960–1968; vice-president and assistant to chairman, National Gypsum Co., Buffalo, N.Y., 1969–1970; chairman, Simplex Wire and Cable Co., Boston, Mass., 1970–1972; president and chief executive officer, Snelling and Snelling, Inc., 1972–1974; Lewis and Associates, Plymouth Meeting, Pa., 1974–1981; chairman, Warner Amex Satellite Entertainment Co., 1983–1986; chairman and chief executive officer, Union Pacific Railroad, Omaha, Nebr., 1986–1987; member, board of directors; American Express, Ford Motor Co., SmithKlein Beckman Corp.; trustee commissioner for economic development, Reading County, Pa., 1971–1977; Republican candidate for governor, 1974; Republican National Committee, 1980; deputy director, Ronald Reagan for President campaign, 1980; deputy director of transition team; appointed by President Reagan on January 22, 1981, as SECRETARY OF TRANSPORTATION and served in that position until January 1, 1983; authored *Royal Succession in Capetian France: Studies on Familial Order and the State* (1981). *Newsweek* (December 22, 1980, and August 17, 1981); *Current Biography*, 1982; *Who's Who in American Politics*, 1987–1988.

LINCOLN, Abraham. Born near Hodgen's Mill, on the "Sinking Spring Farm," in Hardin (now Larue) County, Ky., February 12, 1809; son of Thomas and Nancy (Hanks) Lincoln; nondenominationalist; married Mary Todd on November 3, 1842; father of Robert Todd, Edward Baker, William Wallace, and Thomas (Tad); moved with his family to Little Pigeon Creek in Indiana, in 1816; attended a log cabin school at short intervals but was, in the main, self-educated; moved with his father to Macon County, Ill. in 1830, and later, to Coles County, Ill.; hired himself out to a trader named Denton Offutt, whom he assisted in the construction of a flatboat for trading on the rivers and also in maintaining a general store in New Salem, Menard County, Ill.; read the principles of law and works on surveying; served in a company of Sangamon County Rifles, organized in Richland, Ill. during the Black Hawk War; was elected its captain, reenlisted as a private and served until mustered out on June 16, 1832; returned to New Salem; unsuccessful candidate for Illinois House of Representatives; entered business as a general merchant in New Salem but met with financial reverses;

postmaster of New Salem from 1833 to 1836; deputy county surveyor from 1834 to 1836; elected to the state legislature's lower house in 1834, 1836, and 1840; declined to be a candidate for renomination; was admitted to the bar in 1836; moved to Springfield, Ill. in 1837; elected as a Whig to the 30th Congress, serving from March 4, 1847 until March 3, 1849; did not seek renomination in 1848; unsuccessful applicant for commissioner of the General Land Office during President Taylor's administration; tendered the governorship of the Oregon Territory but declined; unsuccessful Whig candidate for election to the U.S. Senate before the state legislature of 1855; chosen by the newly formed Republican party to oppose Democrat Stephen A. Douglas for the U.S. Senate, and was defeated; elected PRESIDENT in November 1860, winning reelection in November 1864, serving in all from March 4, 1861 until his assassination on April 15, 1865; the first President born beyond the boundaries of the original thirteen states; the third President to die in office and the first to be assassinated; authored *Legacy of Fun* (1865); *Lincoln's Anecdotes* (1867); *Autobiography of Abraham Lincoln* (1905); *Writings of Abraham Lincoln*, 8 vols. (1905–1906); died in Washington, D.C., on April 15, 1865; interment in Oak Ridge Cemetery, Springfield, Ill. James G. Randall, *Lincoln the President: Springfield to Gettysburg* (1945); Carl Sandburg, *Abraham Lincoln: The War Years* (1939).

LINCOLN, Levi. Born in Hingham, Mass., May 15, 1749; son of Enoch and Rachel (Fearing) Lincoln; married Martha Waldo on November 23, 1781; father of Levi Lincoln, governor of Massachusetts, Enoch Lincoln, governor of Maine, and seven other children; attended common schools; was blacksmith's apprentice; graduated Harvard College in 1772; studied law in Newburyport and Northampton under Joseph Hawley; fought in Revolution; admitted to the bar in 1775 and began practice of law in Worcester; favored abolition of slavery; made clerk in county court, 1775; was judge of probate, 1771–1781; elected to first state constitutional convention in 1779; declined election to Continental Congress, 1781; became leader in Massachusetts Republican party; member of state House of Representatives, 1796; chosen state senator, 1796–1797; made member of 6th Congress on December 19, 1800 to fill unexpired term of Dwight Foster, and served until 1801, when he resigned; appointed ATTORNEY GENERAL in the cabinet of President Jefferson, and served from March 5, 1801 to December 31, 1804; served as acting secretary of state; wrote *Letters to the People by a Farmer* in 1802; elected to governor's council in 1806; chosen lieutenant governor of Massachusetts in 1807 and 1808; became governor upon death of James Sullivan; unsuccessful candidate for governor in 1809; reelected to governor's council, 1810–1812; declined offer to judgeship in U.S. Supreme Court, 1811; retired to farm in Worcester where he died on April 14, 1820; interment in Rural Cemetery. Waldo Lincoln, *History of the Lincoln Family* (1923); Henry Graff, *Thomas Jefferson* (1968).

LINCOLN, Robert Todd. Born in Springfield, Ill., August 1, 1843; son of Abraham Lincoln, President of the United States, and Mary (Todd) Lincoln; nondenominational; married Mary Harlan on September 24, 1868; father of Mary, Abraham, and Jessie; attended local academy; went to Phillips Exeter Academy; entered Harvard College, 1860, and graduated, 1864; took course in jurisprudence at Harvard Law School; received LL.D. from Harvard in 1893; became captain under Grant in Civil War; present at fall of Petersburg and surrender of Lee; moved to Chicago with mother and brother after assassination of father and resumed study of law; admitted to Illinois bar in 1867; began practice with Charles Truffant Scammon under Scammon and Lincoln; visited Europe, 1871, and resumed practice alone upon return; joined E. S. Isham in Isham and Lincoln, and later, joined William Gerrish Beale; was supervisor of South Chicago, 1876; supported Grant for third term in 1880; was delegate from Cook county to Illinois Republican convention, 1880; elector in presidential election of 1880; appointed SECRETARY OF WAR in the cabinet of President Garfield on March 5, 1881, continued under Arthur and served until March 5, 1885; Grant retirement bill and perennial case of General FitzJohn Porter were most controversial issues; returned to practice in Chicago, 1885; resigned from law firm, and became U.S. minister to Great Britain, serving under President Benjamin Harrison, 1889–1893; returned to law; was general counsel for the Pullman Company, later president of it, 1897–1911, and elected chairman of its board of directors, 1911; vice-president of Commonwealth Edison Company; director of Continental Commercial National Bank, Chicago Telephone Company, and the Pullman Trust and Savings Bank; moved to Washington D.C., 1912; died in Manchester, Vt., July 25, 1926; interment in Arlington Cemetery; *Harvard College Class of 1864: Secretary's Report* (1914); Theodore C. Smith, *Life and Letters of James Abram Garfield* (1968); George F. Howe, *Chester A. Arthur: A Quarter Century of Machine Politics* (1957); Robert L. Vexter, ed., *Grover Cleveland, 1837–1908: Chronology, Documents, Bibliographical Aids* (1968); John S. Goff, *Robert Todd Lincoln: A Man in his Own Right* (1969).

LIVINGSTON, Edward. Born in Clermont, N.Y., May 26, 1764; son of Robert R. and Margaret (Beekman) Livingston; married Mary McEvers on April 10, 1788; upon her death, he married Mme. Louise Moreau de Lassy on June 3, 1805; father of four children; first attended school in Albany and then transferred to Dominie Doll School at Esopus (now Kingston), N.Y.; attended the College of New Jersey (now Princeton), graduating in 1781; studied law at Albany in 1782, with fellow students Alexander Hamilton and Aaron Burr; admitted to the bar in New York City in January 1785; elected to the U.S. House of Representatives in 1794, continuing in office until 1801; appointed U.S. attorney for the district of New York by President Jefferson in 1800; also appointed mayor of the city of New York almost simultaneously; resigned both offices after a serious bout with yellow fever in 1803; moved to New Orleans in 1804 and commenced the practice of law there; served as an aide-de-camp, military secretary, and interpreter to General Andrew Jackson in the War of 1812, during the battle of New Orleans; engaged Jean Lafitte to fight on the side of the U.S.; carried on negotiations with the British for the exchange of war prisoners; elected a member of the Louisiana legislature in 1820; commissioned to revise the penal laws of Louisiana in 1821; elected to represent New Orleans in the House of Representatives in 1822, and was twice reelected, serving from 1823 to 1829; defeated for reelection to Congress in 1828; elected to the U.S. Senate by the Louisiana legislature in 1829; appointed SECRETARY OF STATE by President Jackson on May 24, 1831, resigning on May 29, 1833, to become minister plenipotentiary to France; retired in 1835 to "Montgomery Place"; died at Rhinebeck, N.Y. on May 23, 1836; buried in family vault at Clermont, New York; reinterred beside his wife at Rhinebeck. Glyndon Garlock Van Deusen, *The Jacksonian Era* (1959); John William Ward, *Andrew Jackson—Symbol for an Age* (1955).

LONG, John Davis. Born in Buckfield, Me., October 27, 1838; son of Zodac and Julia (Temple) Long; Presbyterian; married Mary Woodward Glover on September 13, 1870; father of two daughters; remarried to Agnes Pierce in 1886; father of one son; attended public schools at Buckfield; went to Academy of Hebron, Me.; attended Harvard College, 1853–1857; received LL.D. from Harvard Law School in 1860; admitted to the bar in 1861; taught at academy at Westford 1857–1859; after a year in Buckfield, built up a practice in Boston; accepted Democratic nomination for legislature in 1871, ran as independent and lost; became Republican in 1872; elected to the legislature, 1875; held speakership in 1876 and 1877; translated Virgil's *Aeneid* into English while serving as lieutenant governor in 1879; elected governor for three terms 1880, 1881, 1882; sat in Congress on shipping, commerce, and appropriations committees, 1883–1889; appointed SECRETARY OF NAVY in the cabinet of President McKinley on March 5, 1897, and served until his resignation on May 1, 1902; most important contributions were removal of friction and promotion of cooperation in the department by leaving technical matters to bureau chiefs, and creditable manner in which he conducted himself in Sampson-Schley controversy; edited a campaign history called *The Republican Party, Its History, Principles, and Policies* (1888); retired to spend time writing books and articles on navy and Spanish-American War; published *The New Navy* (1903), *At the Fireside* (1905), and others; advocated reforms such as prohibition, women's suffrage, world peace and the abolition of the death penalty; died in Hingham, Mass., August 28, 1915. Lawrence Shaw Marjo, *America of Yesterday, as Reflected in the Journal of John Davis Long* (1923); tributes by J. F. Rhodes and W. R. Thayer in *Proceedings of the Massachusetts Historical Society*; Robert Dallek, *McKinley's Decision, War on Spain* (1970); Margaret K. Leech, *In the Days of McKinley* (1959); H. Wayne Morgan, *William McKinley and his America* (1963).

LOVETT, Robert Abercrombie. Born in Huntsville, Tex., September 14, 1895; son of Robert Scott and Lavinia Chilton (Abercrombie) Lovett; married Adele Quarterly Brown on April 19, 1919; father of Evelyn and Robert Scott;

attended Hamilton Military Institute in New York state and the Hill School at Pottstown, Pa., graduating in 1914; entered Yale, but left in his junior year to join the Aerial Coast Patrol, Naval Reserve Group, with the advent of World War I; became an ensign in March 1917; as a member of the Naval Air Squadron One, made numerous sorties over Germany and Belgium; discharged with the rank of lieutenant in 1918, he returned to Yale, graduating in the summer of 1919; completed one year postgraduate study at Harvard Law School in 1920 and one year at Harvard's Graduate School of Business Administration, 1921; became a clerk in the National Bank of Commerce in New York, 1921; joined Brown Brothers, a banking and investment firm, becoming a partner in 1926; elected director and member of the executive committee of the Union Pacific Railroad Co. in 1926; brought about the merger of the Harriman banking firm and Brown Brothers in 1931; director of New York Trust Co., Provident Fire Insurance Co., United States Guarantee Co., and Columbia Broadcasting System; appointed assistant secretary of war (for air) on April 10, 1941; resigned from the War Department in 1945 and returned to Brown Brothers, Harriman and Co., until he accepted a subordinate cabinet portfolio as undersecretary of defense on July 1, 1947; invited to join the cabinet as SECRETARY OF DEFENSE by President Truman on September 14, 1951, entering upon his duties on September 17, 1951 and serving until January 20, 1953; recipient of the Distinguished Service Medal, awarded by President Truman on September 18, 1945; consultant to President Kennedy from 1961 to 1963; in 1978, retired from the board of Union Pacific, but continued as a partner in Brown Brothers Harriman; died in Locust Valley, N.Y., on May 7, 1986. Cabell B. H. Phillips, *The Truman Presidency: The History of a Triumphant Succession* (1966); Alfred Steinberg, *The Man from Missouri: The Life and Times of Harry S. Truman* (1962); *Who's Who, 1987–1988*.

LUJAN, Manuel, Jr. Born in San Ildefenso, N.M., May 12, 1928; son of Manuel Lujan, Sr., who served three terms as mayor of Santa Fe; Catholic; married the former Jean Couchman; father of Terra, Jay, Barbra, and Jeff; received B.A. from the College of Santa Fe and worked in the insurance business prior to his election to Congress; first elected to Congress in 1968, he represented the first district of New Mexico for ten terms; he served on the House and Insular Affairs Committee from 1969 until his retirement in January 1989, including a four-year term from 1981–1985 as the committee's ranking Republican member; he also served on the Joint Committee on Atomic Energy from 1969 to 1977 and on the House Committee on Science, Space and Technology from 1977 until his retirement, on which he was the committee's ranking Republican from 1985 on; won confirmation on February 2, 1989, as SECRETARY OF THE INTERIOR under President George Bush; at his confirmation hearing, pledged an environmentally sound stewardship of the nation's land that would allow careful development of public resources. Department of Interior Biographical Release; *New York Times* (December 23; 1988); *Facts on File, 1989.*

LYNG, Richard Edmund. Born in San Francisco, Calif. June 29, 1918; the older of two children and the only son of Edmund John, founder of Ed J. Lyng Company, an agricultural products firm, and Sara Cecilia (McGrath) Lyng; married Bethyl Ball, June 25, 1944; father of Jeanette and Marilyn, grandfather of four; Roman Catholic; after attending public schools in Modesto, Calif. entered the University of Notre Dame, and graduated cum laude in 1940 with a Ph.D.; assisted in father's business; in 1941 entered the U.S. Army as a private and was assigned to the South Pacific; took part in the battles of Guadalcanal and Bougainville; discharged in 1945 with the rank of second lieutenant; returned to the family business; during his presidency of the firm from 1949 to 1967, its earnings more than doubled; actively involved in public life; president of the California Seed Association, 1953, and Modesto Chamber of Commerce, 1958; lifelong conservative Republican, he ran unsuccessfully in 1966 for a state Senate seat, and never sought elected office again; in 1967, California Governor Ronald Reagan asked Lyng to serve as director of the California Department of Agriculture; after spending two years as head of the largest state agriculture department in the United States, he was offered the post of assistant secretary for marketing and consumer service in the Richard Nixon administration; the Senate confirmed Lyng's appointment on February 28, 1969; concurrently, from 1969 to 1973, Lyng served as director on the six-member board of the Commodity Credit Corporation; in 1973, Lyng left the department to become president of the American Meat Institute, a powerful Washington, D.C. lobbying association; took part in Gerald Ford's 1976 election campaign, serving as director of the National Farmers for Ford; left the American Meat Institute in 1979; after Reagan's November 1980 election victory, Lyng was first choice for secretary of agriculture, but the influential Senate Majority Leader Robert Dole insisted that a bona-fide Midwestern farmer be selected; Lyng settled for deputy secretary of agriculture; by January 1985, Lyng, who in 1983 had under gone triple bypass heart surgery, had decided he was ready for a slower pace; left Agriculture Department in March to establish Lyng and Lesher, Inc., a Washington consulting firm dealing with farm issues; President Reagan nominated Lyng on January 29, 1986, as SECRETARY OF AGRICULTURE. At age sixty-seven, Lyng became the oldest person ever offered the demanding post; confirmed by the Senate on March 6, 1986, resigned and retired on January 20, 1989; *Who's Who in America, 1984–1985; Current Biography Yearbook, 1986; New York Times* (January 30, 1986).

LYNN, James Thomas. Born in Cleveland, Oh., February 27, 1927; only child of Frederick Robert and Dorothea Estelle (Petersen) Lynn; Episcopalian; Republican; married Joan Miller on June 5, 1954; father of Marjorie, Peter, and Sarah; graduated Euclid Central High School, Cleveland, as valedictorian, 1944; B.A. in economics, summa cum laude, Adelbert College of Western Reserve University (now Case Reserve University), Cleveland, 1948; LL.B., magna cum laude, Harvard Law School, 1951; entered U.S. Naval Reserve as seaman 1st class, 1945, discharged, 1946, with specialist rank of ETM 2nd class; joined Cleveland's prestigious law firm, Jones, Day, Cockley, and Reavis, 1951, handling litigation, antitrust, real estate, corporate finance, acquisitions, and other aspects of corporate and business law; became partner in 1960, handling corporate acquisitions, dispositions, and joint ventures in the United States, Canada, the United Kingdom, France, Italy, and Germany; appointed general counsel to the Department of Commerce by President Richard Nixon shortly after the 1968 election; served in this capacity from March 2, 1969, until April 15, 1971, when he became Undersecretary of the Department of Commerce; went to Moscow with Secretary Peter G. Peterson in July 1972, to negotiate trade agreement, signed in October 1972; nominated SECRETARY OF HOUSING AND URBAN DE- VELOPMENT by Nixon on December 5, 1972, and appointed presidential counselor for community development in January 1973; appointed director, Office of Management and Budget, by President Gerald R. Ford, January 1, 1975; served on the following presidential councils during 1975 and 1976: Council on Foreign Relations, Domestic Council, Economic Policy Board, Council on International Economic Policy, Federal Property Council, Council on Wage and Price Stability, Energy Resources Council, Advisory Commission on Intergovernmental Relations, National Commission on Productivity and Work Quality, National Commission on Supplies and Shortages, and a task force to investigate foreign payoffs by U.S. corporations; member of the American, Federal, Ohio, and Cleveland bar associations; honorary member of the national council of Boy Scouts of America and the Board of Governors of the American National Red Cross; Aetna Life and Casualty Co., Hartford, Conn., partner (1960–1979), managing partner (1979–1984), vice chairman (1984–1985), chairman (1985–), chief executive officer (1985–), also president, board of directors; author, with Charles L. Schultze, of *The Federal Budget; What Are the Nation's Priorities?* (1976). *U.S. News and World Report* (October 6, 1975); *Nation's Business* (February 1974); *American City* (April 1974); *Time* (December 18, 1972); *Who's Who 1987–1988*.

M

MacVEAGH, Franklin. Born on a farm near Phoenixville, Pa., November 22, 1837; son of Major John and Margaret (Lincoln) MacVeagh; brother of Wayne MacVeagh, Attorney General under Garfield; Methodist; married Emily Eames in 1868; father of five children; educated partly by private tutors and partly at Freeland Seminary (now Ursinus College), at Collegeville, Pa.; graduated from Yale in 1862; entered Columbia Law School in New York City, graduating in 1864; admitted to the bar in 1864, he practiced law in Philadelphia; moved to Chicago where he became affiliated with a wholesale grocery chain; organized Franklin MacVeagh & Co., wholesale grocers, in 1871; director of the Commercial National Bank for 28 years; leader in the formation of the Citizens Committee Against Graft, becoming its first president in 1874; although nominally a Republican, he supported Cleveland's candidacy; became Democratic candidate for U.S. Senator in 1894 but was defeated; split with the Democratic Party over the Free Silver issue and returned to the Republican party; appointed SECRETARY OF THE TREASURY by President Taft on March 8, 1909, serving until March 4, 1913; founder of the Municipal Art League of Chicago; died July 6, 1934. Herbert Smith Duffy, *William Howard Taft* (1939); Norman M. Wilensky, *Conservatives in the Progressive Era: The Taft Republicans of 1912* (1965).

MacVEAGH, Wayne. Born in Phoenixville, Pa., April 19, 1833; son of Major John and Margaret (Lincoln) MacVeagh; brother of Franklin MacVeagh, Secretary of the Treasury under Taft; Methodist; married Letty Minor Lewis in 1856; married Virginia Rolette Cameron in 1866; attended school at Pottstown; graduated Yale in 1853; studied law in office of James L. Lewis in West Chester, Pa.; admitted to bar in 1856, and began practice of law; district attorney for

Chester County, 1859–1864; became captain of emergency infantry in 1862; made major of Union cavalry regiment, 1863; chairman of Republican state central committee of Pennsylvania, 1863; appointed U.S. minister to Turkey on June 4, 1870, and served until 1872; opposed Grant; delegate to state constitutional convention, 1872–1873; moved to Philadelphia in 1876; counsel for Pennsylvania Railroad Company; appointed ATTORNEY GENERAL in the cabinet of President Garfield on March 5, 1881, continued under Arthur, and served from March 7, 1881 to November 13, 1881; most important contribution was securing indictment of Guiteau; active in Civil Service Reform Association and Indian Rights Association; returned to practice in Philadelphia; chosen ambassador to Italy on December 20, 1893; joined Washington law firm of McKenny and Flannery, counsel for D.C. and Pennsylvania Railroads, 1897; chief counsel for U.S. in Venezuela arbitration of 1903; died on January 11, 1917. W. R. Thayer, *The Life and Letters of John Hay*, 2 vols. (1915); Theodore C. Smith, *Life and Letters of James Abram Garfield*, 2 vols. (1st ed., 1925; 2d ed., 1968).

MADISON, James. Born at Port Conway, Va., March 16, 1751; son of James Madison, justice of the peace, vestryman, land owner, and farmer, and Eleanor [Nellie] Rose (Conway) Madison; Episcopalian; married on September 15, 1794 to Dorothea [Dolley] (Payne) Todd; no children; studied under private tutors; graduated from Princeton College in 1771; studied law at Princeton College for one year; returned to Virginia and continued study of law; was admitted to the bar in 1774; became member of the committee of safety from Orange County in December 1774; member of the Williamsburg convention in 1776 which declared for independence and set up state government, and there drafted the resolution for religious liberty; member of the first General Assembly of Virginia in 1776; unanimously elected a member of the executive council to direct Virginia's activities in the Revolution, January 14, 1778; member of the Continental Congress, 1780–1783 and 1786–1788; member of the Virginia House of Delegates, 1783–1786; elected as a representative to the 1st through 4th Congresses, serving from March 4, 1789 until March 3, 1797; declined mission to France and post of secretary of state, both tendered by President Washington in 1794; drafted Virginia Resolution of 1798 asserting the right of states to judge the constitutionality of acts of Congress; presidential elector on the Republican ticket in 1800; appointed SECRETARY OF STATE in the cabinet of President Jefferson on March 5, 1801, entering upon his duties on May 2, 1801; most important contributions were helping to realize the Louisiana Purchase of 1803, presenting legal arguments against British and French violations of American neutrality on the high seas, and supporting the Embargo Act of 1807; served until March 3, 1809; elected PRESIDENT in 1808 and reelected in 1812, serving from March 4, 1809 until March 3, 1817; retired to "Montpelier," his estate in Orange County, Va.; rector of the University of Virginia, 1826; delegate to the Virginia constitutional convention, 1829; contributor to the *Federalist Papers*; died at Montpelier on June 28, 1836; interment in the private cemetery of his estate. Gaillard

Hunt, *The Life of James Madison* (1902); Irving Brant, *James Madison*, 6 vols. (1941–1961); Samuel F. Bemis, *The American Secretaries of State and Their Diplomacy* (1958); Edward M. Burns, *James Madison: Philosopher of the Constitution* (1968).

MANNING, Daniel. Born in Albany, N.Y., August 16, 1831; son of John and Eleanor (Oley) Manning; married Mary Little on October 11, 1853; father of James Hilton, Frederick Clinton, Anastasia, and Mary Elizabeth; married Mary Margaret Fryer on November 19, 1884; attended common schools; became page for state assembly in 1841; was paper boy for Albany *Atlas* (later *Argus*); *Argus* reporter for State Senate, 1858–1871; made Associated Press reporter for State Assembly in 1863; associate editor of *Argus*, 1865; chosen legislative correspondent for *Brooklyn Eagle*; became director of National Commercial Bank of Albany in 1873; made president of *Argus* in 1873; took part in Democratic state convention in Syracuse, 1874; headed New York delegation to Democratic national convention in St. Louis, 1876 and 1880; secretary of Democratic state committee in 1879; chosen vice-president of National Bank of Albany in 1881, and president, 1882; chairman of Democratic state committee, 1881, 1882, and 1883; supported Cleveland, 1884; appointed SECRETARY OF THE TREASURY in the cabinet of President Cleveland on March 6, 1885, and served from March 8, 1885 to May 31, 1887; most important contributions were desire for stoppage of silver coinage and government purchase of silver, and condemnation of reduction of treasury surplus; became director of Albany Electric Illuminating Company; died in Albany, N.Y. on December 24, 1887. Robert McElroy, *Grover Cleveland: The Man and the Statesman* (1923); Robert I. Vexler, ed., *Grover Cleveland, 1837–1908: Chronology, Documents, Bibliographical Aids* (1968).

MARCY, William Learned. Born in Sturbridge (now Southbridge), Mass., December 12, 1786; son of Jedediah and Ruth (Learned) Marcy; married Dolly Newell on September 27, 1812, and after her death married Cornelia Knower in 1825; father of six children; educated at the academy at Leicester and at Woodstock Academy, Union, Conn.; attended Brown University, graduating in 1808; taught school at Newport, R.I.; moved to Troy, N.Y.; studied law and was admitted to the bar in 1811, commencing his practice at Troy; volunteered and served in the War of 1812; recorder of Troy, 1816–1818; adjutant general of New York State Militia in 1821; editor of the *Troy Budget*, which became an organ of the Democratic party; comptroller of New York state in 1823; moved to Albany, N.Y.; associate justice of the New York Supreme Court, 1829–1831; elected to the U.S. Senate as a Democrat on December 5, 1831, serving as chairman of the Judiciary Committee; resigned his Senate seat when he won the governorship of New York in 1832; three-term governor, 1833–1839; appointed commissioner of Mexican claims by President Van Buren, 1839–1842; appointed to the cabinet of President Polk as SECRETARY OF WAR on March 6, 1845, entering upon his duties March 8, 1845 and serving until March 8, 1849; advocated the

Tariff of 1846; appointed SECRETARY OF STATE by President Pierce on March 7, 1853, serving until March 4, 1857; negotiated 24 treaties, including the significant Gadsden Purchase with Mexico and the Reciprocity Treaty with Great Britain; coined the phrase, "To the victor belong the spoils"; died at Ballston Spa, N.Y., July 4, 1857; interment in the Rural Cemetery, Albany, N.Y. Charles Allan McCoy, *Polk and the Presidency* (1957); Roy Franklin Nichols, *Franklin Pierce: Young Hickory of the Granite Hills* (1969).

MARSHALL, Freddie Ray. Born in Oak Grove, La., August 22, 1928; raised in a Baptist orphanage, from which he ran away at age fifteen; after leaving orphanage, overstated his age and enlisted in the U.S. Navy, serving during World War II; A.B. in economics, Millsaps College, Jackson, Miss., 1949; M.A. in economics, Louisiana State University, Baton Rouge, 1950; Ph.D. in economics, University of California, Berkeley, 1954; Fulbright Scholar in Finland, 1955–1956; instructor in economics, San Francisco State College, 1952; associate professor, University of Mississippi, 1953–1954; on the faculty at Louisiana State University, rising to the rank of professor, 1957–1962; professor, University of Texas, Austin, 1962–1967; professor, University of Kentucky, Lexington, 1967–1969; director, Center for the Study of Human Resources, University of Texas, 1970; chairman, Federal Committee on Apprenticeships; member, National Council on Employment Policy; president, National Rural Center; president, Industrial Relations Research Association; chairman, American Economic Association's Committee on Political Discrimination; Democrat; nominated on December 21, 1976, by President-Elect Jimmy Carter as SECRETARY OF LABOR; sworn in on January 27, 1977; contributions included raising safety standards to reduced workers' exposure to various cancer-causing chemicals; worked to make the Occupational Safety and Health Administration (OSHA) a more efficient organization; involved in negotiations that settled the United Coal Miners' strike, between December 1977 and March 1978; left office on January 21, 1981; in fall 1981, became Rapoport Professor of Economics and Public Affairs at the Lyndon B. Johnson School of Public Affairs, University of Texas at Austin; author of *The Negro in Organized Labor* (1965); *The Negro Worker* (1967); *Rural Workers in Rural Labor Markets* (1974); *Human Resources and Labor Markets* (revised 1975); *Labor Economics: Wages, Employment and Trade Unionism* (revised 1976); *The Role of Unions in the American Economy* (1976); *An Economic Strategy For the 1980's* (1981); *Work and Women in the Eighties* (1983); *Unheard Voices: Labor and Economic Policy in a Competitive World* (1987). Congressional Quarterly, *Weekly Report*, Vol. 34 (December 26, 1976); *Time* (December 27, 1976); *Time* (January 3, 1977); *U.S. News and World Report* (January 10, 1977); *Facts on File Yearbook* (1977–1980); *International Who's Who, 1988–1989*.

MARSHALL, George Catlett. Born in Uniontown, Pa., December 31, 1880; son of George Catlett and Laura (Bradford) Marshall; Episcopalian; married Elizabeth Carter Coles on February 11, 1902; married Katherine Boyce (Tupper)

Brown on October 15, 1930; attended public and private schools; entered Virginia
Military Institute in 1897, and graduated, 1901, as senior first captain of corps
of cadets; commissioned second lieutenant in U.S. Army in February 1902, sent
to Philippines, and remained there until November 1903; graduated from Infan-
try-Cavalry School at Fort Leavenworth, 1907; made first lieutenant in March
1907; graduated Army Staff College in 1908, and became instructor there; was
inspector-instructor of Massachusetts National Guard, 1911–1912; officer with
4th Infantry in Arkansas and Texas until 1913; returned to duty in Philippines,
1913–1916; became captain in 1916; went to France with 1st Division, 1917–
1919; was aide de camp to General Pershing from 1919 to 1924; lieutenant
colonel in 1923; assigned to 15th U.S. Infantry in Tientsin, China; taught at
Army War College in Washington, D.C. in 1927; commander of 8th Infantry,
1932–1933; senior instructor of Illinois National Guard from 1933 to 1936;
brigadier general in charge of 5th Infantry Brigade in 1936; assistant chief of
staff in War Plans Division, July 1938, deputy chief of staff in October 1938,
acting chief of staff in July 1939, and chief of staff with rank of general in
September 1939; General of the Army in December 1944; sent to China as
special representative of President Truman in November 1945; appointed SEC-
RETARY OF STATE in the cabinet of President Truman on January 8, 1947, and
served from January 21, 1947 to January 20, 1949; most important contribution
was Marshall Plan; appointed SECRETARY OF DEFENSE by President Truman, and
served from September 21, 1950 to September 17, 1951; most important contributions were establishment of management engineering staff under Defense
Management Committee; awarded Nobel Peace Prize in 1953; died in Washington, D.C., on October 16, 1959. R. Wilson, *General Marshall Remembered*
(1968); Forrest Pogue, *George C. Marshall, Ordeal and Hope, 1939–1943*
(1966).

MARSHALL James William. Born in Clarke County, Va., August 14, 1822;
never married; spent early years in Mount Sterling Ky.; attended local schools
of Clarke County; graduated Dickinson College, Carlisle, Pa., in 1848; became
professor at Dickinson College, 1848–1850, and was made full professor of
foreign languages, 1850–1861; appointed U.S. consul at Leeds, England in 1861,
and served until 1865; chosen first assistant postmaster general in 1869; appointed
POSTMASTER GENERAL in the cabinet of President Grant on July 3, 1874, and
served from July 7, 1874 to August 23, 1874; again made first assistant postmaster
general, and served as such until the end of Grant's administration; became
general superintendent of railway mail service; died in Washington, D.C., on
February 5, 1910. Ulysses S. Grant III, *Ulysses S. Grant, Warrior and Statesman*
(1969); Philip R. Moran, *Ulysses S. Grant, 1822–1885: Chronology, Documents,
Bibliographical Aids* (1968).

MARSHALL, John. Born in Germantown, Va., September 24, 1755; son of
Thomas Marshall, Revolutionary soldier and farmer, and Mary Isham (Keith)
Marshall; Episcopalian; married Mary Willis Ambler on January 3, 1783; edu-

cated by private tutor; attended academy in Westmoreland County, 1769–1770; volunteer in military company at outbreak of Revolution; became first lieutenant in a regiment of minutemen near Norfolk; joined Washington's army in New Jersey, promoted to captain in 1777; while in Virginia attempting to raise troops, attended lectures on law at William and Mary College; resigned commission in January 1781; admitted to bar in 1781 and began practice in Fauquier County; moved practice to Richmond two years later, competing with Patrick Henry, Alexander Cambell, Benjamin Botts, and Edmund Randolph; elected in 1782 to the General Assembly Virginia; Federalist, reelected to the General Assembly from Fauquier County in 1784, and from Henrico County in 1787; elected in 1788 to the Virginia constitutional convention, there opposed Patrick Henry who led those against the Constitution which passed by ten votes; elected to the General Assembly in 1788, holding office until spring 1791; became defender of Washington administration; was offered and declined position as attorney general and a foreign mission; declined reelection in 1792; practiced law until reelected to the General Assembly in 1797; appointed with Charles Pinckney and Francis Dana as envoys extraordinary and ministers plenipotentiary to France by President John Adams in 1797; Talleyrand's suggestion to the envoys led to the statement "Millions for defense, but not a cent for tribute"; declined Adams' offer of a seat on the U.S Surpeme Court to run for Congress; elected to the House of Representatives, seated in December of 1799, and served until 1800; appointed SECRETARY OF STATE in the cabinet of President John Adams on May 13, 1800, entered duties on June 6, 1800; while in office he held the position that the U.S should remain neutral in the conflict between France and England, supported the Ellsworth Commission negotiating with Talleyrand, and dealt with implications of the Jay Treaty in settling financial claims with England; also negotiated conflicts with Spain over Spanish-aided French privateers and interference with American shipping, as well as territorial disputes in the West Indies, Florida, and Louisiana; while Secretary, also appointed chief justice of the U.S. Supreme Court Grant on February 4, 1801, serving until he died and establishing a log of thirty volumes of cases; published *Life of Washington* (1804–1807); presided over the 1807 trial of Aaron Burr; elected to the Virginia state constitutional convention in 1829; died July 6, 1835 in Philadelphia, Pa. William Jones, *Chief Justice John Marshall: A Reappraisal* (1956); Samuel Flagg Bemis, *The American Secretaries of State and Their Diplomacy* (1958); Benjamin Palmer, *Marshall and Taney: Statesman of Law* (1966); John P. Roche, ed., *Major Opinions* (1967); Robert Faulkner, *The Jurisprudence of John Marshall* (1968).

MARSHALL, Thomas Riley. Born at North Manchester, Ind., March 14, 1854; son of Dr. Daniel M. and Martha (Patterson) Marshall: Presbyterian; married Lois Irene Kimsey on October 2, 1895; no children; moved with his family to Illinois, Kansas and Missouri, finally returning to Indiana; after attending the public schools, he entered Wabash College, Crawfordsville, Ind., graduating in 1873; studied law at Fort Wayne, Ind. and was admitted to the bar in 1875, commencing the practice of his profession in Columbia City, Ind.; taught Sunday school at the Presbyterian Church; served on the local school board; nominated and elected governor of Indiana in 1908, serving until 1913; Indiana's favorite son for president of the U.S. at the 1912 Democratic national convention; when the nomination went to Woodrow Wilson, he accepted the vice-presidential nomination; elected VICE-PRESIDENT on the Democratic ticket in November 1912, serving two full terms, from March 4, 1913, until March 3, 1921, having been reelected with President Wilson in November 1916; acted as ceremonial head of the U.S. when the President was out of the country promoting the League of Nations; coined the phrase: "What this country needs is a really good five-cent cigar"; member of the Federal Coal Commission in 1922 and 1923; trustee of Wabash College; upon retiring from political office, he returned to Indiana, making his home in Indianapolis; died in Washington, D.C., on June 1, 1925; buried in Indianapolis. Norman Gordon Levin, *Woodrow Wilson and World Politics* (1968); John Morton Blum, *Woodrow Wilson and the Politics of Morality* (1956).

MASON, John Young. Born near Hicksford (now Emporia), Va., April 18, 1799; son of Edmunds and Frances Ann (Young) Mason; married Mary Anne Port on August 9, 1821; father of eight children; after completing his preparatory education at the local schools, he attended the University of North Carolina at Chapel Hill, graduating in 1816; studied law at the Litchfield Law School, Litchfield, Conn., and was admitted to the bar in 1819, commencing the practice of law in Hicksford, Va.; elected a member of the Virginia General Assembly from 1823 to 1831; represented a Tidewater district at the constitutional convention in 1830; elected as a Democrat to the U.S. House of Representatives, serving from March 4, 1831 to November 11, 1837; a Jacksonian Democrat, he broke with President Jackson by his refusal to vote for the rechartering of the National Bank; chairman of the House committee on foreign affairs; resigned from Congress on November 11, 1837, having been appointed U.S. district judge for the eastern district of Virginia; president of the James River and Kanawha Company in 1849; delegate to the state constitutional convention of 1850; invited to join the cabinet of President Tyler as SECRETARY OF THE NAVY on March 14, 1844, serving until March 10, 1845, 1845; appointed ATTORNEY GENERAL by President Polk on March 6, 1845, entering his duties on March 11, 1845, and terminating the office on September 9, 1846; reappointed SECRETARY OF THE NAVY by President Polk from September 9, 1846 until March 8, 1849; resumed the practice of law in Richmond, Va. from 1849 to 1854; appointed U.S. minister plenipotentiary to France on January 22, 1854, serving until his death; died in Paris, France, on October 31, 1859; interred in Hollywood Cemetery, Richmond, Va. Charles Allan McCoy, *Polk and the Presidency* (1960); Robert J. Morgan, *A Whig Embattled: The Presidency under John Tyler* (1954).

MATTHEWS, Forrest David. Born at Grove Hill, Ala., December 6, 1935; son of Forrest Lee and Doris M. (Pearson) Matthews; married Mary Chapman, January 24, 1960; father of Lee Ann and Lucy McLeod; A.B., University of Alabama, 1958; M.A., University of Alabama, 1959; Ph.D., Columbia University, 1965; served in the U.S. Army, 1958–1959; was at University of Alabama as lecturer, dean of men, executive assistant to the president, executive vice president, and president from 1960 to 1975; board of directors, Alabama Community and Technical Services Agency, 1968; member, Southern Regional Educational Board, 1969 to present; member, National Programming Council for Public Television, 1970 to present; chairman, Committee on Educational Opportunities for Minority Groups, National Association State Universities and Land-Grant Colleges, 1971–1972; member, Internal Program Advisory Committee, American Council on Education, 1970 to present; Phi Beta Kappa; Phi Alpha Theta; Phi Delta Kappa; Omicron Delta Kappa; nominated on June 26, 1975, by President Gerald Ford, to the office of HEALTH, EDUCATION, AND WELFARE, and on July 22, appointment confirmed by the United States Senate; he was more conservative in his views than his predecessor, which was reflected in his opinion on bussing to achieve a racial balance; questioned the "effectiveness" of "lawful" bussing; during administration apparent widespread fraud was uncovered in the federal Medicaid program; left office on January 20, 1977, with the change in presidential administrations. Charles Moritz, ed., *Current Biography Yearbook*, 1976; National Journal, *Ford's Presidency*; Henry H. Schulte, Jr., ed., *Facts on File Yearbook, 1975*; Henry H. Schulte, Jr., ed., *Facts on File Yearbook, 1976.*

MAYNARD, Horace. Born in Westboro, Mass., August 30, 1814; son of Ephraim and Diana (Cogswell) Maynard; Presbyterian; married Laura Ann Washburn on August 30, 1840; father of Edward Maynard, U.S. consul to Turks Island in 1866, and six other children; attended common schools of Westboro; prepared at Milbury Academy; graduated Amherst College in 1838; moved to Knoxville, Tenn.; became tutor at East Tennessee College (now University of Tennessee), and made professor of mathematics, 1842–1843; studied law, was admitted to the bar in 1844, and began practice in Knoxville; candidate for district elector in 1852; was presidential elector on Whig ticket of Scott and Graham; was state elector on Fillmore ticket, 1856; elected to 35th, 36th, and 37th Congresses, and served from March 4, 1857 to March 3, 1863; received LL.D. from Amherst College in 1860; campaigned for Bell and Everett in 1860; fought withdrawal of Tennessee from Union; made attorney general of Tennessee, 1863–1865; was presidential elector on Republican ticket of Lincoln and Andrew Johnson in 1864; became trustee of East Tennessee University in 1865; chosen delegate to South Loyalist convention at Philadelphia in 1866; elected to 39th through 43d Congresses, and served from July 24, 1866 to March 3, 1875; was unsuccessful candidate for governor of Tennessee in 1874; minister to Turkey, March 9, 1875 to May, 1880; appointed POSTMASTER GENERAL in the cabinet of President Hayes on June 2, 1880, and served from August 25, 1880 to March 4, 1881; retired to private life; died in Knoxville, Tenn. on May 3, 1882; interment in Old Gray Cemetery. James Park, *Life and Services of Horace Maynard* (1903); Arthur Bishop, *Rutherford B. Hayes, 1822–1893: Chronology, Documents, Bibliographical Aids* (1969).

McADOO, William Gibbs. Born near Marietta, Ga., October 31, 1863; son of Judge William Gibbs McAdoo, officer in the Mexican War; Episcopalian; married Sarah Houston Fleming on November 18, 1885; father of Harriet, Francis, Nona, William, and Sally; after death of first wife married Eleanor Randolph Wilson, daughter of President Wilson, in a White House ceremony on May 7, 1914; father by second marriage of Ellen and Mary; divorced in 1934; married Doris I. Cross on September 14, 1935; briefly attended University of Tennessee; appointed deputy clerk of 6th U.S. Circuit Court of Appeals in Tennessee in May, 1882; admitted to the bar in 1885; practiced at Chattanooga, Tenn. until 1892 when he moved to New York City and entered into law partnership with William McAdoo (no relation), formerly assistant secretary of the navy; in 1902 became president and director of two companies later consolidated as the Hudson and Manhattan Railroad Company which, on March 8, 1904, completed the first tunnel under the Hudson River; vice-chairman of the Democratic national committee in 1912, and acting chairman for the greater part of the campaign; appointed SECRETARY OF THE TREASURY in the cabinet of President Wilson on March 6, 1913; most important contributions were conducting four successful Liberty Bond drives, establishing war risk insurance law which later was extended to include life insurance for the armed forces, and serving as chairman of the Federal Reserve Board, which he helped institute in 1913; resigned from office on December 16, 1918; served as director general of U.S. railroads during the period of government operation from 1917 to his resignation on January 10, 1919; resumed law practice first in New York and later in Los Angeles, Cal.; was a prominent candidate for the Democratic presidential nomination in the conventions of 1920 and 1924, but failed to secure nomination; chairman of the California delegation to the Democratic national conventions of 1932 and 1936; elected U.S. Senator from California in 1933 and served until his resignation in 1939; retired from political life and became chairman of the board of directors of the American President Steamship Lines; supported the League of Nations, prohibition, and women's suffrage; author of *The Challenge—Liquor and Lawlessness vs. Constitutional Government* (1928); died in Washington, D.C. on February 1, 1941. William Gibbs McAdoo, *Crowded Years* (1931); *Who Was Who in America*, vol. 1 (1943); *Encyclopedia Americana*, vol. 18 (1968).

McCLELLAND, Robert. Born in Greencastle, Pa., August 1, 1807; son of John and Eleanor Bell (McCulloh) McClelland; Methodist; married Sarah E. Sabine in 1837; graduated Dickinson College in 1829; taught; studied law; admitted to Chambersburg bar in 1831; moved to Pittsburgh, and began practice;

moved to Monroe, Mich. in 1833; organized new state government and Democratic party; active in state constitutional convention of 1835; declined offer of
first bank commissioner of state; declined attorney generalship of Michigan; was
member of board of regents of University of Michigan in 1837 and 1850; elected
to 28th, 29th, and 30th Congresses, and served from March 4, 1843 to March
3, 1849; made Cass's chief Michigan lieutenant, and aided him in presidential
campaign of 1848; member of state constitutional convention, 1850; elected
governor of Michigan in 1850 and 1852; appointed SECRETARY OF THE INTERIOR
in the cabinet of President Pierce, and served from March 7, 1853 to March 5,
1857; most important contributions were reduction of corruption in land, Indian
and pension bureaus, efficient operations of bureaus, placing Indians on reservations, settlement of annuities in goods, opposition to homestead legislation,
and making pensions available to only the indigent; returned to Michigan and
practiced law, 1857; member of Michigan constitutional convention in 1867;
toured Europe in 1870; died in Detroit, Mich. on August 30, 1880; interment
in Elwood Cemetery. Alfred Nevin, *Men of Mark of Cumberland Valley, Pennsylvania* (1876); Irving J. Sloan, ed., *Franklin Pierce, 1804–1869: Chronology,
Documents, Bibliographical Aids* (1968).

McCRARY, George Washington. Born near Evansville, Ind., August 29, 1835;
son of James McCrary, farmer, and Matilda (Forest) McCrary; Unitarian; married
Helen Galett in 1857; family moved to Van Buren County, Iowa; studied for
brief intervals at school and academy; taught country school at 18; studied law
in Keokuk with John W. Rankin and Samuel F. Miller; admitted to bar in 1856;
began practice; elected state representative, 1857; became state senator on committee of Indian affairs and judiciary, 1861–1865; entered partnership with Rankin when Miller became justice of Supreme Court, 1862; was representative to
Congress from March 4, 1869 to March 3, 1877; published *A Treatise on the
American Law of Elections*; appointed SECRETARY OF WAR in the cabinet of
President Hayes on March 12, 1877, and served until his resignation on December
11, 1879; most important contributions were withdrawal of support of federal
troops from remaining carpetbag governments in South Carolina and Louisiana,
use of federal troops in railway strike of 1877, order for troops to pursue mar-
auding Mexicans across border, which resulted in American recognition of Diaz
government, and beginning publication of *War of the Rebellion: Official Records*;
was federal judge of 8th Judicial Circuit, 1880–1884; moved to Kansas City,
Mo., 1884, and acted as general counsel for Atchison, Topeka and Sante Fe
Railroad; member of firm of Pratt, McCrary, Hagerman and Pratt; died in St.
Joseph, Mo., July 23, 1890; interment in Oakland Cemetery, Keokuk, Iowa.
B. F. Gue, *History of Iowa* (1903); C. R. Williams, *The Life of Rutherford B.
Hayes* (1914); Arthur Bishop, ed., *Rutherford B. Hayes, 1822–1893: Chronol-
ogy, Documents, Bibliographical Aids*.

McCULLOCH, Hugh. Born at Kennebunk, Me., December 7, 1808; son of Hugh and Abigail (Perkins) McCulloch; married Susan Mann in 1838; father of four children; educated at the academy at Saco, Me.; entered Bowdoin College but left in his sophomore year; Bowdoin subsequently gave him honorary A.M. degree; taught school at age 17; studied law in Boston; admitted to the bar in 1832; moved to Fort Wayne, Ind. in 1833, where he commenced the practice of law; appointed cashier and manager of the Fort Wayne branch of the State Bank of Indiana, holding that position until 1856; became president of the State Bank of Indiana from 1856 to 1863; though an opponent of the National Bank Act of 1863 which established federal control over the issue of currency by state banks, Secretary of the Treasury Chase invited him in April 1863 to assume the new office of federal comptroller of the currency which the act had created to carry out its provisions; appointed SECRETARY OF THE TREASURY by President Lincoln on March 7, 1865 and served until March 4, 1869; labored to reduce the Civil War debt and advocated the retirement of legal tender (greenback) notes and return to specie payments, a program which Congress adopted on a limited scale in 1866 and abandoned again in 1868; advocated return to gold standard; at age 75, he was reappointed SECRETARY OF THE TREASURY by President Arthur, on October 28, 1884, a post he held until the incoming President Cleveland named a successor on March 4, 1885; became a partner in Jay Cook's Banking House in 1869, in charge of the London Branch; authored *Men and Measures of Half a Century* (1888); died at "Holly Hill," Prince Georges County, Md. on May 24, 1895. Jesse Burton Hendrick, *Lincoln's War Cabinet*, (1946); George Frederick Howe, *Chester A. Arthur: A Quarter Century of Machine Politics* (1957).

McELROY, Neil Hosler. Born in Berea, Ohio, October 30, 1904; son of Malcolm Ross McElroy, teacher, and Susan Harriet (Hosler) McElroy; Episcopalian; married Mary Camilla Fry on June 29, 1929; father of Nancy Sue, Barbara Ellen, and Malcolm Neil; attended schools of Berea and Cincinnati, Ohio; received B.A. from Harvard, 1925; employed in advertising department of Proctor and Gamble Co. in Cincinnati; became manager of promotion department in 1929, established new branch in England in 1930, was made advertising and promotion manager in 1940, and was chosen president of advertising and promotion in 1943; was president of Cincinnati Citizens Planning Board in 1946; made assistant to the president of Proctor and Gamble in 1946, became vice-president and general manager, and was made president from 1948 to 1957; member of numerous Cincinnati civic organizations; trustee of Cincinnati Institute of Fine Arts; chairman of White House Conference on Education, 1955; chairman of National Industrial Conference Board in 1956; appointed SECRETARY OF DEFENSE in the cabinet of President Eisenhower, and served from October 9, 1957 to December 1, 1959; most important contributions were appointment of director of guided missiles, establishment of Advanced Research Projects Agency, launching of first successful satellite, and passage of Department of Defense Reorganization Act of 1958; chairman of the board of Proctor and Gamble, 1959–1972; director of General Electric Co., Chrysler Corp., and Equitable Assurance Society; member of National Council, United Negro College Fund; president of Commonwealth Commercial Club, 1960–1961; member of board of American Soap and Glycerine Producers, Inc.; died on November 30, 1972. Carl Borklund, *Men of the Pentagon* (1966); Dean Albertson, *Eisenhower as President* (1963).

McGRANERY, James Patrick. Born in Philadelphia, Pa., July 8, 1895; son of Patrick and Bridget (Gallagher) McGranery; Roman Catholic; married Regina T. Clark on November 29, 1939; father of James Patrick, Jr., Clark, and Regina; after attending the parochial school in his native city and Maher Preparatory School, he entered Temple University in Philadelphia, where he studied law, graduating in 1928; admitted to the bar in 1928 and began practice in Philadelphia; served in the U.S. Air Force as an observation pilot and as an adjutant in the 111th Infantry Division during World War I; worked briefly for the Curtis Publishing Co.; admitted to practice before the U.S. Supreme Court in 1939; member of the Democratic state committee from 1928 to 1932; unsuccessful candidate for district attorney in 1931; unsuccessful candidate for the U.S. House of Representatives in 1934; served as chairman of the registration committee of Philadelphia in 1935; elected as a Democrat to the 75th through 78th Congresses, serving in all from January 3, 1937 until his resignation on November 17, 1943 to accept a presidential appointment in the Justice Department; appointed assistant U.S. attorney general in November 1943, serving until October 9, 1946, at which time he was sworn in as a U.S. district judge for the eastern district of Pennsylvania by appointment of President Truman; served in this capacity until May 26, 1952, when he resigned to accept the position of ATTORNEY GENERAL in the cabinet of President Truman; invited to join on May 21, 1952, he entered upon his duties on May 27, 1952 and served until the termination of the Truman administration on January 20, 1953; upon retirement, he returned to the general practice of law in Washington, D.C.; trustee of Immaculata College, Pa.; member of the Advisory Board of Temple University Law School and Villanova College; member of the American Judicature Society and of the American Catholic Historical Society; died on December 23, 1962. Cabell B. H. Phillips, *The Truman Presidency: The History of a Triumphant Succession* (1966); Alfred Steinberg, *The Man from Missouri: The Life and Times of Harry S. Truman* (1962).

McGRATH, James Howard. Born in Woonsocket, R.I., November 28, 1903; son of James J. and Ida E. (May) McGrath; Roman Catholic; married Estelle A. Cadorette on November 28, 1929; father of David; after receiving his primary education at the Woonsocket parochial school, he entered LaSalle Academy in Providence, R.I., graduating in 1922; matriculated at Providence College, receiving his Ph.B. in 1926; studied law at Boston University, graduating in 1948; admitted to the Rhode Island bar in 1929 and commenced practice in Providence;

employed as assistant to Senator Gerry of Rhode Island; designated city solicitor of Central Falls, R.I., 1930–1934; vice-chairman of the Democratic state committee; president of the Young Men's Democratic League, 1924–1938; chairman of the Rhode Island delegation to the Democratic national convention in 1932; joined the law firm of Senator Green of Rhode Island in 1932; appointed U.S. district attorney for Rhode Island in 1934, serving until 1940; delegate to the Democratic national conventions of 1936, 1944, 1948, 1952, and 1960; associated with J. J. McGrath and Sons, his father's real estate and insurance firm; elected governor of Rhode Island in 1940, and reelected in 1942 and 1944, serving until his resignation in October 1945 to accept the appointment of U.S. solicitor general; resigned his post in October 1946 to become the Democratic candidate for U.S. Senator; elected to the U.S. Senate in November 1946 for the term commencing January 3, 1947, serving until his resignation on August 23, 1949; chairman of the Democratic national committee from 1947 to 1949; selected ATTORNEY GENERAL in the cabinet of President Truman on August 19, 1949, entering upon his duties on August 24, 1949 and serving until his resignation on April 3, 1952; unsuccessful candidate for the nomination of U.S. Senator in 1960; author of *The Power of the People* (1948) and *The Case for Truman* (1948); died on November 11, 1966. Cabell B. H. Phillips, *The Truman Presidency: The History of a Triumphant Succession* (1966); Alfred Steinberg, *The Man from Missouri: The Life and Times of Harry S. Truman* (1962).

McHENRY, James. Born in Ballymena, County Antrim, Ireland, on November 16, 1753; son of Daniel and Agnes McHenry; Roman Catholic; married Margaret Allison Caldwell on January 8, 1784; father of John; educated in Dublin; emigrated to Philadelphia in 1771; attended Newark Academy in Delaware in 1772 where he studied medicine under Dr. Benjamin Rush, and poetry; volunteered for military service in Cambridge, Mass., 1775; assigned to medical staff of a Cambridge hospital in 1776; named surgeon of 5th Pennsylvania Battalion on August 10, 1776; discharged January 27, 1777 after the November capture of Fort Washington; became senior surgeon of the Flying Hospital, Valley Forge and on May 15, 1778 he withdrew from medical practice upon appointment as Washington's secretary; transferred to Lafayette's staff in August 1780; commissioned major on May 30, 1781; resigned from active service upon election to the Maryland Senate in September 1781, where he served five years; appointed to Congress in May 1783, where he served until 1786; Maryland delegate to the 1787 Constitutional Convention; appointed SECRETARY OF WAR in the cabinet of President Washington in January 1796, and served until June 1, 1800, when he resigned at President Adams' request after political disagreements; in defense of his activities he read *A Letter to the Honorable Speaker of the House* on December 28, 1802 (published 1803); served as president of the Baltimore Bible Society, 1813; died in Baltimore, Md. on May 3, 1816. B. C. Steiner, *The Life and Correspondence of James McHenry* (1907).

McKAY, Douglas James. Born in Portland, Ore., June 24, 1893; son of Edwin Donald and Minnie Adele (Musgrove) McKay; Presbyterian; married Mabel Christine Hill on March 31, 1917; father of Douglas, Shirley, and Mary Lou; after attending the public schools of Portland, he entered Oregon State College, graduating in 1917; worked in various positions for the Portland *Oregonian* and *Daily News*; served as a lieutenant with the American expeditionary forces in France and was severely injured during the Meuse-Argonne offensive during World War I; served as captain and then major at Camp Adair, Ore., during World War II; joined the Portland firm of Dooley and Co. as an insurance salesman in 1919; became an automobile salesman for the Francis Motor Co. of Portland, becoming manager in 1932; moved to Salem, Ore. in 1927, establishing his own automobile agency, the Douglas McKay Chevrolet Co., of which he was owner until 1955; became active in Republican party politics in 1932; elected mayor of Salem, 1933–1934; elected Senator in the Oregon state legislature from Marion County in 1934, serving in that capacity, except for his period of military service, until 1949; speaker of the House during 1947 and 1948; elected governor of Oregon in 1948 and reelected in 1950; invited to join the Eisenhower cabinet as SECRETARY OF THE INTERIOR on January 21, 1953, serving until his resignation to run for U.S. Senate on June 8, 1956; during his incumbency, he opposed the transfer of lands from the Wichita Wildlife Refuge for Army use, added nine new wildlife areas, promulgated measures to govern oil and gas leasing on wildlife areas, and embarked on a long-range plan for the integration of Indians into American society, advancing a program of voluntary relocation from marginal economic areas to places where they could earn livelihoods; chairman of the President's Commission on Water Resources Policy; died in Salem, Ore., July 22, 1959. Robert J. Donovan, *Eisenhower, The Inside Story* (1956); Walter Bedell Smith, *Eisenhower's Six Great Decisions* (1956).

McKEAN, Thomas. Born in New London Township, Pa., March 19, 1734; son of William McKean, farmer and tavern keeper, and Letitia (Finney) McKean; married Mary Borden on July 21, 1763 and father of Joseph McKean, jurist; after death of first wife, married Sarah Armitage on September 3, 1774; attended Reverend Francis Allison's academy, New London; studied law; engaged as a clerk to the prothonotary of the court of common pleas, 1750–1752; appointed deputy prothonotary and recorder for the probate of wills for New Castle County, Del., 1752; admitted to the bar in 1755 and began practice in New Castle; appointed deputy attorney general for Sussex County in 1756 and served until his resignation in 1758; clerk of the Delaware House of Assembly, 1757 to 1759; went to England and continued law study at the Middle Temple in London; member of the Delaware House of Assembly, 1762–1775, serving as speaker in 1772; appointed a trustee of the New Castle County loan office in 1764 and served until 1776; member of the Stamp-Act Congress, 1765; delegate from Delaware to the General Congress in New York City in 1765; appointed chief notary for the lower counties of Delaware on July 10, 1765; commissioned a justice of the peace of the court of common pleas and quarter sessions and of the orphan's court for New Castle County, 1765; appointed collector of the port of New Castle, 1771; member of the Continental Congress, 1774–1783; a signer of the Declaration of Independence; member of the Delaware House of Representatives in 1776 and 1777, serving as speaker in 1777; served in the Revolutionary War; commissioned chief justice of Pennsylvania on July 28, 1777, and served until 1799; PRESIDENT OF THE CONTINENTAL CONGRESS from July 10, 1781 to November 5, 1781; member of the convention of Pennsylvania which ratified the U.S. Constitution, December 12, 1787; elected governor of Pennsylvania and served from 1799 to 1808; retired from public life; compiled *The Acts of the General Assembly of Pennsylvania*, 2 vols. (1782), and collaborated with Edmund Physick in *A Calm Appeal to the People of the State of Delaware* (1793); also co-author, with James Wilson, of *Commentaries on the Constitution of the United States of America* (1792); died in Philadelphia, Pa. on June 24, 1817; interment in Laurel Hill Cemetery. J. H. Peeling, *The Public Life of Thomas McKean, 1734–1817* (1929); E. C Burnett, *The Continental Congress* (1964).

McKENNA, Joseph. Born in Philadelphia, Pa., August 10, 1843; son of John and Mary (Johnson) McKenna; Roman Catholic; married Amanda F. Borneman in 1869; father of three girls; attended Catholic seminaries in Benicia, Cal.; graduated Benicia Collegiate Institute, 1865; turned to law after abandoning priesthood; admitted to bar, 1865; began practice in Fairfield, Solano County, Cal.; served as county attorney, 1866–1870; was representative in the state legislature, 1875–1876, and unsuccessful Republican candidate for speakership; defeated, due to religion, as candidate for U.S. House of Representatives in 1876, 1878, and 1880; elected to U.S. House, and served from March 4, 1885 until his resignation on March 28, 1892; appointed by President Benjamin Harrison as U.S. circuit court judge for the 9th circuit, 1892; appointed ATTORNEY GENERAL in the cabinet of President McKinley on March 5, 1897, and served until January 25, 1898; nominated, December 16, 1897, for associate justice of U.S. Supreme Court, confirmed January 21, 1898, and served until his resignation on January 25, 1925; died in Washington, D.C., November 21, 1926. O. T Shuck, *History of the Bench and Bar of California* (1901); H. L Carson, *The History of the Supreme Court of the United States* (1902); Robert Dallek, *McKinley's Decision, War on Spain* (1970); Margaret K. Leech, *In the Days of McKinley* (1959).

McKENNAN, Thomas McKean Thompson. Born in Dragon Neck, New Castle County, Del., March 31, 1794; son of Colonel William McKennan, soldier in the Revolutionary war, and Elizabeth (Thompson) McKennan; Presbyterian; married Matilda Lourie Bowman on December 6, 1815; father of William, Thomas, Isabella, Jacob Bowman, Thomas McKean Thompson, Anne Elizabeth, John Thompson, and Matilda Bowman; moved with family to western Virginia,

1797, and then to Washington, Washington County, Pa.; graduated Washington College (later Washington and Jefferson College) in 1810; tutor of ancient languages, 1813–1814; studied law in the office of Parker Campbell of Washington, Pa.; admitted to the bar, 1814; deputy attorney general for the county, 1815–1817; served as trustee of Washington College, 1818–1852; member of Washington town council, 1818–1831; became official of Washington (Pa.) and Pittsburgh Railroad Company, 1831; member of U.S. House of Representatives from March 4, 1831 to March 3, 1839; was presidential elector on Harrison-Tyler ticket, 1840; was member of Congress, May 3, 1842–March 3, 1843, completing an unexpired term; active Whig in tariff of 1842; headed Pennsylvania's presidential electors, 1848; appointed SECRETARY OF THE INTERIOR in the cabinet of President Fillmore, and served from July 23, 1850 to August 14, 1850, leaving because of disagreement with administration; became first president of Hempfield Railroad Company, Inc., and remained so until death; founder of Washington Female Seminary; founder of Washington County Agricultural Society; died in Reading, Pa., July 9, 1852; interment in Washington Cemetery, Washington, Pa. Boyd Crumrine, *The Courts of Justice, Bench and Bar of Washington County* (1902); Robert J. Rayback, *Millard Fillmore* (1959).

McKINLEY, William, Jr. Born in Neles, Ohio, January 29, 1843; son of William and Nancy Campbell (Allison) McKinley; Methodist Episcopalian; married Ida Saxton on January 25, 1871; father of Katherine and Ida; attended the public schools, Poland Academy, and Allegheny College in Meadville, Pa.; taught school near Poland, Ohio in 1859; enlisted as a private in the 23d Regiment, Ohio Volunteer Infantry, on June 11, 1861; engaged in combat at the Battle of Carnifax Ferry on September 10, 1861; promoted to sergeant; commissioned second lieutenant in September 1862; promoted to first lieutenant, captain, and finally major, in 1865; discharged on July 26, 1865; studied law in Mahoning County, Ohio, and was admitted to the bar in 1867, commencing practice in Canton County, Ohio; elected prosecuting attorney of Stark County, Ohio, from 1869 to 1871; elected as a Republican to the U.S. House of Representatives, serving from March 4, 1877 until March 3, 1883; presented credentials as a member-elect to the 48th Congress, but was unseated by Jonathan H. Wallace, who contested his election; reelected to the U.S. House of Representatives in the 49th, 50th, and 51st Congresses, serving in all from March 4, 1885 to March 3, 1891; unsuccessful candidate for reelection to the 52d Congress in 1890; delegate to the Republican national conventions of 1885, 1888, and 1892; unsuccessful candidate for the Republican presidential nomination in June 1892; elected governor of Ohio in 1891 and reelected in 1893, serving until January 13, 1896; elected PRESIDENT on the Republican ticket in November 1896 and reelected in November 1900; inaugurated on March 4, 1897 and served until he was shot by an anarchist assassin, Leon Czolgosz, on September 6, 1901, while attending the Pan American Exposition in Buffalo, N.Y.; the third President to be assassinated; the fifth President to die in office; died in

Buffalo, September 14, 1901; interment in the McKinley Monument in Canton, Ohio. Margaret K. Leech, *In the Days of McKinley* (1959); Paul W. Glad, *McKinley, Bryan, and the People* (1964).

McLANE, Louis. Born in Smyrna, Del., May 28, 1786; son of Allan McLane, Revolutionary war soldier and speaker of Delaware legislature, and Rebecca (Wells) McLane; married Catherine Mary Milligan in 1812; father of Robert Milligan, Congressman and diplomat; attended private schools; served as midshipman in navy on U.S.S. *Philadelphia* from 1798–1799; entered Newark College in Delaware, 1801, but did not graduate; read law under James A. Bayard; was admitted to the bar in 1807; began practice in Smyrna; joined volunteer company in War of 1812 in defense of home town and Baltimore; elected to Congress as a Jeffersonian Republican, 1816, took seat on March 4, 1817, and served until March 3, 1827; supported Crawford, 1824; was reelected to 20th Congress, but resigned to take seat in Senate, March 4, 1827–March 16, 1829; supported Jackson, 1828; offered post of attorney general, but refused; appointed envoy extraordinary and minister plenipotentiary to Great Britain and served from March 18, 1829 to July 6, 1831; appointed SECRETARY OF THE TREASURY in the cabinet of President Jackson, and served from August 8, 1831 to May 28, 1833; most important contribution was urging Congress to recharter the Bank of the United States although President Jackson opposed it; appointed SECRETARY OF STATE in the cabinet of President Jackson, and served from May 29, 1833 to June 26, 1834; most important contributions were firmness in dealings of claims and boundaries with Mexico, negotiation with Great Britain over Northeast boundary, pressure on France to pay spoilation claims, and introduction of orderly procedure into operation of department; president of Morris Canal and Banking Company; moved to Baltimore, 1837, to accept presidency of Baltimore and Ohio Railroad Company, and remained in that capacity until his resignation in 1847; appointed U.S. minister to Great Britain by President Polk to negotiate Oregon question, June 1845–August 1846; offered position of commissioner to Mexico to gain ratification to Treaty of Guadalupe Hidalgo, 1848, but refused; member of Maryland constitutional convention, 1850–1851; died in Baltimore, Md., October 7, 1857; interment in Greenmount Cemetery. S. F. Bemis, *The American Secretaries of State and Their Diplomacy* (1928); Ronald Shaw, *Andrew Jackson, 1767–1845: Chronology, Documents, Bibliographical Aids* (1969).

McLAUGHLIN, Ann Dore. Born in Chatham, N.J., November 16, 1941; daughter of Edward Joseph and Maria (Koellhofer) Lauenstein; married William Dore in 1963, divorced in 1964; married John J. McLaughlin, August 23, 1975; B.A. Marymount College, 1963, after spending junior year at the University of London; supervised network communications at ABC Television in New York City, 1963–1966; account executive, Myers-Infoplan International, 1969–1971; managed John McLaughlin's unsuccessful race for the Senate seat in Rhode

Island, 1970; director of communications, Presidential Election Commission, 1971–1972; director of office of public information, Environmental Protection Agency, 1973–1974; Union Carbide Corp., 1974–1977; McLaughlin and Co., 1977–1981; assistant secretary for public affairs for the Treasury Department, 1981–1984; undersecretary of the interior, 1984–1987; on October 15, 1987, Secretary of Labor William Brock resigned to manage the presidential bid of Senator Robert Dole, and on December 17, 1987, McLaughlin was sworn in as SECRETARY OF LABOR in the Ronald Reagan administration; remained at the post in the George Bush administration; opposed both increase in the minimum wage and organized labor's demand for plant closing notification; in general supported Reagan-Bush policies toward unions and unionism. *New York Times* (December 18, 1987); *Who's Who, 1988; Ms Magazine* (March 1988).

McLEAN, John. Born in Morris County, N.J., March 11, 1785; son of Fergus McLean, weaver turned farmer, and Sophia (Blockford) McLean; married Rebecca Edwards in 1807; later married Sarah Bella (Ludlow) Garrard in 1843; moved with family to Morgantown, Va., 1789, then to Jessamine, Ky. and later to Maysville, Ky., and settled on a farm near Lebanon, now Warren County, Ohio, 1799; attended schools as opportunity permitted; worked; hired two private tutors at 16 years of age; indentured at 18 for two years to a clerk of Hamilton County court at Cinicinnati, worked, read law with Arthur St. Clair, and joined a debating club; was admitted to the bar, 1807, and began practice of law in Lebanon; founded weekly newspaper, the *Western Star*; elected as War Democrat to Congress from the district of Cincinnati in October 1812, and was reelected in 1814; declined candidacy for Senate, 1815; resigned seat in Congress 1816, and became judge of Supreme Court of Ohio, serving until 1822; appointed commissioner of land office by President Monroe, 1822; appointed POSTMASTER GENERAL in the cabinet of President Monroe, June 26, 1823, and continued under John Quincy Adams, serving from July 1, 1823 to March 9, 1829; most important contributions were removal of unfaithful and incompetent officials and holding of management contractors to agreements; declined cabinet portfolios of Secretary of War and Secretary of the Navy in Jackson's administration; pursued interests in literary field; nominated associate justice of U.S. Supreme Court by President Jackson, confirmed by Senate on March 7, 1829, was assigned to 7th circuit, took seat in January 1830, and served until death; died in Cincinnati, Ohio, April 4, 1861; interment in Spring Grove Cemetery. Charles Warren, *The Supreme Court in United States History* (1922); Ian Elliot, ed., *James Monroe, 1758–1831: Chronology, Documents, Bibliographical Aids* (1969); H. F. Bremer, ed., *John Adams, 1735–1826: Chronology, Documents, Bibliographical Aids* (1967).

McNAMARA, Robert Strange. Born in San Francisco, Cal., June 9, 1916; son of Robert James McNamara, wholesale shoe industry executive, and Clara Nell (Strange) McNamara; Presbyterian; married Margaret Craig on August 13,

1940; father of Margaret Elizabeth, Kathleen, and Robert; attended public schools of Piedmont, Cal.; received B.A. from University of California, Berkeley in 1937; earned M.B.A. from Harvard, 1939; worked for Price Waterhouse and Company; assistant professor of business administration at Harvard, 1940–1943; consultant to U.S. Department of War in 1942; sent to England as civilian consultant in 1943; commissioned captain in U.S. Army Air Force in 1943, rose to lieutenant colonel in 1946, was discharged in April 1946, and was made colonel in Air Force Reserve; became manager in Ford Motor Company, 1946–1949, and was made comptroller in 1949; appointed assistant general manager of Ford division in 1953, elected vice-president and manager in 1955, made director in 1957, and became president, 1960–1961; was director of Scott Paper Company; appointed SECRETARY OF DEFENSE in the cabinet of President Kennedy, continued under Lyndon B. Johnson, and served from January 21, 1961 to February 29, 1968; most important contributions were new planning-program-ming-budget system, increase in nuclear defense bases, preparedness of forces during Berlin crisis and Cuban missile crisis, establishment of Defense Supply Agency and Defense Intelligence Agency with Defense Intelligence School, formation of Office of Education and Manpower Resources; accepted position as president of International Bank for Reconstruction and Development on November 29, 1967, and took over duties in 1968; awarded U.S. Legion of Merit, 1946; in 1972 elected to presidency of the World Bank for the second time and returned for a third term in 1977; during his tenure dealt with the growing inability of the Third World to pay back its debt, and expanded the bank's loans in inflation-adjusted figures from less than $1 billion to $11.5 billion annually; since retirement from the World Bank in 1981, has kept a busy schedule working with nonprofit organizations including the Ford Foundation, the Brookings Institution, and the Barbara Ward Fund, as well as independent efforts on such issues as nuclear arms, the population explosion, world hunger, East-West relations, and the anti-Apartheid movement in South Africa. Robert J. Art, *TFX Decision: McNamara and the Military* (1968); Hugh Sidey, *John F. Kennedy, President* (1963); *Current Biography Yearbook, 1987.*

McREYNOLDS, James Clark. Born in Elkton, Ky., February 3, 1862; son of John Oliver McReynolds, surgeon and gynecologist, and Ellen (Reeves) McReynolds; never married; graduated Vanderbilt University in 1882 and received law degree at the University of Virginia in 1884; served briefly as private secretary to U.S. Senator (later Supreme Court Justice) Howell E. Jackson; began law practice in Nashville, Tenn.; in 1896, was unsuccessful candidate for Congress as a ''gold'' Democrat; professor of law at Vanderbilt University, 1900–1903; appointed assistant U.S. attorney general by President Theodore Roosevelt on June 1, 1903 to serve until January 1, 1907; appointed by the attorney general as special counsel for the government, and from 1907 to 1912 was active in prosecuting violators of the Sherman Anti-trust Act; appointed ATTORNEY GENERAL on March 5, 1913 in the cabinet of President Wilson; most important contributions were dissolving the Union Pacific-Southern Pacific railroad merger, initiating the government case against the alleged monopoly practices of the American Telephone and Telegraph Company, prohibiting price-fixing practices of the Elgin (Ill.) Board of Trade, helping to prepare the Covington Bill to create an Interstate Trade Commission, and prosecuting the monopolies of the National Wholesale Jewelers Association and the New York, New Haven and Hartford Railroad Company; appointed asociate justice of the U.S. Supreme Court in August 1914 by President Wilson to succeed Justice Horace H. Lurton; confirmed by U.S. Senate, and took his seat on October 12, 1914; serving until his retirement on February 1, 1941; during the administration of President Franklin Roosevelt, became known as a staunch defender of states' rights and a literal interpretation of the Constitution, voting against more New Deal measures than any other justice; died in Washington, D.C. on August 24, 1946. Arthur S. Link, *Woodrow Wilson and the Progressive Era, 1910–1917* (1954), and *Woodrow Wilson: The New Freedom* (1965); Leon H. Canfield, *The Presidency of Woodrow Wilson* (1966).

MEESE, Edwin, III. Born in Oakland, Calif. December 2, 1931; son of Edwin Meese, Jr., treasurer and tax collector for Alameda County, and Leone Meese; Lutheran; married Ursula Herrick on September 6, 1959; father of Scott, Dana Lynn, and Michael; attended Oakland High School; obtained B.A. from Yale University in 1953; entered Boalt Law School of the University of California where his legal studies were interrupted by two years of service to the army, as a lieutenant in military intelligence; earned LL.B. degree in 1958; worked as deputy district attorney in Alameda County for eight years, from 1958 to 1967; selected as California Governor Ronald Reagan's secretary on clemency and extradition, November 1966; elected as California legal affairs secretary from 1969 to 1974; was vice-president for administration at Rohr Industries, an aerospace firm located in Chula Vista, Calif., from January 1975 to May 1976; elected as executive assistant and chief of staff to Governor Ronald Reagan, 1975–1976; founded and became the director of the Center for Criminal Justice Policy and Management at the University of San Diego Law School in 1977; was on the Ronald Reagan-George Bush Committee from 1980 to 1981; joined Reagan's staff as an advisor on key political issues, 1980; appointed as counselor to the president on November 14, 1980, and served until 1985; served as director of transition for President-Elect Ronald Reagan from 1981 until 1985; appointed ATTORNEY GENERAL on February 25, 1985, and resigned on August 12, 1988; most important contributions were as a liaison to the grand jury, played an active role in the development of a drug abuse testing program, lobbied before the legislature on behalf of the state district attorney's association, supervised arrests of over seven hundred participants in disturbances associated with the Free Speech Movement at the University of California at Berkeley in December 1964, assisted in putting down antidraft protests in Oakland and Berkeley in the mid–1960s, represented Reagan when violence erupted at San Francisco State College and at the University of California at Berkeley in 1969, reported to the Un-American Activities Committee of the U.S. House of Representatives on the activities of antiwar students and in August 1966 testified in favor of a bill to make the aiding of Communist forces in Vietnam a crime; accomplishments also included abolition of the federal Legal Services Corporation, opposition to a peacetime draft, and disapproval of the insanity defense; he justified preventative detention, complained of the exclusion of illegally gathered evidence from trials, and defended President Reagan's pardon of two FBI officials convicted of un-authorized break-ins; served as director of transition for President-Elect Ronald Reagan from 1981 until 1985; became a fellow at the Heritage Foundation and at the Hoover Institution; honorary LL.D: Delaware Law School, Widener University of San Diego, Valparaiso University, California Lutheran College; vice-president of the First Lutheran Church in El Cajun, Calif.; contributed publications to professional journals. *Current Biography, 1981; Who's Who, 1987; U.S. Government Manual, 1987–1988; Facts on File, 1988.*

MEIGS, Return Jonathan, Jr. Born in Middletown, Conn., November 17, 1764; son of Return Jonathan Meigs, soldier and pioneer, and Joanna (Winborn) Meigs; married Sophia Wright in 1788; father of Mary; graduated Yale College in 1785; studied law, was admitted to the Ohio bar in 1788 and moved to Marietta, Ohio (then Northwest Territory) to practice law; fought in Indian wars of that area; appointed one of judges of territorial government, 1798; elected representative of Marietta region in territorial legislature, 1799; supported statehood in 1801; appointed chief justice of supreme court of new state of Ohio, 1803, and served until his resignation in October 1804; appointed commander of U.S. troops in St. Charles district of Louisiana, brevetted colonel, and served, 1804–1806; judge of supreme court of Louisiana, 1805–1806; returned to Ohio, 1806, and called to Richmond, Va. to participate in Burr's trial; was transferred to serve as U.S. district court judge for Michigan Territory, 1807–1808; resigned to become candidate for governor of Ohio, and was elected, but declared ineligible due to prolonged absence from state; elected U.S. senator to fill vacancy caused by resignation of John Smith, took seat on December 12, 1808, was reelected in 1809, and served until May 1, 1810; ran for governor in 1810, elected, reelected in 1812 and served until his resignation in 1814; appointed POSTMASTER GENERAL in the cabinet of President Madison on March 17, 1814, and continued under President Monroe, serving from April 11, 1814 to June 30, 1823, resigning due to ill health; deficits and irregularities in awarding of mail-contracts led to investigations by Congress in 1816 and 1821, but neither resulted in more than charges of inefficiency; returned to Marietta, Ohio, and died there on March 29, 1824; interment in Mound Cemetery. F. B. Dexter, *Biographical Sketches of the Graduates of Yale College* (1907); Ian Elliot, ed., *James Madison, 1751–1836: Chronology, Documents, Bibliographical Aids* (1969); Ian Elliot, ed., *James Monroe, 1758–1831: Chronology, Documents, Bibliographical Aids* (1969).

MELLON, Andrew William. Born in Pittsburgh, Pa., March 24, 1855; son of Thomas Mellon, judge and banker, and Sara (Negley) Mellon; Presbyterian; married September 12, 1900 to Nora McMullen, and divorced July 1912; father of Alisa and Paul; attended the public schools; studied at the Western University of Pennsylvania until 1872; started a lumber and building business in Mansfield, Pa. in 1872; joined father's banking firm in 1874, becoming owner in 1882; leading organizer in 1889 of the Union Trust Company, and its first president; helped organize the Mellon oil producing and refining enterprises and the Gulf Corporation; one of the founders of the Aluminum Company of America (AL-COA); also engaged in development of coal, coke, and iron enterprises; when the firm of T. Mellon & Sons was incorporated as the Mellon National Bank, he became first president; at one time was director or officer of more than sixty corporations; appointed SECRETARY OF THE TREASURY in the cabinet of President Harding on March 4, 1921, to remain in that office under Presidents Coolidge and Hoover; most important contributions were instituting the "Mellon Plan" of tax revision which reduced corporation and personal taxes, reducing the national debt by nearly $8 billion, serving as chairman of the War Debt Commission, enforcing Prohibition, revising paper currency, and reorganizing the federal farm loan system; resigned from his cabinet post on February 12, 1932 following his appointment as ambassador to Great Britain by President Hoover; served as ambassador until the end of the Hoover administration, resigning on March 7, 1933 and returning to the Mellon National Bank; helped found the National Gallery of Art in Washington, D.C.; author of *Taxation: The People's Business* (1924); died on August 26, 1937 at Southampton, Long Island; interment in Allegheny Cemetery, Pittsburgh, Pa. Philip H. Love, *Andrew Mellon* (1929); Harvey O'Conner, *Mellon's Millions* (1933); William L. Mellon and Boyden Sparkes, *Judge Mellon's Sons* (1948); Joseph Brandes, *Herbert Hoover and Economic Diplomacy* (1962).

MEREDITH, Edwin Thomas. Born on a farm near Avoca, Iowa, December 23, 1876; son of Thomas Oliver and Minerva Jane (Marsh) Meredith; married Edna C. Elliott on January 8, 1896; father of Edwin Thomas, Jr. and Mildred Marie; attended the country schools until he was 16 years of age and then entered the business school of Highland Park College (later Des Moines University) in 1894; worked on the *Farmer's Tribune*, a family-operated farm newspaper devoted to Populism; received the *Farmer's Tribune* from his grandfather as a wedding gift, whereupon he turned it into an organ of statewide circulation; founded *Successful Farming* in 1902, selling his interest in the *Farmer's Tribune*; purchased the *Dairy Farmer* in 1922 and founded *Fruit, Gardens and Home* (later *Better Homes and Gardens*) that same year; an avant-garde believer in truth in advertising, he promised to reimburse any of his subscribers who were defrauded by any of his advertisers, promising to expose the malefactors; initially a Republican, he later became affiliated with the Democratic party; became the Democratic candidate for U.S. Senator in 1914 and Democratic candidate for

Governor in 1916, but was defeated in both contests; appointed director of the Chicago Federal Reserve Bank, 1918–1920; on February 2, 1920, he became SECRETARY OF AGRICULTURE in the cabinet of President Wilson, serving until March 4, 1921; a champion of "farm relief," tariff reform, adequate military preparedness, tax reform, the World Court, and the League of Nations; director of the U.S. Chamber of Commerce, 1915–1919 and 1923–1928; died in Des Moines, Iowa on June 17, 1928. William Diamond, *The Economic Thought of Woodrow Wilson* (1943); John Morton Blum, *Woodrow Wilson and the Politics of Morality* (1956).

MEREDITH, William Morris. Born in Philadelphia, Pa., June 8, 1799; son of William Meredith, lawyer and bank president, and Gertrude Gouverneur (Ogden) Meredith; married Catherine Keppele on June 17, 1834; received B.A. from University of Pennsylvania in 1812 at the age of 13; admitted to Philadelphia bar in December 1817, but because of youth had to wait for successful practice; associated with John Sergeant and Horace Binney; served in the state legislature from 1824 to 1828; became president of select council of Philadelphia, 1834–1849; appointed U.S. attorney for eastern district of Pennsylvania by President William H. Harrison on March 15, 1841; candidate for U.S. Senate, 1849; appointed SECRETARY OF THE TREASURY in the cabinet of President Taylor, continued under Fillmore, and served from March 8, 1849 to July 22, 1850; most important contributions were argument for protective tariff in annual report, and disapproval of compromise measures of 1850; returned to practice of law in Philadelphia; joined new Opposition or People's Party in Pennsylvania; delegate to Peace Convention of 1861; made attorney general of state by Governor Curtin, 1861–1867; first president of Union League Club in Philadelphia; appointed one of counsel of U.S. in *Alabama* claims case; president of state constitutional convention, November 1872–June 1873; died in Philadelphia, August 17, 1873. H. R. Mueller, *The Whig Party in Pennsylvania* (1922); Homan Hamilton, *Soldier in the White House* (1966); Robert J. Rayback, *Millard Fillmore* (1959).

METCALF, Victor Howard. Born in Utica, N.Y., October 10, 1853; son of William Metcalf and Sarah P. (Howard) Metcalf; married Emily Corrine Nicholsen on April 11, 1882; father of two children; attended public schools of Utica; went to Utica Free Academy; attended Russell's Military Institute at New Haven, Conn.; entered Yale College in 1872; graduated Yale Law School, 1876; graduated from law department of Hamilton College in 1877; during college vacations studied law in offices of Francis Kernan and Horatio and John F. Seymour; admitted to practice before Supreme Court of Connecticut, 1876; practiced in Utica, 1877–1879; moved to Oakland, Cal. in 1879; formed law partnership with George D. Metcalf; became prominent in Republican party councils; elected to Congress on Republican ticket, 1898 and reelected, 1900 and 1902; served on committee of ways and means, 59th and 60th Congresses;

appointed SECRETARY OF COMMERCE AND LABOR in the cabinet of President Theodore Roosevelt on July 1, 1904, and served until December 17, 1906; most important contributions were reduction of $300,000 in departmental expenses in one year, catching and breaking up of operations of Japanese trespassers upon Alaskan salmon fisheries, organization of bureau of manufacturers, investigations of exclusion of Japanese students from public schools by San Francisco school board in October 1906; appointed SECRETARY OF THE NAVY by President Roosevelt on December 17, 1906 and served until December 1, 1908; most important contribution was expansion of navy regarding number of ships and men; retired to private life; died February 20, 1936; interment in Mountain View Cemetery. James F. Rhodes, *McKinley and Roosevelt Administrations 1897–1909* in *History of the United States*, vol. 9 (1922); George E. Mowry, *Era of Theodore Roosevelt, 1900–1912* (1958).

MEYER, George von Lengerke. Born in Boston, Mass., June 24, 1858; son of George A. Meyer, an East India merchant, and Helen (Parker) Meyer; Episcopalian; married Marion Alice Appleton on June 25, 1885, father of Julia, Alice, and George von Lengerke, Jr.; attended Nobel's School in Boston; graduated Harvard College with B.A. in 1879; received LL.D. from Harvard, 1911; entered old mercantile house of Alpheus H. Hardy and Company, and remained two years; became member of firm Linder and Meyer, established as East Indian merchant at India Wharf, Mass. by father in 1818; elected to Boston common council and served, 1889–1890; nominated by both parties for member of board of aldermen, 1901, and elected without opposition; Republican representative to state legislature, 1892–1897, and speaker of lower house, 1894–1897; appointed ambassador to Italy by President McKinley, 1900–1905; transferred by President Theodore Roosevelt to Russia in March 1905, and served as ambassador until 1907; appointed POSTMASTER GENERAL in the cabinet of President Roosevelt on March 4, 1907, and served until March 6, 1909; most important contributions were recommendation of the establishment of postal savings banks, put into use experimentally a service of automobile mail collection; appointed SECRETARY OF THE NAVY in the cabinet of President Taft on March 6, 1909, and served until March 1913; trustee of Provident Institution for Savings; died March 9, 1918. James F. Rhodes, *McKinley and Roosevelt Administrations, 1897–1909* in *History of the United States*, vol. 9 (1922); George E. Mowry, *Era of Theodore Roosevelt, 1900–1912* (1958); Norman M. Wilensky, *Conservatives in the Progressive Era* (1965).

MIDDLETON, Henry. Born near Charleston, S.C., in 1717; son of Arthur Middleton, acting colonial governor, and Sarah (Armory) Middleton; married to Mary Williams in 1741 and father of five sons and seven daughters, including Arthur Middleton, Revolutionary leader and signer of the Declaration of Independence, and Thomas Middleton, Revolutionary patriot; after death of first wife, married Maria Henrietta Bull in 1762; later married Lady Mary Mackenzie in January 1776; educated at home and in England; justice of the peace, 1742–1780; member of the provincial House of Commons, 1742–1755, and speaker, 1745–1747, 1754, and 1755; commissioned officer of the horse of the provincial forces in 1743; commissioner of Indian Affairs, 1755; also commissioner of the church act, of free schools, and internal improvements; member of His Majesty's Council for South Carolina from 1755 until his resignation in 1770; member of the provincial convention in 1774; chosen as a representative of the Continental Congress in July 1774; after the resignation of Peyton Randolph, elected second PRESIDENT OF THE CONTINENTAL CONGRESS and served from October 22, 1774 to May 10, 1775; president of the South Carolina Congress and a member of the Council of Safety in 1775 and 1776; appointed, along with his son Arthur, a member of the committee to frame a temporary constitution for the state, 1776; member of the legislative council under the transition government, 1776–1778; member of the state Senate, 1778–1780; large landowner and planter; died on June 13, 1784 in Charleston, S.C.; interment at the Church of St. James Parish, Berkeley County, S. C. Edward McCrady, *The History of South Carolina in the Revolution* (1902); Edmund C. Burnett, *The Continental Congress* (1964).

MIFFLIN, Thomas. Born in Philadelphia, Pa., January 10, 1744; son of John Mifflin, merchant and public official and Elizabeth (Bagnell) Mifflin; Quaker; married to Sarah Morris on March 4, 1767; attended a Quaker school; was graduated from the University of Pennsylvania in 1760; prepared for a mercantile career in the counting house of William Coleman for four years; went to Europe, 1764, returned to the colonies, 1765, and entered business as a merchant in partnership with his brother, George; member of the American Philosophical Society, 1765–1799; member of the colonial legislature, 1772–1774; member of the Continental Congress, 1774–1776; assisted in the recruiting and training of troops for service in the Continental Army; major and chief aide-de-camp to General Washington, July 4, 1775; major and quartermaster general of the Continental Army, 1775; colonel, 1775; brigadier general, 1776; major general, 1777–1779; appointed a member of the board of war, November 7, 1777; trustee of the University of Pennsylvania, 1778–1791; member of the State Assembly, 1778–1779; again a member of the Continental Congress, 1782–1784; elected PRESIDENT OF THE CONTINENTAL CONGRESS on November 3, 1783 and served from December 13, 1783 until June 3, 1784; speaker of the state House of Representatives, 1785–1788; delegate to the federal Constitutional Convention, 1787; elected to the supreme executive council of Pennsylvania in 1788 and served as its president, 1788–1790; president of the state constitutional convention, 1790; elected governor of Pennsylvania and served three terms, 1790–1799; again a member of the state House of Representatives in 1799 and 1800; died on January 19, 1800 in Lancaster, Pa.; interment in the front yard of Trinity Lutheran Church. William Rawle, "Sketch of the Life of Thomas Mifflin," *Memoirs of the Historical Society of Pennsylvania*, vol. 2 (1830); E. C. Burnett,

Letters of Members of the Continental Congress (1921–1931); E. C. Burnett, *The Continental Congress* (1964).

MILLER, G. William. Born in Sapulpa, Okla., March 9, 1925; son of James Dick Miller, a furniture salesman, and Hazel Deane (née Orrick) Miller; married Ariadna Rogojarsky on December 22, 1946; no children; graduated Borger High School, 1941; attended Amarillo Junior College, 1941; entered the U.S. Coast Guard Academy in Connecticut, and received his B.S. degree in marine engineering in 1945; served as U.S. Coast Guard officer, Pacific area, 1945–1949; received his J.D. degree from the University of California School of Law, Berkeley, 1952; admitted to the bar of California, 1952; New York bar, 1953; as a lawyer worked with Cravath, Swaine, and Moore, a prestigious Wall Street firm, 1952–1956; joined Textron Inc., Providence, R.I., 1956; became vice-president, 1957, and treasurer, 1958; became Textron's president and chief operating officer, 1960; in 1966 served as campaign committee chairman for the reelection of U.S. senator Clairborne Pell; he was also a Rhode Island delegate to the Democratic national convention and, subsequently, the national chairman of Businessmen for Hubert Humphrey-Edmund Muskie, 1968; became chief executive of Textron, 1968–1978; Miller's aggressive aquisition techniques gave Textron record sales that year, adding up to $1.7 billion; chairman of the board, 1974–1978; on December 28, 1977, named by Jimmy Carter to be the new chairman of the Board of Governors of the Federal Reserve System on the expiration of Arthur Burn's term on January 31, 1978, and served through 1979; named SECRETARY OF THE TREASURY in the cabinet of President Carter on December 28, 1977, and served from August 6, 1979, until January 21, 1981; after a two-year investigation, beginning in 1978, the Securities and Exchange Commission (SEC) claimed Textron had made improper payments overseas; more specifically, the SEC said that as Textron's chairman, Miller knew that expenses were being padded by unnamed Department of Defense officials; Miller denied all the allegations and Carter did not ask Miller to step down from his position as secretary of the treasury; private investments and ventures, 1981–1983; chairman, G. Miller and Co. Inc., 1982– ; director of Federated Department Stores, Repligen Corp., Private Satellite Network, Georgetown Industries Inc., Harman International, International Power Machines Corp., Kleinwort Benston Australian Income Fund, Inc.; chairman, Supervising Committee, Schroder Venture Trust, 1983– ; chairman, The Conference Board (1977–1978), National Alliance of Business (1978), U.S. Industrial Payroll Savings Committee (1977); member of the state bar of California; clubs; Chevy Chase (Maryland), The Brook (New York), Burning Tree (Maryland), Lyford Cay (Bahamas). New York Times Biographical Service (1977); *Current Biography, 1979; Time* (February 11 and March 24, 1980); *International Who's Who*, 1989.

MILLER, William Henry Harrison. Born in Augusta, N.Y., September 6, 1840; son of Curtis Miller, farmer, and Lucy (Duncan) Miller; married Gertrude A. Bunce in December 1863; father of Florence, Jessie, Samuel, and four other children; raised on father's farm; attended county schools; studied at Whitestown Seminary; graduated Hamilton College, Clinton, N.Y. in 1861; taught school in Maumee, Ohio; joined 84th Ohio Infantry in May 1862, and mustered out in September 1862 as second lieutenant; studied law with Morrison R. Waite in Toledo, Ohio; read law in Peru, Ind. while employed as superintendent of schools; admitted to the bar in 1865, and commenced practice; became county school examiner; moved to Fort Wayne and opened practice in partnership with William H. Coombs, 1866; went into law partnership with Benjamin Harrison and Hines at Indianapolis in 1874; received LL.D. from Hamilton College, 1889; was personal advisor to Harrison; appointed ATTORNEY GENERAL in the cabinet of President Harrison, and served from March 5, 1889 to March 5, 1893; most important contributions were investigation of candidates for federal judicial positions, personal attention given to cases involving anti-lottery laws, interstate commerce act, Sherman anti-trust act and constitutionality of McKinley tariff; practiced law in firm of Miller, Winter and Elam until 1910; died in Indianapolis on May 25, 1917. H. J. Sievers, ed., *Benjamin Harrison, 1833–1901: Chronology, Documents, Bibliographical Aids* (1969).

MILLS, Ogden Livingston. Born in Newport, R.I., August 23, 1884; son of Ogden and Ruth T. (Livingston) Mills; Episcopalian; married Margaret Stuyvesant Rutherford on September 20, 1911, the marriage ending in divorce in 1919; married Mrs. Dorothy (Randolph) Fell on September 2, 1924; no issue from either marriage; after attending the Browning School in New York City, he entered Harvard University, graduating in 1904; entered Harvard Law School, graduating in 1907; admitted to the bar in 1908, commencing the practice of his profession in New York City; unsuccessful candidate for election to 63d Congress in 1912; delegate to the Republican national conventions at Chicago in 1912, 1916 and 1920; elected to the New York State Senate from 1914 to 1917, when he resigned to enlist in the U.S. Army; served with the rank of captain until the close of hostilities; president of the New York Tax Association; elected to U.S. House of Representatives on the Republican ticket to the 67th, 68th and 69th Congresses, serving in all from March 4, 1921 to March 3, 1927; unsuccessful candidate for the governorship of New York in 1926; appointed under-secretary of the treasury by President Coolidge on February 1, 1927, serving from March 4, 1927 until February 11, 1932; invited to join President Hoover's cabinet as SECRETARY OF THE TREASURY on February 12, 1932, serving until March 3, 1933; engaged as an author and a lecturer following his political career; authored *What Of Tomorrow?* (1935); *Liberalism Fights On* (1936); *The Seventeen Million* (1937); died in New York City on October 11, 1937; interment in St. James Churchyard, Staatsburg, N.Y. Eugene Lyons, *Our Unknown Ex-President, A Portrait of Herbert Hoover*; Dorothy Horton McGee, *Herbert Hoover: Engineer, Humanitarian, Statesman* (1965).

MITCHELL, James Paul. Born in Elizabeth, N.J., November 12, 1900; son of Peter J. and Anna C. (Driscoll) Mitchell; Roman Catholic; married Isabelle Nulton on January 22, 1923; father of Elizabeth; attended St. Patrick's parochial school and Batten High School in Elizabeth, from which he graduated in 1917; worked in a grocery store and then opened a store of his own in Rahway, N.J.; became an expeditor in the Western Electric Co. plant at Kearny, N.J. in 1926; assisted the New Jersey Relief Administration in directing the relief and work activities of Union County, 1931; took charge of labor relations in the New York City division of the Works Program Administration, 1936; director of industrial personnel for the War Department, 1941; member of the National Building Trades Stabilization Board; alternate for the undersecretary of war in the War Manpower Commission; director of personnel and industrial relations for R. H. Macy and Co. of New York City, 1945; vice-president in charge of labor relations and operations at Bloomingdale Brothers, New York City, in 1947; served on the personnel advisory board of the Hoover Commission on the organization of the Executive Branch of the government in 1948; chairman of the executive committee of the Retail Labor Standards Association of New York; designated assistant secretary of the Army in charge of manpower and reserve forces affairs, July 1953; joined the Eisenhower cabinet as SECRETARY OF LABOR on January 20, 1954, serving until the termination of that administration on January 20, 1961; during his incumbency, he established the new career service position of deputy undersecretary of labor and three positions of deputy assistant secretary of labor, also adding an office of research and development to the Department; he was the first secretary to determine prevailing minimum wages for the soft coal industry and later for other industries, under the provisions of the Walsh-Healey Act; died on October 19, 1964. Emmett John Hughes, *The Ordeal of Power: A Political Memoir of the Eisenhower Years* (1963); Arthur Larson, *Eisenhower: The President Nobody Knew* (1968).

MITCHELL, John Newton. Born in Detroit, Mich., September 15, 1913; son of Joseph Charles and Margaret Agnes (McMahon) Mitchell; Presbyterian; married Martha (Beall) Jennings in 1955; father of John and Jill by a previous marriage and of Martha by his second wife; moved as a child to Long Island, N.Y. and attended the public schools of Blue Point and Patchogue; attended Jamaica High School, Queens, N.Y.; attended Fordham University, 1932–1934, and was admitted to the law school before completing the requirements for the bachelor's degree; graduated from Fordham Law School in 1938 and was admitted to the bar that same year; attended St. John's University Law School, 1938–1939; associate in the law firm of Caldwell and Raymond, 1938–1942, becoming a partner in 1942; during World War II commanded several squadrons of torpedo boats in the U.S. Navy; returned to his law firm which merged in 1967 with the firm of Richard M. Nixon to become Nixon, Mudge, Rose, Guthrie, Alexander, and Mitchell; campaign manager for Nixon in the 1968 presidential race; appointed ATTORNEY GENERAL in the Cabinet of President

Nixon on December 11, 1968, and took the oath of office on January 22, 1969; most important contributions have been seeking expansion of legal telephone wiretapping, submitting a proposal to extend the 1965 Voting Rights Act, submitting proposed legislation for the enactment and enforcement of stronger narcotics laws, and urging law enforcement on college campuses; resigned on February 1, 1972, to help work for the reelection of President Nixon; subsequently indicted for criminal actions during the Watergate affair; found guilty of five counts of criminal violations and sentenced to four years in prison; after serving most of his sentence, he returned to private life; died on November 9, 1988, in New York City. *U.S. News and World Report*, vol. 65 (December 23, 1968), p. 21; *N.Y. Times Magazine* (August 10, 1969), pp. 10–11; *U.S. News and World Report*, vol. 67 (July 28, 1969), pp. 9–10; Earl Mazo and Stephen Hess, *Nixon: A Political Portrait* (1969); John J. Sirica, *To Set the Record Straight* (1979); *New York Times* (November 10, 1988).

MITCHELL, William DeWitt. Born at Winona, Minn., September 9, 1874; son of William Mitchell, jurist, and Frances (Merritt) Mitchell; Presbyterian; married to Gertrude Bancroft on June 27, 1901; father of William and Bancroft; attended the Lawrenceville School, N.J.; studied electrical engineering at the Sheffield Scientific School of Yale University for two years; attended the University of Minnesota and was graduated in 1895; studied law and received his degree from the University of Minnesota in 1896; admitted to the bar and began practice with the firm of Stringer and Seymour; second lieutenant in the 15th Minnesota Volunteer Infantry during the Spanish-American War, also acting judge advocate for the 2d U.S. Army Corps, 1898, engineer officer, 1899, and captain and adjutant in the Minnesota national guard, 1899–1901; resumed law practice in St. Paul and became partner in the firm of Butler, Mitchell, and Doherty; colonel in the Minnesota infantry during World War I; regional counsel for the U.S. Railroad Administration, 1919; resumed law practice and became head of the firm of Mitchell, Doherty, Rumble, Bunn, and Butler, 1922; appointed solicitor general on June 4, 1925 by President Coolidge; appointed ATTORNEY GENERAL in the cabinet of President Hoover on March 5, 1929; most important contributions were successfully arguing before the U.S. Supreme Court his contentions that the Jay Treaty of 1794 was abrogated by the War of 1812 and that in the case of a Presidential "pocket veto" the bill in question does not become law, and supervising Prohibition legislation; served until the end of the Hoover administration, March 3, 1933; joined the New York law firm of Taylor, Capron, and Marsh, April 1933; headed the court cases against Germany in the Black Tom and Kingsland sabotage cases, 1939; special prosecutor in the federal grand jury investigation of publication of alleged confidential Navy information; appointed chief counsel for the Congressional Pearl Harbor investigating committee, 1945; member of a panel of jurists upholding the right of the United Nations Secretary General to fire staff employees belonging to the American Communist Party, December 1952; died in Syosset, Long Island, N.Y. on

August 24, 1955. Albert U. Romasco, *Poverty of Abundance: Hoover, the Nation, the Depression* (1965); Harris G. Warren, *Herbert Hoover and the Great Depression* (1967).

MONDALE, Walter Frederick. Born in Ceylon, Minn., January 5, 1928; son of Theodore Sigvaard, a minister, and Claribel Hope (Cowan) Mondale; Presbyterian; married Joan Adams, December 27, 1955; father of Theodore, Eleanor, and William; attended the public schools of Martin County, and Macalester College in St. Paul, Minn.; B.A. cum laude, University of Minnesota, 1951; served in U.S. Army as corporal, 1951–1953; graduated LL.B., University of Minnesota Law School, 1956; admitted to the Minnesota bar in 1956 and practiced law in Minneapolis, 1956–1960; served as attorney general for the state of Minnesota, 1960–1964; member of the President's Consumer Advisory Council, 1960–1964; appointed as a Democrat to the U.S. Senate, December 30, 1964, to fill the vacancy caused by the resignation of Hubert H. Humphrey for the term ending January 3, 1967; elected Senator of the United States, 1966 and 1972; served 1967–1976; elected VICE-PRESIDENT OF THE UNITED STATES, November 2, 1976; served from January 21, 1977, to January 20, 1981; was the most active vice-president up to that time; was fully briefed on all issues including being the first vice-president to be trained in how to respond in a nuclear war situation should the president be incapacitated; ran as Democratic nominee for president in 1984, winning only the state of Minnesota and the District of Columbia; member of Washington, D.C., law firm Winston and Strawn since 1981; currently regent Smithsonian Institution; member of American, Minnesota, and Hennepin County bar associations; member Minnesota Safety Council, American Association for the United Nations, American Legion, and Democratic Farm Labor Party; on editorial board of *Minnesota Law Review*, 1955–1956; authored "Accountability of Power: Toward a Responsible Presidency" (1976). George Douth, "Leaders in Profile of the United States Senate" (1972); *Atlantic Monthly* (December 1974); *Biographical Directory of the American Congress* (1774–1971); *Who's Who in America, 1975–1976; Congressional Quarterly Weekly* (July 19, 1976); *New York Times* (July 16, 1976); Jimmy Carter, *Keeping Faith* (1982); *Who's Who in American Politics, 1987–1988.*

MOODY, William Henry. Born on a farm at Newbury, Mass., December 23, 1853; son of Henry L. and Melissa Augusta (Emerson) Moody; unmarried; graduated Phillips Andover Academy, 1872; received B.A. from Harvard College in 1876; studied law in office of Richard H. Dana of Boston; admitted to bar, 1878, and began practice in Haverhill; city solicitor, 1888–1890; elected U.S. district attorney for eastern district of Massachusetts in 1890, and served until 1895; elected to the 54th Congress, and reelected in 1896, 1898, and 1900, serving in all from 1895 to 1902; appointed SECRETARY OF THE NAVY in the cabinet of President Theodore Roosevelt on May 1, 1902, and served until June 30, 1904; most important contributions were establishment of naval bases at

Guantanamo, Cuba, and at Subig Bay in the Philippines, and establishment of first joint army and navy board to simplify and harmonize work; appointed ATTORNEY GENERAL by President Roosevelt on July 1, 1904, and served until December 16, 1906; most important contributions were securement of decision from U.S. Supreme Court to the effect that officers of a corporation cannot refuse to testify on a plea that they may incriminate the corporation nor withhold books and papers in proper legal proceedings, broke up "peonage," and instituted famous suit against the government by Standard Oil Company in 1906; became associate justice of the Supreme Court on December 17, 1906, and served until ill health forced his resignation on November 20, 1910; retired to Haverhill, Mass., where he died on July 2, 1917. George Whitelock in *Green Bag* (June 1909); Theodore Roosevelt, in *Outlook* (November 5, 1910); James F. Rhodes, *McKinley and Roosevelt Administrations, 1897–1909* in *History of the United States*, vol. 9 (1922); George E. Mowry, *Era of Theodore Roosevelt, 1900–1912* (1958).

MONROE, James. Born in Westmoreland County, Va., April 28, 1758; son of Spence and Elizabeth (Jones) Monroe; Episcopalian; married Elizabeth Kortright in 1785; father of Eliza Kortright and Maria Hester; attended private school operated by Parson Archibald Campbell; pursued classical studies; attended William and Mary College in Williamsburg, Va., leaving to enter the Continental Army in 1776; became a lieutenant in the 3d Virginia Regiment on June 24, 1776; severely wounded in the Battle of Harlem Heights; military commissioner for Virginia in 1780, with rank of lieutenant colonel; elected to the State Assembly in 1782; member of the Continental Congress from 1783 until 1786; resumed the study of law; admitted to the bar in 1786; commenced his practice at Fredericksburg, Va.; reelected to the State Assembly in 1786; delegate to the state convention to consider the federal constitution in 1788; elected to the U.S. Senate on November 9, 1790, resigning on May 27, 1794, upon his designation as minister plenipotentiary to France, by George Washington, on May 28, 1794; elected governor of Virginia from 1799 until 1802; reappointed minister plenipotentiary to France by President Jefferson on January 12, 1803; appointed minister plenipotentiary to Great Britain by President Jefferson, serving from 1803 until 1807; returned to America in 1808; reelected to State Assembly in 1810 and 1811; elected governor of Virginia again in 1811; appointed SECRETARY OF STATE in the cabinet of President Madison on April 2, 1811, entering his duties on April 6, 1811 and serving until March 3, 1817; appointed secretary of war, *ad interim*, by President Madison on January 1, 1813 and served until October 1, 1814; the War of 1812 broke out during his secretaryship and he continually justified war with Great Britain on the grounds of impressments of seamen; elected fifth PRESIDENT of the United States, serving two terms, from March 4, 1817 until March 3, 1825; became regent of the University of Virginia in 1826; member and president of the Virginia constitutional convention of 1829; moved to New York City in 1831 and died there on July 4, 1831; interment in

Marble Cemetery in New York City; reinterment in Hollywood Cemetery, Richmond, Va. on July 4, 1858. Arthur Styron, *The Last of the Cocked Hats; James Monroe and the Virginia Dynasty* (1945); William Penn Cress, *James Monroe* (1946).

MORGENTHAU, Henry, Jr. Born in New York, N.Y. on May 11, 1891; son of Henry Morgenthau, ambassador to Turkey, and Josephine (Sykes) Morgenthau; Jewish; married Elinor Fatman on April 17, 1916; father of Henry, Robert, and Joan; married Marcelle Puthon on November 21, 1951; attended private schools; went to Exeter Academy; studied at Cornell University, 1909–1910 and 1912–1913; served in World War I as lieutenant in U.S. Navy; received LL.D. from Temple University in 1938; published *American Agriculturalist*, 1922–1933; chairman of Governor Roosevelt's Agricultural Advisory Commission, 1929; member, then chairman, of Taconic State Park Commission, 1929–31; member of New York State Conservation Commission, 1931; member of Washington Farm Board; headed Farm Credit Administration in 1933; chosen acting secretary of the treasury in 1933; was undersecretary of the treasury in 1934; Secretary of the Treasury *ad interim* from January 1, 1934 to January 8, 1934; appointed SECRETARY OF TREASURY in the cabinet of President Franklin Roosevelt on January 8, 1934, continued under Truman, and served until July 17, 1945; most important contributions were plan to transform Germany from an industrial power to an agricultural country, defense of dollar devaluation against competitive devaluation of foreign nations, and buying and selling foreign money to obtain monetary stabilization; general chairman of United Jewish Appeal, 1947–1950; member of American Financial and Development Corps for Israel from 1951 to 1954; died on February 6, 1967. John M. Blum, *From the Diaries of Henry Morgenthau, Jr.*, 3 vols. (1959–1967); H. F. Bremer, ed., *Franklin D. Roosevelt, 1882–1954: Chronology, Documents, Bibliographical Aids* (1969).

MORRILL, Lot Myrick. Born in Belgrade, Me., May 3, 1812; son of Peaslee and Nancy (Macomber) Morrill; Methodist; married Charlotte Holland Vance in 1845; father of four daughters; after attending the local schools and nearby academy, he taught school in order to obtain the tuition to attend Waterville (now Colby) College, 1830–1831; studied law in Readfield, Me.; admitted to the bar in 1839; moved to Augusta in 1841; became chairman of the state Democratic committee in 1849, retaining that office until 1856; elected to the Maine House of Representatives in 1854; elected to the State Senate in 1856 and elected president of that body by the Democratic majority; converted to the Republican party in 1856; elected Republican governor in 1858, 1859, and 1860; by appointment of the state legislature, he was sent to the U.S. Senate to succeed Hannibal Hamlin; popularly reelected to the Senate, he served from 1861 to 1869; member of the Peace Convention of 1861; led the debate which resulted in the act emancipating the slaves in the District of Columbia; advocate of an act giving suffrage to the black residents of the District; voted for the impeachment of President Andrew Johnson; reelected to the U.S. Senate in 1869, he resigned on July 7, 1876 to join the cabinet of President Grant as SECRETARY OF THE TREASURY, which post he held until March 9, 1877; appointed collector of customs in Portland, Me. by President Hayes on March 13, 1877; died in Augusta, Me., January 10, 1883; interment in Forest Grove Cemetery, Augusta. William Best Hesseltine, *Ulysses S. Grant, Politician* (1953); Allan Nevins, *Hamilton Fish: The Inner History of the Grant Administration* (1936).

MORTON, Julius Sterling. Born in Adams, N.Y., April 22, 1832; son of Julius Dewey and Emeline (Sterling) Morton; Episcopalian; married Caroline Joy French on October 30, 1854; father of four sons, one of whom, Paul, was Secretary of the Navy under Theodore Roosevelt; attended the University of Michigan, 1852–1853, and was expelled for his independence of constituted authorities; received B.A. from Union College in Schenectady, N.Y. in 1856; moved to Nebraska in 1854 and became editor of the *Nebraska City News*; member of Nebraska territorial legislature in the 2d assembly, 1855–1856, and in the 4th assembly, 1857–1858; served as acting governor; ran two times for territorial delegate to Congress; was four times Democratic nominee for governor; Nebraska legislature delegated April 22, his birthday, Arbor Day, for the purpose of encouraging tree planting; appointed SECRETARY OF AGRICULTURE in the cabinet of President Cleveland on March 6, 1893 and served in that office until March 4, 1897; most important contributions were emphasis on economy and temporary elimination of free distribution of seeds by congressmen as waste of money; undertook editorship of *The Illustrated History of Nebraska* in 1897; began publication of the *Conservative*, 1898; died in Lake Forest, Ill., April 27, 1902. J. M. Woolworth, *In Memory of Caroline Joy French Morton* (1882); R. W. Furnas, *Arbor Day* (1888); Henry J. Ford, *Cleveland Era* (1921); Margaret Leech, *In the Days of McKinley* (1959).

MORTON, Levi Parsons. Born in Shoreham, Vt., May 16, 1824; son of Rev. Daniel Oliver and Lucretia (Parsons) Morton; Episcopalian; married Lucy Young Kimball on October 15, 1856; father of three children; attended public schools; studied at Shoreham Academy; was clerk in general store in Enfield, Mass. from 1838 to 1840; taught school in Boscawen, N.H., 1840 to 1841; pursued mercantile interests in Hanover, N.H., 1845; moved to Boston in 1850; dealt in dry goods in New York City in 1854; became head of Morton, Grinnell and Company on January 1, 1855; banker in New York City firm of Drexel, Morgan and Company in 1870; unsuccessful candidate for Congress in 1876; chosen commissioner to Paris Exposition in 1878; elected to U.S. House of Representatives in 1878, reelected 1880, and served from March 4, 1879 to March 21, 1881; made U.S. minister to France, August 5, 1881 to May 14, 1885; elected VICE-PRESIDENT in the administration of President Benjamin Harrison, and served from March 4, 1889 to March 3, 1893; governor of New York, 1895–1897; founded Morton Trust Company in 1899; joined Guaranty Trust Company in

1909; traveled; died in Rhinebeck, N.Y. on May 16, 1920; interment in Rhinebeck Cemetery. J. G. Leach, *Memoranda Relating to the Ancestry and Family of Hon. Levi Parsons Morton, Vice President of the United States, 1889–93* (1894); H. J. Sievers, ed., *Benjamin Harrison, 1833–1901: Chronology, Documents, Bibliographical Aids* (1969).

MORTON, Paul. Born in Detroit, Mich., May 22, 1857; son of Julius Sterling Morton, Secretary of Agriculture under Cleveland, and Caroline Joy (French) Morton; Episcopalian; married Charlotte Goodridge on October 13, 1880; father of Caroline and Pauline; attended public schools in Nebraska City, Neb.; clerk in land office of Burlington and Missouri River Railroad at Burlington, Iowa, for two years; moved to Chicago, where he became clerk in general freight office of Chicago, Burlington and Quincy Railroad, and by 1890 had become general freight agent; became vice-president of Colorado Fuel and Iron Co., 1890; was president of Whitebreast Fuel Co., 1890–1896; became third vice-president of Atchison, Topeka and Santa Fe Railroad in 1896, and became second vice-president in 1898; originally a Democrat, he became a Republican in 1896; appointed SECRETARY OF THE NAVY in the cabinet of President Theodore Roosevelt on July 1, 1904, and served until July 1, 1905; devoted rest of life to rehabilitation of Equitable Co.; died in New York City, February 19, 1911. Obituary, New York *Evening Post* (January 20, 1911); *Nation* (June 3, 1904 and June 22, 1905); Edwin Lefevre, "Paul Morton—Human Dynamo," *Cosmopolitan Magazine* (October 1905); James F. Rhodes, *McKinley and Roosevelt Administrations, 1897–1909* in *History of the United States*, vol. 9 (1922); George E. Mowry, *Era of Theodore Roosevelt, 1900–1912* (1958).

MORTON, Rogers Clark Ballard. Born in Louisville, Ky., September 14, 1914; son of David C. and Mary (Ballard) Morton; married Anne Jones on May 27, 1939; father of David and Anne; attended Woodbury Forest Preparatory School until June 1933; graduated Yale in June 1937 with a B.A. in business and political science; entered the U.S. Army in 1941 as a private and was discharged four years later with the rank of captain; helped manage his father's milling business, Ballard and Ballard, and served as the firm's president from October 1947 through June 1951; upon merger of the company with Pillsbury in July 1951, became vice-president of Pillsbury; served as U.S. Representative from Maryland 1st district during the 88th through 91st Congresses; delegated a representative to the Republican national convention of 1968, and was appointed chairman of the 1969 convention; chosen by President Nixon to succeed Walter Hickel as SECRETARY OF THE INTERIOR on December 11, 1970 and took office January 29, 1971; resigned to accept position as SECRETARY OF COMMERCE on April 25, 1975, serving until November 3, 1975, at which time he resigned to work for the reelection of President Gerald Ford; served as campaign chairman from March 30 to August 25, 1976, after which he continued to work for the President; reentered private business in November 1976; director and member of the Executive Committee of the Civil Advisory Board Air Training Command of the Air Force, and director of Atlas Chemical Industries, Inc., died April 19, 1979. *New York Times* (December 12–15, 1970); *Who's Who in America; Who's Who in American Politics; New York Times* (April 20, 1979).

MOSBACHER, Robert Adam. Born in Mt. Vernon, N.Y., March 11, 1927; Presbyterian; son of Emil and Gertrude (Schwartz) Mosbacher; children from his first marriage are Diane, Robert, Kathryn, and Lisa Mosbacher Mears; married Georgette Paulsin in 1985; B.S., Washington and Lee University, 1947; independent oil and gas producer since 1948; chairman and chief executive officer, Mosbacher Energy Co., Houston, Tex., director, Texas Commerce Bancshares, Houston, Tex., Director N.Y. Life Insurance Co.; N.Y. board of directors, Choate School, Wallingford, Conn.; director Aspen Institute, Center for Strategic and International Studies; chairman Board of Visitors M. D. Anderson Hospital; cochairman, National Finance Committee of the Republican party; national finance chairman, George Bush for President committee; director Texas Heart Institute; member and past chairman; Mid-Continent Oil and Gas association; director, executive committee, American Petroleum Institute; past chairman, National Petroleum Council; past chairman, All American Wildcatters Association; past president, American Association Petroleum Landmen; appointed by President Bush as SECRETARY OF COMMERCE on January 31, 1989; articles include "How Business Can Help," *New York Times* (1981); "Standing Tall in Texas," *Forbes* (September 12, 1983); "Congress Needs to Clean House," *Dallas Morning News* (1984); "Heading Off a Political Tragedy," *Houston Chronicle. Who's Who in America, 1985; New York Times* (November 8, 1988 and January 1989); *Washington Post* (January 30, 1989).

MUELLER, Frederick Henry. Born in Grand Rapids, Mich., November 22, 1893; son of John Frederick and Emma Matilde (Oesterle) Mueller; Episcopalian; married Mary Darrah on November 6, 1915; father of Marcia Joan and Frederick Eugene; while still attending the public schools, he began an apprenticeship at age 13 in his father's furniture-manufacturing company; entered Michigan State University in East Lansing, graduating with a B.S. in mechanical engineering in 1914; became a partner in his father's business in 1914, advancing to general manager in 1922, and later, president, which position he held until his retirement in 1955; president of the Furniture Mutual Insurance Company from 1936 to 1946; served as president and general manager of Grand Rapids Industries, Inc. from 1941 to 1946; president of the United Hospital Fund, Inc. from 1948 to 1955, and of Butterworth Hospital from 1945 to 1955; director of the People's National Bank of Grand Rapids; named assistant secretary of commerce for domestic affairs by President Eisenhower on November 22, 1958; promoted to undersecretary of commerce in November 1958; invited to join the Eisenhower cabinet as SECRETARY OF COMMERCE on August 6, 1959, serving until January 20, 1961; member of the governing board of Michigan State University; founder of the Grand Rapids Furniture Makers Guild, serving as its president from its inception until 1941; after leaving government became a member of the boards of directors of Fruehauf Trailer Co. and Detroit Edison Co.; retired 1974; died August 31, 1976. Arthur Larson, *Eisenhower: The President Nobody Knew* (1968); Emmett John Hughes, *The Ordeal of Power: A Political Memoir of the Eisenhower Years* (1963); *New York Times* (September 2, 1976).

MURPHY, Frank. Born in Harbor Beach, Mich., April 13, 1890; son of John T. and Mary (Brennan) Murphy; Roman Catholic; bachelor; after receiving his elementary and secondary education at Harbor Beach public schools, he entered the University of Michigan at Ann Arbor, graduating in 1912; studied law at the University of Michigan, receiving his LL.B. in 1914, and was admitted to the bar that same year; pursued graduate studies at Lincoln's Inn, London and at Trinity College, Dublin; became clerk in law office of Monaghan and Monaghan of Detroit; enlisted in the U.S. Army during World War I, serving as a first lieutenant and then as a captain of the infantry with the American expeditionary forces in France and with the army of occupation in Germany following the Armistice; designated chief assistant U.S. attorney of the eastern district of Michigan, 1919–1920; resumed private practice, 1920–1923; instructor in law at the University of Detroit, 1923–1927; judge of the recorder's court of Detroit, 1923–1930; elected mayor of Detroit in 1930, resigning on May 1, 1933 to accept appointment as governor general of the Philippine Islands, serving during 1935 and 1936; appointed the first U.S. high commissioner to the Philippines; elected governor of Michigan, serving from 1936 to 1938; appointed ATTORNEY GENERAL by President Franklin D. Roosevelt on January 17, 1939, serving until January 17, 1940, when he joined the U.S. Supreme Court; while attorney general, he created a Civil Liberties Unit in the Criminal Division of the Justice Department; died while still a Supreme Court justice, in Detroit, on July 19, 1949. Leonard Baker, *Back to Back: The Duel Between FDR and the Supreme Court* (1967); Paul K. Conkin, *The New Deal* (1967).

MUSKIE, Edmund Sixtus. Born in Rumford, Me., March 28, 1914; son of Stephen Muskie, a tailor, and Josephine (Czarnecki) Muskie; Roman Catholic; married Jane Frances Gray on May 29, 1948; father of Stephen Oliver, Ellen Muskie Allen, Melinda Muskie Stanton, Martha, and Edmund Sixtus, Jr.; graduated from Stephens High School, 1932; attended Bates College, 1932–1936; elected to Phi Beta Kappa and became class president; received his B.A. degree cum laude, in 1936, and was awarded a scholarship to Cornell University Law School; earned his LL.B. degree in 1939; was admitted to the Massachusetts bar later in the year and to the Maine bar in 1940; U.S. District Court, 1941, N.Y. state 1981; U.S. Supreme Court, 1981, Washington D.C., 1981; took over a law practice in Waterville, Me., 1940; enlisted in the U.S. Naval Reserve in 1942, and was released to inactive duty as lieutenant in 1945; returned to Waterville, Me., to practice law, 1945–1955; was elected to the Maine House of

Representatives in 1946 and served 1947–1951; Democratic floor leader, 1949–1951; district director for Maine Office of Price Stabilization, 1951–1952; executive director American Veterans, 1951; city solicitor, Waterville, Me., 1954–1955; Democratic candidate for the governorship of Maine against Burton M. Cross, 1954; won the election in September 1954, despite state's Republican orientation; served as governor of the State of Maine, 1955–1959; former chairman and member, Democratic Senatorial Campaign Committee; chairman, Senate subcommittees on Environmental Pollution, Senate Environment, and Public Works Committee; member, Intergovernmental Relations, Senate Governmental Affairs Committee, 1959–1978; U.S. senator from Maine, 1959–1980; Senate assistant majority whip, 1966–1980; won Democratic vice-presidential nomination, 1968; chairman, Senate Budget Committee, 1974–1980; member, Senate Foreign Relations Committee, 1970–1974, 1979–1980; appointed SECRETARY OF STATE on May 8, 1980, and served in office until January 21, 1981; partner, Chadbourne and Parke, Washington, D.C., 1982–   ; named director of Nestle infant formula panel, May 4, 1982; named to National Security Council review board November 26, 1986; former member, Special Committee on Aging, Executive Committee of National Governors' Conference; chairman, Roosevelt Campobello International Park Commission; received thirty honorary degrees from various colleges and universities; awards include Presidential Medal of Freedom (1981), Notre Dame Laetre Medal, (1981); member, Academy of Arts and Sciences, Maine and Massachusetts bar associations, Lions, Amvets, VFW, and American Legion; legal residence, Bethesda, Md.; author of *Journeys*, 1972.

Current Biography, 1968; David Nevin, *Muskie of Maine* (1972); *Facts on File* (1982 and 1986); *Who's Who in the East, 1986; New York Times Biographical Service* (1987); *Who's Who in American Politics, 1987–1988; Who's Who in America, 1988; Who's Who, 1989.*

N

NAGEL, Charles. Born on a farm in Colorado County, Tex., August 9, 1849; son of Dr. Hermann F. and Friedericke (Litzmann) Nagel; married first to Fannie Brandeis, on August 4, 1876, and upon her death, to Anne Shepley on May 5, 1895; father of Hildegard, Mary Shepley, Edith, Charles, Jr., and Anne Dorothea; educated in a boy's boarding school and a high school in St. Louis, Mo.; studied law at Washington University and graduated in 1872; traveled to Europe, where he pursued his education, studying Roman law and political economy at the University of Berlin in Germany; returning to St. Louis in 1873, he was admitted to the bar and commenced his practice there; elected to the Missouri state legislature in 1881; elected judge of the Supreme Court of Missouri in 1893; lecturer at the St. Louis Law School from 1886 until 1910; member of the Republican national committee from 1908 to 1912; invited to join the cabinet of President Taft as SECRETARY OF COMMERCE AND LABOR on March 5, 1909, a position he held until March 1913; president of the Boy Scouts of St. Louis in 1918; died in St. Louis, Mo. on June 5, 1940. Norman M. Wilensky, *Conservatives in the Progressive Era: The Taft Republicans of 1912* (1965); Henry Fowler Pringle, *The Life and Times of William Howard Taft* (1930).

NELSON, John. Born in Fredericktown, Md., June 1, 1794; son of Roger Nelson, brigadier general in Revolutionary army and member of Congress; never married; graduated William and Mary College in 1811; admitted to bar in 1813, and began practice in Fredericktown; held local offices; elected to U.S. Congress, and served from March 4, 1821 to March 3, 1823; made chargé d'affaires to the Two Sicilies, October 24, 1831 to October 15, 1832; appointed ATTORNEY GENERAL in the cabinet of President Tyler, and served from July 1, 1843 to March 5, 1845; while attorney general, served as secretary of state *ad interim*,

February 29–March 6, 1844, following the death of Secretary Upshur in the U.S.S. *Princeton* disaster; died in Baltimore, Md. on January 28, 1860; interment in Greenmount Cemetery. Robert Seager, *And Tyler Too* (1963); Hugh R. Fraser, *Democracy in the Making: The Jackson-Tyler Era* (1938).

NEW, Harry Stewart. Born in Indianapolis, Ind., December 31, 1858; son of John Chalfont New, who held several important government positions under Presidents Grant, Arthur, and W. H. Harrison, and of Melissa New; member of the Central Christian Church; married first to Kathleen Virginia Mulligan on October 18, 1888, and after her death to Catherine McLaen on August 18, 1891; attended the public schools and, in 1880, Butler University in Indianapolis; served with the *Indianapolis Journal* as reporter, editor, part owner, and publisher, 1878–1903; member of the Indiana State Senate, 1896–1900; captain and assistant adjutant general in the Army during the Spanish-American War; president of Bedford Stone and Construction Co., 1903; delegate to the Republican national conventions of 1896, 1912, 1920, and 1924; member of the Republican national committee, 1900–1912, and served as its chairman in 1907 and 1908; elected as a Republican to the U.S. Senate and served from March 4, 1917 to March 3, 1923; member of the Committee on Military Affairs and the Committee on Foreign Relations; unsuccessful candidate for renomination in 1922; first candidate to use radio in a political campaign; appointed POSTMASTER GENERAL in the cabinet of President Harding on February 27, 1923; reappointed by President Coolidge in 1925 and served until March 4, 1929; most important contributions were expanding the airmail service by substituting private airline contracts for government-owned planes, and the establishment of a government-owned and -operated postal motor service; retired from active business pursuits and resided in Washington, D.C.; U.S. Commissioner to the Century of Progress Exposition in Chicago, 1933; died in Baltimore, Md. on May 9, 1937; interment in Crown Hill Cemetery, Indianapolis, Ind. Edward Elwell Whiting, *President Coolidge: A Contemporary Estimate* (1923); Francis Russell, *The Shadow of Blooming Grove: Warren G. Harding and His Times* (1968).

NEWBERRY, Truman Handy. Born in Detroit, Mich., November 5, 1864; son of John Stoughton Newberry, elected to Congress in 1878, and Helen Parmelee (Handy) Newberry; married Harriet Josephine Bornes on February 7, 1888; father of Carol B. and Phelps; attended Michigan Military Academy at Orchard Lake; went to Charlie Institute in New York City; attended Reed's School at Lakeville, Conn.; graduated Yale University, 1885; assisted in father's business and took over Newberry interests upon his death; superintendent of construction, payment, and freight and passenger agent of Detroit, Bay City, and Alpena Railroad, 1885–1887; succeeded his father as president of Detroit Steel Spring Company, 1887–1901; director of Union Trust Company, States Savings Bank, Union Elevator Company, Detroit Steel Casting Company, Parke, Davis, and Company, the Union Station and Depot Company, and Michigan State Telephone

Company; vice-president of Grave Hospital; elected estimator-at-large for Detroit, 1891; undertook formation of naval militia in 1893; first landsman, then ensign on staff of 1st Battalion of Michigan state naval brigade, 1894; promoted to lieutenant and navigating and ordinance office in 1895; became lieutenant junior grade in U.S. Navy when Michigan reserves entered war with Spain, 1898; director of Packard Motor Car Company in 1903; appointed assistant secretary of the navy by President Theodore Roosevelt in 1905; appointed SECRETARY OF THE NAVY in the cabinet of President Theodore Roosevelt on December 1, 1908, and served until March 4, 1909; most important contributions were reorganization of the department, and creation of general staff; member of the U.S. Senate from Michigan, 1919–1922; died on October 3, 1945. James F. Rhodes, *McKinley and Roosevelt Administrations 1897–1909* in *History of the United States*, vol. 9 (1922).

NILES, John Milton. Born in Poquonnock, Conn., August 20, 1787; son of Moses and Naomi (Marshall) Niles; married Sarah Robinson on June 17, 1824, and following her death, married Jane Pratt on November 26, 1845; common school education; admitted to the Hartford bar in 1817 and began practice; founded and edited the Hartford *Times* in 1817; Republican and Tolerationist; supported General Jackson; judge for Hartford County, 1821–1829; ran for state legislature in 1826; appointed postmaster of Hartford in 1829; published *The Independent Whig* (1816), *Gazatteer of Connecticut and Rhode Island* (1819), *History of the Revolution in Mexico and South America with a View of Texas* (1829); chosen by Governor Henry W. Edwards to fill the U.S. Senate vacancy of Nathan Smith in 1835, reelected and served until March 1839; ran unsuccessfully in 1833 and 1840 for the governorship of Connecticut; appointed POSTMASTER GENERAL in the cabinet of Martin Van Buren on May 25, 1840, serving until March 3, 1841; elected to a second term as senator 1843–1849; became a horticulturist; toured Europe, 1851–1852; died in Hartford, Conn. on May 31, 1856. Denis Tilden Lynch, *An Epoch and a Man: Martin Van Buren and His Times* (1941).

NIXON, Richard Milhous. Born in Yorba Linda, Cal., January 9, 1913; son of Francis Anthony Nixon, small merchant and farmer, and Hannah (Milhous) Nixon; Quaker; married Thelma [Pat] Ryan on June 21, 1940; father of Patricia and Julie; worked in father's gas station; delivered groceries; graduated Whittier College in California in 1934; received degree from Duke University Law School, 1937, was admitted to the bar, and began practice in Whittier, Cal.; joined Wingert and Bewley in 1942 and then became a junior member of the firm of Bewley, Knoop and Nixon; was attorney with Office of Emergency Management in Washington, D.C., January-August 1942; served in the South Pacific as a lieutenant j.g. with the U.S. Navy from 1942 to 1946; elected to the U.S. House of Representatives from California in 1946, and served from January 3, 1947, to November 1950, being reelected in 1948; elected to the U.S. Senate on

November 7, 1950 for the term beginning January 3, 1951, took office in early December 1950 by appointment of Governor Earl Warren to fill a vacancy, and served until January 20, 1953; elected VICE-PRESIDENT in the administration of President Eisenhower in 1952 and served two terms until January 20, 1961; unsuccessful candidate for presidency on Republican ticket in 1960; counsel in law firm of Adams, Duque and Hazeltine, 1961–1963; unsuccessful candidate for governor of California, 1962; author of *Six Crises* (1962); moved to New York where he joined the law firm of Mudge, Stern, Baldwin, and Todd, 1963–1964; director of Hosco Corp., elected PRESIDENT in 1968 on the Republican ticket, and took office on January 20, 1969; reelected PRESIDENT in 1972; resigned from the presidency August 9, 1974; resides in New Jersey; author of *Memoirs* (1978); *The Real War* (1980); *Leaders* (1982); *Real Peace* (1983); and *No More Viet Nams* (1985). Earl Mazo and Stephan Hess, *Nixon: A Political Portrait* (1969); Gary Wills, *Nixon Agonistes: The Crisis of the Self-Made Man* (1969); David A. Frier, *Conflict of Interest in the Eisenhower Administration* (1969); Robert Woodward and Carl Bernstein, *All the President's Men* (1975); *Who's Who in American Politics, 1987–1988.*

NOBLE, John Willock. Born in Lancaster, Ohio, October 26, 1831; son of John and Catherine (McDill) Noble; Presbyterian; married Lisabeth Halstead, February 8, 1864; attended Cincinnati public schools and University of Ohio for three years; graduated Yale College in 1851; graduated from Cincinnati Law School in 1852; studied in the offices of Henry Stanbery; moved to St. Louis in 1855, later moving to Keokuk, Iowa; practiced law in Keokuk, 1856–1861, sharing leadership of the Iowa state bar with Samuel Freeman Miller; enlisted as a private in the 3d Iowa Cavalry of the Union army in August 1861, commissioned brigadier general in 1865 when he resigned; following service in Civil War, served as judge advocate general of the Army of the Southwest; returned to St. Louis in 1865; appointed U.S. district attorney for the eastern district of Missouri in 1867; resumed private practice in 1870; appointed SECRETARY OF THE INTERIOR in the cabinet of President Benjamin Harrison on March 5, 1889, entering upon duties on March 7, 1889, and serving until his retirement on March 6, 1893; in this office he supported the tariff act of 1890, interpreted land laws in the settlers' favor, and most important, introduced forest reserve sections in the 1891 land laws, withdrawing millions of valuable acres for national forests; upon retirement returned to St. Louis where he died on March 22, 1912. Arthur W. Dunn, *From Harrison to Harding*, 2 vols. (1922).

O

O'BRIEN, Lawrence Francis. Born in Springfield, Mass., July 7, 1917; son of Lawrence F. O'Brien, Sr., hotel owner and real estate dealer, and Myra (Sweeney) O'Brien; Roman Catholic; married Elva I. Brassard on May 30, 1944; father of Lawrence Francis, III; attended local schools and Cathedral High School; worked for Springfield Democrats; tended bar and was active in Hotel and Restaurant Employees Union; received B.A. from Northeastern University, Boston, in 1942; served as sergeant in U.S. Army, 1943–1945; managed O'Brien Realty Co.; directed Foster Furcolo's congressional campaigns of 1946 and 1948 and went to Washington as Furcolo's assistant in 1948; worked in John F. Kennedy's senatorial campaigns of 1952 and 1958; made director of organization for Kennedy team, 1959; chosen national director of organization on Democratic national committee in 1960; appointed White House assistant for congressional relations and personnel on January 2, 1961; appointed POSTMASTER GENERAL in the cabinet of President Lyndon Johnson, and served from November 3, 1965 to January 20, 1969; most important contribution was proposal that post office department be replaced by a nonprofit government corporation; chosen president of McDonald and Co., Inc., January 7, 1969; member of citizens' group for postal reform, September 1969; made Democratic national chairman on March 5, 1970; on June 17, 1972, police arrested five men for breaking into O'Brien's office in the Watergate complex, thus beginning the Watergate affair; resigned as Democratic National Committee chairman to serve as George McGovern's national campaign chairman for the 1972 presidential election; signed three-year contract as the commissioner of the National Basketball Association, 1975; currently working in the field of public relations; author of *No Final Victories; A Life in Politics—from John F. Kennedy to Watergate* (1974); Rowland Evans and Robert Novak, *Lyndon B. Johnson: The Exercise of Power* (1966); Hugh

Sidey, *A Very Personal Presidency: Lyndon Johnson in the White House* (1968); *Current Biography Yearbook, 1977*.

OLNEY, Richard. Born in Oxford, Mass., September 15, 1835; son of Wilson and Eliza L. (Butler) Olney; Presbyterian; married Agnes Thomas on March 6, 1861; father of two daughters; attended Leicester Academy; graduated from Brown University in 1856; received his law degree from Harvard Law School in 1858; admitted to the bar in 1859 and entered the law office of Benjamin F. Thomas, to whose practice he succeeded; in 1873 he was elected to the Massachusetts state legislature, but after repeated defeats in attempts at reelection, he temporarily gave up politics; appointed ATTORNEY GENERAL on March 6, 1893 by President Cleveland, and served until June 9, 1895; in 1894 he prevented Coxey's "revolution" from assuming greater proportions by protecting the railroads from rebel takeover; in that same summer he thwarted a strike against the railroads by taking strict action against the American Railway Union, arresting union leader Eugene V. Debs and his lieutenants; afterwards, he backed the Arbitration Act of 1898; appointed SECRETARY OF STATE on June 10, 1895; his major contributions in this office included arbitration of the Venezuela-British Guiana boundary dispute, which culminated in the award of 1899, and recommendations to Spain on how a revolution in Cuba might be avoided; retired from politics on March 5, 1897 and resumed his law practice; served on the boards of many foundations; died April 8, 1917. *Who Was Who in America*; Henry James, *Richard Olney and his Public Service* (1923).

OSGOOD, Samuel. Born in Andover, Mass., February 3, 1748; son of Peter and Sarah Osgood; Episcopalian; married Martha Brandon, January 4, 1775; remarried to Maria Bowne Franklin, May 24, 1786; graduated Harvard, 1770, studied theology; became merchant with his brother; at outbreak of Revolution joined army as captain of a company of minutemen; became major and aide-de-camp of General Artemis Ward; delegate to Essex County Convention, 1774; served in Provincial Congress, 1775; member of Massachusetts legislature; captain at Lexington and Cambridge, Mass. in April 1775; left army in 1776 with the rank of colonel and assistant assistant commissary; member Massachusetts board of war, 1776; delegate to Constitutional Convention of 1779; member of Massachusetts legislature until 1780 entrance to State Senate, where he served until 1781; Massachusetts delegate to Continental Congress, 1781–1784; appointed director of Bank of North America by Congress, December 1, 1781; chairman of delegation to Rhode Island to secure support for Hamilton's proposed import duty, 1782; first commissioner of the United States Treasury, 1785–1789; appointed POSTMASTER GENERAL in the cabinet of President Washington, September 26, 1789, serving until his resignation on August 12, 1791; continued living in New York when the government moved to Philadelphia; served in New York legislature, 1800–1803; founder of Society for Establishment of a Free School for the Education of Poor Children, and the American Academy of Fine

Arts; supervisor of New York State, 1801–1803; appointed naval officer of the port of New York, May 10, 1803, serving until his death; died August 12, 1813 in New York City; interment in Brick Presbyterian Church, New York City. J. G. Wilson, *The Memorial History of the City of New York* (1893); Ira Osgood and Eben Putnam, *A Genealogy of the Descendents of John Christopher, and William Osgood* (1894).

P

PALMER, Alexander Mitchell. Born at Moosehead, Pa., May 4, 1872; son of Samuel Bernard Palmer, engineer; Quaker; married on November 23, 1898 to Roberta Bartlett Dixon; father of Mary; following death of first wife, married Margaret Fallon Burrall on August 29, 1923; attended public schools and the Moravian Parochial School, Bethlehem, Pa.; graduated from Swarthmore College in 1891; appointed official stenographer of the 43d judicial district of Pennsylvania, 1892; studied law under Judge John B. Strom of Stroudsburg, Pa., and admitted to the bar in 1893; began practice at Stroudsburg; director of various banks and public service corporations; member of the Democratic state executive committee of Pennsylvania; elected as a Democrat to the 61st, 62d, and 63d Congresses, serving from March 4, 1909 to March 3, 1915; co-sponsored an anti-child-labor bill and served on the Ways and Means Committee; delegate to the Democratic national convention at Baltimore in 1912 and at St. Louis in 1916; ran unsuccessfully for the Senate in 1914; member of the Democratic national committee, 1912–1920; appointed by President Wilson as alien property custodian on October 22, 1917 and served until his resignation on March 4, 1919; appointed ATTORNEY GENERAL in the cabinet of President Wilson on March 4, 1919; most important contributions were establishment of price fixing committees and the use of anti-trust laws to help combat inflationary trends and profiteering, dissolution of the "beef trust," prosecution of alleged radicals and anarchists and deportation of many to Russia, and usage of the injunction against striking mineworkers in 1919; left office with the outgoing administration on March 4, 1921; was a leading contender for the Democratic presidential nomination in 1920; retired from public life in 1921 and resumed law practice in Stroudsburg and Washington, D.C.; delegate to the 1932 Democratic national convention, serving on the resolutions committee; died on May 11, 1936 in

Washington; interment in Laurelwood Cemetery, Stroudsburg, Pa. J. M. Blum, *Joe Tumulty and the Wilson Era* (1951); Arthur S. Link, *Woodrow Wilson: The New Freedom* (1956); Leon H. Canfield, *The Presidency of Woodrow Wilson* (1966).

PATTERSON, Robert Porter. Born in Glens Falls, N.Y., February 12, 1891; son of Charles R. and Lodice E. (Porter) Patterson; Presbyterian; married Margaret Tarleton Winchester on January 3, 1920; father of Robert Porter, Aileen W., Susan Hand, and Virginia D.; after completing his preliminary and secondary education at the local schools, he entered Union College, graduating in 1912; studied law at Harvard, graduating in 1915; admitted to the bar in 1915, commencing practice in New York City; served as a private in the 7th Regiment of the New York National Guard; became a captain and then a major during World War I, serving in the 306th Infantry Division, U.S. Army; resumed his law practice in New York following the close of hostilities; became a member of the law firm of Webb, Patterson and Hadley from 1920 to 1930; appointed judge of the U.S. district court, southern New York district, in 1930; appointed judge of the circuit court of appeals in 1939, resigning in July 1940 to accept a presidential appointment; named assistant secretary of war by President Franklin D. Roosevelt in December 1940; named SECRETARY OF WAR by President Truman on September 26, 1945, entering upon his duties on September 27, 1945 and serving until his resignation on July 1, 1947; director of the Federal Reserve Bank of New York; president of Practicing Law Institute; trustee of Union College; president of Harvard Law School Association, 1937–1949; president of Freedom House; chairman of the Commission on Organized Crime; recipient of the Distinguished Service Medal for his exemplary service to the nation; died in Elizabeth, N.J. on January 22, 1952; buried at Arlington National Cemetery, Arlington, Va. Cabell B. H. Phillips, *The Truman Presidency: The History of a Triumphant Succession* (1966); Alfred Steinber, *The Man from Missouri: The Life and Times of Harry S. Truman* (1962).

PAULDING, James Kirke. Born in Great Nine Partners, N.Y., August 22, 1778; son of William and Catherine (Ogden) Paulding; married Gertrude Kemble, sister of Governor Kemble, in 1818; educated in country schools in Westchester County; resided in Tarrytown; acquainted with Washington Irving through his brother-in-law, William Irving, and collaborated with the author on "Salamagundi" in 1807–1808; wrote *The Diverting History of John Bull and Brother Jonathan*, a comic treatment of early United States History (1812), *The Lay of the Scottish Fiddle*, a parody of Scott's "Lay of the Last Minstrel" (1813), and *The Backwoodsman* (1818); *The United States and England*, written in 1815, brought him an appointment by President Madison as secretary of the Board of Naval Commissioners; wrote three documentaries; *Letters from the South by a Northern Man*, written after an 1816 Virginia tour (1817), *A Sketch of Old England* (1822), and *John Bull in America*, a satire (1825); appointed naval agent for the port of New York in 1824; resided in New York until 1837; wrote *Konigsmarke* (1823), *The Dumb Girl* (1830), *The Dutchman's Fireside* (1831), *Westward Ho!* (1832), *The Old Continental* (1846), *The Puritan and his Daughter* (1846); appointed SECRETARY OF THE NAVY in the cabinet of President Van Buren on June 25, 1838, entering upon duties July 1, 1838 and serving until March 4, 1841, when the administration ended; during his period of service he sent a South Seas exploring expedition on a four-year mission to explore the Oregon coast and Antarctica, and attempted to reform the Navy Department; following his wife's death, he toured the west with Van Buren in 1842; retired to his home, "Placentia," in Hyde Park, N.Y. in 1846 and died there on April 6, 1860; interment in Greenwood Cemetery, Brooklyn, N.Y. Denis Tilden Lynch, *An Epoch and a Man: Martin Van Buren and his Times* (1929); Robert V. Remini, *Martin Van Buren and the Making of the Democratic Party* (1951).

PAYNE, Henry Clay. Born in Ashfield, Mass., November 23, 1843; son of Orrin Pierre and Eliza Etta (Ames) Payne; Methodist; married Lydia Wood Van Dyke on October 15, 1869; childless; attended local schools at Ashfield, Mass.; went to Shelburne Falls Academy; moved to Milwaukee, Wis., and entered wholesale dry goods house of Sherwin, Nowell and Pratt, 1863; took up insurance business in 1868; organized Young Men's Republican Club, and took part in Grant-Greeley campaign, 1872; chairman, Republican State Central Committee; was postmaster of Milwaukee, 1875–1885; secretary and chairman of Republican state central committee; member of Republican national committee, 1880–1904; became vice-president of Wisconsin Telephone Company, 1886, and president, 1889; became vice-president of Milwaukee Street Railway Company in 1890, and acting president, 1892–1895; elected president of Milwaukee Northern Railroad Company, 1890–1893; president of Chicago and Calumet Terminal Railway, 1893–1894; chairman of Republican county committee of Milwaukee County; organized Milwaukee Light, Heat and Traction Company; president of Fox River Electric Company; vice-president of Milwaukee Electric Railway and Light Company, 1896; charge of Republican western headquarters in Chicago; supported Theodore Roosevelt for vice-president; appointed POSTMASTER GENERAL in the cabinet of President Theodore Roosevelt on January 9, 1902, and served until his death on October 4, 1904; most important contributions were concluding of parcel post conventions with Japan, Germany, and other foreign countries, organization of postal service into fifteen "battalions" and rural free delivery into eight, free transmission of literature for the blind through the mails; died in Washington, D.C., October 4, 1904. W. W. Wright, *Henry Clay Payne, A Life* (1907); *Railway Age* (October 7, 1904); James F. Rhodes, *McKinley and Roosevelt Administrations 1897–1909* in *History of the United States*, vol. 9 (1922).

PAYNE, John Barton. Born in Pruntytown, Va., (now W.Va.), January 26, 1855; son of Amos Payne, physician and farmer; Trinity Methodist Episcopalian; married on October 17, 1878 to Kate Bunker; after her death, married to Jennie

Byrd Bryan on May 1, 1913; attended school and studied under tutors at Orleans, Va.; became clerk in general store in Warrentown in 1870; hired as manager of a general store, freight, and express office at Thoroughfare Gap, Prince William County, Va., in 1873; later that year entered the employ of Adolphus Armstrong, clerk of county and circuit courts at Pruntytown, and studied law; admitted to the bar in 1876 and began practice in Kingswood, W. Va.; published a newspaper, the *West Virginia Argus*; served as chairman of the Preston County Democratic committee; in 1880, appointed special judge of the circuit court of Tucker County; elected mayor of Kingswood, 1882; moved to Chicago; president of Chicago Law Institute, 1889; elected judge of the superior court of Cook County in 1893, resigning in 1898 to become a trial lawyer; president of the board of South Park Commissioners, 1911–1924; offered the position of U.S. solicitor general by President Wilson in 1913, but declined; in 1917, accepted post of arbitrator in shipbuilding strikes on West Coast; moved to Washington, D.C.; appointed general counsel of the U.S. Shipping Board Emergency Fleet Corporation in 1917, and became its chairman in 1919; appointed SECRETARY OF THE INTERIOR in the cabinet of President Wilson on February 28, 1920, serving until the end of the Wilson administration on March 4, 1921; most important contributions were development of national parks and conservation of the navy's petroleum reserves; drafted the legislation under which the government took over the railroads, and served as director general of railroads from May 1920 to April 1921; appointed chairman of the American Red Cross by President Harding on October 15, 1921, and reappointed by Presidents Coolidge, Hoover, and Roosevelt; chairman of the board of governors of the League of Red Cross Societies, 1922; appointed by President Harding commissioner for furthering better relations with Mexico, 1923; died on January 24, 1935; interment in Washington, D.C. *The Book of Chicagoans* (1905, 1911); *Red Cross Courier* (March 1935); Leon H. Canfield, *The Presidency of Woodrow Wilson* (1966).

PERKINS, Frances. Born in Boston, Mass., April 10, 1882; daughter of Frederick Winslow and Susan (Wright) Perkins; Episcopalian; married Paul Caldwell Wilson in 1913; mother of Susanna Perkins; after receiving her preliminary and secondary education at the local schools, she entered Mount Holyoke College, graduating in 1905; continued the study of sociology and economics at the Universities of Chicago, Pennsylvania, and Columbia, receiving an A.M. from Columbia University in 1910; worked at Hull House in Chicago; became secretary of the Research and Protective Association in Philadelphia, Pa.; moved to New York City in 1909; in 1912, became executive secretary of the Commission of Safety which secured the adoption of some thirty bills designed to prevent sweatshop fires; executive director of the New York Council of Organization for War Service, 1917–1919; appointed commissioner of the New York State Industrial Commission in 1919, serving until 1921 and again from 1929 to 1933; member of the New York State Industrial Board from 1922 to 1933 and its chairman from 1926 to 1929; appointed by President Franklin D. Roosevelt as

SECRETARY OF LABOR on March 4, 1933, and continued in office under President Truman, serving until May 31, 1945; she became the first woman ever to serve in a presidential cabinet; under her administration a public works program was begun, minimum wage standards and improved working conditions were provided in the Wages and Hours Act, and old-age insurance and unemployment compensation laws were enacted; civil service commissioner from 1945 to 1953; awarded the medal for eminent achievement by the American Women's Association; author of *Women As Employers* (1919), *A Social Experiment Under The Workmen's Compensation Jurisdiction* (1921), *People At Work* (1934), *The Roosevelt I Knew* (1946); died in New York City, May 14, 1965; buried in Newcastle, Me. Don Lawson, *Frances Perkins: First Lady of the Cabinet* (1960); Rexford Guy Tugwell, *Democratic Roosevelt: A Biography of Franklin Delano Roosevelt* (1957).

PETERSON, Peter George. Born June 5, 1926, in Kearny, Neb.; son of George and Venet (Paul) Peterson; attended Nebraska State Teachers College for one year and transferred to Massachusetts Institute of Technology in 1944; in 1945 transferred to Northwestern University, where he received his B.S. degree summa cum laude in 1947; attended night school at the University of Chicago and received M.B.A. with honors in only thirteen months; Beta Gamma Sigma, Alpha Tau Omega; married Sally Hornbagen on May 9, 1953; father of John Scott, James, David, Holly and Michael; began working in 1947 for Market Facts, Inc.; by 1949 was assistant director and in 1951 was appointed vice-president; chairman of the Planning Committee for the Illinois Citizens for Eisenhower, 1952; hired by McCann-Erickson in 1953 as director of marketing services; vice-president, 1958; joined Bell and Howell in 1958, was executive vice-president and director by 1961, was president from 1961 to 1963; president and chief executive officer from 1963 to 1968; and chairman of the board and executive officer from 1968 to 1971; while at Bell and Howell, Peterson doubled sales and quadrupled operating earnings; Republican; in February 1971, appointed head of the newly formed Cabinet-level Council on International Economic Affairs by President Richard Nixon and asked to serve as a presidential advisor; besides being advisor, he was to "prepare the basis for new policies in trade based on his concept of a changed world"; after eleven months, President Nixon appointed him SECRETARY OF COMMERCE; as Secretary of Commerce, he negotiated trade agreements with both Poland and the Soviet Union; called "the innovator" because he was "a reshaper of trade policies and initiator of new ways by which the government can spur productivity and technology"; "ungracefully let go" in December 1972; accepted chairmanship of Wall Street's Lehman Brothers in June 1973; a former director of the American Express Co., First National Bank of Chicago and the Bell Telephone Company; former trustee of Brookings Institution, National Educational T.V., and the Committee for Economic Development; on the board of trustees for the University of Chicago; member of Economic Club of Chicago, the Burning Tree Club and the Chevy

Chase Club; in 1952 was a contributing editor to *Readings in Market Organizing and Price Policies*; in 1961 named by the U.S. Junior Chamber of Commerce as one of the "Ten Outstanding Young Men" in the nation; in 1962 was cited by *Life* magazine as one of the 100 most important American men under forty; Chairman, Lehman Brothers, 1973–1983; resigned on July 26, 1983; became consultant to Shearson-Lehman American Express in 1984; formed, and became chairman of, the Blackstone Group, an investment firm, in October 1985; member, Independent Committee on International Development Issues, Trilateral Commission, since 1980; member, Council on Foreign Relations, since 1985; serves on the board of directors of numerous corporations, universities, and institutions, including Federated Department Stores, the Lehman Corporation, RCA Corp., Black and Decker Manufacturing, Cities Service Co., University of Chicago, Museum of Modern Art, N.Y.; author of *On Borrowed Time* (1988). *Current Biography* (1972); *Who's Who in American Politics* (1975–1976); *Time* (January 8, 1973, and August 13, 1973); *New York* (January 26, 1971; September 3, 1972; May 23, 1976; April 14, 1984; February 24, 1985; October 22, 1985; and November 13, 1987); *Facts on File Yearbook* (1983); *International Who's Who* (1988–89).

PICKERING, Timothy. Born in Salem, Mass., July 17, 1745; son of Timothy and Mary (Wingate) Pickering; Puritan; married Rebecca White on April 8, 1776; father of John, Henry, and Octavius; graduated Harvard in 1763; appointed registrar of deeds for Essex; commissioned lieutenant in militia, 1766; admitted to bar in 1768; elected colonel in 1775; appointed judge of Essex court of common pleas and judge of the district maritime court including Boston and Salem in 1775; published "An Essay of Discipline for the Militia" in 1775; became representative to general court in May 1776; commanded Essex regiment and joined Washington at Morristown in February 1777; made adjutant general and member of the board of war; succeeded General Greene as quartermaster general in August 1780, held post until resigning in 1785 when the post was abolished; member of the Pennsylvania constitutional convention in 1789; concluded treaty with the six Indian Nations in 1791; appointed POSTMASTER GENERAL in the cabinet of President Washington, serving from August 12, 1791 to February 24, 1795, when he succeeded General Knox as SECRETARY OF WAR, serving from January 2, 1795 to January 26, 1796; aided in organization of West Point and supervised the building of frigates *Constitution, Constellation* and *United States*; placed in charge of the Department of State following Edmund Randolph's resignation on August 19, 1795; appointed SECRETARY OF STATE in the cabinet of President Washington on December 10, 1795 and served until removed from office by President Adams on May 12, 1800; settled as a farmer in Danvers, Mass.; appointed chief justice of court of common pleas at Essex in 1802; elected to the U.S Senate in 1803 where he served until 1811; retired from the Senate in 1811 to a farm in Wentham, Mass.; wrote "Political Essays: A Series of Letters Addressed to the People of the United States" in 1812; elected member of Congress, serving from 1813 to 1817; elected member of the Massachusetts executive council in 1817; wrote *A Review of the Correspondence between Honorable John Adams . . . and the Late William Cunningham, Esq.* in 1824; died in Salem, Mass., on January 29, 1829. Octavius Pickering, *The Life of Timothy Pickering* (1867–1873); Ellery Harrison and C. P. Bowditch, *The Pickering Genealogy* (1897).

PIERCE, Franklin. Born in Hillsborough (now Hillsboro), N.H., November 23, 1804; son of General Benjamin and Elizabeth (Andrews) Pierce; Episcopalian; married Jane Means Appleton on November 10, 1834; father of Franklin, Robert, Frank, and Benjamin; attended the academies of Hancock and Francestown, N.H., and the preparatory school at Exeter, N.H.; entered Bowdoin College, Brunswick, Me., graduating in 1824; studied law and was admitted to the bar in 1827, commencing the practice of his profession in Hillsborough; elected to the New Hampshire House of Representatives, serving from 1829 to 1833; speaker of the House from 1832 and 1833; elected as a Democrat to the U.S. House of Representatives in the 23d and 24th Congresses, serving in all from March 4, 1833 until March 3, 1837; elected to the U.S. Senate, serving from March 4, 1837 until February 28, 1842, when he resigned to resume the practice of law at Concord, N.H.; declined the appointment of Attorney General tendered by President Polk in 1846; enlisted as a private in the Mexican War, rising to the rank of brigadier general on March 3, 1847; resigned from army on March 20, 1848; member of the New Hampshire constitutional convention held in 1850, serving as its president; elected PRESIDENT on the Democratic ticket in November 1852; inaugurated on March 4, 1853, serving until March 3, 1857; unsuccessful candidate for the Democratic nomination for the presidency in 1856; upon his retirement he made a European tour, 1857, and then returned to Concord, N.H. and resumed the practice of law; died on October 8, 1869 in Concord; interment in Old North Cemetery, Concord. Roy F. Nichols, *Franklin Pierce: Young Hickory of the Granite Hills* (1969).

PIERCE, S. R., Jr. Born in Glen Cove, N.Y., September 8, 1922; son of Samuel R. and Hettie E. (Armstrong) Pierce; married Barbara Penn Wright on April 1, 1948; Methodist; father of Victoria Wright; received A.B. with honors, Cornell University, 1947; J.D., post-graduate, Ford Foundation Fellowship; LL.M. taxation, New York University, 1952; Yale Law School, 1957–1958; LLD, 1972; admitted to New York bar, 1949; private law practice 1957–1959, 1961–1970, 1973–1981; faculty at New York University School of Law, 1958–1970; partner, Battle, Fowler, Joffin, Pierce, and Kheel; served with army of the United States, 1943–1946; as first lieutenant Judge Advocate General Corps, Reserve, 1950–1952; served as assistant district attorney, New York, 1949–1953; assistant U.S. attorney, Southern District, New York, 1953–1955; assistant undersecretary of labor, Washington, D.C., 1955–1956; appointed to the Supreme Court in 1956; served as associate counsel, Council of Judicial Subcommittee on Antitrust; elected to House of Representatives, 1956–1957; judge, New York Court of General Sessions, 1959–1961; member, council on Fundamental International and Social Economic Education, 1961–1967; chairman, Impartial Disciplinary Review Board, New York City Transit System, 1968–1981; general counsel and head legal director, U.S. Treasury, Washington, D.C., 1970–1973; nominated by President Ronald Reagan on December 22, 1980, as SECRETARY OF HOUSING AND URBAN DEVELOPMENT, and confirmed by the Senate on January 2, 1981; served until February 5, 1989; named New York City Junior Chamber of Commerce Annual Distinguished Service Award, 1958; Alexander Hamilton Award, Treasury Department, 1973; Fellow American College of Trial Lawyers; member, Cornell Association of Class Secretaries, Telluride Association Alumni, Cornell Alumni Association, New York County Lawyers Association, Institute of Judicial Administration; Phi Beta Kappa, Phi Kappa Phi, Alpha Phi Alpha, and Alpha Phi Omega. *Newsweek* (January 5, 1971); *Time* (January 5, 1981); *Current Biography: 1982; Who's Who in America, 1982–1983; Who's Who in American Politics; 1987–1988.*

PIERREPONT, Edwards. Born at North Haven (now New Haven), Conn., March 4, 1817; son of Giles and Eunice (Munson) Pierpont; married Margaretta Willoughby on May 27, 1846; educated at the schools of his native town and graduated from Yale College in 1837; studied law at the New Haven Law School; admitted to the bar in 1840; tutored at Yale College in 1840 and 1841; moved to Columbus, Ohio, and pursued the practice of law there; moved to New York City in 1846; became active in the campaigns of the Democratic party; elected judge of the superior court of the city of New York in 1857, but resigned in 1860 to resume his law practice; helped organize the War Democrats in support of the reelection of President Lincoln in 1864; approved President Andrew Johnson's policies of Reconstruction; appointed U.S. district attorney for the southern district of New York in 1869 and 1870, by President Grant; became director, counsel, and treasurer of the Texas and Pacific Railroad in 1871; appointed minister to Russia in 1873 but declined to serve; invited to serve in the cabinet of President Grant as ATTORNEY GENERAL on April 26, 1875, took office on May 15, 1875; and served until May 31, 1876; during his incumbency, he prosecuted members of the "Whiskey Ring"; appointed minister to Great Britain in 1876 by President Grant, serving until December 1877; member of the state constitutional convention of 1867 and 1868 and one of the Committee of Seventy in 1870 which assisted in ridding New York of the "Tweed Ring"; died in New York City, March 6, 1892. John Y. Simon, ed., *The Papers of Ulysses S. Grant* (1967); Courtlandt Canby, ed., *Lincoln and the Civil War: A Profile and a History* (1960).

PINKNEY, William. Born in Annapolis, Md., March 17, 1764; son of Jonathan and Ann (Rind) Pinkney; married Maria Rodgers on March 16, 1789; father of ten children, among them Edward Coate, author; entered office of Judge Samuel

Chase in 1783 at Baltimore, after attending the King William School; admitted to bar in 1786; began practice in Hartford County, Md., practiced two years; elected to the U.S. constitutional convention in 1788, voted against ratification; representative to the Maryland House of Delegates, 1788–1792; resisted anti-slavery legislation; in 1792 elected member of the executive council of Maryland, serving until his resignation in 1795; Anne Arundel County delegate to the state legislature, 1795; appointed commissioner of the U.S. under the seventh article of Jay's Treaty to settle United States' claims against Great Britain in 1796; returned to the U.S. in 1804, moving from Annapolis to Baltimore; appointed attorney general of Maryland in 1805; sent to London with Minister James Monroe in 1806 regarding reparations and impressment, retained in 1807 when Monroe resigned, returned in 1811; elected to the State Senate in September 1811; appointed ATTORNEY GENERAL in the cabinet of President Madison on December 11, 1811, resigned on February 10, 1814; while in office he advocated the War of 1812; commanded a battalion in the War of 1812; congressional representative of Baltimore, March 4, 1815 to April 18, 1816, when he resigned to accept an appointment as minister plenipotentiary to Russia and special envoy to Naples to negotiate compensation for United States' losses in 1809; returned to the U.S., 1818; elected U.S. senator to fill a vacancy, serving from 1819 to 1822; pro-slavery attitudes instrumental in the Missouri Compromise; died in Washington, D.C., February 25, 1822; interment in the Congressional Cemetery. Abbot Emerson Smith, *James Madison, Builder: A New Estimate of a Memorable Career* (1937); Irving Brant, *James Madison: The President 1809–1812* (1956); Irving Brant, *James Madison: Commander in Chief, 1812–1836* (1961); Gaillard Hunt, *The Life of James Madison* (1968).

POINSETT, Joel Roberts. Born in Charlestown (now Charleston), S.C., March 2, 1779; son of Dr. Elisha and Ann (Roberts) Poinsett; Baptist; married Mrs. Mary (Izard) Pringle on October 24, 1833; spent his early childhood in England, returning to the U.S. in 1788; attended private schools at Greenfield Hill, Conn., and, later, in Wandsworth, near London, England; studied medicine at St. Paul's School in Edinburgh, Scotland; attended the military academy at Woolwich, England; studied law briefly; travelled extensively in Europe from 1801 to 1809; sent to South America by President Madison in 1809, to investigate revolutionary struggles for independence from Spain; returned to Charleston in 1816; elected to the state House of Representatives from 1816 to 1820; served as president of the Board of Public Works; elected as a Democrat to the 17th, 18th, and 19th Congresses, serving from 1821 to 1825, when he resigned to enter the diplomatic service; appointed minister to Mexico from 1825 to 1829; invited to join the cabinet of President Martin Van Buren as SECRETARY OF WAR on March 7, 1837, entering upon his duties on March 14, 1837 and serving until March 4, 1841; during his secretaryship, he improved the status of the regular army, proposed a plan for universal training and frontier defense, organized a general staff, improved the artillery, broadened the course of study at the West Point Military

Academy, moved more than 40,000 Indians west of the Mississippi River, and directed the war against the Seminoles in Florida; retired to his South Carolina plantation in 1841; opposed the Mexican War and the secessionist movement of 1847–1852; the *Poinsettia Pulcherina*, an indigenous Mexican flower, was named for him on his introducing it to the U.S.; founded the Academy of Fine Arts in Charleston, S.C.; authored *Notes On Mexico, Made in 1822, With An Historical Sketch Of the Revolution* (1824); died near what is now Statesburg, S.C., on December 12, 1851; interment in the Church of the Holy Cross (Episcopal) Cemetery, Statesburg, S.C. Robert Vincent Remini, *Martin Van Buren and the Making of the Democratic Party* (1959); Edwin Palmer Hoyt, *Martin Van Buren* (1964).

POLK, James Knox. Born near Little Sugar Creek, N.C., November 4, 1795; son of Samuel and Jane (Knox) Polk; Presbyterian; married Sarah Childress on January 1, 1824; no children; moved to Tennessee with his family in 1806, settling in what is now Maury County; attended the common schools and was privately tutored briefly; entered the University of North Carolina at Chapel Hill, graduating in 1818; studied law at Portsmouth, N.H., and Northampton, Mass., and was admitted to the bar in 1820, commencing practice in Columbia, Tenn.; became chief clerk of the Tennessee Senate from 1821 to 1823; served in the Tennessee House of Representatives from 1823 to 1825; elected as a Democrat to the U.S. House of Representatives in the 19th through 25th Congresses, serving in all from March 4, 1825 until March 3, 1839; served as speaker of the House during the sessions of the 24th and 25th Congresses; did not seek renomination in 1838, having become a candidate for governor; elected governor of Tennessee from 1839 to 1841; elected PRESIDENT on the Democratic ticket November 1844; inaugurated on March 4, 1845, serving until March 3, 1849; he did not seek a second term; upon retiring from the White House, he returned to Nashville, where he died on June 15, 1849; interment within the grounds of the State Capitol, Nashville, Tenn. Charles Allan McCoy, *Polk and the Presidency* (1960).

PORTER, James Madison. Born in Selma, Pa., January 6, 1793; son of Andrew and Elizabeth (Parker) Porter and brother of David Rittenhouse Porter and Robert Porter; married Eliza Michler on September 18, 1821; studied law in Lancaster, Pa., in 1809 and later with his brother Robert in Reading, Pa.; in 1812 served as a clerk in a prothonotary's office in Philadelphia; organized a volunteer force to fight the British and served as second lieutenant; discharged with the rank of colonel; admitted to the bar on April 23, 1813, and began his own law practice; in 1818 moved to Easton to serve as deputy attorney general of Northampton County; he returned to private practice in 1821 and maintained one of the largest practices in that vicinity; active member of the founding committee of Lafayette College, chartered in 1826; served as president of the board of trustees of Lafayette from 1826 to 1852 and as professor of jurisprudence and political economy from 1837 to 1852; appointed in June 1839 to serve as presiding judge of the

12th District; resigned in 1840 to resume his legal practice; in 1843, President Tyler appointed him SECRETARY OF WAR; he was to assume the duties of that office on March 8, 1843, but Congress rejected his nomination on January 30, 1844, after he had served almost ten months; in 1847 he became the first president of the Schuylkill and Susquehanna Railroad, and when its name was changed in 1853 to Lehigh Valley Railroad he became president of the new company; in 1849 he was elected to the state legislature where he became chairman of the judiciary committee; elected president judge of the 22d Judicial district, 1853, and served until March 1855, when he was forced to resign following a stroke; died on November 11, 1862; interment in Easton, Pa. *Dictionary of American Biography*; Charles H. Hart, *James Madison Porter* (1856); *Who Was Who in American Politics*.

PORTER, Peter Buell. Born in Salisbury, Conn., August 14, 1773; son of Colonel Joshua and Abigail Buell Porter; married to Letitia Breckinridge in 1818; was graduated from Yale College in 1791; studied law in Litchfield, Conn.; admitted to the bar and began practice in Canandaigua, N.Y., in 1795; appointed clerk of Ontario County, 1797, serving until 1805 when he was removed by Governor Morgan Lewis because of his identification with the Burr faction of the Republican party; member of the New York State Assembly in 1802 and again in 1828; removed to Black Rock, N.Y.; in 1809 and engaged in transportation enterprises; elected as a Democrat to the 11th and 12th Congresses, serving from March 4, 1809 until March 3, 1813; appointed canal commissioner by the New York state legislature in 1811; served in the War of 1812 as major general of New York Volunteers, 1812–1815; elected to the 14th Congress and served from March 4, 1815 to January 23, 1816; secretary of State of New York, 1815–1816; appointed member of the Northwestern Boundary Commission, 1816; unsuccessful candidate for governor of New York, 1817; regent of the University of the State of New York, 1824–1830; appointed SECRETARY OF WAR in the cabinet of President John Quincy Adams on June 21, 1828; most important contribution was advocating moving all Indians residing in the eastern states to west of the Mississippi; served until March 3, 1829; moved to Niagara Falls, N.Y., in 1836 where he died on March 20, 1844; interment in Oakwood Cemetery. D. S. Alexander, *A Political History of the State of New York*, vol. 1 (1906); Robert A. East, *John Q. Adams: The Critical Years* (1962); F. Clarke, *John Quincy Adams* (1966).

PRESTON, William Ballard. Born in Smithfield, Va., November 29, 1805; son of James Patton Preston, governor of Virginia, and Ann (Taylor) Preston; married to Lucinda Staples Redd on November 21, 1839; father of Walter, Nannie, James, Lucy, Jane, and Keziah; attended the common schools; attended William and Mary College, Williamsburg, Va., and graduated in 1823; studied law at the University of Virginia at Charlottesville in 1825; admitted to the bar and began practice in 1826; member of the Virginia House of delegates, 1830–

1832 and 1844–1845; served in the State Senate from 1840 until 1844; elected in 1846 as a Whig to the 30th Congress, serving from March 4, 1847 until March 3, 1849; appointed SECRETARY OF THE NAVY in the cabinet of President Taylor to serve from March 7, 1849 until July 19, 1850, when the cabinet was reorganized by President Fillmore; resumed law practice; sent to France in 1858 to negotiate the establishment of a commercial steamship line between Virginia and France, but was unsuccessful due to the outbreak of the Civil War; opposed Virginia's secession from the Union but defended its right to secede and thus was elected from Montgomery County to the secession convention of Virginia in February 1861; elected senator from Virginia to the Confederate Congress and served in that body until his death on November 16, 1862 in Smithfield, Va.; interment probably in the cemetery of the Old Brick Church, Smithfield. L. A. Wilson, ed., *The Preston Genealogy* (1900); Holman Hamilton, *Zachary Taylor: Soldier in the White House* (1966); Brainerd Dyer, *Zachary Taylor* (1967).

PROCTOR, Redfield. Born in Proctorsville, Vt., July 1, 1831; son of Jabez Proctor, farmer, merchant, and manufacturer, and Betsey (Parker) Proctor; married Emily J. Dutton on May 26, 1858; father of five children; was graduated from Dartmouth College in 1851; studied law at the Albany Law School, graduating in 1859; admitted to the bar and began practice in Boston, Mass., in 1860; during the Civil War, attained the rank of major in the 5th Vermont Regiment; discharged due to ill health in 1863, but later returned as colonel of the 15th Vermont Regiment and participated in the battle of Gettysburg; returned to Vermont and the practice of law; pursued business interests in the marble industry and became president of the Vermont Marble Company in 1880; member of the Vermont House of Representatives, 1867–1868; served in the State Senate and was president *pro tempore* in 1874 and 1875; lieutenant governor of Vermont, 1876–1878; governor of Vermont, 1878–1880; delegate to the Republican national conventions of 1884, 1888, and 1896; reelected to the state House of Representatives in 1888; appointed SECRETARY OF WAR in the cabinet of President Benjamin Harrison on March 5, 1889; most important contributions were revision of court martial system, institution of system of efficiency records and examinations for officers' promotions, organization of a record and pension division in the department, all of which influenced the decline in the rate of desertions; resigned on November 2, 1891 to enter the U.S. Senate; subsequently reelected in 1892, 1898, and 1904, serving in all from 1891 to 1908; in 1904, edited from the original manuscripts in the Library of Congress the *Records of Conventions in the New Hampshire Grants for the Independence of Vermont*; died in Washington, D.C., on March 4, 1908; interment in the City Cemetery, Proctor, Vt. F. C. Partridge, "Redfield Proctor," *Vermont Historical Society, 1913–1914* (1915); Harry J. Sievers, *Benjamin Harrison: Hoosier President*, vol. 3 (1966).

Q

QUAYLE, Danforth. Born in Indianapolis, Ind., February 4, 1947; son of James C. Quayle, publisher of the *Huntington Herald Press*, and Corinne (Pulliam) Quayle; Presbyterian; married Marilyn Tucker on November 18, 1972; father of Tucker Danforth, Benjamin Eugene, and Mary Corinne; graduated from Huntington High School, 1965; graduated from DePauw University with a B.A. in political science, 1969; was vice-president of Delta Kappa Epsilon at DePauw University; rejected by Indiana University Law School, he managed to get in under an affirmative action program after he visited the dean of admissions; while a law student he was appointed a member of the Indiana governor's executive committee; received his J.D. from Indiana University Law School, 1974; admitted to the bar in 1974; opened up a law practice with his wife and called it Quayle and Quayle, 1974; court reporter, *Huntington Herald Press*, Indiana, 1965–1969; served in Indiana National Guard, 1969–1975; associate publisher of *Huntington Herald Press*, 1974–1976; member of the Consumer Protection Division, Office of Attorney General, State of Indiana, 1970–1971; administrative assistant to the Governor of Indiana, 1971–1973; director of Indiana Inheritance Tax Division, 1973–1974; teacher of business law at Huntington College, 1975; representative from Indiana, 1976–1980; Senator from Indiana; 1981–1988; elected to Senate November 4, 1980, for a six-year term beginning January 3, 1981 and reelected by a landslide margin on November 4, 1986; Quayle's biggest single achievement in the Senate was the Training Act of 1982; he was head of an Armed Services task force in 1984 that investigated Defense Department procurements; in the ninety-ninth Congress, Quayle pushed two pet Pentagon reorganization projects—the "enterprise program," a designation for weapon systems allowing defense officials to streamline development and production, and creation of the "procurement czar," who would have absolute authority over military purchasing; most of his domestic policy-making efforts were geared to employment and health matters; the first Indiana Senator of either party to break 60 percent in the history of popular Senate elections; Republican running mate to George Bush in the presidential election, 1988; nominated for vice-president on September 3, 1988; biggest problems throughout his campaign dealt with his qualifications to become vice-president, and the extent to which family influence helped him avoid serving in the Vietnam War, as well as helping him get elected to various political positions; elected VICE-PRESIDENT of the United States on November 8, 1988; member of Rotary, Huntington Chamber of Commerce, Hoosier State Press, and Huntington Bar Association; received honorary degrees from Tri-State University, Indiana Institute of Technology; Vincennes University; L.H.D., De Pauw University, 1982; awards: One of Ten Outstanding Young Men in America, U.S. Jaycees, Taxpayers' Best Friend, National Taxpayers Union; Golden Bulldog, Watch Dog of the Treasury; Guardian of Small Businesses, National Federation of Independent Business; National Security Leadership Award, Coalition for Peace through Strength, 1985; author of various articles for the *New York Times, Washington Post*, and other publications. *Time* (August 29, 1988); *The New Republic* (October 31, 1988); *International Who's Who in American politics, (1987); Politics in America (1987); Who's Who, 1989; Who's Who in the Midwest, 1987; International Who's Who 1988–1989*; *New York Times Biographical Service* (August 1988); Richard F. Fenno, *The Making of a Senator: Dan Quayle (1989)*.

R

RAMSEY, Alexander. Born near Harrisburg, Pa., September 8, 1815; son of Thomas and Elizabeth (Kelker) Ramsey; Methodist; married to Anna Earl Jenks on September 10, 1845; father of three children; worked as a store clerk and carpenter while attending the common schools; studied law at Lafayette College, Easton, Pa.; admitted to the bar in 1839 and began practice in Harrisburg; became active in the Whig party; secretary of the Pennsylvania electoral college, 1840; chief clerk of the Pennsylvania House of Representatives in 1841; elected as a Whig to the 28th and 29th Congresses, serving from March 4, 1843 until March 3, 1847; chairman of the Whig central committee of Pennsylvania, 1848; Commissioned governor of the Minnesota territory by President Taylor on April 2, 1849 and served until 1853; pursued real estate interests in St. Paul, Minn.; mayor of St. Paul in 1855; unsuccessful Republican candidate for governor of Minnesota in 1857; secured governorship in 1859 and was reelected in 1861; elected in 1863 to the U.S. Senate as a Republican and reelected in 1869, serving until 1875; appointed SECRETARY OF WAR in the cabinet of President Hayes on December 10, 1879, and served until the close of the Hayes administration, March 4, 1881; appointed by President Arthur as chairman of the commission to carry out the provisions of the Edmunds bill dealing with Mormonism in Utah, and served in this capacity until 1886; first president of the Minnesota Historical Society from 1849 to 1863; was author of several papers in the Minnesota Historical Collections; 1891–1903; delegate to the centennial celebration of the adoption of the federal Constitution in 1887; died in St.Paul, Minnesota on April 22, 1903; interment in Oakland Cemetery. J. H. Baker, *Lives of the Governors of Minnesota* (1908); Arthur Bishop, ed., *Rutherford B. Hayes, 1822–1893: Chronology, Documents, Bibliographical Aids* (1969); T. Harry Williams, ed., *Hayes: The Diary of a President, 1875–1881* (1964).

RANDALL, Alexander Williams. Born at Ames, N.Y., October 31, 1819; son of Phineas Randall, lawyer, and Sarah (Beach) Randall; married to Mary C. Van Vechten in 1842; after death of first wife, married Helen M. Thomas in 1863; attended Cherry Valley Academy; studied law; admitted to the bar in 1840 and began practice in the new village of Prairieville in Wisconsin Territory; formerly a Whig, became a Democrat by 1845; appointed by President Polk as postmaster of Prairieville; delegate to the Wisconsin constitutional convention, 1846; member of the Wisconsin Assembly, 1848; associate justice of the Milwaukee circuit court, 1855–1857; elected governor of Wisconsin as a Republican in 1857 and reelected in 1859; appointed minister to Italy by President Lincoln, serving from 1862–1863; appointed first assistant postmaster general in 1863 in the cabinet of President Lincoln; appointed POSTMASTER GENERAL in the cabinet of President Andrew Johnson on July 25, 1866 and remained in that post until the close of that administration, March 3, 1869; settled in Elmira, N.Y., and resumed law practice; died on July 26, 1872. H. A. Tenney and David Atwood, *Memorial Record of the Fathers of Wisconsin* (1880); "Reminiscences of Alex W. Randall," *Milwaukee Sentinel* (November 14, 1897); Eric L. McKitrick, *Andrew Johnson and Reconstruction* (1960).

RANDOLPH, Edmund Jennings. Born in Williamsburg, Va., August 10, 1753; son of John Randolph, King's attorney for Virginia, and Ariana (Jennings) Randolph; nephew of Peyton Randolph, President of the Continental Congress in 1774 and 1775; married Elizabeth Nicholas in 1776; father of Lucy and Peyton; attended William and Mary College, studied law in his father's office, 1773; became an aide-de-camp for George Washington in 1775; elected to Virginia convention in 1776, assisted in writing of Virginia constitution and bill of rights; elected attorney general of state of Virginia, 1776–1782; member of Continental Congress 1779–1782; governor of Virginia 1786–1788; delegate to 1787 Constitutional Convention; wrote "Letter . . . on the Federal Constitution" in 1787; entered the Virginia Assembly in 1788; appointed ATTORNEY GENERAL in the cabinet of President Washington on February 2, 1790, and served until January 28, 1794; reported on the judiciary system and defended foreigners' right to sue the state; appointed SECRETARY OF STATE in the cabinet of President Washington on January 2, 1794; instrumental in developing Jay Treaty with England while maintaining relations with France and the 1795 Treaty of San Lorenzo (Pinckney Treaty) with Spain regarding free navigation of the Mississippi River; resigned from office on August 19, 1795; wrote "Democratic Societies," 1795, and "Political Truth," 1796; resumed law practice, acting as senior counsel at Aaron Burr's trial for treason in 1807; died in Millwood, Va., September 13, 1813. Wirt, *British Spy* (1803); Jonathan Eliot, *The Debates in the Several States on the Adoption of the Federal Constitution* (1836); M. D. Conoway, *Omitted Chapters of History* (1888); S. F. Bemis, "Edmund Randolph" in *The American Secretaries of State and Their Diplomacy* (1927); H. J. Eckenrode, *The Ran-*

dolphs: The Story of a Virginia Family (1928); Nathan Schachner, *The Founding Fathers* (1954).

RANDOLPH, Peyton. Born in Williamsburg, Va., in September 1721; son of Sir John Randolph, King's attorney of Virginia, diplomat, and speaker of the House of Burgesses, and Susanna (Beverly) Randolph; uncle of Edmund Randolph, Attorney General and Secretary of State under Washington; member of Bruton Parish Church; married to Elizabeth Harrison on March 8, 1745; no children; studied under private tutors; attended the College of William and Mary; began study of law at the Inner Temple, London, 1739, and admitted to the bar in February 10, 1744; appointed King's attorney for the province in 1748; member of the House of Burgesses representing Williamsburg, 1748–1749 and 1758–1775, and representing the College of William and Mary, 1752–1758; elected speaker of the House of Burgesses in November 1766 and reelected in successive assemblies until the Revolution; member of the Virginia Committee of Correspondence, 1759–1767; chairman of the Committee of Correspondence, 1773; president of the Virginia revolutionary conventions in 1774 and 1775; appointed by the Virginia convention to the first session of the Continental Congress; elected first PRESIDENT OF THE CONTINENTAL CONGRESS on September 5, 1774; resigned on October 22, 1774 to attend the state legislature; reelected PRESIDENT OF THE CONTINENTAL CONGRESS in Philadelphia, and served from May 10 to May 24, 1775; resigned on account of ill health; died in Philadelphia on October 22, 1775; interment in the chapel of the College of William and Mary, Williamsburg, Va. H. J. Eckenrode, *The Revolution in Virginia* (1916); *Virginia Magazine of History and Biography* (January 1924); Edmund C. Burnett, *The Continental Congress* (1964).

RAWLINS, John Aaron. Born in Galena, Ill., February 13, 1831; son of James Dawson Rawlins, farmer, and Lovisa (Collier) Rawlins; married to Emily Smith on June 5, 1856; after death of first wife married Mary E. Hurlburt on December 23, 1863; father of three children; attended local schools and the Rock River Seminary at Mount Morris, Ill.; studied law in Galena; admitted to the bar in 1854; elected attorney for Galena in 1857; nominated for the electoral college on the Douglas ticket; at the start of the Civil War, played an active part in the organization of the 45th Illinois Infantry, becoming a major in that regiment in 1861; aide-de-camp to General Ulysses S. Grant; commissioned a lieutenant, August 1861; became captain and assistant adjutant general of U.S. Volunteers as a member of General Grant's staff, August 30, 1861; editor of Grant's papers; promoted to brigadier general of the Volunteers, August 11, 1863; became brigadier general and chief of staff of the Army following the creation of that permanent position by Congress on March 3, 1865; promoted to major general on April 9, 1865; appointed SECRETARY OF WAR in the cabinet of President Grant on March 11, 1869; attempted to annex Cuba to the United States; after five months in office, died in Washington on September 6, 1869. Ulysses Simpson

Grant, *Personal Memoirs of U.S. Grant* (1885); J. H. Wilson, *The Life of John A. Rawlins* (1916); John Y. Simon, ed., *The Papers of Ulysses S. Grant* (1967); Philip R. Moran, ed., *Ulysses S. Grant, 1822–1885: Chronology, Documents, Bibliographical Aids* (1968).

REAGAN, Ronald Wilson. Born in Tampico, Ill., February 6, 1911; son of John Edward Reagan, a shoe salesman, and Nelle Clyde (Wilson) Reagan; Presbyterian (according to most sources); his father came from Irish ancestry with a Catholic backround and his mother, Nelle, was of Protestant Scots-English descent; his family had little money and his father suffered from alcoholism; married Jane Wyman on January 26, 1940; officially divorced on July 19, 1948; married Nancy Davis on March 4, 1952; father of Maureen Elizabeth, Michael Edward (adopted), Patricia Ann, and Ronald Prescott; graduated from Dixon High School in 1928; in high school he was president of the student body and received his first acting part; attended Eureka College in 1928, belonged to Tau Kappa Epsilon, and graduated with a B.A. in economics and sociology, June 7, 1932; during his freshman year at Eureka, he was the spokesman for a strike committee; received his first broadcasting job with WOC, a radio station in Davenport, Iowa, in 1933; WOC was consolidated with WHO in Des Moines, and "Dutch" Reagan (the nickname he was often known by) became increasingly popular; his sportscaster career, 1932–1937, prompted him to pursue a career in acting; signed a contract with Warner Brothers in 1937; later signed on with Universal, and continued his acting career until 1954; entered as second Lieutenant in the U.S. Army's Cavalry Reserve on April 14, 1942; served in the eighteenth Army Air Force Base Unit, Fort Mason, and was released as captain on December 9, 1945; returned to Hollywood in 1948; became president of the Screen Actors Guild on two separate occasions, November 17, 1947–1952, and 1959–June 1960; host and production supervisor for General Electric Theatre, 1954–1962; host and part-time performer in the T.V. series, "Death Valley Days," 1962–1966; member of California's Republican Central Committee, 1964–1966; the Republicans for Ronald Reagan organization formed October 28, 1964; ran for governor of California in December 1964; won a victory over Governor Edmund Brown in November 1966; sworn in January 2, 1967; won reelection and sworn in for a second term on January 4, 1971; held position as governor of California through 1975; achievements as governor included budget surpluses so great that in 1973 Reagan was able to institute generous programs of income tax rebates and property tax relief, and to establish the California Welfare Reform Act of 1971; delegate to the Republican national convention, 1968 and 1972; chairman, Republican Governor's Association, 1968–1973; member of the Presidential Commission on CIA activities within the United States, 1975; candidate for the Republican nomination for president, 1976; member of the board of directors for the Committee on the Present Danger, Washington, D.C., 1977; nominated for president at the Republican national convention on July 16, 1980; Reagan's campaign supported a conservative platform stressing issues of family, work, neighborhood, peace, and freedom; swamped Jimmy Carter at the polls with 51 percent of the popular vote to 41 percent (the remaining 8 percent went to John Anderson), and received 489 electoral votes as compared to Carter's 49 votes, on November 4, 1980; elected fortieth PRESIDENT on November 4, 1980; inaugurated on January 20, 1981; the oldest president ever to be elected in U.S. history; wanted to improve foreign affairs, and shortly after his inaugural address on January 21, 1981, Iran had released the 52 American hostages which had been held for 444 days; only two months later, on March 20, 1981, John Hinkley, Jr., tried to assassinate Reagan in Washington D.C., Reagan made an excellent recovery; strategic arms reduction talks (START) were inaugurated on January 29, 1982; reelected PRESIDENT on November 6, 1984 and inaugurated January 20, 1985; Iran-Contra scandal and other various covert actions led up to an intense investigation, 1986; Reagan's major achievements as president include the success of U.S.-Soviet relations and revival of confidence in the presidency; Reagan did not suceed in cutting government spending throughout his career—the deficit was his greatest failure; the Iran-Contra scandal left the American people hesitant about Reagan's choice of George Bush for his successor; he left office on January 20, 1989; presently resides in Santa Barbara, Calif.; member of American Federation of Radio and Television Artists, Screen Actors Guild, Lions, Friars; honors and awards include Great American of the Decade Award, Virginia Young American for Freedom (1960 and 1970), Man of the Year Free Enterprise Award (1965), Horatio Alger Award (1969), and George Washington Honor Medal Award, Freedoms Foundation, Valley Forge, Pa. (1971); author of *Where's the Rest of Me* (1965). Joseph Nathan Kane, *Facts about Presidents* (1981); *Current Biography Yearbook, 1982; National Cyclopedia of American Biography; 1984*; Anne Edwards, *Early Reagan: The Rise to Power* (1987); *Who's Who in American Politics, 1987–1988; Newsweek* (January 9, 1989).

REDFIELD, William Cox. Born in Albany, N.Y., June 18, 1858; son of Charles Bailey Redfield; Episcopalian; married to Elise Mercein Fuller on April 8, 1885; father of Elsie and Humphrey; moved with his parents to Pittsfield, Mass. in 1867; attended the public schools and received home instruction; worked in the Pittsfield post office and as a traveling salesman for a paper company; went to New York City in 1877 and was employed in the stationery and printing business; in 1883 began work with J. H. Williams and Company of Brooklyn, making steel and iron forgings, becoming treasurer and later president of the firm; elected to the board of the Equitable Life Insurance Company, through the influence of Grover Cleveland, in 1905, and served as director until 1913; delegate to the Gold Democrat national convention at Indianapolis in 1896; unsuccessful candidate as Gold Democrat for election to Congress in 1896; appointed commissioner of public works for Brooklyn in 1902 and 1903; elected as a Democrat to the 62d Congress, serving from March 4, 1911 until March 3, 1913; appointed SECRETARY OF COMMERCE in the cabinet of President Wilson on March 4, 1913; most important contributions were reorganization and enlargement of the Bureau of Foreign and Domestic Commerce, institution of the commercial attaché service, strengthening of the Bureau of Standards; resigned on November 1, 1919; engaged in banking and insurance concerns in New York City; active in civic organizations and philanthropic enterprises; author of *The New Industrial Day* (1912), *With Congress and Cabinet* (1924), *Dependent America* (1926), *We And The World* (1927), and an extended series of articles, "Glimpses of Our Government," appearing in the *Saturday Evening Post* (May 1924–January 1925); died in New York City on June 13, 1932; interment in the Albany Rural Cemetery, Albany, N.Y. William C. Redfield, *With Congress and Cabinet* (1924); R. S. Baker and W. E. Dodd, *The Public Papers of Woodrow Wilson*, vol. 2 (1925); Arthur S. Link, *Woodrow Wilson: The New Freedom* (1956); Leon H. Canfield, *The Presidency of Woodrow Wilson* (1966).

REGAN, Donald Thomas. Born in Cambridge, Mass., December 21, 1918; son of William F. Regan, a policeman and railroad worker, and Kathleen (Ahern) Regan; Catholic; married Ann G. Buchanan on July 11, 1942; father of Donna, Donald, Richard, and Diane; attended Cambridge Latin School; graduated with B.A. in English from Harvard University, 1940; served in the U.S. Marine Corps, 1940–1946; retired as lieutenant colonel, Marine Corps Reserve; after the war he could not afford to resume his law studies and instead attended Merrill Lynch's course for stockbrokers; graduated from the company's trainee class in 1946 and worked for Merrill Lynch, Pierce, Fenner, and Smith, Inc., 1946–1981; became their vice-president, 1959–1964; executive vice-president, 1964–1968; president, 1968–1971; chairman of the board, 1971–1980; chairman of the board and chief executive officer, Merrill Lynch and Co., Inc., 1973–1981; served as vice-chairman of the board of directors of the New York Stock Exchange, 1972–1975; on December 11, 1980, nominated by president-elect Ronald Reagan as the sixty-sixth SECRETARY OF THE TREASURY; served in office from January 21, 1981, until January 8, 1985; White House chief of staff, Washington, from January 8, 1985, to February 27, 1987; chairman of the board of trustees, University of Pennsylvania, 1974–1979, and life trustee 1978–1981; Honorary degrees include LL.D., Hahnemann Medical College and Hospital (1968), Tri-State College (1969), University of Pennsylvania (1972); Hon. Dr. of Commercial Science, Pace University (1973), Hon. D.H.L., Colgate University (1984); member of Policy Commission, Business Roundtable, 1978–1980; trustee commission for Economic Development, 1978–1980; clubs: Army-Navy, Metropolitan (Washington, D.C.); Economic (New York City); Baltusrol Golf (Maryland); author of *A View from the Street* (1972); *For the Record* (1988). *Current Biography, 1981*; Ronald Brownstein and Nina Easton, *Reagan's Ruling Class* (1982); *Who's Who in the East; 1986; New York Times Biographical Service* (January 1987); *Who's Who in America, 1988; Who's Who, 1989.*

RIBICOFF, Abraham Alexander. Born in New Britain, Conn., April 9, 1910; son of Samuel and Rose (Sable) Ribicoff; Jewish; married Ruth Siegel on June 28, 1931; second wife Lois Mathes, married on August 4, 1972; father of Peter and Jane; attended public schools of New Britain; employed by G. E. Prentice Company; studied at New York University, 1928–1929; headed Chicago office of G. E. Prentice Company, 1920–1931; received LL.B. from University of Chicago in 1933, was admitted to the Connecticut bar, and began practice of law with A. S. Bordon, becoming partner in Bordon and Ribicoff in 1938; elected to lower house of the Connecticut state legislature, 1938–1942; member of American Arbitration Association, 1941; was chairman of Connecticut assembly of municipal court judges, 1941–1942; joined brother in establishing Hartford law office of Ribicoff, Ribicoff and Kotkin, 1941–1954; served as judge for Hartford municipal court, 1941–1943 and 1945–1947; made chairman of Commission for the Study of Alcoholism and Crime in 1943; member of bipartisan Hartford Charter Revision Committee, 1945–1947; became hearing examiner on Connecticut Interracial Commission, 1947–1948; elected to U.S. House of Representatives in 1948, was reelected in 1950, and served from 1949 to 1953; delegate to San Francisco Peace Conference in 1951; elected governor of Connecticut in 1954, was reelected, and served until 1961; appointed SECRETARY OF HEALTH, EDUCATION AND WELFARE in the cabinet of President Kennedy, and served from January 21, 1961 to July 30, 1962; most important contributions were proposal for federal funds to better educational resources and offer educational opportunities to larger numbers of people, appropriations for dental research, licensing and use of Sabin oral polio vaccine, increase in radiation screening of milk, water, air and other foodstuffs, liberalization of Social Security legislation; elected U.S. senator from Connecticut in 1962, and took office January 3, 1963; served as U.S. senator until 1981, declining to seek reelection in 1980; since 1981 has practiced law with the firm of Kaye, Scholer, Fireman, Hays, and Handler; appointed in 1983 to the Senate Rules and Administration Commission with other former senators, and charged with studying the ways by which the Senate passes legislation and develops recommendations for change; in 1988, headed a bipartisan commission to determine which military bases should be closed; author of *Politics: The American Way* (1967); *America Can Make It* (1972); *The American Military Machine* (1972); coauthor, *American Hostages in Iran: The Conduct of a Crisis* (1980). James MacGregor Burns, *John Kennedy: A Political Profile* (1959); New York Times, *The Kennedy Years* (1964); Eleanora W. Schoenebaum, ed., *Facts on File: Political Profiles: The Nixon/Ford Years* (1979); *New York Times* (November 20, 1980; April 8, 1983; June 6, 1985; and July 13, 1988).

RICHARDSON, Elliot Lee. Born in Boston, Mass., July 20, 1920; son of Dr. Edward P. and Clara (Shattuck) Richardson; Episcopalian; married to Anne Francis Hazard on August 2, 1952; father of Henry, Anne, and Michael; graduated from Harvard College in 1941; first lieutenant of the 4th Infantry Division,

U.S. Army, 1942–1945; studied law at Harvard Law School and received his degree in 1947; served as a law clerk to Judge Learned Hand of the U.S. Court of Appeals, 1947–1948, and then to Justice Felix Frankfurter of the U.S. Supreme Court, 1948–1949; admitted to the Massachusetts bar, 1950; associate in the law firm of Ropes, Gray, Best, Coolidge, and Rugg, 1949–1953 and 1954–1956; law lecturer at Harvard, 1952; assistant to Senator Leverett Saltonstall of Massachusetts, 1953–1954; assistant secretary for legislation of the department of Health, Education, and Welfare, 1957–1959, and served as acting secretary from April to July 1958; U.S. attorney, Massachusetts, 1959–1961; special assistant to the U.S. Attorney General, 1961; partner in the Boston law firm of Ropes and Gray, 1961–1964; lieutenant governor of Massachusetts, serving from 1965–1967; Massachusetts attorney general, 1967–1969; appointed undersecretary of state in the cabinet of President Nixon on January 4, 1969; appointed SECRETARY OF HEALTH, EDUCATION AND WELFARE in the cabinet of President Nixon on June 6, 1970, to fill the vacancy caused by the resignation of Robert Finch; appointment was confirmed by the U.S. Senate on June 16; while Secretary of Health, Education, and Welfare, he sought to simplify the processing of grants, consolidate existing programs, and to transfer greater administrative responsibility to state and local governments; in August 1970 he announced an end to the policy of cutting off federal funds to school districts that refused to desegregate; in January 1973, was nominated by President Nixon as SECRETARY OF DEFENSE of the United States, and his appointment was confirmed by the U.S. Senate on January 29; served as Secretary of Defense for approximately three months, and on April 30, 1974, he was named by President Nixon as ATTORNEY GENERAL of the United States; confirmed by the U.S. Senate on May 23, he served until October 20, 1974, when he resigned after the firing of Archibald Cox, director of the Office of the Watergate Special Prosecuting Force; returned to his private law practice in Washington, D.C.; on January 9, 1975, named U.S. Ambassador to the United Kingdom by President Gerald R. Ford and his appointment was confirmed by the U.S. Senate on February 19; on November 3, 1975, nominated by President Ford as SECRETARY OF COMMERCE of the United States, and his appointment was confirmed by the U.S. Senate on December 11; while Secretary of Commerce, he headed the probe of alleged payoffs by American corporations to secure foreign contracts; remained in office until the end of the Ford administration on January 20, 1977; nominated by President Jimmy Carter for U.S. ambassador-at-large, United Nations Law of the Sea Conference, January 25, 1977; confirmed February 24, 1977; served in that capacity until end of conference in 1980; became resident partner in Washington, D.C., law firm of Milbank, Tweed, Hadley, and McCloy in 1980; in August 1983, named trustee for National Public Radio (NPR) Satellite Equipment as part of a compromise to save NPR from bankruptcy; named to board of directors, Ecumed, in 1984; ran unsuccessfully for U.S. Senate as candidate from Massachusetts in 1984; became member of the Chatam House Foundation to improve Anglo-American relations, June 1985; appointed by the government of the Peoples'

Republic of China in February 1986 to conduct a comprehensive study of China's commercial relations with the United States; named to special U.N. Crisis Panel on September 16, 1987, to discover how the U.N. could increase its authority during international crises; currently practicing law with Milbank, Tweed, Hadley, and McCloy; Lasker Award, 1978; honorary degree, University of Vermont, 1983; member, board of directors of numerous companies; authored *The Creative Balance* (1976). *Time*, (June 15, 1970); *Newsweek* (June 15, 1970); *Who's Who in America, 1976–1977*; Charles Moritz, ed., *Current Biography Yearbook, 1971; Facts on File Yearbook* (1971–1975, 1977–1987); *New York Times* (February 12, March 20, September 16, and December 13, 1984; March 12, 1985; February 2 and November 13, 1986; and January 24, 1987).

RICHARDSON, William Adams. Born in Tyngsborough, Mass., November 2, 1821; son of Daniel and Mary (Adams) Richardson; Unitarian; married Anna Maria Marston on October 29, 1849; father of one daughter; received his preparatory education at Pinkerton Academy in Derry, N.H. and at Lawrence Academy in Groton, Mass.; graduated Harvard in 1843; studied law at the Harvard Law School and was admitted to the bar in July 1846, commencing his legal practice in Lowell, Mass.; initially a Whig, he became a Republican in 1855; appointed to compile and index the statute laws of Massachusetts, 1856; became judge of probate for Middlesex County in 1856; appointed assistant secretary of the treasury by President Grant on March 20, 1869, at the recommendation of Treasury Secretary Boutwell; tendered a full cabinet portfolio as SECRETARY OF THE TREASURY by President Grant on March 17, 1873, and served until June 3, 1874; appointed to the Massachusetts court of appeals in June 1874, and was elevated to chief justiceship in 1885; overseer of Harvard University, 1863 to 1875; lecturer and professor at Georgetown Law School in Washington, D.C.; authored *The Banking Laws of Massachusetts* (1855), *Practical Information Covering the Debt of the United States* (1872), *National Banking Laws* (1872), *History, Jurisdiction and Practice of the Court of Claims* (1885); died in Washington, D.C., on October 19, 1896. William Best Hesseltine, *Ulysses S. Grant, Politician* (1953); Louis Arthur Coolidge, *Ulysses S. Grant* (1917).

ROBESON, George. Born at Oxford Furnace, N.J., March 16, 1829; son of William Penn Robeson, iron manufacturer, and Ann (Maxwell) Robeson; married to Mary Isabelle (Ogston) Aulick in 1872; father of one daughter; graduated from Princeton College in 1847; studied law with Chief Justice Hornblower; admitted to the bar in 1850; licensed as a counselor, 1854; practiced in Newark, N.J., and later in Camden; appointed prosecuting attorney for Camden County in 1858; during the Civil War was commissioned a brigadier-general and took an active part in the organization of the state troops; attorney general of New Jersey from 1867 until his resignation in 1869; appointed SECRETARY OF THE NAVY in the cabinet of President Grant on June 25, 1869 to fill the vacancy caused by the resignation of A. E. Borie; most important contribution was securing the federal appropriation for the ill-fated North Polar Expedition of Captain C. F. Hall, who named Robeson Channel in northern Greenland after the Secretary; served until the end of President Grant's second term, resigning on March 12, 1877; resumed practice of law; unsuccessful candidate for U.S. Senator in 1877; elected as a Republican to the 46th and 47th Congresses from the 1st New Jersey district, and served from March 4, 1879 until March 3, 1883; unsuccessful candidate for reelection in 1882 to the 48th Congress; resumed practice of law in Trenton, N.J.; died in Trenton on September 27, 1897; interment in Belvidere Cemetery, Belvidere, N.J. Adam Badeau, *Grant in Peace* (1888); William Best Hesseltine, *Ulysses S. Grant, Politician* (1957); John Y. Simon, ed., *The Papers of Ulysses S. Grant* (1967).

ROCKEFELLER, Nelson Aldrich. Born in Bar Harbor, Me., July 8, 1908; son of John Davison, Jr., and Abby Greene (Aldrich) Rockefeller; married Mary Todhunter Clark, June 23, 1930 (divorced in 1962); father of Rodman, Ann (Coste), Steven, Michael (deceased), Mary (Morgan); married Margaretta Fitler Murphy, May 1963; father of Nelson Aldrich and Mark Fitler; attended Lincoln School of Teachers College, New York City, 1917–1926; B.A., Dartmouth, 1930; director of Rockefeller Center, Inc., 1931–1958, president, 1938–1945, 1948–1951, chairman, 1945–1953, 1956–1958; co-ordinator, Office of Inter-American Affairs, 1940–1944; assistant Secretary of State for American Republics Affairs, December 1944 to August 1945; Undersecretary of Health, Education and Welfare, 1953–1954; special assistant to President Eisenhower, 1954–1955; elected GOVERNOR of New York in 1959 and resigned December 1973; president of Rockefeller Brothers Fund, Inc., 1956–1958; nominated by President Gerald Ford to be VICE-PRESIDENT of United States, confirmed by the Senate on December 19, 1974, and served to January 20, 1977, when President Jimmy Carter took office; announced on November 3, 1975, that he would not run as President Ford's running mate in 1976, but would continue in office for his term; campaigned unsuccessfully for the Republican presidential nomination in 1964 and 1968; trustee of New York's Museum of Modern Art, 1932, treasurer, 1937–1939, president, 1939–1941 and 1946–1953; trustee, Dartmouth College, Metropolitan Museum of Art, 1946–1951; honorary M.A., Dartmouth College, 1942; L.L.D. degrees by Fordham University, 1941, and Jewish Theological Seminary, 1950; awarded Chile's Order of Merit, October 1945, Brazilian National Order of the Southern Cross, November 1946, Mexican Order of the Aztec Eagle, February 1949, citations by National Conference of Christians and Jews for work in field of human relations, 1948 and 1950, Thomas F. Cunningham Award for contributions toward betterment of Inter-American Relations, 1964, Gold Medal, National Institution of Social Sciences, 1967; concentrated on his art collection after leaving the vice-presidency, and on writing about that collection; opened a retail art dealership in 1978; died of a heart attack in New York City on January 26, 1979; author of *The Future of Federalism* (1962), *Unity, Freedom and Peace* (1968), *Our Environment Can Be Saved*

(1970). James Poling, *The Rockefeller Record; A Political Self-Portrait* (1960); Frank Gervasi, *The Real Rockefeller* (1964); Michael Kramer, *I Never Wanted to Be Vice-President of Anything* (1976); *Current Biography* (1951); *Facts on File, 1976; Who's Who, 1976; Who's Who in America, 1976; New York Times* (January 2, May 10, and October 27, 1977; January 27 and 28, 1979); Michael Turner, *The Vice President as Policy Maker: Rockefeller in the Ford White House* (1982).

RODNEY, Caesar Augustus. Born in Dover, Del., January 4, 1772; son of Thomas and Elizabeth (Fisher) Rodney; married Susan Hunn; father of ten daughters and five sons; family settled in Wilmington, Del., in 1780; after completing preparatory studies, he entered the University of Pennsylvania, graduating in 1789; studied law, was admitted to the bar, and commenced practice in Wilmington in 1793; elected as a Democrat to the 8th Congress, serving from March 4, 1803 to March 3, 1805; one of managers appointed in January 1804 to conduct impeachment proceedings against Judges John Pickering and Samuel Chase; invited to join the cabinet of President Jefferson as ATTORNEY GENERAL on January 20, 1807, and was continued in that office by President Madison, serving until his resignation on December 5, 1811; served in the War of 1812, and was commissioned as captain on April 7, 1813; member of the Delaware Committee of Safety in 1813; elected to the State Senate in 1815; was sent to South America by President Monroe as one of the commissioners to investigate and report on the propriety of recognizing the independence of the Spanish-American republics, 1817; elected as a Democrat to the 17th Congress, serving from March 4, 1821 to January 24, 1822, when he resigned; elected to the U.S. Senate, serving from January 24, 1822 to January 29, 1823, when he resigned; appointed minister plenipotentiary to Argentina on January 27, 1923, and served until his death in Buenos Aires on June 10, 1824; interment in the English Churchyard, Buenos Aires, Argentina. Max Beloff, *Thomas Jefferson and American Democracy* (1949); Leonard Patrick O'Connor Wibberly, *Time of the Harvest: Thomas Jefferson, The Years 1801–1826* (1966).

ROGERS, William Pierce. Born in Norfolk, N.Y., June 23, 1913; son of Harrison Alexander and Myra (Beswick) Rogers; married Adele Langston on June 27, 1936; father of Dale, Anthony Wood, Jeffrey Langston, and Douglas Langston; after attending the local schools, he moved to Canton, N.Y., attending the high school there; entered Colgate University in 1930, graduating with an A.B. in 1934; entered Cornell Law School, where he was editor of the *Cornell Law Quarterly* in 1935, 1936, and 1937; graduated in 1937; appointed assistant district attorney of New York by District Attorney Thomas E. Dewey in 1938; entered the U.S. Navy as a lieutenant in August 1942, serving first as a division officer at the Naval Air Station at Anacostia, Washington, D.C., and later as administrative officer of Carrier Group Ten; released in January 1946 as a lieutenant commander, he returned to the New York district attorney's office, but left in April 1947 to become counsel to the Senate's special committee to investigate the national defense program, becoming its chief counsel in July 1947; resigned his position to join the Washington office of the New York law firm of Dwight, Harris, Koegel and Caskey; appointed deputy attorney general by President Eisenhower in 1952; joined the Eisenhower cabinet as ATTORNEY GENERAL on January 27, 1958, serving until January 20, 1961; he advocated a constitutional amendment to deal with the question of presidential disability or inability to perform the functions of the office, sent a group of deputy U.S. marshals to Little Rock, Ark., to insure enforcement of the desegregation orders of the federal courts, and created a special unit to fight syndicated crime and racketeering in 1958; resumed private practice upon leaving government service; joined the Nixon cabinet as SECRETARY OF STATE on January 23, 1969; resigned that post as of September 3, 1973, and returned to private law practice; played role of President Ronald Reagan in mock nuclear war drill to test U.S. readiness for a nuclear crisis, March 1–5, 1983; testified before the U.S. National Bipartisan Commission on Central America, 1983; headed the commission appointed by Reagan on February 3, 1986, to investigate the January 28 explosion of the space shuttle *Challenger*; led the February 15, 1986, assertion that the *Challenger* launch decision "may have been flawed"; charged that space agency officials had abandoned good judgment in handling safety problems with the space shuttle, February 27, 1986; testified before the Foreign Relations Commission on January 27, 1988, in support of the INF Treaty, insisting that to let the treaty fail would be a serious setback to U.S. foreign policy. Arthur Larson, *Eisenhower: The President Nobody Knew* (1968); Emmett John Hughes, *The Ordeal of Power; A Political Memoir of the Eisenhower Years* (1963); *Facts on File Yearbook* (1982; 1983; and 1986).

ROMNEY, George Wilcken. Born in Chihuahua, Mexico, on July 8, 1907; son of Gaskell Romney, contractor, and Anna (Pratt) Romney; Mormon; married to Lenore La Fount on July 2, 1931; father of Lynn, Jane, Scott, and Willard; began work at age 11 as a sugar harvester and then as a lath and plaster workman; attended Latter Day Saints University in Salt Lake City, Utah, 1922–1926; Mormon missionary in Scotland and England, 1927–1928; attended the University of Utah, 1929, and George Washington University, 1929–1930; tariff specialist for U.S. Senator David I. Walsh, 1929–1930; apprentice, Aluminum Company of America, 1930, and salesman, 1931; Washington representative, Aluminum Company of America and Aluminum Wares Association, 1932–1938; management member of the War Manpower Commission, the Labor-Management Commission, and president of the Washington Trade Association, 1937–1938; Detroit manager of the Automobile Manufacturers Association, 1939–1941, and served as general manager, 1942–1948; president of the Detroit Trade Association, 1941; director of the American Trade Association Executives, 1944–1947; managing director of Automotive Council War Production, 1942–1945; U.S. employer delegate to Metal Trades Industry Conferences, 1946–1949; vice-president of the Nash-Kelvinator Corp., 1950–1953, and served as executive vice-president and director, 1953–1954; president, chairman of the board, and general manager of the American Motors Corporation, 1954–1962; vice-chairman and director (on leave) until 1962; elected as Republican governor of Michigan and served from 1963 to 1968; candidate for the Republican presidential nomination in 1968 until his withdrawal that year; appointed SECRETARY OF HOUSING AND URBAN DEVELOPMENT in the cabinet of President Nixon on December 11, 1968, and took the oath of office on January 22, 1969; most important contributions were reorganizing the Model Cities program and initiating "Operation Breakthrough" to help secure mass housing for the poor; resigned his post on November 22, 1972, and returned to private business interests in Michigan. D. Duane Angel, *Romney: A Political Biography* (1967), G. Harris, *Romney's Way* (1967); Gerald O. Plas, *Romney Riddle* (1967).

ROOSEVELT, Franklin Delano. Born near Hyde Park, N.Y., January 30, 1882; son of James and Sara (Delano) Roosevelt; Episcopalian; married Anna Eleanor Roosevelt, niece of President Theodore Roosevelt and a distant cousin, on March 17, 1905; father of Anna Eleanor, James, Franklin, Jr., Elliott, and John Aspinall; educated by private tutors until the age of 14, when he entered Groton School, graduating in 1900; attended Harvard University, graduating in 1904; attended Columbia Law School in New York City, attending until 1907; admitted to the bar in 1907, he commenced the practice of his profession in New York City with the firm of Carter, Ledyard and Milburn; elected to the New York State Senate from Dutchess County; reelected, serving from 1911 until March 17, 1913, when he resigned, having been tendered an appointment as assistant secretary of the navy by President Wilson; served in that post until 1920; received the Democratic nomination for the vice-presidency at the San Francisco convention as a running mate of James M. Cox in July 1920; resumed his New York law practice, joining the firm of Emmet, Marvin and Roosevelt in 1920; vice-president of the Fidelity and Deposit Company of Maryland from 1920 to 1928; stricken with infantile paralysis at his summer home in Campobello, New Brunswick, Canada, in August 1921; president of the Woodrow Wilson Foundation, the Boy Scouts Foundation and the Seaman's Institute; chairman of the Taconic Park Commission; trustee of Vassar College; became member of the law firm of Roosevelt and O'Connor in 1924; elected governor of New York in 1928 and reelected in 1930, serving until 1933; nominated for the presidency at the Democratic national convention at Chicago in June 1932; elected PRESIDENT in November 1932; inaugurated on March 4, 1933, reelected three times and served until his death in office on April 12, 1945; he was the seventh President to die in office, the fourth of these to die a natural death; authored *Government, Not Politics* (1932), *Looking Forward*, (1933), *On Our Way* (1934); died in Warm Springs, Ga., April 12, 1945; interment in the family plot at Hyde Park, N.Y. Arthur M. Schlesinger, *The Politics of Upheaval* (1960); Rexford Tugwell, *The Democratic Roosevelt* (1965).

ROOSEVELT, Theodore. Born in New York, N.Y., October 27, 1858; son of Theodore and Martha (Bulloch) Roosevelt; married Alice Hathaway Lee on October 27, 1880; married Edith Kermit Carow on December 2, 1886; father of Alice Lee, Theodore, Jr., Kermit, Ethel Carow, Archibald Bulloch, and Quentin; educated by private tutors; entered Harvard University, graduating in 1880; studied law; travelled abroad extensively; elected to the New York State Assembly from 1882 to 1884; delegate to the Republican national convention at Chicago, 1884; moved to North Dakota and lived on his ranch; returned to New York City in 1886; appointed a member of the U.S. Civil Service Board in 1889, by President Benjamin Harrison; became president of the New York state Board of Police Commissioners in 1895, resigning in 1897 upon being tendered the position of assistant secretary of the navy by President McKinley, in April 1897; served until 1898, when he resigned to enter the war with Spain; organized the 1st Regiment, U.S. Volunteer Cavalry; appointed lieutenant colonel and then colonel of this regiment; elected governor of New York in 1898; elected VICE-PRESIDENT on the Republican ticket headed by William McKinley in 1900, and was inaugurated on March 4, 1901; upon the assassination of President McKinley on September 14, 1901, he succeeded to the Presidency, serving that term until March 1905; elected PRESIDENT in 1904, being inaugurated on March 4, 1905, and serving until March 3, 1909; organized a scientific expedition to South Africa under the auspices of the Smithsonian Institution, to gather natural history materials for the new U.S. Natural History Museum at Washington, D.C., in 1910; unsuccessful candidate of the Progressive Party for reelection to the presidency in 1912; headed an exploring party to South America in 1914; engaged in literary pursuits; his published works include *Essays on Practical Politics* (1888), *The Winning of the West* (1889), *American Ideals and Other Essays, Social and Political* (1897), *History as Literature, and Other Essays* (1913); *The Great Adventure: Present Day Studies in American Nationalism* (1918); died at Oyster Bay, New York, on January 6, 1919; interment in Young's Memorial Cemetery, Oyster Bay. William Henry Harbaugh, *Power and Responsibility: The Life and Times of Theodore Roosevelt* (1961); Edward Charles Wagenknecht, *Seven Worlds of Theodore Roosevelt* (1958).

ROOT, Elihu. Born in Clinton, N.Y., February 15, 1845; son of Oren Root, professor at Hamilton College, and Nancy Whitney (Buttrick) Root; married Clara Wales on January 8, 1878; father of Edith, Elihu, and Edward Wales; graduated from Hamilton College in 1864; taught at the Rome Academy in 1865; received LL.B. from New York University Law School in 1867 and was admitted to the bar that same year; began practicing as corporation lawyer in New York; United States district attorney for southern district of New York, 1883–1885; chairman of the judiciary committee in the New York constitutional convention of 1894; appointed SECRETARY OF WAR in the cabinet of President McKinley on August 1, 1899, and continued in President Theodore Roosevelt's cabinet until February 1, 1904; most important contributions were reorganization of the administration of the army and establishment of governments in territories newly acquired from Spain; appointed SECRETARY OF STATE in the cabinet of President Roosevelt on July 1, 1905, and served until his resignation on January 27, 1909; most important contributions were efforts to improve deteriorating relations with Latin America, and obtainment of Japanese adherence to the Open Door policy; elected U.S. senator from New York in January 1909, and served until March 4, 1915; acted as U.S. counsel in North Atlantic fisheries dispute in 1910; sat on the Hague Tribunal, 1910; headed the Carnegie Endowment for International Peace, 1910; won Nobel peace prize in 1912; headed U.S. diplomatic mission to Russia in an attempt to keep Russia fighting for the Allies, 1917; work on Permanent Court of International Justice plans led to its establishment; author of *Experiment in Government and the Essentials of the Constitution* (1913), *Russia and the United States* (1917), and other books; U.S. commissioner plenipotentiary at Washington Conference on Limitations of Armaments, 1921–1922; received doctorate degrees in law and political sciences from twenty colleges and universities, 1894–1929; died in New York, N.Y., February 7, 1939. Richard William Leopold, *Elihu Root* (1954); P. C. Jessup, *Elihu Root* (1938).

ROPER, Daniel C. Born in Marlboro County, S.C., April 1, 1867; son of John Wesley Roper, farmer, merchant, and Confederate officer during the Civil War, and Henrietta Virginia (McLaurin) Roper; member of the Methodist Episcopal Church; married to Lou McKenzie in 1889; father of Margaret May, James Hunter, Daniel Calhoun, Grace Henrietta, John Wesley, Harry McKenzie, and Richard Frederick; attended Wofford College, Spartansburg, S.C. and then Trinity College, from which he was graduated in 1888; taught school, worked as a farmer, and wrote life insurance, 1888–1892; elected to the state House of Representatives, 1892; appointed clerk of the U.S. Senate Committee on Interstate Commerce in 1893 and served for three years; engaged in private business in New York City, 1896–1898; life insurance agent in Maryland and Washington, D.C., studied law at the National Law School, Washington, D.C., and received his degree in 1901; special agent of the federal Bureau of the Census, 1900–1911; appointed clerk of the U.S. House of Representatives Ways and Means Committee, 1911; appointed first assistant postmaster general, 1913, and served until 1916; chairman of the organization bureau of the Democratic national committee, 1916; appointed vice-chairman of the U.S. Tariff Commission, 1917; appointed by President Wilson as commissioner of Internal Revenue in 1917, and served until his resignation in 1920; president of the Marlin-Rockwell Corporation, 1920–1921; engaged in law practice in Washington, D.C., 1921–1933 as head of the firm of Roper, Hagerman, Hurrey, and Parks, and later of Roper, Hurrey, and Dudley; appointed SECRETARY OF COMMERCE in the cabinet of President Franklin D. Roosevelt on March 4, 1933; most important contributions were establishing a business advisory council, helping to organize and administer many early reform measures of the New Deal, and reorganizing the department to reduce expenditures; resigned on December 23, 1938 and resumed law practice in Washington; appointed temporary U.S. minister to Canada by President Roosevelt in May 1939 and resigned from that post after four months of service; director of the Atlantic Coast Line Railroad; author of *The United States Post Office* (1917) and an autobiography; died in Washington, D.C. on April 11, 1943. Daniel C. Roper, *Fifty Years of Public Life* (1942); Barry Karl, *Executive Reorganization and Reform in the New Deal* (1963).

ROYALL, Kenneth Claiborne. Born in Goldsboro, N.C., July 24, 1894; son of George and Clara Howard (Jones) Royall; Episcopalian; married Margaret Best on August 18, 1917; father of Kenneth Claiborne, Jr., Margaret, and George Pender; after completing his preliminary education in the local school, he attended the Episcopal High School in Alexandria, Va., and then entered the University of North Carolina, graduating in 1914; studied law at Harvard, graduating in 1917; associate editor of the *Harvard Law Review* from 1915 to 1917; admitted to the bar in 1917, practicing his profession in Goldsboro and Raleigh, N.C.; elected to the North Carolina legislature as state senator in 1927; author of the North Carolina bank liquidation statute; presidential elector from North Carolina in 1914; served as second lieutenant in the field artillery during 1917 and 1918, and later, as first lieutenant, in France, during 1918 and 1919; served in the U.S. Army during World War II as a colonel and, finally, as a brigadier general; appointed special assistant to the Secretary of War during 1944 and 1945; invited to join the Truman Cabinet as SECRETARY OF WAR on July 21, 1947, entering upon his duties on July 25, 1947, serving until September 17, 1947; appointed the first secretary of the army under the unification of the armed forces, serving from 1947 to 1949; delegate-at-large to the Democratic national convention in 1964; member of the Presidential Racial Commission held in Birmingham, Ala., in 1963; national chairman for the lawyer's committee for the Johnson and Humphrey national ticket in 1964; trustee of the John Fitzgerald Kennedy Memorial Library; member of the General Alumni Association of the University of North Carolina and its president during 1959 and 1960; lives in retirement at his home at 1040 Fifth Avenue, New York City. Cabell B. H. Phillips, *The Truman Presidency: The History of a Triumphant Succession* (1966); Alfred Steinberg, *The Man from Missouri: The Life and Times of Harry S. Truman* (1962).

RUMSFELD, Donald. Born in Chicago, Ill., July 9, 1932; son of George Donald and Jeannette R. (Huster) Rumsfeld; married Joyce Pierson, December 27, 1954; father of Valerie Jeanne, Marcy Kay, and Donald Nicholas; received A.B. degree from Princeton University in 1954; served in the U.S. Navy, 1954–1957; administrative assistant, U.S. Congress, 1958; staff assistant, U.S. Congress, 1959; representative, A. G. Becker and Company of Chicago, 1960–1962; member, U.S. Congress, 1965–1971; director, Office of Economic Opportunity, 1969–1970; counselor to the President, 1970–1973; director, Cost of Living Council, 1971–1973; U.S. ambassador to NATO, 1973–1974; member, Council for Urban Affairs; member, Rural Affairs Council; Cabinet Commission on Civil Rights and Education; chairman, Property Revaluation Board, 1971–1973; board of directors, National Center for Volunteer Action; member, Advisory Committee, Fellowship Program, American Political Science Association; Republican; in November 1975, nominated by President Gerald Ford to the office of SECRETARY OF DEFENSE, and on November 11, appointment was confirmed by the U.S. Senate; took office on November 20, 1975; a staunch defender of the nation's defense budget, and strong resister of congressional efforts at budget cutting; supported development of the Cruise Missile as means to offset the striking power of the Soviet Union; left office on January 20, 1977, with the change in presidential administrations; named as special envoy to the Middle East by President Ronald Reagan, November 3, 1983; resigned from position as envoy to the Middle East on May 18, 1984, to join the board of directors of G. D. Searle and Company; served on General Advisory Committee on Arms Control and Disarmament, January 1984; named as chairman of Searle and Company, the first chairman who was not a Searle family member, on June 1, 1985; on August 22, 1985, announced he was leaving Searle and Company effective September 1, 1985, as the company completed a merger with Monsanto Co.; joined board of directors of Westmark Systems, Inc., a military electronics development company, in 1986; on March 2, 1987, decided not to run for president of the United States, citing his conclusion that he could not raise sufficient campaign funding to compete effectively against better-known candidates in the early primaries. *Facts on File Yearbook* (1973; 1975–1976, 1983–1987); National Journal, *Ford's Presidency* (1976).

RUSH, Richard. Born in Philadelphia, Pa., August 29, 1780; son of Dr. Benjamin and Julia (Stockton) Rush; married Catherine E. Murray on August 29, 1809; father of ten children; raised in a cultured home, he entered the College of New Jersey (now Princeton) at the age of 14 in 1794, graduating in 1797; studied law and was admitted to the bar in December 1800; appointed attorney general of Pennsylvania in January 1811; became comptroller of the treasury in November 1811, by appointment of President Madison; invited to join the cabinet of President Monroe on February 10, 1814, as ATTORNEY GENERAL, and served until November 12, 1817; during his incumbency, he superintended the publication of *The Laws of the United States from 1789 to 1815* (1815); appointed secretary of state, *ad interim*, on October 30, 1817, by President Monroe, pending the return of John Quincy Adams from Europe to assume that office; during his secretaryship, he negotiated the Rush–Bagot Convention on April 28, 1817, establishing a limitation of naval armaments on the Great Lakes; appointed minister to Great Britain on October 31, 1817; appointed SECRETARY OF THE TREASURY by President John Quincy Adams on March 7, 1825, serving until March 3, 1829; unsuccessful candidate for vice-president on Adams' ticket in 1828; appointed by President Jackson to adjust the dispute concerning the boundaries between Ohio and Michigan in 1835; sent to England in 1836 by President Jackson to obtain the legacy bequeathed the U.S. by the late James Smithson, which legacy resulted in the erection in Washington, D.C. of the Smithsonian Institution in August 1846; appointed minister to France on March 3, 1847, by President Polk; author of *Memoranda of a Residence at the Court of London* (1833) and *Occasional Productions, Political, Diplomatic and Miscellaneous* (1860); died in Philadelphia, Pa., July 30, 1859, Irving Brant, *James Madison and American Nationalism* (1968); John William Ward, *Andrew Jackson, Symbol for an Age* (1955).

RUSK, David Dean. Born in Cherokee County, Ga., February 9, 1909; son of Robert Hugh Rusk, farmer and mail carrier, and Frances Elizabeth (Clotfelter) Rusk; Presbyterian; married Virginia Foisie on June 19, 1937; father of David Patrick, Richard Geary, and Margaret Elizabeth; attended public schools of Atlanta, Ga.; worked two years in Atlanta law office; graduated Davidson College in 1931; received B.A. from St. Johns College, Oxford University, in 1933, and M.A. in 1934; studied at University of Berlin and several other German colleges during vacations; became associate professor of government and international relations at Mills College, Oakland, Cal., 1934, and was made dean of faculty in 1938; studied law at University of California, Berkeley, 1937–1940; became infantry reserve officer in 1931, and was called to active duty in 1941; sent to China-Burma-India theater of operations as part of war plans department of general staff; became deputy chief of staff to General Joseph W. Stilwell; assistant chief, operations division of U.S. War Department general staff; attained rank of colonel; made assistant chief of international security affairs in Department of State, 1948; recalled to Pentagon as special assistant to coordinate war and state departments on common matters; director of Office of Special Political Affairs and Office of United Nations Affairs, 1947–1949; chosen assistant secretary of state in February 1949; made deputy undersecretary of state in May 1949; assistant secretary of state for far eastern affairs, 1950–1951; president of Rockefeller Foundation, 1952–1961; appointed SECRETARY OF STATE in the cabinet of President Kennedy, continued under President Johnson and served from January 21, 1961 to January 21, 1969; most important contributions were negotiations for test ban treaty, conferences on Berlin situation, support of United Nations action in Congo, economic and military aid to Republic of Korea, helped formulate American policy toward Viet Nam and was leading administration defender of policy of intervention; upon leaving office accepted a post as professor of law in the University of Georgia Law School; testified before the U.S. National Bipartisan Commission on Central America, on September 1, 1983, advocating economic and social aid to Central American countries; member of a group organized to "save" the ABM (antiballistic missile) treaty, June 19, 1984. Dean Rusk, *The Winds of Freedom* (1963); Hugh Sidey, *John F. Kennedy, President* (1963).

RUSK, Jeremiah McLain. Born on a farm at Malta, Ohio, June 17, 1830; son of Daniel and Jane (Faulkner) Rusk; married to Mary Martin on April 5, 1849, and after her death, to Elizabeth M. Johnson in 1856; father of five children;

received a limited education at the local schools; moved to Vernon County, Wis., in 1853, and engaged in agricultural pursuits; became owner of a stagecoach line and part owner of a bank; became sheriff of Viroqua, Wis., 1855–1857; became coroner in 1857; elected to the State Assembly in 1862; served as a combatant in the Civil War, rising to the rank of major in the 28th Regiment of the Wisconsin Volunteer Infantry, advanced to lieutenant colonel, to colonel, and finally to brigadier general on March 13, 1856; mustered out on June 7, 1865; bank comptroller of Wisconsin, 1866–1869; elected as a Republican to the 42d, 43d, and 44th Congresses, serving from 1871 to 1877; declined the appointment of minister to Uruguay and Paraguay tendered by President Garfield; elected governor of Wisconsin, 1882–1889; in connection with his orders to shoot strikers in Milwaukee in May 1866, he remarked, "I seen my duty and I done it"; appointed to the cabinet of President Benjamin Harrison as SECRETARY OF AGRICULTURE on March 5, 1889, serving until March 5, 1893; died in Viroqua, Wis., November 21, 1893; interment in Viroqua Cemetery. Robert Granville Caldwell, *James A. Garfield, Party Chieftain* (1931); Theodore Clarke Smith, *The Life and Letters of James Abram Garfield* (1925).

S

ST. CLAIR, Arthur. Born in Thurso, Caithness, Scotland on March 23, 1734; probably the son of William Sinclair, merchant, and Elizabeth (Balfour) Sinclair; married to Phoebe Bayard on May 15, 1760; father of seven children; attended the University of Edinburgh; studied medicine; became an ensign in the British Army, May 13, 1757; resigned on April 16, 1762 with the commission of lieutenant; purchased an estate and settled in Ligonier Valley, Pennsylvania, 1764; erected mills; surveyor of the district of Cumberland, 1770; justice of the court of quarter sessions and of common pleas; member of the proprietary council, justice, recorder, and clerk of the orphans' court; prothonotary of Bedford and Westmoreland Counties; colonel of the Pennsylvania Militia, 1775; became brigadier general in the Continental Army, August 9, 1776; became major general on February 19, 1777; recalled from service by Congress after his evacuation of Fort Ticonderoga; exonerated of charges by court martial, September 1778, and served until the end of the Revolutionary War; member of the military tribunal which tried Major André, 1780; member of the Pennsylvania council of censors, 1783; member of the Continental Congress from November 2, 1785 to November 28, 1787; elected PRESIDENT OF THE CONTINENTAL CONGRESS and served from February 2, 1787 to January 21, 1788; appointed governor of the Northwest Territory in 1787 and served until 1802; major general and commander of the U.S. Army, March 4, 1791 to March 5, 1792; retired to his home, "Hermitage," near Ligonier, Pa.; author of *A Narrative of the Manner in which the Campaign Against the Indians in . . . [1791] was Conducted Under the Command of Major General St. Clair . . .*; died near Youngstown, Pa. on August 31, 1818; interment in General St. Clair Cemetery, Greensburg, Pa. W. H. Smith, *The St. Clair Papers* (1882); E. C. Burnett, *The Continental Congress* (1964).

SARGENT, John Garibaldi. Born in Ludlow, Vt., October 13, 1860; son of John Henmon and Ann Eliza (Hanley) Sargent; Universalist; married Mary Lorraine Gordon on August 4, 1887; father of Gladys Gordon; attended the Vermont Liberal Institute, Plymouth, Vt., and the Black River Academy, Ludlow, Vt., graduating the latter in 1883; entered Tufts College, receiving an A.B. Degree in 1887; studied law and was admitted to the Vermont Bar in 1890; became a member of the law firm of Stickney, Sargent and Skeels; state's attorney of Windsor County, Vt. from 1898 to 1900; appointed secretary of civil and military affairs of Vermont by Governor Stickney from 1900 to 1902; returned to private practice from 1902 to 1908; attorney general of Vermont from 1908 to 1912; invited to join the Coolidge cabinet as ATTORNEY GENERAL on March 17, 1925, entering upon his duties on March 18, 1925, and serving until March 4, 1929; during his incumbency, he vigorously supported enforcement of Prohibition, and upheld the validity of evidence secured by wiretapping; resumed private practice after his retirement; appointed referee in the reorganization of the railroads of Vermont in 1935; director of the Vermont Valley, Boston and Maine Railroad and the Central Vermont Railroad from 1935 until his death; served as president of the Ludlow Savings Bank and Trust Company; chairman of the Vermont Commission on Uniform State Laws; trustee of the Black River Academy; member of the Vermont Historical Society; died in Ludlow, Vt. on March 5, 1939. Jules Abel, *In the Time of Silent Cal* (1969); Donald R. McCoy, *Calvin Coolidge: The Quiet President* (1967).

SAWYER, Charles. Born in Cincinnati, Ohio, February 10, 1887; son of Edward Milton and Caroline (Butler) Sawyer; Episcopalian; married to Margaret Sterrett on July 15, 1918, and after her death married Elizabeth De Veyrac on June 10, 1942; father of Anne Johnston, Charles, Jean Johnston, John, and Edward; after receiving his education at the local public schools, he entered Oberlin College in Ohio, graduating in 1908; studied law at the University of Cincinnati, graduating in 1911; admitted to the bar in 1911, commencing practice in Cincinnati; elected to the Cincinnati city council in 1911; delegate to the Democratic national convention in 1912; reelected in 1913; enlisted in the U.S. Army as a private in 1917; subsequently commissioned a captain and promoted to major; delegate to the Democratic national convention in 1932 and again in 1936, at Philadelphia, at which time he was elected the Democratic national committeeman from Ohio; elected lieutenant governor of Ohio in 1933 and 1934; unsuccessful Democratic nominee for the office of governor in 1938; appointed U.S. ambassador to Belgium and Luxemburg in 1944 by President Franklin D. Roosevelt, serving until his resignation in 1946; named SECRETARY OF COMMERCE by President Truman on May 6, 1948, serving until January 20, 1953; during his tenure, he broadened the activities of the department by the addition of the Bureau of Public Roads to its jurisdiction and the creation of a new agency, the Maritime Administration; trustee of Oberlin College; member of the National Council of Boy Scouts of America; recipient of the Freedom Foundation Award in 1949; upon retiring from public service, he resumed the practice of law in Glendale, Ohio; chairman, Cincinnati Community Chest, 1954; Cincinnati United Fund, 1955–1960; in 1955, appointed to the Overseas Economic Operations Task Force of the Hoover Commission and charged with recommending policy changes concerning foreign aid; served on the Commission on Money and Credit, created by the Committee for Economic Development, between May 1958 and June 1961; upon retirement from government service, practiced law as a senior partner for the law firm of Taft, Stettinius, and Hollister; died on April 7, 1979 in Palm Beach, Fla.; wrote autobiography *Concerns of a Conservative Democrat* (1968). William Hillman, *Mr. President* (1952); Cabell B. H. Phillips, *The Truman Presidency: The History of a Triumphant Succession* (1966); *New York Times* (January 29, 1953; June 18, 1961; and April 9, 1979). *Who's Who in America, 1976–1977*; Maeva Marius, *Truman and the Steel Seizure Case* (1977); Eleanora W. Schoenebaum, ed., *Facts on File: Political Profiles: The Truman Years* (1978).

SAXBE, William. Born in Mechanicsburg, Oh., on June 24, 1916; son of Bart Rockwell and Faye Henry (Carey) Saxbe; Episcopalian; married Ardath Louise Kleinhans on September 14, 1940; father of William Bart, Juliet Louise and Charles Rockwell; B.A., Ohio State University, 1940; a member of Ohio National Guard, served for five years in the Army Air Force during World War II; while studying law at Ohio State, elected to the Ohio House of Representatives for four terms, 1947–1954, during third term (1951–1952) was a majority leader, during fourth term (1953–1954) was a speaker; elected to four terms as State Attorney General, 1957–1958, 1963–1968; ran as Republican candidate for U.S. SENATOR from Ohio, won, and served from 1969 to 1974; offered the post of U.S. ATTORNEY GENERAL by Richard Nixon and was sworn into office on January 4, 1974; as Attorney General pushed for legislation to limit access to criminal records of arrested and convicted persons; favored capital punishment as deterrent and stiff prison sentences for gun-related crimes; in keeping with reputation for accessibility and candor with the press, instituted weekly news conferences at the Department of Justice; referred to Patty Hearst as a "common criminal" and to the "Jewish intellectual" of the 1950s as being "enamored" of the Communist party; on April 24, 1974, in the wake of uproars caused by his explosive statements, he suspended his weekly meetings with the journalists; gradually learned to control his tongue, and soon accomplished many things using surprisingly liberal views; investigated Cointelpro, the FBI's counter-intelligence program, and declared that it had been used in "reprehensible" fashion to harass left-wing groups, black leaders, and campus radicals; came down hard on antitrust matters, presiding over two of the biggest antitrust suits in history, against IBM and AT&T; in December 1974, resigned post as Attorney General to accept nomination as AMBASSADOR to India, 1975–1977; partner in law firm of Chester, Saxbe, Hoffman, and Wilcox, Columbus, Ohio, 1977–1981; of counsel, Jones, Day Reavis, and Pogue, Cleveland, Ohio, 1981–1984; of counsel, Pearson, Ball, and Dowd, Washington, D.C., since 1984; became independent special counsel for Central States Teamsters Pension Fund in December 1982. *Newsweek* (December 23, 1974); *New York Post* (April 27, 1974); *New York Times* magazine (May 5, 1974); *New York Times* (December 5, 1982); *Who's Who in America, 1988–1989.*

SCHLESINGER, James Born on February 15, 1929, in New York City; son of Julius and Rhea (Rogen) Schlesinger; Lutheran; married Rachel Mellinger on June 19, 1954; father of Cara K., Charles L., Ann R., William F., Emily, Thomas S., Clara, and James Rodney; received his A.B. summa cum laude, Harvard, 1950; A.M. in economics, 1952; Ph.D. in economics, 1956; served as assistant professor, and then as associate professor of economics at the University of Virginia, 1955–1963; senior staff member, Rand Corp., 1963–1967; director of strategic studies, 1967–1969; visiting scholar, Johns Hopkins University, 1976–1977; currently senior advisor, strategic and international studies office, Georgetown University, and senior advisor, Lehman Brothers Kuhn Loeb, Inc.; academic consultant, Naval War College, 1957; consultant to board of governors, Federal Reserve Board, 1962–1963; consultant, Bureau of Budget, 1965–1969; assistant director, Office of Management and Budget, 1970–1971; appointed by President Richard Nixon as chairman of the Atomic Energy Commission on July 21, 1971, and served in that position until January 22, 1973; confirmed as director of the Central Intelligence Agency on January 23, 1973; served in that position until May 1, 1973; then nominated on May 10, 1973, by President Nixon to serve as SECRETARY OF DEFENSE, and was confirmed by the Senate on June 28, 1973; resigned that office on November 3, 1975; later served in the newly created Department of Energy under President Jimmy Carter as the first SECRETARY OF ENERGY, nominated and confirmed on August 4, 1977; resigned from that position on July 19, 1979, after President Carter called for resignations of a number of cabinet positions. Received a number of awards, including Distinguished Intelligence Service Medal (1975), Distinguished Public Service Medal, Department of the Navy (1976), Exceptional Citizen Service Medal, Department of the Air Force (1976), and National Security Medal (1979); authored *The Political Economy of National Security: A Study of the Economic Aspects of the Contemporary Power Struggle* (1960); coauthored *Issues in Defense Economics* (1967). *Current Biography, 1973; Facts on File Yearbook* (1971, 1973, 1975, 1977, 1979); *Who's Who in American Politics, 1987–1988.*

SCHOFIELD, John McAllister. Born in Gerry, N.Y., September 29, 1831; son of James Schofield, Baptist clergyman, and Caroline (McAllister) Schofield; married Harriet Bartlett in June 1857; father of two sons and one daughter; married Georgia Kilbourne in 1891; moved with family to Freeport, Ill. in 1843; attended public schools; was surveyor of public lands in northern Wisconsin during summers; taught district school; appointed cadet at West Point, 1849–1853; brevetted second lieutenant of 2d Artillery at Fort Moultrie, S.C.; commissioned second lieutenant of 1st Artillery in Florida, and dealt with Seminole Indian troubles; made first lieutenant in 1855, and sent to West Point as assistant professor of philosophy; took leave of absence, 1860, and was professor of physics at Washington University, Mo.; became mustering officer for Missouri in 1861; made major in 1st Missouri Volunteer Infantry; chosen chief of staff to General Nathaniel Lyon in June 1861, and assumed command upon Lyon's death, August 10, 1861; made captain, and later brigadier general of volunteers; headed "Army of the Frontier," October 1862 to April 1863; appointed major general, and took command of Department of the Missouri in St. Louis; commanded 23d Corps of Department of Army of the Ohio, February 1864; made brigadier general in regular army in November 1864, and brevetted major general in March 1865; headed Department of North Carolina; went on mission to France, 1865–1866; commanded Department of Potomac; appointed SECRETARY OF WAR in the cabinet of President Andrew Johnson on May 28, 1868, and served from July 1, 1868 to March 10, 1869; most important contributions were organization of light artillery school at Fort Riley, Mounted Service School, and U.S. Cavalry School; commanded Department of the Missouri from March 20, 1869 to May 3, 1870; went on mission to Hawaii in 1872; superintendent of U.S. Military Academy, 1876–1881; spent one year in Europe; took command of Division of Pacific on October 15, 1882, Division of Missouri on November 1, 1883, and Division of Atlantic on April 2, 1886; made commanding general of the army on August 14, 1888; became lieutenant general in February 1895; retired in September 1895; wrote *Forty-Six Years in the Army* (1897); died in St. Augustine, Fla., on March 4, 1906. J. D. Cox, *The March to the Sea* (1906).

SCHURZ, Carl. Born in Liblar-am-Rhein, near Cologne, Germany, March 2, 1829; son of Christian Schurz, village schoolmaster and businessman, and Marianne (Jussen) Schurz; married Margarethe Meyer on July 6, 1852; father of two sons and two daughters; attended gymnasium at Cologne, 1839–1846; was candidate for doctorate at University of Bonn in 1847; took part in revolution of 1848; became lieutenant and staff officer in revolutionary army; fled Germany, and joined refugees in Switzerland; was newspaper correspondent in Paris in 1851; taught in London; moved to United States in August 1852, and settled in Philadelphia until 1855; bought farm in Watertown, Wis., 1856; admitted to bar, 1856, and began practice in Milwaukee; was anti-slavery Republican; unsuccessful candidate for lieutenant governor in 1857; spoke for Lincoln against Douglas in Illinois, 1858; unsuccessful candidate for governor of Wisconsin; chairman of Wisconsin delegation to Chicago Republican convention in 1860; appointed minister to Spain in 1862; made brigadier general in charge of a division in Frémont's Army on June 10, 1862; became major general on March 14, 1863; was chief of staff to Major General Slocum in Sherman's army; Washington correspondent for *New York Tribune*, 1865–1866; became editor-in-chief of Detroit *Post* in 1866; made joint editor with Emil Pretorius on St. Louis *Westliche Post*, 1867; delegate to Republican national convention of 1868;

elected U.S. senator from Missouri in 1868, and served from March 4, 1869 to March 3, 1875; was permanent president of Cincinnati convention to form Liberal Republican party in 1872; appointed SECRETARY OF THE INTERIOR in the cabinet of President Hayes, and served from March 12, 1877 to March 4, 1881; most important contributions were use of merit system in department, development of national parks, enlightened treatment of Indians, and preservation of public domain; published *The New South* (1885) and *Life of Henry Clay* (1887); became counselor for *Evening Post*; wrote essay on Lincoln in *Atlantic Monthly* (June 1891); president of National Service Reform League, 1892–1900; contributed articles to *Harper's Weekly* from 1892 to 1898; president of Civil Service Reform Association of New York, 1893–1906; died in New York City on May 14, 1906; interment in Sleepy Hollow Cemetery, Tarrytown, N.Y. C. R. Goedsche and Walter E. Glaettle, *Carl Schurz* (1963); James P. Terzian, *Defender of Human Rights: Carl Schurz* (1965).

SCHWEIKER, Richard Born in Norristown, Pa., June 1, 1926; son of Malcolm Schweiker and Blanche Schultz Schweiker (deceased); Schwenkfelder Church; married Claire Joan Coleman on June 18, 1955; father of Malcolm C., Lani I., Kyle C., Richard S., Jr., and Lara Kristi; earned B.A. Phi Beta Kappa at Pennsylvania State University; was selected as an alternate delegate to the Republican national convention in 1952 and 1956, and as a delegate in 1972 and 1980; served in the U.S. House of Representatives, thirteenth district of Pennsylvania, 1961–1969; while in the House of Representatives, served on the House Armed Services Committee and the Government Operations Committee; served as U.S. Senator from Pennsylvania, 1969–1981; while in the Senate he became the ranking Republican member on the Labor Committee, the Human Resources Committee, the Health Subcommittee, and the Labor-HEW Subcommittee, and a member of the Appropriations and Rules committees; appointed SECRETARY OF HEALTH AND HUMAN SERVICES by President Ronald Reagan and served from January 21, 1981, to January 13, 1983; as secretary he strengthened the Social Security System, put more emphasis on preventative medicine, cut Medicare and food stamp grants to the states, and tightened the welfare eligibility rules. *Congressional Record* (January 21, 1981); *New York Times* (January 7, 1981, and January 13, 1983); *Who's Who in American Politics, 1987–1988*.

SCHWELLENBACH, Lewis Baxter. Born in Superior, Wis., September 20, 1894; son of Francis William and Martha (Baxter) Schwellenbach; Episcopalian; married Anne Duffy on December 30, 1935; no children; moved to Spokane, Wash. with his parents in 1902; after attending the public schools of Spokane, he entered the University of Washington at Seattle, and was graduated with a law degree in 1917; assistant instructor at the University of Washington in 1916 and 1917; during World War I, he served as a private in the 1st Regiment, U.S. Infantry and then as a corporal, being discharged on February 2, 1919; was admitted to the bar in 1919 and commenced the practice of his profession in

Seattle; state commander of the American Legion in 1922; member of the Board of Regents of the University of Washington during 1933 and 1934, serving as president in 1933; chairman of the Democratic state convention in 1924; chairman of the King County Democratic committee from 1928 to 1930; unsuccessful candidate for nomination for governor in 1932; delegate to the Interparliamentary Union at The Hague in 1936; elected as a Democrat to the U.S. Senate, serving from January 3, 1935 to December 6, 1940, when he resigned to enter the judiciary; appointed U.S. district judge for the eastern district of Washington, in which capacity he served until tendered a cabinet portfolio; invited to join the Truman cabinet as SECRETARY OF LABOR on June 1, 1945, entering upon his duties on July 1, 1945, serving continuously until his death; during his incumbency, he helped to end the wartime government controls over management-labor relations and to restore free bargaining between management and labor, and was a vigorous foe of the Taft-Hartley Law; died in Washington, D.C., on June 10, 1948; interment in Washelli Cemetery, Seattle, Wash. Cabell B. H. Phillips, *The Truman Presidency: The History of a Triumphant Succession* (1966); Alfred Steinberg, *The Man from Missouri: The Life and Times of Harry S. Truman* (1962).

SEATON, Frederick Andrew. Born in Washington, D.C., December 11, 1909; son of Fay Noble and Dorothea Elizabeth (Schmidt) Seaton; Methodist; married Gladys Hope Dowd on January 23, 1931; father of Donald Richard, Johanna Christine, Monica Margaret and Alfred Noble; moved with his family to Manhattan, Kans. in 1915; after attending the local public schools, he entered the Kansas State Agricultural College in Manhattan, Kans., graduating in 1931; while in college, he became a sports announcer over radio stations KSAC and WIBW, continuing until 1937; became associated with his father's newspaper business in 1931; wire news editor on the Manhattan *Morning Chronicle* in 1932; city editor of the *Mercury* in 1933; associate editor of Seaton Publications in 1933, remaining in that capacity until 1937; elected chairman of the Young Republicans, becoming national committeeman for Kansas in 1935; vice chairman of the Kansas Republican national convention delegation in 1936; vice chairman of the Kansas Republican state committee from 1934 to 1937; secretary to Alfred M. Landon, the Republican presidential candidate in 1936; member of the Republican National Speakers Bureau from 1936 to 1940; moved to Hastings, Neb. in 1937, where he became publisher of the *Daily Tribune* and president of the Seaton Publishing Company; named a director of the Nebraska State Grain Improvement Association in 1945; served for two terms, from 1945 to 1949, in Nebraska's legislature; chairman of the Nebraska Legislative Council from 1947 to 1949; manager of Harold E. Stassen's presidential primary campaign in Nebraska; appointed to the U.S. Senate by Governor Peterson to fill a vacancy on December 10, 1951, serving until January 3, 1953; appointed assistant secretary of defense for legislative affairs in September 1953; promoted to presidential administrative assistant for congressional liaison on February 19,

1955, rising to deputy assistant to President Eisenhower on June 15, 1955; invited to join the Eisenhower cabinet as SECRETARY OF THE INTERIOR on June 6, 1956, entering upon his duties on June 8, 1956, and serving until the close of that administration on January 20, 1961; during his secretaryship, he engaged in a program to extract drinking water from the sea via a saline water conversion program; considered for Richard Nixon's vice-presidential running mate in 1960; ran unsuccessfully for governor of Kansas in 1962, defeated by incumbent Frank B. Morrison; member, board of directors, Investors Life Insurance Co., Omaha, Nebr., 1961–1974; member, board of directors, First National Bank, Hastings, Nebr., 1961–1974; worked for Seaton Publishing Co., 1962–1974; served as Kansas state chairman, Radio Free Europe Fund, 1965; served as chairman of the Senior Advisors to the Nixon Campaign, 1968; chairman, President Nixon's Committee on Timber and the Environment, 1973; director of the Nebraska State Reclamation Association; trustee of the University of Nebraska Foundation and of Hastings College; member of the National Editorial Association and the American Academy of Political and Social Science; upon his retirement from government service, he resumed his interest in the Seaton Publishing Company; died January 16, 1974, in Minneapolis. Robert J. Donovan, *Eisenhower: The Inside Story* (1956); Arthur Larson, *Eisenhower: The President Nobody Knew* (1968); *New York Times* (January 18, 1974); Eleanora W. Schoenebaum, ed., *Facts on File: Political Profiles: The Eisenhower Years* (1977).

SEWARD, William Henry. Born in Florida, N.Y., May 6, 1801; son of Dr. Samuel S. and Mary (Jennings) Seward; married Frances Miller on October 20, 1824; father of five children; attended Farmer's Hall Academy in Goshen, N.Y.; entered Union College in 1815 and left to teach school in 1819 and 1820, returning to college and graduating in 1820; studied law and was admitted to the bar in 1823, commencing his legal practice in Auburn, N.Y.; elected senator in the New York state legislature from 1830 to 1834; governor of New York, 1838–1842; elected as a Whig to the U.S. Senate in 1849; reelected to his Senate seat as a Republican in 1855, serving until March 3, 1861; aspirant for the Republican presidential nomination in 1860; invited to join the cabinet of President Lincoln as SECRETARY OF STATE on March 5, 1861, and continued in office under President Andrew Johnson, serving until March 3, 1869; during his incumbency, concluded the convention with Great Britain for the settlement of the *Alabama* claims, completed a treaty with Russia on March 30, 1867 by which Alaska was purchased by the U.S. (purchase known as "Seward's Folly"), asserted the Monroe Doctrine to force withdrawal of French troops from Mexico; on the night of Lincoln's assassination, an unsuccessful attempt was made on Seward's life; after retiring from the cabinet, made a tour of the world; author of *Travels Around the World* (1873); died in Auburn, N.Y., October 16, 1872; interment in Fort Hill Cemetery, Auburn. Jesse Burton Hendrick, *Lincoln's War Cabinet* (1946); Courtlandt Canby, ed., *Lincoln and the Civil War: A Profile and a History* (1960).

SHAW, Leslie Mortier. Born in Morristown, Vt., November 2, 1848; son of Boardman O. and Louise (Spaulding) Shaw; Methodist; married Alice Crenshaw on December 6, 1877; father of one son and two daughters; attended village academy in Stowe; taught school; went to uncle's farm in Iowa, 1869; graduated Cornell College in 1874; completed course at Iowa College of Law, Des Moines, 1876, and started practice at Dennison, Iowa; organized bank and mortgage loan business, 1880; champion of gold standard in campaign of 1896; elected governor of Iowa and served two terms, 1898–1902; became permanent chairman of International Monetary Convention, 1898; campaigned for Theodore Roosevelt, 1900; appointed SECRETARY OF THE TREASURY in the cabinet of President Theodore Roosevelt on January 9, 1902, and served until March 3, 1907; most important contributions were liberalizing security and waiving reserve requirements for government bank deposits, withholding funds for deposit in time of need, artificially stimulating gold importation, and regulating note issues by executive decree; head of Carnegie Trust Company of New York, 1907–1908; head of First Mortgage Guarantee and Trust Company of Philadelphia, 1909–1913; moved to Washington to write and lecture, 1913; published *Current Issues* (1908) and *Vanishing Landmark: The Trend Toward Bolshevism* (1919); died in Washington, D.C., March 28, 1932. B. F. Shambaugh, *The Messages and Proclamations of the Governors of Iowa* (1905); *Annual Reports of the Secretary of the Treasury* (1902–1906); James F. Rhodes, *McKinley and Roosevelt Administrations, 1897–1909* in *History of the United States*, vol. 9 (1922).

SHERMAN, James Schoolcraft. Born in Utica, N.Y., October 24, 1855; son of Richard U. Sherman, newspaper editor, Democratic politician, and member of the state legislature, and Mary Frances (Sherman) Sherman; Dutch Reformed; married on January 26, 1881 to Carrie Babcock; father of Sherrill, Richard, and Thomas; attended the public schools of New Hartford, Utica Academy, and Whitestone Seminary; was graduated from Hamilton College in 1878; studied law and received his degree from Hamilton College in 1879; admitted to the bar and began practice with his brother-in-law, Henry J. Cookinham; elected as a Republican mayor of Utica in 1884, serving until 1886; elected to the U.S. House of Representatives in 1886 and served until 1891, and again from 1893 to 1909; in 1895 became president of the New Hartford Canning Company; helped form the Utica Trust and Deposit Company, becoming its president in 1900; presided over three New York state Republican conventions, and chairman of the congressional campaign committees in 1906; nominated for the vice-presidency at the Republican national Convention in Chicago, June 1908, and elected VICE-PRESIDENT with President Taft on November 3, 1908, taking office on March 4, 1909; renominated in 1912 but died before the close of the campaign on October 30, 1912 in Utica, N.Y.; interment in Utica. Henry F. Pringle, *Life and Times of William H. Taft* (1939); Norman M. Wilensky, *Conservatives in the Progressive Era* (1965).

SHERMAN, John. Born in Lancaster, Ohio, May 10, 1823; son of Charles Robert and Mary (Hoyt) Sherman; younger brother of William Tecumseh Sherman; Methodist; married Margaret Sarah Cecelia Stewart on August 31, 1848; father of an adopted daughter; after attending the common schools, he entered Horner Academy in Lancaster, Ohio, from 1835 to 1837; became junior rodman of an Engineers Corps in 1839; studied law and was admitted to the bar in 1844, commencing his practice at Mansfield, Ohio; delegate to the Whig national conventions at Philadelphia in 1848 and at Baltimore in 1852, serving as secretary to the 1848 convention; moved to Cleveland, Ohio, in 1853; president of the first Ohio Republican state convention in 1855; elected as a representative to the 34th through 37th Congresses, serving from March 4, 1855 to March 21, 1861, when he resigned; elected as a Republican to the U.S. Senate in 1861 and was reelected in 1866 and 1872, serving from March 21, 1861 until his resignation on March 8, 1877; was president *pro tempore* in the Senate from 1885 to 1887; invited to join the cabinet of President Hayes as SECRETARY OF THE TREASURY on March 8, 1877 and served until March 3, 1881; as secretary, his main objectives were the resumption of specie payments and the funding of the public debt and settling the silver question without banishing gold or displacing paper; elected to the U.S. Senate in the place of James A. Garfield, who had been elected President, on March 4, 1881, reelected in 1886 and 1892, and served until his resignation on March 4, 1897; appointed SECRETARY OF STATE in the cabinet of President McKinley, serving from March 5, 1897 until his resignation on April 25, 1900; retired to private life; died in Washington, D.C., on October 22, 1900; interment in Mansfield Cemetery, Mansfield, Ohio. T. Harry Williams, ed., *Hayes, The Diary of a President, 1875–1881* (1964); Richard Shuster, *The Selfish and the Strong* (1958).

SHERMAN, William Tecumseh. Born in Lancaster, Ohio, on February 8, 1820; son of Charles Robert Sherman, lawyer and state supreme court judge, and Mary (Hoyt) Sherman; Methodist; married Eleanor Boyle Ewing on May 1, 1850; father of eight children; after death of father in 1829, raised by Thomas Ewing; attended local academy; received appointment to West Point in 1836, graduated in 1840, and appointed second lieutenant, 3d Artillery, in Florida; became first lieutenant in 1841; studied law while stationed at Fort Moultrie, S.C.; aide to Philip Kearney, adjutant to Richard Barnes Mason, and then adjutant general to Persifer Frazer Smith in Mexican War; made captain of subsistence department until resignation on September 6, 1853; became partner in branch bank in San Francisco; bank representative in New York, 1857; law partnership with Thomas and Hugh Boyle Ewing in Leavenworth, Kans.; was superintendent of military college at Alexandria, La. from October 1859 to January 18, 1861; president of Louisiana street railway; named colonel of 13th Infantry in 1861; fought on Union side in Civil War; named major general of volunteers in May 1862; became major general in 1864 and lieutenant general in 1866; temporarily put in command of army; sent on mission to Mexico, 1866; made general in

command of army on March 4, 1869; appointed SECRETARY OF WAR in the
cabinet of President Grant on September 9, 1869, and served from September
11, 1869 to October 25, 1869; toured Europe, 1871–1872; established school
at Fort Leavenworth; retired from active duty on November 1, 1883; settled in
St. Louis; moved to New York, 1889; died in New York City on February 14,
1891. Henry Hitchcock, *Marching with Sherman* (1927); E. S. Miers, ed., *General
Who Marched to Hell* (1965).

SHULTZ, George Pratt. Born in New York, N.Y., December 13, 1920; son
of Birl E. Shultz, personnel director and founder of the New York Stock Exchange Institute, and Margaret (Pratt) Shultz; Episcopalian; married to Helena
Maria O'Brien on February 16, 1946; father of Margaret Ann, Kathleen Pratt,
Peter Milton, Barbara Lennox, and Alexander George; attended Loomis Institute
in Windsor, Conn., and graduated in 1938; studied economics at Princeton
University from 1938 to 1942, when he graduated; World War II Marine officer,
1942–1945; entered Massachusetts Institute of Technology for postgraduate
study, 1945; teaching assistant in economics, 1946–1947, and instructor, 1948–
1949; received Ph.D., 1949; assistant professor of industrial relations, 1949–
1954; began to serve on arbitration panels for labor-management disputes, 1953;
acting director of the industrial relations section at M.I.T., 1954–1955; promoted
to associate professor, 1955; served as senior staff economist for the President's
Council of Economic Advisors, 1955; resigned from M.I.T. faculty to accept
appointment as professor of industrial relations at the University of Chicago
Graduate School of Business, 1957; appointed dean, 1962; consultant to the
office of Secretary of Labor Mitchell, 1960; appointed by President Kennedy as
consultant to the President's Advisory Committee on Labor-Management Policy,
1961 and 1962; member of the Governor's Committee on Unemployment in
Illinois, 1961 and 1962; chairman of the task force of the U.S. Employment
Service, 1962; member of the National Manpower Policy task force, 1963;
member of the board of directors of Borg-Warner Corp., Stein, Roe, and Farnham, and the General Transportation Company; fellow of the Center for Advanced Study in the Behavioral Sciences at Stratford, Conn., 1968; appointed
by President-elect Nixon as chairman of a task force to study manpower, labor-
management relations, and wage-price policy in 1968; appointed SECRETARY OF
LABOR in the cabinet of President Nixon on December 11, 1968, and took the
oath of office on January 22, 1969; most important contributions were opposing
an increase in the minimum wage rate, helping to avert a national rail strike in
April 1969, ordering into effect the "Philadelphia Plan" to increase minority
group employment, and helping to negotiate a settlement during the postal workers strike, 1970; member of the American Economic Association, the Economic
Club, and the Research Advisory Board of the Committee for Economic Development; president in 1968 of the Industrial Relations Association; relinquished
office on June 10, 1970, to become head of office of Management and the
Budget, part of the Nixon "Supercabinet"; sworn in as SECRETARY OF THE

TREASURY on June 12, 1973, serving until April 30, 1974; in this post he helped formulate Nixon and Ford responses to inflationary pressures and unemployment; professor of management and public policy, Graduate School of Business, Stanford University 1974–1982; executive vice-president, Bechtel Corporation (1974–1975), president (1975–1980); President, Bechtel Group Inc., 1981–1982; member of the Treasury Advisory Committee on reform of the international monetary system, 1975– ; chairman of the President's Economic Policy advisory board, February 10, 1982; director, G.M. Corp. (1981–1982), Dillon, Read, and Co., Inc. (1981–1982); named SECRETARY OF STATE on June 25, 1982, and served from July 16, 1982, to November 9, 1988; assassination attempt against him in South America, August 1988; elected director to Boeing Co., March 1989. Coauthor of *The Dynamics of a Labor Market* with Charles A. Myers (1951), *Management Organization and the Computer* with Thomas L. Whisler (1960), *Strategies for the Displaced Worker* with Arnold A. Weber (1966), and *Economic Policy beyond the Headlines* with Kenneth W. Dam (1978); coeditor with Robert Z. Aliber of *Guidelines, Informed Controls, and the Market Place* (1966). *U.S. News and World Report*, vol. 65 (December 23, 1968); Earl Mazo and Stephan Hess, *Nixon: A Political Portrait* (1969). *Facts on File, 1981; Who's Who in American Politics; 1987–1988 Current Biography; 1988; International Who's Who; 1988–1989; Who's Who, 1989.*

SIMON, William Edward. Born in Paterson, N.J., November 27, 1927; son of Charles and Eleanor (Kearns) Simon; married in 1950 to Carol Girard; father of two sons and five daughters; attended schools in Spring Lake, N.J., and Blair Academy and Newark Academy, graduating from the latter in 1946; U.S. Army, 1946–1948, member U.S. Army swimming team in Japan; B.A., Lafayette College, 1952; began career in finance, 1952, with Union Securities (N.Y.), became assistant vice-president and manager of firm's Municipal Trading Department; joined Weeden and Company in 1955, as vice-president through 1963; began working with banking firm of Salomon Brothers in January 1964 and became partner in charge of federal bonds and securities nine months later; elected the first president of the newly formed Association of Primary Dealers in U.S. Government Securities in 1969; appointed deputy of the Department of the Treasury in December 1972; director of Federal Energy Office, December 1973; has been very active in many public and private organizations, past chairman, Oil Policy Committee Economy Policy Board (1974), East-West Foreign Trade Board (1975), National Advisory Council on International Monetary and Financial Policies, Federal Financing Bank-Emergency Loan Guarantee Board, U.S. Olympic Committee, Public Finance Council; Trustee of Lafayette College, Mannes College of Music (New York City), Newark Academy; term of office as head of the Federal Energy Office began with the oil shortage of 1973; when Arab oil embargo ended in March 1974, named SECRETARY OF THE TREASURY; as Secretary, he faced a growing economic slump which was characterized by inflation and a recession; left office on January 20, 1977; senior advisor, Blyth

Eastman Dillon and Co. Inc., 1977–1980; deputy chairman, Olayan Investments Co. Est., 1980; chairman, Crescent Diversified Ltd., 1980; member of the Committee to Fight Inflation, 1980; Economic Policy Advisory Board, 1981– ; chairman, Wesray Corporation, Morristown, 1981–1986, now emeritus; Wesray Capital Corporation, 1984–1986; appointed to head the Productivity Panel, January 1, 1982; honorary Dr. of Laws: Manhattanville College, 1978; Washington and Boston, 1980; Rider College, Seton Hall, and Fairleigh Dickenson, 1984; Rutgers and Rochester, 1985; investment banker–consultant on Wall Street, 1987– ; author of *A Time for Truth* (1978); *A Time for Action* (1980); presently resides in Morris County, N.J. *Who's Who in America, 1976–1977; Who's Who, 1976; Current Biography, 1974; Facts on File, 1974; New York Times Biographical Service* (1987); *International Who's Who, 1988–1989.*

SKINNER, Samuel Knox. Born in Chicago, Ill., June 10, 1938; son of Vernon Orlo and Imelda Jane (Curran) Skinner; Presbyterian; married Susan Ann Thomas; father of Thomas, Steven, and Jane; received B.S. from University of Illinois , 1960; J.D., DePaul University, 1966; served as first lieutenant, U.S. Army, 1960–1961; admitted to the bar in Illinois, 1966; served as assistant U.S. attorney, Northern District, Chicago, Ill., 1968–1974; first assistant U.S. attorney, 1974–1975; U.S. attorney, 1975–1977; partner, Sidley and Austin, Chicago, Ill., 1977–1984; chairman, Regional Transportation Authority, Chicago, Ill., 1984; chairman, Illinois Capitol Development Board, 1977–1984; nominated as SECRETARY OF TRANSPORTATION by President George Bush and confirmed by the Senate on February 1, 1989; *Who's Who in American Law, 1977–1978.*

SMITH, Caleb Blood. Born in Boston, Mass., April 16, 1808; son of Blood Smith; married Elizabeth B. Walton on July 18, 1831; father of three children; moved with his parents to Cincinnati, Ohio in 1814; attended the College of Cincinnati, 1823–1825, and Miami University, Oxford, Ohio, 1825–1826, but did not graduate; studied law in Cincinnati and in Connorsville, Ind.; admitted to the bar and began practice in 1828 in Connorsville; founded and edited the *Indiana Sentinel* in 1832; elected as a Whig to the state House of Representatives in 1832; reelected each year until 1837, and elected again in 1840 and 1841; served as Speaker of the House in 1836; presidential elector on the Whig ticket of 1840; elected as a Whig to the 28th, 29th and 30th Congresses, serving from March 4, 1843 to March 3, 1849; appointed by President Taylor as member of the board investigating American claims against Mexico, and served until 1851; moved to Cincinnati and resumed law practice; president of the Cincinnati and Chicago Railroad Company, 1854; presidential elector on the Republican ticket of 1856; moved to Indianapolis, Ind. in 1859; delegate to the Republican national convention in Chicago in 1860; Indiana delegate to the peace convention held in Washington in 1861 to attempt to avert war; appointed SECRETARY OF THE INTERIOR in the cabinet of President Lincoln and served from March 5, 1861 until January 1, 1863 when he resigned; appointed judge of the U.S. District

Court for Indiana, serving from 1863 until his death; died in Indianapolis, Ind. on January 7, 1864; interment in the City Cemetery, Connorsville, Ind. L. J. Bailey, "Caleb Blood Smith," *Indiana Magazine of History* (September 1933); Burton J. Hendrick, *Lincoln's War Cabinet* (1946); Noah Brooks, *Mr. Lincoln's Washington* (1967).

SMITH, Charles Emory. Born in Mansfield, Conn., February 18, 1842; son of Emory Boutelle and Arvilla Topliff (Royce) Smith; married Ella Huntly on June 3, 1863; married Nettie Nichols on October 3, 1907; childless; moved to Albany, N.Y. at age seven; attended public schools of Albany; graduated from Albany Academy at age 16; began journalistic career while still in school by writing for *Albany Evening Transcript;* entered Union College as a junior, graduating in 1861; received LL.D. from Union College, 1889; granted LL.D. from Lafayette, 1900; received LL.D. from Wesleyan, 1901; became military secretary to Brigadier General John F. Rathbone at beginning of Civil War, and resigned, 1862; became instructor in Albany Academy, 1862; joined staff of *Albany Express* in 1865; became associate editor of leading Republican newspaper, the *Albany Evening Journal*, 1870, served as editor, 1874–1880; president of New York State Press Association, 1874; wrote nearly all state Republican platforms, 1874–1880, and most of national, 1876; chairman of committee on resolutions of the Republican state conventions, 1874–1880; president of Republican state convention, 1879; elected member of board of regents of the University of the State of New York, 1879–1880; became editor of *Philadelphia Press* in 1880; trustee of Union College, 1881; U.S. minister to Russia, 1890–1892; appointed POSTMASTER GENERAL in the cabinet of President McKinley on April 21, 1898, continued under Theodore Roosevelt, and served until his resignation on January 15, 1902; most important contributions were advice on political problems of Spanish-American War period, prevention of use of mails for fraudulent purposes, extension and popularization of rural free delivery service, and elimination of corruption in postal service established by his department in Cuba; died in Philadelphia, Pa., January 19, 1908. S. W. Pennypacker, *The Autobiography of a Pennsylvanian* (1894); *New York Times* (January 20, 1908); Dorothy G. Fowler, *The Cabinet Politician: The Postmasters General, 1829–1900* (1943); Margaret K. Leech, *In the Days of McKinley* (1859); H. Wayne Morgan, *William McKinley and His America* (1963).

SMITH, Cyrus Rowlett. Born in Minerva, Tex., September 9, 1899; son of Roy Edgerton and Marion (Burck) Smith; Baptist; married Elizabeth L. Manget on December 29, 1934; father of Douglas; employed as accountant with Peat, Marwick, Mitchell and Company, 1921–1926; received B.A. in business administration from University of Texas in 1924; was assistant treasurer of Texas-Louisiana Power Company, 1926–1928; became vice-president of Texas Air Transport, Inc., 1926–1928; made vice-president of American Airlines 1930–1933; chosen president and chief executive of American Airlines in 1934; commissioned colonel in U.S., Army Air Forces in 1942, and moved through the ranks to become major general; served as deputy commander of Air Transport Command, 1942–1945; became chairman of the board of American Airlines in 1964, and retired in 1968; appointed SECRETARY OF COMMERCE in the cabinet of President Lyndon Johnson, and served from March 1, 1968 to January 20, 1969; general partner; Lazard Freres, N.Y., 1969 to 1973; D.S.M. Legion of Merit, honorary Commander of the Order of the British Empire; named to Aviation Hall of Fame, 1974; Business Hall of Fame, 1975; Democrat; Baptist. Hugh Sidney, *A Very Personal Presidency: Lyndon Johnson in the White House* (1968); "Commerce's Rugged New Pilot," *Chemical Week*, vol. 102 (March 2, 1968); *U.S. News* (March 22, 1968); *International Who's Who* (1979–1982); *Who's Who in America, 1984*.

SMITH, Hoke. Born in Newton, N.C., September 2, 1855; son of Professor H. H. Smith, educator, and Mary Brent (Hoke) Smith; Presbyterian; married Birdie Cobb on December 19, 1885; father of one son and three daughters; married Mazie Crawford on August 27, 1924; tutored by his father; read law in offices of Collier, Mynatt, and Collier in Atlanta, Ga. while teaching in Waynesboro, Ga., 1872; admitted to the bar at the age of 17, in 1873; began practice; chairman of Fulton County Democratic executive committee, 1876; delegate to state Democratic convention, 1882; president of Young Men's Library, 1881, 1882, and 1883; organized and became president of Atlanta *Evening Journal* in June 1887; delegate to Democratic national convention in 1892; appointed SECRETARY OF THE INTERIOR in the cabinet of President Cleveland on March 6, 1893, and served until resignation on September 1, 1896; most important contributions were furthering the cause of conservation, purging the pension list of fraud, and upholding Cleveland's effort to maintain the gold standard; offered himself as candidate for governor of Georgia, 1906; served as governor from July 1907 to July 1909, and July 1911 to November 1911; elected by the legislature to fill unexpired term of U.S. Senator A. S. Clay, 1911; reelected to U.S. Senate in 1914, and served until 1921; chairman of commission on national aid to vocational education created by a joint resolution of Congress on January 20, 1914; responsible for Smith-Hughes bill which provided for studies of agriculture, home economics, trade, and industry in public schools and vocational education of the disabled, February 23, 1917; chairman of Board of Education in Atlanta; organized Piedmont Hotel and Fulton National Bank; died on November 27, 1931. A. D. Candler and C. A. Evans, eds., *Georgia* (1906); Clark Howell, *History of Georgia* (1926); Dewey Grantham, *Hoke Smith and the Politics of the New South* (1958); Robert L. Vexter, ed., *Grover Cleveland, 1837–1908: Chronology, Documents, Bibliographical Aids* (1968).

SMITH, Robert. Born in Lancaster, Pa., November 3, 1757; married distant cousin Margaret Smith on December 7, 1790; father of eight children; graduated from the College of New Jersey in 1781; studied law in Baltimore, Md., and was admitted to bar in 1786; served in Maryland Senate from 1793 until 1795; member of Maryland House of Delegates, 1796–1800; served on Baltimore City Council from 1798 until 1801; accepted appointment by President Jefferson as SECRETARY OF THE NAVY on July 15, 1801, served July 27, 1801 until March 8, 1809; confirmed as ATTORNEY GENERAL in 1805, only to return to Navy secretary position after a few months and served out his term without recommission; accomplishments include maintenance of blocking squadron in Mediterranean during war on Barbary States, conscientiously enforcing Embargo despite personal disapproval; appointed SECRETARY OF STATE by President Madison, served March 6, 1809 until his resignation under pressure from President Madison on April 1, 1811; declined President Madison's offer of the position of minister to Russia in March 1811; published *Robert Smith's Address to the People of the United States* in June 1811, as an attempted defense of the actions which had caused President Madison to seek his resignation; retired to private business in Baltimore; died November 26, 1842. C. C. Tansill, "Robert Smith," in S. F. Bemis, *The American Secretaries of State and Their Diplomacy*, vol. 3 (1927); G. E. Davies, "Robert Smith and the Navy," *Maryland Historical Magazine* (December 1919).

SMITH, William French. Born in Wilton, N.H., August 26, 1917; son of William French Smith, president of the Mexican Telephone and Telegraph Company, and Margaret (Dawson) Smith; married Jean Webb Vaughan on November 6, 1964; father of William French, Stephanie Oakes, Scott Cameron, and Gregory Hale from previous marriage; graduated summa cum laude and received his A.B. from University of California at Berkeley in 1939; LL.B. from Harvard Law School, 1942; served in the U.S. Naval Reserve from 1942 to 1946; admitted to the California bar in 1942; Republican; became a senior partner for Gibson, Dunn, and Crutcher law firm, Los Angeles, from 1946 to 1981; appointed to the California Board of Regents in 1968, chaired the board from 1970 to 1972, and was reelected, 1974–1976; elected president of the California Chamber of Commerce in 1979; served as chairman of California's delegation to the Republican national convention in 1968, and as vice-chairman in 1976 and 1980; nominated as ATTORNEY GENERAL under President Ronald Reagan, on December 11, 1980; assumed post at the Department of Justice on January 23, 1981, serving until February 25, 1985; major contributions were: supported Reagan's welfare reform program; recommended a comprehensive crime package of more than 150 administrative and legislative initiatives which included a federal death penalty, the denial of bail for certain types of crime, the modification of the rule barring the use of illegally seized evidence in criminal trials, mandatory prison sentences for crimes involving the use of guns, and the use of private Internal Revenue Service information in combating organized crime; designed an immigration and refugee policy; announced a more lenient attitude toward corporate mergers in order to make government more responsive to the concerns of business; opposed anticompetitive practices; modified the Freedom of Information

Act of 1966; advocated repeal of the 1978 Ethics in Government Act; enforced laws that forbid federal employees from striking; opposed the distortion of the meaning of equal protection by courts that mandate counterproductive busing and quotas; selected appointees to the federal bench who believed in judicial restraint; director of Pacific Lighting Corporation, American International Group, Inc., General Electric Company, National Broadcasting Corporation, Earle M. Jorgensen Company, H. F. Ahmanson and Company, Pacific Telesis Group, Inc., and Weintraub Entertainment Group, Inc.; recipient of American Jewish Committee Human Relations Award, University of California Outstanding University Service Award, and University of California Alumnus of the Year Award; trustee of Claremont Men's College, Cale School, Northrop Institute of Technology, Ronald Reagan Presidential Foundation, and the Henry E. Huntington Library and Art Gallery; member of President's Foreign Intelligence Advisory Board, 1971– ; U.S. Advisory Commission on International Educational, and Cultural Affairs, 1971 to 1978; served on the Los Angeles World Affairs Council, 1970– ; board of the Legal Aid Foundation of Los Angeles; advisory board of the Center for Strategic and International Studies, Georgetown University; advisory board of the Stanton Panel on International Information, Education, and Cultural Relations; Performing Arts Council; Los Angeles Music Center; American Law Institute; American Judicature Society; American Bar Association; American Bar Foundation; received Golden Plate Award for American Academy of Achievement in 1984; Franklin Social Award; Federation for American Immigrations Reform (1986). *Current Biography, 1982; Facts on File, 1985.*

SNYDER, John Wesley. Born in Jonesboro, Ark., June 21, 1895; son of Jesse Hartwell and Ellen (Hatcher) Synder; Episcopalian; married Evlyn Cook on January 5, 1920; father of Edith Drucie; after receiving his early education in the local public schools, he entered Vanderbilt University in 1914; joined the U.S. Army in World War I and was commissioned a second lieutenant in the Field Artillery; subsequently promoted to the rank of captain; served with Army of Occupation until June 1919; served in various banks in Arkansas and Missouri from 1919 to 1930; national bank receiver from 1930 to 1936, in the office of the Comptroller of Currency, Washington, D.C.; manager of the St. Louis branch of the Reconstruction Finance Corp. from 1937 to 1943; special assistant to the board of directors of the Reconstruction Finance Corp., and director of Defense Plants Corp., a subsidiary of RFC, from 1940 to 1944; vice-president of the First National Bank of St. Louis, Mo., in 1943; appointed Federal Loan Administrator by President Truman in April 1945, and in July 1945, was promoted to director of war mobilization and reconversion, playing a leading part in the transition of the nation's economy from a wartime to a peacetime basis; joined the Truman cabinet as SECRETARY OF THE TREASURY on June 12, 1946, entering upon his duties on June 25, 1946, serving until the termination of the Truman administration on January 20, 1953; during his tenure the national debt was reduced by approximately $15 billion; he instituted a vigorous campaign for the sale of U.S., savings bonds; chairman of the board of trustees of the endowment fund of the American on National Red Cross, and Library of Congress fund board, and the National Advisory Council on International Monetary and Financial Problems; U.S. Governor of the International Monetary Fund and the International Bank for Reconstruction and Development; trustee of the Federal old age and survivors insurance trust fund; trustee of the postal savings system, the National Gallery of Art, the National Archives Council, and the Franklin Delano Roosevelt Library; director of the Federal Farm Mortgage Corporation; member of the National Park Trust Fund Board, Defense Mobilization Board, Smithsonian Institution, and the National Securities Resources Board; colonel in the U.S. army field artillery reserve; died on October 8, 1985, on Seabrook Island, S.C., at the age of 90. Alfred Steinberg, *The Man from Missouri: The Life and Times of Harry S. Truman* (1962); Cabell B. H. Phillips, *The Truman Presidency: The History of a Triumphant Succession* (1966); *Facts on File Yearbook*, (1985).

SOUTHARD, Samuel Lewis. Born in Basking Ridge, N.J., June 9, 1787; son of Henry Southard, Congressman, and Sarah (Lewis) Southard; married Rebecca Harrow in 1811; attended the school conducted by the Rev. Robert Finley at Basking Ridge; entered the College of New Jersey (now Princeton), graduating in 1804; engaged as a private tutor by a family near Fredericksburg, Va., in 1805; studied law and was admitted to the bar in Virginia in 1809; returned to New Jersey and commenced practice in Flemington in 1811; appointed law reporter of the Supreme Court by the state legislature in 1814; elected to the N.J. General Assembly in 1815, resigning upon his designation to the state Supreme Court bench; associate justice of the N.J. Supreme Court from 1815 to 1820; moved to Trenton, N.J., becoming city recorder; was a presidential elector on the Democratic ticket of Monroe and Tompkins in 1820; appointed and subsequently elected to the U.S. Senate, serving from January 26, 1821 to March 3, 1823, when he resigned, having been tendered a cabinet portfolio; appointed SECRETARY OF THE NAVY by President Monroe, September 6, 1823, holding the office until the close of President John Quincy Adams' administration on March 3, 1829; during his incumbency, he began the program of building naval hospitals in 1828 and also advocated the construction of a naval academy, a thorough charting of the American coastline, a naval criminal code, a reorganization and increase of the Marine Corps, and the establishment of regular communication across Panama; he and his father both served in the 16th Congress; appointed Secretary of the Treasury, *ad interim*, by President John Quincy Adams, on March 7, 1825; appointed Secretary of War, *ad interim*, by President Adams on May 26, 1828; attorney general of New Jersey from 1829 to 1833; elected governor of New Jersey on October 26, 1832, serving until February 23, 1833, when he resigned to become a senator; elected as a Whig to the U.S. Senate in 1833 and reelected in 1839, serving from March 4, 1833 until his death; was president *pro tempore* of the Senate from March 4, 1841 to May 31,

1842, when he resigned; died in Fredericksburg, Va. on June 26, 1842; interment in the Congressional Cemetery, Washington, D.C. Arthur Styron, *The Last of the Cocked Hats: James Monroe and the Virginia Dynasty* (1945); Robert Abraham East, *John Quincy Adams: The Critical Years, 1785–1794* (1962).

SPEED, James. Born in Farmington, Ky., March 11, 1812; son of John and Lucy Gelmer (Fry) Speed; married Jane Cochran in 1841; father of seven sons; attended local schools and St. Joseph College in Bardstown, Ky., graduating in 1828; clerk in the circuit and county courts, 1828–1830; studied law at Transylvania University in Lexington, Ky.; admitted to the bar and began practice in Louisville in 1833; elected to the Kentucky state legislature in 1847; defeated as delegate to the state constitutional convention in 1849; staunch advocate of Negro emancipation; taught law at the University of Louisville, 1856–1858; elected in 1861 to the state Senate and continued in that capacity until July 1863; appointed ATTORNEY GENERAL in the cabinet of President Lincoln on December 2, 1864 and continued under Andrew Johnson; most important contributions were advocating Negro suffrage, supporting the Fourteenth Amendment; resigned on July 17, 1866 as a result of policy disagreement with President Johnson; returned to Louisville; chairman of the Southern Radical convention in Philadelphia in 1866; defeated in contests for vice-president in 1868 and for congressman in 1870; delegate to the Republican national conventions of 1872 and 1876; continued law practice and taught law again at the University of Louisville from 1872 to 1879; died in Louisville, Ky. on June 25, 1887; interment in Cave Hill Cemetery, Louisville. James Speed, *James Speed, A Personality* (1914); Burton J. Hendrick, *Lincoln's War Cabinet* (1946); James G. Randall, *Constitutional Problems Under Lincoln* (1964); Ernest S. Cox, *Lincoln's Negro Policy* (1968).

SPENCER, John Canfield. Born in Hudson, N.Y., January 8, 1788; son of Ambrose and Laura (Canfield) Spencer; Methodist; married Elizabeth Scott Smith in 1809; father of three children; after attending the common schools, he entered Williams College at Williamstown, Mass., remained there a year and then transferred to Union College, Schenectady, N.Y., graduating in 1806; studied law and was admitted to the bar in 1809, commencing his legal practice in Canandaigua, N.Y.; served as a combatant in the War of 1812; appointed judge advocate general in 1813; appointed postmaster of Canandaigua, 1814; designated assistant attorney general for western New York in 1815; elected as a Democrat to the 15th Congress, serving from March 4, 1817 to March 3, 1819; elected to the New York State Assembly in 1820 and 1821, serving one year as Assembly speaker; elected to the New York State Senate from 1824 to 1828; charged by Governor De Witt Clinton with the task of revising the statutes of New York State, his efforts culminating in *The Revised Statutes of the State of New York*, 3 vols. (1829); reelected to the New York State Assembly in 1831 and 1832; appointed special Attorney General to prosecute the abductors of

Morgan, 1839; designated secretary of state of New York in 1839; invited to join the cabinet of President Tyler as SECRETARY OF WAR on October 12, 1841, serving until March 3, 1843; assigned a new cabinet portfolio by President Tyler, that of SECRETARY OF THE TREASURY, serving from March 3, 1843 to May 2, 1844 when, because of his opposition to the annexation of Texas, he resigned; nominated by President Tyler to become associate justice of the U.S. Supreme Court in January 1844, a position subsequently denied him by the U.S. Senate; died in Albany, N.Y. on May 18, 1855; interment in the Rural Cemetery, Albany, New York. Robert J. Morgan, *A Whig Embattled: The Presidency under John Tyler* (1954); Oscar Doane Lambert, *Presidential Politics in the United States 1840–1844* (1936).

STANBERY, Henry. Born in New York, N.Y., February 20, 1803; son of Dr. Jonas and Ann Lucy (Seaman) Stanbery; Presbyterian; married to Frances E. Beecher in 1829, and upon her death in 1840, married Cecelia Bond; father of five children; moved with his family to Ohio in 1814, settling in Zanesville; graduated from Washington College (now Washington and Jefferson College), Pa., at the age of 16; studied law and was admitted to the bar in 1824, commencing the practice of law at Lancaster, Ohio; elected the first attorney general of Ohio, 1846; a member of the state constitutional convention of 1850; transferred his law office to Cincinnati in 1853; invited to join the cabinet of President Andrew Johnson on July 23, 1866, as ATTORNEY GENERAL; a moderate, he interpreted the Reconstruction legislation as liberally as the language of the acts permitted; with the initiation of proceedings against President Johnson, he resigned on March 12, 1868 to serve as the President's chief counsel; at the close of the trial, President Johnson renominated him Attorney General but the Senate refused to confirm his appointment; resumed his law practice in Cincinnati; became president of the Law Association of Cincinnati; retired from active practice in 1878; died in New York City on June 26, 1881. Margaret Green, *Defender of the Constitution: Andrew Johnson* (1962); Eric L. McKitrick, *Andrew Johnson and Reconstruction* (1960).

STANS, Maurice Hubert. Born in Shakopee, Minn., March 22, 1908; son of J. Hubert and Mathilda (Nyseen) Stans; Roman Catholic; married to Kathleen Carmody on September 7, 1933; father of Steven, Maureen, Theodore, and Terrell; attended the public schools and Shakopee High School; moved to Chicago and worked as a stenographer while attending Northwestern University, 1925–1928; attended Columbia University, 1928–1930; joined the accounting firm of Alexander Grant and Co. as an office boy, 1928, becoming a partner in 1931 and an executive partner in 1938; chairman of the board of the Moore Corporation, stove manufacturers, 1942–1945; established the Stans Foundation to assist charitable institutions, 1940; consultant to the U.S. House of Representatives appropriations committee, 1953; financial consultant to U.S. Postmaster General Summerfield, 1953–1955; appointed deputy postmaster general by President Eisenhower in September 1955, serving until 1957; deputy director of the Bureau of the Budget, 1957–1958, becoming director on March 13, 1958 and serving until 1961; president of the Western Bank Corp., Los Angeles, 1961–1962; vice-chairman of the United California Bank, 1961–1962; syndicated columnist, 1961–1962; senior partner in William R. Staats & Co., 1963–1964, and president, 1964–1965; president of Glore Forgan, William R. Staats & Co., Inc., New York, 1965–1968; appointed SECRETARY OF COMMERCE in the cabinet of President Nixon on December 11, 1968 and took the oath of office on January 22, 1969; most important contribution was heading a U.S. trade mission to Europe in April 1969; resigned his post on January 28, 1972, to take charge of Committee to Reelect the President; involved in Watergate affair and indicted for criminal conduct; currently finance chairman for the Nixon Library and a business consultant in Pasadena, Calif. *Time*, vol. 71 (March 24, 1958); *U.S. News and World Report*, vol. 44 (March 21, 1958); *Time*, vol. 92 (December 20, 1968); Earl Mazo and Stephan Hess, *Nixon: A Political Portrait* (1969); *Personal Biography, 1989.*

STANTON, Edwin McMasters. Born in Steubenville, Ohio, December 19, 1814; son of Dr. David and Lucy (Norman) Stanton; Quaker; married to Mary Ann Lamson on December 31, 1834, and upon her death, married Ellen M. Hutchinson on June 25, 1856; father of six children; he was obliged to withdraw from school due to lack of funds; clerked in a local bookstore, studying in his spare time; entered Kenyon College in 1831, but his funds ran out and he was unable to complete his academic career studied law and was admitted to the bar in 1836, commencing his practice in Cadiz, Ohio; moved to Steubenville in 1839 and then to Pittsburgh, Pa. in 1847; moved to Washington, D.C., in 1856, where he won a national reputation by his astute handling of the fraudulent land claims in California, serving as special counsel for the U.S. government; invited to join the cabinet by appointment of President Buchanan as ATTORNEY GENERAL on December 20, 1860, entering upon his duties on December 22, 1860 and serving until March 3, 1861; though a staunch Unionist, and averse to the institution of slavery, he contended that all laws constitutionally enacted for the protection of slavery should be rigidly enforced; though an outspoken critic of President Lincoln and of his administration, he was invited to join the Lincoln cabinet as SECRETARY OF WAR on January 15, 1862, entering upon his duties on January 20, 1862; during his secretaryship, he scrutinized all war department contracts, prosecuting those tainted with fraud; persuaded Congress to authorize the taking over of the railroads and telegraph lines where necessary; continued in office by President Andrew Johnson, he directed the demobilization of the Union armies; on August 5, 1867, President Johnson requested his resignation; when that request by the President was ignored, he was suspended forthwith, and General Grant was appointed Secretary of War, *ad interim*; Stanton resigned May 26, 1868; gave active support to Grant's candidacy in 1868 and subsequently was nominated and confirmed for a justiceship on the U.S. Supreme Court on

December 20, 1869, but died before he could occupy his seat; died in Wash-
ington,D.C., on December 24, 1869. William Severn, *In Lincoln's Footsteps:
The Life of Andrew Johnson* (1960); Benjamin Platt Thomas and Harold M.
Hyman, *Stanton: The Life and Times of Lincoln's Secretary of War* (1962).

STETTINIUS, Edward Reilley, Jr. Born in Chicago, Ill., October 22, 1900;
son of Edward Reilley and Judith (Carrington) Stettinius; Episcopalian; married
Virginia Gordon Wallace on May 15, 1926; father of Edward Reilley III, Wallace, and Joseph; attended the Pomfret School in Connecticut, 1907–1919; entered University of Virginia in 1919; briefly studied law and considered the
clergy; elected president of Young Men's Christian Society in 1921; organized
an employment agency and paid needy students' tuition; left University of Virginia in 1924 and became a stockboy for Hyatt Roller Bearing Works; became
assistant to the vice-president of General Motors Corp. in 1926, and in 1931
was appointed vice-president in charge of industrial and public relations; named
vice-president of United States Steel Corp. in 1934, and in 1938, became chairman of the board; left United States Steel in the same year to chair President
Franklin Roosevelt's War Resources Board, and on May 28, 1940, he resigned
all business affiliations and entered government service; appointed director of
the Office of Production Management under President Roosevelt and served from
January to September 1941; special assistant to the President, October 1941–
September 1943, and chief legislator of the Lend Lease Policy; played a vital
role at the Dumbarton Oaks Conference, August 1944; appointed undersecretary
of state and served in that position from September 25, 1943 to November 30,
1944; named SECRETARY OF STATE in Roosevelt's cabinet on November 30,
1944; chief advisor to President Roosevelt at the Yalta Conference, January
1945,and continued under Harry Truman, serving until July 2, 1945; chairman
of the U.S. delegation to the United Nations Conference on International Organization at San Francisco, April–June 1945; resigned his post as Secretary of
State in December 1945 to serve as first U.S. delegate to the United Nations, a
post held until 1946; became rector of the University of Virginia, 1946; was
also director of the Foreign Policy Administration, Thomas Jefferson and Patrick
Henry Memorial Organization, General Electric, and the Federal Reserve Bank
of Richmond, Va.; member of the governing board of the Pan American Union
and the American Red Cross; died in Greenwich, Conn., October 31, 1949;
interment in Locust Valley Cemetery, Locust Valley, N.Y. *New York Times*,
Obituary (November 1, 1949); *Who Was Who in America*.

STEVENSON, Adlai Ewing. Born in Christian County, Ky., October 23, 1835;
son of John Turner Stevenson, small planter, and Ann Eliza (Ewing) Stevenson;
married Letitia Grenn on December 20, 1866; father of Louis Green, Mary,
Julia, and Letitia; attended local schools and was preparatory student for two
years at Illinois Wesleyan University; attended Centre College for two years;
taught; read law under Judge Davis and Robert E. Williams; admitted to the

bar, 1857; opened law office at Metamora, Ill., 1858; was master in chancery, 1860–1964; was state district attorney of Illinois and master of circuit court, 1865–1869; elected to U.S. Congress in 1874 and served from 1875 to 1877; candidate for reelection in 1876, but was defeated; member of board to inspect military academy at West Point, 1877; reelected to Congress with Greenback support in 1878 and served from 1879 to 1881; appointed assistant postmaster general under Cleveland in 1885, serving until 1889; headed Illinois delegation to Democratic national convention in 1892, and helped nominate Cleveland for president; elected VICE-PRESIDENT under Grover Cleveland, serving from March 4, 1893 to March 3, 1897; appointed member of monetary commission to Europe, 1897; was Bryan's running mate in 1900; ran unsuccessfully for governor of Illinois in 1908; published *Something of Men I Have Known* (1909); died in Chicago, Ill., June 14, 1914; interment in Bloomington, Ill. Robert L. Vexter, *Grover Cleveland, 1837–1908: Chronology, Documents, Bibliographical Aids* (1968); Henry J. Ford, *Cleveland Era* (1921).

STIMSON, Henry Lewis. Born in New York, N.Y., September 21, 1867; son of Lewis Atterbury Stimson, surgeon, and Candace (Wheeler) Stimson; Presbyterian; married on July 6, 1893 to Mabel Wellington White; attended Phillips Academy, Andover, Mass.; graduated Yale in 1888; studied at Harvard, 1888–1889 and attended Harvard Law School, 1889–1890; admitted to the bar in 1891 and began practice in New York City with the firms of Root and Clark (1893), Root, Howard, Winthrop, and Stimson (1897), and Winthrop and Stimson (1901); appointed U.S. attorney by President Theodore Roosevelt in 1906; resigned in 1909 but continued to serve in federal anti-trust prosecutions as special counsel by appointment of President Taft; unsuccessful Republican candidate for governor of New York in 1910; appointed SECRETARY OF WAR in the cabinet of President Taft on May 16, 1911; most important contribution was reorganizing the Army through more efficient grouping of its forces; served until the end of the Taft administration, resigning March 4, 1913; delegate to the New York constitutional convention in 1915; during World War I, served overseas and was commissioned lieutenant colonel in the 305th Field Artillery; later promoted to colonel of the 31st Field Artillery; after the war resumed law practice in New York City; appointed by President Coolidge in 1927 as special peace envoy to Nicaragua; appointed by President Coolidge as governor general of the Philippine Islands in 1927, and served until March 1929; appointed SECRETARY OF STATE in the cabinet of President Hoover on March 4, 1929; most important contributions were supporting naval armament limitations, serving as chairman of the American delegation to the London Naval Conference of 1930 and to the General Conference for the reduction and limitation of armaments at Geneva in 1932, and issuing the "Stimson Doctrine" in January 1932 condemning Japan's occupation of Manchuria and all other such territorial gains based on force; resigned with the outgoing administration on March 3, 1933; resumed law practice in New York City; appointed by President Franklin Roosevelt a member of the

International Court of Arbitration at The Hague, 1938; appointed SECRETARY OF WAR in the cabinet of President Franklin Roosevelt on July 10, 1940 and continued in that post in the cabinet of President Truman; most important contributions were urging the enactment of the first compulsory service law in a time of peace, helping to establish the autonomy of the U.S. Air Corps, leading the support of the Lend-Lease Act, participating in Allied conferences during World War II, reorganizing the Army command, serving as advisor to the President on atomic energy, and recommending the use of the first atomic bomb on Japan; also was member of such governmental bodies as the Council of National Defense, the War Production Board, and the Foreign Trade Zones Board; retired from office on September 21, 1945; received the Distinguished Service Medal from President Truman on September 28, 1945; author of *American Policy in Nicaragua* (1927), *Democracy and Nationalism in Europe* (1934), *My Vacations* (1949), an autobiography, and several articles; member of the editorial advisory board of *Foreign Affairs*; died in Huntington, N.Y., October 20, 1950. Henry L. Stimson, (with McGeorge Bundy) *On Active Service in Peace and War* (1948); Elting E. Morison, *Turmoil and Tradition: A Study of the Life and Times of Henry L. Stimson* (1960); Armin Rappaport, *Henry L. Stimson and Japan, 1931–1933* (1963).

STODDERT, Benjamin. Born in Charles County, Md. in 1751; son of Captain James Stoddert, officer in French and Indian War, and Sarah (Marshall) Stoddert; married Rebecca Lowndes on June 17, 1781; educated as a merchant; joined Pennsylvania regiment at outbreak of Revolution, became cavalry captain, gained rank of major; wounded in battle of Brandywine and forced to retire; unanimously elected secretary of the Board of War on September 1, 1779, serving until 1781; settled in Georgetown, District of Columbia, as a merchant; organizer and later president of Bank of Columbia in January 1794; appointed SECRETARY OF THE NAVY in the cabinet of President John Adams on May 21, 1798, entering upon duties June 1, 1798, and serving until March 1, 1801, when he retired to private life; during period of cabinet service, faced war with France, built up naval forces and recommended them reduced following the war, drafted bill for government of Marine Corps, and began construction of a naval hospital at Newport, R.I.; died in Bladensburg, Md. on December 18, 1813. Manning J. Daver, *The Adams Federalists* (1953); Stephen G. Kurtz, *The Presidency of John Adams* (1957).

STONE, Harlan Fiske. Born in Chesterfield, N.H., October 11, 1872; son of Frederick Lauson and Ann Sophia (Butler) Stone; married Agnes Harvey on September 7, 1899; father of Marshall Harvey and Lauson Harvey; after attending the local school and Amherst High School, he entered the Massachusetts Agricultural College in Amherst and later enrolled at Amherst College, receiving a B.S. in 1894 and an M.A. in 1897; entered Columbia University School of Law in New York City, graduating in 1898; taught at Adelphi Academy in

Brooklyn, N.Y.; admitted to the bar in 1898; lecturer on law at Columbia University, 1899–1902, and professor of law, 1902–1905; dean of the Columbia University School of Law, 1910–1923; member of the law firm of Sullivan and Cromwell of New York City; invited to join the Coolidge cabinet as ATTORNEY GENERAL on April 7, 1924, entering upon his duties on April 9, 1924 and serving until March 2, 1925; during his incumbency, he created a precedent by taking personal charge of many of the more important cases; appointed associate justice of the U.S. Supreme Court by President Coolidge on March 2, 1925, serving in that capacity until June 1941, when he was named chief justice by President Franklin D. Roosevelt; vice-president of the American Red Cross and of the Washington Monument Society; honorary president of the National Association of Legal Aid Organizations in 1941; trustee of Amherst College; chairman of the board of trustees of the National Gallery of Art; chancellor of the Smithsonian Institution; president of the Association of American Law Schools; fellow of the American Academy of Arts and Sciences; died in Washington, D.C. on April 22, 1946. Edward Connery Latham, ed., *Meet Calvin Coolidge: The Man Behind the Myth* (1960); Leonard Baker, *Back to Back: The Duel Between FDR and the Supreme Court* (1967).

STRAUS, Oscar Solomon. Born in Otterberg, Rhenist Bavaria, Germany, December 23, 1850; son of Lazarus and Sara (Straus) Straus; Jewish; married Sarah Lavanburg on April 19, 1882; father of three children; family migrated to the U.S. in 1854, first settling in Talbotton and Columbus, Ga., and later in New York City; studied at private schools preparatory to his attendance at Columbia College, where he graduated in 1871; entered Columbia Law School, graduating in 1873; admitted to the bar and commenced practice in New York City; abandoned the law and became a partner in L. Straus and Sons, merchants in china and glassware; a progressive Democrat in politics, he drew the notice of President Cleveland who, in 1887, appointed him minister to Turkey, a post he held until 1889; reappointed minister to Turkey by President McKinley in 1898, resigning in 1900; appointed a member of the permanent court of arbitration at The Hague, Netherlands, in 1902, and was subsequently reappointed in 1908, 1912 and 1920; invited to join the cabinet of President Theodore Roosevelt as SECRETARY OF COMMERCE AND LABOR, on December 12, 1906, serving until March 4, 1909; again designated minister to Turkey by President William Howard Taft in 1909, this time as the first American ambassador to the Ottoman Empire; his service under both Republican and Democratic administrations made him one of the earliest American career diplomats; resigned his mission to Turkey in December 1910; unsuccessful candidate for the governorship of New York on the Theodore Roosevelt Progressive Ticket, in 1912; appointed chairman of the New York Public Service Commission by Governor Whitman, 1915–1918; member of the League to Enforce Peace; authored *The Origin of the Republican Form of Government in the United States* (1885), *Reform in the Consular Service* (1894), *The American Spirit* (1913), and his autobiographical memoirs, *Under Four*

Administrations: From Cleveland To Taft (1922); died in New York City on January 11, 1931. Norman M. Wilensky, *Conservatives in the Progressive Era: The Taft Republicans of 1912* (1965); James L. Penick, Jr., *Progressive Politics and Conservatives* (1968).

STRAUSS, Lewis Lichtenstein. Born in Charleston, W. Va., January 31, 1896; son of Lewis S. Strauss, businessman, and Rosa (Lichtenstein) Strauss, artist; Jewish; married to Alice Hanauer on March 5, 1923; father of two sons; attended the public schools; was graduated from John Marshall High School, Richmond, Va.; worked as a traveling salesman; volunteer staff member to Herbert Hoover, who was then chairman of the commission for relief of Belgium, 1917–1919; personal secretary to Hoover when the latter became head of the U.S. Food Administration; member of the Belgian–American Educational Foundation from 1920; one of the four American delegates to the final Armistice convention at Brussels, 1919; declined the position of comptroller of the League of Nations, 1919; joined the banking firm of Kuhn, Loeb, and Co. of New York City, 1919, and became a partner in 1928; commissioned lieutenant commander in the U.S. Navy Reserve, 1926; vice-treasurer of the Republican national committee, 1928; called to active naval duty in February 1941 and became staff assistant to the chief of ordnance, serving until 1943; represented the Navy on the Interdepartmental Committee on Atomic Energy and on the Army-Navy Munitions Board; became special assistant to Secretary of the Navy James Forrestal in 1944; named rear admiral by President Truman in November 1945; appointed to the Navy's Civilian Research Advisory Committee after World War II; returned briefly to Kuhn, Loeb, and Co.; appointed by President Truman to the Atomic Energy Commission in 1946 and served until his resignation in 1950; appointed special assistant on atomic energy matters to President Eisenhower in February 1953; became chairman of the Atomic Energy Commission on July 2, 1953, and served until June 30, 1958; continued to serve as a presidential assistant for the Atoms for Peace program; appointed SECRETARY OF COMMERCE by President Eisenhower in October 1958 to fill the vacancy caused by the resignation of Sinclair Weeks; served on an interim basis until June 30, 1959, when his appointment failed to receive Senate confirmation; head of a space study group under Senator Barry Goldwater, 1964; helped form the Free Society Association chaired by Goldwater in 1965; author of *Men and Decisions* (1962). David A. Frier, *Conflict of Interest in the Eisenhower Administration* (1969).

STUART, Alexander Hugh Holmes. Born in Staunton, Va., April 2, 1807; son of Archibald and Eleanor (Briscoe) Stuart; Episcopalian; married Frances Cordelia Baldwin on August 1, 1833; father of nine children; after attending Staunton Academy, he entered William and Mary College, Williamsburg, Va., and later the University of Virginia at Charlottesville, graduating in 1828; studied law and was admitted to the bar in 1828, commencing his practice in Staunton; became a Whig and a champion of Henry Clay; elected to the Virginia House of Delegates, 1836–1839; elected as a Whig to the 27th Congress, serving from March 4, 1841 to March 3, 1843; presidential elector on the Whig ticket of Clay and Freylinghuysen in 1844, and of Taylor and Fillmore in 1848; invited to join the cabinet of President Fillmore as SECRETARY OF THE INTERIOR, serving from September 16, 1850 to March 6, 1853; elected to the State Senate from 1857 to 1861; member of the state secession convention in 1861; delegate to the national convention of conservatives, held in Philadelphia in 1866; presented credentials as a member-elect to the 39th Congress in 1865, but was not seated; chairman of the Committee of Nine, which was responsible for the restoration of Virginia to the Union in 1870; again elected to the Virginia House of Delegates from 1874 to 1877; rector of the University of Virginia from 1874 to 1882; president of the Virginia Historical Society; resumed the practice of law; authored *The Recent Revolution, Its Causes and Its Consequences* (1866); died in Staunton, Va. on February 13, 1891; interment in Thornrose Cemetery, Staunton. Robert J. Rayback, *Millard Fillmore: Biography of a President* (1959); Philip Shriver Klein, *President James Buchanan, A Biography* (1962).

SULLIVAN, Louis W. Born in Atlanta, Ga., on November 3, 1934; married; father of three children; attended Morehouse College, graduated magna cum laude in 1954 with a B.S.; attended Boston University, graduated cum laude in 1958 with an M.D.; did his internship (1958–1959) and medical residency (1960–1961) at New York Hospital's Cornell Medical Center; pathology fellowship, Massachusetts General Hospital, 1960–1961; fellow in hematology, Thorndike Research Laboratories of Harvard Medical School at the Boston City Hospital; instructor of medicine, Harvard Medical School, 1963–1964; assistant professor of medicine, New Jersey College of Medicine, 1964–1966; codirector of hematology, Boston University Medical Center, 1966; successive posts as assistant professor of medicine, associate professor of medicine, and professor of medicine at Boston University School of Medicine, 1966–1975; co–project director and project director, Boston Sickle Cell Center, and director of hematology, Boston City Hospital, 1972–1975; professor of biology and medicine, Morehouse School of Medicine, 1975; founding dean and director of the medical education program at Morehouse College, July 1975; associate editor, *Nutrition Reports International*, 1969–1973; on the editorial boards of the *American Journal of Hematology*, 1975–1977, and the *Journal of Medical Education*, 1977–1978; elected to fellowship in the American College of Physicians, 1980; first dean and president of Morehouse School of Medicine, July 1, 1981; nominated as SECRETARY OF HEALTH AND HUMAN SERVICES in the cabinet of President George Bush on January 20, 1989; confirmed by the Senate on March 1, 1989, and sworn in on March 10, 1989; confirmed after debate regarding his conflicting statements about his views on abortion; also at issue was the propriety of sabbatical and severance payments he was to receive from the Morehouse School of Medicine, due to possible conflict of interests because of the large grants Morehouse receives from the Department of Health and Human Services; this position marks his entrance into politics; member, American Medical Association, National Medical Association, Atlanta Medical Association, Medical Association of Atlanta, Medical Association of Georgia, Georgia State Medical Association; founding president of Association of Minority Health Professional Schools; recipient of the Boston University Alumni Award for Distinguished Public Service, 1985; Outstanding Alumnus Award from New York University's Cornell Medical Center, 1984; honoree of the National Association of Minority Medical Educators (NAMME), 1984; recipient of the first Martin Luther King Visiting Professorship at the University of Michigan, 1986; awarded the Equitable Southeastern Regional Black Achievement Award for Education, 1986; member of then–Vice President George Bush's official twelve-member delegation to seven African countries, 1982; member, Alpha Omega Alpha Honor Medical Society, Phi Beta Kappa, American Society of Clinical Investigation, National Academy of Sciences, Atlanta Rotary Club; board member, Friends of the National Library of Medicine, Boy Scouts of America. *Facts on File, 1989.*

SUMMERFIELD, Arthur Ellsworth. Born in Pinconning, near Bay City, Mich., March 17, 1899; son of William Henry and Cora Edith (Ellsworth) Summerfield; married Miriam W. Graim on July 22, 1918; father of Gertrude Miriam and Arthur E., Jr.; after completing grammar school, worked on a factory production line, followed by a job as inspector in the ammunition department of the Chevrolet plant in Flint, Mich.; entered the real estate business in 1919; became distributor for the Pure Oil Co. in Flint, developing his company into the largest distributorship in Michigan; launched the Summerfield Chevrolet Co. in September 1929, and has been the company's president since its establishment; president of the Bryant Properties Corp.; member of the Board of Directors of the American Motorists Insurance Co. as well as of the Lumbermen's Mutual Insurance Co.; entered politics to aid the presidential aspirations of Wendel Willkie in 1940; Michigan director of the National Dealers Association from 1942 to 1949, and its one-time regional vice-president; chairman of the National Auto Dealers of America Postwar Planning Committee during 1943 and 1944; appointed finance director of the Republican state central committee in 1943; elected committeeman from Michigan at the 1944 Republican national convention; regional vice-chairman of the Republican party's national finance committee in 1946; organized the Michigan Republicans for Vandenberg for President in 1946; chairman of the Republican strategy committee in July 1949; succeeded in keeping the Michigan delegation to the 1952 Republican national convention uncommitted and was thus instrumental in throwing the eventual nomination to General Eisenhower; joined the Eisenhower cabinet as POSTMASTER GENERAL on January 21, 1953, and was recommissioned on February 4, 1957, serving until the termination of the Eisenhower administration on January 20, 1961; during his incumbency, rural mail delivery services were extended to an additional 300,000 farm families and the first large-scale automation and mechanization program to modernize the Post Office system was initiated; director of the Boys

Club of America; member of the Board of Trustees of Cleary College, Ypsilanti, Mich.; upon his retirement from political service, he resumed his interests in the automobile business; died on April 26, 1972. Arthur Larson, *Eisenhower: The President Nobody Knew* (1968); Emmett John Hughes, *The Ordeal of Power: A Political Memoir of the Eisenhower Years* (1963).

SWANSON, Claude Augustus. Born in Swansonville, near Danville, Va., March 31, 1862; son of John Muse Swanson, farmer and tobacco manufacturer, and Catherine (Pritchett) Swanson; married to Lizzie Deane Lyons on December 11, 1894, and after her death married Lulie (Lyons) Hall on October 27, 1923; no children; attended the public schools; worked on farm; taught school; attended the Virginia Agricultural and Mechanical College at Blacksburg; worked as grocer's clerk; was graduated from Randolph-Macon College in 1885; received law degree from the University of Virginia in 1886; admitted to the bar and began practice in 1886 in Chatham, Va.; elected as a Democrat to the 53d through 59th Congresses, serving from March 4, 1893 until his resignation on January 30, 1906; unsuccessful candidate for governor in 1901; elected governor of Virginia to serve from 1906 until 1910; appointed on August 1, 1910 to the U.S. Senate to fill the vacancy caused by the death of Senator John W. Daniel; reappointed on February 28, 1911, and subsequently reelected as Senator in 1916, 1922, and 1928, serving until March 3, 1933; appointed by President Hoover as delegate to the General Disarmament Conference in Geneva, 1932; appointed SECRETARY OF THE NAVY in the cabinet of President Franklin Roosevelt on March 4, 1933; most important contribution was urging expansion of the navy to the limits established by the London Naval Treaty of 1930; died in office while on a visit to Rapidan Camp in the Blue Ridge Mountains, near Criglersville, Va., on July 7, 1939; funeral services held in the Senate chamber; interment in Hollywood Cemetery, Richmond, Va. C. P. Hill, *Franklin Roosevelt* (1966); A. J. Wann, *The President as Chief Administrator: A Study of Franklin D. Roosevelt* (1968).

T

TAFT, Alphonso. Born at Townshend, Vt., November 5, 1810; son of Peter Rawson Taft, member of the Vermont legislature and judge, and Sylvia (Howard) Taft; married to Fanny Phelps on August 29, 1841; father of five children, the eldest being Charles Phelps, lawyer, publisher, and philanthropist; after death of first wife, married Louisa Torrey on December 26, 1853; father of William Howard Taft, U.S. President and Chief Justice, and of Henry, Horace, Fanny, and Alphonso; attended local schools; taught school; studied at Amherst Academy; entered Yale College in 1829, graduating in 1833; taught in the high schools of Ellington, Conn., 1833–1835; studied law and admitted to the bar in 1838; moved to Cincinnati, Ohio, and there began law practice; became member of the city council; connected with railroad development; appointed to the superior court of Cincinnati to fill a vacancy in 1865 and was elected to the bench for two terms, resigning to resume law practice on January 1, 1872; appointed SECRETARY OF WAR in the cabinet of President Grant on March 8, 1876; served until May 22, 1876 when he was appointed ATTORNEY GENERAL in Grant's cabinet; most important contribution was assisting in drafting a bill which established the commission to settle the Hayes-Tilden election; continued in this post until the end of the Grant administration, March 3, 1877; resumed law practice; appointed minister to Austria-Hungary by President Arthur; transferred to St. Petersburg, Russia on July 4, 1884, where he remained until August 1885; died in San Diego, Cal. on May 21, 1891. Mabel T. R. Washburn, *Ancestry of William Howard Taft* (1908); L. A. Leonard, *The Life of Alphonso Taft* (1920); Ishbel Ross, *American Family: The Tafts, 1678–1964* (1964).

TAFT, William Howard. Born in Cincinnati, Ohio, September 15, 1857; son of Alphonso Taft, Secretary of War and Attorney General in Grant's cabinet, and Louisa Maria (Torrey) Taft; Unitarian; married Helen Herron on June 19,

1886; father of Robert Alphonso Taft, U.S. Senator, and two other children; attended local schools and Woodward High School; entered Yale, 1874, and graduated, 1878; received law degree from Cincinnati Law School and was admitted to the bar, 1880; while studying, served as court reporter for *Cincinnati Commercial*; appointed prosecuting attorney of Hamilton County, 1881; appointed collector of internal revenue for Cincinnati in 1882; resumed practice of law; toured Europe; appointed judge of superior court of Ohio in March 1887; elected judge of superior court for five-year term in April 1888; received post of U.S. solicitor general from President Benjamin Harrison, 1890; became federal circuit court judge on March 17, 1892, and served until March 1900; became president of Philippine Commission in March 1900; appointed SECRETARY OF WAR in the cabinet of President Theodore Roosevelt on February 1, 1904 and served until June 28, 1908; most important contributions were trip to Canal Zone to investigate start of construction of Panama Canal, trip to Cuba to effect peace when revolution threatened; elected PRESIDENT of the United States on November 1, 1908 on the Republican ticket; nominated to run for a second term in 1912, but lost to Wilson; returned to Yale as Kent Professor of Constitutional Law in March 1913; served as joint chairman of National War Labor Board, 1918–1919; named by President Harding chief justice of the U.S. Supreme Court on June 3, 1921; served until ill health forced his retirement on February 3, 1930; died in Washington, D.C., March 8, 1930; interment in Arlington National Cemetery. William Smith, *The Taft Story* (1954); Henry F. Pringle, *William Howard Taft* (1939); Ishbel Ross, *American Family: The Tafts, 1678–1964* (1964); Norman M. Wilensky, *Conservatives in the Progressive Era* (1965).

TANEY, Roger Brooke. Born in Calvert County, Md., March 17, 1777; son of Michael and Monica (Brooke) Taney; Roman Catholic; married Anne P. C. Key, sister of Francis Scott Key, on January 7, 1806; father of six daughters and one son; graduated from Dickinson College in 1795; studied law under Judge Jeremiah Townley Chase; admitted to practice in 1799; elected to state legislature in 1799; moved in 1801 to Frederick, Md., where he established a law practice; elected in 1816 to a five-year term in the State Senate; moved to Baltimore in 1823; appointed attorney general of Maryland in 1827; appointed chairman of the state committee for the election of Andrew Jackson in 1828; accepted recess appointment from President Jackson in 1831 as ATTORNEY GENERAL, took oath on July 20, 1831, was confirmed in December 1831, and served until September 23, 1833; most important contributions include advising President Jackson to veto proposed law which would grant a charter to the Second Bank of the United States, aiding him in redrafting this veto message when all others refused, and advising President Jackson to withdraw government deposits from the Second Bank of the United States; accepted recess appointment from President Jackson as SECRETARY OF TREASURY on September 23, 1833; most important contribution was the withdrawal of federal funds from the Second Bank of the United States and redistributing them in specified state banks; confirmation of his appointment was rejected by a hostile Senate on June 24, 1834; nomination for associate justice of the Supreme Court was defeated on March 3, 1835; nominated for chief justice of the Supreme Court on December 28, 1835 to fill vacancy left by Chief Justice Marshall; appointment was confirmed on March 15, 1836; most significant ruling was in connection with *Dred Scott v. Sandford*, when he proposed that Congress had no power to ban slavery from the territories; died in Washington, D.C. on October 12, 1864. J. Herman Schauinger, *Profiles in Action* (1966); Walker Lewis, *Without Fear or Favor* (1965).

TAYLOR, Zachary. Born in Montebello, Va., November 24, 1784; son of Lieutenant Colonel Richard and Sarah Dabney (Strother) Taylor; Episcopalian; married Margaret Mackall Smith on June 21, 1810; father of Anne Margaret Mackall, Sarah, Knox, Octavia Pannel, Margaret Smith, Mary Elizabeth, and Richard; moved with his family to Muddy Fork in Jefferson County, Ky. in 1785; received his only formal education from a tutor; assisted his father on the family plantation during his formative years; appointed first lieutenant in the 7th Infantry in 1806 and promoted to captain in 1810; advanced to the rank of major; transferred to the 26th Infantry Division on May 15, 1814; commanded the 3d Infantry Division at Green Bay, Wis.; also in command of Fort Winnebago; appointed lieutenant colonel of the 4th Infantry Division on April 20, 1819; commanded Fort Snelling in the unorganized Territory of Minnesota in 1828; commanded Fort Crawford in the Michigan Territory (now the state of Wisconsin) in 1829; promoted to full colonel of the 1st Regiment on April 4, 1832; advanced to brigadier general for his distinguished service during the Battle of Okeechobee against the Seminole Indians on August 21, 1832; assumed full command of Fort Jesup on June 17, 1844; promoted to major general during the Mexican campaigns, on May 28, 1846; established his residence at Baton Rouge, La. in 1840; defeated Santa Anna at the Battle of Buena Vista on February 23, 1847; nominated for the presidency by the Whigs on July 18, 1848, and subsequently resigned from the U.S. Army on January 31, 1849; elected PRESIDENT in November 1848; inaugurated on March 4, 1849, serving until his death in office on July 9, 1850; the first President representing a state west of the Mississippi River; the second President to die in the White House; died in Washington, D.C. on July 19, 1850; interment in Springfield, Ky. Holman Hamilton, *Zachary Taylor: Soldier in the White House* (1960).

TELLER, Henry Moore. Born on a farm in Granger, N.Y., May 23, 1830; son of John and Charlotte (Moore) Teller; Methodist; married Harriet M. Bruce on June 7, 1862; father of three children; after attending the rural schools and the academy at Rushford, he entered Alfred University at Alfred, N.Y., graduating in 1852; taught school; studied law at Angelica, N.Y., and was admitted to the bar in 1858; moved to Morrison, Ill. in 1858 and then to Central City, Colo. in 1861; major general of the Colorado militia from 1862 to 1864; upon the admission of Colorado to the Union, he was elected to the U.S. Senate, serving from November 15, 1876 until his resignation on April 17, 1882, to accept a cabinet portfolio; appointed SECRETARY OF THE INTERIOR by President Arthur, serving from April 17, 1882 to March 4, 1885; elected as a Republican to the U.S. Senate in 1885 and reelected in 1891; elected to the Senate again as an Independent Republican in 1897 and as a Democrat in 1903, serving in all from March 4, 1885 to March 3, 1909; secured the adoption of the Teller Resolution which pledged the U.S. to an independent Cuba in 1898; appointed a member of the U.S. Monetary Commission in 1908; resumed the private practice of law until his death in Denver, Colo., February 23, 1914; interment in Fairmount Cemetery, Denver. George Frederick Howe, *Chester A. Arthur: A Quarter Century of Machine Politics* (1957); Allan Nevins, *Grover Cleveland, A Study in Courage* (1932).

THOMAS, Philip Francis. Born in Easton, Md., September 12, 1810; son of Dr. Tristam and Maria (Francis) Thomas; married Sarah Maria Kerr on February 5, 1835, and upon her death, married Mrs. Clintonia (Wright) May in 1876; father of thirteen children; attended the Easton Academy and then entered Dickinson College, Carlisle, Pa., graduating in 1830; studied law and was admitted to the bar in 1831, commencing his legal practice in Easton, Md.; delegate to the state constitutional convention in 1836; elected to the Maryland House of Delegates in 1838, 1843, and 1845; elected as a Democrat to the 26th Congress, serving from March 4, 1839 to March 3, 1841; declined renomination in 1840, resuming the practice of law; judge of the Land Office Court of eastern Maryland, 1841; elected governor of Maryland from 1848 to 1851; declined the governorship of the Utah Territory offered by President Buchanan; comptroller of the U.S. Treasury from 1851 to 1853; collector of the Port of Baltimore from 1853 to 1860; declined the position of Treasurer of the United States tendered to him by President Buchanan; U.S. commissioner of patents from February 16, 1860 until December 10, 1860, resigning to accept a cabinet portfolio; appointed SECRETARY OF THE TREASURY by President Buchanan on December 10, 1860, serving until his resignation on January 11, 1861, because of his Southern sympathies; again elected to the Maryland House of Delegates in 1863; presented credentials as a Senator-elect to the U.S. Senate for the term beginning March 4, 1867, but was not seated on the grounds of disloyalty, because of his earlier Confederate sympathies; elected as a Democrat to the 44th Congress, serving from March 4, 1875 to March 3, 1877; unsuccessful candidate for election to the U.S. Senate in 1878; elected a member of the Maryland House of Delegates from 1878 to 1883; delegate to the Democratic state convention in 1883; resumed the practice of law in Easton, Md.; died in Baltimore, Md. on October 2, 1890; interment in Spring Hill Cemetery, Easton, Md. Philip Gerald Auchampaugh, *James Buchanan and his Cabinet on the Eve of Secession* (1926); Philip Shriver Klein, *President James Buchanan, A Biography* (1962).

THOMPSON, Jacob. Born in Leasburg, N.C., May 15, 1810; son of Nicholas and Lucretia (Van Hook) Thompson; married Catherine Jones; father of one son; attended the public schools and Bingham Academy in Orange County; entered the University of North Carolina, at Chapel Hill, graduating in 1831; member of the faculty of the University of North Carolina in 1831 and 1832; studied law and was admitted to the bar in 1834; commenced the practice of law in Pontatoc, Miss. in 1835; elected as a Democrat to the 26th through 31st Congresses, serving from March 4, 1839 to March 3, 1851; appointed SECRETARY OF THE INTERIOR by President Buchanan, serving from March 6, 1857 until his resignation on January 8, 1861; served as inspector general for the Confederate Army during the Civil War; confidential agent of the Confederacy to Canada in 1864 and 1865; traveled throughout Europe in 1866 and 1867; settled in Memphis, Tenn. in 1868 and died there on March 24, 1885; interment in Elmwood Cemetery, Memphis. Philip Gerald Auchampaugh, *James Buchanan and his Cabinet on the Eve of Secession* (1926); Philip Shriver Klein, *President James Buchanan, A Biography* (1962).

THOMPSON, Richard Wigginton. Born in Culpeper County, Va., June 9, 1809; son of William and Catherine Wigginton (Broadus) Thompson; married Harriet Eliza Gardiner on May 5, 1836; father of eight children; pursued classical studies; moved to Louisville, Ky. in 1831; clerked in a store; moved to Lawrence County, Ind. in 1831; taught school; studied law and was admitted to the bar in 1834, commencing his legal practice in Bedford, Ind.; elected to the Indiana House of Representatives, 1834–1836; elected to the state Senate, 1836–1838, serving as president *pro tempore* for a short time; elected as a Whig to the 27th Congress, serving from March 4, 1841 to March 3, 1843; moved to Terre Haute, Ind. in 1843; Terre Haute city attorney in 1846 and 1847; elected as a Whig to the 30th Congress, serving from March 4, 1847 to March 3, 1849; declined several presidential appointments; commander of Camp Thompson, Ind., and provost marshall, 1861–1865; appointed collector of internal revenue by President Lincoln for the seventh district of Indiana, serving one term; presidential elector on the Republican ticket of Lincoln and Johnson in 1864; delegate to the Republican national convention of Chicago in 1868 and of Cincinnati in 1876; judge of the fifth Indiana circuit court, 1867–1869; joined the cabinet of President Hayes as SECRETARY OF THE NAVY, serving from March 12, 1877 until his forced resignation on November 21, 1880 because of an economic "conflict of interests"; chairman of the American committee of the Panama Canal Company in 1881; director of the Panama Railroad from 1881 to 1888; author of *The Papacy and the Civil Power* (1876), *The History of Protective Tariff Laws* (1888), *Recollections of Sixteen Presidents* (1894), and *The Footprints of the Jesuits* (1894); died in Terre Haute, Ind., February 9, 1900; interment in High Lawn Cemetery, Terre Haute. George Frederick Howe, *Chester A. Arthur: A Quarter Century of Machine Politics* (1957); Courtlandt Canby, ed., *Lincoln and the Civil War: A Profile and a History* (1960).

THOMPSON, Smith. Born in Dutchess County, N.Y., January 17, 1768; son of Ezra and Rachel (Smith) Thompson; Presbyterian; married Sarah Livingston in 1794; father of two sons and two daughters; remarried to Eliza Livingston in 1836; father of one son and two daughters; graduated from the College of New Jersey (now Princeton) in 1788; studied law in Poughkeepsie, N.Y. under James Kent while teaching school; admitted to the bar in 1792 and began law practice in Troy, N.Y.; returned to Poughkeepsie in 1793 and practiced there; elected to the state legislature in 1800; represented Dutchess County in constitutional convention of 1801; appointed district attorney for the middle district, 1801, but did not serve; appointed associate justice of the New York Supreme Court on January 8, 1802, and served until 1814; made chief justice on February 25, 1814; became regent of the University of the State of New York in 1813; appointed SECRETARY OF THE NAVY in the cabinet of President Monroe on November 9, 1818, and served from January 1, 1819 until August 31, 1823; accepted appointment of associate justice in New York State Supreme Court left vacant by the death of Henry Livingston, and served from 1823 to 1843; received honorary LL.D.s from Yale and Princeton, 1824; ran unsuccessfully for governor of New York in 1828; received honorary LL.D. from Harvard, 1835; was vice-president of the American Bible Society; died in Poughkeepsie, N.Y., December 18, 1843. Charles Warren, *The Supreme Court in United States History* (1922); Ian Elliot, *James Monroe, 1758–1831: Chronology, Documents, Bibliographical Aids* (1969).

THORNBURGH, Richard Lewis. Born in Rosslyn Farms, Pa., July 16, 1932; son of Charles Garland Thornburgh, an engineer and Alice (Sanborn) Thornburgh; Episcopalian; married Virginia Hooton in 1955; father of John, David, and Peter; Virginia Thornburgh was killed in a car accident in 1960; remarried on October 12, 1963, to Virginia ("Ginny") Walton Judson, a schoolteacher, father of William; attended Mercersburg Academy, a private preparatory school; graduated from Yale University, 1954, with a degree in engineering; went on to University of Pittsburgh School of Law, and graduated with high honors in 1957; hired as legal counsel for the Aluminum Company of America and in 1959 joined the firm of Kirkpatrick Pomeroy Lockhart and Johnson in Pittsburgh; in 1966 he ran unsuccessfully for a seat in the U.S. House of Representatives; Richard Nixon appointed Richard Thornburgh U.S. attorney for Western Pennsylvania in 1969; during the following six years, he earned a reputation as a resourceful and aggressive prosecutor in pursuit of mobsters, drug traffickers, corporate polluters, and corrupt public officials; in 1975 he was appointed by Gerald Ford as assistant attorney general in charge of the criminal division; he returned to Kirkpatrick and Lockhart in Pittsburgh in 1977; Thornburgh was elected governor in 1978, and sworn in on January 16, 1979, as forty-first governor of Pennsylvania; ten weeks later, he was faced with the Three Mile Island Nuclear Power Plant accident; praised by President Jimmy Carter for a "superlative job" in handling the crisis, he led the fight to postpone reopening of the power plant; reelected to a second term in 1982; in 1987, named director of the Institute of Politics at the John F. Kennedy School of Government at Harvard University; Appointed by Ronald Reagan as ATTORNEY GENERAL, he was confirmed by the Senate on August 11, 1988, and sworn in on August 12, 1988; retained by George Bush. *Current Biography Yearbook, 1988. Who's Who in America, 1989.*

TOBIN, Maurice Joseph. Born in Boston, Mass., May 22, 1901; son of James Tobin, carpenter, and Margaret M. (Daly) Tobin; Roman Catholic; married Helen M. Noonan on November 19, 1932; father of Helen Louise, Carol Ann, and Maurice Joseph; attended Our Lady of Perpetual Help elementary school and High School of Commerce in Boston; studied at Boston College; worked for Conway Leather Company, 1919–1922; became district traffic manager of New England Telephone and Telegraph Co., 1928–1937; elected to Massachusetts House of Representatives for a two-year term in 1926; member of Boston School Committee, 1931–1934 and 1935–1937; elected mayor of Boston in 1937 and reelected 1942; chosen governor of Massachusetts in 1944 and took office in January 1945; appointed SECRETARY OF LABOR in the cabinet of President Truman on February 1, 1949, having previously served in the interim of August 13, 1948 to February 1, 1949, and served until January 20, 1953; most important contributions were establishment of Federal Safety Council in Bureau of Labor Standards, increase in minimum wage through Fair Labor Standards Amendment of 1949, and extension of Wagner-Peysen Act to Puerto Rico and Virgin Islands; died in Jamaica Plain, Mass., July 19, 1953; interment in Holyhood Cemetery. Barton J. Bernstein and A. J. Matusow, *Truman Administration: A Documentary History* (1966); Howard Furrer, ed., *Harry S. Truman 1884– : Chronology, Documents, Bibliographical Aids* (1969).

TOMPKINS, Daniel D. Born in Scarsdale, N.Y., June 21, 1774; son of Jonathon G. Tompkins, Revolutionary patriot, and Sarah (Hyatt) Tompkins; brother of Caleb Tompkins, member of Congress; Presbyterian; married Hannah Minthorne about 1797; father of seven children; completed preparatory studies; was graduated from Columbia College in 1795; studied law and was admitted to the bar in 1797; began practice in New York City; member of the state constitutional convention in 1801; member of the State Assembly in 1803; elected as a Democrat to the 9th Congress in 1804, but resigned before the beginning of his term to accept appointment as an associate justice of the New York State Supreme Court, serving from 1804 to 1807; elected governor of New York in 1807 and reelected in 1810, 1813, and 1816; as governor, was responsible for the passage of a law ending slavery in the state, and also urged improvements in the state school system, liberalization of its criminal code, and reform of the militia system; declined an appointment as secretary of state in 1814; elected VICE-PRESIDENT under President Monroe in 1816 and reelected with Monroe in 1820, serving from March 4, 1817 to March 3, 1825; president of the New York state constitutional convention of 1821; one of the founders of the New York Historical Society; died in Tompkinsville, Staten Island, N.Y. on June 11, 1825; interment in the Minthorne vault in St. Mark's Churchyard, New York City. P. J. Van Pelt, *An Oration Containing Sketches of the Life, Character, and Services of the Late Daniel D. Tompkins* (1843); J. L. Jenkins, *Lives of the Governors of New York State* (1851).

TOUCEY, Isaac. Born in Newtown, Conn., November 5, 1796; son of Zalmon and Phebe (Booth) Toucey; married Catherine Nichols on October 28, 1827; childless; educated by private tutors; studied law in office of Asa Chapman; admitted to the bar in Hartford in 1818 and began the practice of law; became state attorney for Hartford County, 1822–1835; elected to the 24th and 25th Congresses, serving from March 4, 1835 to March 3, 1839; unsuccessful candidate for reelection in 1838; made state attorney, 1842–1844; unsuccessful Democratic candidate for governor in 1845; elected governor of Connecticut, 1846–1847, but failed to be reelected; appointed ATTORNEY GENERAL in the cabinet of President Polk on June 21, 1848, and served from June 29, 1848 to March 7, 1849; acting Secretary of State, 1849–1850; member of Connecticut Senate in 1850; elected to state House of Representatives in 1852; became member of U.S. Senate in 1852, and served from May 12, 1852, to March 3, 1857; appointed SECRETARY OF THE NAVY in the cabinet of President Buchanan, and served from March 6, 1857 to March 3, 1861; most important contribution was supervision of expedition to Paraguay; returned to law practice in Hartford; benefactor of Trinity College; died in Hartford, Conn., July 30, 1869; interment in Cedar Hill Cemetery. Irving J. Sloan, ed., *James Buchanan, 1791–1868: Chronology, Documents, Bibliographical Aids* (1968).

TRACY, Benjamin Franklin. Born in Oswego, N.Y., April 26, 1830; son of Benjamin Franklin Tracy; married Delinda E. Catlin in 1851; attended common schools of Owego; went to Owego Academy; studied in law office of N. W. Davis; admitted to the bar in May 1851; elected district attorney of Tioga county as Whig in November 1853, reelected in 1856; chosen member of New York State Assembly as Republican and War Democrat, 1861; recruited two regiments of state volunteers in 1862, and became colonel of 109th regiment; fought in battle of the Wilderness, 1864; became colonel of 127th U.S. Negro troops; commanded military post at Elmira, N.Y., and was in charge of prison camps; brevetted brigadier general; discharged on June 3, 1865; entered law firm of Benedict, Burr and Benedict in New York City; appointed U.S. district attorney for eastern district of New York, 1866–1873; returned to practice in Brooklyn, N.Y., 1873; made associate justice of state Court of Appeals, December 1881 to January 1883; went into law partnership with his son, F. B. Tracy, and with William C. DeWitt; appointed SECRETARY OF THE NAVY in the cabinet of President Benjamin Harrison, and served from March 5, 1889 to March 5, 1893; most important contributions were plans for rehabilitation and increase of naval force; was counsel for Venezuela in boundary arbitration; chairman of commission which formed charter of Greater New York, 1896; bred trotters on Tioga County farm; died August 6, 1915. D. S. Alexander, *Four Famous New Yorkers* (1923); H. J. Sievers, ed., *Benjamin Harrison, 1833–1901*; *Chronology, Documents, Bibliographic Aids* (1969).

TROWBRIDGE, Alexander Buel. Born in Englewood, N.J., December 12, 1929; son of Alexander Buel Trowbridge, college history professor, and Julie (Chamberlain) Trowbridge; Presbyterian; married Nancy Horst on July 2, 1955; father of Stephen, Scott, and Kimberley; graduated Philips Academy, Andover, Mass. in 1947; volunteered for reconstruction work in western Europe; member of International Intern Program of United Nations headquarters in Lake Success, N.Y., 1948; assistant to Congressman Franklin D. Roosevelt, Jr. in 1950; received B.A. from Princeton University, 1951; employed by Central Intelligence Agency, 1951; joined Marine Corps in 1951; commissioned second lieutenant, and served with 1st division in Korea until 1953; joined California Texas Oil Company, and made marketing assistant for petroleum products, 1954–1958; with Esso Standard Oil, S. A., Ltd. in Cuba, 1959–1960; moved to San Juan, Puerto Rico, to become president and division manager of Esso Standard Oil Co., 1961–1963; director of Federation of YMCA; director of Better Business Bureau; chosen assistant secretary of commerce on May 6, 1965; made acting secretary of commerce on January 18, 1967; appointed SECRETARY OF COMMERCE in the cabinet of President Lyndon Johnson, and served from May 23, 1967 to March 1, 1968; most important contributions were support of merger with department of labor and organization of office of foreign direct investment to curb deficit in balance of payments; became president of American Management Association in May 1968; member of Council on Foreign Relations in New York City and Federal City Club of Washington, D.C.; co-author with H. Cleveland, et al., of *The Overseas Americans* (1960), and aided in preparation of *Spearheads of Democracy—Labor in the Developing Countries* (1962). *New York Times* (June 9, 1967); "New Man at Commerce," *Newsweek* (February 26, 1968); Rowland Evans and Robert Novak, *Lyndon B. Johnson: The Exercise of Power* (1966).

TRUMAN, Harry S[hippe]. Born in Lamar, Mo., May 8, 1884; son of John Anderson Truman, farmer and livestock dealer, and Martha Ellen (Young) Truman; Baptist; married Elizabeth Virginia (Bess) Wallace on June 28, 1919; father of (Mary) Margaret; moved with family to Harrisonville, Mo., in 1886, to a farm in Grandview, Mo., in 1888, and to Independence, Mo., on December 28, 1890; attended public schools; worked in mail room of Kansas City *Star*; became timekeeper for contractor of Santa Fe Railroad, 1902; employed by National Bank of Commerce in Kansas City, 1903–1905; worked at Union National Bank of Kansas City in 1905; joined National Guard of Missouri as a corporal on June 14, 1905; worked on family farm as a partner, 1906–1917; organized 2d Missouri

Field Artillery, 1917, and later 129th Artillery, 35th Division; commissioned first lieutenant on June 22, 1917, and first lieutenant of field artillery on September 26, 1917; sent overseas on March 30, 1918; attended 2d Corps Artillery School at Chantillon-sur-Seine, France, from April 20, 1918, to June 18, 1918; rejoined regiment to become adjutant, 2d Battalion; went to Artillery School at Coetquidan, France, July 5, 1918; put in command of Battery D., 129th Field Artillery, on July 12, 1918; returned to New York on April 20, 1919, and was discharged as a major on May 6, 1919; went into haberdashery business in Kansas City, 1919–1921; was administrative judge in Jackson County Court, Missouri, 1922–1924; attended Kansas City Law School, 1923–1925; presiding judge of Jackson County Court from 1926 to 1934; elected to U.S. Senate and served from January 3, 1935, to January 17, 1945; elected VICE-PRESIDENT on Democratic ticket with President Franklin D. Roosevelt in November 1944 and was inaugurated on January 20, 1945, serving until April 12, 1945, when he became PRESIDENT upon the death of Roosevelt; was reelected in 1948 and served until January 20, 1953; during his presidency he authorized the atomic bombing of Japan to end World War II, and sent the military into Korea to fight communism; tried and failed to establish some sort of national health insurance, but was honored by President Johnson when the latter traveled to Independence, Mo., to sign Medicare; promoted the formation of NATO and aided the European economic recovery through the Marshall Plan; died in Kansas City, Mo., on December 26, 1972; buried at the Truman Library; wrote *Years of Decisions* (vol. 1, 1955); *Years of Trial and Hope* (vol. 2, 1956); *Mr. Citizen* (vol. 3, 1960). Howard Furer, ed., *Harry S. Truman, 1884– : Chronology, Documents, Bibliographical Aids* (1969); *Colliers Encyclopedia* (1972 yearbook); *Current Biography, 1972; NY Times* (December 27, 1972; Richard Goodwin, *Remember America* (1988).

TYLER, John. Born at Greenway, Va., March 29, 1790; son of John Tyler, judge, member and Speaker of the Virginia House of Delegates, and fourteenth governor of Virginia, and Mary Marot (Armstead) Tyler; Episcopalian; married to Letitia Christian on March 29, 1813 and father of seven children; after death of first wife in 1842, married Julia Gardiner on June 26, 1844, and was father of seven more children including David Gardiner Tyler, member of Congress; attended private schools; graduated from William and Mary College in 1807; studied law; admitted to the bar in 1809 and began practice in Charles City County, Va.; captain of a military company, 1813; elected to the Virginia House of Delegates and served from 1811 to 1816; member of Virginia executive council, 1815–1816; elected in 1816 as a Democratic-Republican to the 14th Congress to fill a vacancy; reelected to the 15th and 16th Congresses and served from December 16, 1817 until March 3, 1821; member of the Virginia House of Delegates, 1823–1825; elected governor of Virginia in 1825, and served until 1827; elected to the U.S. Senate in 1827 and reelected in 1833, serving from March 4, 1827 until his resignation on February 29, 1836; elected president *pro* *tempore* of the Senate on March 3, 1835; member of the state constitutional convention, 1829 and 1830; nominated for U.S. Vice-President, 1835; again elected to the state House of Delegates, 1838; elected VICE-PRESIDENT on the Whig ticket with William H. Harrison in 1840, and took office on March 4, 1841; upon the death of President Harrison, took the oath of office as PRESIDENT on April 6, 1841, becoming the first vice-president to assume the presidency by right of succession; served until March 3, 1845; chairman of the Washington, D.C. peace convention in February 1861; member of the Virginia secessional convention, 1861; member of the Confederate provisional congress in 1861; elected to the House of Representatives of the Confederate congress, but died before serving; died in Richmond, Va. on January 18, 1862; interment in Hollywood Cemetery, Richmond, where a monument has been erected by the U.S. Congress. Hugh Russell Fraser, *Democracy in the Making: The Jackson-Tyler Era* (1938); Robert J. Morgan, *A Whig Embattled: The Presidency Under John Tyler* (1954); Robert Seager, *And Tyler Too* (1963).

TYNER, James Noble. Born in Brookville, Ind., January 17, 1826; pursued academic studies, and graduated from Brookville Academy, 1844; went into business with father, 1846–1854; studied law, was admitted to the bar in 1857, and began practice in Peru, Ind.; secretary of Indiana State Senate; presidential elector on Lincoln-Hamlin Republican ticket, 1860; special agent for post office department, 1861–1866; chosen member of Congress to fill vacancy, and served from March 4, 1869 to March 3, 1875; appointed second assistant postmaster general, and served from February 26, 1875 to July 11, 1876; appointed POST-MASTER GENERAL in the cabinet of President Grant, and continued under the administration of President Hayes, serving from July 12, 1876 to March 11, 1877; was first assistant postmaster general from April 1877 to October 1881; delegate from U.S. to International Postal Congresses of 1878 in Paris; assistant attorney general for post office department, March 21, 1889–May 27, 1893, and May 6, 1897–April 27, 1903; died in Washington, D.C., December 5, 1904; interment in Oak Hill Cemetery. Allan Nevins, *Hamilton Fish: The Inner History of the Grant Administration* (n.d.).

U

UDALL, Stewart Lee. Born in Saint Johns, Ariz., January 31, 1920; son of Levi Stuart Udall, chief justice of Supreme Court of Arizona, and Louise (Lee) Udall; Mormon; married Ermalee Webb on August 1, 1947; father of Thomas, Scott, Lynn, Lori, Dennis, and James; attended public schools of St. Johns; studied at Eastern Arizona Junior College; received LL.B. from University of Arizona in 1948; served in U.S. Army Air Forces in Italy during World War II; admitted to the Arizona bar in 1948; practiced law in Tucson with brother Morris, 1948–1954; elected to U.S. House of Representatives in 1954, was reelected three times, and served from 1955 to 1961; appointed SECRETARY OF THE INTERIOR in the cabinet of President Kennedy, continued under Lyndon Johnson, and served from January 21, 1961 to January 23, 1969; most important contributions were eighteen-month moratorium on sale of public lands, study of Bureau of Indian Affairs, establishment of manufacturing plants to provide employment for Indians; headed Overseer Group at New School for Social Research in New York City; authored *The Quier Crisis* (1963, 1970); *1976: Agenda for Tomorrow* (1968); *America's Natural Treasures; National Nature Monuments and Seashores* (1971); *The Energy Balloon* (1974). New York Times, *The Kennedy Years* (1964); Hugh Sidey, *John F. Kennedy, President* (1963); *Who's Who* (1987–1988).

UPSHUR, Abel Parker. Born in Northampton County, Va., June 17, 1790; son of Littlejohn Upshur, planter, Federalist member of Virginia legislature in 1809, and captain in the War of 1812, and Ann (Parker) Upshur; married Elizabeth Dennis, February 26, 1817; after her death in childbirth in October 1817, remarried to Elizabeth Ann Brown Upshur, his second cousin, March 24, 1824; father of one daughter; received classical education under tutors; attended Yale and Princeton; studied law and was admitted to the bar in 1810; began practice in Richmond, Va.; elected to the Virginia House of Delegates in 1812 and served until 1813; served as commonwealth attorney for Richmond from 1816 until his resignation in 1823; was also elected to the Common Hall (city council), and continued his law practice; retired to "Vaucluse," his plantation in Northampton County; elected again to the House of Delegates in 1824, to serve there until 1827; justice in the General Court of Virginia, 1826 to 1841; member of the Virginia constitutional convention from 1829 to 1830; a former Federalist, he supported the Whig Party in the election of 1840; appointed SECRETARY OF THE NAVY on September 13, 1841 in the cabinet of President Tyler, and served until July 23, 1843; most important contributions were reorganization of the department into bureaus to promote efficiency, initiation of expansion and modernization measures, the construction of the first iron-hulled steamship in the U.S. Navy, and reform of some disciplinary abuses; appointed SECRETARY OF STATE by Tyler on June 23, 1843; most important contributions were urging of the annexation of Texas as a slaveholding state and authorizing negotiations for that purpose in October 1843, and opening up negotiations with Britain to solve Oregon dispute, efforts eventually leading to the acquisition of both territories by the U.S.; wrote many essays, addresses, and pamphlets, including "A Brief Inquiry into the True Nature and Character of Our Federal Government: A Review of Judge Joseph Story's Commentaries on the Constitution" (Petersburg, Va., 1840); killed February 28, 1844, along with several other Cabinet members when a gun of the new steamer *Princeton* exploded upon being fired during a demonstration cruise on the Potomac River; interment in Congressional Cemetery, Washington, D.C. Claude H. Hall, *Abel Parker Upshur: Conservative Virginian* (1964); R. G. Adams, "Abel Parker Upshur," in S. F. Bemis, ed., *The American Secretaries of State*, vol. 5 (1928); *Cyclopedia of American Biography*, vol. 6 (1899); *Dictionary of American Biography*, vol. 10 (1936); *Who Was Who in America*, Historical Volume (1967).

USERY, Willie J., Jr. Born in Hardwick, Ga., December 21, 1923; son of Willie J. and Effie Mae (Williamson) Usery; Baptist; married Gussie Mae Smith, June 14, 1942; father of Melvin J.; served in the U.S. Naval Reserve, 1943–1946; attended Mercer University, Macon, Ga., 1951–1952; worked as machinist, 1946–1956; Grand Lodge representative, International Association Machinist and Aerospace Workers, AFL-CIO, 1956–1969; chairman, Cape Kennedy Management Relations Council, 1968; Department of Labor, Assistant Secretary for Labor-Management Relations, 1969–1973; director, Federal Mediation and Concilliation Service, 1973–1976; Mason; Elk; nominated to the office of SECRETARY OF LABOR, on January 22, 1976, by President Gerald Ford and confirmed by the U.S. Senate on February 4; sworn into office on February 10, 1976; during his administration the nation continued its gradual economic recovery from the recession; however, the recovery rate was not as fast as anticipated; many union contracts renegotiated to increase wages and offset the effects of inflation; left office on January 20, 1977, with the change of presidential administrations. Henry H. Schulte, Jr., ed., *Facts on File Yearbook, 1976*; National Journal, *Ford's Presidency; Who's Who in America, 1976*.

USHER, John Palmer. Born in Brookfield, N.Y., January 9, 1816; son of Dr. Nathaniel and Lucy (Palmer) Usher; married Margaret Patterson on January 26, 1844; father of four sons; attended the common schools; studied law in the office of Henry Bennett of New Berlin, N.Y.; was admitted to the bar in 1839; moved to Terre Haute, Ind., 1840, and began practice of law; served in the Indiana legislature, 1850–1851; appointed attorney general of Indiana in November of 1861, and resigned four months later; became assistant secretary of the interior at Washington in 1862; appointed SECRETARY OF THE INTERIOR *ad interim* in the cabinet of President Lincoln, January 1, 1863 to January 7, 1863; appointed SECRETARY OF THE INTERIOR by President Lincoln, and continued under Johnson, serving from January 8, 1863 to May 14, 1865; most important contributions were recommendation of small tax on net profits of larger Indian reservations and silver and gold mines, request for greater appropriations for Indians, and report on public lands; resumed practice of law; moved to Lawrence, Kansas and accepted appointment as chief counsel for Union Pacific Railroad; died in Philadelphia, Pa., April 13, 1889. A. T. Rice, *President Lincoln's Cabinet* (1925); Elmo R. Richardson and Alan W. Farley, *John Palmer Usher, Lincoln's Secretary of the Interior* (1960).

V

VAN BUREN, Martin. Born in Kinderhook, N.Y., December 5, 1782; son of Abraham Van Buren, farmer and innkeeper, and Maria Goes Hoes (Van Allen) Van Buren; Dutch Reform; married Hannah Hoes on February 21, 1807; father of Abraham, John, Martin, and Smith Thompson; attended local schools; went to Kinderhook Academy; worked in law office of Francis Sylvester, 1796–1802; studied law in New York City with William P. Van Ness in 1802; admitted to bar in 1803, and began practice in Kinderhook; counselor for Superior Court of New York, 1807; appointed surrogate of Columbia County, N.Y. on February 20, 1808, and remained in that capacity until 1813; moved to Hudson, N.Y., 1809; member of New York State Senate from 1813 to 1820; was attorney general of New York State, 1815–1819; elected U.S. Senator from New York, and served from March 4, 1821 to December 20, 1828; delegate to third New York State constitutional convention, August 28, 1821; served as governor of New York from January 1, 1829 until his resignation on March 12, 1829; appointed SECRETARY OF STATE in the cabinet of President Jackson on March 6, 1829, and served from March 28, 1829 to May 23, 1831; commissioned minister to Great Britain on January 25, 1831, but returned after January 25, 1832 when Senate rejected the nomination; elected VICE-PRESIDENT in the administration of President Jackson, and served from March 4, 1833 to March 3, 1837; elected PRESIDENT and served from March 4, 1837 to March 3, 1841; was unsuccessful Democratic nominee for reelection in 1840 and 1844; unsuccessful Free Soil nominee for presidential election in 1848; returned to Lindewald, Kinderhook, N.Y. and retired; died in Kinderhook, July 24, 1862; interment in Kinderhook Cemetery. Robert V. Remini, *Martin Van Buren and the Making of the Democratic Party* (1959); Irving J. Sloan, ed., *Martin Van Buren, 1782–1862: Chronology, Documents, Bibliographical Aids* (1969).

VANCE, Cyrus Roberts. Born in Clarksburg, W.V., March 27, 1917; son of John Carl and Amy (Roberts) Vance; Episcopalian; married Grace Elsie Sloane, a painter, on February 15, 1947; father of Elsie Nicoll, Amy Sloane, Grace Roberts, Camilla and Cyrus Roberts, Jr.: attended Kent school in Kent, Conn.; B.A. in economics, Yale, 1939; Yale Law School, with honors, 1942; enlisted in U.S. Navy, 1942; served as gunnery officer on *USS Hale* and *USS Henderson* during World War II; discharged in 1946 as lieutenant j.g.; assistant to the president of the Mead Corp., paper products manufacturers, 1946–1947; joined New York law firm of Simpson, Thacher and Bartlett in 1947; Democrat; entered government service in 1957 as special counsel to the Senate Preparedness Investigating Subcommittee; counsel to government committees until appointed Secretary of the Army in 1961; Deputy Defense Secretary, 1964; undertook successful peacemaking missions for President Lyndon Johnson during anti-American crisis in the Canal Zone, 1964, civil war in Santo Domingo, 1965, army occupation of Detroit during 1967 race riots, and Cyprus dispute between Greece and Turkey, 1967; served as deputy ambassador, under Averill Harriman, to Paris negotiations on the Vietnam War, 1968–1969; returned to law practice in 1969 as partner in the firm of Simpson and Thacher; Medal of Freedom, 1969; selected to be SECRETARY OF STATE by President-Elect Jimmy Carter on December 3, 1976; served until April 21, 1980; dealt with Iran revolution, Iranian hostage crisis, the Camp David Accords which led to the Israeli-Egyptian peace treaty, the new Panama Canal treaties, and the deployment of the neutron bomb in Europe; member Century Association and Links Clubs, New York City, and Metropolitan Club, Washington, D.C.; member board of directors, I.B.M., Pan American World Airways and the *New York Times*; trustee of Yale University, the Rockefeller Foundation, the Urban Institute and the New York Presbyterian Hospital. *New Republic* (December 18, 1976); *New York Times* (December 4, 1976); *Time* (December 13, 1976); *U.S. News & World Report* (December 13, 1976); Jimmy Carter, *Keeping Faith* (1982).

VERITY, C(alvin) William, Jr. Born in Middletown, Ohio, January 26, 1917; son of Calvin W. Verity and Elizabeth (O'Brien) Verity; married Margaret (Peggy) Burnley Wymond on April 19, 1941; father of Jonathan George, Peggy Wymond, and William Wymond; Episcopalian; student at the Choate School in Wallingford, Conn.; transferred to Phillips Exeter Academy in Exeter, N.H., graduating in 1935; B.A. in economics from Yale University, 1939; after graduating he traveled the Far East but the trip was cut short by the outbreak of World War II; moved to New York City and worked for Young and Rubican (advertising) and then for Hapsburg House (restaurant) as a manager; returned to Ohio and Armco, the business founded by his grandfather; started as a laborer in the Hamilton plant; continued in the public relations department in Middletown; joined the navy in 1942 and served in the Pacific as a lieutenant; returned to Armco after release in 1946; began as an assistant safety advisor at Middletown; assistant to the plant officer in charge of personnel, grievances, and labor relations, 1948; transferred to Ashland, Ky.; plant in charge of personnel and labor negotiations, 1950; assistant to the works manager responsible for all staff operations, 1953; returned to Middletown as director of Armco's organizational planning and development, 1957; director of public relations, 1961; vice-president and general manager of steel, 1964; executive vice-president of Armco (fourth largest steel company at that time), 1965; during the 1970s he became a spokesman to make U.S. businesses more competitive abroad; chairman of the board at Armco, 1971; chairman, U.S. Chamber of Commerce, 1980–1981; chairman, President Ronald Reagan's bipartisan Task Force on Private Sector Initiatives, 1981; cochairman of the U.S.-USSR Trade Economic Council, 1979–1984; nominated by President Regan as SECRETARY OF COMMERCE on August 11, 1987, and confirmed on October 13, 1987; served until January 31, 1989. *NY Times Biographical Service* (August 1987); *Current Biography* (Yearbook 1988); *Who's Who in America, 1988–1989; Facts on File* (1987 and 1989).

VILAS, William Freeman. Born in Chelsea, Vt., July 9, 1840; son of Levi B. and Esther G. (Smilie) Vilas; married Anna M. Fox on January 3, 1866; father of Mary Esther; moved with his parents to Madison, Wis., in 1851; attended the common schools; entered the University of Wisconsin, at Madison, graduating in 1858; graduated from the University of Albany School of Law, Albany, N.Y., in 1860; was admitted to the bar and commenced his legal practice in Madison, on July 9, 1860; enlisted in the Union Army during the Civil War; Captain of Company A, 23d Regiment, Wisconsin Volunteer Infantry; later promoted to major and then lieutenant colonel; professor of law at the University of Wisconsin; regent of the University of Wisconsin from 1880 to 1885; appointed by the Wisconsin Supreme Court to prepare a revised body of the statute law which was subsequently adopted in 1878; elected to the Wisconsin State Assembly in 1885; delegate to the Democratic national convention in 1876, 1880, 1884, 1892; and 1896; invited to join the cabinet as POSTMASTER GENERAL by appointment of President Cleveland on March 7, 1885, serving until January 16, 1888, when President Cleveland commissioned him SECRETARY OF THE INTERIOR, a portfolio he held until March 6, 1889; elected as a Democrat to the U.S. Senate from Wisconsin on January 28, 1891, serving from March 4, 1891 to March 3, 1897; again designated regent of the University of Wisconsin, a position he held from 1896 to 1905, whereupon he resumed the practice of law; died in Madison, Wis. on August 28, 1908; interment Forest Hills Cemetery, Madison. Horace Samuel Merrill, *Bourbon Leader: Grover Cleveland and the Democratic Party* (1957); Allan Nevins, *Grover Cleveland: A Study in Courage* (1932).

VINSON, Frederick Moore. Born in Louisa, Ky., January 22, 1890; son of James Vinson, county jailer, and Virginia (Ferguson) Vinson; Methodist; married to Roberta Dixon on January 24, 1923; father of Frederick Moore and James Robert; attended the local schools; was graduated from Kentucky Normal College in Louisa in 1908; was graduated from the law department of Centre College, Danville, Ky., in 1911; admitted to the bar in 1911 and began practice in Louisa; city attorney of Louisa, 1914 and 1915; also engaged in grocery, milling, and banking enterprises; served in the U.S. Army during World War I; elected commonwealth attorney for the 32d judicial district of Kentucky in 1921 and served until January, 1924; elected as a Democrat to the 68th Congress in 1924 to fill a vacancy; reelected to the 69th and 70th Congresses and served until March 3, 1929; resumed law practice in Ashland, Ky.: elected to the 72d through 75th Congresses, serving from March 4, 1931 until May 12, 1938; appointed associate justice of the U.S. Circuit Court of Appeals for the District of Columbia by President Franklin Roosevelt in December 1937; subsequently appointed on March 2, 1942 as chief judge of the U.S. Emergency Court of Appeals by Chief Justice Harlan Stone; served in each capacity until his resignation on May 27, 1943 to accept an appointment by the President as Director of the Office of Economic Stabilization, and in that capacity was vice-chairman of the U.S. delegation to the United Nations Monetary and Financial Conference in July 1944; served until March 5, 1945 when he became Federal Loan Administrator; appointed director of War Mobilization and Reconversion and served from April 4 to July 22, 1945; appointed SECRETARY OF THE TREASURY in the cabinet of President Truman on July 18, 1945; most important contributions were supervising the last of the great war bond drives, recommending the Revenue Act of 1945 to relieve tax burdens, serving as the first chairman of the boards of governors of both the International Monetary Fund and the International Bank for Reconstruction and Development, serving as chairman of the National Advisory Council on International Monetary and Financial Problems, and urging the extension of credit to Great Britain; served until June 23, 1946 when he resigned following his appointment by President Truman as chief justice of the United States to succeed Harlan F. Stone; received the Medal of Merit of the United States in 1947; died in Washington, D.C. on September 8, 1953. Glendon Schubert, *Judicial Mind: Attitudes and Ideologies of Supreme Court Justices, 1946–1963* (1965); Barton J. Bernstein and A. J. Matusow, *The Truman Administration: A Documentary History* (1966); Cabell Phillips, *The Truman Presidency* (1966).

VOLPE, John Anthony. Born in Wakefield, Mass., December 8, 1908; son of Vito and Filomena (Benedetto) Volpe; Roman Catholic; married to Jennie Benedetto on June 18, 1934; father of Jean and John Anthony; attended Malden High School in Boston; worked as a journeyman plasterer, 1926–1928; attended the Wentworth Institute in Boston from 1928 until his graduation in 1930; timekeeper of a residential and commercial construction firm in 1930 and was assistant superintendent of construction until 1932; formed the John A. Volpe Construction Company in March 1933, and became its president; lieutenant with the Civil Engineer Corps of the U.S. Navy during World War II; elected deputy chairman of the Republican state committee in 1950 and was an alternate delegate to the Republican national convention in 1952; appointed a member of the Massachusetts commission of public works, serving from 1953 to 1956; appointed by President Eisenhower the first federal highway administrator in 1956 and served until 1957; elected governor of Massachusetts in 1960; unsuccessful candidate for reelection in 1962, but ran successfully in 1966 and served again as governor in 1967 and 1968; appointed SECRETARY OF TRANSPORTATION in the cabinet of President Nixon on December 11, 1968 and took the oath of office on January 22, 1969; attempted without success to prevent Penn Central bankruptcy; resigned on January 1, 1973, and subsequently named to become Ambassador to Italy; served in this post until January 20, 1977, and then returned to private business interests. Earl Mazo and Stephen Hess, *Nixon: A Political Portrait* (1969).

W

WALKER, Frank Comerford. Born in Plymouth, Pa., May 30, 1886; son of David Walker, merchant and copper mine operator and Ellen (Comerford) Walker; Roman Catholic; married on November 11, 1914 to Hallie Victoria Boucher; father of Thomas Joseph and Laura Hallie; attended parochial schools in Butte, Mont.; attended Gonzaga University, 1903–1906; studied law at the University of Notre Dame, graduating in 1909; admitted to the bar in 1909 and began practice in Butte with his brother Thomas Joseph; assistant district attorney of Silver Bow County, 1909–1912; member of the Montana legislature, 1913; first lieutenant in the U.S. Army during World War I; moved to New York City, 1925; became vice-president and general counsel of Comerford Theaters, Inc., and general counsel of the Meco Realty Co. and the Comerford Publix Corp., all of Scranton, Pennsylvania; treasurer of the Democratic national committee, 1932–1933; appointed executive secretary of President Franklin Roosevelt's Executive Council in 1933; appointed executive director of the National Emergency Council, and served, 1933–1935; engaged in business pursuits; named chairman of the finance committee of the Democratic campaign of 1938; appointed POST-MASTER GENERAL in the cabinet of President Roosevelt on September 10, 1940, continued under President Truman, and served until May 8, 1945; most important contributions were establishing the V-mail system to reduce weight and bulk of mail to U.S. servicemen abroad, and initiating helicopter and bus delivery of mail in rural areas; chairman of the Democratic national committee, 1943–1944; attended the first session of the United Nations General Assembly as an alternate U.S. delegate in 1946 and served as a U.S. representative on the Assembly's legal committee; served as director of the First National Bank, Scranton, and the Grace National Bank, New York; died in New York City on September 13,

1959. Rexford G. Tugwell, *FDR: Architect of an Era* (1967); A. J. Wann, *The President as Chief Administrator: A Study of Franklin D. Roosevelt* (1968).

WALKER, Robert James. Born in Northumberland, Pa., July 19, 1801; son of Jonathan Hoge Walker, a jurist, and Lucretia (Duncan) Walker; married Mary Blechynder Bacle, granddaughter of Benjamin Franklin, on April 4, 1825; father of eight children; attended town schools; studied under private tutors; graduated University of Pennsylvania in 1819; was admitted to the bar in 1821; moved to Natchez, Miss. in 1826, and entered law practice with Duncan Walker, his brother; elected judge of state Supreme Court, 1828, but declined to serve; became member of U.S. Senate on February 22, 1835, was reelected, and served from March 4, 1835 to March 5, 1845; appointed SECRETARY OF THE TREASURY in the cabinet of President Polk on March 5, 1845, and served from March 8, 1845 to March 5, 1849; most important contributions were establishment of independent treasury system to deal with public funds, favoring of free trade and financing of Mexican War; attended to business interests and lands in Mississippi, Louisiana and Wisconsin, 1849–1857; sold securities of Illinois Central Railroad in England, 1851–1852; appointed governor of Kansas Territory, serving from April 10, 1857 to his resignation in December 1857; part owner of and contributor to *Continental Monthly* with F. P. Stanton in 1862; went to Europe as U.S. financial agent, 1863 and 1864; acted as lobbyist of Russian minister and Seward in passing bill of Alaskan purchase; wrote on advantages of annexation of Nova Scotia; died in Washington, D.C., November 11, 1869; interment in Oak Hill Cemetery. W. E. Dodd, *Robert J. Walker: Imperialist* (1914); G. W. Brown, *Reminiscences of Governor R. J. Walker* (1902).

WALLACE, Henry Agard. Born on a farm near Orient, Iowa, October 17, 1888; son of Henry Cantwell Wallace, Secretary of Agriculture in the Harding and Coolidge administrations, and May (Broadhead) Wallace; Presbyterian; married Ilo Browne on May 20, 1914; father of Henry B., Robert B., and Jean B.; after attending the public schools and West Des Moines High School, he entered Iowa State College at Ames, Iowa, graduating in 1910; served on the editorial staff of *Wallaces' Farmer*, Des Moines, Iowa, from 1910 to 1924, becoming its editor from 1924 to 1929; editor of *Wallaces' Farmer and Iowa Homestead* from 1929 until 1933; experimented with high yielding strains of corn from 1913 through 1933; devised the first corn-hog rates charts indicating the probable course of the markets; chairman of the Agricultural Round Table, Williamstown, Mass. in 1927; delegate to the International Conference of Agricultural Economics held at South Devon, England, in 1929; delegate to the Democratic national conventions at Chicago in 1940 and 1944; joined cabinet of President Franklin Roosevelt as SECRETARY OF AGRICULTURE on March 4, 1933, serving until September 2, 1940, when he resigned upon receiving the Democratic nomination for vice-president of the United States; during his secretaryship, he set up the Agricultural Adjustment Administration to operate the farm support program; elected VICE-PRESIDENT on November 5, 1940, with Franklin D. Roosevelt at the head of the Democratic ticket, serving from his inauguration on January 20, 1941 until January 20, 1945; from 1942 to 1944 was head of the Board of Economic Warfare; appointed SECRETARY OF COMMERCE by President Roosevelt on March 21, 1945, and continued under President Truman until September 20, 1946, when he was requested to resign because of a speech attacking the Truman administration's foreign policy toward the Soviet Union; unsuccessful Progressive Party candidate for President in 1948; upon his retirement, he resumed his farming interest; editor of the *New Republic* in 1946; authored *America Must Choose* (1934), *Statesmanship and Religion* (1934), *Technology, Corporations and the General Welfare* (1937), *The Century of the Common Man* (1948); died in Danbury, Conn. on November 18, 1965; Dwight Macdonald, *Henry Wallace, The Man and the Myth* (1948); Paul K. Conkin, *The New Deal* (1967).

WALLACE, Henry Cantwell. Born in Rock Island, Ill., May 11, 1866; son of Henry and Nannie (Cantwell) Wallace; Presbyterian; married Carrie May Broadhead; father of Henry Agard Wallace, Vice-President under Franklin Roosevelt, and five other children; learned the printer's trade in the newspaper offices in Winterset; attended the Iowa State Agricultural College (now the Iowa State College of Agriculture) from 1885 to 1887; returned to college in 1891, graduating in 1892; became part owner and publisher of the *Farm and Dairy* in Ames, Iowa; purchased the publication outright with his father and brother, moving the plant to Des Moines and changing the name to *Wallaces' Farm and Dairy*, and later to *Wallaces' Farmer*; this farm journal eventually became one of the leading agricultural periodicals in the U.S.; secretary of the Cornbelt Meat Producers Association for fourteen years; invited to join the cabinet of President Harding as SECRETARY OF AGRICULTURE on March 5, 1921, and was continued in office by President Coolidge, remaining in that post until his death; during his incumbency, he urged the Department of Agriculture not only to assist the farmer in increasing the efficiency of production but also to develop improved systems of marketing, emphasized the adjustment of production to the needs of consumption as a proper function of the Department, established the Bureau of Agricultural Economics and the Bureau of Home Economics, and inaugurated the radio service for market reports; authored *Our Debt and Duty to the Farmers* (1925); died in Washington, D.C. on October 25, 1924; funeral services held at the White House; interment in Des Moines; Iowa, Edward Connery Latham, ed., *Meet Calvin Coolidge: The Man Behind the Myth* (1960); Harold Underwood Faulkner, *From Versailles to the New Deal: A Chronicle of the Harding, Coolidge, Hoover Era* (1958).

WANAMAKER, John. Born in Philadelphia, Pa., July 11, 1838; son of Nelson Wanamaker, a brickmaker, and Elizabeth Deshong (Kochersperger) Wanamaker; married Mary Erringer Brown in 1860; father of Lewis Podman and Thomas B., and two daughters; attended public schools; moved to farm near Leesburg,

Ind., 1850; returned to Philadelphia, 1851, and became errand boy for publishing house; turned to men's clothing business, and advanced to become salesman; in 1857 became secretary of Young Men's Christian Association in Philadelphia; founded Bethany Sunday School in Bethany, N.Y. in 1858; invested in men's clothing business, 1861; began money-back guarantee, 1865; opened John Wanamaker and Company, 1869; converted an old freight depot of the Pennsylvania Railroad into the Grand Depot, dealing in dry goods and clothing, in 1876; began new type of store gathering various kinds of shops under one roof on March 12, 1877, forerunner of modern department store; started employees' mutual benefit association, 1881; considered for Republican nomination for mayor in 1886; appointed POSTMASTER GENERAL in the cabinet of President Benjamin Harrison, serving from March 5, 1889 to March 5, 1893; most important contributions were experiments with rural free delivery, advocation of parcel post and postal savings, favor of government ownership of telegraph and telephone, establishment of sea post offices, and improvement of immediate mail delivery system; began John Wanamaker Commercial Institute in 1896; trained employees for military duty and offered them to the government, 1898–1917; used store editorials to support American entry into World War I; died at "Lindenhurst," Philadelphia, Pa., December 12, 1922. H. A. Gibbons, *John Wanamaker*, 2 vols. (1926); H. J. Sievers, ed., *Benjamin Harrison, 1833–1901: Chronology, Documents, Bibliographical Aids* (1969).

WASHBURNE, Elihu Benjamin. Born in Livermore, Me., September 23, 1816; son of Israel Washburn, farmer and small storeowner, and Martha (Benjamin) Washburn; brother of Israel Washburn, governor of Maine, and Cadwallader Washburn, governor of Wisconsin; Presbyterian; married Adele Gratiot on July 31, 1845; father of seven children; left home at age 14; added "e" to surname; worked on a farm; taught school for three months; was apprentice for newspaper publisher; became typesetter; decided to study law; attended Maine Wesleyan Seminary at Kent's Hill; apprenticed in law office in Boston; was admitted to Massachusetts bar in 1840 and settled in Galena, Ill.; went into a quasi-partnership with Charles S. Hempstead to practice law, then practiced alone, 1841–1845; entered into actual partnership with Hempstead, 1845; invested in western lands; supported Whigs; unsuccessful candidate for Congress, 1848; elected to 33d through 41st Congresses, serving from March 4, 1853 to March 6, 1869; supported Lincoln during the Civil War but was kept out of army because of health; supported Grant in campaign of 1868; appointed SECRETARY OF STATE in the cabinet of President Grant, serving from March 5, 1869 until his resignation on March 16, 1869, after serving only eleven days (resignation was tendered on March 10); became minister of France on March 17, 1869 and served until 1877; almost nominated for presidency in 1880; member of Chicago Historical Society; published *Recollections of a Minister to France 1869–1877* (1877); wrote and published articles in *Scribner's Magazine* and *The Edwards Papers*; died in Chicago, Ill., October 22, 1887; interment in Greenwood Cemetery, Galena, Ill. Gaillard Hunt, *Israel, Elihu and Cadwallader Washburn* (1925); S. F. Bemis, *The American Secretaries of State* (1928); Allan Nevins, *Hamilton Fish: The Inner History of the Grant Administration* (n.d.).

WASHINGTON, George. Born at "Wakefield," near Pope's Creek Va., February 22, 1732; son of Augustine and Mary (Ball) Washington; Episcopalian; married Mrs. Martha (Dandridge) Custis on January 6, 1759; no children; moved with his parents to an estate in Stafford County, Va., on the east side of the Rappahannock River, opposite Fredericksburg; obtained education at the "Old Field" Schoolhouse; learned surveying through self-study, and at the age of 16, undertook to survey the lands of Lord Fairfax, occupying himself in that endeavor for three years; appointed adjutant of a provincial troop with the rank of major in 1752; sent on an expedition by Governor Dinwiddie in 1753, to ascertain the number and force of the French stationed in the Ohio Valley; promoted to the rank of lieutenant colonel in 1754, and served in the French and Indian War, becoming an aide-de-camp to General Braddock in 1755; elected to the House of Burgesses at Williamsburg, Va. in April 1759; continued to raise crops of wheat and tobacco on his estate; justice of the peace for Fairfax County in 1770; delegate to the General Congress held in Philadelphia in 1774 and in Richmond in 1775; appointed Commander-in-Chief of the Army by the legislature; took formal control of the Army of the United Colonies on July 3, 1775; resigned on December 23, 1783, returning to private life at Mount Vernon; delegate to and president of the national convention which framed the federal Constitution in Philadelphia; unanimously elected PRESIDENT, taking his oath of office at City Hall, in New York City, on April 30, 1789; unanimously reelected to a second term, he served until March 3, 1797; appointed lieutenant general and commander of the U.S. Army on July 3, 1798, serving in that post until his death; died in Mount Vernon, Va., December 14, 1799; interment at Mount Vernon. Marcus Cunliffe, *George Washington and the Making of a Nation* (1966).

WATKINS, James D. Born in Alhambra, Calif., March 7, 1927; son of Edward Francis and Louise (Whipple) Watkins; Roman Catholic; married Sheila Jo McKinney, August 19, 1950; children are Katherine Marie, Laura Jo, Charles, Susan, James, and Edward; graduate of the U.S. Naval Academy, 1949; M.S. Naval Postgraduate School (mechanical engineering) 1958; commissioned ensign in the U.S. Navy, 1949; advanced to admiral, 1979; headed submarine/nuclear power distribution control branch of the Bureau of Naval Personnel, 1971–1972, working under Admiral Hyman Rickover; assistant chief of naval personnel, 1972–1973; deputy chief of naval operations, 1975–1978; commander of the sixth fleet, 1978–1979; vice-chief of naval operations, 1979–1981; commander of Pacific Fleet, 1981–1982; chief of naval operations, 1982–1986, during which time he presided over a major expansion of the navy and was a leader in Strategic Defense Initiative or the " Star Wars" program; retired from the navy in 1986; named to commission to study Acquired Immune Deficiency Syndrome (AIDs) by President Ronald Reagan in 1986; chosen to be SECRETARY OF ENERGY by President George Bush on January 20, 1989. *Saturday Evening Post*, (May-June 1988); *Who's Who in America, 1988–1989; Current Biography* (March 1989).

WATSON, William Marvin, Jr. Born in Oakhurst, Tex., June 6, 1924; son of William Marvin, Sr., and Lillie Mae (Anderson) Watson; married Marion Baugh; father of Winston Lee, Kimberly Baugh, and William Marvin III; received B.B.A. from Baylor University in 1949 and M.A. in 1950; entered U.S. Marine Corps as private in World War II and was discharged as a sergeant; made manager of Daingerfield, Tex., Chamber of Commerce; was Daingerfield city secretary, 1954, and city judge, 1958; executive assistant to the president of Lone Star Steel from 1956 to 1965; member of Texas state Democratic executive committee, and chairman from 1964 to 1965; special assistant to President Lyndon Johnson, 1965–1968; appointed POSTMASTER GENERAL in the cabinet of President Johnson, and served from April 10, 1968 to January 21, 1969; granted honorary L.H.D. from Ouachita Baptist University in 1968; was state vice-president of Red River Valley Association; secretary to the president of Northeast Texas Municipal Water District; president of Occidental Interest Corp., 1969–   ; Senior Vice-President, Occidental Petroleum Corp. 1971–72; Executive Vice-President, Corporate Affairs, Occidental Petroleum 1972–76; pleaded guilty on September 23, 1976 to helping Armand Hammer, Chairman of Occidental Petroleum Corp., cover up illegal contributions made during President Nixon's 1972 re-election campaign; resigned immediately afterwards; Honorary LL.B. degree Hardin-Simmons Univ., 1972. Rowland Evans and Robert Novak, *Lyndon B. Johnson: The Exercise of Power* (1965); Ronnie Dugger, *Johnson: From Poverty to Power* (1968); *Who's Who in America; 1975–1976; Facts on File Yearbook, 1976; Standard and Poor's Register of Corporations, Directors and Executives* (1976 and 1977).

WATT, James Gaius. Born in Lusk, Wyo. January 31, 1938; son of William G., attorney, and Lois M. (Williams) Watt; manager of the thirty room Globe Hotel in Wheatland, Wyo.; married Leilani Bomgardner, November 2, 1957; father of Erin Gaia and Eric Gaius; Born-Again Christian affiliated with the Assemblies of God; varsity high-school athlete and member of the school honor society; entered College of Commerce and Industry of the University of Wyoming, where he served successively as president of the Sophomore, Junior, and Senior Honor Society; obtained a B.S. degree with honors in 1960; in the fall of 1960, entered the university's College of Law and eventually became an editor of the *Wyoming Law Journal*. In July 1962, after obtaining his J.D. degree and gaining admittance to the Wyoming State bar, Watt became a personal assistant to Milward L. Simpson, at the time a Republican candidate for the U.S. Senate; after Simpson was elected in 1962, Watt accompanied him to Washington, D.C., and served as his legislative assistant and counsel until September 1966; while in Washington, D.C., he was admitted to the bar of the U.S. Supreme Court;

from September 1966 to January 1969, Watt served as secretary to the Natural Resources Committee and the environmental pollution advisory panel of the U.S. Chamber of Commerce; toward the end of 1968, Watt became special assistant and consultant to former Alaska Governor Walter J. Hickel, who had been nominated as secretary of the interior by President-Elect Richard M. Nixon; in January 1969, when the Nixon administration took over, Watt became the undersecretary of the interior; in May 1969, he was appointed deputy assistant secretary, with special responsibility for water and power resources; in 1971, he was a U.S. delegate to the Economic Commission for Europe in Geneva and went to Israel to take part in a conference on desalination; in July 1972, Watt was appointed director of the Interior Department's Bureau of Outdoor Recreation; he left the Interior Department in November 1975 when President Gerald R. Ford appointed him to the Federal Power Commission; in July 1977 Watt became the president and chief legal officer of the Denver-based Mountain State Legal Foundation, founded in 1977 by Colorado brewer Joseph Coors as a nonprofit public-interest law center; on December 22, 1980, after a twenty-minute interview, President-Elect Ronald Reagan designated Watt to become the forty-third SECRETARY OF THE INTERIOR; Watt was confirmed by the Senate on January 22, 1981; he also became chairman of the new administration's Cabinet Council on Natural Resources and Environment and of the Advisory Commission of Intergovernment Relations; from the beginning of his tenure, Watt was embroiled in controversy; in February 1982, he was cited for contempt by the House Energy and Commerce Committee after he had invoked executive privilege in refusing to supply the committee with documents concerning Canadian energy policy; the charges were later dropped when the White House agreed to make the documents available to the committee; in July 1982, he went under fire because of a letter he had sent to the Israeli ambassador in Washington, D.C., warning that opposition by '' liberal Jews'' to the administration's energy policy could weaken the U.S. ''ability to be a good friend to Israel''; angry reactions from Jewish leaders and members of Congress prompted Watt to issue an apology; resigned October 10, 1983; now working as a private consultant. *New York Times* (December 23, 1980); *Current Biography Yearbook, 1982; Who's Who in America, 1982–1983.*

WEAVER, Robert Clifton. Born in Washington, D.C. December 29, 1907; son of Mortimer G. and Florence (Freeman) Weaver; Methodist; married Ella V. Hiath on July 19, 1935; father of Robert; attended local schools of Washington, D.C.; received B.A. from Harvard University in 1929, M.A. in 1931 and Ph.D. in 1934; was advisor on Negro affairs for Department of the Interior as member of Franklin Roosevelt's ''Black Cabinet,'' 1933–1937; made special assistant for administration of U.S. Housing Authority, 1937–1940; made administrative assistant of OPM and WPR, 1940–1942; became visiting professor at Columbia Teacher's College in 1947; appointed professor at New York University School of Education, 1947–1949; director of opportunity fellowships of

J. H. Whitney Foundation, 1949–1954; made deputy commissioner of New York State Division of Housing, 1954–1955; was rent administrator for New York State, 1955–1959; consultant for Ford Foundation, 1959–1960; chosen vice-chairman of Housing and Redevelopment of Roads in New York City, 1960–1961; made administrator of federal Housing and Home Finance Agency, 1961–1966; chairman of NAACP; appointed SECRETARY OF HOUSING AND URBAN DEVELOPMENT in the cabinet of President Lyndon Johnson, and served from January 18, 1966 to January 1, 1969; most important contribution was lobbying for "demonstration cities" bill; president of Bernard M. Baruch College, 1969–1970; Distinguished Professor of Urban Affairs, Hunter College, 1970–1978; since 1978, Distinguished Professor Emeritus, Hunter College; president, National Commission against Discrimination in Housing, Inc., 1973–1987; director, Urban Programs, Brookdale Center on Aging, 1978; director, Metropolitan Life Insurance Co., 1969–1978; member of several New York City and New York State committees on housing, transportation, and rent policies between 1974 and 1984; trustee, Bowery Savings Bank, 1969–1980; consultant, Government Accounting Office, since 1973; author of *Negro Labor: A National Problem* (1946), *The Negro Ghetto* (1948), *The Urban Complex* (1964), and *Dilemma of Urban America* (1965). Rowland Evans and Robert Novak, *Lyndon B. Johnson: The Exercise of Power* (1966); Hugh Sidey, *A Very Personal Presidency: Lyndon Johnson in the White House* (1968); *Who's Who in America, 1988–1989*.

WEBSTER, Daniel. Born in Salisbury (now Franklin), N.H., January 18, 1782; son of Ebenezer Webster, a Revolutionary leader, and Abigail (Eastman) Webster; Presbyterian; married Grace Fletcher on May 29, 1808; attended local schools; enrolled in Phillips Exeter Academy, 1796; studied under Rev. Samuel Wood of Boscawen; graduated Dartmouth College, 1801; studied law in the office of Thomas W. Thompson of Salisbury; became principal in an academy at Fryeburg; returned to law office of Thompson to study, September 1802; became clerk for Christopher Gore in Boston; was admitted to the bar in March 1805; recalled to Boscawen to practice law because of father's illness; moved practice to Portsmouth, September 1807–1816; elected Federalist representative of New Hampshire to 13th and 14th Congresses, serving from March 4, 1813 to March 3, 1817; moved to Boston; was presidential elector on Monroe-Tompkins ticket, 1820; delegate to New Hampshire state constitutional convention of 1820; elected to 18th, 19th and 20th Congresses as representative from Massachusetts, and served from March 4, 1823 to May 30, 1827; elected U.S. Senator on March 4, 1827, was reelected in 1833 and 1839, and served until his resignation took effect on February 22, 1841; appointed SECRETARY OF STATE in the cabinet of President William H. Harrison, continued under Tyler, and served from March 5, 1841 to May 8, 1843; most important contributions were Webster-Ashburton Treaty of 1842 dealing with Maine boundary, successful negotiations with Portugal, discussions with Mexico, settlement of preliminaries to opening of diplomatic relations with China which led to commercial treaty negotiations by Caleb Cushing in 1844, and enactment of Whig Tariff, 1842; elected as Whig member of U.S. Senate, and served from March 4, 1845 to July 22, 1850; appointed SECRETARY OF STATE in the cabinet of President Fillmore, and served from July 22, 1850 until his death on October 24, 1852; most important contributions were support of legislation covering ground of Clay's compromise measures, letters denouncing right of secession as revolution, and Hulsemann letter; died in Marshfield, Mass., October 24, 1852; interment in Winslow Cemetery. Fletcher Webster, *The Private Correspondence of Daniel Webster* (1857); F. A. Ogg. *Daniel Webster* (1914); S. H. Adams, *The Godlike Daniel* (1930); Daniel Webster, *Speak for Yourself Daniel: A Life of Webster in His Own Words*, ed. Walker Lewis (1969).

WEEKS, John Wingate. Born near Lancaster, N.H., April 11, 1860; son of William Dennis Weeks, farmer and county probate judge; married on October 7, 1885 to Martha A. Sinclair; father of Katherine and Charles Sinclair (Secretary of Commerce under President Eisenhower); attended local schools; received appointment to the U.S. Naval Academy in 1877, and graduated in 1881; continued in the navy until 1883; engaged in land surveying in Florida, and served as assistant land commissioner of the Florida Southern Railway until 1888; removed to Boston, Mass. and formed a banking and brokerage firm, Hornblower and Weeks; served in Massachusetts naval brigade, 1890–1900, and was commanding officer for last six years; lieutenant in the Volunteer Navy during Spanish-American War, and later rear admiral in Massachusetts naval reserve; alderman of Newton, Mass., 1900–1902; elected mayor of Newton in 1903, and served for two terms; chairman of the Republican state convention, 1905; elected to Congress as a Republican from the 12th Massachusetts district, and reelected four times, serving from 1905 until 1913; named to the U.S. Senate in 1913 by the Massachusetts legislature to succeed Winthrop Murray Chase, and served until 1919; candidate for presidential nomination at the 1916 Republican national convention; member of Republican national committee in 1920 and a manager of the Harding presidential campaign; appointed SECRETARY OF WAR in the cabinet of President Harding on March 4, 1921, continuing under Coolidge until his resignation on October 13, 1925 due to ill health; most important contributions were contradicting charges of Brigadier Gen. William Mitchell concerning the adequacy of the nation's air defenses, putting into effect the National Defense Act of 1920, disposing of war equipment, and establishing in 1924 a National Defense Day; attacked Prohibition, women's suffrage, and the primary election system; died at Mount Prospect near Lancaster, N.H. on July 12, 1926; ashes interred in Arlington National Cemetery, Fort Myer, Va. Jacob Chapman, *Leonard Weeks and His Descendants* (1889); C. G. Washburn, *The Life of John W. Weeks* (1928); Samuel Hopkins Adams, *The Incredible Era* (1939); Donald R. McCoy, *Calvin Coolidge, The Quiet President* (1967).

WEEKS, (Charles) Sinclair. Born in West Newton, Mass., June 15, 1893; son of John Wingate Weeks, Secretary of War under Presidents Harding and Coolidge, and Martha Aroline (Sinclair) Weeks; married Beatrice Dowse on December 4, 1915; father of Frances Lee, John Wingate, Sinclair, Beatrice, and William Dowse; married Jane (Tompkins) Rankin on January 3, 1948; attended Newton public schools; received B.A. from Harvard University in 1914; served in World War I as lieutenant and later captain; lieutenant colonel in National Guard, 1918; vice-president, president, and later chairman of the board of Reed and Barton Corp., 1923–1953; president and chairman of the board of United Carr Fastener Corp., director of Gillette Safety Razor Co., Prellman Co., and First National Bank of Boston; served as alderman of Newton, 1923–1929; mayor of Newton, 1930–1935; chairman of Republican state committee, 1936–1938; member of national committee, 1940–1953; treasurer of Republican national committee, 1941–1942; appointed U.S. Senator from Massachusetts to fill seat vacated by Henry Cabot Lodge in February 1944, serving until December 1944; did not seek reelection to the vacancy; chairman of finance committee, 1949–1952; appointed SECRETARY OF COMMERCE in cabinet of President Eisenhower and served from January 21, 1953 to November 12, 1958; most important contributions were expansion of services of department while decreasing budget, increased interest and defense highways, largest peacetime shipbuilding program of merchant ships, increased safety of jet age travel; director of Wentworth Institute; trustee of Fessenden School in West Newton, Mass.; was director and honorary vice-president of National Association of Manufacturers; died on February 7, 1972. Dean Albertson, ed., *Eisenhower as President* (1963); David A. Frier, *Conflict of Interest in the Eisenhower Administration* (1959).

WEINBERGER, Caspar Willard. Born in San Francisco, Calif., August 18, 1917; son of Herman and Cerise Carpenter (Hampson) Weinberger; Episcopalian; married Jane Calton, August 12, 1942; father of Arlin Cerise and Caspar Willard; A.B., magna cum laude, Harvard University, 1938; LL.B., Harvard University, 1941; entered U.S. Army as private in 1941 and left the service as captain in 1945; winner of the Bronze Star; law clerk to U.S. Judge William E. Orr, 1945–1947; member, Heller, Ehrman, White and McAuliffe Legal Firm, 1947–1969; member, California Legislature, 1952–1958; vice chairman, California Republican Central Committee, 1960–1962; chairman, California Republican Central Committee, 1962–1964; chairman, Committee on California Government Organization and Economics, 1967–1968; California director of finance, 1968–1969; chairman, Federal Trade Commission, 1970; deputy director, Office of Management and Budget, 1970–1972; director, Office of Management and Budget, 1972–1973; councilor to the president, 1973; chairman, President's Committee on Mental Retardation; Republican; nominated for the office of SECRETARY OF THE DEPARTMENT OF HEALTH, EDUCATION, AND WELFARE in November 1972, by President Richard Nixon, and on February 8, 1973, appointment was confirmed by the U.S. Senate; while serving as HEW Secretary, he proposed a series of cuts in the department's programs; however, Congress blocked his efforts; when Nixon created "Super Cabinet" to oversee the actions of the ordinary Cabinet, he joined Secretary of Housing and Urban Development James Lynn and Secretary of Agriculture Earl L. Butz as Presidential Counselors on Human Resources; resigned his office on June 26, 1975; general counsel, vice-president, and director, Bechtel Power Corp., Bechtel Incorporated, and Bechtel Corp., San Francisco, 1975–1980; nominated by President-Elect Ronald Reagan for SECRETARY OF DEFENSE on December 12, 1980; confirmed on January 21, 1981; contributions include: presided over largest peacetime military spending increase in the nation's history; fought for huge budgets for the defense department, and spent over 2 trillion dollars during his seven-year tenure; was leading advocate of proposed strategic defense initiative or "star wars," space-based defense system against enemy ballistic missiles; favored building up the U.S. nuclear arsenal; pushed for new weapons systems such as the MX missile and B–1 bomber, to update older systems; second in duration of tenure as defense secretary only to Robert S. McNamara; sparred frequently with Secretary of State George Schultz over arms control policies; resigned on November 5, 1987, due to wife's illness with cancer; awarded Presidential Medal of Freedom and Distinction upon resignation; joined Washington, D.C., law firm, Rogers and Wells, on March 1, 1988; has served on the board of directors of numerous cultural institutions, including the J. F. Kennedy Center for the Performing Arts, San Francisco Symphony, National Symphony, Yosemite Institute, and St. Luke's Hospital, San Francisco; former member, Trilateral Commission. *Business World* (May 20, 1972); *New York Times* (November 29, 1972); *Time* (December 11, 1972); Congressional Quarterly Staff, *New York Times* (December 12, 1980; November 3, 4, and 6, 1987; March 1, 1988); *Who's Who in America, 1988–1989*.

WELLES, Gideon. Born in Glastonbury, Conn., July 1, 1802; son of Samuel and Ann (Hale) Welles; Episcopalian; married to Mary Jane Hale on June 16, 1835; father of nine children; attended the Episcopalian academy at Cheshire, Conn., 1819–1821, and the American Literary, Scientific, and Military Academy at Norwich, Vt., 1823–1825; studied law and was admitted to the bar in 1834; part owner and editor of the *Hartford Times*, 1826–1836; member of the Connecticut legislature, 1827–1835; elected state comptroller of public accounts in 1935, 1842, and 1843; appointed postmaster of Hartford by President Jackson in 1836, and served until 1841; chief of the Bureau of Provisions and Clothing for the U.S. Navy, 1846–1849; left the Democratic party on the slavery issue and helped organize the Republican party in 1855 when the Democrats supported the Kansas-Nebraska bill; helped establish and was a contributor to the *Hartford Evening Press*, a Republican organ, in 1856; member of the Republican national committee and the national executive committee, 1856–1864; chairman of the Connecticut delegation to the Chicago convention of 1860; appointed SECRETARY OF THE NAVY in the cabinet of President Lincoln on March 5, 1861 and continued in that office in the cabinet of President Andrew Johnson, serving until March 3, 1869; most important contributions were reorganizing the Navy upon the outbreak of the Civil War, sponsoring the construction of the first ironclad ships, supervising experiments in guns and naval tactics, ordering naval commanders to give protection to runaway slaves, issuing orders to enlist former slaves in the navy, and urging enlargement and modernization of navy yards after the war; in 1868 returned to the Democratic party; became a Liberal Republican in 1872; author of a diary, several articles, and *Lincoln and Seward* (1874); died in Hartford, Conn. on February 11, 1878. J. C. Nicolay and John Hay, *Abraham Lincoln: A History*, vol. 3 (1897); Gideon Welles, *Diary of Gideon Welles* (1911); H. K. Beale, *The Critical Year: A Study of Andrew Johnson and Reconstruction* (1930); Noah Brooks, *Mr. Lincoln's Washington* (1967).

WEST, Roy Owen. Born in Georgetown, Ill., October 27, 1868; son of Pleasant and Helen Anna (Yapp) West; member of the Methodist Episcopal Church; married to Louisa Augustus on June 11, 1898, and upon her death, married Louise McWilliams on June 8, 1904; father of two children; after receiving his preliminary education in the public schools at Georgetown, he entered De Pauw University, graduating in 1890; studied law and was admitted to the bar in 1890, commencing his practice in Chicago; became a leader in state and national Republican party affairs; served as assistant attorney of Cook County in 1893; elected city attorney of Chicago from 1895 to 1897; elected a member of the Cook County board of review of assessments from 1898 to 1914; member of the Cook County Republican committee from 1900 to 1928; chairman of the Illinois Republican state central committee from 1904 to 1914; secretary of the Republican state central committee from 1924 to 1928; Western treasurer of the Republican national committee in 1928; delegate to the Republican national convention in 1908, 1912, 1916 and 1928; appointed SECRETARY OF THE IN-TERIOR, *ad interim*, by President Calvin Coolidge on July 25, 1928; elevated to full cabinet status by President Coolidge on January 21, 1929, serving until March 3, 1929; became head of the national Republican party, a conservative group, which opposed the progressive Republicans of 1932; alumni trustee of De Pauw University in 1914; president of the Board of Trustees of De Pauw University in 1928; special assistant to the U.S. Attorney General in 1941, a position he held continuously until 1953; died in Chicago, Ill. on November 29, 1958. Jules Abel, *In the Time of Silent Cal* (1969); Edward Connery Latham, ed., *Meet Calvin Coolidge: The Man Behind the Myth* (1960).

WHEELER, William Almon. Born in Malone, N.Y., June 30, 1819; son of Almon Wheeler, lawyer, and Eliza (Woodworth) Wheeler; Presbyterian; married Mary King on September 17, 1845; no children; attended Franklin Academy; taught school; attended the University of Vermont, 1838–1840; studied law in Malone, 1840–1844, and admitted to the bar in 1845; while studying law, was elected town clerk, then appointed school commissioner and school inspector;

elected district attorney, serving from 1846 to 1849; member of the State Assembly in 1850 and 1851; appointed trustee for mortgage holders of the Northern Railway, 1853; state senator and president *pro tempore* of the State Senate, 1858–1860; elected as a Republican from New York to the 37th Congress, serving from March 4, 1861 to March 3, 1863; president of the state constitutional conventions in 1867 and 1868; elected to the 41st through 44th Congresses, serving from March 4, 1869 to March 3, 1877; nominated as the Republican candidate for vice-president in 1876; elected VICE-PRESIDENT in 1876 under President Hayes and took the oath of office on March 5, 1877; left office with the outgoing administration on March 3, 1881; retired from public life and active business pursuits due to ill health; died in Malone, N.Y., June 4, 1887; interment in Morningside Cemetery. A. G. Wheeler, *The Genealogical and Encyclopedic History of the Wheeler Family in America* (1914); C. R. Williams, ed., *Diary and Letters of Rutherford Birchard Hayes*, vols. 3 (1924) and 4 (1925); E. P. Myers, *Rutherford B. Hayes* (1969).

WHITING, William Fairfield. Born at Holyoke, Mass., July 20, 1864; son of William Whiting, U.S. Congressman (1883–1889) and paper manufacturer, and Anne Maria (Fairfield) Whiting; Congregationalist; married to Anne Chapin on October 19, 1892; father of William, Edward, Fairfield, and Ruth; attended the Holyoke schools and Williston Academy, Easthampton, Mass.; graduated from Amherst College in 1886; worked in father's paper business; served as president of the Whiting Paper Company, 1911–1928; delegate to the Republican national conventions of 1920, 1924, 1928, and 1932; appointed SECRETARY OF COMMERCE in the cabinet of President Coolidge on August 21, 1928 to fill the vacancy caused by the resignation of Herbert Hoover; served until the end of the Coolidge administration, March 3, 1929; in this post, he served as chairman of the U.S. section, inter-American High Commission; member of the Federal Narcotics Control Board, the Federal Oil Conservation Board, the U.S. Council of National Defense, the National Board for Vocational Education, and the Foreign Service Buildings Commission; died on August 31, 1936; interment in Holyoke, Mass. Donald R. McCoy, *Calvin Coolidge* (1967); Jules Abel, *In the Time of Silent Cal* (1969).

WHITNEY, William Collins. Born in Conway, Mass., July 5, 1841; son of Brigadier General James Scollay and Laurinda (Collins) Whitney; married Flora Payne on October 13, 1869, and after her death, married Mrs. Edith Sibyl (May) Randolph sometime between 1893 and 1899; father of four children; after being educated by private tutors, he entered Yale, graduating in 1863; attended Harvard Law School in 1863 and 1864 and was admitted to the bar in 1865; took part in the action against the "Tweed Ring" in New York City; became corporation counsel in New York City, 1875–1882; supported Grover Cleveland in 1884, and was subsequently appointed SECRETARY OF THE NAVY by President Cleveland, serving from March 6, 1885 to March 4, 1889; during his incumbency, he inaugurated the Naval War College at Newport, R.I.; supported Cleveland again in 1892; fought free silver ideology at the Democratic convention of 1896; declined to accept further public office; became a horse-breeder in Lexington, Ky., operating a racing stable in 1898; director of Consolidated Gas Co. of New York, Fifth Avenue Trust Co., and Mutual Life Insurance Co. of New York; author of *The Whitney Stud* (1902); died in New York City, February 2, 1902. Horace Samuel Merrill, *Bourbon Leader: Grover Cleveland and the Democratic Party* (1957); Allan Nevins, *Grover Cleveland, A Study in Courage* (1932).

WICKARD, Claude Raymond. Born on a farm in Carroll County, Ind., February 28, 1893; son of Andrew Jackson and Iva Lenora (Kirkpatrick) Wickard; member of the United Brethren Church; married to Louise Eckert in 1918; father of Betty Jane and Ann Louise; was graduated from the agricultural college of Purdue University in 1915; elected to the Indiana Senate, 1932; gave up his office to work for the Agricultural Adjustment Administration in 1933, becoming chief of its corn-hog section; also served as assistant director of the Administration's central division in 1937, and as its director from 1937 to 1940; undersecretary of agriculture from February to August 1940; appointed SECRETARY OF AGRICULTURE in the cabinet of President Franklin Roosevelt on August 27, 1940, and continued under President Truman, serving until June 2, 1945; most important contributions were offering many proposals for conservation and restoration of farm and forests to be put into effect after the war, and urging that the U.S. develop export markets for its agricultural products while retaining price supports; administrator of the Rural Electrification Administration under President Truman, 1945–1953; headed an executive committee of farmers supporting Senator John. F. Kennedy in the 1960 presidential election; member of the Indiana Farm Bureau Federation and the national Farm Bureau Federation; received Master Farmer of Indiana award; killed in an automobile accident in Delphi, Ind. on April 29, 1967; interment in Deer Creek, Ind. Dean Albertson, *Roosevelt's Farmer: Claude R. Wickard in the New Deal* (1961); A. J. Wann, *President as Chief Administrator: A Study of Franklin D. Roosevelt* (1968).

WICKERSHAM, George. Born in Pittsburgh, Pa., September 19, 1858; son of Samuel Morris Wickersham, inventor in the iron and steel industry, and Elizabeth Cox (Woodward) Wickersham; Quaker as a youth, but later Episcopalian; married Mildred Wendell on September 19, 1883; father of Cornelius Wendell, Mildred, Gwendolyn, and Constance; studied civil engineering at Lehigh University, 1873–1875; studied law at the University of Pennsylvania, graduating in 1880; admitted to the bar in 1880 and began practice in Philadelphia; editor of "The Weekly Notes of Cases" of Pennsylvania; moved to New York City in 1882; became managing clerk in the law firm of Strong and Cadwallader in 1883, and became a partner in 1887; appointed ATTORNEY GENERAL in the cabinet of President Taft on March 5, 1909, serving until March 5, 1913; most important contributions were initiating many suits against monopolistic practices of corporations, proposing the creation of a body similar to the Interstate Commerce Commission, drawing, drawing up the original draft of the Mann-Elkins Railroad Act (1910), and assisting with the corporation tax provision in the Payne-Aldrich Tariff Act; retired with the outgoing administration and resumed law practice; floor leader of the New York State Constitutional Convention in 1915, and chairman of the judiciary committee; commissioner of the War Trade Board to Cuba, August-September 1918, by appointment of President Wilson; special correspondent for the *New York Tribune* in Paris, 1919, to cover the Peace Conference; American member of the League of Nations committee to codify international law; president of the international arbitral tribunal under the Young Plan; president of the American Law Institute; member of the commission for the reorganization of the New York State government, 1925; appointed head of the National Commission on Law Observance and Enforcement by President Hoover in 1929; author of *The Changing Order* (1914) and *Some Legal Phases of Corporate Financing, Reorganization and Regulation* (1917); died in New York City, January 26, 1936; interment in Rockside Cemetery, Englewood, N.J. Robert C. McManus, "Unhappy Warrior: A Portrait of George Wickersham," *Outlook and Independent* (September 17, 1930); Henry F. Pringle, *The Life and Times of William H. Taft* (1939); Norman M. Wilensky, *Conservatives in the Progressive Era* (1965).

WICKLIFFE, Charles Anderson. Born near Springfield, Ky., June 8, 1788; son of Charles and Lydia (Hardin) Wickliffe; married Margaret Crepps in 1813; father of eight children; after completing preparatory education, studied law and was admitted to the bar in 1809, commencing practice in Bardstown, Ky.; served in the War of 1812; elected to the Kentucky House of Representatives in 1812 and 1813; again entered the Army as an aide to general Caldwell; reelected to the state legislature in 1822, 1823, 1833, and 1835, serving as speaker of the House in 1834; elected as a Democrat to the 18th through 22d Congresses, serving in all from March 4, 1823 to March 3, 1833; chosen to conduct impeachment proceedings against Judge James H. Peck, 1830; elected lieutenant governor of Kentucky in 1836, and upon the death of Governor Clark, succeeded to the governorship, serving from March 5, 1839 to September 1840; invited to join the cabinet of President Tyler as POSTMASTER GENERAL on September 13, 1841, entering upon his duties on October 13, 1841 and serving until March 6, 1845; was the first postmaster general to appoint a woman to office in the postal service; sent on a secret mission by President Polk to the Republic of Texas in 1845, in connection with the annexation of Texas to the Union; delegate to the Kentucky constitutional convention in 1849; member of the Peace Conference of 1861; opposed the movement for the secession of Kentucky in 1861; elected as a Union Whig to the 37th Congress, serving from March 4, 1861 to March 3, 1863; delegate to the Democratic national convention at Chicago in 1864; died near Ilchester, Md., October 31, 1869; interment in Bardstown Cemetery,

Bardstown, Ky. Robert Seager, *And Tyler Too: A Biography* (1963); Charles Allan McCoy, *Polk and the Presidency* (1960).

WILBUR, Curtis Dwight. Born in Boonesboro, Iowa, May 10, 1867; son of Dwight Locke and Edna Maria (Lyman) Wilbur; brother of Ray Lyman Wilbur, Secretary of the Interior under Hoover; Congregationalist; married to Ella T. Chilson on November 9, 1893, and upon her death to Olive Doolittle on January 13, 1898; father of Edna May, Lyman Dwight, Paul Curtis, and Leonard Fiske; after completing his preliminary and secondary education at rural schools, he entered the U.S. Naval Academy at Annapolis, graduating in 1888; resigned his commission and moved to Los Angeles, Cal.; studied law and was admitted to the bar in 1890; designated chief deputy district attorney of Los Angeles County, serving from 1899 to 1903; appointed judge of the Superior Court of California, serving from 1919 to 1921; became chief justice of the Supreme Court of California in 1922, serving until his resignation in 1927; joined the Coolidge cabinet as SECRETARY OF THE NAVY on March 18, 1924, serving until March 4, 1929; during his secretaryship he advocated a larger navy and greater use of heavier-than-air craft; judge of the 9th U.S. Circuit Court of Appeals in 1929; senior circuit judge from 1931 to 1945, when he retired to his estate, "Pine Lane," Los Altos, Cal.; organized the Juvenile Court of Los Angeles and drafted several juvenile laws in California; died in Los Altos on September 8, 1954. Jules Abel, *In the Time of Silent Cal* (1969); Edward Latham, ed., *Meet Calvin Coolidge: The Man Behind the Myth* (1960).

WILBUR, Ray Lyman. Born in Boonesboro, Iowa, April 13, 1875; son of Dwight Locke and Edna Maria (Lyman) Wilbur; brother of Curtis Dwight, Secretary of the Navy under Coolidge; Congregationalist; married Marguerite May Blake on December 5, 1898; father of three sons; moved to California, where he graduated from Riverside High School in 1892; attended Stanford University, earning his B.A. in 1896 and his M.A. in 1897; received his M.D. from Cooper Medical College in 1899; served as dean of the Stanford University medical school, 1911–1916; served as president of Stanford University, 1916–1943; elected lifetime chancellor of Stanford in 1943; served as chief of the Conservation Division of the Food Administration in 1917; U.S. delegate to the 6th Pan American Congress in Havana in 1928; headed committee on the costs of medical care, 1928; appointed SECRETARY OF THE INTERIOR by President Hoover, serving from March 5, 1929 to March 4, 1933; accomplishments include announcement that no new leases for naval oil reserves would be awarded, the allocation of 36 percent of the power of the projected Hoover Dam to Arizona and 64 percent to California for the period 1930–1980, advocating the return of public land to state control, reorganization of Indian Affairs favoring freedom from the restriction of reservation life in order to foster a more self-supporting citizenry; served as chairman of the White House Conferences on Child Health and Protection, 1929–1931; served as co-chairman of the Conference on Home

Building and Home Ownership, 1931; chairman of the National Advisory Commission on Illiteracy, 1930–1931; chairman of the National Advisory Commission on Illiteracy, 1930–1931; chairman of the federal Oil Conservation Board, 1929–1933; elected president of the American Social Hygiene Association, 1936; received the Dr. William F. Snow medal for distinguished service to humanity, 1943; returned to Stanford University to continue work in the field of medicine; died on June 26, 1949 in Stanford, Cal. A. Guerard, "Ray Lyman Wilbur," *Nation* (June 30, 1949); Edgar Eugene Robinson and Paul Carrol Edwards, eds., *Ray Lyman Wilbur* (1960).

WILKINS, William. Born in Carlisle, Pa., December 20, 1779; son of John and Catherine (Rowan) Wilkins; married to Catherine Holmes in 1815, and after her death, to Matilda Dallas on October 1, 1818; father of four daughters and three sons; after attending the local schools, he entered Dickinson College in Carlisle; studied law and was admitted to the bar on December 28, 1801, commencing the practice of law in Pittsburgh; president of the Pittsburgh Common Council, 1816–1819; elected to the Pennsylvania House of Representatives in 1820, resigning on December 18, 1820; president judge of the 5th judicial district of Pennsylvania, 1821–1824; judge of the U.S. district court for western Pennsylvania, 1824–1831; elected to the 21st Congress, but resigned before qualifying; elected as a Democrat and Anti-Mason to the U.S. Senate, serving from March 4, 1831 to June 30, 1834, when he resigned upon being tendered a diplomatic post; appointed U.S. minister to Russia, serving from June 1834 to December 1835; received the Pennsylvania electoral vote for vice-president in 1833; elected as a Democrat to the 28th Congress, serving from March 4, 1843 to February 14, 1844, when he resigned to accept a cabinet portfolio; appointed SECRETARY OF WAR by President Tyler on February 14, 1844, entering upon his duties on February 20, 1844 and serving until March 6, 1845; Pennsylvania state senator, 1855–1857; major general of the Pennsylvania Home Guards in 1862; one of the founders and first president of the Bank of Pittsburgh; died at "Homewood," near Pittsburgh, Pa., June 23, 1865; interment in Homewood Cemetery, Wilkinsburgh, Pa., Oliver Perry Chitwood, *John Tyler, Champion of the Old South* (1964); Robert J. Morgan, *A Whig Embattled: The Presidency Under John Tyler* (1954).

WILLIAMS, George Henry. Born in New Lebanon, N.Y., March 23, 1823; son of Taber and Lydia (Goodrich) Williams; Episcopalian; married to Kate Van Antwerp in 1850, and after her death, to Kate (Hughes) George in 1867; father of one daughter and two adopted children; attended the district schools and Pompey Academy at Pompey Hills, N.Y. until the age of 17; studied law and was admitted to the bar in 1844; moved to Iowa Territory and commenced the practice of law in Fort Madison in 1844; after the admission of Iowa to the Union, he was elected a district judge, serving from 1847 to 1852; presidential elector on the Democratic ticket of Pierce and King, 1852; appointed chief justice of the Oregon Territory by President Pierce, 1853–1857; member of the state constitutional convention of Oregon in 1858; elected as a Union Republican to the U.S. Senate, serving from March 4, 1865 to March 3, 1871; voted "guilty" in the impeachment trial of President Andrew Johnson; appointed a member of the Joint High Commission in February 1871, which negotiated the Treaty of Washington with Great Britain; invited to join the cabinet as ATTORNEY GENERAL by President Grant on December 14, 1871, entering upon his duties on January 10, 1872 and serving until May 15, 1875; nominated as chief justice of the U.S. Supreme Court by President Grant but asked that his name be withdrawn in face of protest from the opposition; twice elected mayor of Portland, Ore., serving from 1902 to 1905; president of Boys' and Girls' Aid Society and of the Patton Home for the Aged; died in Portland, Ore., April 4, 1910; interment in Riverview Cemetery, Portland. William Best Hesseltine, *Ulysses S. Grant, Politician* (1957).

WILSON, Charles Erwin. Born in Minerva, Ohio, July 18, 1890; son of Thomas E. Wilson, principal of a local school, and Rosilynd (Unkfer) Wilson; married Jessie Ann Curtis in 1912; father of Edward, Thomas Erwin, Charles Erwin Jr., and three daughters; moved to Mineral City with family at the age of 4; graduated Carnegie Institute of Technology in 1909; worked for Westinghouse Corp., and designed first motor for auto starters; went to Washington on a series of special assignments for Army, Navy, and Air Corps during World War I; became chief engineer for Remy Electric Co.; moved to Detroit, 1919, and later to Anderson, Ind.; became president of Delco-Remy Corp., 1926; vice-president of General Motors Corp., 1929–1939; appointed SECRETARY OF DEFENSE in the cabinet of President Eisenhower, and served from January 28, 1953 to October 8, 1957; most important contributions were narrow-base defense plans; returned to business interests; member of board of trustees of General Motors; chairman of Michigan advisory committee to U.S. Commission of Civil Rights, died in Norwood, La., on September 26, 1961; interment in Acadia Park Cemetery. Carl W. Borklund, *Men of the Pentagon* (1966); Dean Albertson, ed., *Eisenhower as President* (1963).

WILSON, Henry. Born in Farmington, N.H., February 16, 1812; son of Winthrop and Abigail (Witham) Colbaith; originally named Jeremiah Jones Colbaith, he changed his name legally upon attaining his majority; Congregationalist; married Harriet Malvina Howe in 1840; father of one son; attended the common schools; soon after his tenth birthday, he was bound by indenture to work for a neighboring farmer; moved to Natick, Mass. in 1833, where he learned the shoemaker's trade; traveled through the South in 1836; returned to New Hampshire where he attended the Strafford, Wolfsboro, and Concord Academies for short periods; taught school in Natick; elected to the Massachusetts House of Representatives in 1841 and 1842; served in the State Senate, 1844–1846 and 1850–1852; delegate to the Whig convention in Philadelphia in 1848, but withdrew from the party upon its rejection of the anti-slavery resolutions; owner and editor of the *Boston Republican*, 1848–1851; delegate to the Free Soil convention in Pittsburgh, 1852; delegate to the state constitutional convention in 1852; elected to the U.S. Senate in 1854 and reelected in 1859, 1865, and 1871, serving from January 31, 1855 to March 3, 1873; elected VICE-PRESIDENT under President Grant, serving from March 4, 1873 until his death; authored *History of the Anti-Slavery Measures of the Thirty-seventh and Thirty-eighth United States Congresses* (1864), *History of the Reconstruction Measures of the Thirty-ninth and Fortieth Congress* (1868), and *History of the Rise and Fall of the Slave Power in America*, 3 vols. (1872–1877); died in Washington, D.C., November 22, 1875; interment in Old Dell Park Cemetery, Natick, Mass. William Best Hesseltine, *Ulysses S. Grant, Politician* (1957); Louis Arthur Coolidge, *Ulysses S. Grant* (1917).

WILSON, James. Born on a farm in Ayrshire, Scotland, August 16, 1835; son of John and Jean (McCosh) Wilson; married Esther Wilbur on May 7, 1863; father of eight children; immigrated to the U.S. in 1852, settling in Norwich, Conn.; moved to Iowa in 1855, locating in Traer, Tama County; attended the public schools and Grinnell College, Grinnell, Iowa; engaged in agricultural pursuits; taught school; elected to the Iowa House of Representatives from 1867 to 1871, serving as speaker in 1870 and 1871; designated regent of the State University from 1870 to 1874; elected as a representative on the Republican ticket to the 43d and 44th Congresses, serving in all from March 4, 1873 until March 3, 1877; member of the Iowa Railway Commission from 1878 to 1883; presented credentials as a member-elect to the 48th Congress and served from March 4, 1883 until March 3, 1885; director of the Agricultural Experiment Station and professor of agriculture at the Iowa Agricultural College at Ames, Iowa, from 1891 to 1897; invited to join the cabinet as SECRETARY OF AGRICULTURE by President McKinley on March 5, 1897, and subsequently retained in that capacity by President Theodore Roosevelt and President Taft, serving for sixteen years, until March 3, 1913; during his incumbency, the department extended its activities into many fields: experiment stations were established in all parts of the United States, farm demonstration work was inaugurated in the South, cooperative extension work in agriculture and home economics was begun, experts and scientists were enlisted to obtain information from all over the world for the promotion of agriculture; editor of the *Agricultural Digest*; died in Traer, Iowa, on August 26, 1920; interment in Buckingham Cemetery, Buckingham, Iowa. William Henry Harbaugh, *Power and Responsibility: The Life and Times of Theodore Roosevelt* (1961); Norman M. Wilensky, *Conservatives in the Progressive Era: The Taft Republicans of 1912* (1965).

WILSON, William Bauchop. Born in Blantyre, Scotland on April 2, 1862; son of Adam Wilson, miner; married on June 7, 1883 to Agnes Williamson; father of eleven children; emigrated with his parents to Arnot, Pa. in 1870;

attended the common schools until the age of 9, when he began work in Pennsylvania coal mines; president of the district miners' union, 1888–1890; member of the national executive board of the miners' union which organized the United Mine Workers of America in 1890; secretary-treasurer of that body from 1900 until 1908, and was prominently connected with coal strikes of 1899 and 1902; appointed member of a Pennsylvania commission in 1891 to revise state laws relating to coal mining; elected to the 60th Congress, and served three successive terms from 1907 to 1913; appointed the first SECRETARY OF LABOR on March 5, 1913 in the cabinet of President Wilson; most important contributions were reorganization of the Bureau of Immigration and Naturalization, the development of agencies to mediate in industrial disputes, and the formation of the U.S. Employment Service to handle the problems of wartime employment and transfer of workers; resigned with outgoing administration on March 5, 1921; during World War 1, member of the Council for National Defense; president of the International Labor Conference, 1919; member, Federal Board for Vocational Education, 1914–1921, and chairman, 1920–1921; appointed member of the International Joint Commission, 1921; engaged in mining and agricultural pursuits near Blossburg, Pa.; died on a train near Savannah, Ga. on May 25, 1934; interment in Arbon Cemetery, Blossburg, Pa. R. W. Babson, *William B. Wilson and the Department of Labor* (1919); Chris Evans, *History of the United Mine Workers of America*, 2 vols. (1918, 1920); Ray Stannard Baker, *Woodrow Wilson, Life and Letters—President, 1913–1914* (1931); Arthur S. Link, *Woodrow Wilson: The New Freedom* (1956).

WILSON, William Lyne. Born at Middleway, Jefferson County, Va. (now W. Va.), May 3, 1843; son of Benjamin and Mary Whiting (Lyne) Wilson; married Nannine Huntington on August 6, 1868; father of six children; attended Charles Town Academy and then entered Columbian College (now George Washington University), Washington, D.C., graduating in 1860; also studied at the University of Virginia at Charlottesville; served in the Confederate Army as a private during the Civil War, in the 12th Virginia Cavalry; taught for several years at Columbian College, during which time he was graduated from its school; was admitted to the bar in 1869 and commenced the practice of law in Charles Town, W.Va.; delegate to the Democratic national convention at Cincinnati in 1880; presidential elector on the Democratic ticket of Hancock and English in 1880; elected president of the University of West Virginia, at Morgantown, in 1882; elected as a Democrat to the 48th Congress and to the five succeeding Congresses, serving from March 4, 1883 until March 3, 1895; inviting to join the cabinet as POST-MASTER GENERAL by President Cleveland, serving from April 4, 1895 until March 5, 1897; during his secretaryship inaugurated the rural free delivery and enlarged the classified civil service; president of Washington and Lee University, Lexington, Va.; permanent chairman of the Democratic national convention in 1892; died in Lexington, Va. on October 17, 1900; interment in Edgehill Cemetery, Charles Town, W.Va. Horace Samuel Merrill, *Bourbon Leader: Grover Cleve-*

land and the Democratic Party (1957) Allan Nevins, *Grover Cleveland: A Study in Courage* (1932).

WILSON, Woodrow. Born in Staunton, Va., December 28, 1856, with the given name Thomas Woodrow; son of Reverend Joseph Ruggles and Jessie Janet (Woodrow) Wilson; Presbyterian; married to Ellen Louise Axson on June 24, 1885, and after her death in 1914, married Edith (Bolling) Galt on December 18, 1915; father of Margaret Woodrow, Jesse Woodrow, and Eleanor Randolph; moved with his family to Augusta, Ga. in 1856; received his preliminary and secondary education at the local schools; moved with his family to Columbia, S.C. in 1870; entered Davidson College, Davidson, N.C. in 1873, withdrawing in 1874 because of ill health; entered the College of New Jersey (now Princeton) in September 1875, graduating on June 18, 1879; entered the University of Virginia Law School, graduating on June 30, 1881; admitted to the bar in 1882, commencing practice in Atlanta, Ga.; taught history and political science at Bryn Mawr College, Bryn Mawr, Pa., in 1885; received a Ph.D. in political science from Johns Hopkins University, Baltimore, Md., in 1886; taught at Wesleyan University, Middletown, Conn. from 1888 to 1890; professor of jurisprudence and political economy at Princeton University from 1890 to 1902; elected president of Princeton University on June 9, 1902, serving in that post until October 23, 1910, having been nominated by the Democrats for governor of New Jersey; elected governor of New Jersey, serving from January 7, 1911 until March 1, 1913; nominated by the Democrats for the presidency on July 2, 1912, and elected PRESIDENT on November 5, 1912; reelected in November 1916, serving in all from March 4, 1913 until March 3, 1921; awarded the Nobel Peace Prize on December 10, 1920; following the inauguration of President Harding, he retired to his Washington, D.C., residence; authored *Congressional Government* (1885), *The State* (1889), *State and Federal Government of the United States* (1889), *Division and Reunion* (1893), *When a Man Comes to Himself* (1901), *History of the American People* (1902), *Constitutional Government* (1911), *New Freedom* (1913), *Robert E. Lee, An Interpretation* (1924); died in Washington, D.C., on February 3, 1924; interment in the National Cathedral, Washington, D.C. John Morton Blum, *Woodrow Wilson and the Politics of Morality* (1956).

WINDOM, William. Born in Belmont County, Ohio, May 10, 1827; son of Hezekiah and Mary (Spencer) Windom; Quaker; married Ellen P. Hatch on August 20, 1856; father of three children; pursued an academic course at Martinsburg, Ohio, and at the academy at Mount Vernon, Ohio; studied law and was admitted to the bar in 1850, commencing the practice of his profession in Mount Vernon; elected prosecuting attorney of Knox County in 1852, on the Whig ticket; moved to Winona, Minn. in 1855; elected as a Republican to the 36th through 40th Congresses, serving from March 4, 1859 until March 3, 1869; appointed to the U.S. Senate to fill a vacancy, serving from July 15, 1870 to January 22, 1871; popularly elected to full six-year term in the Senate in 1871 and was reelected in 1877, serving until March 7, 1881, when he resigned to accept a cabinet portfolio; appointed SECRETARY OF THE TREASURY by President Garfield on March 5, 1881, entered upon his duties on March 8, 1881, and was continued in office by President Arthur, serving until he resigned on November 14, 1881, having been reelected U.S. Senator on October 26, 1881; served from November 15, 1881 until March 3, 1883; moved to New York City where he resumed the practice of law; invited to join the cabinet of President Benjamin Harrison as SECRETARY OF THE TREASURY on March 5, 1889, serving from March 7, 1889 until his death; he was a high tariff man and generally an advocate of sound money, although he was a believer in international bimetallism; died in New York City on January 29, 1891; interment in Rock Creek Cemetery, Washington, D.C. Richard Shuster, *The Selfish and the Strong* (1958); George Frederick Howe, *Chester A. Arthur: A Quarter Century of Machine Politics* (1957).

WIRT, William. Born at Bladensburg, Md., November 8, 1772; son of Jacob and Henrietta Wirt; Presbyterian; married to Mildred Gilmer on May 28, 1795, and upon her death, married Elizabeth Washington, on September 7, 1802; father of twelve children; attended school at Georgetown, District of Columbia, and then at the academy operated by Reverend James Hunt in Montgomery County, Md.; acted as a private tutor while he pursued his studies; studied law and was admitted to the bar in 1792, opening a law office at the Court House, Culpeper, Va.; moved to Richmond in 1799; designated clerk of the House of Delegates; became chancellor of the eastern district of Virginia in 1802; by appointment of President Jefferson, was named prosecuting attorney in the trial of Aaron Burr, in 1807; appointed U.S. district attorney for Virginia by appointment of President Madison in 1816; invited to join the cabinet of President Monroe as ATTORNEY GENERAL on November 13, 1817, entering upon his duties on November 15, 1817, and was continued in that office by President John Quincy Adams, serving until March 3, 1829; moved to Baltimore, Md. in 1829; he was the first Attorney General to organize the work of the office and to make a systematic practice of preserving his official opinions so that they might serve as precedents for his successors; he took an active part in the U.S. Supreme Court cases of *McCulloch v. Maryland* and the Dartmouth College Case, both landmark decisions; authored *Letters of a British Spy* (1803), *The Rainbow* (1808), *The Old Bachelor* (1812); died in Washington, D.C., on February 18, 1834; interment in the National Cemetery, Washington, D.C., John Dos Passos, *The Shackles of Power: Three Jeffersonian Decades* (1966); Merrill D. Peterson, *The Jefferson Image in the American Mind* (1960); Irving Brant, *James Madison and American Nationalism* (1968).

WIRTZ, William Willard. Born in DeKalb, Ill., March 14, 1912; son of William Willard Wirtz, educator and businessman, and Alpha Belle (White) Wirtz; Methodist; married Mary Jane Quisenberry on September 8, 1936; father of Richard and Philip; attended public schools of DeKalb; studied at Northern Illinois State Teachers College, 1928–1930; went to University of California at

Berkeley from 1930 to 1931; received B.A. from Beloit College in 1933; taught at Kewanee High School in Illinois, 1933–1934; earned LL.B. from Harvard in 1937; was assistant professor of law at State University of Iowa, 1937–1939; admitted to bar in 1939; became assistant professor of law at Northwestern University School of Law, 1939–1942; was associate general counsel for Board of Economic Warfare from 1942 to 1943; made general counsel and public member of War Labor Board, 1943–1945; became chairman of National Wage Stabilization Board in 1946; made professor at Northwestern University School of Law, 1946–1954; member of Illinois Liquor Control Commission from 1950 to 1956; was advisor to Adlai Stevenson during presidential campaign of 1952; joined Stevenson in forming Chicago law firm of Stevenson and Wirtz in 1955; combined firm with that of Paul, Weiss, Rifkind, Wharton and Garrison ; chosen undersecretary of labor in 1961; appointed SECRETARY OF LABOR in the Cabinet of President Kennedy on August 30, 1962, continued under Johnson, and served from September 25, 1962 to January 20, 1969; most important contributions were backing of trade expansion bill, Manpower Development and Training Act, and fight against public apathy regarding unemployed; partner in Washington, D.C., law firm, Friedman and Wirtz, since 1984; professor of law, University of San Diego, since 1988. New York Times, *The Kennedy Years* (1964); Hobart Rowen, *The Free Enterprisers: Kennedy, Johnson and the Business Establishment* (1964); *Who's Who in America*, 1988–1989).

WOLCOTT, Oliver. Born in Litchfield, Conn., January 11, 1760; son of General and Governor Oliver Wolcott and Laura (Collins) Wolcott; Congregationalist; married Elizabeth Stoughton on June 1, 1785; father of five sons and two daughters; entered Litchfield Grammar School at age 11, leaving at age 13 to enter Yale, from which he graduated in 1778; studied law under Judge Tapping Reeve at Litchfield; served as aide de camp to his father in 1779; admitted to the bar in January 1781; moved to Hartford and became a clerk in the financial office of the Connecticut department of state; appointed member of central board of accountants, January 1782, serving until the office was abolished in May 1788; member of the literary circle of John Trumbull and Joel Barlow; assisted in organization of the Hartford County bar, November 1783; commissioned with Oliver Ellsworth in May 1784 to settle claims of Connecticut against the federal government; headed office of comptroller of public accounts until September 1789, when the new national constitution became effective; appointed auditor of the U.S. Treasury, 1789–1791; became comptroller of the Treasury in the spring of 1791 after refusing the presidency of the United States Bank; appointed SECRETARY OF THE TREASURY in the cabinet of President Washington on February 2, 1795, continuing in office under President John Adams; accused with other Federalists, by Republicans, of setting fire to the State Department, he resigned on November 8, 1800 in protest against the investigation; appointed by President Adams as judge of the U.S. Supreme Court for the second district, including Vermont, New York, and Connecticut; served until 1802 when the judiciary act under which he was appointed was repealed; moved to New York City in 1802 and entered mercantile business; became president of the Merchant's Bank in 1803; founder and president of the Bank of North America, 1812–1814; returned to Litchfield in 1815 as a gentleman farmer and began manufacturing textiles with his brother, Frederick, in Wolcottville; defeated for the governorship of Connecticut in 1816; presided over convention for constitutional revisions on August 26, 1818; conferred honorary LL.D. degrees by Yale, Princeton, and Brown; died in New York City, June 1, 1833; interment in Litchfield, Conn. George Gibbs, *Memoirs of the Administrations of Washington and John Adams, Edited from the Papers of Oliver Wolcott* (1846); Samuel Wolcott, *Memorial of Henry Wolcott* (1881).

WOOD, Robert Coldwell. Born in Saint Louis, Mo., September 16, 1923; son of Thomas Frank and Mary (Bradshaw) Wood; married Margaret Byers on March 22, 1952; father of Frances, Margaret, and Frank Randolph; served in the Army during World War II; received B.A. from Princeton in 1946; M.A. from Harvard in 1947, M.B.A. in 1948, and Ph.D in 1950; became associate director of Florida Legislative Bureau, 1949–1951; made management organization expert for U.S. Bureau of the Budget from 1951 to 1954; became lecturer, then assistant professor at Harvard, 1954; assistant professor of political science at Massachusetts Institute of Technology, 1957–1959, became associate professor, 1959–1962, full professor, 1962–1966, and made head of department, 1965–1966; chosen undersecretary of Department of Housing and Urban Development, 1966–1968; appointed SECRETARY OF HOUSING AND URBAN DEVELOPMENT in the cabinet of President Lyndon Johnson, and served from January 2, 1969 to January 21, 1969; head of department of political science at Massachusetts Institute of Technology, 1969–1970; president of the University of Massachusetts at Boston, 1970–1977; superintendent, Boston Public Schools, 1978–1980; professor of political science, University of Massachusetts at Boston, 1980–1983; chairman, Twentieth Century Task Force on Federal Educational Policy, 1983; author of *Suburbia—Its People and Their Politics* (1958); *Metropolis against Itself* (1959); *1400 Governments: The Political Economy of the New York Region* (1960); and *The Necessary Majority: Middle America and the Urban Crisis* (1972); co-authored *Schoolmen and Politics* with S. K. Bailey (1962) and *Government and Politics of the United States* (1965). Hugh Sidney, *A Very Personal Presidency: Lyndon Johnson in the White House* (1968); Rowland Evans and Robert Novak, *Lyndon B. Johnson: The Exercise of Power* (1966); *Who's Who in America, 1984; The Writers Directory, 1988–1989.*

WOODBURY, Levi. Born in Francestown, N.H., December 22, 1789; son of Peter and Mary (Woodbury) Woodbury; married Elizabeth Williams Clapp in June 1819; father of five children; after attending the village schools, he entered Dartmouth College, graduating in 1809; studied law and was admitted to the bar in 1812, and practiced his profession in Francestown from 1813 to 1816; appointed judge of the Superior Court of New Hampshire in 1816; moved to

Portsmouth, N.H., in 1819; designated governor of New Hampshire in 1823 and 1824; elected to the state House of Representatives in 1825, where he served as Speaker of the House; elected as a Democrat to the U.S. Senate for the term beginning March 4, 1825, serving until March 3, 1831; invited to join the cabinet of President Jackson as SECRETARY OF THE NAVY on May 23, 1831, serving until June 30, 1834, when President Jackson appointed him SECRETARY OF THE TREASURY, a post he held until March 3, 1841; during his administration, he favored the independent treasury, maintaining that the government needed no banks to care for its funds; believed that Congress had no power to recharter the bank; again elected to the U.S. Senate, serving from March 4, 1841 to November 20, 1845, when he resigned; appointed associate justice of the U.S. Supreme Court, serving from November 20, 1845, until his death; died in Portsmouth, N.H., on September 4, 1851; interment in Harmony Grove Cemetery, Portsmouth. Harold Coffin Syrett, *Andrew Jackson: His Contributions to the American Tradition* (1953); John William Ward, *Andrew Jackson—Symbol for an Age* (1955).

WOODIN, William Hartman. Born in Berwick, Pa., May 27, 1868; son of Clemuel Ricketts and Mary Louise (Dickerman) Woodin; Presbyterian; married Annie Jessup on October 9, 1899; father of Mary, Anne Jessup, William Hartman, Jr., and Elizabeth Foster; after attending the New York Latin School and the Woodbridge School, he attended the School of Mines of Columbia University in 1890; entered the plant of the Jackson and Woodin Manufacturing Co., makers of railroad cars and railroad equipment, working as a day laborer for one year; became general superintendent of the company in 1892, vice-president in 1895, and upon his father's death, president in 1899; after a merger with the American Car and Foundry Co., became district manager in charge of the Berwick plant; advanced to president and member of the executive board of the American Car and Foundry Co. in 1916; president of the American Locomotive Company during 1925 and 1926 and from 1927 to 1929; chairman of the board of the Brill Co., the Montreal Locomotive Works, and the Railway Steel Co.; director of the Cuba Railroad Company, Compania Cubana, and the Remington Arms Company; trustee of the American Surety Co.; appointed New York State fuel administrator in 1922; though nominally a Republican, he supported the candidacy of Al Smith for the presidency in 1928, on the Prohibition issue; appointed a member of a committee to study and revise the banking laws of New York in 1929 by Governor Roosevelt; supported Franklin Roosevelt for the presidency in 1932; joined the Roosevelt cabinet as SECRETARY OF THE TREASURY on March 4, 1933, serving until illness forced his resignation on January 1, 1934; during his incumbency, he played a conspicuous part in formulating and putting into effect the measures adopted to meet the financial crisis of 1933; devised and promulgated the regulations permitting the banks to resume operations following the banking moratorium and also undertook to prevent the hoarding of gold; trustee of the Georgia Warm Springs Foundation and of Lafayette College,

Easton, Pa.; studied music in Vienna, Berlin, and Paris and became a composer; among his works was the "Franklin D. Roosevelt March" which was played at the presidential inauguration in 1933; authored *The United States Pattern—Trial and Experimental Pieces* (1913), a standard work on American coinage; died in New York City, May 3, 1934. Paul K. Conkin, *The New Deal* (1967).

WOODRING, Henry H. Born in Elk City, Kans., May 31, 1890; son of Hines Woodring, farmer and soldier in the Union Army during the Civil War; Congregationalist; married to Helen Coolidge in 1933; father of two children; attended the high schools of Elk City and Independence but did not graduate; completed one-year business and commerce course at Lebanon University, Lebanon, Ind.; worked in an Elk City bank, and later as a bookkeeper; removed to Neodesha and became a bank cashier; served as a second lieutenant in the U.S. Tank Corps during World War I; resumed banking career in Kansas City; bought a controlling interest in the Neodesha bank, and sold it in 1929; served as state commander of the American Legion, 1929; elected Democratic governor of Kansas, 1930; appointed assistant secretary of war in the cabinet of President Franklin Roosevelt, 1932; took over duties of assistant secretary of war for air when that cabinet post was abolished in 1933; appointed SECRETARY OF WAR in the cabinet of President Roosevelt on September 25, 1936; most important contributions were opposing the draft and any commitment of American troops to Europe, instituting competitive bidding as the new policy for government airplane purchases, and recommending the appointment of General George C. Marshall as Army Chief of Staff over the objections of prominent Congressmen; resigned from office on June 19, 1940; opposed Roosevelt's fourth presidential campaign and headed the American Democratic National Committee; died in Topeka, Kans. on September 9, 1967; Robert A. Divine, *Roosevelt and World War II* (1969); A. J. Wann, *President as Chief Administrator: A Study of Franklin D. Roosevelt* (1968).

WORK, Hubert. Born at Marion Center, Pa., July 3, 1860; son of Moses Thompson Work; Presbyterian; married in 1887 to Laura M. Arbuckle who died in 1924; father of Philip, Doris, and Robert; married in December 1933 to Ethel Reed Gano; studied at the Pennsylvania State Normal School, the Medical School of the University of Michigan, 1882–1884, and the University of Pennsylvania, receiving M.D. degree in 1885 from the latter institution; began medical practice in 1885 in Greeley, Colo.; moved to Pueblo, Colo. in 1896 and there founded the Woodcroft Hospital for Mental and Nervous Diseases; delegate-at-large to the Republican national convention of 1908; chairman of the Colorado Republican state central committee, 1912; during World War I, served in the U.S. Army Medical Corps; commissioned as a major by President Wilson and assigned to the staff of the provost marshal; later promoted to colonel; president of the American Medical Association, 1920; served as Colorado member of the Republican national committee, 1920; became the first assistant postmaster general of the United States on March 4, 1921 in the cabinet of President Harding, serving until March 4, 1922; appointed POSTMASTER GENERAL by President Harding on March 4, 1922; served until March 4, 1923; appointed SECRETARY OF THE INTERIOR on March 5, 1923 in the cabinet of President Harding; continued to serve under President Coolidge until his resignation on July 24, 1928; most important contributions were reorganization of the department, decreasing its budget by $129 million, and granting citizenship to non-citizen American Indians born in the United States; chairman of the Republican national committee, 1928–1929; died in South Denver, Colo. on December 14, 1942. Samuel Hopkins Adams, *The Incredible Era* (1939); Francis Russell, *The Shadow of Blooming Grove: Warren G. Harding and His Times* (1968).

WRIGHT, Luke Edward. Born in Memphis, Tenn., August 29, 1846; son of Archibald and Mary Elizabeth (Elderidge) Wright; married Kate Semmes on December 15, 1869; father of Elderidge, Anna, Luke E., Semmes, and Katrina; attended local schools; attended University of Mississippi, 1867–1868; enlisted in Confederate Army at outset of Civil War, and eventually became captain; admitted to Tennessee bar in 1870; opened office in Memphis; attorney general of Tennessee 1870–1878; appointed member of U.S. Philippine commission in 1900, and served as president until 1904; appointed vice-governor of Philippine Islands by President Theodore Roosevelt on October 29, 1901; governor general, 1904–1906; became American ambassador to Japan on March 30, 1906, and served until resignation on September 1, 1907; returned to law practice; appointed SECRETARY OF WAR in the cabinet of President Theodore Roosevelt on July 1, 1908, and served until March 5, 1909; died November 17, 1922. J. T. Moore, *Tennessee, The Volunteer State* (1923); J. M. Keating, *History of Memphis* (1888); James F. Rhodes, *McKinley and Roosevelt Administrations, 1897–1909* in *History of the United States*, vol. 9 (1922); George E. Mowry, *Era of Theodore Roosevelt, 1900–1912* (1958).

WYNNE, Robert John. Born in New York, N.Y., November 18, 1851; son of John and Mary Wynne; married Mary McCabe on July 7, 1875; attended public schools in New York City; moved to Philadelphia, Pa. and learned telegraphy; employed by Bankers and Brokers Telegraph Co., 1870; went to Washington, D.C. to become assistant correspondent of Cincinnati *Gazette*, 1880; private secretary to Charles Foster, secretary of the treasury under Benjamin Harrison, 1891–1893; at accession of Cleveland, returned to journalism as Washington correspondent of Cincinnati *Tribune* and Philadelphia *Bulletin*; became Washington correspondent for New York *Press*: appointed POSTMASTER GENERAL in the cabinet of President Theodore Roosevelt on October 4, 1904, and served until March 4, 1905; became consul-general to Great Britain, 1905; president of First National Fire Insurance Company in 1915; died March 11, 1922; James F. Rhodes, *McKinley and Roosevelt Administrations, 1897–1909* in *History of the United States*, vol. 9 (1922); George E. Mowry, *Era of Theodore Roosevelt, 1900–1912* (1958).

Y

YEUTTER, Clayton Keith. Born December 10, 1930, in Eustis, Nebr.; married Jeanne Vierk; father of Brad, Gregg, Kim, and Jan; graduated Eustis High School, 1948; graduated University of Nebraska, Lincoln, B.S. in 1952 with High Distinction, the highest scholastic honor given by the University of Nebraska; University of Nebraska Law School, J.D. 1963, cum laude, ranked first in graduating class; received Ph.D. in 1966, University of Nebraska; named Outstanding Graduate Student in Agriculture Economics; U.S. Air Force, 1952 to 1957, enlisted as a basic airman upon graduation from the University of Nebraska; later received a direct commission in medical administration; recipient of numerous military awards; continued in active reserve until 1977; presently a lieutenant colonel in the inactive reserve; from 1957 to 1975, operator of a twenty-five-hundred-acre farming, ranching, and cattle feeding enterprise in central Nebraska; active in law practice in Lincoln, Nebr., 1963–1968; faculty member, Department of Agricultural Economics, University of Nebraska, 1960–1966; executive assistant to the governor of Nebraska, 1966–1968; director, University of Nebraska mission in Colombia, 1968–1970; administrator, Consumer and Marketing Service, U.S. Department of Agriculture 1970–1971; regional director, Committee for the reelection of the president, 1972; assistant secretary of agriculture for marketing and consumer services, 1973–1974; assistant secretary of agriculture for international affairs and commodity programs 1974–1975; deputy special trade representative, Executive Office of the President, 1975–1977; senior partner of the law firm Nelson, Harding, Yeutter, and Leonard in Lincoln, Nebr., 1977–1978; president and chief executive officer, Chicago Mercantile Exchange, 1978–1985; U.S. trade representative, Executive Office of the President, 1985–1989; chairman, Agricultural Development Task Force to Peru, appointed by President Ronald Reagan; chairman, Transition Task

Force on Agricultural Policy, Reagan administration; first American businessman invited to Japan in 1982 under Japanese government program to improve trade relations with the United States; confirmed unanimously by the Senate on February 8, 1989, as SECRETARY OF AGRICULTURE under President George Bush; pledged to Senate to reduce trade barriers and create a "level playing field" for farm commodity and food exports; one of his first tests came when he was a negotiator in resolving a trade war with the European Economic Community caused by hormone-treated beef; on February 18, 1989, a seventy-five-day truce was declared. *New York Times* (December 15, 1988); *Facts on File, 1989*; Personal biographical release from the Department of Agriculture.

Appendixes

Presidential Administrations

FIRST ADMINISTRATION OF GEORGE WASHINGTON
(1789–1793)

Office	Name
Pres.	Washington, George
Vice-Pres.	Adams, John
Secy. State *ad int.*, 1789	Jay, John
Secy. State, 1789–93	Jefferson, Thomas
Secy. Treas.	Hamilton, Alexander
Secy. War	Knox, Henry
Atty. Gen.	Randolph, Edmund J.
Postm. Gen., 1789–91	Osgood, Samuel
Postm. Gen., 1791–93	Pickering, Timothy

SECOND ADMINISTRATION OF GEORGE WASHINGTON
(1793–1797)

Office	Name
Pres.	Washington, George
Vice-Pres.	Adams, John
Secy. State, 1793–94	Jefferson, Thomas
Secy. State, 1794	Randolph, Edmund J.
Secy. State *ad int.*, 1795; Secy. State, 1795–97	Pickering, Timothy
Secy. Treas., 1793–95	Hamilton, Alexander
Secy. Treas., 1795–97	Wolcott, Oliver, Jr.

Secy. War, 1793–95	Knox, Henry
Secy. War *ad int.*, 1795–96	Pickering, Timothy
Secy. War, 1796–97	McHenry, James
Atty. Gen., 1793–94	Randolph, Edmund J.
Atty. Gen., 1794–95	Bradford, William
Atty. Gen., 1795–97	Lee, Charles
Postm. Gen., 1793–95	Pickering, Timothy
Postm. Gen., 1795–97	Habersham, Joseph

ADMINISTRATION OF JOHN ADAMS (1797–1801)

Office	Name
Pres.	Adams, John
Vice-Pres.	Jefferson, Thomas
Secy. State, 1797–1800	Pickering, Timothy
Secy. State *ad int.*, 1800	Lee, Charles
Secy. State, 1800; *ad int.*,* 1800–01	Marshall, John
Secy. Treas., 1797–1801	Wolcott, Oliver, Jr.
Secy. Treas. *ad int.*, 1801	Dexter, Samuel
Secy. War, 1797–1800	McHenry, James
Secy. War *ad int.*, 1800	Stoddert, Benjamin
Secy. War, 1800–01	Dexter, Samuel
Atty. Gen.	Lee, Charles
Postm. Gen.	Habersham, Joseph
Secy. War, 1798–1801	Stoddert, Benjamin

FIRST ADMINISTRATION OF THOMAS JEFFERSON (1801–1805)

Office	Name
Pres.	Jefferson, Thomas
Vice-Pres.	Burr, Aaron
Secy. State *ad int.*, 1801	Lincoln, Levi
Secy. State, 1801–05	Madison, James
Secy. Treas., 1801	Dexter, Samuel
Secy. Treas., 1801–05	Gallatin, Albert
Secy. War	Dearborn, Henry
Atty. Gen.	Lincoln, Levi
Postm. Gen., 1801	Habersham, Joseph
Postm. Gen., 1801–05	Granger, Gideon
Secy. Navy, 1801	Stoddert, Benjamin

* While Chief Justice.

Secy. Navy *ad int.*, 1801
Secy. Navy, 1801–05

Dearborn, Henry
Smith, Robert

SECOND ADMINISTRATION OF THOMAS JEFFERSON
(1805–1809)

Office	Name
Pres.	Jefferson, Thomas
Vice-Pres.	Clinton, George
Secy. State	Madison, James
Secy. Treas.	Gallatin, Albert
Secy. War, 1805–09	Dearborn, Henry
Atty. Gen., 1805–06	Breckinridge, John
Atty. Gen., 1807–09	Rodney, Caesar A.
Postm. Gen.	Granger, Gideon
Secy. Navy	Smith, Robert

FIRST ADMINISTRATION OF JAMES MADISON (1809–1813)

Office	Name
Pres.	Madison, James
Vice-Pres.	Clinton, George
Secy. State, 1809–11	Smith, Robert
Secy. State, 1811–13	Monroe, James
Secy. Treas.	Gallatin, Albert
Secy. War, 1809–12	Eustis, William
Secy. War *ad int.*, 1813	Monroe, James
Secy. War, 1813	Armstrong, John
Atty. Gen., 1809–11	Rodney, Caesar A.
Atty. Gen., 1812–13	Pinkney, William
Postm. Gen.	Granger, Gideon
Secy. Navy, 1809	Smith, Robert
Secy. Navy, 1809–12	Hamilton, Paul
Secy. Navy, 1813	Jones, William

SECOND ADMINISTRATION OF JAMES MADISON (1813–1817)

Office	Name
Pres.	Madison, James
Vice-Pres., 1813–14	Gerry, Elbridge
Secy. State, 1813–14; *ad int.*, 1814–15; Secy. State, 1815–17	Monroe, James
Secy. Treas., 1813–14	Gallatin, Albert
Secy. Treas. *ad int.*, 1814	Jones, William

Secy. Treas., 1814	Campbell, George W.
Secy. Treas., 1814–16	Dallas, Alexander J.
Secy. Treas., 1816–17	Crawford, William M.
Secy. War, 1813–14	Armstrong, John
Secy. War *ad int.*, 1814–15	Monroe, James
Secy. War *ad int.*, 1815	Dallas, Alexander J.
Secy. War, 1815–16	Crawford, William H.
Secy. War *ad int.*, 1816–17	Graham, George
Atty. Gen., 1813–14	Pinkney, William
Atty. Gen., 1814–17	Rush, Richard
Postm. Gen., 1813–14	Granger, Gideon
Postm. Gen., 1814–17	Meigs, Return J., Jr.
Secy. Navy, 1813–14	Jones, William
Secy. Navy, 1815–17	Crowninshield, Benjamin W.

FIRST ADMINISTRATION OF JAMES MONROE (1817–1821)

Office	Name
Pres.	Monroe, James
Vice-Pres.	Tompkins, Daniel D.
Secy. State *ad int.*, 1817	Rush, Richard
Secy. State, 1817–21	Adams, John Q.
Secy. Treas.	Crawford, William H.
Secy. War, 1817–21	Calhoun, John C.
Atty. Gen., 1817	Rush, Richard
Atty. Gen., 1817–21	Wirt, William
Postm. Gen.	Meigs, Return J., Jr.
Secy. Navy, 1817–18	Crowninshield, Benjamin W.
Secy. Navy *ad int.*, 1818–19	Calhoun, John C.
Secy. Navy, 1819–21	Thompson, Smith

SECOND ADMINISTRATION OF JAMES MONROE (1821–1825)

Office	Name
Pres.	Monroe, James
Vice-Pres.	Tompkins, Daniel D.
Secy. State	Adams, John Q.
Secy. Treas.	Crawford, William H.
Secy. War	Calhoun, John C.
Atty. Gen.	Wirt, William
Postm. Gen., 1821–23	Meigs, Return J., Jr.
Postm. Gen., 1823–25	McLean, John

Secy. Navy, 1821–23   Thompson, Smith
Secy. Navy, 1823–25   Southard, Samuel L.

ADMINISTRATION OF JOHN QUINCY ADAMS (1825–1829)

Office	Name
Pres.	Adams, John Q.
Vice-Pres.	Calhoun, John C.
Secy. State	Clay, Henry
Secy. Treas.	Rush, Richard
Secy. War, 1825–28	Barbour, James
Secy. War *ad int.*, 1828	Southard, Samuel L.
Secy. War, 1828–29	Porter, Peter B.
Atty. Gen.	Wirt, William
Postm. Gen.	McLean, John
Secy. Navy	Southard, Samuel L.

FIRST ADMINISTRATION OF ANDREW JACKSON (1829–1833)

Office	Name
Pres.	Jackson, Andrew
Vice-Pres., 1829–32	Calhoun, John C.
Secy. State, 1829–31	Van Buren, Martin
Secy. State, 1831–33	Livingston, Edward
Secy. Treas., 1829–31	Ingham, Samuel D.
Secy. Treas., 1831–33	McLane, Louis
Secy. War, 1829–31	Eaton, John H.
Secy. War *ad int.*, 1831	Taney, Roger B.
Secy. War, 1831–33	Cass, Lewis
Atty. Gen., 1829–31	Berrien, John M.
Atty. Gen., 1831–33	Taney, Roger B.
Postm. Gen.	Barry, William T.
Secy. Navy, 1829–31	Branch, John
Secy. Navy, 1831–33	Woodbury, Levi

SECOND ADMINISTRATION OF ANDREW JACKSON (1833–1837)

Office	Name
Pres.	Jackson, Andrew
Vice-Pres.	Van Buren, Martin
Secy. State, 1833	Livingston, Edward
Secy. State, 1833–34	McLane, Louis
Secy. State, 1834–37	Forsyth, John

Secy. Treas., 1833   McLane, Louis
Secy. Treas., 1833   Duane, William J.
Secy. Treas., 1833–34   Taney, Roger B.
Secy. Treas., 1834–37   Woodbury, Levi
Secy. War, 1833–36   Cass, Lewis
Secy. War *ad int.*, 1836–37   Butler, Benjamin F.
Atty. Gen., 1833   Taney, Roger B.
Atty. Gen., 1833–37   Butler, Benjamin F.
Postm. Gen., 1833–35   Barry, William T.
Postm. Gen., 1835–37   Kendall, Amos
Secy. Navy, 1833–34   Woodbury, Levi
Secy. Navy, 1834–37   Dickerson, Mahlon

ADMINISTRATION OF MARTIN VAN BUREN (1837–1841)

Office	Name
Pres.	Van Buren, Martin
Vice-Pres.	Johnson, Richard M.
Secy. State	Forsyth, John
Secy. Treas.	Woodbury, Levi
Secy. War	Poinsett, Joel R.
Atty. Gen., 1837–38	Butler, Benjamin F.
Atty. Gen., 1838–39	Grundy, Felix
Atty. Gen., 1840–41	Gilpin, Henry D.
Postm. Gen., 1837–40	Kendall, Amos
Postm. Gen., 1840–41	Niles, John M.
Secy. Navy, 1837–38	Dickerson, Mahlon
Secy. Navy, 1838–41	Paulding, James K.

ADMINISTRATION OF WILLIAM HENRY HARRISON (1841)

Office	Name
Pres.	Harrison, William H.
Vice-Pres.	Tyler, John
Secy. State	Webster, Daniel
Secy. Treas.	Ewing, Thomas
Secy. War	Bell, John
Atty. Gen.	Crittenden, John J.
Postm. Gen.	Granger, Francis
Secy. Navy	Badger, George E.

ADMINISTRATION OF JOHN TYLER (1841–1845)

Office	Name
Pres.	Tyler, John
Secy. State, 1841–43	Webster, Daniel

Secy. State *ad int.*, 1843	Legaré, Hugh S.
Secy. State *ad int.*, 1843; Secy. State, 1843–44	Upshur, Abel P.
Secy. State *ad int.*, 1844	Nelson, John
Secy. State, 1844–45	Calhoun, John C.
Secy. Treas., 1841	Ewing, Thomas
Secy. Treas., 1841–43	Forward, Walter
Secy. Treas., 1843–44	Spencer, John C.
Secy. Treas., 1844–45	Bibb, George M.
Secy. War, 1841	Bell, John
Secy. War, 1841–43	Spencer, John C.
Secy. War, 1843–44	Porter, James M.
Secy. War, 1844–45	Wilkins, William
Atty. Gen., 1841	Crittenden, John J.
Atty. Gen., 1841–43	Legaré, Hugh S.
Atty. Gen., 1843–45	Nelson, John
Postm. Gen., 1841	Granger, Francis
Postm. Gen., 1841–45	Wickliffe, Charles A.
Secy. Navy, 1841	Badger, George E.
Secy. Navy, 1841–43	Upshur, Abel P.
Secy. Navy, 1843–44	Henshaw, David
Secy. Navy, 1844	Gilmer, Thomas W.
Secy. Navy, 1844–45	Mason, John Y.

ADMINISTRATION OF JAMES K. POLK (1845–1849)

Office	Name
Pres.	Polk, James K.
Vice-Pres.	Dallas, George M.
Secy. State	Buchanan, James
Secy. Treas.	Walker, Robert J.
Secy. War	Marcy, William L.
Atty. Gen., 1845–46	Mason, John Y.
Atty. Gen., 1846–48	Clifford, Nathan
Atty. Gen., 1848–49	Toucey, Isaac
Postm. Gen.	Johnson, Cave
Secy. Navy, 1845–46	Bancroft, George
Secy. Navy, 1846–49	Mason, John Y.

ADMINISTRATION OF ZACHARY TAYLOR (1849–1850)

Office	Name
Pres.	Taylor, Zachary
Vice-Pres.	Fillmore, Millard
Secy. State	Clayton, John M.

Secy. Treas.	Meredith, William M.
Secy. War *ad int.*, 1849	Johnson, Reverdy
Secy. War, 1849–50	Crawford, George W.
Atty. Gen.	Johnson, Reverdy
Postm. Gen., 1849–50	Collamer, Jacob
Secy. Navy	Preston, William B.
Secy. Interior	Ewing, Thomas

ADMINISTRATION OF MILLARD FILLMORE (1850–1853)

Office	Name
Pres.	Fillmore, Millard
Secy. State, 1850	Clayton, John M.
Secy. State, 1850–52	Webster, Daniel
Secy. State *ad int.*, 1852	Conrad, Charles M.
Secy. State, 1852–53	Everett, Edward
Secy. Treas., 1850	Meredith, William M.
Secy. Treas., 1850–53	Corwin, Thomas
Secy. War, 1850	Crawford, George W.
Secy. War, 1850–53	Conrad, Charles M.
Atty. Gen., 1850	Johnson Reverdy
Atty. Gen., 1850–53	Crittenden, John J.
Postm. Gen., 1850	Collamer, Jacob
Postm. Gen., 1850–52	Hall, Nathan K.
Postm. Gen., 1852–53	Hubbard, Samuel D.
Secy. Navy, 1850	Preston, William B.
Secy. Navy, 1850–52	Graham, William A.
Secy. Navy, 1852–53	Kennedy, John P.
Secy. Interior, 1850	Ewing, Thomas
Secy. Interior, 1850	McKennan, Thomas M. T.
Secy. Interior, 1850–53	Stuart, Alexander H. H.

ADMINISTRATION OF FRANKLIN PIERCE (1853–1857)

Office	Name
Pres.	Pierce, Franklin
Vice-Pres.	King, William R.
Secy. State	Marcy, William L.
Secy. Treas.	Guthrie, James
Secy. War	Davis, Jefferson
Atty. Gen.	Cushing, Caleb
Postm. Gen.	Campbell, James
Secy. Navy	Dobbin, James C.
Secy. Interior	McClelland, Robert

ADMINISTRATION OF JAMES BUCHANAN (1857–1861)

Office	Name
Pres.	Buchanan, James
Vice-Pres.	Breckinridge, John C.
Secy. State, 1857–60	Cass, Lewis
Secy. State, 1860–61	Black, Jeremiah S.
Secy. Treas., 1857–60	Cobb, Howell
Secy. Treas. *ad int.*, 1860	Toucey, Isaac
Secy. Treas., 1860–61	Thomas, Philip F.
Secy. Treas., 1861	Dix, John A.
Secy. War, 1857–61	Floyd, John B.
Secy. War *ad int.*, 1861; Secy. War, 1861	Holt, Joseph
Atty. Gen., 1857–60	Black, Jeremiah S.
Atty. Gen., 1860–61	Stanton, Edwin M.
Postm. Gen., 1857–59	Brown, Aaron V.
Postm. Gen., 1859–61	Holt, Joseph
Postm. Gen., 1861	King, Horatio
Secy. Navy, 1857–61	Toucey, Isaac
Secy. Interior, 1857–61	Thompson, Jacob

FIRST ADMINISTRATION OF ABRAHAM LINCOLN (1861–1865)

Office	Name
Pres.	Lincoln, Abraham
Vice-Pres.	Hamlin, Hannibal
Secy. State	Seward, William H.
Secy. Treas., 1861–64	Chase, Salmon P.
Secy. Treas., 1864–65	Fessenden, William P.
Secy. War, 1861–62	Cameron, Simon
Secy. War, 1862–65	Stanton, Edwin M.
Atty. Gen., 1861–64	Bates, Edward
Atty. Gen., 1864–65	Speed, James
Postm. Gen., 1861–64	Blair, Montgomery
Postm. Gen., 1864–65	Dennison, William
Secy. Navy	Welles, Gideon
Secy. Interior, 1861–63	Smith, Caleb B.
Secy. Interior *ad int.*, 1863; Secy. Interior, 1863–65	Usher, John P.

SECOND ADMINISTRATION OF ABRAHAM LINCOLN (1865)

Office	Name
Pres.	Lincoln, Abraham
Vice-Pres.	Johnson, Andrew

Secy. State	Seward, William H.
Secy. Treas.	McCulloch, Hugh
Secy. War	Stanton, Edwin M.
Atty. Gen.	Speed, James
Postm. Gen.	Dennison, William
Secy. Navy	Welles, Gideon
Secy. Interior	Usher, John P.

ADMINISTRATION OF ANDREW JOHNSON (1865–1869)

Office	Name
Pres.	Johnson, Andrew
Secy. State	Seward, William H.
Secy. Treas.	McCulloch, Hugh
Secy. War, 1865–(68)*	Stanton, Edwin M.
Secy. War *ad int.*, 1867–68	Grant, Ulysses S.
Secy. War, 1868–69	Schofield, John M.
Atty. Gen., 1865–66	Speed, James
Atty. Gen., 1866–68	Stanbery, Henry
Atty. Gen. *ad int.*, 1868	Browning, Orville H.
Atty. Gen., 1868–69	Evarts, William M.
Postm. Gen., 1865–66	Dennison, William
Postm. Gen. *ad int.*, 1866;	Randall, Alexander W.
Postm. Gen., 1866–69	
Secy. Navy	Welles, Gideon
Secy. Interior, 1865	Usher, John P.
Secy. Interior, 1865–66	Harlan, James
Secy. Interior, 1866–69	Browning, Orville H.

FIRST ADMINISTRATION OF ULYSSES S. GRANT (1869–1873)

Office	Name
Pres.	Grant, Ulysses S.
Vice-Pres.	Colfax, Schuyler
Secy. State, 1869	Washburne, Elihu B.
Secy. State, 1869–73	Fish, Hamilton
Secy. Treas., 1869–73	Boutwell, George S.
Secy. War, 1869	Rawlins, John A.
Secy. War, 1869	Sherman, William T.
Secy. War, 1869–73	Belknap, William W.
Atty. Gen., 1869–70	Hoar, Ebenezer R.
Atty. Gen., 1870–71	Akerman, Amos T.
Atty. Gen., 1872–73	Williams, George H.

* See biography for details.

Office	Name
Postm. Gen.	Creswell, John A. J.
Secy. Navy, 1869	Borie, Adolph E.
Secy. Navy, 1869–73	Robeson, George M.
Secy. Interior, 1869–70	Cox, Jacob D.
Secy. Interior, 1870–73	Delano, Columbus

SECOND ADMINISTRATION OF ULYSSES S. GRANT
(1873–1877)

Office	Name
Pres.	Grant, Ulysses S.
Vice-Pres., 1873–75	Wilson, Henry
Secy. State	Fish, Hamilton
Secy. Treas., 1873–74	Richardson, William A.
Secy. Treas., 1874–76	Bristow, Benjamin H.
Secy. Treas., 1876–77	Morrill, Lot M.
Secy. War, 1873–76	Belknap, William W.
Secy. War, 1876	Robeson, George M.
Secy. War, 1876	Taft, Alphonso
Secy. War, 1876–77	Cameron, James D.
Atty. Gen., 1873–75	Williams, George H.
Atty. Gen., 1875–76	Pierrepont, Edwards
Atty. Gen., 1876–77	Taft, Alphonso
Postm. Gen., 1873–74	Creswell, John A. J.
Postm. Gen., 1874	Marshall, James W.
Postm. Gen., 1874–76	Jewell, Marshall
Postm. Gen., 1876–77	Tyner, James N.
Secy. Navy, 1873–77	Robeson, George M.
Secy. Interior, 1873–75	Delano, Columbus
Secy. Interior, 1875–77	Chandler, Zachariah

ADMINISTRATION OF RUTHERFORD B. HAYES (1877–1881)

Office	Name
Pres.	Hayes, Rutherford B.
Vice-Pres.	Wheeler, William A.
Secy. State	Evarts, William M.
Secy. Treas.	Sherman, John
Secy. War, 1877–79	McCrary, George W.
Secy. War, 1879–81	Ramsey, Alexander
Atty. Gen.	Devens, Charles
Postm. Gen., 1877–1880	Key, David M.
Postm. Gen., 1880–81	Maynard, Horace
Secy. Navy, 1877–80	Thompson, Richard W.
Secy. Navy ad int., 1880–81	Ramsey, Alexander

Secy. Navy, 1881   Goff, Nathan, Jr.
Secy. Interior   Schurz, Carl

ADMINISTRATION OF JAMES A. GARFIELD
(1881)

Office	Name
Pres.	Garfield, James A.
Vice-Pres.	Arthur, Chester A.
Secy. State	Blaine, James G.
Secy. Treas.	Windom, William
Secy. War	Lincoln, Robert T.
Atty. Gen.	MacVeagh, Wayne
Postm. Gen.	James, Thomas L.
Secy. Navy	Hunt, William H.
Secy. Interior	Kirkwood, Samuel J.

ADMINISTRATION OF CHESTER A. ARTHUR (1881–1885)

Office	Name
Pres.	Arthur, Chester A.
Secy. State, 1881	Blaine, James G.
Secy. State, 1881–85	Frelinghuysen, Frederick T.
Secy. Treas., 1881	Windom, William
Secy. Treas., 1881–84	Folger, Charles J.
Secy. Treas., 1884	Gresham, Walter Q.
Secy. Treas., 1884–85	McCulloch, Hugh
Secy. War	Lincoln, Robert T.
Atty. Gen., 1881	MacVeagh, Wayne
Atty. Gen., 1882–85	Brewster, Benjamin H.
Postm. Gen., 1881–82	James, Thomas L.
Postm. Gen., 1882–83	Howe, Timothy O.
Postm. Gen., 1883–84	Gresham, Walter Q.
Postm. Gen. *ad int.*, 1883; *ad int.*, 1884; Postm. Gen., 1884–85	Hatton, Frank
Secy. Navy, 1881–82	Hunt, William H.
Secy. Navy, 1882–85	Chandler, William E.
Secy. Interior, 1881–82	Kirkwood, Samuel J.
Secy. Interior, 1882–85	Teller, Henry M.

FIRST ADMINISTRATION OF GROVER CLEVELAND
(1885–1889)

Office	Name
Pres.	Cleveland, Grover
Vice-Pres.	Hendricks, Thomas A.

Secy. State	Bayard, Thomas F.
Secy. Treas., 1885–87	Manning, Daniel
Secy. Treas., 1887–89	Fairchild, Charles S.
Secy. War	Endicott, William C.
Atty. Gen.	Garland, Augustus H.
Postm. Gen., 1885–88	Vilas, William F.
Postm. Gen., 1888–89	Dickinson, Donald M.
Secy. Navy	Whitney, William C.
Secy. Interior, 1885–88	Lamar, Lucius Q. C.
Secy. Interior, 1888–89	Vilas, William F.
Secy. Agricult., 1889	Colman, Norman J.

ADMINISTRATION OF BENJAMIN HARRISON (1889–1893)

Office	Name
Pres.	Harrison, Benjamin
Vice-Pres.	Morton, Levi P.
Secy. State, 1889–92	Blaine, James G.
Secy. State, 1892–93	Foster, John W.
Secy. Treas., 1889–91	Windom, William
Secy. Treas., 1891–93	Foster, Charles
Secy. War, 1889–91	Proctor, Redfield
Secy. War, 1891–93	Elkins, Stephen B.
Atty. Gen.	Miller, William H. H.
Postm. Gen.	Wanamaker, John
Secy. Navy	Tracy, Benjamin F.
Secy. Interior	Noble, John W.
Secy. Agricult.	Rusk, Jeremiah M.

SECOND ADMINISTRATION OF GROVER CLEVELAND (1893–1897)

Office	Name
Pres.	Cleveland, Grover
Vice-Pres.	Stevenson, Adlai E.
Secy. State, 1893–95	Gresham, Walter Q.
Secy. State, 1895–97	Olney, Richard
Secy. Treas.	Carlisle, John G.
Secy. War	Lamont, Daniel S.
Atty. Gen., 1893–95	Olney, Richard
Atty. Gen., 1895–97	Harmon, Judson
Postm. Gen., 1893–95	Bissell, Wilson S.
Postm. Gen., 1895–97	Wilson, William L.
Secy. Navy	Herbert, Hilary A.
Secy. Interior, 1893–96	Smith, Hoke

Secy. Interior, 1896–97   Francis, David R.
Secy. Agricult.   Morton, Julius S.

FIRST ADMINISTRATION OF WILLIAM McKINLEY (1897–1901)

Office	Name
Pres.	McKinley, William
Vice-Pres.	Hobart, Garret A.
Secy. State, 1897–98	Sherman, John
Secy. State, 1898	Day, William R.
Secy. State, 1898–1901	Hay, John
Secy. Treas.	Gage, Lyman J.
Secy. War, 1897–99	Alger, Russell A.
Secy. War, 1899–1901	Root, Elihu
Atty. Gen., 1897–98	McKenna, Joseph
Atty. Gen., 1898–1901	Griggs, John W.
Postm. Gen., 1897–98	Gary, James A.
Postm. Gen., 1898–1901	Smith, Charles E.
Secy. Navy	Long, John D.
Secy. Interior, 1897–99	Bliss, Cornelius N.
Secy. Interior, 1899–1901	Hitchcock, Ethan A.
Secy. Agricult.	Wilson, James

SECOND ADMINISTRATION OF WILLIAM McKINLEY (1901)

Office	Name
Pres.	McKinley, William
Vice-Pres.	Roosevelt, Theodore
Secy. State	Hay, John
Secy. Treas.	Gage, Lyman J.
Secy. War	Root, Elihu
Atty. Gen. (Jan.–Mar.)	Griggs, John W.
Atty. Gen. (Apr.–Sept.)	Knox, Philander C.
Postm. Gen.	Smith, Charles E.
Secy. Navy	Long, John D.
Secy. Interior	Hitchcock, Ethan A.
Secy. Agricult.	Wilson, James

FIRST ADMINISTRATION OF THEODORE ROOSEVELT
(1901–1905)

Office	Name
Pres.	Roosevelt, Theodore
Secy. State	Hay, John

Office	Name
Secy. Treas., 1901–02	Gage, Lyman J.
Secy. Treas., 1902–05	Shaw, Leslie M.
Secy. War, 1901–04	Root, Elihu
Secy. War, 1904–05	Taft, William H.
Atty. Gen., 1901–04	Knox, Philander C.
Atty. Gen., 1904–05	Moody, William H.
Postm. Gen., 1901–02	Smith, Charles E.
Postm. Gen., 1902–04	Payne, Henry C.
Postm. Gen., 1904–05	Wynne, Robert J.
Secy. Navy, 1901–02	Long, John D.
Secy. Navy, 1902–04	Moody, William H.
Secy. Navy, 1904–05	Morton, Paul
Secy. Interior	Hitchcock, Ethan A.
Secy. Agricult.	Wilson, James
Secy. Comm. and Labor, 1903–04	Cortelyou, George B.
Secy. Comm. and Labor, 1904–05	Metcalf, Victor H.

SECOND ADMINISTRATION OF THEODORE ROOSEVELT
(1905–1909)

Office	Name
Pres.	Roosevelt, Theodore
Vice-Pres.	Fairbanks, Charles W.
Secy. State, 1905	Hay, John
Secy. State, 1905–09	Root, Elihu
Secy. State, 1909	Bacon, Robert
Secy. Treas., 1905–07	Shaw, Leslie M.
Secy. Treas., 1907–09	Cortelyou, George B.
Secy. War, 1905–08	Taft, William H.
Secy. War, 1908–09	Wright, Luke E.
Atty. Gen., 1905–06	Moody, William H.
Atty. Gen., 1906–09	Bonaparte, Charles J.
Postm. Gen., 1905–07	Cortelyou, George B.
Postm. Gen., 1907–09	Meyer, George von L.
Secy. Navy, 1905	Morton, Paul
Secy. Navy, 1905–06	Bonaparte, Charles J.
Secy. Navy, 1906–08	Metcalf, Victor H.
Secy. Navy, 1908–09	Newberry, Truman H.
Secy. Interior, 1905–07	Hitchcock, Ethan A.
Secy. Interior, 1907–09	Garfield, James R.
Secy. Agricult.	Wilson, James
Secy. Comm. and Labor, 1905–06	Metcalf, Victor H.
Secy. Comm. and Labor, 1906–09	Straus, Oscar S.

ADMINISTRATION OF WILLIAM H. TAFT (1909–1913)

Office	Name
Pres.	Taft, William H.
Vice-Pres.	Sherman, James S.
Secy. State	Knox, Philander C.
Secy. Treas.	MacVeagh, Franklin
Secy. War, 1909–11	Dickinson, Jacob M.
Secy. War, 1911–13	Stimson, Henry L.
Atty. Gen.	Wickersham, George W.
Postm. Gen.	Hitchcock, Frank H.
Secy. Navy	Meyer, George von L.
Secy. Interior, 1909–11	Ballinger, Richard A.
Secy. Interior, 1911–13	Fisher, Walter L.
Secy. Agricult.	Wilson, James
Secy. Comm. and Labor	Nagel, Charles

FIRST ADMINISTRATION OF WOODROW WILSON (1913–1917)

Office	Name
Pres.	Wilson, Woodrow
Vice-Pres.	Marshall, Thomas R.
Secy. State, 1913–15	Bryan, William J.
Secy. State *ad int.*, 1915; Secy. State, 1915–17	Lansing, Robert
Secy. Treas.	McAdoo, William G.
Secy. War, 1913–16	Garrison, Lindley M.
Secy. War, 1916–17	Baker, Newton D.
Atty. Gen., 1913–14	McReynolds, James C.
Atty. Gen., 1914–17	Gregory, Thomas W.
Postm. Gen.	Burleson, Albert S.
Secy. Navy	Daniels, Josephus
Secy. Interior	Lane, Franklin K.
Secy. Agricult.	Houston, David F.
Secy. Comm.	Redfield, William C.
Secy. Labor	Wilson, William B.

SECOND ADMINISTRATION OF WOODROW WILSON (1917–1921)

Office	Name
Pres.	Wilson, Woodrow
Vice-Pres.	Marshall, Thomas R.
Secy. State, 1917–20	Lansing, Robert

Office	Name
Secy. State, 1920–21	Colby, Bainbridge
Secy. Treas., 1917–18	McAdoo, William G.
Secy. Treas., 1918–20	Glass, Carter
Secy. Treas., 1920–21	Houston, David F.
Secy. War	Baker, Newton D.
Atty. Gen., 1917–19	Gregory, Thomas W.
Atty. Gen., 1919–21	Palmer, A. Mitchell
Postm. Gen.	Burleson, Albert S.
Secy. Navy	Daniels, Josephus
Secy. Interior, 1917–20	Lane, Franklin K.
Secy. Interior, 1920–21	Payne, John B.
Secy. Agricult., 1917–20	Houston, David F.
Secy. Agricult., 1920–21	Meredith, Edwin T.
Secy. Comm., 1917–19	Redfield, William C.
Secy. Comm., 1919–21	Alexander, Joshua W.
Secy. Labor	Wilson, William B.

ADMINISTRATION OF WARREN G. HARDING (1921–1923)

Office	Name
Pres.	Harding, Warren G.
Vice-Pres.	Coolidge, Calvin
Secy. State	Hughes, Charles E.
Secy. Treas.	Mellon, Andrew W.
Secy. War	Weeks, John W.
Atty. Gen.	Daugherty, Harry M.
Postm. Gen., 1921–22	Hays, Will H.
Postm. Gen., 1922–23	Work, Hubert
Postm. Gen., 1923	New, Harry S.
Secy. Navy	Denby, Edwin
Secy. Interior, 1921–23	Fall, Albert B.
Secy. Interior, 1923	Work, Hubert
Secy. Agricult.	Wallace, Henry C.
Secy. Comm.	Hoover, Herbert C.
Secy. Labor	Davis, James J.

FIRST ADMINISTRATION OF CALVIN COOLIDGE (1923–1925)

Office	Name
Pres.	Coolidge, Calvin
Secy. State	Hughes, Charles E.
Secy. Treas.	Mellon, Andrew W.
Secy. War	Weeks, John W.
Atty. Gen., 1923–24	Daugherty, Harry M.
Atty. Gen., 1924–25	Stone, Harlan F.

Postm. Gen.   New, Harry S.
Secy. Navy, 1923–24   Denby, Edwin
Secy. Navy, 1924–25   Wilbur, Curtis D.
Secy. Interior   Work, Hubert
Secy. Agricult., 1923–24   Wallace, Henry C.
Secy. Agricult. *ad int.*, 1924; Secy.   Gore, Howard M.
  Agricult., 1924–25
Secy. Comm.   Hoover, Herbert C.
Secy. Labor   Davis, James J.

SECOND ADMINISTRATION OF CALVIN COOLIDGE
(1925–1929)

Office   **Name**

Pres.   Coolidge, Calvin
Vice-Pres.   Dawes, Charles G.
Secy. State   Kellogg, Frank B.
Secy. Treas.   Mellon, Andrew W.
Secy. War, 1925   Weeks, John W.
Secy. War, 1925–29   Davis, Dwight F.
Atty. Gen.   Sargent, John G.
Postm. Gen.   New, Harry S.
Secy. Navy   Wilbur, Curtis D.
Secy. Interior, 1925–28   Work, Hubert
Secy. Interior *ad int.*, 1928–29; Secy.   West, Roy O.
  Interior, 1929
Secy. Agricult.   Jardine, William M.
Secy. Comm., 1925–28   Hoover, Herbert C.
Secy. Comm. *ad int.*, 1928; Secy.   Whiting, William F.
  Comm., 1928–29
Secy. Labor   Davis, James J.

ADMINISTRATION OF HERBERT C. HOOVER (1929–1933)

Office   **Name**

Pres.   Hoover, Herbert C.
Vice-Pres.   Curtis, Charles
Secy. State   Stimson, Henry L.
Secy. Treas., 1929–32   Mellon, Andrew W.
Secy. Treas., 1932–33   Mills, Ogden L.
Secy. War, 1929   Good, James W.
Secy. War, 1929–33   Hurley, Patrick J.
Atty. Gen.   Mitchell, James D.
Postm. Gen.   Brown, Walter F.
Secy. Navy   Adams, Charles F.

Office	Name
Secy. Interior	Wilbur, Ray L.
Secy. Agricult.	Hyde, Arthur M.
Secy. Comm., 1929–32	Lamont, Robert P.
Secy. Comm. *ad int.*, 1932; Secy. Comm., 1932–33	Chapin, Roy D.
Secy. Labor, 1929–30	Davis, James J.
Secy. Labor, 1930–33	Doak, William N.

FIRST ADMINISTRATION OF FRANKLIN DELANO ROOSEVELT (1933–1937)

Office	Name
Pres.	Roosevelt, Franklin D.
Vice-Pres.	Garner, John N.
Secy. State	Hull, Cordell
Secy. Treas., 1933–34	Woodin, William H.
Secy. Treas. *ad int.*, 1934; Secy. Treas., 1934–37	Morgenthau, Henry, Jr.
Secy. War, 1933–36	Dern, George H.
Secy. War *ad int.*, 1936–37	Woodring, Henry H.
Atty. Gen.	Cummings, Homer S.
Postm. Gen.	Farley, James A.
Secy. Navy	Swanson, Claude A.
Secy. Interior	Ickes, Harold L.
Secy. Agricult.	Wallace, Henry A.
Secy. Comm.	Roper, Daniel C.
Secy. Labor	Perkins, Frances

SECOND ADMINISTRATION OF FRANKLIN DELANO ROOSEVELT (1937–1941)

Office	Name
Pres.	Roosevelt, Franklin D.
Vice-Pres.	Garner, John N.
Secy. State	Hull, Cordell
Secy. Treas.	Morgenthau, Henry, Jr.
Secy. War, 1937–40	Woodring, Henry H.
Secy. War, 1940–41	Stimson, Henry L.
Atty. Gen., 1937–39	Cummings, Homer S.
Atty. Gen. *ad int.*, 1939; Atty. Gen., 1939–40	Murphy, Frank
Atty. Gen., 1940–41	Jackson, Robert H.
Postm. Gen., 1937–40	Farley, James A.
Postm. Gen., 1940–41	Walker, Frank C.
Secy. Navy, 1937–39	Swanson, Claude A.

Office	Name
Secy. Navy, 1939 (acting); *ad int.*, 1939–40; Secy. Navy, 1940	Edison, Charles
Secy. Navy, 1940–41	Knox, Frank
Secy. Interior	Ickes, Harold L.
Secy. Agricult., 1937–40	Wallace, Henry A.
Secy. Agricult., 1940–41	Wickard, Claude R.
Secy. Comm., 1937–38	Roper, Daniel C.
Secy. Comm. *ad int.*, 1938–39; Secy. Comm., 1939–40	Hopkins, Harry L.
Secy. Comm., 1940–41	Jones, Jesse H.
Secy. Labor	Perkins, Frances

THIRD ADMINISTRATION OF FRANKLIN DELANO ROOSEVELT (1941–1945)

Office	Name
Pres.	Roosevelt, Franklin D.
Vice-Pres.	Wallace, Henry A.
Secy. State, 1941–44	Hull, Cordell
Secy. State, 1944–45	Stettinius, Edward R.
Secy. Treas.	Morgenthau, Henry, Jr.
Secy. War	Stimson, Henry L.
Atty. Gen., 1941	Jackson, Robert H.
Atty. Gen., 1941–45	Biddle, Francis
Postm. Gen.	Walker, Frank C.
Secy. Navy, 1941–44	Knox, Frank
Secy. Navy, 1944–45	Forrestal, James V.
Secy. Interior	Ickes, Harold L.
Secy. Agricult.	Wickard, Claude R.
Secy. Comm.	Jones, Jesse H.
Secy. Labor	Perkins, Frances

FOURTH ADMINISTRATION OF FRANKLIN DELANO ROOSEVELT (January–April 1945)

Office	Name
Pres.	Roosevelt, Franklin D.
Vice-Pres.	Truman, Harry S.
Secy. State	Stettinius, Edward R.
Secy. Treas.	Morgenthau, Henry, Jr.
Secy. War	Stimson, Henry L.
Atty. Gen.	Biddle, Francis
Postm. Gen.	Walker, Frank C.
Secy. Navy	Forrestal, James V.
Secy. Interior	Ickes, Harold L.

Office	Name
Secy. Agricult.	Wickard, Claude R.
Secy. Comm., Jan.–March	Jones, Jesse H.
Secy. Comm., March–April	Wallace, Henry A.
Secy. Labor	Perkins, Frances

FIRST ADMINISTRATION OF HARRY S. TRUMAN (1945–1949)

Office	Name
Pres.	Truman, Harry S.
Secy. State, 1945	Stettinius, Edward R.
Secy. State, 1945–47	Byrnes, James F.
Secy. State, 1947–49	Marshall, George C.
Secy. Treas., 1945	Morgenthau, Henry, Jr.
Secy. Treas., 1945–46	Vinson, Fred M.
Secy. Treas., 1946–49	Snyder, John W.
Secy. War, 1945	Stimson, Henry L.
Secy. War, 1945–47	Patterson, Robert P.
Secy. War, 1947	Royall, Kenneth C.
Secy. Defense, 1947–49	Forrestal, James
Atty. Gen., 1945	Biddle, Francis
Atty. Gen., 1945–49	Clark, Tom C.
Postm. Gen., 1945	Walker, Frank C.
Postm. Gen., 1945–47	Hannegan, Robert E.
Postm. Gen., 1947–49	Donaldson, Jesse M.
Secy. Navy, 1945–47	Forrestal, James
Secy. Interior, 1945–46	Ickes, Harold L.
Secy. Interior, 1946–49	Krug, Julius A.
Secy. Agricult., 1945	Wickard, Claude R.
Secy. Agricult., 1945–48	Anderson, Clinton P.
Secy. Agricult., 1948–49	Brannan, Charles F.
Secy. Comm., 1945–46	Wallace, Henry A.
Secy. Comm. *ad int.*, 1946–47; Secy. Comm., 1947–48	Harriman, W. Averill
Secy. Comm., 1948–49	Sawyer, Charles
Secy. Labor, 1945	Perkins, Frances
Secy. Labor, 1945–48	Schwellenbach, Lewis B.
Secy. Labor *ad int.*, 1948–49	Tobin, Maurice J.

SECOND ADMINISTRATION OF HARRY S. TRUMAN (1949–1953)

Office	Name
Pres.	Truman, Harry S.
Vice-Pres.	Barkley, Alben W.
Secy. State	Acheson, Dean G.

Secy. Treas.	Snyder, John W.
Secy. Defense, 1949	Forrestal, James
Secy. Defense, 1949–50	Johnson, Louis A.
Secy. Defense, 1950–51	Marshall, George C.
Secy. Defense, 1951–53	Lovett, Robert A.
Atty. Gen., 1949	Clark, Tom C.
Atty. Gen., 1949–52	McGrath, J. Howard
Atty. Gen., 1952–53	McGranery, James P.
Postm. Gen.	Donaldson, Jesse M.
Secy. Interior, 1949	Krug, Julius A.
Secy. Interior *ad int.*, 1949–50; Secy. Interior, 1950–53	Chapman, Oscar L.
Secy. Agricult.	Brannan, Charles F.
Secy. Comm.	Sawyer, Charles
Secy. Labor	Tobin, Maurice J.

FIRST ADMINISTRATION OF DWIGHT DAVID EISENHOWER (1953–1957)

Office	Name
Pres.	Eisenhower, Dwight D.
Vice-Pres.	Nixon, Richard M.
Secy. State	Dulles, John F.
Secy. Treas.	Humphrey, George M.
Secy. Defense	Wilson, Charles E.
Atty. Gen.	Brownell, Herbert, Jr.
Postm. Gen.	Summerfield, Arthur E.
Secy. Interior, 1953–56	McKay, Douglas
Secy. Interior, 1956–57	Seaton, Frederick A.
Secy. Agricult.	Benson, Ezra T.
Secy. Comm.	Weeks, Sinclair
Secy. Labor, 1953	Durkin, Martin P.
Secy. Labor *ad int.*, 1953–54; Secy. Labor, 1954–57	Mitchell, James P.
Secy. Health, Education and Welfare, 1953–55	Hobby, Oveta Culp
Secy. HEW, 1955–57	Folsom, Marion B.

SECOND ADMINISTRATION OF DWIGHT DAVID EISENHOWER (1957–1961)

Office	Name
Pres.	Eisenhower, Dwight D.
Vice-Pres.	Nixon, Richard M.
Secy. State, 1957–59	Dulles, John F.

Secy. State, 1959–61	Herter, Christian A.
Secy. Treas., 1957	Humphrey, George M.
Secy. Treas., 1957–61	Anderson, Robert B.
Secy. Defense, 1957	Wilson, Charles E.
Secy. Defense, 1957–59	McElroy, Neil H.
Secy. Defense *ad int.*, 1959–60, Secy. Defense, 1960–61	Gates, Thomas S., Jr.
Atty. Gen., 1957	Brownell, Herbert, Jr.
Atty. Gen. *ad int.*, 1957–58; Atty. Gen., 1958–61	Rogers, William P.
Postm. Gen.	Summerfield, Arthur E.
Secy. Interior	Seaton, Frederick A.
Secy. Agricult.	Benson, Ezra T.
Secy. Comm., 1957–58	Weeks, Sinclair
Secy. Comm. *ad int.*, 1958–59	Strauss, Lewis L.
Secy. Comm. *ad int.*, 1959; Secy. Comm., 1959–61	Mueller, Frederick H.
Secy. Labor	Mitchell, James P.
Secy. HEW, 1957–58	Folsom, Marion B.
Secy. HEW, 1958–61	Flemming, Arthur S.

ADMINISTRATION OF JOHN F. KENNEDY (1961–1963)

Office	Name
Pres.	Kennedy, John F.
Vice-Pres.	Johnson, Lyndon B.
Secy. State	Rusk, D. Dean
Secy. Treas.	Dillon, C. Douglas
Secy. Defense	McNamara, Robert S.
Atty. Gen.	Kennedy, Robert F.
Postm. Gen., 1961–63	Day, J. Edward
Postm. Gen., 1963	Gronouski, John A.
Secy. Interior	Udall, Stewart L.
Secy. Agricult.	Freeman, Orville L.
Secy. Comm.	Hodges, Luther H.
Secy. Labor, 1961–62	Goldberg, Arthur J.
Secy. Labor, 1962–63	Wirtz, W. Willard
Secy. HEW, 1961–62	Ribicoff, Abraham A.
Secy. HEW, 1962–63	Celebrezze, Anthony J.

FIRST ADMINISTRATION OF LYNDON B. JOHNSON (1963–1965)

Office	Name
Pres.	Johnson, Lyndon B.
Secy. State	Rusk, D. Dean

Secy. Treas.	Dillon, C. Douglas
Secy. Defense	McNamara, Robert S.
Atty. Gen.	Kennedy, Robert F.
Postm. Gen.	Gronouski, John A.
Secy. Interior	Udall, Stewart L.
Secy. Agricult.	Freeman, Orville L.
Secy. Comm., 1963–65	Hodges, Luther A.
Secy. Comm., 1965	Connor, John T.
Secy. Labor	Wirtz, W. Willard
Secy. HEW	Celebrezze, Anthony J.

SECOND ADMINISTRATION OF LYNDON B. JOHNSON (1965–1969)

Office	Name
Pres.	Johnson, Lyndon B.
Vice-Pres.	Humphrey, Hubert H.
Secy. State	Rusk, D. Dean
Secy. Treas., 1965	Dillon, C. Douglas
Secy. Treas., 1965–69	Fowler, Henry H.
Secy. Defense, 1965–68	McNamara, Robert S.
Secy. Defense, 1968–69	Clifford, Clark M.
Atty. Gen., 1965–67	Katzenbach, Nicholas de B.
Atty. Gen., 1967–69	Clark, Ramsey
Postm. Gen., 1965	Gronouski, John A.
Postm. Gen., 1965–68	O'Brien, Lawrence F.
Postm. Gen., 1968–69	Watson, William M.
Secy. Interior	Udall, Stewart L.
Secy. Agricult.	Freeman, Orville L.
Secy. Comm., 1965–67	Connor, John T.
Secy. Comm., 1967–68	Trowbridge, Alexander G.
Secy. Comm., 1968–69	Smith, Cyrus R.
Secy. Labor	Wirtz, W. Willard
Secy. HEW, 1965	Celebrezze, Anthony J.
Secy. HEW, 1965–68	Gardner, John W.
Secy. HEW, 1968–69	Cohen, Wilbur J.
Secy. Housing and Urban Development, 1966–69	Weaver, Robert C.
Secy. HUD, 1969	Wood, Robert C.
Secy. Transport., 1966–69	Boyd, Alan S.

FIRST ADMINISTRATION OF RICHARD M. NIXON (1969–1973)

Office	Name
Pres.	Nixon, Richard M.
Vice-Pres.	Agnew, Spiro T.

Office	Name
Secy. State, 1969–73	Rogers, William P.
Secy. State, 1973	Kissinger, Henry A.
Secy. Treas., 1969–70	Kennedy, David M.
Secy. Treas., 1970–72	Connally, John B.
Secy. Treas., 1972–73	Shultz, George P.
Secy. Defense, 1969–73	Laird, Melvin R.
Atty. Gen., 1969–72	Mitchell, John N.
Atty. Gen., 1972–73	Kleindienst, Richard G.
Postm. Gen.	Blount, Winton
Secy. Interior, 1969–71	Hickel, Walter J.
Secy. Interior, 1971–73	Morton, Rogers C. B.
Secy. Agricult., 1969–71	Hardin, Clifford M.
Secy. Agricult., 1971–73	Butz, Earl L.
Secy. Comm., 1969–72	Stans, Maurice H.
Secy. Comm., 1972–73	Peterson, Peter G.
Secy. Labor, 1969–70	Shultz, George P.
Secy. Labor, 1970–73	Hodgson, James D.
Secy. HEW, 1969–70	Finch, Robert H.
Secy. HEW, 1970–73	Richardson, Elliot L.
Secy. HUD, 1969–73	Romney, George W.
Secy. Transport., 1969–73	Volpe, James A.

SECOND ADMINISTRATION OF RICHARD M. NIXON (1973–1974)

Office	Name
Pres.	Nixon, Richard M.
Vice-Pres., 1973	Agnew, Spiro T.
Vice-Pres., 1973–74	Ford, Gerald R.
Secy. State	Kissinger, Henry A.
Secy. Treas., 1973–74	Shultz, George P.
Secy. Treas., 1974	Simon, William E.
Secy. Defense, 1973	Richardson, Elliot L.
Secy. Defense, 1973–74	Schlesinger, James R.
Atty. Gen., 1973–74	Richardson, Elliot L.
Atty. Gen., 1974	Saxbe, William B.
Secy. Interior	Morton, Rogers C. B.
Secy. Agricult.	Butz, Earl L.
Secy. Comm.	Dent, Frederick B.
Secy. Labor	Brennan, Peter J.
Secy. HEW	Weinberger, Caspar W.
Secy. HUD	Lynn, James T.
Secy. Transport.	Brinegar, Claude S.

ADMINISTRATION OF GERALD R. FORD (1974–1977)

Office	Name
Pres.	Ford, Gerald R.
Vice-Pres.	Rockefeller, Nelson A.

Office	Name
Secy. State	Kissinger, Henry A.
Secy. Treas.	Simon, William E.
Secy. Defense, 1974–76	Schlesinger, James R.
Secy. Defense, 1976–77	Rumsfeld, Donald
Atty. Gen., 1974–75	Saxbe, William B.
Atty. Gen., 1975–77	Levi, Edward H.
Secy. Interior, 1974–75	Morton, Rogers C. B.
Secy. Interior, 1975	Hathaway, Stanley K.
Secy. Interior, 1975–77	Kleppe, Thomas
Secy. Agricult., 1974–76	Butz, Earl L.
Secy. Agricult., 1976–77	Knebel, John
Secy. Comm., 1974–75	Dent, Frederick B.
Secy. Comm., 1975–76	Morton, Rogers C. B.
Secy. Comm., 1976–77	Richardson, Elliot L.
Secy. Labor, 1974–75	Brennan, Peter J.
Secy. Labor, 1975–76	Dunlop, John T.
Secy. Labor, 1976–77	Usery, Willie J., Jr.
Secy. HEW, 1974–75	Weinberger, Caspar W.
Secy. HEW, 1975–77	Matthews, Forrest D.
Secy. HUD, 1974–75	Lynn, James T.
Secy. HUD, 1975–77	Hills, Carla
Secy. Transport., 1974–75	Brinegar, Claude S.
Secy. Transport., 1975–77	Coleman, William

ADMINISTRATION OF JIMMY CARTER (1977–1981)

Office	Name
Pres.	Carter, Jimmy
Vice-Pres.	Mondale, Walter F.
Secy. State, 1977–80	Vance, Cyrus R.
Secy. State, 1980–81	Muskie, Edmund S.
Secy. Treas., 1977–79	Blumenthal, W. Michael
Secy. Treas., 1979–81	Miller, G. William
Secy. Defense	Brown, Harold
Atty. Gen., 1977–79	Bell, Griffin B.
Atty. Gen., 1979–81	Civiletti, Benjamin R.
Secy. Interior	Andrus, Cecil D.
Secy. Agricult.	Bergland, Bob S.
Secy. Comm., 1977–79	Kreps, Juanita M.
Secy. Comm., 1979–81	Klutznick, Philip M.
Secy. Labor	Marshall, Freddie R.
Secy. HEW, 1977–79	Califano, Joseph A., Jr.
Secy. HEW, 1979–81	Harris, Patricia R.
Secy. HUD, 1977–79	Harris, Patricia R.
Secy. HUD, 1979–81	Landrieu, Moon E.
Secy. Transport., 1977–79	Adams, Brockman

Office	Name
Secy. Transport., 1979–81	Goldschmidt, Neil E.
Secy. Energy, 1977–79	Schlesinger, James R.
Secy. Energy, 1979–81	Duncan, Charles W., Jr.
Secy. Health and Human Svcs.	Harris, Patricia R.
Secy. Education	Hufstedler, Shirley M.

FIRST ADMINISTRATION OF RONALD REAGAN (1981–1985)

Office	Name
Pres.	Reagan, Ronald W.
Vice-Pres.	Bush, George H.
Secy. State, 1981–82	Haig, Alexander M., Jr.
Secy. State, 1982–85	Shultz, George P.
Secy. Treas., 1981–85	Regan, Donald T.
Secy. Treas., 1985	Baker, James A., III
Secy. Defense	Weinberger, Caspar W.
Atty. Gen.	Smith, William French
Secy. Interior, 1981–83	Watt, James G.
Secy. Interior, 1983–85	Clark, William P.
Secy. Agricult.	Block, John R.
Secy. Labor	Donovan, Raymond J.
Secy. Commerce	Baldridge, Malcolm
Secy. HUD	Pierce, Samuel R., Jr.
Secy. Transport., 1981–83	Lewis, Andrew
Secy. Transport., 1983–85	Dole, Elizabeth H.
Secy. Energy, 1981–82	Edwards, James
Secy. Energy, 1982–85	Hodel, Donald P.
Secy. Health and Human Svcs., 1981–83	Schweiker, Richard
Secy. Health and Human Svcs., 1983–85	Heckler, Margaret M.
Secy. Education	Bell, Terrel H.

SECOND ADMINISTRATION OF RONALD REAGAN (1985–1989)

Office	Name
Pres.	Reagan, Ronald W.
Vice-Pres.	Bush, George H.
Secy. State, 1982–85	Shultz, George P.
Secy. Treas., 1985	Regan, Donald T.
Secy. Treas., 1985–88	Baker, James A., III
Secy. Treas., 1988–89	Brady, Nicholas F.
Secy. Defense, 1985–87	Weinberger, Caspar W.
Secy. Defense, 1987–89	Carlucci, Frank C., III
Atty. Gen., 1985	Smith, William French

Atty. Gen., 1985–88   Meese, Edwin, III
Atty. Gen., 1988–89   Thornburgh, Richard L.
Secy. Interior, 1985   Clark, William P.
Secy. Interior, 1985–89   Hodel, Donald P.
Secy. Agricult., 1985–86   Block, John R.
Secy. Agricult., 1986–89   Lyng, Richard E.
Secy. Labor, 1985   Brock, William E., III
Secy. Labor, 1985–89   McLaughlin, Ann D.
Secy. Commerce, 1985–87   Baldridge, Malcolm
Secy. Commerce, 1987–89   Verity, C. William, Jr.
Secy. HUD   Pierce, Samuel R., Jr.
Secy. Transport., 1985–87   Dole, Elizabeth H.
Secy. Transport., 1987–89   Burnley, James H., IV
Secy. Energy, 1985   Hodel, Donald P.
Secy. Energy, 1985–89   Herrington, John
Secy. Health and Human Svcs., 1985   Heckler, Margaret M.
Secy. Health and Human Svcs., 1985–   Bowen, Otis R.
  89
Secy. Education, 1985   Bell, Terrel H.
Secy. Education, 1985–88   Bennett, William John
Secy. Education, 1988–89   Cavazos, Lauro F.

ADMINISTRATION OF GEORGE BUSH (1989–   )

Office   **Name**

Pres.   Bush, George H.
Vice-Pres.   Quayle, Danforth
Secy. State   Baker, James A., III
Secy. Treas.   Brady, Nicholas F.
Secy. Defense   Cheney, Richard B.
Atty. Gen.   Thornburgh, Richard L.
Secy. Interior   Lujan, Manuel, Jr.
Secy. Agricult.   Yeutter, Clayton K.
Secy. Labor   Dole, Elizabeth H.
Secy. Commerce   Mosbacher, Robert A.
Secy. HUD   Kemp, Jack
Secy. Transport.   Skinner, Samuel K.
Secy. Energy   Watkins, James D.
Secy. Health and Human Svcs.   Sullivan, Louis W.
Secy. Education   Cavazos, Lauro F.
Secy. Veteran Affairs   Derwinski, Edward J.

Heads of State and Cabinet Officials

PRESIDENTS OF THE CONTINENTAL CONGRESS
(1774–1789)

Name	Date Elected
Elias Boudinot	Nov. 4, 1782
Nathaniel Gorham	June 6, 1786
Cyrus Griffin	Jan. 22, 1788
John Hancock	May 24, 1775
John Hancock	Nov. 23, 1785
John Hanson	Nov. 5, 1781
Samuel Huntington	Sept. 28, 1779
John Jay	Dec. 10, 1778
Henry Laurens	Nov. 1, 1777
Richard Henry Lee	Nov. 30, 1784
Thomas McKean	July 10, 1781
Henry Middleton	Oct. 22, 1774
Thomas Mifflin	Nov. 3, 1783
Peyton Randolph	Sept. 5, 1774
Peyton Randolph	May 10, 1775
Arthur St. Clair	Feb. 2, 1787

PRESIDENTS

Name	Dates
Adams, John	1797–1801
Adams, John Q.	1825–29

Arthur, Chester A.	1881–85
Buchanan, James	1857–61
Bush, George H.	1989–
Carter, Jimmy	1977–1981
Cleveland, Grover	1885–89; 1893–97
Coolidge, Calvin	1923–29
Eisenhower, Dwight D.	1953–61
Fillmore, Millard	1850–53
Ford, Gerald R.	1974–77
Garfield, James A.	1881–85
Grant, Ulysses S.	1869–77
Harding, Warren G.	1921–23
Harrison, Benjamin	1889–93
Harrison, William H.	1841
Hayes, Rutherford B.	1877–81
Hoover, Herbert C.	1929–33
Jackson, Andrew	1829–37
Jefferson, Thomas	1801–09
Johnson, Andrew	1865–69
Johnson, Lyndon B.	1963–69
Kennedy, John F.	1961–63
Lincoln, Abraham	1861–65
McKinley, William, Jr.	1897–1901
Madison, James	1809–17
Monroe, James	1817–25
Nixon, Richard M.	1969–74
Pierce, Franklin	1853–57
Polk, James K.	1845–49
Reagan, Ronald W.	1981–89
Roosevelt, Franklin D.	1933–45
Roosevelt, Theodore	1901–09
Taft, William H.	1909–13
Taylor, Zachary	1849–50
Truman, Harry S.	1945–53
Tyler, John	1841–45
Van Buren, Martin	1837–41
Washington, George	1789–97
Wilson, Woodrow	1913–21

VICE-PRESIDENTS

Name	Dates	President
Adams, John	1789–97	Washington
Agnew, Spiro T.	1969–74	Nixon
Arthur, Chester A.	1881	Garfield
Barkley, Alben W.	1949–53	Truman

Breckinridge, John C.	1857–61	Buchanan
Burr, Aaron	1801–05	Jefferson
Bush, George H.	1981–89	Reagan
Calhoun, John C.	1825–29	J. Q. Adams
Calhoun, John C.	1929–32	Jackson
Clinton, George	1805–09	Jefferson
Clinton, George	1809–13	Madison
Colfax, Schuyler	1869–73	Grant
Coolidge, Calvin	1921–23	Harding
Curtis, Charles	1929–33	Hoover
Dallas, George M.	1845–49	Polk
Dawes, Charles G.	1924–29	Coolidge
Fairbanks, Charles W.	1905–09	T. Roosevelt
Fillmore, Millard	1849–50	Taylor
Ford, Gerald R.	1973–74	Nixon
Garner, John N.	1933–41	F. D. Roosevelt
Gerry, Elbridge	1813–14	Madison
Hamlin, Hannibal	1861–65	Lincoln
Hendricks, Thomas A.	1885	Cleveland
Hobart, Garret A.	1897–99	McKinley
Humphrey, Hubert H., Jr.	1964–69	L. B. Johnson
Jefferson, Thomas	1797–1801	Adams
Johnson, Andrew	1865	Lincoln
Johnson, Lyndon B.	1961–63	Kennedy
Johnson, Richard M.	1837–41	Van Buren
King, William R. deV.	1853	Pierce
Marshall, Thomas R.	1913–21	Wilson
Mondale, Walter	1977–1981	Carter
Morton, Levi P.	1889–93	B. Harrison
Nixon, Richard M.	1953–61	Eisenhower
Quayle, Danforth	1989–	Bush
Rockefeller, Nelson A.	1974–77	Ford
Roosevelt, Theodore	1901	McKinley
Sherman, James S.	1908–12	Taft
Stevenson, Adlai E.	1893–97	Cleveland
Tompkins, Daniel D.	1817–25	Monroe
Truman, Harry S.	1945	F. D. Roosevelt
Tyler, John	1841	W. H. Harrison
Van Buren, Martin	1833–37	Jackson
Wallace, Henry A.	1941–45	F. D. Roosevelt
Wheeler, William A.	1877–81	Hayes
Wilson, Henry	1873–75	Grant

SECRETARIES OF STATE

Name	Dates	President
Acheson, Dean G.	1949–53	Truman
Adams, John Q.	1817–25	Monroe

Bacon, Robert	1909	T. Roosevelt
Baker, James A., III	1989–	Bush
Bayard, Thomas F.	1885–89	Cleveland
Black, Jeremiah	1860–61	Buchanan
Blaine, James G.	1881	Garfield
Blaine, James G.	1889–92	B. Harrison
Bryan, William J.	1913–15	Wilson
Buchanan, James	1845–49	Polk
Byrnes, James F.	1945–47	Truman
Calhoun, John C.	1844–45	Tyler
Cass, Lewis	1857–60	Buchanan
Clay, Henry	1825–29	J. Q. Adams
Clayton, John M.	1849–50	Taylor
Colby, Bainbridge	1920–21	Wilson
Conrad, Charles M.	*ad int.*, 1852	Fillmore
Day, William R.	1898	McKinley
Dulles, John F.	1953–59	Eisenhower
Evarts, William M.	1877–81	Hayes
Everett, Edward	1852–53	Fillmore
Fish, Hamilton	1869–77	Grant
Forsyth, John	1834–37	Jackson
Forsyth, John	1837–41	Van Buren
Foster, John W.	1892–93	B. Harrison
Frelinghuysen, Frederick T.	1881–85	Arthur
Gresham, Walter Q.	1893–95	Cleveland
Haig, Alexander M., Jr.	1981–82	Reagan
Hay, John M.	1898–1905	McKinley
Herter, Christian A.	1959–61	Eisenhower
Hughes, Charles E.	1921–25	Harding
Hull, Cordell	1933–44	F. D. Roosevelt
Jay, John	1789–90	Washington
Jefferson, Thomas	1790–94	Washington
Kellogg, Frank B.	1925–29	Coolidge
Kissinger, Henry A.	1973–74	Nixon
Kissinger, Henry A.	1974–77	Ford
Knox, Philander C.	1909–13	Taft
Lansing, Robert	1915–20	Wilson
Lee, Charles	*ad int.*, 1800	J. Adams
Legaré, Hugh S.	*ad int.*, 1843	Tyler
Levi, Lincoln	*ad int.*, 1801	Jefferson
Livingston, Edward	1831–33	Jackson
McLane, Louis	1833–34	Jackson
Madison, James	1801–09	Jefferson
Marcy, William L.	1853–57	Pierce
Marshall, George C.	1947–49	Truman
Marshall, John	1800; *ad int.*,	J. Adams
Marshall, John	1800–01	
Monroe, James	1811–17	Madison

Muskie, Edmund S.	1980–81	Carter
Olney, Richard	1895–97	Cleveland
Pickering, Timothy	1795–97	Washington
Pickering, Timothy	1797–1800	J. Adams
Randolph, Edmund J.	1794	Washington
Rogers, William P.	1969–73	Nixon
Root, Elihu	1905–09	T. Roosevelt
Rush, Richard	*ad int.*, 1817	Monroe
Rusk, D. Dean	1961–63	Kennedy
Rusk, D. Dean	1963–69	L. B. Johnson
Seward, William H.	1861–65	Lincoln
Seward, William H.	1865–69	A. Johnson
Sherman, John	1897–1900	McKinley
Shultz, George P.	1982–89	Reagan
Smith, Robert	1809–11	Madison
Stettinius, Edward R., Jr.	1944–45	F. D. Roosevelt
Stimson, Henry L.	1929–33	Hoover
Upshur, Abel P.	1843–44	Tyler
Van Buren, Martin	1829–31	Jackson
Vance, Cyrus	1977–80	Carter
Washburne, Elihu B.	1869	Grant
Webster, Daniel	1841–43	W. H. Harrison
Webster, Daniel	1850–52	Fillmore

SECRETARIES OF THE TREASURY

Name	Dates	President
Anderson, Robert B.	1957–61	Eisenhower
Baker, James A., III	1985–89	Reagan
Bibb, George H.	1844–45	Tyler
Blumenthal, Michael W.	1977–79	Carter
Boutwell, George S.	1869–73	Grant
Brady, Nicholas F.	1989–	Bush
Bristow, Benjamin H.	1874–76	Grant
Campbell, George W.	1814	Madison
Carlisle, John G.	1893–97	Cleveland
Chase, Salmon P.	1861–64	Lincoln
Cobb, Howell	1857–60	Buchanan
Connally, John B.	1970–72	Nixon
Cortelyou, George B.	1907–09	T. Roosevelt
Corwin, Thomas	1850–53	Fillmore
Crawford, William H.	1816–17	Madison
Crawford, William H.	1817–25	Monroe
Dallas, Alexander	1814–16	Madison
Dexter, Samuel	*ad int.*, 1801	Adams
Dillon, C. Douglas	1961–63	Kennedy

Dillon, C. Douglas	1963–65	L. B. Johnson
Dix, John A.	1861	Buchanan
Duane, William J.	1833	Jackson
Ewing, Thomas	1841	W. H. Harrison
Fairchild, Charles S.	1887–89	Cleveland
Fessenden, William P.	1864–65	Lincoln
Folger, Charles J.	1881–84	Arthur
Forward, Walter	1841–43	Tyler
Foster, Charles	1891–93	B. Harrison
Fowler, Henry H.	1965–69	L. B. Johnson
Gage, Lyman J.	1901–02	McKinley
Gallatin, Albert	1801–09	Jefferson
Gallatin, Albert	1809–14	Madison
Glass, Carter	1918–20	Wilson
Gresham, Walter Q.	1884	Arthur
Guthrie, James	1853–57	Pierce
Hamilton, Alexander	1789–95	Washington
Houston, David F.	1920–21	Wilson
Humphrey, George M.	1953–57	Eisenhower
Ingham, Samuel D.	1829–31	Jackson
Jones, William	*ad int.*, 1814	Madison
Kennedy, David M.	1969–70	Nixon
McAdoo, William G.	1913–18	Wilson
McCulloch, Hugh	1865	Lincoln
McCulloch, Hugh	1865–69	A. Johnson
McCulloch, Hugh	1884–85	Arthur
McLane, Louis	1831–33	Jackson
MacVeagh, Franklin	1909–13	Taft
Manning, Daniel	1885–87	Cleveland
Mellon, Andrew W.	1921–23	Harding
Mellon, Andrew W.	1923–29	Coolidge
Meredith, William M.	1849–50	Taylor
Miller, G. William	1977–79	Carter
Mills, Ogden L.	1932–33	Hoover
Morgenthau, Henry, Jr.	1934–45	F. D. Roosevelt
Morrill, Lot M.	1876–77	Grant
Regan, Donald T.	1981–85	Reagan
Richardson, William A.	1873–74	Grant
Rush, Richard	1825–29	J. Q. Adams
Shaw, Leslie M.	1902–07	T. Roosevelt
Sherman, John	1877–81	Hayes
Shultz, George P.	1972–74	Nixon
Simon, William E.	1974	Nixon
Simon, William E.	1974–77	Ford
Snyder, John W.	1946–53	Truman
Spencer, John C.	1825	Tyler
Taney, Roger B.	1833–34	Jackson
Thomas, Philip F.	1860–61	Buchanan

Vinson, Frederick M.	1945–46	Truman
Walker, Robert J.	1845–49	Polk
Windom, William	1881	Garfield
Windom, William	1889–91	B. Harrison
Wolcott, Oliver, Jr.	1795–1800	Washington
Woodbury, Levi	1834–37	Jackson
Woodbury, Levi	1837–41	Van Buren
Woodin, William H.	1933–34	F. D. Roosevelt

SECRETARIES OF WAR*

Name	Dates	President
Alger, Russell A.	1897–99	McKinley
Armstrong, John	1813–14	Madison
Baker, Newton D.	1916–21	Wilson
Bancroft, George	(acting) 1845	Polk
Barbour, James	1825–28	J. Q. Adams
Belknap, William W.	1869–76	Grant
Bell, John	1841	W. H. Harrison
Butler, Benjamin F.	*ad int.*, 1836–37	Jackson
Calhoun, John C.	1817–25	Monroe
Cameron, James D.	1876–77	Grant
Cameron, Simon	1861–62	Lincoln
Cass, Lewis	1831–36	Jackson
Conrad, Charles M.	1850–53	Fillmore
Crawford, George W.	1849–50	Taylor
Crawford, William H.	1815–16	Madison
Dallas, Alexander	*ad int.*, 1815	Madison
Davis, Dwight F.	1925–29	Coolidge
Davis, Jefferson	1853–57	Pierce
Dearborn, Henry	1801–09	Jefferson
Dern, George H.	1933–36	F. D. Roosevelt
Dexter, Samuel	1800–01	Adams
Dickinson, Jacob M.	1909–11	Taft
Eaton, John H.	1829–31	Jackson
Elkins, Stephen B.	1891–95	B. Harrison
Endicott, William C.	1885–89	Cleveland
Eustis, William	1809–12	Madison
Floyd, John B.	1857–61	Buchanan
Garrison, Lindley M.	1913–16	Wilson
Good, James W.	1929	Hoover
Grant, Ulysses S.	*ad int.*, 1867–68	A. Johnson
Holt, Joseph	*ad int.*, 1861	Buchanan

*Position merged with that of Secretary of the Navy into the National Military Establishment under Department of Defense by the National Security Act of 1947.

Hurley, Patrick J.	1929–33	Hoover
Johnson, Reverdy	*ad int.*, 1849	Taylor
Knox, Henry	1785–94	Washington
Lamont, Daniel S.	1893–97	Cleveland
Lincoln, Robert T.	1881	Garfield
Lincoln, Robert T.	1881–85	Arthur
McCrary, George W.	1877–79	Hayes
McHenry, James	1796–1800	Washington
Marcy, William L.	1845–49	Polk
Monroe, James	1813–14; *ad int.*,	Madison
Monroe, James	1814–15	
Patterson, Robert P.	1945–47	Truman
Pickering, Timothy	*ad int.*, 1795–96	Washington
Poinsett, Joel R.	1837–41	Van Buren
Porter, James M.	1843–44	Tyler
Porter, Peter B.	1828–29	J. Q. Adams
Proctor, Redfield	1889–91	B. Harrison
Ramsey, Alexander	1879–81	Hayes
Rawlins, John A.	1869	Grant
Root, Elihu	1899–1904	McKinley
Royall, Kenneth C.	1947	Truman
Schofield, John M.	1868–69	A. Johnson
Sherman, William T.	1869	Grant
Southard, Samuel L.	*ad int.*, 1828	J. Q. Adams
Spencer, John C.	1841–43	Tyler
Stanton, Edwin M.	1862–65	Lincoln
Stanton, Edwin M.	1865–67; 1868	A. Johnson
Stimson, Henry L.	1940–45	F. D. Roosevelt
Stimson, Henry L.	1945	Truman
Stoddert, Benjamin	*ad int.*, 1800	J. Adams
Taft, Alphonso	1876	Grant
Taft, William H.	1904–08	T. Roosevelt
Taney, Roger B.	*ad int.*, 1831	Jackson
Weeks, John W.	1921–23	Harding
Weeks, John W.	1923–25	Coolidge
Wilkins, William	1844–45	Tyler
Woodring, Henry H.	1936–40	F. D. Roosevelt
Wright, Luke E.	1908–09	T. Roosevelt

SECRETARIES OF THE NAVY*

Name	Dates	President
Adams, Charles F.	1929–33	Hoover
Badger, George E.	1841	W. H. Harrison

*Positions merged with that of Secretary of War into the National Military Establishment under Department of Defense by the National Security Act of 1947.

Bancroft, George	1845–46	Polk
Bonaparte, Charles J.	1905–06	T. Roosevelt
Borie, Adolph	1869	Grant
Branch, John	1829–31	Jackson
Calhoun, John C.	*ad int.*, 1818–19	Monroe
Chandler, William E.	1882–85	Arthur
Crowninshield, Benjamin W.	1815–17	Madison
Crowninshield, Benjamin W.	1817–18	Monroe
Daniels, Josephus	1913–21	Wilson
Dearborn, Henry	*ad int.*, 1801	Jefferson
Denby, Edwin	1921–24	Harding
Dickerson, Mahlon	1834–38	Jackson
Dobbin, James C.	1853–57	Pierce
Edison, Charles	1939–40	F. D. Roosevelt
Forrestal, James V.	1944–47	F. D. Roosevelt
Gilmer, Thomas W.	1844	Tyler
Goff, Nathan, Jr.	1881	Hayes
Graham, William A.	1850–52	Fillmore
Hamilton, Paul	1809–12	Madison
Henshaw, David	1843–44	Tyler
Herbert, Hilary A.	1893–97	Cleveland
Hunt, William H.	1881–82	Garfield
Jones, William	1813–14	Madison
Kennedy, John P.	1852–53	Fillmore
Knox, W. Frank	1940–44	F. D. Roosevelt
Long, John D.	1897–1902	McKinley
Mason, John Y.	1844–45	Tyler
Mason, John Y.	1846–49	Polk
Metcalf, Victor H.	1906–08	T. Roosevelt
Meyer, George Von L.	1909–13	Taft
Moody, William H.	1902–04	T. Roosevelt
Morton, Paul	1904–05	T. Roosevelt
Newberry, Truman H.	1908–09	T. Roosevelt
Paulding, James K.	1838–41	Van Buren
Preston, William B.	1849–50	Taylor
Ramsey, Alexander	*ad int.*, 1880–81	Hayes
Robeson, George M.	1869–77	Grant
Smith, Robert	1801–09	Jefferson
Southard, Samuel L.	1823–25	Monroe
Southard, Samuel L.	1825–29	J. Q. Adams
Stoddert, Benjamin	1798–1801	J. Adams
Swanson, Claude	1933–39	F. D. Roosevelt
Thompson, Richard W.	1877–80	Hayes
Thompson, Smith	1819–23	Monroe
Toucey, Isaac	1857–61	Buchanan
Tracy, Benjamin F.	1889–93	B. Harrison

Upshur, Abel P.	1841–43	Tyler
Welles, Gideon	1861–65	Lincoln
Welles, Gideon	1865–69	A. Johnson
Whitney, William C.	1885–89	Cleveland
Wilbur, Curtis D.	1924–29	Coolidge
Woodbury, Levi	1831–34	Jackson

SECRETARIES OF DEFENSE*

Name	Dates	President
Brown, Harold	1977–81	Carter
Carlucci, Frank C., III	1987–88	Reagan
Cheney, Richard B.	1989–	Bush
Clifford, Clark M.	1968–69	L. B. Johnson
Forrestal, James V.	1947–49	Truman
Gates, Thomas S., Jr.	1959–61	Eisenhower
Johnson, Louis M.	1949–50	Truman
Laird, Melvin R.	1969–73	Nixon
Lovett, Robert A.	1951–53	Truman
McElroy, Neil H.	1957–59	Eisenhower
McNamara, Robert S.	1961–63	Kennedy
McNamara, Robert S.	1963–68	L. B. Johnson
Marshall, George C.	1950–51	Truman
Richardson, Elliot L.	1973–74	Nixon
Schlesinger, James R.	1974	Nixon
Schlesinger, James R.	1974–76	Ford
Weinberger, Caspar W.	1981–87	Reagan
Wilson, Charles E.	1953–57	Eisenhower

ATTORNEYS GENERAL

Name	Dates	President
Akerman, Amos J.	1870–71	Grant
Bates, Edward	1861–64	Lincoln
Bell, Griffin B.	1977–79	Carter
Berrien, John M.	1829–31	Jackson
Biddle, Francis B.	1941–45	F. D. Roosevelt
Black, Jeremiah	1857–60	Buchanan
Bonaparte, Charles J.	1906–09	T. Roosevelt
Bradford, William	1794–95	Washington

*Position created by the National Security Act of 1947, merging Departments of War and Navy into the National Military Establishment under Department of Defense.

Breckinridge, John	1805–06	Jefferson
Brewster, Benjamin H.	1882–85	Arthur
Brownell, Herbert, Jr.	1953–58	Eisenhower
Browning, Orville H.	*ad int.*, 1868	A. Johnson
Butler, Benjamin	1833–37	Jackson
Civiletti, Benjamin R.	1979–81	Carter
Clark, Tom C.	1945–49	Truman
Clark, W. Ramsey	1967–69	L. B. Johnson
Clifford, Nathan	1846–48	Polk
Crittenden, John J.	1841	W. H. Harrison
Crittenden, John J.	1850–53	Fillmore
Cummings, Homer S.	1933–39	F. D. Roosevelt
Cushing, Caleb	1853–57	Pierce
Daugherty, Harry M.	1921–24	Harding
Devens, Charles	1877–81	Hayes
Evarts, William M.	1868–69	A. Johnson
Garland, Augustus H.	1885–89	Cleveland
Gilpin, Henry D.	1840–41	Van Buren
Gregory, Thomas W.	1914–19	Wilson
Griggs, John W.	1898–1901	McKinley
Grundy, Felix	1838–39	Van Buren
Harmon, Judson	1895–97	Cleveland
Hoar, Ebenezer R.	1869–70	Grant
Jackson, Robert H.	1940–41	F. D. Roosevelt
Johnson, Reverdy	1849–50	Taylor
Katzenbach, Nicholas De B.	1965–67	L. B. Johnson
Kennedy, Robert F.	1961–63	Kennedy
Kennedy, Robert F.	1963–65	L. B. Johnson
Kleindienst, Richard G.	1972–73	Nixon
Knox, Philander C.	1901–04	McKinley
Lee, Charles	1795–97	Washington
Lee, Charles	1797–1801	J. Adams
Legaré, Hugh S.	1841–43	Tyler
Levi, Edward H.	1975–77	Ford
Lincoln, Levi	1801–04	Jefferson
McGranery, James P.	1952–53	Truman
McGrath, James H.	1949–52	Truman
McKenna, Joseph	1897–98	McKinley
McReynolds, James C.	1913–14	Wilson
MacVeagh, Wayne	1881	Garfield
MacVeagh, Wayne	1881	Arthur
Mason, John Y.	1845–46	Polk
Meese, Edwin, III	1985–88	Reagan
Miller, William H.	1889–93	B. Harrison
Mitchell, John N.	1969–72	Nixon
Mitchell, William D.	1929–33	Hoover
Moody, William H.	1904–06	T. Roosevelt
Murphy, Frank	1939–40	F. D. Roosevelt

Nelson, John	1843–45	Tyler
Olney, Richard	1893–95	Cleveland
Palmer, Alexander M.	1919–21	Wilson
Pierrepont, Edwards	1875–76	Grant
Pinkney, William	1811–14	Madison
Randolph, Edmund J.	1789–94	Washington
Richardson, Elliot L.	1973–74	Nixon
Rodney, Caesar A.	1807–11	Jefferson
Rogers, William P.	1958–61	Eisenhower
Rush, Richard	1814–17	Madison
Rush, Richard	*ad int.*, 1817	Monroe
Sargent, John G.	1925–29	Coolidge
Saxbe, William B.	1974	Nixon
Saxbe, William B.	1974–75	Ford
Smith, William French	1981–85	Reagan
Speed, James	1864–66	Lincoln
Stanbery, Henry	1866–68	A. Johnson
Stanton, Edwin M.	1860–61	Buchanan
Stone, Harlan F.	1924–25	Coolidge
Taft, Alphonso	1876–77	Grant
Taney, Roger B.	1831–33	Jackson
Thornburgh, Richard L.	1988–89	Reagan
Thornburgh, Richard L.	1989–	Bush
Toucey, Isaac	1848–49	Polk
Wickersham, George W.	1909–13	Taft
Williams, George H.	1872–75	Grant
Wirt, William	1817–25	Monroe
Wirt, William	1825–29	J. Q. Adams

POSTMASTERS GENERAL

Name	Dates	President
Barry, William T.	1829–35	Jackson
Bissell, Wilson S.	1893–95	Cleveland
Blair, Montgomery	1861–64	Lincoln
Blount, Winton M.	1969–73	Nixon
Brown, Aaron V.	1857–59	Buchanan
Brown, Walter F.	1929–33	Hoover
Burleson, Albert S.	1913–21	Wilson
Campbell, James	1853–57	Pierce
Collamer, Jacob	1849–50	Taylor
Cortelyou, George B.	1905–07	T. Roosevelt
Creswell, John A. J.	1869–70	Grant
Day, J. Edward	1960–63	Kennedy
Dennison, William	1864–66	Lincoln
Dickinson, Donald M.	1887–89	Cleveland

Donaldson, Jesse M.	1947–53	Truman
Farley, James A.	1933–40	F. D. Roosevelt
Gary, James A.	1897–98	McKinley
Granger, Francis	1841	W. H. Harrison
Granger, Gideon	1801–14	Jefferson, Monroe
Gresham, Walter Q.	1883–84	Arthur
Gronouski, John A.	1963	Kennedy
Gronouski, John A.	1963–65	L. B. Johnson
Habersham, Joseph	1795–97	Washington
Habersham, Joseph	1797–1801	J. Adams
Hall, Nathan K.	1850–52	Fillmore
Hannegan, Robert E.	1945–47	Truman
Hatton, Frank	1884–85	Arthur
Hays, William H.	1921–22	Harding
Hitchcock, Frank H.	1909–13	Taft
Holt, Joseph	1859–61	Buchanan
Howe, Timothy O.	1882–83	Arthur
Hubbard, Samuel D.	1852–53	Fillmore
James, Thomas L.	1881–82	Garfield
Jewell, Marshall	1874–76	Grant
Johnson, Cave	1845–51	Polk
Kendall, Amos	1835–37	Jackson
Kendall, Amos	1837–40	Van Buren
Key, David M.	1877–80	Hayes
King, Horatio	1861	Buchanan
McLean, John	1823–25	Monroe
McLean, John	1825–29	J. Q. Adams
Marshall, James W.	1874	Grant
Maynard, Horace	1880–81	Hayes
Meigs, Return J., Jr.	1814–17	Madison
Meigs, Return J., Jr.	1817–23	Monroe
Meyer, George von L.	1907–09	T. Roosevelt
New, Harry S.	1923	Harding
New, Harry S.	1923–29	Coolidge
Niles, John M.	1840–41	Van Buren
O'Brien, Lawrence F.	1965–69	L. B. Johnson
Osgood, Samuel	1789–91	Washington
Payne, Henry C.	1902–04	T. Roosevelt
Pickering, Timothy	1791–95	Washington
Randall, Alexander W.	1866–69	A. Johnson
Smith, Charles E.	1898–1902	McKinley
Summerfield, Arthur E.	1953–61	Eisenhower
Tyner, James N.	1876–77	Grant
Vilas, William F.	1885–88	Cleveland
Walker, Frank C.	1940–45	F. D. Roosevelt
Wanamaker, John	1889–93	B. Harrison
Watson, William M.	1968–69	L. B. Johnson
Wickliffe, Charles A.	1841–45	Tyler

Wilson, William L.	1895–97	Cleveland
Work, Hubert	1922–23	Harding
Wynne, Robert J.	1904–05	T. Roosevelt

SECRETARIES OF THE INTERIOR

Name	Dates	President
Andress, Cecil	1977–1981	Carter
Bollinger, Richard A.	1909–11	Taft
Bliss, Cornelius N.	1897–99	McKinley
Browning, Orville H.	1866–69	A. Johnson
Chandler, Zachariah	1875–77	Grant
Chapman, Oscar L.	1950–53	Truman
Clark, William P.	1983–85	Reagan
Cox, Jacob D., Jr.	1869–70	Grant
Delano, Columbus	1870–75	Grant
Ewing, Thomas	1849–50	Taylor
Fall, Albert B.	1921–23	Harding
Fisher, Walter L.	1911–13	Taft
Francis, David R.	1896–97	Cleveland
Garfield, James R.	1907–09	T. Roosevelt
Harlan, James	1865–66	A. Johnson
Hathaway, Stanley K.	1975	Ford
Hickel, Walter J.	1969–71	Nixon
Hitchcock, Ethan A.	1898–1907	McKinley
Hodel, Donald P.	1985–89	Reagan
Ickes, Harold L.	1933–46	F. D. Roosevelt
Kirkwood, Samuel J.	1881–82	Garfield
Kleppe, Thomas	1975–77	Ford
Krug, Julius A.	1946–49	Truman
Lamar, Lucius Q. C.	1885–88	Cleveland
Lane, Franklin K.	1913–20	Wilson
Lujan, Manuel, Jr.	1989	Bush
McClelland, Robert	1853–57	Pierce
McKay, Douglas J.	1953–56	Eisenhower
McKennan, Thomas M. T.	1850	Fillmore
Morton, Rogers C. B.	1971–73	Nixon
Morton, Rogers C. B.	1974–75	Ford
Noble, John W.	1889–93	B. Harrison
Payne, John B.	1920–21	Wilson
Schurz, Carl	1877–81	Hayes
Seaton, Frederick A.	1956–61	Eisenhower
Smith, Caleb	1861–63	Lincoln
Smith, Hoke	1893–96	Cleveland
Stuart, Alexander H. H.	1850–53	Fillmore

Teller, Henry M.	1882–85	Arthur
Thompson, Jacob	1857–61	Buchanan
Udall, Stewart L.	1961–63	Kennedy
Udall, Stewart L.	1963–69	L. B. Johnson
Usher, John P.	1863–65	Lincoln
Vilas, William F.	1888–89	Cleveland
Watt, James G.	1981–83	Reagan
West, Roy O.	1928–29	Coolidge
Wilbur, Ray L.	1929–33	Hoover
Work, Hubert	1923–28	Coolidge

SECRETARIES OF AGRICULTURE

Name	Dates	President
Anderson, Clinton B.	1945–48	Truman
Benson, Ezra T.	1953–61	Eisenhower
Bergland, Robert S.	1977–81	Carter
Block, John R.	1981–86	Reagan
Brannan, Charles F.	1948–53	Truman
Butz, Earl L.	1971–74	Nixon
Butz, Earl L.	1974–76	Ford
Colman, Norman J.	1889	Cleveland
Freeman, Orville L.	1961–63	Kennedy
Freeman, Orville L.	1963–69	L. B. Johnson
Gore, Howard M.	1924–25	Coolidge
Hardin, Clifford M.	1969–71	Nixon
Houston, David F.	1913–20	Wilson
Hyde, Arthur M.	1929–31	Hoover
Jardine, William M.	1928–29	Coolidge
Knebel, John	1976–77	Ford
Lyng, Richard E.	1986–89	Reagan
Meredith, Edwin T.	1920–21	Wilson
Morton, Julius S.	1893–97	Cleveland
Rusk, Jeremiah M.	1889–93	B. Harrison
Wallace, Henry A.	1933–40	F. D. Roosevelt
Wallace, Henry C.	1921–23	Harding
Wallace, Henry C.	1923–24	Coolidge
Wickard, Claude R.	1940–45	F. D. Roosevelt
Wilson, James	1897–1901	McKinley
Wilson, James	1901–09	T. Roosevelt
Wilson, James	1909–13	Taft
Yeutter, Clayton K.	1989–	Bush

SECRETARIES OF COMMERCE AND LABOR*

Name	Dates	President
Cortelyou, George B.	1903–04	T. Roosevelt
Metcalf, Victor H.	1904–05	T. Roosevelt
Nagel, Charles	1909–13	Taft
Strauss, Oscar S.	1906–09	T. Roosevelt

SECRETARIES OF COMMERCE**

Name	Dates	President
Alexander, Joshua W.	1919–21	Wilson
Baldridge, Malcolm	1981–87	Reagan
Chapin, Roy D.	1932–33	Hoover
Connor, John T.	1965–67	L. B. Johnson
Dent, Frederick B.	1973–74	Nixon
Dent, Frederick B.	1974–75	Ford
Harriman, W. Averill	1947–48	Truman
Hodges, Luther H.	1961–63	Kennedy
Hodges, Luther H.	1963–65	L. B. Johnson
Hoover, Herbert C.	1921–23	Harding
Hoover, Herbert C.	1923–28	Coolidge
Hopkins, Harry L.	1938–40	F. D. Roosevelt
Jones, Jesse H.	1940–45	F. D. Roosevelt
Klutznick, Philip M.	1979–81	Carter
Kreps, Juanita	1977–79	Carter
Lamont, Robert P.	1929–32	Hoover
Morton, Rogers C. B.	1975–76	Ford
Mosbacher, Robert A.	1989–	Bush
Mueller, Frederick H.	1959–61	Eisenhower
Peterson, Peter G.	1972–73	Nixon
Redfield, William C.	1913–19	Wilson
Richardson, Elliot L.	1976–77	Ford
Roper, Daniel C.	1933–38	F. D. Roosevelt
Sawyer, Charles	1948–53	Truman
Smith, Cyrus R.	1968–69	L. B. Johnson
Stans, Maurice H.	1969–72	Nixon
Strauss, Oscar S.	*ad int.*, 1958	Eisenhower
Trowbridge, Alexander B.	1967–68	L. B. Johnson
Verity, C. William, Jr.	1987–89	Reagan

*Department established by Congress, February 1903; split into Department of Commerce and Department of Labor, March 1913.

**Established following dissolution of Department of Commerce and Labor, March 1913.

Name	Dates	President
Wallace, Henry A.	1945–48	Truman
Weeks, Sinclair	1953–58	Eisenhower
Whiting, William F.	1928–29	Hoover

SECRETARIES OF LABOR*

Name	Dates	President
Brennan, Peter J.	1973–74	Nixon
Brennan, Peter J.	1974–75	Ford
Brock, William E., III	1985–87	Reagan
Davis, James J.	1921–23	Harding
Davis, James J.	1923–29	Coolidge
Davis, James J.	1929–30	Hoover
Doak, William N.	1930–33	Hoover
Dole, Elizabeth H.	1989–	Bush
Donovan, Raymond J.	1981–85	Reagan
Dunlop, John T.	1975–76	Ford
Durkin, Martin P.	1953	Eisenhower
Goldberg, Arthur J.	1961–62	Kennedy
Hodgson, James D.	1970–73	Nixon
McLaughlin, Ann D.	1987–89	Reagan
Marshall, F. Ray	1977–81	Carter
Mitchell, James P.	1954–61	Eisenhower
Perkins, Frances	1933–45	F. D. Roosevelt
Schwellenbach, Lewis B.	1945–48	Truman
Shultz, George P.	1969–70	Nixon
Tobin, Maurice J.	1948–53	Truman
Usery, Willie J., Jr.	1976–77	Ford
Wilson, William B.	1913–21	Wilson
Wirtz, William W.	1962–63	Kennedy
Wirtz, William W.	1963–69	L. B. Johnson

SECRETARIES OF HEALTH, EDUCATION, AND WELFARE

Name	Dates	President
Califano, Joseph	1977–79	Carter
Celebrezze, Anthony J.	1962–63	Kennedy
Celebrezze, Anthony J.	1963–65	L. B. Johnson
Cohen, Wilbur J.	1968–69	L. B. Johnson
Finch, Robert H.	1969–70	Nixon
Flemming, Arthur S.	1958–61	Eisenhower
Folsom, Marion B.	1955–58	Eisenhower

*Established following dissolution of Department of Commerce and Labor, March 1913.

Gardner, John W.	1965–69	L. B. Johnson
Hobby, Oveta C.	1953–55	Eisenhower
Matthews, Forrest D.	1975–77	Ford
Ribicoff, Abraham A.	1961–62	Kennedy
Richardson, Elliot L.	1970–73	Nixon
Weinberger, Caspar W.	1973–74	Nixon
Weinberger, Caspar W.	1974–75	Ford

SECRETARIES OF HOUSING AND URBAN DEVELOPMENT

Name	Dates	President
Harris, Patricia R.	1977–79	Carter
Hills, Carla	1975–77	Ford
Kemp, Jack	1989–	Bush
Landrieu, Moon E.	1979–81	Carter
Lynn, James T.	1973–74	Nixon
Lynn, James T.	1974–75	Ford
Pierce, Samuel R., Jr.	1981–89	Reagan
Romney, George W.	1969–73	Nixon
Weaver, Robert C.	1966–69	L. B. Johnson
Wood, Robert C.	1969	L. B. Johnson

SECRETARIES OF TRANSPORTATION

Name	Dates	President
Adams, Brockman	1977–79	Carter
Boyd, Alan S.	1967–69	L. B. Johnson
Brinegar, Claude S.	1973–74	Nixon
Brinegar, Claude S.	1974–75	Ford
Burnley, James H., IV	1987–89	Reagan
Coleman, William	1975–77	Ford
Dole, Elizabeth H.	1983–87	Reagan
Goldschmidt, Neil E.	1979–81	Carter
Lewis, Andrew	1981–83	Reagan
Skinner, Samuel K.	1989–	Bush
Volpe, John A.	1969–73	Nixon

SECRETARIES OF EDUCATION

Name	Dates	President
Bell, Terrel H.	1981–84	Reagan
Cavasos, Lauro F.	1988–89	Reagan

Cavasos, Lauro F.	1989–	Bush
Bennett, William J.	1985–88	Reagan
Hufstedler, Shirley M.	1979–81	Carter

SECRETARIES OF HEALTH AND HUMAN SERVICES

Name	Dates	President
Bowen, Otis R.	1985–89	Reagan
Heckler, Margaret	1983–85	Reagan
Schweiker, Richard	1981–83	Reagan
Sullivan, Louis W.	1989–	Bush

SECRETARIES OF ENERGY

Name	Dates	President
Duncan, Charles W., Jr.	1979–81	Carter
Edwards, James	1981–82	Reagan
Watkins, James D.	1989–	Bush
Hodel, Donald P.	1982–85	Reagan
Herrington, John	1985–89	Reagan
Schlesinger, James	1977–79	Carter

SECRETARIES OF VETERAN AFFAIRS

Name	Dates	President
Derwinski, Edward J.	1989–	Bush

Other Federal Government Service

U. S. SENATE

Name	State	Dates
Adams, John Q.	Mass.	1801–08; 1831–48
Alger, Russell A.	Mich.	1902–07
Anderson, Clinton P.	N.M.	1948–50; 1954–67
Armstrong, John	N.Y.	1800–02; 1803–04
Badger, George E.	N.C.	1846–55
Barbour, James	Va.	1815–25
Barkley, Alben W.	Ky.	1927–49; 1955–56
Bayard, Thomas F.	Del.	1869–85
Bell, John	Tenn.	1947–59
Berrien, John M.	Ga.	1825–29; 1841–52
Bibb, George M.	Ky.	1811–14; 1828–34
Blaine, James G.	Me.	1876–81
Boutwell, George S.	Mass.	1873–77
Brady, Nicholas F.	N.J.	1982
Branch, John	N.C.	1823–29
Breckinridge, John	Ky.	1801–05
Breckinridge, John C.	Ky.	1861
Browning, Orville H.	Ky.	1861–63
Buchanan, James	Pa.	1835–45
Burr, Aaron	N.Y.	1791–97
Byrnes, James F.	S.C.	1931–41
Calhoun, John C.	S.C.	1832–43; 1845–50
Cameron, James D.	Pa.	1877–97
Cameron, Simon	Pa.	1845–49; 1857–61; 1867–77

Campbell, George W.	Tenn.	1811–14; 1815–18
Carlisle, John G.	Ky.	1890–93
Cass, Lewis	Mich.	1845–48; 1849–57
Chandler, William E.	N.H.	1887–91; 1895–1901
Chandler, Zachariah	Mich.	1857–75; 1879
Chase, Salmon P.	Ohio	1849–55; 1861*
Clay, Henry	Ky.	1806–07; 1810–11; 1831–42; 1849–52
Clayton, John M.	Del.	1829–36; 1845–49; 1853–56
Collamer, Jacob	Vt.	1855–65
Conrad, Charles M.	La.	1842–43
Corwin, Thomas	Ohio	1845–50
Crawford, William H.	Ga.	1807–13
Creswell, John A. J.	Md.	1865–67
Crittenden, John J.	Ky.	1817–19; 1835–41; 1843–48; 1855–61
Curtis, Charles	Kans.	1907–13; 1915–29
Dallas, George M.	Pa.	1831–33
Davis, James J.	Pa.	1930–45
Davis, Jefferson	Miss.	1847–51; 1857–61
Dexter, Samuel	Mass.	1799–1800
Dickerson, Mahlon	N.J.	1817–29;1829–33
Dix, John A.	N.Y.	1845–49
Dulles, John F.	N.Y.	1949
Eaton, John H.	Tenn.	1818–29
Elkins, Stephen B.	N.M.	1895–1911
Evarts, William M.	N.Y.	1885–91
Everett, Edward	Mass.	1853–54
Ewing, Thomas	Ohio	1831–37; 1850–51
Fairbanks, Charles W.	Ind.	1897–1905
Fall, Albert B.	N.M.	1912–21
Fessenden, William P.	Me.	1854–64; 1865–69
Fish, Hamilton	N.Y.	1851–57
Forsyth, John	Ga.	1818–19; 1823–27
Frelinghuysen, Frederick T.	N.J.	1866–69; 1871–77
Gallatin, Albert	Pa.	1795–1801
Garland, Augustus H.	Ark.	1877–85
Glass, Carter	Va.	1920–46
Goff, Nathan	W.Va.	1913–19
Graham, William A.	N.C.	1840–43
Grundy, Felix	Tenn.	1829–38; 1839–40
Guthrie, James	Ky.	1865–68
Hamlin, Hannibal	Me.	1848–56; 1857–61; 1869–81
Harding, Warren G.	Ohio	1915–21
Harlan, James	Iowa	1855–57; 1857–65; 1867–73
Harrison, Benjamin	Ind.	1881–87

*Resigned after 2 days.

Harrison, William H.	Ohio	1825–28
Hendricks, Thomas A.	Ind.	1863–69
Howe, Timothy O.	Wisc.	1861–79
Hull, Cordell	Tenn.	1930–33
Humphrey, Hubert H.	Minn.	1948–64
Jackson, Andrew	Tenn.	1797–98; 1823–25
Johnson, Andrew	Tenn.	1857–62; 1875
Johnson, Lyndon B.	Tex.	1948–61
Johnson, Reverdy	Md.	1845–49; 1863–68
Johnson, Richard M.	Ky.	1819–29
Kellogg, Frank B.	Minn.	1917–23
Kennedy, John F.	Mass.	1953–65
Kennedy, Robert F.	N.Y.	1965–68
Key, David M.	Tenn.	1875–77
King, William R. deV.	Ala.	1819–44; 1848–52
Kirkwood, Samuel J.	Iowa	1866–67; 1877–81
Knox, Philander C.	Pa.	1904–09; 1917–21
Lamar, Lucius Q. C.	Miss.	1877–85
Lee, Richard H.	Va.	1789–92
Livingston, Edward	La.	1829–31
McAdoo, William G.	Calif.	1933–39
McGrath, James H.	R.I.	1947–49
McLane, Louis	Del.	1827–29
Marcy, William L.	N.Y.	1831–32
Meigs, Return J., Jr.	Ohio	1808–10
Mills, Ogden L.	N.Y.	1921–27
Mondale, Walter F.	Minn.	1964–76
Monroe, James	Va.	1790–94
Morrill, Lot M.	Me.	1861–76
Muskie, Edmund S.	Me.	1959–80
New, Harry S.	Ind.	1917–23
Niles, John M.	Conn.	1835–39; 1843–49
Nixon, Richard M.	Calif.	1950–53
Pickering, Timothy	Mass.	1803–11
Pierce, Franklin	N.H.	1837–42
Pinkney, William	Md.	1819–22
Proctor, Redfield	Vt.	1891–1908
Quayle, Danforth	Ind.	1981–89
Ramsey, Alexander	Minn.	1863–75
Ribicoff, Abraham A.	Conn.	1963–89
Rodney, Caesar A.	Del.	1822–23
Root, Elihu	N.Y.	1910–15
Saxbe, William	Ohio	1969–74
Schurz, Carl	Mo.	1869–75
Schweiker, Richard	Pa.	1969–81
Schwellenbach, Lewis B.	Wash.	1935–40
Seaton, Frederick A.	Nebr.	1951–53
Seward, William H.	N.Y.	1850–61

Sherman, John	Ohio	1881–97
Smith, Hoke	Ga.	1911–21
Southard, Samuel L.	N.J.	1821–23; 1834–42
Swanson, Claude	Va.	1910–33
Teller, Henry M.	Col.	1876–82; 1885–1909
Toucey, Isaac	Conn.	1852–57
Truman, Harry S.	Mo.	1935–45
Tyler, John	Va.	1827–36
Van Buren, Martin	N.Y.	1821–28
Vilas, William F.	Wisc.	1891–97
Walker, Robert J.	Miss.	1835–45
Webster, Daniel	Mass.	1827–41; 1845–50
Weeks, John W.	Mass.	1913–19
Weeks, Sinclair	Mass.	1944
Wilkins, William	Pa.	1831–34
Williams, George H.	Ore.	1865–71
Wilson, Henry	Mass.	1855–73
Windom, William	Minn.	1870–81; 1881–83
Woodbury, Levi	N.H.	1825–31; 1841–45

U.S. HOUSE OF REPRESENTATIVES

Name	State	Dates
Adams, Brockman	Wash.	1965–77
Alexander, Joshua W.	Mo.	1907–19
Anderson, Clinton P.	N.M.	1941–45
Barkley, Alben W.	Ky.	1913–27
Bates, Edward	Mo.	1827–29
Bell, John	Tenn.	1827–41
Bergland, Robert S.	Minn.	1970–77
Blaine, James G.	Me.	1863–69
Boutwell, George S.	Mass.	1863–69
Boudinot, Elias	N.J.	1789–95
Branch, John	N.C.	1831–33
Breckinridge, John	Va.	1792
Breckinridge, John C.	Ky.	1851–55
Brock, William E., III	Tenn.	1963–71
Brown, Aaron V.	Tenn.	1839–45
Bryan, William J.	Nebr.	1891–95
Buchanan, James	Pa.	1821–31
Burleson, Albert S.	Tex.	1899–1913
Bush, George H.	Tex.	1967–71
Byrnes, James F.	S.C.	1911–25
Calhoun, John C.	S.C.	1811–17
Campbell, George W.	Tenn.	1803–09
Carlisle, John G.	Ky.	1877–90

Cheney, Richard B.	Wyo.	1979–88
Clay, Henry	Ky.	1811–14; 1815–21; 1823–25
Clifford, Nathan	Me.	1839–43
Cobb, Howell	Ga.	1843–51; 1855–57
Colfax, Schuyler	Ind.	1855–69
Collamer, Jacob	Vt.	1843–49
Conrad, Charles M.	La.	1849–50
Corwin, Thomas	Ohio	1831–40; 1859–61
Crawford, George W.	Ga.	1843 (Jan. 7–Mar. 4)
Creswell, John A. J.	Md.	1863–65
Crittenden, John J.	Ky.	1861–63
Crowninshield, Benjamin W.	Mass.	1823–31
Curtis, Charles	Kans.	1893–1907
Cushing, Caleb	Mass.	1835–43
Davis, Jefferson	Miss.	1845–46
Dearborn, Henry	Me.	1793–97
Delano, Columbus	Ohio	1845–47
Denby, Edwin	Mich.	1905–11
Derwinski, Edward J.	Ill.	1959–79
Dexter, Samuel	Mass.	1793–95
Elkins, Stephen B.	N.M.	1873–77
Eustis, William	Mass.	1801–05; 1820–23
Fessenden, William P.	Me.	1841–43
Fillmore, Millard	N.Y.	1833–35; 1837–43
Fish, Hamilton	N.Y.	1843–45
Ford, Gerald R., Jr.	Mich.	1949–73
Forsyth, John	Ga.	1813–18
Forward, Walter	Pa.	1822–25
Foster, Charles	Ohio	1871–79
Garner, John N.	Tex.	1903–33
Glass, Carter	Va.	1902–18
Goff, Nathan	W.Va.	1883–89
Good, James W.	Iowa	1909–21
Granger, Francis	N.Y.	1835–37; 1839–41; 1841–43
Grundy, Felix	Tenn.	1811–14
Harrison, William H.	Ohio	1816–19
Hayes, Rutherford B.	Ohio	1865–67
Heckler, Margaret M.	Mass.	1967–83
Hendricks, Thomas A.	Ind.	1851–54
Herter, Christian A.	Mass.	1942–53
Hoar, Ebenezer R.	Mass.	1973–75
Hull, Cordell	Tenn.	1906–21; 1923–31
Ingham, Samuel D.	Pa.	1822–29
Jackson, Andrew	Tenn.	1796–97
Johnson, Andrew	Tenn.	1843–53
Johnson, Cave	Tenn.	1829–37; 1839–45
Johnson, Lyndon B.	Tex.	1937–48

Johnson, Richard M.	Ky.	1807–19; 1829–37
Jones, William	Pa.	1801–03
Kemp, Jack	N.Y.	1971–89
Kennedy, John F.	Mass.	1947–53
Kennedy, John P.	Md.	1838–40; 1841–45
King, William R. deV.	N.C.	1811–16
Kleppe, Thomas S.	N.D.	1967–71
Knebel, John A.	D.C.	1968–71
Laird, Melvin R.	Wisc.	1952–69
Lamar, Lucius Q. C.	Miss.	1857–60; 1873–77
Legaré, Hugh S.	S.C.	1837–39
Lincoln, Abraham	Ill.	1847–49
Lincoln, Levi	Mass.	1800–01
Livingston, Edward	N.Y.	1794–1801
Livingston, Edward	La.	1823–29
Long, John D.	Mass.	1883–89
Lujan, Manuel, Jr.	N.M.	1969–89
McClelland, Robert	Mich.	1843–49
McCrary, George W.	Iowa	1869–77
McGranery, James P.	Pa.	1937–49
McKenna, Joseph	Calif.	1885–92
McKennan, Thomas M. T.	Pa.	1831–39
McKinley, William, Jr.	Ohio	1877–83; 1885–91
McLane, Louis	Del.	1817–27
McLean, John	Ohio	1813–16
Madison, James	Va.	1789–97
Marshall, John	Va.	1799–1800
Mason, John Y.	Va.	1831–37
Maynard, Horace	Tenn.	1857–63; 1866–75
Metcalf, Victor H.	Calif.	1899–1904
Moody, William H.	Mass.	1895–1902
Morton, Levi P.	N.Y.	1879–81
Morton, Rogers C. B.	Md.	1963–69
Nelson, John	Md.	1821–23
Nixon, Richard M.	Calif.	1947–50
Palmer, Alexander M.	Pa.	1909–15
Pickering, Timothy	Mass.	1813–17
Pierce, Franklin	N.H.	1833–37
Pinkney, William	Md.	1815–16
Poinsett, Joel R.	S.C.	1821–25
Polk, James K.	Tenn.	1825–39
Porter, Peter B.	N.Y.	1809–13; 1815–16
Preston, William B.	Va.	1847–49
Quayle, Danforth	Ind.	1977–81
Ramsey, Alexander	Pa.	1843–47
Redfield, William C.	N.Y.	1911–13
Ribicoff, Abraham A.	Conn.	1949–53
Robeson, George	N.J.	1879–83

Rodney, Caesar A.	Del.	1803–05; 1821–22
Rumsfeld, Donald	Ill.	1965–71
Rusk, Jeremiah M.	Wisc.	1871–77
Schweiker, Richard	Pa.	1961–69
Sherman, James S.	N.Y.	1887–97; 1893–1909
Sherman, John	Ohio	1855–61
Smith, Caleb	Ind.	1843–49
Spencer, John C.	N.Y.	1817–19
Stevenson, Adlai E.	Ill.	1875–77; 1879–81
Stuart, Alexander H. H.	Va.	1841–43
Swanson, Claude	Va.	1893–1906
Thomas, Philip F.	Md.	1839–41; 1975–77
Thompson, Jacob	Miss.	1839–51
Toucey, Isaac	Conn.	1835–39
Tyler, John	Va.	1817–21
Tyner, James N.	Ind.	1869–75
Udall, Stewart L.	Ariz.	1955–61
Vinson, Frederick M.	Ky.	1924–29
Washburne, Elihu B.	Ill.	1853–59
Webster, Daniel	N.H.	1813–17
Webster, Daniel	Mass.	1823–27
Weeks, John W.	Mass.	1905–13
Wheeler, William A.	N.Y.	1861–63; 1869–77
Wickliffe, Charles A.	Ky.	1823–33; 1861–63
Wilkins, William	Pa.	1843–44

U.S. SUPREME COURT

Name	**Dates**
Byrnes, James F.	1941–42
Chase, Salmon P.	1864–73 (Chf. Justice)
Clark, Tom C.	1949–67
Clifford, Nathan	1858–81
Day, William R.	1903–22
Goldberg, Arthur J.	1962–65
Hughes, Charles E.	1910–16
Hughes, Charles E.	1930–41 (Chf. Justice)
Jay, John	1789–95 (Chf. Justice)
Jackson, Robert H.	1941–54
McKenna, Joseph	1898–1925
McLean, John	1830–61
McReynolds, James C.	1914–41
Marshall, John	1801–35
Moody, William H.	1906–10
Stone, Harlan F.	1925–46 (Chf. Justice, 1941–46)
Taft, William H.	1921–30 (Chf. Justice)

Taney, Roger B.	1836–64 (Chf. Justice)
Vinson, Frederick M.	1946–53
Wolcott, Oliver, Jr.	1800–02
Woodbury, Levi	1845–51

OTHER FEDERAL JUDICIAL SERVICE

Name	Office	Dates
Akerman, Amos T.	Dist. Atty.	1867–70
Alexander, Joshua W.	Judge, Circ. Ct.	1901–07
Barry, William T.	Judge, Circ. Ct.	1816–17
Bates, Edward	Cir. Pros. Atty.	1818–20
Bates, Edward	Dist. Atty.	1821–26
Bayard, Thomas F.	Dist. Atty.	1853–54
Bell, Griffin B.	Judge, Circ. Ct. of Appeals	1961–76
Biddle, Francis B.	Chf. Counsel to Investigate TVA	1938–39
Biddle, Francis B.	Judge, Circ. Ct. of Appeals	1939–40
Biddle, Francis B.	Solicitor Gen.	1940–41
Black, Jeremiah	Judge, Dist. Ct.	1842
Blair, Montgomery	Dist. Atty.	1839
Blair, Montgomery	First Solicitor Ct. of Claims	1855
Brannan, Charles F.	Asst. Reg. Atty., U.S. Dept. of Agricult. Resettlement Admin.	1935
Brannan, Charles F.	Reg. Atty., U.S. Dept. of Agricult. Resettlement Admin.	1937
Bristow, Benjamin H.	Dist. Atty.	1866–70
Bristow, Benjamin H.	Solicitor Gen.	1870–72
Butler, Benjamin	Dist. Atty.	1838–41
Campbell, George W.	Judge, Dist. Ct.	*ca.* 1821–1830
Chandler, William E.	Solicitor, Navy Dept.	1865
Civiletti, Benjamin R.	Judge, Dist. Ct.	1961
Collamer, Jacob	Judge, Circ. Ct.	1850–54
Connor, John T.	Gen. Counsel, Ofc. of Scientif. Rsch. and Devel.	1942
Connor, John T.	Counsel, Ofc. of Naval Rsch.	1946

Crawford, William H.	Judge, Circ. Ct.	1827–34
Crittenden, John J.	Dist. Atty.	1827–29
Dallas, Alexander	Dist. Atty.	1801–04
Dallas, George M.	Solicitor, U.S. Bank	1815–17
Dallas, George M.	Dist. Atty.	1829–31
Day, William R.	Judge, Circ. Ct. of Appeals	1899–1903
Dickerson, Mahlon	Judge, Dist. Ct.	1840
Elkins, Stephen B.	Dist. Atty.	1867–70
Evarts, William M.	Asst. Atty.	1849–53
Fowler, Henry	Counsel for Fed. Power Comm.	1941
Fowler, Henry	Counsel for Ofc. of Prod. Mgmt.	1941
Gilpin, Henry D.	Solicitor, U.S. Treas.	1837
Goff, Nathan	Dist. Atty.	1868–81; 1881–82
Gresham, Walter Q.	Dist. Judge	1869–82
Gresham, Walter Q.	Circ. Judge	1884–93
Griffin, Cyrus	Judge, Dist. Ct.	1789–1810
Hall, Nathan K.	Dist. Judge	1852–74
Hills, Carla A.	Asst. Atty. Gen.	1974–75
Hufstedler, Shirley M.	Ct. of Appeals	1968–79
Hunt, William H.	Judge, Ct. of Claims	1878–81
Jackson, Robert H.	Gen. Counsel, Bur. of Internal Rev.	1933
Jackson, Robert H.	Spec. Counsel, Sec. & Exch. Comm.	1935
Jackson, Robert H.	Solicitor Gen.	1938
Johnson, Cave	Circ. Judge	1850–51
Kellogg, Frank B.	Federal Prosecutor	1905
Kellogg, Frank B.	Spec. Counsel to Interstate Commerce Comm.	1906
Kellogg, Frank B.	Govt. Counsel	1909
Kennedy, Robert F.	Atty, Justice Dept.	1951–52
Kennedy, Robert F.	Asst. Counsel, Sen. Investig. Subcomt.	1953
Kennedy, Robert F.	Minority Counsel, Sen. Subcomt.	1953
Kennedy, Robert F.	Chf. Counsel, Sen. Investig. Subcomt.	1955
Kennedy, Robert F.	Chf. Counsel, Sen. Subcomt. to Investig. Labor— Mgmt. Relations	1957–59
Knox, Philander C.	Asst. Dist. Atty.	1876
Lansing, Robert	Counselor, Dept. State	1914–15

Lee, Charles	Circ. Judge	1801–02
Livingston, Edward	Dist. Atty.	1800–03
McCrary, George W.	Circ. Judge	1880–84
McGranery, James P.	Dist. Judge	1946–52
McGrath, James H.	Dist. Atty.	1934–40
McGrath, James H.	Solicitor Gen.	1945–46
McKenna, Joseph	Circ. Judge	1892–97
McReynolds, James C.	Spec. Counsel for U.S. Govt.	1907–12
Mason, John Y.	Dist. Judge	1837
Meigs, Return J.	Dist. Judge	1807–08
Meredith, William M.	Dist. Atty.	1841–49
Mitchell, William D.	Solicitor Gen.	1925–29
Mitchell, William D.	Spec. Pros., Fed. Grand Jury	1929–33
Mitchell, William D.	Chf. Counsel, Cong. Pearl Harbor Investig. Comt.	1945
Moody, William H.	Dist. Atty.	1890–95
Murphy, Frank	Asst. Dist. Atty.	1919–20
Noble, John W.	Dist. Atty.	1867–70
Patterson, Robert P.	Dist. Judge	1930–39
Patterson, Robert P.	Circ. Judge	1939–40
Pierce, Samuel R., Jr.	Asst. Dist. Atty.	1949–52
Pierce, Samuel R., Jr.	U.S. Atty.	1953–55
Pierrepont, Edwards	Dist. Atty.	1869–70
Richardson, Elliot L.	U.S. Atty.	1959–61
Rogers, William P.	Counsel, Sen. Comm. to Investig. Natl. Defense	1947
Root, Elihu	Dist. Atty.	1838–85
Saxbe, William	Atty. Gen.	1974–75
Schwellenbach, Lewis B.	Dist. Judge	1940–45
Skinner, Samuel K.	Asst. U.S. Atty.	1968–74
Skinner, Samuel K.	1st Asst. U.S. Atty.	1974–75
Skinner, Samuel K.	U.S. Atty.	1975–77
Smith, Caleb	Dist. Judge	1863–64
Stanton, Edwin McM.	Spec. Counsel for U.S. Govt.	1856
Stimson, Henry L.	U.S. Atty.	1906–09
Taft, William H.	Solicitor Gen.	1890–92
Taft, William H.	Judge, Circ. Ct.	1892
Thornburgh, Richard L.	U.S. Atty.	1966–75
Tracy, Benjamin F.	Dist. Atty.	1866–73
Vinson, Frederick M.	Judge, Circ. Ct.	1937–43
Vinson, Frederick M.	Judge, Emerg. Ct. of Appeals	1942–43

Wilbur, Curtis D.	Judge, Circ. Ct. of Appeals	1929–31
Wilbur, Curtis D.	Senior Cir. Judge	1931–35
Wilkins, Wilbur	Judge, Dist. Ct.	1824–31
Wirt, William	Pros. Atty., Aaron Burr Trial	1807
Wirt, William	Dist. Atty.	1816–17
Wirtz, William W.	Assoc. Gen. Counsel, Bd. of Econ. Warfare	1942–43
Wirtz, William W.	Gen. Counsel, War Labor Bd.	1943–45

OTHER EXECUTIVE BRANCH SERVICE

Name	Office	Dates
Acheson, Dean G.	Undersecy. Treas.	1933
Acheson, Dean G.	Asst. Secy. State	1941–45
Acheson, Dean G.	Undersecy. State	1945–47
Bacon, Robert	Asst. Secy. State	1905
Baker, James A., III	Undersecy. Commerce	1975–76
Baker, James A., III	White House Chief of Staff	1980–85
Barr, Joseph W.	Undersecy. Treas.	1965–68
Blumenthal, W. Michael	Dep. Asst. Secy. State	1961; 1963–67
Boutwell, George S.	Comr. of Int. Revenue	1862–63
Boyd, Alan S.	Undersecy. Commerce	1965–67
Brannan, Charles F.	Reg. Dir., Farm Security Admin.	1941–45
Brannan, Charles F.	Asst. Secy. Agric.	1944–48
Brock, William E., III	U.S. Trade Rep.	1981–85
Brown, Harold	Secy. A.F.	1965–69
Brown, Walter F.	Asst. Secy. Commerce	1927–29
Burnley, James H., IV	Dir. Vista	1981–82
Bush, George H.	Dir. CIA	1976–77
Butz, Earl L.	Asst. Secy. Agric.	1954–57
Chandler, William E.	Asst. Secy. Treas.	1865–67
Chapman, Oscar L.	Asst. Secy. Interior	1933
Chapman, Oscar L.	Undersecy. Interior	1946
Cheney, Richard B.	White House Chief of Staff	1975–77
Clark, Tom C.	Asst. Atty. Gen.	1943–45
Clark, W. Ramsey	Asst. Atty. Gen.	1961–65

Clark, W. Ramsey	Acting Atty. Gen.	1966–67
Clifford, Clark McA.	Pres. Naval Aide	1946
Clifford, Clark McA.	Spec. Counsel to Pres.	1946–50
Clifford, Clark McA.	Adv. to Pres.	1963–65
Cohen, Wilbur J.	Social Security Admin., Dir. of Rsch. and Statistics Bureau	1953–56
Cohen, Wilbur J.	Consultant to White House Conf. on Aging	1959–60
Cohen, Wilbur J.	Asst. Secy. HEW	1961–65
Cohen, Wilbur J.	Undersecy. HEW	1965–67
Cohen, Wilbur J.	Acting Secy. HEW	1968
Colby, Bainbridge	Spec. Asst. to Atty. Gen.	1917
Colby, Bainbridge	Comr., U.S. Shipping Bd. Emer. Fleet	1917–19
Colman, Norman J.	U.S. Comr. Agric.	1885–89
Connally, John B.	Secy. of the Navy	1961–62
Connor, John T.	Spec. Asst. to Secy. Navy	1946
Daniels, Josephus	Chf. Clerk, U.S. Dept. Interior	1893–95
Davis, Dwight F.	Mbr., War Finance Corp.	1921–23
Davis, Dwight F.	Asst. Secy. War	1923–25
Davis, Dwight F.	Acting Secy. War	1925
Davis, Dwight F.	Gov. Gen., Philippines	1929–32
Davis, Dwight F.	Dir. Gen., Army Spec. Corps	1942
Dawes, Charles G.	Comp. of the Currency	1898–1901
Dawes, Charles G.	Dir., Bureau of Budget	1921–23
Dawes, Charles G.	Recon. Finance Corp.	1932
Delano, Columbus	Comr. of Int. Revenue	1869–70
Devens, Charles	U.S. Marshal	1849–53
Dillon, C. Douglas	Dep. Undersecy. State	1957–58
Dillon, C. Douglas	Undersecy. State for Econ. Affairs	1958–59
Dillon, C. Douglas	Undersecy. State	1959–60
Donaldson, Jesse M.	Dep. Asst. Postm. Gen.	1933–45

Donaldson, Jesse M.	Chf. Post Ofc. Inspector	1945–46
Donaldson, Jesse M.	Asst. Postm. Gen.	1946–47
Dulles, John F.	Spec. Agt., Dept. of State	1917
Dulles, John F.	Consultant to Secy. State	1951–52
Duncan, Charles W., Jr.	Dep. Secy. Defense	1977–79
Edison, Charles	Natl. Recovery Bd.	1935
Edison, Charles	Asst. Secy. Navy	1936–39
Edison, Charles	Acting Secy. Navy	1939
Eisenhower, Dwight D.	Asst. Exec. to Asst. Secy. War	1929–33
Fairchild, Charles S.	Asst. Secy. Treas.	1885–86
Fairchild, Charles S.	Acting Secy. Treas.	1886–87
Forrestal, James V.	Acting Secy. Navy	1944
Fowler, Henry H.	Undersecy. Treas.	1961–64
Gates, Thomas S., Jr.	Undersecy. of Navy	1955–57
Gates, Thomas S., Jr.	Secy. of Navy	1957–59
Gates, Thomas S., Jr.	Undersecy. of Defense	1959–60
Gilpin, Henry D.	Dir. Bank of U.S.	1833
Gore, Howard M.	Asst. of U.S. Food Admin.	1917
Gore, Howard M.	Chf. of Trade Practices, Dept. of Agric.	1921
Gore, Howard M.	Asst. Secy. Agric.	1923–24
Gregory, Thomas W.	Spec. Asst. to U.S. Atty. Gen.	1912–14
Griffin, Cyrus	Comr. to Creek Nation	1789
Haig, Alexander M., Jr.	White House Chief of Staff	1973–74
Hannegan, Robert E.	Dist. Collector of Int. Revenue	1942
Hannegan, Robert E.	Comr. of Int. Revenue	1943–44
Hatton, Frank	Asst. Postm. Gen.	1881
Harriman, William A.	Business Adv. Council, Dept. Commerce	1933–40
Harriman, William A.	Asst. Admin. of NRA	1934
Harriman, William A.	Ofc. of Prod. Mgmt.	1941
Harriman, William A.	Spec. Asst. to Pres.	1950–51
Harriman, William A.	Asst. Secy. State, Far Eastern Affairs	1961–63

Harriman, William A.	Undersecy. State, Political Affairs	1963–65
Harrison, William H.	Comr. of Indian Affairs	1801
Hendricks, Thomas A.	Comr. of Gen. Land Ofc.	1855–59
Herrington, John	Asst. Chief of Staff	1983
Herter, Christian A.	Amer. Relief Admin.	1919
Herter, Christian A.	Asst. Secy. Commerce	1919–24
Herter, Christian A.	European Relief Council	1920–21
Herter, Christian A.	Undersecy. State	1957–59
Herter, Christian A.	Planner on Foreigner Trade	1962
Hitchcock, Frank H.	Chf. Clerk, Dept. Commerce and Labor	1903–04
Hitchcock, Frank H.	Asst. Postm. Gen.	1905–08
Hodgson, James D.	Undersecy. of Labor	1969–70
Hobby, Oveta C.	War Dept., Bureau Public Relations	1941
Hobby, Oveta C.	Dir., Women's Auxiliary Army Corps	1942
Hodel, Donald P.	Dep. Dir. Bonneville Power Admin.	1969–72
Hodel, Donald P.	Undersecy. Interior	1981–82
Hodges, Luther H.	Ofc. of Price Admin.	1944
Hodges, Luther H.	Consultant of Secy. Agric.	1945
Holt, Joseph	Comr. of Patents	1857
Hoover, Herbert C.	U.S. Food Admin.	1917–19
Hughes, Charles E.	Spec. Asst. to Atty. Gen.	1906
Hurley, Patrick J.	Asst. Secy. War	1928
Ickes, Harold L.	Fed. Admin. of Public Works	1933
Jackson, Robert H.	Asst. Atty. Gen.	1937
Johnson, Louis A.	Aide to Secy. War	1933
Johnson, Louis A.	Adv. Council, U.S. Employ. Service	1934
Johnson, Louis A.	Asst. Secy. War	1937–40
Johnson, Reverdy	Peace Conf.	1861
Katzenbach, Nicholas de B.	Asst. Atty. Gen.	1961
Katzenbach, Nicholas de B.	Dep. Atty. Gen.	1962
Katzenbach, Nicholas de B.	Acting Atty. Gen.	1964
Katzenbach, Nicholas de B.	Undersecy. State	1966

Kellogg, Frank B.	Gov. Del. to Cong. of Lawyers and Jurists	1904
Kendall, Amos	Aud. of the Treas.	1832–35
Kennedy, David M.	Bd. of Gov., Fed. Reserve System	1930–46
Kennedy, David M.	Spec. Asst. to Secy. Treas.	1953–54
King, Horatio	First Asst. to Postm. Gen.	1854–61
King, Horatio	Acting Postm. Gen.	1861
Kleindienst, Richard G.	Atty. Gen.	1972–73
Kleppe, Thomas S.	Head, Sm. Bus. Adm.	1971
Klutznick, Philip M.	Federal Housing Comm.	1944–46
Knebel, John A.	Undersecy. Agric.	1975–76
Krug, Julius A.	Public Utilities Expert, FCC	1935
Krug, Julius A.	Chf. Power Engineer, TVA	1938
Krug, Julius A.	Head of Power Branch, Ofc. of Prod. Mgmt.	1941
Lamont, Daniel S.	Private Secy. to Pres. Cleveland	1885
Lamont, Robert P.	Procurement Div., Army Ordnance Dept.	1919
Levi, Edward H.	Spec. Asst. to Atty. Gen.	1940–45
Levi, Edward H.	Atty. Gen.	1975–77
Lovett, Robert A.	Asst. Secy. War	1941–45
Lovett, Robert A.	Undersecy. Defense	1947–51
Lovett, Robert A.	Consultant to Pres. Kennedy	1961–63
Lyng, Richard E.	Dir. Commodity Credit Corp.	1969–73
Lyng, Richard E.	Dep. Secy. Agriculture	1981–86
Lynn, James T.	Undersecy. Dept. Comm.	1971–72
McAdoo, William G.	Dir. Gen., U.S. Railroads	1917–19
McCulloch, Hugh	Comp. of the Currency	1863
McGranery, James P.	Asst. Atty. Gen.	1943–46
McLaughlin, Ann D.	Dir. EPA Office of Pub. Info.	1973–74

McLaughlin, Ann D.	Asst. Secy. Public Affairs, Treasury	1981–84
McLaughlin, Ann D.	Undersecy. Interior	1984–87
McNamara, Robert S.	Consultant to War Dept.	1942
McReynolds, James C.	Asst. Atty. Gen.	1903–07
McReynolds, James C.	Spec. Counsel for the Govt.	1907–12
Marshall, James W.	Asst. Postm. Gen.	1869–74
Meese, Edwin, III	Counselor	1980–85
Mills, Ogden L.	Undersecy. Treas.	1927–32
Mitchell, James P.	WPA	1936
Mitchell, James P.	Dir. of Indus. Personnel, War Dept.	1941
Mitchell, James P.	Asst. Secy. Army	1953–54
Morgenthau, Henry	Farm Credit Admin.	1933
Morgenthau, Henry	Acting Secy. Treas.	1933
Morgenthau, Henry	Undersecy. Treas.	1934
Morgenthau, Henry	Secy. Treas. *ad int.*	1934
Mueller, Frederick H.	Asst. Secy. Commerce	1958
Mueller, Frederick H.	Undersecy. Commerce	1958
Murphy, Frank	Gov. Gen. Philippines	1935–36
New, Harry S.	U.S. Comr. to Chicago Exposition	1933
Newberry, Truman H.	Asst. Secy. Navy	1905–08
O'Brien, Lawrence F.	White House Asst. For Congressional Relations and Personnel	1961
Osgood, Samuel	Comr., U.S. Treas.	1785–89
Palmer, Alexander M.	Alien Property Custodian	1917–19
Patterson, Robert P.	Asst. Secy. War	1940–45
Paulding, James K.	Secy., Bd. of Naval Comrs.	1815
Perkins, Frances	Civil Service Comr.	1945–53
Pierce, Samuel R., Jr.	Asst. Undersecy. Labor	1955–56
Pierce, Samuel R., Jr.	Gen. Counsel, Treasury	1970–73
Randall, Alexander W.	Asst. Postm. Gen.	1863–66
Richardson, Elliot L.	Asst. Secy., Dept. HEW	1957–59
Richardson, Elliot L.	Acting Secy., HEW	1958
Richardson, Elliot L.	Spec. Asst., U.S. Atty. Gen.	1961

Richardson, Elliot L.	Undersecy. State	1969–70
Richardson, William A.	Asst. Secy. Treas.	1869–73
Rockefeller, Nelson A.	Asst. Secy. State	1944–45
Rockefeller, Nelson A.	Undersecy. HEW	1953–54
Rogers, William P.	Dep. Atty. Gen.	1952–58
Roosevelt, Franklin D.	Asst. Secy. Navy	1913–20
Roosevelt, Theodore	U.S. Civil Service Bd.	1889
Roosevelt, Theodore	Asst. Secy. Navy	1897–98
Roper, Daniel C.	Spec. Agt., Fed. Bureau of Census	1900–11
Roper, Daniel C.	Asst. Postm. Gen.	1913–16
Roper, Daniel C.	Comr. of Int. Revenue	1917–20
Royall, Kenneth C.	Spec. Asst. to Secy. War	1944–45
Rumsfeld, Donald	Dir., OEO	1967–70
Rumsfeld, Donald	Dir., Cost of Living Council	1971–73
Rush, Richard	Comp. of the Treas.	1811–14
Rusk, D. Dean	Asst. Chf., Intl. Security Affairs, Dept. State	1948
Rusk, D. Dean	Dir. Ofc. Spec. Political Affairs and Ofc. UN Affairs	1947–49
Rusk, D. Dean	Asst. Secy. State	1949
Rusk, D. Dean	Dep. Undersecy. State	1949
Rusk, D. Dean	Asst. Secy. State for Far Eastern Affairs	1950
Seaton, Frederick A.	Asst. Secy. Defense	1953–55
Seaton, Frederick A.	Pres. Asst. for Congressional Liaison	1955–56
Schlesinger, James R.	Dir., CIA	1973
Schlesinger, James R.	Secy. Defense	1973–75
Shultz, George P.	Consultant to Ofc. of Secy. Labor	1960
Shultz, George P.	Consultant to Pres. Comt. on Labor-Mgmt. Policy	1961–62
Shultz, George P.	U.S. Employ. Service Task Force	1964
Shultz, George P.	Natl. Manpower Policy Task Force	1964
Shultz, George P.	Nixon Task Force	1968
Simon, William E.	Dep., Dept. of Treas.	1972
Simon, William E.	Secy. Treas.	1974–77

Snyder, John W.	Natl. Bank Receiver	1930–36
Snyder, John W.	Fed. Loan Admin.	1945
Stans, Maurice H.	Financial Consultant to Postm. Gen.	1953–55
Stans, Maurice H.	Dep. Postm. Gen.	1955–57
Stans, Maurice H.	Dep. Dir., Bureau of Budget	1957–58
Stans, Maurice H.	Dir., Bureau of Budget	1958–61
Stettinius, Edward R.	Dir., Ofc. of Prod. Mgmt.	1941
Stettinius, Edward R.	Spec. Asst. to Pres.	1941–43
Stettinius, Edward R.	Undersecy. State	1943–44
Stettinius, Edward R.	Pres. Adv. at Yalta Conf.	1945
Stevenson, Adlai E.	Asst. Postm. Gen.	1885–89
Strauss, Lewis L.	Spec. Asst. to Secy. Navy	1944
Strauss, Lewis L.	Navy Civilian Rsch. Adv. Comt.	1945
Stimson, Henry L.	Gov. Gen. Philippines	1927–29
Thomas, Philip F.	Comp. of U.S. Treas.	1851–53
Thomas, Philip F.	Comr. of Patents	1860
Thompson, Richard W.	Collector of Int. Revenue	1861–65
Thornburgh, Richard L.	Asst. Atty. Gen.	1975–77
Toucey, Isaac	Acting Secy. State	1849–50
Trowbridge, Alexander B.	Employee of CIA	1951
Trowbridge, Alexander B.	Asst. Secy. Commerce	1965
Trowbridge, Alexander B.	Acting Secy. Commerce	1967
Tyner, James N.	Spec. Agt. for Post Ofc. Dept.	1861–66
Tyner, James N.	Second Asst. Postm. Gen.	1875–76
Tyner, James N.	First Asst. Postm. Gen.	1877–81
Tyner, James N.	Del. to Intl. Postal Congresses	1878; 1897
Tyner, James N.	Asst. Atty. Gen. for Post Ofc. Dept.	1890–93; 1897–1903
Usery, Willie J., Jr.	Secy. of Labor	1976–77
Usher, John P.	Asst. Secy. Interior	1862–63
Vance, Cyrus R.	Secy. Army	1961
Vance, Cyrus R.	Dep. Def. Secy.	1964
Vance, Cyrus R.	Secy. State	1977–80

Vinson, Frederick M.	Dir., Ofc. of Econ. Stabilization	1943–45
Vinson, Frederick M.	Fed. Loan Admin.	1945
Volpe, John A.	Fed. Highway Admin.	1956–57
Walker, Frank C.	Exec. Dir., Natl. Emer. Council	1933–35
Watson, William M.	Spec. Asst. to Pres.	1965–68
Watt, James G.	Undersecy. Interior	1969–72
Watt, James G.	Interior Dept. Bureau of Outdoor Recreation	1972–75
Watt, James G.	Federal Power Comm.	1975–77
Weaver, Robert C.	Adv. of Negro Affairs, Dept. of Interior	1933–37
Weeks, Sinclair	Chmn. of Finance Comt.	1949–52
Weinberger, Caspar W.	Dep. Dir., Off. Mgmt. and Budg.	1972–73
Weinberger, Caspar W.	Secy. HEW	1973–75
West, Roy O.	Spec. Asst. to U.S. Atty. Gen.	1941–53
Wickard, Claude R.	Agric. Adjust. Admin.	1933
Wickard, Claude R.	Asst. Dir., Central Div., Agric. Adjust. Admin.	1937
Wickard, Claude R.	Dir., Agric. Adjust. Admin.	1937–40
Wickard, Claude R.	Undersecy. Agric.	1940
Wickard, Claude R.	Admin., Rural Electrification Admin.	1945–53
Wilbur, Ray L.	Conservation Div., Food Admin.	1917
Wirtz, William W.	Chmn., Natl. Wage Stabilization Bd.	1946
Wirtz, William W.	Undersecy. Labor	1961
Wolcott, Oliver, Jr.	Aud., U.S. Treas.	1789–91
Wolcott, Oliver, Jr.	Comp. of U.S. Treas.	1791–95
Wood, Robert C.	Mgmt. Org. Expert, Bureau of Budget	1951–54
Wood, Robert C.	Undersecy. HUD	1966–68
Woodring, Henry H.	Asst. Secy. War	1932
Woodring, Henry H.	Asst. Secy. War for Air	1933–36

Work, Hubert	Asst. Postm. Gen.	1921–22
Yeutter, Clayton K.	Consumer and Marketing Svc. Dept. of Agriculture	1972–75
Yeutter, Clayton K.	Asst. Secy. Agriculture	1975–77
Yeutter, Clayton K.	Dep. Trade Rep.	1977–78

FEDERAL COMMISSIONS AND COMMITTEES

Name	Commission or Committee	Dates
Acheson, Dean G.	Exec. Admin. Investig. Comm.	1939
Acheson, Dean G.	Comm. for Org. of Exec. Branch (Hoover Comm.)	1947–49
Acheson, Dean G.	U.S.–Canadian Defense Bd.	1947–48
Adams, Brockman	Chmn., House Budget Comm.	1974
Adams, Brockman	Interst. and For. Commerce Comm.	n.d.
Adams, Brockman	Science and Tech. Comm.	n.d.
Alexander, Joshua W.	Comm. of U.S. to Intl. Conf. on Safety at Sea	1913–14
Anderson, Clinton P.	U.S. Coronado Exposition Comm.	1939–40
Ballinger, Richard A.	Commr., Gen. Land Office	1907
Baker, Newton D.	Natl. Comm. on Law Enforcemt. and Observ.	1929
Bayard, Thomas F.	Chf. Counsel to Investig. TVA	1938–39
Biddle, Francis B.	Chmn., Natl. Labor Relations Bd.	1934–35
Bonaparte, Charles J.	Bd. of Indians Comrs.	1902–04
Boutwell, George S.	Comm. to edit statutes at large	1877
Boyd, Alan S.	Civil Aero. Bd.	1959–61

Brady, Nicholas F.	National Bipartisan Comm. on Central America	1983
Brady, Nicholas F.	Comm. on Executive, Legislative and Judicial Salaries	1985
Brady, Nicholas F.	Stock Market Crisis Comm.	1987–88
Brewster, Benjamin H.	Commr. for Cherokee Indians	1846
Burleson, Albert S.	U.S. Comm. to Intl. Wire Communications Conf.	1920
Carlucci, Frank C., III	Dir. Office of Econ. Opportunity	1971–72
Carlucci, Frank C., III	Dep. Dir. CIA	1978–81
Chapman, Oscar L.	Comm. to Coord. Health and Welfare Svcs.	1935
Chapman, Oscar L.	Comm. on Voc. Education	1936
Chapman, Oscar L.	Comm. to Review Charges of Subversive Activities Against Fed. Empls.	1941–42
Clay, Henry	Commr., negot. of Treaty of Ghent	1814
Clifford, Clark M.	Comm. on Defense Estab.	1960
Clifford, Clark M.	Foreign Adv. Bd.	1961
Clifford, Clark M.	Foreign Intel. Adv. Bd.	1963–68
Creswell, John A. J.	Counsel for U.S. to *Alabama* Claims Comm.	1874–76
Cushing, Caleb	Counsel for U.S. to *Alabama* Claims Comm.	1872–74
Dawes, Charles G.	Reparations Comt.	1923
Day, William R.	Mixed Claims Comm.	1922
Dole, Elizabeth H.	Dep. Dir. Office of Consumer Affairs	1971
Dulles, John F.	War Trade Bd.	1918
Durkin, Martin P.	Defense Mobil Bd.	1953
Durkin, Martin P.	Natl. Security Resources Bd.	1953

Durkin, Martin P.	Natl. War Labor Bd.	*ca.* 1950
Farley, James A.	Comm. on Org. of Exec. Branch	1953
Fish, Hamilton	Comm. for Relief of Civil War Pris.	1867–69
Flemming, Arthur S.	Civil Service Comm.	1939–48
Flemming, Arthur S.	War Manpower Comm.	1942–45
Flemming, Arthur S.	Comm. for Org. of Exec. Branch (Hoover Comm.)	1947
Flemming, Arthur S.	Atomic Energy Comm.	1948
Flemming, Arthur S.	Asst. to Dir., Defense Mobil.	1951
Flemming, Arthur S.	Pres. Adv. Comm. on Govt. Org.	1953
Flemming, Arthur S.	Dir., Ofc. of Defense Mobil.	1953
Flemming, Arthur S.	Natl. Security Council	1953
Flemming, Arthur S.	Natl. Adv. Comm. on Peace Corps	1961
Folsom, Marion B.	Business Adv. Council	1936–48
Folsom, Marion B.	Adv. Council on Social Security	1937–38
Folsom, Marion B.	Reg. War Manpower Comt.	1942–45
Folsom, Marion B.	Adv. Comm. on Merchant Marine	1947–48
Fowler, Henry H.	War Prod. Bd.	1942–44
Fowler, Henry H.	Natl. Prod. Auth.	1951–52
Fowler, Henry H.	Defense Prod. Admin.	1952–53
Fowler, Henry H.	Natl. Comm. on Money and Credit	n.a.
Gardner, John W.	Adv. Comm. on Intl. Educ. and Cultural Affairs	1962–64
Gardner, John W.	White House Conf. on Ed.	1965
Garfield, James R.	Civil Service Comm.	1902–03
Garfield, James R.	Commr. of Corporations, Dept.of Commerce and Labor	1903
Griffin, Cyrus	Commr. to Creek Nation	1789

Hardin, Clifford M.	Foreign Aid Review Comt.	1962
Hardin, Clifford M.	Agricul. Dept. Task Force	1968
Harrison, William H.	Commr., Ofc. of Indian Affairs	1800–13
Hendricks, Thomas A.	Commr., General Land Ofc.	1855–59
Hoar, Ebenezer R.	Comm. on *Alabama* Claims	1871–72
Hobby, Oveta C.	Comm. for Org. of Exec. Branch (Hoover Comm.)	1948
Hobby, Oveta C.	Security Admin.	1953
Hodges, Luther H.	Intl. Mgmt. Conf.	1951
Hoover, Herbert C.	Indust. Conf.	1920
Hopkins, Harry L.	Fed. Emer. Relief Admin.	1933
Hopkins, Harry L.	Adm., Lend Lease Prog.	1940–41
Hopkins, Harry L.	War Prod. Bd.	1942–44
Hopkins, Harry L.	War Resources Bd.	1942–45
Humphrey, Hubert H., Jr.	WPA Admin. Staff	1941–43
Humphrey, Hubert H., Jr.	Asst. Reg. Dir., War Manpower Comm.	1943
Jackson, Robert H.	Spec. Counsel, Sec. & Exch.	1935
Jones, Jesse	War Prod. Bd.	1942–44
Kendall, Amos	Indian Agt. for Collection of Claims	1843
Kennedy, David M.	Comm. on Fed. Budget Drafting	1967
Krug, Julius	War Prod. Bd.	1942–44
Krug, Julius	Dir., Ofc. of War Utilities	1943
Krug, Julius	Acting Head, War Prod. Bd.	1944
Krug, Julius	Permanent Chmn., War Prod. Bd	1944–45
Lane, Franklin K.	Member, Interstate Commerce Comm.	1906–13
Lane, Franklin K.	Chmn., Interstate Commerce Comm.	1913
McElroy, Neil H.	Chmn., White House Conf. on Ed.	1955
McLean, John	Commr., Land Ofc.	1822–23

Marcy, William L.	Commr. on Mexican Claims	1839–42
Marshall, Freddie R.	Chmn., Comm. on Apprenticeships	n.a.
Marshall, Thomas R.	Fed. Coal Comm.	1922–23
Miller, G. William	Chmn., Federal Reserve Bank	1978–79
Mitchell, James P.	Comm. for Org. of Exec. Branch (Hoover Comm.)	1948
Peterson, Peter G.	Chmn., Council on Int'l Econ. Affairs	1971
Porter, Peter B.	Northwestern Boundary Comm.	1816
Ramsey, Alexander	Chmn., Edmunds Comm.	1882–86
Roper, Daniel C.	Clerk, Sen. Comm. on Interstate Commerce	1893–96
Roper, Daniel C.	Clerk, House Ways and Means Comt.	1911
Roper, Daniel C.	Tariff Comm.	1917
Royall, Kenneth C.	Pres. Race Comm.	1963
Schlesinger, James R.	Chmn., Atomic Ener. Comm.	1971–73
Simon, William E.	Dir., Fed. Energ. Off.	1973–74
Smith, Caleb	Mexican Claims Bd.	1849–51
Smith, Hoke	Jt. Comm. on Natl. Aid to Voc. Ed.	1914
Snyder, John W.	Dir., War Mobil. and Reconversion	1945–46
Stans, Maurice H.	Consultant, Hse. Approp. Comt.	1953
Stettinius, Edward R., Jr.	War Resources Bd.	1938–51
Strauss, Lewis L.	Navy Civilian Rsch. Adv. Comm.	1945
Strauss, Lewis L.	Member, Atomic Energy Comm.	1946–50
Strauss, Lewis L.	Chmn., Atomic Energy Comm.	1953–58
Taft, William H.	Jt. Chmn., Natl. War Labor Conf. Bd.	1918–19
Teller, Henry M.	Monetary Comm.	1908
Usery, Willie J., Jr.	Dir., Med. and Concil. Serv.	1973–76
Verity, C. William, Jr.	Bipartisan Task Force on Private Sector Initiatives	1981

Verity, C. William, Jr.	U.S.-U.S.S.R. Trade Council	1979–84
Vinson, Frederick M.	Dir., War Mobil. and Reconversion	1945
Weaver, Robert	Housing & Home Finance Comm.	1961–66
Weinberger, Caspar W.	Chmn., FTC	1970
Wickersham, George	War Trade Bd. to Cuba	1918
Wickersham, George	Natl. Comm. on Law Observ. Enforcemt.	1929
Wilson, William B.	Intl. Jr. Comm.	1921
Wirtz, William W.	Assoc. Gen. Counsel, Bd. of Economic Warfare	1942–43
Wirtz, William W.	Gen. Counsel, War Labor Bd.	1943–45
Wright, Luke E.	Member, Philippine Comm.	1900
Wright, Luke E.	Pres., Philippine Comm.	1900–04

DIPLOMATIC CORPS

Name	Office	Dates
Acheson, Dean G.	Del. to U.N. Monetary and Financial Conference	1944
Adams, John Q.	Min. to Netherlands	1794
Adams, John Q.	Min. to Russia	1808
Armstrong, John	Min. to France	1804–10
Armstrong, John	Acting Min. to Spain	1806
Bacon, Robert	Amb. to France	1909–12
Baker, Newton D.	Del. Permanent Court of Arbitration, The Hague	1928
Bancroft, Robert	Min. to Great Britain	1846
Barbour, James	Min. to Great Britain	1828–29
Barry, William T.	Min. to Spain	1835
Bayard, Thomas F.	Amb. to Great Britain	1893–97
Biddle, Francis B.	Del., Permanent Court of Arbitration, The Hague	n.a.
Blumenthal, W. Michael	Sp. Rep. for Trade	1963–67
Borie, Adolph	Consul to Belgium	1843

Buchanan, James	Min. to Russia	1832–34
Buchanan, James	Min. to Great Britain	1853–56
Bush, George H.	Amb. to U.N.	1971–73
Bush, George H.	Liaison Office to China	1974–75
Cameron, Simon	Min. to Russia	1862–63
Campbell, George W.	Min. to Russia	1818–20
Carlucci, Frank C., III	Vice Consul, Union of South Africa	1956–60
Carlucci, Frank C., III	Vice Consul, Congo	1960–62
Carlucci, Frank C., III	Head, Congo Desk	1962–65
Carlucci, Frank C., III	Amb. to Brazil	1965–69
Carlucci, Frank C., III	Amb. to Portugal	1974–77
Carlucci, Frank C., III	Deputy Dir. CIA	1978–81
Cass, Lewis	Min. to France	1836–42
Clifford, Nathan	Min. to Mexico	1848–53
Cohen, Wilbur J.	Consultant to U.N.	1956–57
Corwin, Thomas	Min. to Mexico	1861–64
Crawford, William H.	Min. to France	1813–15
Cushing, Caleb	Min. to China	1843–45
Cushing, Caleb	Min. to Spain	1874–77
Dallas, George M.	Min. to Russia	1837–39
Dallas, George M.	Min. to Great Britain	1856–61
Daniels, Josephus	Amb. to Mexico	1933–41
Davis, Dwight F.	Gov.-Gen., Philippines	1929–32
Dawes, Charles G.	Amb. to Great Britain	1929–32
Dawes, Charles G.	Del. to London Naval Conf.	1930
Dearborn, Henry	Min. to Portugal	1822–24
Dickinson, Donald McD.	Counsel to Comm. on Bering Sea Claims	1896
Dickinson, Donald McD.	U.S.-El Salvador Court of Arbitration	1902
Dickinson, Jacob McG.	U.S. Counsel to Alaskan Boundary Tribunal	1903
Dillon, C. Douglas	Amb. Extraordinary Plenipot. to France	1953–57
Dix, John A.	Min. to France	1866–69
Dulles, John F.	Amer. Comt. to Negotiate Peace	1918–19
Dulles, John F.	Reparations Comt.	1919
Dulles, John F.	Supreme Economic Council	1919
Dulles, John F.	Berlin Dept. Conference	1933

Dulles, John F.	San Fran. Conference on World Organization	1945
Dulles, John F.	Advisor, Council of Foreign Ministers, London	1945
Dulles, John F.	Advisor, Council of Foreign Ministers, Moscow and London	1947
Dulles, John F.	Council of Foreign Ministers, Paris	1949
Dulles, John F.	U.N. Representative	1946–49
Dulles, John F.	U.S. Del. to France	1948; 1950
Dulles, John F.	Amb. to Peace Treaty Negotiations	1950–51
Eaton, John H.	Min. to Spain	1836–40
Evarts, William M.	Envoy to Great Britain	1863–64
Evarts, William M.	Del. to International Monetary Conference, Paris	1881
Everett, Edward	Min. to Great Britain	1841–45
Fairbanks, Charles W.	U.S.-British Joint High Comm.	1898
Folsom, Marion B.	Del. to International Labor Conference, Geneva	1936
Forsyth, John	Min. to Spain	1819–23
Forward, Walter	Chargé d'affaires, Denmark	1849–51
Foster, John W.	Min. to Mexico	1873
Foster, John W.	Min. to Russia	1880–81
Foster, John W.	Min. to Spain	1883
Foster, John W.	Agent to Madrid Treaty Negotiations	1890
Foster, John W.	Agent to Bering Sea Arbitration	n.a.
Foster, John W.	Second Hague Conference	1907
Fowler, Henry H.	U.S. Mission of Economic Affairs in London	1944
Fowler, Henry H.	Foreign Economic Admin.	1945
Francis, David R.	Amb. to Russia	1916
Gallatin, Albert	Negotiator for Treaty of Ghent	1814

Gallatin, Albert	Min. to France	1815–23
Goldberg, Arthur J.	U.N. Representative	1965–68
Gregory, Thomas W.	Advisor to Versailles Peace Conference	*ca.* 1917
Griggs, John W.	Permanent Court of Arbitration, The Hague	1901–02
Hamlin, Hannibal	Min. to Spain	1881–82
Hardin, Clifford M.	Del. to International Conference of Agricultural Economists	1947
Harriman, William A.	Amb. to U.S.S.R.	1943–46
Harriman, William A.	Amb. to Great Britain	1946
Harriman, William A.	U.S. Representative in Europe	1946
Harriman, William A.	Amb. Extraordinary	1948–50
Harriman, William A.	NATO Defense Representative	1951
Harriman, William A.	Amb.-at-large	1961; 1965
Harriman, William A.	Peace talks Representative on Vietnam	1968–69
Harris, Patricia R.	Amb. to Luxembourg	1965–67
Harrison, William H.	Min. to Columbia	1828–29
Hay, John M.	Min. to Great Britain	1897–98
Herter, Christian A.	Del. in Brussels	1917
Herter, Christian A.	American Comm. for Peace with Germany	1918
Hitchcock, Ethan A.	Min. to Russia	1897
Hoover, Herbert C.	American Relief Comt., London	1914–15
Hoover, Herbert C.	Comm. for Relief of Belgium	1915–19
Hoover, Herbert C.	Supreme Economic Conference, Paris	1919
Hopkins, Harry L.	Del. to London	1940; 1941
Hopkins, Harry L.	Del. to U.S.S.R.	1941
Hughes, Charles E.	Del., Permanent Court of Arbitration, The Hague	1926–30
Hughes, Charles E.	Del. to Pan-American Conference	1928
Hull, Cordell	Pan-American Conference	1940

Hull, Cordell	Del. to U.N. Conf., San Francisco	1945
Humphrey, Hubert H., Jr.	Del. to U.N.	1956–58
Hunt, William H.	Min. to Russia	1882–84
Hurley, Patrick J.	Min. to New Zealand	1942
Hurley, Patrick J.	Presidential Rep. to U.S.S.R.	n.a.
Hurley, Patrick J.	Amb. to China	1944–45
Jardine, William M.	Min. to Egypt	1930–33
Jay, John	Min. to Spain	1780
Jay, John	British peace negotiations	1782
Jay, John	Envoy to Great Britain	1794
Jefferson, Thomas	Min. Plenipot. to France	1784–87
Jewell, Marshall	Min. to Russia	1873
Johnson, Cave	Commr., U.S.-Paraguay Dispute	1860
Johnson, Louis A.	Rep. to India	1942
Johnson, Reverdy	Min. to Great Britain	1868–69
Kellogg, Frank B.	Del. to International Conference on American States	1923
Kellogg, Frank B.	Min. to Great Britain	1923–25
Kellogg, Frank B.	Del., Permanent Court for International Justice	1930–35
King, William R. deV.	Secy. of U.S. Legation, Naples	1816
King, William R. deV.	Secy. of U.S. Legation, Russia	1818
King, William R. deV.	Min. to France	1844–46
Klutznick, Philip M.	U.N. Delegate	1957
Klutznick, Philip M.	U.N. Amb.	1961–63
Lansing, Robert	Anglo-American Claims Arbitration	1912–14
Lansing, Robert	American Comm. to negotiate peace	1918–19
Legaré, Hugh S.	Chargé d'affaires, Belgium	1832–36
Lincoln, Robert T.	Min. to Great Britain	1889–93
Livingston, Edward	Min. to France	1833–35
McLane, Louis	Min. to Great Britain	1829–31; 1845–46

MacVeagh, Wayne	Min. to Turkey	1870–72
MacVeagh, Wayne	Amb. to Italy	1893–97
MacVeagh, Wayne	Counsel to Venezuela Arb.	1903
Marshall, James W.	Consul at Leeds, England	1861–65
Marshall, John	Min. to France	1797
Mason, John Y.	Min. to France	1854–59
Maynard, Horace	Min. to Turkey	1875–80
Mellon, Andrew W.	Amb. to Great Britain	1932–33
Meyer, George von L.	Amb. to Italy	1900–05
Meyer, George von L.	Amb. to Russia	1905–07
Monroe, James	Min. to France	1794–99
Monroe, James	Min. to Great Britain	1803–07
Morton, Levi P.	Commr. to Paris Exhibition	1878
Morton, Levi P.	Min. to France	1881–85
Murphy, Frank	Gov.-Gen. of Philippines	1935–36
Nelson, John	Chargé d'affaires, Two Sicilies	1831–32
Payne, John B.	Commr. to Mexico	1923
Pierrepont, Edward S.	Min. to Great Britain	1876–77
Pinkney, William	Commr. to Great Britain	1796
Pinkney, William	Min. to London	1807–11
Pinkney, William	Min. to Russia	1816–18
Pinkney, William	Spec. envoy to Naples	1816–18
Poinsett, Joel R.	Min. to Mexico	1825–29
Preston, William B.	Envoy to France	1858
Randall, Alexander W.	Min. to Italy	1862–63
Rodney, Caesar A.	Commr. to South America	n.a.
Rodney, Caesar A.	Min. to Argentina	1823–24
Root, Elihu	U.S. Counsel, North Atlantic Fisheries Dispute	1910
Root, Elihu	Envoy to Russia	1917
Root, Elihu	Commr. at Washington Conf. on Armaments Limitations	1921–22
Roper, Daniel C.	Min. to Canada	1839
Rumsfeld, Donald	Amb. to NATO	1973–74
Rush, Richard	Min. to Great Britain	1817
Rush, Richard	Min. to France	1847
Sawyer, Charles	Amb. to Belgium and Luxembourg	1944–46

Saxbe, William	Amb. to India	1974–
Schofield, John McA.	Mission to France	1865–66
Schofield, John McA.	Mission to Hawaii	1872
Schurz, Carl	Min. to Spain	1862
Schwellenbach, Lewis B.	Del. to Interparliamentary Union, The Hague	1936
Sherman, William T.	Envoy to Mexico	1866
Smith, Charles Emory	Min. to Russia	1890–92
Stettinius, Edwin R., Jr.	Chief U.S. del. to U.N. Conf., San Francisco	1945
Stettinius, Edwin R., Jr.	Del. to U.N.	1945–46
Stimson, Henry L.	Envoy to Nicaragua	1927
Stimson, Henry L.	Gov.-Gen., Philippines	1927–29
Stimson, Henry L.	Del., Intl. Ct. of Arbitration, The Hague	1938–40
Straus, Oscar S.	Min. to Turkey	1887–89; 1898– 1900; 1902; 1908; 1909–10
Straus, Oscar S.	Del., Permanent Ct. of Arbitration, The Hague	1912; 1920
Strauss, Lewis L.	Del. to Armistice Convention, Brussels	1919
Swanson, Claude	Del. to Gen. Disarmament Conference	1932
Taft, Alphonso	Min. to Austria-Hungary	n.a.
Taft, Alphonso	Min. to Russia	1884–85
Van Buren, Martin	Min. to Great Britain	1831–32
Walker, Frank C.	Alt. Del. to U.N.	1946
Walker, Frank C.	Rep. to U.N. Legal Comt.	1946
Walker, Robert J.	Financial agt. to Europe	1863–64
Washburne, Elihu B.	Min. to France	1869–72
Wickersham, George	League of Nations Comt. to Codify Internatl. Law	n.a.
Wickersham, George	Pres., Internatl. Arbitral Tribunal, Young Plan	n.a.

Wickliffe, Charles A.	Envoy to Repub. of Texas	1845
Wilbur, Ray L.	Del. to Pan-American Conf.	1928
Wilkins, William	Min. to Russia	1834–35
Williams, George H.	Joint High Comm.	1871
Wright, Luke E.	Vice-Gov., Philippines	1901–04
Wright, Luke E.	Gov.-Gen., Philippines	1904–06
Wright, Luke E.	Amb. to Japan	1906–07
Wynne, Robert J.	Consul-Gen. to Great Britain	1905

State, County, and Municipal Government Service

STATE ADMINISTRATIVE SERVICE

Name	Office	State	Dates
Agnew, Spiro T.	Governor	Md.	1967–69
Alger, Russell A.	Governor	Mich.	1885–87
Anderson, Clinton P.	Treasurer	N.M.	1933–34
Anderson, Robert B.	Asst. Atty. Gen.	Tex.	1933–34
Andrus, Cecil D.	Governor	Ida.	1970–77
Armstrong, John	Secy.	Pa.	1783–87
Barbour, James	Governor	Va.	1813–15
Barry, William T.	Lt. Governor	Ky.	1820–22
Barry, William T.	Secy. of State	Ky.	1824–25
Bates, Edward	State's Atty.	Mo.	1820–22
Bell, Griffin B.	Chf. of Staff	Ga.	1959–61
Bell, Terrel H.	Comm. of Education	Utah	1976–80
Block, John R.	Dir. Dept. of Agric.	Ill.	1977–80
Boutwell, George S.	Governor	Mass.	1851–52
Bowen, Otis R.	Governor	Ind.	1973–81
Bradford, William	Atty. Gen.	Pa.	1780–91
Branch, John	Governor	N.C.	1817–20

Branch, John	Territorial Governor	Fla.	1844–45
Breckinridge, John	Atty. Gen.	Ky.	1795–97
Brewster, Benjamin H.	Atty. Gen.	Pa.	1867–68
Brown, Aaron V.	Governor	Tenn.	1845–47
Burleson, Albert S.	Dist. Atty.	Tex.	1891–98
Burr, Aaron	Atty. Gen.	N.Y.	1789–90
Byrnes, James F.	Solicitor of 2d Judicial Court	S.C.	1908
Byrnes, James F.	Governor	S.C.	1950–53
Campbell, James	Atty. Gen.	Pa.	1852
Carlisle, John G.	Lt. Governor	Ky.	1871–75
Carter, Jimmy	Governor	Ga.	1971–74
Chase, Salmon P.	Governor	Ohio	1855–59
Clayton, John M.	Secy. of State	Del.	1826–28
Cleveland, Grover	Governor	N.Y.	1883–85
Clifford, Nathan	Atty. Gen.	Me.	1834–38
Clinton, George	Governor	N.Y.	1777–97
Connally, John B.	Governor	Tex.	1962–69
Coolidge, Calvin	Lt. Governor	Mass.	1916–18
Coolidge, Calvin	Governor	Mass.	1919–20
Corwin, Thomas	Governor	Ohio	1840–42
Cox, Jacob Dolson	Governor	Ohio	1866–68
Crawford, G. W.	Atty. Gen.	Ga.	1827–31
Crittenden, John J.	Governor	Ky.	1848–50
Crittenden, John J.	Territorial Atty. Gen.	Ill.	1809–10
Dallas, Alexander	Secy. of State	Pa.	1791–1801
Dern, George H.	Governor	Utah	1924–32
Dickerson, Mahlon	Adj. Gen.	Pa.	1805–08
Dickerson, Mahlon	Governor	N.J.	1815–17
Dix, John A.	Adj. Gen.	N.Y.	1830
Dix, John A.	Secy. of State	N.Y.	1833–39
Dix, John A.	Postmaster	N.Y.	1860–61
Dix, John A.	Governor	N.Y.	1872–74
Eaton, John H.	Territorial Governor	Fla.	1834–36
Edison, Charles	Governor	N.J.	1940–44
Edwards, James	Governor	S.C.	1975–78
Eustis, William	Governor	Mass.	1823–25
Everett, Edward	Governor	Mass.	1836–40
Fairchild, Charles S.	Dep. Atty. Gen.	N.Y.	1874–75
Fairchild, Charles S.	Atty. Gen.	N.Y.	1875–77

Fillmore, Millard	Comptroller	N.Y.	1847–49
Finch, Robert H.	Lt. Governor	Calif.	1966–68
Fish, Hamilton	Lt. Governor	N.Y.	1847
Fish, Hamilton	Governor	N.Y.	1849–51
Floyd, John B.	Governor	Va.	1850–52
Forsyth, John	Atty. Gen.	Va.	1808
Forsyth, John	Governor	Ga.	1827–29
Foster, Charles	Governor	Ohio	1879–81
Francis, David R.	Governor	Mo.	1888–93
Freeman, Orville L.	Governor	Minn.	1955–61
Frelinghuysen, Frederick T.	Atty. Gen.	N.J.	1861–66
Garland, Augustus H.	Acting Secy. of State	Ark.	1874
Garland, Augustus H.	Governor	Ark.	1875–77
Gerry, Elbridge	Governor	Mass.	1810–12
Gilmer, Thomas W.	Governor	Va.	1840–41
Gore, Howard M.	Governor	W.Va.	1925–29
Graham, William A.	Governor	N.C.	1845–49
Griggs, John W.	Governor	N.J.	1896–98
Guthrie, James	Commonwealth Atty.	Ky.	1820
Hamilton, Paul	Comptroller	S.C.	1799–1804
Hamilton, Paul	Governor	S.C.	1804–06
Hamlin, Hannibal	Governor	Me.	1856–57
Hancock, John	Governor	Mass.	1780–85 1787–93
Harding, Warren G.	Lt. Governor	Ohio	1904–05
Harmon, Judson	Governor	Ohio	1908–13
Hathaway, Stanley K.	Governor	Wyo.	1962–64
Hayes, Rutherford B.	Governor	Ohio	1868–77; 1876–77
Hendricks, Thomas A.	Governor	Ind.	1873–77
Herter, Christian A.	Governor	Mass.	1953–57
Hickel, Walter J.	Governor	Alaska	1966–68
Hodges, Luther H.	Lt. Governor	N.C.	1952–54
Hodges, Luther H.	Governor	N.C.	1954–61
Hughes, Charles E.	Governor	N.Y.	1906–10

Hunt, William H.	Atty. Gen.	La.	1876
Huntington, Samuel	Lt. Governor	Conn.	1785
Huntington, Samuel	Governor	Conn.	1786–96
Hyde, Arthur M.	Governor	Mo.	1921–25
Ingham, Samuel D.	Secy. of Commonwealth	Pa.	1819–20
Jardine, William M.	Treasurer	Kans.	1933–34
Jay, John	Governor	N.Y.	1795–1801
Jefferson, Thomas	Governor	Va.	1779–81
Jewell, Marshall	Governor	Conn.	1869–74
Johnson, Andrew	Governor	Tenn.	1853–57
Johnson, Reverdy	Dep. Atty. Gen.	Md.	1816–17
Key, David McK.	Chancellor	Tenn.	1870–75
Kirkwood, Samuel J.	Governor	Iowa	1859–63; 1875–77
Landrieu, Moon E.	House of Rep.	La.	1959–53; 1966–70
Legaré, Hugh S.	Atty. Gen.	S.C.	1830–32
Lincoln, Levi	Lt. Governor	Mass.	1807–08
Lincoln, Levi	Governor	Mass.	1808–09
Lincoln, Levi	Governor's Council	Mass.	1806; 1810–12
Long, John D.	Lt. Governor	Mass.	1879
Long, John D.	Governor	Mass.	1880–82
Lyng, Richard E.	Dir. Dept. of Agric.	Calif.	1967–69
McClelland, Robert	Governor	Mich.	1850–54
McGrath, James H.	Governor	R.I.	1940–45
McKay, Douglas J.	Governor	Ore.	1948–52
McKean, Thomas	Governor	Pa.	1799–1808
McKennan, Thomas M. T.	Dep. Atty. Gen.	Pa.	1815–17
McKinley, William, Jr.	Governor	Ohio	1892–96
Marcy, William L.	Comptroller	N.Y.	1823
Marcy, William L.	Governor	N.Y.	1833–39
Marshall, Thomas R.	Governor	Ind.	1908–13
Maynard, Horace	Atty. Gen.	Tenn.	1863–65
Meese, Edwin, III	Chf. of Staff	Calif.	1975–76
Meigs, Return J., Jr.	Governor	Ohio	1808*; 1810–14

*Elected but never served.

Meredith, William M.	Atty. Gen.	Pa.	1861–67
Mifflin, Thomas	Governor	Pa.	1790–99
Monroe, James	Governor	Va.	1799–1802; 1811
Morrill, Lot M.	Governor	Me.	1858–61
Morton, Julius S.	Secy. of the Territory	Nebr.	1858–61
Muskie, Edmund S.	Governor	Me.	1955–59
Osgood, Samuel	State Supervisor	N.Y.	1801–03
Pinkney, William	Exec. Council	Md.	1792–95
Polk, James K.	Governor	Tenn.	1839–41
Porter, Peter B.	Secy. of State	N.Y.	1815–16
Proctor, Redfield	Lt. Governor	Vt.	1876–78
Proctor, Redfield	Governor	Vt.	1878–80
Quayle, Danforth	Consumer Protect. Agency	Ind.	1970–71
Quayle, Danforth	Admin. Assist. to Governor	Ind.	1971–73
Ramsey, Alexander	Territorial Governor	Minn.	1849–53
Ramsey, Alexander	Governor	Minn.	1859–63
Randall, Alexander W.	Governor	Wisc.	1857–61
Randolph, Edmund J.	Atty. Gen.	Va.	1776–82
Randolph, Edmund J.	Governor	Va.	1786–88
Reagan, Ronald W.	Governor	Calif.	1967–75
Richardson, Elliot L.	Lt. Governor	Mass.	1965–67
Richardson, Elliot L.	Atty. Gen.	Mass.	1967–69
Robeson, George	Atty. Gen.	N.J.	1867–69
Rockefeller, Nelson A.	Governor	N.Y.	1959–73
Romney, George W.	Governor	Mich.	1963–68
Roosevelt, Franklin D.	Governor	N.Y.	1928–33
Rush, Richard	Atty. Gen.	Pa.	1811
Rusk, Jeremiah McL.	Bank Comptroller	Wisc.	1866–69
Rusk, Jeremiah McL.	Governor	Wisc.	1882–89
St. Clair, Arthur	Territorial Governor Terr.	N.W.	1787–1802

Sargent, John G.	Secy. of Civil and Military Affairs	Vt.	1900–02
Sawyer, Charles	Lt. Governor	Ohio	1933–34
Seward, William H.	Governor	N.Y.	1838–42
Smith, Hoke	Governor	N.C.	1907–09; 1911
Southard, Samuel L.	Atty. Gen.	N.J.	1829–33
Southard, Samuel L.	Governor	N.J.	1832–33
Spencer, John C.	Asst. Atty. Gen.	N.Y.	1815
Spencer, John C.	Secy. of State	N.Y.	1839
Stanbery, Henry	Atty. Gen.	Ohio	1846
Stevenson, Adlai E.	Dist. Atty.	Ill.	1865–69
Swanson, Claude	Governor	Va.	1906–10
Taney, Roger	Atty. Gen.	Md.	1827
Thomas, Philip F.	Governor	Md.	1848–51
Thornburgh, Richard L.	Governor	Pa.	1979–87
Tobin, Maurice J.	Governor	Mass.	1945–48
Tompkins, Daniel D.	Governor	N.Y.	1807–16
Toucey, Isaac	State Atty.	Conn.	1842–44
Toucey, Isaac	Governor	Conn.	1846–47
Tyler, John	Exec. Council	Va.	1815–16
Tyler, John	Governor	Va.	1825–27
Van Buren, Martin	Atty. Gen.	N.Y.	1815–19
Van Buren, Martin	Governor	N.Y.	1829
Vinson, Frederick M.	Dist. Atty.	Ky.	1921–24
Volpe, John A.	Governor	Mass.	1960–62; 1967–68
Walker, Robert J.	Territorial Governor	Kans.	1857
Welles, Gideon	Comptroller of Public Accounts	Conn.	1835; 1842; 1843
Wheeler, William A.	Dist. Atty.	N.Y.	1846–49
Wickliffe, Charles A.	Lt. Governor	Mo.	1836–39
Wickliffe, Charles A.	Governor	Mo.	1839–40
Wilson, Woodrow	Governor	N.J.	1911–13
Wirt, William	Chancellor	Va.	1802
Woodbury, Levi	Governor	N.H.	1823–24
Woodring, Henry H.	Governor	Kans.	1930–32
Wright, Luke E.	Atty. Gen.	Tenn.	1870–78

| Yeutter, Clayton K. | Asst. to Governor | Nebr. | 1968–70 |

STATE LEGISLATIVE SERVICE

Name	Office	State	Dates
Alexander, Joshua W.	House	Mo.	1883–87
Barbour, James	House	Va.	1798–1812
Barry, William T.	House	Ky.	1809–12; 1814–15
Barry, William T.	Senate	Ky.	1817–20
Bates, Edward	House	Mo.	1822; 1834
Bates, Edward	Senate	Mo.	1830–34
Belknap, William W.	House	Iowa	1857–58
Bell, John	Senate	Tenn.	1817
Berrien, John M.	Senate	Ga.	1822–23
Bibb, George M.	House	Ky.	1817
Blaine, James G.	House	Me.	1859–62
Boutwell, George S.	House	Mass.	1842–50
Branch, John	Senate	N.C.	1811; 1813–17
Breckinridge, John	House	Ky.	1798–1800
Breckinridge, John C.	House	Ky.	1849–51
Bristow, Benjamin H.	Senate	Ky.	1863–65
Brown, Aaron V.	Senate	Tenn.	1821–25; 1826–27
Brown, Aaron V.	House	Tenn.	1831
Brownell, Herbert, Jr.	Assembly	N.Y.	1933–37
Browning, Orville H.	Senate	Ill.	1836–43
Buchanan, James	House	Pa.	1814–15
Burr, Aaron	Assembly	N.Y.	1784
Butler, Benjamin F.	Assembly	N.Y.	1827–33
Calhoun, John C.	House	S.C.	1808
Carlisle, John G.	House	Ky.	1859–61
Carlisle, John G.	Senate	Ky.	1867–71
Carter, Jimmy	Senate	Ga.	1962–66
Cass, Lewis	House	Ohio	1806
Celebrezze, Anthony J.	Senate	Ohio	1951–53
Chandler, William E.	House	N.H.	1863–67

Clay, Henry	House	Ky.	1803; 1808–09
Clayton, John M.	House	Del.	1824
Clifford, Nathan	House	Me.	1830–34
Colby, Bainbridge	Assembly	N.Y.	1901
Collamer, Jacob	House	Vt.	1821–22; 1827–28
Colman, Norman J.	House	Mo.	1865
Conrad, Charles M.	House	La.	1830–42
Coolidge, Calvin	House	Vt.	1907–08
Coolidge, Calvin	Senate	Mass.	1912–15
Corwin, Thomas	House	Ohio	1821; 1822; 1829
Cox, Jacob D., Jr.	Senate	Ohio	1858
Crawford, George W.	House	Ohio	1837–42
Crawford, William H.	House	Ga.	1803–07
Creswell, John A. J.	House	Md.	1861–62
Crittenden, John J.	House	Ky.	1811–17; 1825; 1829
Crowninshield, Benjamin W.	House	Mass.	1811; 1833
Crowninshield, Benjamin W.	Senate	Mass.	1812; 1822
Cushing, Caleb	House	Mass.	1825; 1850
Cushing, Caleb	Senate	Mass.	1826
Daugherty, Harry	House	Ohio	1890–94
Davis, Dwight F.	House	Mo.	1907–09
Delano, Columbus	House	Ohio	1863
Denby, Edwin	House	Mich.	1903
Dennison, William	Senate	Ohio	1848
Dern, George H.	Senate	Utah	1914–23
Derwinski, Edward J.	House	Ill.	1957–58
Dexter, Samuel	House	Mass.	1788–90
Devens, Charles	Senate	Mass.	1848–49
Dickerson, Mahlon	Assembly	N.J.	1811–13
Dix, John A.	Assembly	N.Y.	1841
Dobbin, James C.	House (of Commons)	N.C.	1848; 1850; 1852
Duane, William J.	House	Pa.	1809; 1819
Eaton, John H.	House	Tenn.	1815; 1816
Edwards, James	Senate	S.C.	1972–74
Eustis, William	House	Mass.	1788–94
Fessenden, William P.	House	Me.	1831; 1839
Fillmore, Millard	Assembly	N.Y.	1829–31

Floyd, John B.	House	Va.	1847–49
Folger, Charles J.	Senate	N.Y.	1861–69
Gallatin, Albert	House	Pa.	1790–92
Garfield, James R.	Senate	Ohio	1896–99
Garner, John N.	House	Tex.	1898–1902
Gerry, Elbridge	House	Mass.	1786
Gilmer, Thomas W.	House	Va.	1829–36; 1838–39
Glass, Carter	Senate	Va.	1889; 1901
Goff, Nathan	House	Va.	1867
Graham, William A.	House	N.C.	1833–40; 1854
Granger, Francis	Assembly	N.Y.	1826–28; 1830–32
Granger, Gideon	House	Conn.	1792–1801
Granger, Gideon	Senate	N.Y.	1820–21
Gresham, Walter Q.	House	Ind.	1860
Griggs, John W.	Assembly	N.J.	1876–78
Griggs, John W.	Senate	N.J.	1882–86
Grundy, Felix	House	Ky.	1800–05
Grundy, Felix	House	Tenn.	1819–25
Gorham, Nathaniel	Senate	Mass.	1780–81
Gorham, Nathaniel	House	Mass.	1781–87
Guthrie, James	House	Ky.	1827–29
Guthrie, James	Senate	Ky.	1831–40
Habersham, Joseph	House	Ga.	1785; 1790
Hall, Nathan K.	Assembly	N.Y.	1846
Hamilton, Alexander	Assembly	N.Y.	1787
Hamilton, Paul	House	S.C.	1787–89
Hamilton, Paul	Senate	S.C.	1794; 1798–99
Hamlin, Hannibal	House	Me.	1836–41; 1847
Hannegan, Robert E.	House	Mo.	1935
Hanson, John	Assembly	Md.	1756–77
Hanson, John	Senate	Md.	n.a.
Harding, Warren G.	Senate	Ohio	1899–1903
Hendricks, Thomas A.	House	Ind.	1848
Henshaw, David	House	Mass.	1826; 1830; 1839
Herter, Christian A.	House	Mass.	1931–43
Hoar, Ebenezer R.	Senate	Mass.	1846
Hobart, Garret A.	Assembly	N.J.	1872–76
Hobart, Garret A.	Senate	N.J.	1876–82
Hobby, Oveta C.	House	Tex.	1925–31; 1939–41
Howe, Timothy O.	House	Me.	1845

Hull, Cordell	House	Tenn.	1893–97
Ingham, Samuel D.	House	Pa.	1806
Johnson, Andrew	House	Tenn.	1835–37; 1838–41
Johnson, Louis A.	House	W.Va.	1916–24
Johnson, Reverdy	Senate	Md.	1824–28
Johnson, Richard M.	House	Ky.	1804–07; 1819; 1841–42; 1850
Kennedy, John P.	House	Md.	1821–23
King, William R. deV.	House	N.C.	1807–09
Kirkwood, Samuel J.	Senate	Iowa	1856–59
Kleindienst, Richard G.	House	Ariz.	1953–54
Laird, Melvin R.	Senate	Wisc.	1946–50
Lee, Charles	Assembly	Va.	1793–95
Legaré, Hugh S.	House	S.C.	1820–22; 1824–29
Lincoln, Abraham	House	Ill.	1834–42
Lincoln, Levi	House	Mass.	1796
Lincoln, Levi	Senate	Mass.	1797–98
Livingston, Edward	House	La.	1820
Long, John D.	House	Mass.	1875–77
McCrary, George W.	House	Iowa	1857–59
McCrary, George W.	Senate	Iowa	1861–65
McHenry, James	Senate	Md.	1781–86
McKay, Douglas J.	Senate	Ore.	1934–49
Madison, James	House	Va.	1783–86
Marshall, John	Assembly	Va.	1782–87; 1788–91; 1797
Mason, John Y.	Assembly	Va.	1823–31
Meigs, Return J., Jr.	Rep. to Terr. Legislature	Ohio	1799
Meredith, William M.	House	Pa.	1824–28
Meyer, George von L.	House	Mass.	1892–97
Middleton, Henry	Congress	S.C.	1775–76
Middleton, Henry	Senate	S.C.	1778–80
Mifflin, Thomas	House	Pa.	1785–88; 1799–1800
Mills, Ogden L.	Senate	N.Y.	1914–17
Monroe, James	Assembly	Va.	1782; 1786; 1810–11

Morrill, Lot M.	House	Me.	1854–56
Morrill, Lot M.	Senate	Me.	1856–58
Morton, Julius S.	Territorial	Nebr. Legislature	1855–56; 1857–58
Muskie, Edmund S.	House	Me.	1947–51
Nagel, Charles	Legislature	Mo.	1881
New, Harry S.	Senate	Ind.	1896–1900
Olney, Richard	Legislature	Mass.	1873
Osgood, Samuel	Legislature	Mass.	*ca.* 1775–80
Osgood, Samuel	Senate	Mass.	1780–81
Osgood, Samuel	House	Mass.	1784
Osgood, Samuel	Assembly	N.Y.	1800–03
Pierce, Franklin	House	N.H.	1829–33
Pinkney, William	House of Delegates	Md.	1788–92
Pinkney, William	Legislature	Md.	1795
Pinkney, William	Senate	Md.	1811
Poinsett, Joel R.	House	S.C.	1816–20
Polk, James K.	House	Tenn.	1823–25
Porter, James M.	House	Pa.	1849–53
Porter, Peter B.	Assembly	N.Y.	1802; 1828
Preston, William B.	House of Delegates	Va.	1830–32; 1844–45
Preston, William B.	House of Delegates	Va.	1830–32; 1844–45
Preston, William B.	Senate	Va.	1840–45
Proctor, Redfield	House	Vt.	1867–68; 1888–89
Proctor, Redfield	Senate	Vt.	1874–75
Randolph, Edmund J.	Assembly	Va.	1888–89
Randolph, Peyton	Legislature	Va.	1774–75
Ribicoff, Abraham A.	House	Conn.	1938–42
Rodney, Caesar A.	Senate	Del.	1815
Roosevelt, Franklin D.	Senate	N.Y.	1911–13
Roosevelt, Theodore	Assembly	N.Y.	1882–84
Roper, Daniel C.	House	S.C.	1892–93
Royall, Kenneth C.	Senate	N.C.	1927
Rusk, Jeremiah McL.	Assembly	Wisc.	1862
Saxbe, William	House	Ohio	1947–54
Seaton, Frederick A.	Legislature	Nebr.	1945–49
Seward, William H.	Senate	N.Y.	1830–34

Smith, Caleb	House	Ind.	1832–37; 1840–41
Smith, Robert	Senate	Md.	1793–95
Smith, Robert	House of Delegates	Md.	1796–1800
Southard, Samuel L.	General Assembly	N.J.	1815
Speed, James	Legislature	Ky.	1847
Speed, James	Senate	Ky.	1861–63
Spencer, John C.	Assembly	N.Y.	1820–21; 1830–31
Spencer, John C.	Senate	N.Y.	1824–28
Stuart, Alexander H. H.	House of Delegates	Va.	1836–39; 1847–82
Taney, Roger	Legislature	Md.	1799–1801
Taney, Roger	Senate	Md.	1816–21
Thomas, Philip F.	House	Md.	1838; 1843; 1845; 1863; 1878–83
Thompson, Richard W.	House	Ind.	1834–36
Thompson, Richard W.	Senate	Ind.	1836–38
Thompson, Smith	Legislature	N.Y.	1800
Tobin, Maurice J.	House	Mass.	1926–28
Tompkins, Daniel D.	Assembly	N.Y.	1803
Toucey, Isaac	Senate	Conn.	1850–52
Toucey, Isaac	House	Conn.	1852–57
Tracy, Benjamin F.	Assembly	N.Y.	1861
Tyler, John	House of Delegates	Va.	1811–16; 1823–25; 1838–40
Upshur, Abel P.	House of Delegates	Va.	1812–13; 1824–27
Upshur, John P.	Legislature	Ind.	1850–51
Van Buren, Martin	Senate	N.Y.	1813–20
Vilas, William F.	Assembly	Wisc.	1885
Walker, Frank C.	Legislature	Mont.	1913
Weinberger, Caspar W.	Legislature	Calif.	1952–58
Welles, Gideon	Legislature	Conn.	1827–35
Wheeler, William A.	State Assembly	N.Y.	1850–51
Wheeler, William A.	Senate	N.Y.	1858–60
Wickliffe, Charles A.	House	Ky.	1812–13; 1822; 1823; 1833; 1835
Wilkins, William	House	Pa.	1820
Wilkins, William	Senate	Pa.	1855–57
Wilson, Henry	House	Mass.	1841–42
Wilson, Henry	Senate	Mass.	1844–46; 1850–52

Wilson, James	House	Iowa	1867–71
Woodbury, Levi	House	N.H.	1825

STATE JUDICIAL SERVICE

Name	Office	State	Dates
Badger, George E.	Superior Ct.	N.C.	1820–25
Barry, William T.	Ct. of Appeals (Chf. Justice)	Ky.	1825–29
Berrien, John M.	Supreme Ct.	Ga.	1845
Bibb, George M.	Ct. of Appeals (Chf. Justice, 1809–10)	Ky.	1808–10
Bibb, George M.	Ct. of Appeals (Chf. Justice)	Ky.	1828
Black, Jeremiah	Supreme Ct. (Chf. Justice, 1851–54)	Pa.	1851–57
Bradford, William	Supreme Ct.	Pa.	1791–94
Branch, John	Territorial Judge	Fla.	1822
Campbell, George W.	Supreme Ct. of Errors and Appeals	Tenn.	1809–11
Campbell, James	Ct. of Common Pleas	Pa.	1842–52
Clayton, Henry M.	Chf. Justice	Del.	1837–39
Collamer, Jacob	Supreme Ct.	Vt.	1833–42
Day, William R.	Ct. of Common Pleas	Ohio	1886
Devens, Charles	Superior Ct.	Mass.	1867–73
Devens, Charles	Supreme Ct.	Mass.	1873–77; 1881–91
Dickinson, Jacob M.	Supreme Ct.	Tenn.	1891–93
Endicott, William C.	Supreme Ct.	Mass.	1873–82
Folger, Charles S.	State Ct. of Appeals	N.Y.	1870
Garrison, Lindley M.	Vice-chancellor	N.J.	1904–13
Grundy, Felix	Supreme Ct. of Errors and Appeals	Ky.	1806
Grundy, Felix	Supreme Ct. (Chf. Justice)	Ky.	1807
Hall, Nathan K.	Master in Chancery	N.Y.	1839

Harlan, James	2d Ct. of Claims	Ala.	1882–86
Hoar, Ebenezer R.	Ct. of Common Appeals	Mass.	1849–55
Hoar, Ebenezer R.	Supreme Judicial Ct.	Mass.	1859–69
Howe, Timothy O.	4th Circ. and Supreme Ct.	Wisc.	1850–53
Hufstedler, Shirley M.	Los Angeles Superior Ct.	Calif.	1961–66
Hufstedler, Shirley M.	Calif. Ct. of Appeals	Calif.	1966–68
Hull, Cordell	5th State Judicial Ct.	Tenn.	1903–07
Jackson, Andrew	Supreme Ct.	Tenn.	1798–1804
Jay, John	Supreme Ct.	N.Y.	1877–78
Johnson, Cave	Circ. Ct.	Tenn.	1820–29
Lincoln, Levi	Probate Ct.	Mass.	1771–81
McLean, John	Supreme Ct.	Ohio	1816–22
Marcy, William L.	Supreme Ct.	N.Y.	1829–31
Meigs, Return J., Jr.	Territorial Judge	Ohio	1798
Meigs, Return J., Jr.	Supreme Ct. (Chf. Justice)	Ohio	1803–04
Meigs, Return J., Jr.	Supreme Ct.	La.	1805–06
Nagel, Charles	Supreme Ct.	Mo.	1893
Pierce, Samuel R., Jr.	Court of General Sessions	N.Y.	1959–61
Porter, James M.	Dist. Ct.	Pa.	1839–40; 1853–55
Richardson, William A.	Ct. of Appeals	Mass.	1874
Southard, Samuel L.	Supreme Ct.	N.J.	1915–20
Spencer, John C.	Judge Advocate General	N.Y.	1813
Taft, William H.	Superior Ct.	Ohio	1887–90
Thomas, Philip F.	Land Office Ct.	Md.	1841
Thompson, Smith	Supreme Ct.	N.Y.	1802–19; 1823–43
Tompkins, Daniel D.	Supreme Ct.	N.Y.	1804–07
Tracy, Benjamin F.	Ct. of Appeals	N.Y.	1881–83
Upshur, Abel P.	General Ct.	Va.	1826–41
Wilbur, Curtis D.	Superior Ct.	Calif.	1919–21
Wilbur, Curtis D.	Supreme Ct.	Calif.	1922–27
Wilkins, William	Dist. Ct.	Pa.	1824
Williams, George H.	Dist. Ct.	Iowa	1847–52

Williams, George H.	Territorial Chf. Justice	Ore.	1853–57
Woodbury, Levi	Superior Ct.	N.H.	1816

STATE COMMISSIONS AND COMMITTEES

Commission or Name	Committee	State	Dates
Alexander, Joshua W.	Bd. of Mgrs., State Hospital	Mo.	1893–96
Alexander, Joshua W.	State Const. Conv.	Mo.	1922
Anderson, Clinton P.	Relief Admin.	N.M.	1935–36
Anderson, Clinton P.	Dir., Unemployment Compensation Comm.	N.M.	1936–38
Anderson, Robert B.	State Tax Comm.	Tex.	1934
Anderson, Robert B.	Dir., Unemployment Comm.	Tex.	1936
Anderson, Robert B.	Economy Comm.	Tex.	1938
Anderson, Robert B.	Chmn., Bd. of Education	Tex.	1949
Baldridge, Malcolm	Comm. on Status of Women	Conn.	1968
Bates, Edward	State Const. Conv.	Mo.	1820
Bell, Griffin B.	Chmn., Comm. on Crime Delinq.	Ga.	1965–66
Bergland, Robert S.	Chmn., Agric. Stabil. and Cons. Serv. Comm.	Minn.	1963–68
Boutwell, George S.	State Bank Comm.	Mass.	1849–51
Bowen, Otis R.	Public Health	Ind.	1961–65
Boyd, Alan S.	Railroad and Public Util. Comm.	Fla.	1957–58
Cavazos, Lauro F.	Higher Ed. Mgmt.	Tex.	1980–82
Conrad, Charles M.	State Const. Conv.	La.	1844

Day, James E.	Comm. on Intergov. Cooperation	Ill.	1949–53
Day, James E.	Insurance Comm.	Ill.	1950–53
Day, James E.	Gov.'s Comm. on Metropolitan Area Problems	Calif.	1959–61
Dickerson, Mahlon	Comm. on Bankruptcy	Pa.	1802
Dickerson, Mahlon	State Const. Conv.	N.J.	1844
Dix, John A.	Supt. of Common Schools	N.Y.	1833–39
Edison, Charles	State Recovery Bd.	N.J.	1933
Edwards, James	Comm. for Health Care Planning	S.C.	1968–72
Fall, Albert B.	State Const. Conv.	N.M.	1911
Gallatin, Albert	State Const. Conv.	Pa.	1790
Glass, Carter	State Const. Conv.	Va.	1901–02
Gore, Howard	Bd. of Education	W.Va.	1920–25
Gore, Howard	Commr. of Agriculture	W.Va.	1931–33
Gorham, Nathaniel	Bd. of War	Mass.	1778–81
Gronouski, John	Commr. of Taxation	Wisc.	1960–63
Grundy, Felix	State Const. Conv.	Ky.	1799
Hancock, John	State Const. Conv.	Mass.	1780
Hendricks, Thomas A.	State Const. Conv.	Ind.	1850
Hodges, Luther H.	Vocational Ed. Bd.	N.C.	1929–33
Hodges, Luther H.	State Highway Comm.	N.C.	1933–37
Hopkins, Harry L.	Depty. Chmn./ Chmn., Temp. Emergency Relief Admin.	N.Y.	1931–33
Jackson, Andrew	State Const. Conv.	Tenn.	1796
Jones, Jesse H.	Tex. Comm. for N.Y. World's Fair	Tex.	1939
Jones, Jesse H.	Tex. Cent. Celeb.	Tex.	1926–34
Key, David McK.	State Const. Conv.	Tenn.	1870
Kirkwood, Samuel J.	State Const. Conv.	Ohio	1850–51
Knox, W. Frank	State Publicity Comm.	N.H.	1922–24
Krug, Julius A.	Public Util. Comm.	Wisc.	1932

Krug, Julius A.	Public Serv. Comm.	Ky.	1937
Lincoln, Levi	State Const. Conv.	Mass.	1779
McClelland, Robert	State Const. Conv.	Mich.	1835; 1850; 1867
McLane, Louis	State Const. Conv.	Md.	1850–51
MacVeagh, Wayne	State Const. Conv.	Pa.	1872–73
Madison, James	Exec. Council	Va.	1778
Madison, James	State Const. Conv.	Va.	1829
Marshall, John	State Const. Conv.	Va.	1788; 1829
Mason, John Y.	State Const. Conv.	Va.	1850
Meredith, William M.	State Const. Conv.	Pa.	1872–73
Middleton, Henry	Const. Comt.	S.C.	1776
Middleton, Henry	Leg. Council	S.C.	1776–78
Mitchell, James P.	Relief Admin.	N.J.	1931
Monroe, James	State Const. on Fed. Conv.	Va.	1788
Monroe, James	State Const. Conv.	Va.	1829
Morgenthau, Henry	Agricult. Adv. Comm.	N.Y.	1929
Morgenthau, Henry	Taconic State Park Comm.	N.Y.	1929–31
Morgenthau, Henry	Conservation Comm.	N.Y.	1931
Osgood, Samuel	Bd. of War	Mass.	1776
Perkins, Frances	Comm. of Safety	N.Y.	1912
Perkins, Frances	Council of Org. for War Serv.	N.Y.	1917–19
Perkins, Frances	Indust. Comm.	N.Y.	1919–21; 1929–33
Perkins, Frances	Indust. Bd.	N.Y.	1922–33
Pickering, Timothy	Const. Conv.	Pa.	1789
Pierce, Franklin	Const. Conv.	N.H.	1850
Pierrepont, Edwards	Const. Conv.	N.Y.	1867–68
Porter, Peter B.	Canal Comm.	N.Y.	1811
Ribicoff, Abraham A.	Comm. on Alcoholism and Crime	Conn.	1943
Ribicoff, Abraham A.	Inter-racial Comm.	Conn.	1947–48
Rodney, Caesar A.	Comt. of Safety	Del.	1813
Roosevelt, Theodore	Bd. of Police Comm.	N.Y.	1895–97
Root, Elihu	State Const. Conv.	N.Y.	1894
Shultz, George P.	Gov.'s Comt. on Unemployment	Ill.	1961–62

Stanbery, Henry	State Const. Conv.	Ohio	1850
Stimson, Henry L.	State Const. Conv.	N.Y.	1915
Straus, Oscar S.	Public Serv. Comm.	N.Y.	1915–18
Thomas, Philip F.	State Const. Conv.	Md.	1836
Thompson, Smith	State Const. Conv.	N.Y.	1801
Tompkins, Daniel D.	State Const. Conv.	N.Y.	1801
Tyler, John	State Const. Conv.	Va.	1829–30
Upshur, Abel P.	State Const. Conv.	Va.	1829–30
Van Buren, Martin	State Const. Conv.	N.Y.	1821
Volpe, John A.	Public Wks. Comm.	Mass.	1953–56
Weaver, Robert C.	Dpty. Comm., Div. of Housing	N.Y.	1954–55
Weaver, Robert C.	Rent Admin.	N.Y.	1955–59
Webster, Daniel	State Const. Conv.	N.H.	1820
Weinberger, Caspar W.	Chmn., Comm. on Govt. Org. and Econ.	Calif.	1967–68
Weinberger, Caspar W.	Dir. of Fin.	Calif.	1968–69
Wheeler, William A.	State Const. Conv.	N.Y.	1867–68
Wickersham, George	State Const. Conv.	N.Y.	1915
Wickersham, George	Govt. Reorg. Comm.	N.Y.	1925
Wickliffe, Charles A.	State Const. Conv.	Ky.	1849
Williams, George H.	State Const. Conv.	Ore.	1858
Wilson, Henry	State Const. Conv.	Mass.	1853
Wilson, James	Railway Comm.	Iowa	1878–83
Wilson, William B.	Coal Laws Comm.	Pa.	1891
Wirtz, William W.	Liquor Control Comm.	Ill.	1950–56
Wolcott, Oliver, Jr.	State Const. Conv.	N.Y.	1818
Wood, Robert C.	Assoc. Dir., Legisl. Bureau	Fla.	1949–51
Woodin, William H.	Fuel Administrator	N.Y.	1922
Woodin, William H.	Banking Laws Comt.	N.Y.	1929

COUNTY SERVICE

County & Name	Office	State	Dates
Agnew, Spiro T.	Chmn., Zoning Bd. of Appeals	Balt., Md.	1957–61
Agnew, Spiro T.	Chf. Exec.	Balt., Md.	1962–67
Alexander, Joshua W.	Pub. Admin.	Davies, Mo.	1877–81
Barkley, Alben W.	Pros. Atty. for County Ct.	McCracken, Ky.	1905–09
Barkley, Alben W.	Judge, County Ct.	McCracken, Ky.	1909–13
Black, Jeremiah S.	Dep. Atty. Gen.	Somerset, Pa.	1831
Clark, Tom C.	Civ. Dist. Atty.	Dallas, Tex.	1927–32
Cleveland, Grover	Asst. Dist. Atty.	Erie, N.Y.	1863–65
Cleveland, Grover	Sheriff	Erie, N.Y.	1871–73
Collamer, Jacob	State Atty.	Windsor, Vt.	1822–24
Corwin, Thomas	Pros. Atty.	Warren, Ohio	1818–28
Cummings, Homer S.	State Atty.	Fairfield, Conn.	1914–24
Curtis, Charles	Pros. Atty.	Shawnee, Kan.	1885–89
Davis, James J.	Recorder	Madison, Ind.	1903–07
Delano, Columbus	Pros. Atty.	Knox, Ohio	1832
Folger, Charles J.	Judge, Ct. of Common Pleas	Ontario, N.Y.	1844
Folger, Charles J.	County Judge	Ontario, N.Y.	1851–55
Garner, John N.	County Judge	Uvalde, Tex.	1893–96
Hall, Nathan K.	Judge, Ct. of Common Pleas	Erie, N.Y.	1841
Harding, Warren G.	Auditor	Marion, Ohio	1895
Hays, William H.	City Atty.	Sullivan, Ind.	1910–13
Johnson, Cave	County Pros. Atty.	Montgomery, Tenn.	1817–20
Kellogg, Frank B.	City Atty.	Olmstead, N.Y.	1882–87
Kirkwood, Samuel J.	Pros. Atty.	Richland, Ohio	1845–49
Lane, Franklin K.	County Atty.	San Fran., Calif.	1899–1904
Lincoln, Abraham	Dep. County Surveyor	Hardin, Ill.	1834–36
McKenna, Joseph	County Atty.	Solano, Calif.	1866–70
McKinley, William, Jr.	Pros. Atty.	Stark, Ohio	1869–71

MacVeagh, Wayne	Dist. Atty.	Chester, Pa.	1859–64
Meese, Edwin, III	Dep. Dist. Atty.	Calif.	1958–67
Payne, John B.	Special Judge, Circ. Ct.	Tucker, W.Va.	1880–82
Payne, John B.	Judge, Superior Ct.	Cook, Ill.	1893–98
Porter, James M.	Dep. Atty. Gen.	Northampton, Pa.	1818–21
Richardson, William A.	Probate Judge	Middlesex, Mass.	1856
Robeson, George	Pros. Atty.	Camden, N.J.	1858
Sargent, John G.	State Atty.	Windsor, Vt.	1898–1900
Taft, William H.	Pros. Atty.	Hamilton, Ohio	1881–82
Toucey, Isaac	State Atty.	Hartford, Conn.	1822–35
Truman, Harry S.	Judge, County Ct.	Jackson, Mo.	1922–24; 1926–34
Van Buren, Martin	Surrogate Ct.	Columbia, N.Y.	1808–13
Walker, Frank C.	Asst. Dist. Atty.	Silver Bow, Mont.	1909–12
West, Roy O.	Asst. Atty.	Cook, Ill.	1893
Wilbur, Curtis D.	Dep. Dist. Atty.	Los Angeles, Calif.	1899–1903
Windom, William	Pros. Atty.	Knox, Ohio	1852

MUNICIPAL SERVICE

Name	Office	City & State	Dates
Adams, Charles F.	Councilman	Quincy, Mass.	*ca.* 1895
Adams, Charles F.	Mayor	Quincy, Mass.	1896–97
Alexander, Joshua W.	Secy. and Pres., Board of Ed.	Gallatin, Mo.	1882–1901
Alexander, Joshua W.	Mayor	Gallatin, Mo.	1891–92
Arthur, Chester A.	Port Collector	N.Y., N.Y.	1871–78
Baker, Newton D.	Asst. Dir., Law Dept.	Cleveland, Ohio	1902
Baker, Newton D.	City Solicitor	Cleveland, Ohio	1903–12
Baker, Newton D.	Mayor	Cleveland, Ohio	1912–16
Ballinger, Richard A.	City Atty.	Kankakee, Ill.	1888
Ballinger, Richard A.	Judge, Superior Ct.	Port Townsend, Wash.	1894–97

Ballinger, Richard A.	Mayor	Seattle, Wash.	1904–06
Bancroft, George	Port Collector	Boston, Mass.	1832–34
Bates, Edward	Judge, Land Ct.	St. Louis, Mo.	1853–56
Bibb, George M.	Chancellor, Ct. of Chancery	Louisville, Ky.	1835–44
Blair, Montgomery	Mayor	St. Louis, Mo.	1842–43
Blair, Montgomery	Judge, Ct. of Common Pleas	St. Louis, Mo.	1843–49
Burleson, Albert S.	Asst. City Atty.	Austin, Tex.	1885–90
Butler, Benjamin F.	Dist. Atty.	Albany, N.Y.	1821–24
Celebrezze, Anthony S.	Mayor	Cleveland, Ohio	1950–62
Chandler, Zachariah	Mayor	Detroit, Mich.	1851–52
Chapman, Oscar L.	Chf. Probation Officer, Juvenile Ct.	Denver, Colo.	1921–29
Cleveland, Grover	Mayor	Buffalo, N.Y.	1882
Colman, Norman J.	Dist. Atty.	New Albany, Ind.	1852
Coolidge, Calvin	City Council	Northampton, Mass.	1899
Coolidge, Calvin	City Solicitor	Northampton, Mass.	1900–01
Coolidge, Calvin	Clerk of the Cts.	Northampton, Mass.	1904
Coolidge, Calvin	Mayor	Northampton, Mass.	1910–11
Cummings, Homer S.	Mayor	Stamford, Conn.	1900–02; 1904–06
Cushing, Caleb	Mayor	Newburyport, Mass.	1851–52
Dallas, George M.	Dep. Atty. Gen.	Philadelphia, Pa.	1817
Dallas, George M.	Mayor	Philadelphia, Pa.	1829
Daugherty, Harry M.	Town Clerk	Washington Ct. House, Ohio	1882
Davis, Dwight F.	Public Rec. Comm.	St. Louis, Mo.	1906–07
Davis, Dwight F.	Park Comm.	St. Louis, Mo.	1911–15
Davis, James J.	City Clerk	Elwood, Ind.	1898–1902
Dearborn, Henry	Port Collector	Boston, Mass.	1809
Devens, Charles	City Solicitor	Worcester, Mass.	1856–58
Dickerson, Mahlon	City Recorder	Philadelphia, Pa.	1808–10

Duane, William J.	Pros. Atty., Mayor's Ct.	Philadelphia, Pa.	1820
Duane, William J.	Select Council	Philadelphia, Pa.	1829
Endicott, William C.	Common Council	Salem, Mass.	1857–58
Endicott, William C.	City Solicitor	Salem, Mass.	1858–63
Farley, James A.	Town Clerk	Stony Point, N.Y.	n.a.
Fisher, Walter C.	Special Assessment Atty.	Chicago, Ill.	1889
Fisher, Walter C.	Special Transportation Counsel	Chicago, Ill.	1907
Francis, David R.	Mayor	St. Louis, Mo.	1885
Frelinghuysen, Frederick T.	City Atty.	Newark, N.J.	1849
Frelinghuysen, Frederick T.	City Council	Newark, N.J.	1850–61
Glass, Carter	City Council Clerk	Lynchburg, Va.	1881–1901
Goldschmidt, Neil E.	Mayor	Portland, Ore.	1973–79
Good, James W.	City Atty.	Cedar Rapids, Iowa	1906–08
Gregory, Thomas W.	Asst. City Atty.	Austin, Tex.	1891–94
Griggs, John	City Counsel	Paterson, N.J.	1879–82
Hall, Nathan K.	City Atty.	Buffalo, N.Y.	1833–34
Hall, Nathan K.	Mbr., Bd. of Aldermen	Buffalo, N.Y.	1837
Hamlin, Hannibal	Port Collector	Boston, Mass.	1865
Harmon, Judson	Mayor	Wyoming, Ohio	1875–76
Harmon, Judson	Judge, Superior Ct.	Wyoming, Ohio	1877–87
Hatton, Frank	Postmaster	Burlington, Iowa	1879–81
Hayes, Rutherford B.	City Solicitor	Cincinnati, Ohio	1857–59
Henshaw, David	Port Collector	Boston, Mass.	1827–30
Hobart, Garret A.	City Counsel	Paterson, N.J.	1871
Humphrey, Hubert H.	Mayor	Minneapolis, Minn.	1945–48
Hyde, Arthur M.	Mayor	Princeton, Mo.	1908–12
James, Thomas L.	Insp. of Customs	N.Y., N.Y.	1864–70
James, Thomas L.	Dep. Collector of Port	N.Y., N.Y.	1870–73
James, Thomas L.	Mayor	Tenafly, N.J.	1896
Johnson, Andrew	Alderman	Greenville, Tenn.	1828–30
Johnson, Andrew	Mayor	Greenville, Tenn.	1830–33
Jones, William	Collector of Customs	Philadelphia, Pa.	1827–29

Kellogg, Frank B.	City Atty.	Rochester, N.Y.	1878–81
King, William R. deV.	City Solicitor	Wilmington, N.C.	1810–11
Landrieu, Moon E.	Mayor	New Orleans, La.	1970–78
Lane, Franklin K.	City Atty.	San Fran., Calif.	1899–1904
Lee, Charles	Collector of Port	Alexandria, Va.	1789–93
Lincoln, Abraham	Postmaster	New Salem, Ill.	1833–36
Livingston, Edward	Mayor	N.Y., N.Y.	1800–03
McGrath, James H.	City Solicitor	Central Falls, R.I.	1930–34
McKay, Douglas J.	Mayor	Salem, Ore.	1933–34
Marcy, William L.	Recorder	Troy, N.Y.	1816–18
Meredith, William M.	Select Council	Philadelphia, Pa.	1834–49
Meyer, George von L.	Common Council	Boston, Mass.	1889–90
Meyer, George von L.	Bd. of Aldermen	Boston, Mass.	1891
Moody, William H.	City Solicitor	Haverhill, Mass.	1888–90
Murphy, Frank	Judge, Recorder's Ct.	Detroit, Mich.	1923–30
Murphy, Frank	Mayor	Detroit, Mich.	1930–33
Muskie, Edmund S.	City Solicitor	Waterford, Me.	1954–55
Paulding, James K.	Naval Agent	N.Y., N.Y.	1824
Payne, Henry C.	Postmaster	Milwaukee, Wisc.	1875–85
Payne, John B.	Mayor	Kingswood, W.Va.	1889
Pickering, Timothy	Judge, Ct. of Common Pleas	Essex, Mass.	1802–03
Pierrepont, Edwards	Superior Ct.	N.Y., N.Y.	1857–60
Ramsey, Alexander	Mayor	St. Paul, Minn.	1855
Randall, Alexander W.	Postmaster	Prairieville, Wisc.	1845
Randall, Alexander W.	Judge, Circuit Ct.	Milwaukee, Wisc.	1855–57
Redfield, William C.	Comm. of Public Wks.	Brooklyn, N.Y.	1902–03
Ribicoff, Abraham A.	Judge, Municipal Ct.	Hartford, Conn.	1941–43; 1945–47
Ribicoff, Abraham A.	Charter Revision Comt.	Hartford, Conn.	1945–47

Rusk, Jeremiah McL.	Sheriff	Viroqua, Wisc.	1855–57
Rusk, Jeremiah McL.	Coroner	Viroqua, Wisc.	1857
Sawyer, Charles	City Council	Cincinnati, Ohio	1911–15
Sherman, James S.	Mayor	Utica, N.Y.	1884–86
Smith, Robert	City Council	Baltimore, Md.	1798–1801
Spencer, John C.	Postmaster	Canandaigua, N.Y.	1814
Taft, Alphonso	Judge, Superior Ct.	Cincinnati, Ohio	1865–72
Taft, William H.	Collector of Int. Revenue	Cincinnati, Ohio	1882
Thomas, Philip F.	Collector of Port	Baltimore, Md.	1853–60
Thompson, Richard W.	City Atty.	Terre Haute, Ind.	1846–47
Tobin, Maurice J.	Mayor	Boston, Mass.	1938–46
Tracy, Benjamin F.	Charter Comm.	N.Y., N.Y.	1896
Upshur, Abel P.	City Council	Richmond, Va.	1816
Upshur, Abel P.	Atty.	Richmond, Va.	1816–23
Vinson, Frederick M.	City Atty.	Louisa, Ky.	1914–15
Watson, William M.	City Secy.	Daingerfield, Tex.	1954
Watson, William M.	City Judge	Daingerfield, Tex.	1958
Weaver, Robert C.	Vice-chmn., Housing and Redevelopment of Roads	N.Y., N.Y.	1960–61
Weeks, John W.	Alderman	Newton, Mass.	1900–02
Weeks, John W.	Mayor	Newton, Mass.	1903–05
Weeks, Sinclair	Alderman	Newton, Mass.	1923–29
Weeks, Sinclair	Mayor	Newton, Mass.	1930–35
Welles, Gideon	Postmaster	Hartford, Conn.	1836–41
West, Roy O.	City Atty.	Chicago, Ill.	1895–97
Wilkins, William	Common Council	Pittsburgh, Pa.	1816–19
Williams, George H.	Mayor	Portland, Ore.	1902–05

Military Service by Branch

ARMY

Highest Rank Name	War or Dates Served	Attained
Agnew, Spiro T.	World War II	co. combat cmdr.
Alger, Russell A.	Civil War	maj. gen.
Armstrong, John	War of 1812	brig. gen.
Bacon, Robert	World War I	lt. col.
Baldridge, Malcolm	World War II	capt.
Barry, William T.	War of 1812	ADC
Bates, Edward	War of 1812	sgt.
Belknap, William W.	Civil War	brig. gen.
Bell, Griffin B.	1941–46	maj.
Berrien, John MacP.	War of 1812	capt.
Blair, Montgomery	1835–36	lt.
Block, John R.	1957–60	capt.
Blount, Winton M.	World War II	lt.
Boudinot, Elias	Revolutionary War	commissary gen.
Bowen, Otis R.	World War II	capt.
Boyd, Alan S.	World War II	maj.
Bradford, William	Revolutionary War	col.
Breckinridge, John C.	Mexican War	maj.
Bristow, Benjamin H.	Civil War	maj. gen.
Browning, Orville H.	1832	n.a.
Bryan, William J.	1898	col.
Buchanan, James	War of 1812	n.a.
Burr, Aaron	Revolutionary War	lt. col.
Cass, Lewis	War of 1812	brig. gen.
Clark, Tom C.	World War I	sgt.
Coleman, William T., Jr.	World War II	n.a.

Cox, Jacob D., Jr.	Civil War	maj. gen.
Crittenden, John J.	War of 1812	ADC
Cushing, Caleb	Mexican War	brig. gen.
Davis, Dwight F.	World War I	col.
Davis, Jefferson	1828–35; Mexican War	col.
Dawes, Charles G.	World War I	brig. gen.
Dearborn, Henry	Revolutionary War	maj.
Dearborn, Henry	War of 1812	maj. gen.
Derwinski, Edward J.	World War II	sgt.
Devens, Charles	Civil War	maj. gen.
Dix, John A.	War of 1812	maj.
Dix, John A.	Civil War	maj. gen.
Dulles, John F.	World War I	maj.
Durkin, Martin P.	World War I	pvt.
Eisenhower, Dwight D.	1915–48	chief of staff
Elkins, Stephen B.	Civil War	capt.
Eustis, William	Revolutionary War	physician
Fall, Albert B.	Spanish-American War	capt.
Folsom, Marion B.	World War I	capt.
Foster, John W.	Civil War	brig. gen.
Garfield, James A.	1861–70	maj. gen.
Goff, Nathan	Civil War	maj.
Grant, Ulysses S.	1843–54; 1861–67	general of the army
Gresham, Walter Q.	Civil War	maj. gen.
Gronouski, John A.	World War II	1st lt.
Habersham, Joseph	Revolutionary War	lt. col.
Haig, Alexander M., Jr.	1947–79	gen.
Hamilton, Alexander	Revolutionary War	capt.
Harrison, Benjamin	Civil War	brig. gen.
Harrison, William H.	1791–98; 1811–14	maj. gen.
Hathaway, Stanley K.	1943–45	n.a.
Hatton, Frank	Civil War	1st lt.
Hayes, Rutherford B.	Civil War	maj. gen.
Hobby, Oveta C.	World War II	maj. (WAAC)
Hodges, Luther H.	1919	2d lt.
Hull, Cordell	Spanish-American War	capt.
Hurley, Patrick J.	World War I	col.
Hurley, Patrick J.	World War II	brig. gen.
Jackson, Andrew	1814–16	maj. gen.
Johnson, Andrew	Civil War	brig. gen.
Johnson, Louis A.	World War I	maj.
Johnson, Richard M.	War of 1812	col.
Jones, William	Revolutionary War	pvt.
Katzenbach, Nicholas de B.	World War II	navigator, army air force

Kemp, Jack	1958	pvt.
Kennedy, John P.	War of 1812	n.a.
Kissinger, Henry A.	1943–46	st. sgt.
Kleindienst, Richard G.	World War II	lt.
Kleppe, Thomas S.	1942–46	war. off.
Knox, Henry	Revolutionary War	maj. gen.
Landrieu, Moon E.	1955–57	capt.
Lincoln, Robert T.	Civil War	capt.
Livingston, Edward	War of 1812	ADC
McHenry, James	Revolutionary War	maj.
McKay, Douglas J.	World War I	maj.
McKay, Douglas J.	World War II	maj.
McKinley, William, Jr.	Civil War	maj.
McNamara, Robert S.	World War II	col.
MacVeagh, Wayne	Civil War	capt.
Marcy, William L.	War of 1812	adj. gen.
Marshall, George C.	1901–45	gen. & chief of staff
Marshall, John	Revolutionary War	capt.
Matthews, Forrest D.	1958–59	n.a.
Meese, Edwin, III	1956–57	lt.
Meigs, Return J., Jr.	1804–06	cmdr.
Mifflin, Thomas	Revolutionary War	maj. gen.
Miller, William H. H.	Civil War	2d lt.
Mills, Ogden L.	World War I	capt.
Mitchell, William D.	Spanish-American War	2d lt.
Mondale, Walter F.	1951–53	corp.
Monroe, James	Revolutionary War	lt. col.
Morton, Rogers C. B.	World War II	capt.
Murphy, Frank	World War I	capt.
Noble, John W.	Civil War	brig. gen.
O'Brien, Lawrence F.	World War II	sgt.
Osgood, Samuel	Revolutionary War	col.
Patterson, Robert P.	World War I	maj.
Pickering, Timothy	Revolutionary War	quartermaster gen.
Pierce, Franklin	1846–48	brig. gen.
Pierce, Samuel R., Jr.	World War II	lt.
Porter, James M.	War of 1812	col.
Proctor, Redfield	Civil War	col.
Randolph, Edmund J.	Revolutionary War	ADC
Rawlins, John A.	Civil War	maj. gen.
Reagan, Ronald W.	World War II	capt.
Richardson, Elliot L.	World War II	1st lt.
Robeson, George	Civil War	brig. gen.
Roosevelt, Theodore	Spanish-American War	col.
Royall, Kenneth C.	World War I	brig. gen.
Royall, Kenneth C.	World War II	brig. gen.

Rusk, D. Dean	1931–41	infantry res. off.
Rusk, D. Dean	World War II	col.
Rusk, Jeremiah McL.	Civil War	brig. gen.
St. Clair, Arthur	Revolutionary War	maj. gen.
Sawyer, Charles	World War I	maj.
Saxbe, William	World War II	n.a.
Schofield, John McA.	Civil War	maj. gen.
Schurz, Carl	Civil War	maj. gen.
Schwellenbach, Lewis B.	World War I	cpl.
Sherman, William T.	1840–69	general in command
Simon, William E.	1946–48	n.a.
Skinner, Samuel K.	1960–61	lt.
Smith, Cyrus R.	World War II	maj. gen.
Snyder, John W.	World War I	capt.
Spencer, John C.	War of 1812	brigade judge advocate
Stoddert, Benjamin	Revolutionary War	maj.
Taylor, Zachary	1806–49	maj. gen.
Thompson, Richard W.	Civil War	camp cmdr.
Tracy, Benjamin F.	Civil War	brig. gen.
Truman, Harry S.	World War I	maj.
Udall, Stewart L.	World War II	gunner, army air force
Vilas, William F.	Civil War	lt. col.
Vinson, Frederick M.	World War I	pvt.
Walker, Frank C.	World War I	1st lt.
Washington, George	Revolutionary War	lt. gen. & comdr.
Weeks, Sinclair	World War I	capt.
Weinberger, Caspar W.	World War II	capt.
Wolcott, Oliver, Jr.	Revolutionary War	ADC
Wood, Robert C.	World War II	gen.
Woodring, Henry H.	World War I	2d lt.
Work, Hubert	World War I	col.

NAVY

Name	**War or Dates Served**	**Highest Rank Attained**
Acheson, Dean G.	World War I	ens.
Adams, Brockman	World War II	n.a.
Andrus, Cecil D.	1951–55	n.a.
Brennan, Peter J.	1943–53	lt. comdr.
Brock, William E., III	Korean War	lt. (jg)
Bush, George H.	World War II	lt.
Califano, Joseph Anthony	1955–58	lt.

Carter, Jimmy	1944–?	petty of., 2nd cl.
Celebrezze, Anthony J.	World War II	seaman
Chapman, Oscar L.	World War I	pharm. mate
Clifford, Clark McA.	World War II	capt.
Connally, John B.	World War II	en., res.
Day, James E.	World War II	lt.
Denby, Edwin	Spanish-American War	gunner's mate, 3rd d.
Dent, Frederick B.	1943–46	n.a.
Dillon, C. Douglas	World War II	lt. cmdr.
Ford, Gerald R., Jr.	1942–46	lt. cmdr.
Forrestal, James V.	World War I	lt.
Gates, Thomas S., Jr.	World War II	comdr., res.
Hodgson, James D.	World War II	intell. ofcr.
Johnson, Lyndon B.	1941–48	cmdr.
Kennedy, John F.	World War II	lt.
Laird, Melvin R.	World War II	n.a.
Lovett, Robert A.	World War I	lt.
Lynn, James T.	1945–46	ETM 2nd cl.
McLane, Louis	1798–99	midshipman
Marshall, Freddie R.	World War II	n.a.
Mitchell, John N.	World War II	cmdr.
Morgenthau, Henry	World War I	lt.
Muskie, Edmund S.	World War II	lt.
Newberry, Truman H.	1894–99	lt. (jg)
Nixon, Richard M.	World War II	lt (jg)
Rogers, William P.	World War II	lt. cmdr.
Rumsfeld, Donald	1954–57	n.a.
Strauss, Lewis L.	World War II	rear adm.
Usery, Willie J., Jr.	1943–46	n.a.
Vance, Cyrus R.	1942–46	lt. (jg)
Verity, C. William, Jr.	World War II	lt.
Volpe, John A.	World War II	lt.
Watkins, James D.	1949–86	adm.
Weeks, John W.	1881–83	midshipman

MARINE CORPS

Name	War or Dates Served	Highest Rank Attained
Baker, James A., III	1952–54	capt.
Bell, Terrel H.	World War II	sgt.
Clark, W. Ramsey	1945–46	cpl.
Connor, John T.	World War II	2d lt.
Denby, Edwin	World War I	maj.
Finch, Robert H.	World War II	1st lt.
Finch, Robert H.	Korean War	1st lt.

Freeman, Orville L.	World War II	maj.
Gardner, John W.	World War II	capt.
Regan, Donald T.	World War II	lt. col.
Shultz, George P.	World War II	capt.
Trowbridge, Alexander B.	Korean War	2d lt.
Watson, William M., Jr.	World War II	sgt.

AIR FORCE

Name	War or Dates Served	Highest Rank Attained
Brinegar, Claude Stout	1945–47	n.a.
Knebel, John A.	1959–62	1st lt.
McGranery, James P.	World War I	adj.
Yeutter, Clayton K.	1952–57	lt. col.

COAST GUARD

MILITIA/NATIONAL GUARD

Name	War or Dates Served	Highest Rank Attained
Arthur, Chester A.	1857–62	brig. gen.
Badger, George E.	1814–16	maj.
Clinton, George	Revolutionary War	brig. gen.
Collamer, Jacob	War of 1812	lt.
Colman, Norman J.	Civil War	lt. col.
Dearborn, Henry	Revolutionary War	maj. gen.
Edwards, James	World War II	deck off.
Eustis, William	Revolutionary War	surgeon
Fillmore, Millard	Civil War	cmdr., Home Guard
Hamilton, Paul	Revolutionary War	n.a.
Hurley, Patrick J.	1902–07	capt.
Hyde, Arthur M.	1904–05	capt.
Jackson, Andrew	1812–14	cmdr.
Knox, W. Frank	World War I	col.
Lee, Richard H.	1781	col.
Lincoln, Abraham	1832	capt.
Marcy, William L.	1821	adj. gen.
Miller, G. William	1945–49	lt. (jg)
Mitchell, William D.	1899–1901	capt. & adj.
Patterson, Robert P.	World War I	maj.
Porter, James M.	War of 1812	2d lt.
Quayle, Danforth	1969–75	corp.
Rodney, Caesar A.	1813–14	capt.

St. Clair, Arthur	1775	col.
Teller, Henry M.	Civil War	maj. gen.
Truman, Harry S.	1905–11	cpl.
Weeks, Sinclair	1918	lt. col.

Education

Name	Highest Level Attained (Univ.)	Read Law	Year Completed
Acheson, Dean G.	Harvard (L)		1918
Adams, Brockman	Harvard (L)	passed bar	1952
Adams, Charles F.		passed bar	1893
Adams, John		passed bar	1758
Adams, John Q.		passed bar	1790
Agnew, Spiro T.		passed bar	1949
Akerman, Amos T.		passed bar	1844
Alexander, Joshua W.		passed bar	1875
Alger, Russell A.		passed bar	1859
Anderson, Clinton B.	Univ. of Michigan (U)		no degree
Anderson, Robert B.	Univ. of Texas (L)		1932
Andrus, Cecil D.	Oregon State (U)		no degree
Armstrong, John	Princeton (U)		no degree
Arthur, Chester A.	Union Coll. (U)		1848
Bacon, Robert	Harvard (U)		1880
Badger, George E.		passed bar	1811
Baker, James A., III	Univ. of Texas (L)		1957
Baker, Newton D.	Washington & Lee Univ. (L)		1894
Baldridge, Malcolm	Yale (U)		1944

Ballinger, Richard A.		passed bar	1886
Bancroft, George	Harvard (U)		1817
Barbour, James		passed bar	1794
Barkley, Alben W.	Univ. of Virginia (L)		1901
Barr, Joseph W.	Vincennes Univ. (L)		1966
Barry, William T.		passed bar	1805
Bates, Edward		passed bar	1817
Bayard, Thomas F.		passed bar	1851
Belknap, William W.		passed bar	1851
Bell, Griffin B.	Mercer Univ. (L)	passed bar	1967
Bell, John		passed bar	1817
Bell, Terrel H.	Univ. of Utah (U)		1946
Bennett, William J.	Harvard (L)		1971
Benson, Ezra T.	Iowa State Coll. (G)		1927
Bergland, Robert S.	Univ. of Minn.		no degree
Berrien, John M.		passed bar	1799
Bibb, George M.		passed bar	1798
Biddle, Francis B.	Harvard (L)		1911
Bissell, Wilson S.		passed bar	1871
Bissell, Wilson S.	Yale (L)		1893
Black, Jeremiah		passed bar	1830
Blaine, James G.	Washington Coll. (U)		1847
Blair, Montgomery	Transylvania Coll. (L)		1839
Block, John R.	West Point (U)		1957
Blount, Winton M.	Univ. of Alabama		no degree
Blumenthal, W. Michael	Princeton (G)		1956
Bonaparte, Charles J.	Harvard (L)		1874
Borie, Adolph	Univ. of Pennsylvania (U)		1825
Boudinot, Elias		passed bar	1760
Boutwell, George S.		passed bar	1862
Bowen, Otis R.	Indiana Univ. (M)		1942
Boyd, Alan S.	Univ. of Virginia (L)		1948
Bradford, William		passed bar	1779 (?)

Brady, Nicholas F.	Harvard (G)		1954
Branch, John		passed bar	n.a.
Brannan, Charles F.	Univ. of Denver (L)		1929
Breckinridge, John		passed bar	1785
Breckinridge, John C.	Transylvania Univ. (L)		1841
Brennan, Peter J.	Coll. of City of N.Y. (U)		no degree
Brewster, Benjamin H.		passed bar	1838
Brinegar, Claude S.	Stanford (G)		1954
Bristow, Benjamin H.		passed bar	1853
Brock, William E., III	Washington & Lee		1953
Brown, Aaron V.		passed bar	1816
Brown, Harold	Univ. of California (L)		1969
Brown, Walter F.	Harvard (L)		1894
Brownell, Herbert, Jr.	Yale (L)		1927
Browning, Orville H.		passed bar	1831
Bryan, William J.	Union Coll. (L)		1883
Buchanan, James		passed bar	1812
Burleson, Albert S.	Univ. of Texas (L)		1884
Burnley, James H., IV	Harvard (L)		1973
Burr, Aaron		passed bar	1780
Bush, George H.	Yale (U)		1948
Butler, Benjamin F.		passed bar	1817
Butz, Earl L.	Purdue Univ. (G)		1937
Byrnes, James F.		passed bar	1903
Calhoun, John C.		passed bar	1807
Califano, Joseph A., Jr.	Harvard (L)	passed bar	1955
Cameron, James D.	Princeton Coll. (U)		1852
Campbell, George W.	Princeton Coll. (U)		1794
Campbell, James		passed bar	1833
Carlisle, John G.		passed bar	1858
Carter, Jimmy	U.S. Naval Acad. (U)		1946

Cass, Lewis		passed bar	1802
Cavazos, Lauro F.	Iowa State (G)		1954
Celebrezze, Anthony J.	Ohio Northern Univ. (L)		1936
Chandler, William E.	Harvard (L)		1854
Chapin, Roy D.	Univ. of Michigan (U)		no degree
Chapman, Oscar L.	Westminster Law Sch. (L)		1929
Chase, Salmon P.		passed bar	1829
Cheney, Richard B.	Univ. of Wisconsin		1968
Civiletti, Benjamin R.	Univ. of Maryland		1961
Clark, Tom C.	Univ. of Texas (U)		1921
Clark, W. Ramsey	Univ. of Chicago (G)		1950
Clay, Henry		passed bar	1797
Clayton, John M.	Litchfield Law Sch. (L)		1819
Cleveland, Grover		passed bar	1859
Clifford, Clark M.	Washington Univ. (L)		1928
Clifford, Nathan		passed bar	1824
Clinton, George		passed bar	*ca.* 1762
Cobb, Howell		passed bar	1836
Cohen, Wilbur J.	Univ. of Wisconsin (U)		1934
Colby, Bainbridge	New York Univ. (L)		1892
Coleman, William T., Jr.	Harvard (L)	passed bar	1946
Collamer, Jacob		passed bar	1813
Colman, Norman J.	Univ. of Louisville (L)		1851
Connally, John B.	Univ. of Texas (L)		1941
Connor, John T.	Harvard (L)		1939
Conrad, Charles M.		passed bar	1828
Coolidge, Calvin		passed bar	1897
Cortelyou, George B.	George Washington Univ. (L)		1896
Corwin, Thomas		passed bar	1817
Cox, Jacob D., Jr.		passed bar	1853
Crawford, George W.		passed bar	1822

Crawford, William H.		passed bar	1799
Creswell, John A. J.		passed bar	1850
Crittenden, John J.		passed bar	1807
Cummings, Homer S.	Yale (L)		1893
Curtis, Charles		passed bar	1881
Cushing, Caleb		passed bar	1822
Dallas, Alexander		passed bar	1785
Dallas, George M.		passed bar	1813
Daniels, Josephus		passed bar	1885
Daugherty, Harry M.	Univ. of Michigan (L)		1881
Davis, Dwight F.	Washington Univ. (L)		1903
Davis, James J.	Sharon Business Coll.		no degree
Davis, Jefferson	West Point		1828
Dawes, Charles G.	Cincinnati Law Sch. (L)		1886
Day, James E.	Harvard (L)		1938
Day, William R.		passed bar	1872
Delano, Columbus		passed bar	1831
Denby, Edwin	Univ. of Michigan (L)		1896
Dennison, William		passed bar	1840
Dent, Frederick B.	Yale (U)		1943
Dern, George H.	Univ. of Nebraska (U)		no degree
Derwinski, Edward J.	Loyola (U)		1951
Devens, Charles	Harvard (L)		1840
Dexter, Samuel		passed bar	1784
Dickerson, Mahlon		passed bar	1793
Dickinson, Donald M.	Univ. of Michigan (L)		1867
Dickinson, Jacob M.	Univ. of Paris (L)		1874
Dillon, C. Douglas	Harvard (U)		1931
Dix, John A.		passed bar	1824
Doak, William N.	(business coll.)		no degree
Dobbin, James C.		passed bar	1835
Dole, Elizabeth H.	Harvard (L)		1966
Donaldson, Jesse M.	Sparks Business Coll.		n.a.
Donovan, Raymond J.	Notre Dame Seminary (U)		1952

Duane, William J.		passed bar	1815
Dulles, John F.	George Washington Univ. (L)		1911
Dulles, John F.	Sorbonne (Paris)		no degree
Duncan, Charles W., Jr.	Rice (U)		1947
Dunlop, John T.	Univ. of Chicago		1968
Eaton, John H.		passed bar	1808
Edison, Charles	Mass. Inst. of Technology (U)		1913
Edwards, James	Univ. of Louisville (D)		1955
Eisenhower, Dwight D.	Army War Coll. (G)		1928
Elkins, Stephen B.	Univ. of Missouri (G)		1868
Endicott, William C.		passed bar	1850
Eustis, William	Harvard (U)		1772
Evarts, William M.		passed bar	1841
Everett, Edward	Harvard (U)		1811
Ewing, Thomas		passed bar	1816
Fairbanks, Charles W.		passed bar	1874
Fairchild, Charles S.	Harvard (L)		1865
Fall, Albert B.		passed bar	1891
Fessenden, William P.		passed bar	1823
Fillmore, Millard		passed bar	1823
Finch, Robert H.	Univ. of Southern California (L)		1951
Fish, Hamilton		passed bar	1830
Fisher, Walter L.		passed bar	1888
Flemming, Arthur S.	Ohio Wesleyan Univ. (L)		1941
Flemming, Arthur S.	American Univ. (L)		1942
Floyd, John B.		passed bar	1835
Folger, Charles J.		passed bar	1839
Folsom, Marion B.	Harvard (G)		1914
Ford, Gerald R., Jr.	Yale (L)	passed bar	1941
Forrestal, James V.	Princeton (U)		1915
Forsyth, John		passed bar	1802
Forward, Walter		passed bar	1806

Foster, John W.		passed bar	1857
Fowler, Henry H.	Yale (L)		1932, 1933
Francis, David R.	Washington Univ. (U)		1870
Freeman, Orville L.	Univ. of Minnesota (L)		1946
Frelinghuysen, Frederick T.		passed bar	1839
Gage, Lyman J.	Beloit Coll. (L)		1897
Gage, Lyman J.	New York Univ. (L)		1903
Gardner, John W.	Univ. of California (G)		1938
Garfield, James A.		passed bar	1860
Garfield, James R.		passed bar	1888
Garland, Augustus H.		passed bar	1853
Garner, John N.		passed bar	1890
Garrison, Lindley M.	Univ. of Pennsylvania (L)		1886
Gary, James A.	Allegheny Coll. (U)		1854
Gates, Thomas S.	Univ. of Pennsylvania (U)		1928
Gerry, Elbridge	Harvard (U)		1762
Gilmer, Thomas W.		passed bar	1828
Gilpin, Henry D.		passed bar	1822
Goff, Nathan	New York Univ. (L)		1866
Goldberg, Arthur	Northwestern Univ. (L)		1930
Goldschmidt, Neil E.	Univ. of Oregon (U)		1963
Good, James W.	Univ. of Michigan (L)		1893
Gore, Howard M.	West Virginia Univ. (U)		1900
Graham, William A.		passed bar	1826
Granger, Francis	Yale Coll. (U)		1811
Granger, Gideon		passed bar	1787
Grant, Ulysses S.	West Point (U)		1843
Gregory, Thomas W.	Univ. of Texas		1885
Gresham, Walter Q.		passed bar	1854
Griffin, Cyrus	Edinburgh Univ.		*ca.* 1770

Griffin, Cyrus	Middle Temple (London)		*ca.* 1770
Griggs, John W.		passed bar	1871
Gronouski, John A.	Univ. of Wisconsin (G)		1955
Grundy, Felix		passed bar	1797
Guthrie, James		passed bar	1817
Haig, Alexander M., Jr.	West Point (U)		1947
Hall, Nathan K.		passed bar	1832
Hamlin, Hannibal		passed bar	1833
Hamilton, Alexander		passed bar	*ca.* 1780
Hancock, John	Harvard (U)		1754
Hannegan, Robert E.	St. Louis Univ. (L)		1925
Hardin, Clifford M.	Purdue Univ. (G)		1941
Harding, Warren G.		passed bar	1882
Harlan, James		passed bar	1848
Harmon, Judson	Cincinnati Law Sch. (L)		1869
Harriman, W. Averill	Yale (U)		1913
Harris, Patricia R.	American Univ. (L)	passed bar	1950
Harrison, Benjamin		passed bar	1853
Harrison, William H.	Hampden-Sidney Coll. (U)		1790
Hathaway, Stanley K.	Univ. of Nebraska (L)	passed bar	1950
Hay, John M.	Brown Univ. (U)		1858
Hayes, Rutherford B.	Harvard (L)		1845
Hays, William H.	Wabash Coll. (G)		1904
Heckler, Margaret M.	Boston College (L)		1956
Hendricks, Thomas A.		passed bar	1843
Herbert, Hilary A.		passed bar	1857
Herrington, John	Univ. of California (L)		1964
Herter, Christian A.	Columbia Univ. Sch. of Arch. (G)		1916
Hills, Carla A.	Yale (L)	passed bar	1958

Hitchcock, Ethan A.	Univ. of Missouri (L)		1902
Hitchcock, Ethan A.	Harvard (L)		1906
Hitchcock, Ethan A.	Washington Univ. (L)		1907
Hitchcock, Frank H.	George Washington Univ. (L)		1895
Hoar, Ebenezer R.		passed bar	1840
Hobart, Garret A.		passed bar	1866
Hobby, Oveta C.	Univ. of Texas (L)		1927
Hodel, Donald P.	Univ. of Oregon (L)		1960
Hodges, Luther H.	Univ. of North Carolina (U)		1919
Hodgson, James D.	Univ. of California/ L.A. (G)		1948
Holt, Joseph		passed bar	1831
Hoover, Herbert C.	Stanford Univ. (U)		1895
Hopkins, Harry L.	Grinnell Coll. (U)		1935
Houston, David F.	Harvard (G)		1892
Howe, Timothy O.		passed bar	1839
Hubbard, Samuel D.		passed bar	n.a.
Hufstedler, Shirley M.	Stanford Univ. (L)		1949
Hughes, Charles E.	Columbia Univ. (L)		1884
Hull, Cordell	Cumberland Univ. (L)		1891
Humphrey, George M.		passed bar	1912
Humphrey, Hubert H.	Univ. of Louisiana (G)		1940
Hunt, William H.		passed bar	1844
Huntington, Samuel		passed bar	1758
Hurley, Patrick J.	George Washington Univ. (L)		1912
Hyde, Arthur M.	Univ. of Iowa (L)		1900
Ickes, Harold L.	Univ. of Chicago (L)		1907
Jackson, Andrew		passed bar	1787
Jackson, Robert H.		passed bar	1913

Jardine, William H.	Grad. Sch. of Utah (G)		1906
Jay, John		passed bar	1768
Jefferson, Thomas		passed bar	1762
Johnson, Cave		passed bar	1814
Johnson, Louis A.	Univ. of Virginia (L)		1912
Johnson, Lyndon B.	Georgetown Univ. (L)		no degree
Johnson, Reverdy		passed bar	1815
Johnson, Richard M.	Transylvania Univ. (L)		1800
Katzenbach, Nicholas de B.	Yale (L)		1947
Kellogg, Frank B.		passed bar	1877
Kemp, Jack	Occidental (U)		1957
Kendall, Amos		passed bar	1814
Kennedy, David M.	George Washington Univ. (L)		1935
Kennedy, John F.	Harvard (U)		1940
Kennedy, John P.		passed bar	1816
Kennedy, Robert F.	Univ. of Virginia (L)		1951
Key, David M.		passed bar	1850
King, William R. deV.		passed bar	1806
Kirkwood, Samuel J.		passed bar	1843
Kissinger, Henry A.	Harvard (G)		1954
Kleindienst, Richard G.	Susquehanna Univ.	passed bar	1950
Kleppe, Thomas S.	Valley City Teachers Col. (U)		no degree
Klutznick, Philip M.	Creighton (L)		1929
Knebel, John A.	Amer. Univ. (L)	passed bar	1965
Knox, Philander C.	Mount Union (U)	passed bar	1875
Kreps, Juanita M.	Duke Univ. (G)		1948
Krug, Julius A.	Univ. of Wisconsin (G)		1930
Laird, Melvin	Carleton Coll. (U)		1942
Lamar, Lucius Q. C.		passed bar	1847

Lamont, Daniel S.	Cortland Normal Coll. (U)		1871
Lamont, Robert P.	Univ. of Michigan (U)		1891
Landrieu, Moon E.	Loyola Univ., New Orleans (L)		1954
Lane, Franklin K.	Hastings Law Sch. (L)		1888
Lansing, Robert		passed bar	1889
Lee, Charles		passed bar	1794
Lee, Richard H.		studied law	no degree
Legaré, Hugh S.		passed bar	1822
Levi, Edward H.	Yale (L)	passed bar	1938
Lewis, Andrew	Harvard (G)		1955
Lincoln, Abraham		passed bar	1836
Lincoln, Levi		passed bar	1775
Lincoln, Robert T.	Harvard (L)		1893
Livingston, Edward			1785
Long, John D.	Harvard (L)		1860
Lovett, Robert A.	Harvard (L)		1920
	Harvard (Bus. Adm.) (G)		1921
Lujan, Manuel, Jr.	College of Santa Fe (U)		1950
Lyng, Richard E.	Univ. of Notre Dame (U)		1940
Lynn, James T.	Harvard (L)	passed bar	1951
McAdoo, William G.		passed bar	1885
McClelland, Robert		passed bar	1831
McCrary, George W.		passed bar	1856
McCulloch, Hugh		passed bar	1832
McElroy, Neil H.	Harvard (U)		1925
McGranery, James P.	Temple Univ. (L)		1928
McGrath, James H.	Boston Univ. (L)		1928
McKay, Douglas J.	Oregon State Coll. (U)		1917
McKean, Thomas		passed bar	1755
McKenna, Joseph		passed bar	1865
McKennan, Thomas M. T.		passed bar	1814

McKinley, William, Jr.		passed bar	1867
McLane, Louis		passed bar	1807
McLaughlin, Anne D.	Marymount (U)		1963
McLean, John		passed bar	1807
McNamara, Robert S.	Harvard (G)		1939
McReynolds, James C.	Vanderbilt Univ. (U)		1882
MacVeagh, Franklin	Yale (U)		1862
MacVeagh, Wayne	Yale (U)		1853
Madison, James	Princeton (U)	passed bar	1774
Marcy, William L.	Brown (U)	passed bar	1811
Marshall, Freddie R.	Univ. of California (G)		1954
Marshall, George C.	Virginia Military Inst. (U)		1901
Marshall, James W.	Dickinson Coll. (U)		1848
Marshall, John		passed bar	1781
Marshall, Thomas R.	Wabash Coll. (U)		1873
Mason, John Y.	Litchfield Law Sch. (L)	passed bar	1819
Matthews, Forrest D.	Columbia Univ. (G)		1965
Maynard, Horace		passed bar	1844
Meese, Edwin, III	Univ. of California (L)		1958
Meigs, Return J., Jr.		passed bar	1788
Mellon, Andrew W.	Western Univ. of Pennsylvania (U)		1872
Meredith, Edwin T.	Des Moines Univ. (U)		1894
Meredith, William M.		passed bar	1817
Metcalf, Victor H.	Yale (L)		1876
Meyer, George von L.	Harvard (L)		1911
Mifflin, Thomas	Univ. of Pennsylvania (U)		1760
Miller, G. William	Univ. of California (L)		1952

Miller, William H., Jr.	Hamilton Coll. (L)		1889
Mills, Ogden L.	Harvard (L)		1907
Mitchell, John N.	Fordham Univ. (L)		1938
Mitchell, William D.	Univ. of Minnesota (L)		1896
Mondale, Walter F.	Univ. of Minnesota (L)	passed bar	1956
Monroe, James		passed bar	1786
Moody, William H.		passed bar	1878
Morgenthau, Henry	Cornell Univ. (U)		no degree
Morrill, Lot M.		passed bar	1839
Morton, Julius S.	Univ. of Michigan (U)		1858
Morton, Rogers C. B.	Yale (L)		1937
Mosbacher, Robert A.	Washington & Lee Univ. (U)		1947
Mueller, Frederick H.	Michigan State Univ. (U)		1914
Murphy, Frank	Univ. of Michigan (L)		1914
Muskie, Edmund S.	Cornell (L)		1939
Nagel, Charles	Washington Univ. (L)		1872
Nelson, John		passed bar	1813
New, Harry S.	Butler Univ. (U)		1880
Newberry, Truman H.	Yale (U)		1885
Niles, John M.		passed bar	1817
Nixon, Richard M.	Duke Univ. (L)		1937
Noble, John W.	Yale (U)		1851
O'Brien, Lawrence F.	Northeastern Univ. (U)		1942
Olney, Richard	Harvard (L)		1858
Osgood, Samuel	Harvard (U)		1770
Palmer, Alexander M.		passed bar	1893
Patterson, Robert P.	Harvard (L)		1915
Payne, John B.		passed bar	1876
Perkins, Frances	Columbia Univ. (G)		1910

Peterson, Peter G.	Univ. of Chicago (G)		1948
Pickering, Timothy		passed bar	1768
Pierce, Franklin		passed bar	1827
Pierce, Samuel R., Jr.	Yale (L)		1949
Pierrepont, Edwards	New Haven Law Sch. (L)		1840
Pinkney, William		passed bar	1786
Poinsett, Joel R.		studied for bar	no degree
Polk, James K.	Univ. of North Carolina (U)	passed bar	1820
Porter, James M.		passed bar	1813
Porter, Peter B.		passed bar	1795
Preston, William B.	Univ. of Virginia (L)		1826
Proctor, Redfield	Albany Law Sch. (L)		1859
Quayle, Danforth	Univ. of Indiana (L)		1974
Ramsey, Alexander	Lafayette Coll. (L)		1839
Randolph, Edmund J.		studied law	no degree
Randolph, Peyton		passed bar	1744
Rawlins, John A.		passed bar	1854
Reagan, Ronald W.	Eureka (U)		1928
Regan, Donald T.	Harvard (U)		1940
Ribicoff, Abraham A.	Univ. of Chicago (L)		1933
Richardson, Elliot L.	Harvard (L)		1947
Richardson, William A.	Harvard (L)		1846
Robeson, George		passed bar	1850
Rockefeller, Nelson A.	Dartmouth (U)		1930
Rodney, Caesar A.		passed bar	1793
Rogers, William P.	Cornell Univ. (L)		1937
Romney, George W.	George Washington Univ. (G)		1930
Roosevelt, Franklin D.	Columbia Univ. (L)		1907
Roosevelt, Theodore	Harvard (U)		1880

Root, Elihu	New York Univ. (L)		1867
Roper, Daniel G.	National Law Sch. (L)		1901
Royall, Kenneth C.	Harvard (L)		1917
Rumsfeld, Donald	Princeton (U)		1954
Rush, Richard		passed bar	1800
Rusk, D. Dean	Oxford Univ. {England} (G)		1934
St. Clair, Arthur	Univ. of Edinburgh (U)		no degree
Sargent, John G.	Tufts Coll. (U)		1887
Sawyer, Charles	Univ. of Cincinnati (L)		1911
Saxbe, William	Ohio State (L)		
Schlesinger, James R.	Harvard (G)		1956
Schurz, Carl		passed bar	1856
Schweiker, Richard	Pennsylvania State (U)		1949
Schwellenbach, Lewis B.	Univ. of Washington (L)		1917
Seaton, Frederick A.	Kansas State Agricult. Coll. (U)		1931
Seward, William H.	Union Coll. (U)		1820
Shaw, Leslie M.	Iowa Coll. of Law (L)		1876
Sherman, James S.	Hamilton Coll. (L)		1879
Sherman, William T.	West Point (U)		1840
Shultz, George P.	Mass. Inst. of Technology (G)		1949
Simon, William E.	Lafayette Coll. (U)		1952
Skinner, Samuel K.	DePaul Univ. (L)		1966
Smith, Caleb		passed bar	1828
Smith, Charles E.	Wesleyan Univ. (L)		1901
Smith, Cyrus R.	Univ. of Texas (U)		1924
Smith, Hoke		passed bar	1873
Smith, Robert		passed bar	1786
Smith, William French	Harvard (L)		1942
Snyder, John W.	Vanderbilt Univ. (U)		no degree

Southard, Samuel L.	Princeton (U)		1804
Speed, James	Transylvania Univ. (L)		1833
Spencer, John C.		passed bar	1809
Stanbery, Henry		passed bar	1824
Stans, Maurice H.	Columbia Univ. (U)		1930
Stanton, Edwin M.		passed bar	1836
Stettinius, Edward R., Jr.	Univ. of Virginia (U)		no degree
Stevenson, Adlai E.	Center College (U)	passed bar	1857
Stimson, Henry L.	Harvard (L)		1891
Stone, Harlan F.	Amherst Coll. (G)		1897
Straus, Oscar S.	Columbia Univ. (L)		1873
Stuart, Alexander A. H.		passed bar	1828
Sullivan, Louis W.	Boston Univ. (M)		1958
Swanson, Claude	Univ. of Virginia (L)		1886
Taft, Alphonso		passed bar	1838
Taft, William H.	Cincinnati Law Sch. (L)		1880
Taney, Roger R.		passed bar	1799
Teller, Henry M.		passed bar	1858
Thomas, Philip F.		passed bar	1831
Thompson, Jacob		passed bar	1834
Thompson, Richard W.		passed bar	1834
Thompson, Smith		passed bar	1792
Thornburgh, Richard	Univ. of Pittsburgh (L)		1957
Tobin, Maurice J.	Boston Coll. (U)		n.a.
Tompkins, Daniel D.		passed bar	1797
Toucey, Isaac		passed bar	1818
Tracery, Benjamin F.		passed bar	1851
Trowbridge, Alexander B.	Princeton (U)		1951
Truman, Harry S.	Kansas City Law Sch. (L)		no degree
Tyler, John		passed bar	1809
Tyner, James N.	William and Mary (U)	passed bar	1857
Udall, Stewart L.	Univ. of		1948

	Arizona (L)		
Upshur, Abel P.		passed bar	1810
Usery, Willie J., Jr.	Mercer Univ. (U)		no degree
Usher, John P.		passed bar	1839
Van Buren, Martin		passed bar	1803
Vance, Cyrus R.	Yale (L)		1942
Verity, C. William, Jr.	Yale (U)		1939
Vilas, William F.	Univ. of Albany (L)		1850
Vinson, Frederick M.	Centre Coll. (L)		1911
Walker, Frank C.	Univ. of Notre Dame (L)		1909
Walker, Robert J.		passed bar	1821
Wallace, Henry A.	Iowa State Coll. (U)		1910
Wallace, Henry C.	Iowa State Coll. of Agricult. (U)		1892
Washburne, Elihu B.	Harvard (L)		1940
Watkins, James D.	U.S. Naval Acad. (G)		1958
Watson, William M., Jr.	Baylor Univ. (G)		1950
Watson, William M., Jr.	Machita Univ. (L)		1968
Watt, James G.	Univ. of Wyoming (L)		1962
Weaver, Robert C.	Harvard (G)		1934
Webster, Daniel		passed bar	1805
Weeks, Sinclair	Harvard (U)		1914
Weinberger, Caspar	Harvard		1941
Welles, Gideon		passed bar	1834
West, Roy O.	De Pauw Univ. (U)		1890
Wheeler, William A.		passed bar	1845
Whiting, William F.	Amherst Coll. (U)		1886
Whitney, William C.	Harvard (L)		1865
Wickard, Claude R.	Purdue Univ. (U)		1915
Wickersham, George	Univ. of Pennsylvania (L)	passed bar	1880

Wickliffe, Charles A.		passed bar	1890
Wilbur, Curtis D.		passed bar	1890
Wilbur, Ray L.	Cooper Medical Coll. (M.D.)		1899
Wilkins, William		passed bar	1801
Williams, George H.		passed bar	1844
Wilson, Charles E.	Carnegie Inst. of Tech. (U)		1909
Wilson, James	Grinnell Coll. (U)		n.a.
Wilson, William L.	George Washington Univ. (L)		1869
Wilson, Woodrow	Univ. of Virginia (L)		1881
Windom, William		passed bar	1850
Wirt, William		passed bar	1792
Wirtz, William W.	Harvard (L)		1937
Wolcott, Oliver, Jr.		passed bar	1781
Wood, Robert C.	Harvard (G)		1950
Woodbury, Levi		passed bar	1812
Woodin, William H.	Columbia Univ. Sch. of Mines (U)		1890
Woodring, Henry H.	Lebanon Univ. (Ind.) (U)		no degree
Wright, Luke E.		passed bar	1870
Yeutter, Clayton K.	Univ. of Nebraska		1963

Place of Birth

ALABAMA

Name	Birthdate	City or County
Blount, Winton M.	Feb. 1, 1921	Union Springs
Hitchcock, Ethan A.	Sept. 19, 1835	Mobile
Matthews, Forrest D.	Dec. 6, 1935	Grove Hill

ALASKA

Name	Birthdate	City or County
Udall, Stewart L.	Jan. 31, 1920	Saint Johns

ARIZONA

Name	Birthdate	City or County
Finch, Robert H.	Oct. 9, 1925	Tempe
Kleindienst, Richard G.	Aug. 1923	Winslow

ARKANSAS

Name	Birthdate	City or County
Snyder, John W.	June 21, 1895	Jonesboro

CALIFORNIA

Name	Birthdate	City or County
Brinegar, Claude S.	Dec. 16, 1926	Rockport
Dunlop, John T.	July 5, 1914	Placerville
Gardner, John W.	Oct. 8, 1912	Los Angeles
Herrington, John	May 31, 1939	Los Angeles
Hills, Carla A.	Jan. 3, 1934	Los Angeles
Kemp, Jack	July 13, 1935	Los Angeles
Lyng, Richard E.	June 29, 1918	San Francisco
McNamara, Robert S.	June 9, 1916	San Francisco
Meese, Edwin, III	Dec. 2, 1931	Oakland
Nixon, Richard M.	Jan. 9, 1913	Yorba Linda
Watkins, James D.	Mar. 7, 1927	Alhambra
Weinberger, Caspar W.	Aug. 18, 1917	San Francisco

COLORADO

Name	Birthdate	City or County
Brannan, Charles F.	Aug. 23, 1903	Denver
Hufstedler, Shirley M.	Aug. 24, 1925	Denver

CONNECTICUT

Name	Birthdate	City or County
Acheson, Dean G.	Apr. 11, 1893	Middletown
Forward, Walter	Jan. 24, 1786	East Granby
Gary, James A.	Oct. 22, 1833	Uncasville
Granger, Francis	Dec. 1, 1792	Suffield
Granger, Gideon	Sept. 19, 1767	Suffield
Hubbard, Samuel D.	Aug. 10, 1799	Middletown
Huntington, Samuel	July 3, 1731	Windham
Meigs, Return J., Jr.	Nov. 17, 1764	Middletown
Niles, John M.	Aug. 20, 1787	Poquonnock
Pierrepont, Edwards	Mar. 4, 1817	New Haven
Porter, Peter B.	Aug. 14, 1773	Salisbury
Ribicoff, Abraham A.	Apr. 9, 1910	New Britain
Smith, Charles E.	Feb. 18, 1842	Mansfield
Toucey, Isaac	Nov. 5, 1796	Newtown
Welles, Gideon	July 1, 1802	Glastonbury
Wolcott, Oliver, Jr.	Jan. 11, 1760	Litchfield

DELAWARE

Name	Birthdate	City or County
Bayard, Thomas F.	Oct. 29, 1828	Wilmington
Clayton, John M.	July 24, 1796	Dagsborough
McKennan, Thomas M. T.	Mar. 31, 1794	Dragon Neck
McLane, Louis	May 28, 1786	Smyrna
Rodney, Caesar A.	Jan. 4, 1772	Dover

DISTRICT OF COLUMBIA

Name	Birthdate	City or County
Dulles, John F.	Feb. 25, 1888	D.C.
Seaton, Frederick A.	Dec. 11, 1909	D.C.
Weaver, Robert C.	Dec. 29, 1907	D.C.

FLORIDA

Name	Birthdate	City or County
Boyd, Alan S.	July 20, 1922	Jacksonville
Edwards, James	June 24, 1927	Hawthorne

GEORGIA

Name	Birthdate	City or County
Adams, Brockman	Jan. 13, 1927	Atlanta
Bell, Griffin B.	Oct. 13, 1918	Americus
Carter, Jimmy, Jr.	Oct. 1, 1924	Plains
Cobb, Howell	Sept. 7, 1815	Cherry Hill
Crawford, George W.	Dec. 22, 1798	Augusta
Folsom, Marion B.	Nov. 23, 1893	McRae
Habersham, Joseph	July 28, 1751	Savannah
Lamar, Lucius Q. C.	Sept. 17, 1825	Putnam Co.
Rusk, D. Dean	Feb. 9, 1909	Cherokee Co.
Sullivan, Louis W.	Nov. 3, 1944	Atlanta
Usery, Willie J., Jr.	Dec. 21, 1923	Hardwick

HAWAII

IDAHO

Name	Birthdate	City or County
Bell, Terrel H.	Nov. 11, 1921	Lava Hot Springs
Benson, Ezra T.	Aug. 4, 1899	Whitney
Jardine, William M.	Jan. 16, 1879	Oneida Co.

ILLINOIS

Name	Birthdate	City or County
Block, John R.	Feb. 15, 1935	Galesburg
Bryan, William J.	Mar. 19, 1860	Salem
Cummings, Homer S.	Apr. 30, 1870	Chicago
Day, James E.	Oct. 11, 1914	Jacksonville
Derwinski, Edward J.	Sept. 15, 1926	Chicago
Donaldson, Jesse M.	Aug. 17, 1885	Shelbyville
Durkin, Martin P.	Mar. 18, 1894	Chicago
Goldberg, Arthur J.	Aug. 8, 1908	Chicago
Harlan, James	Aug. 26, 1820	Clark Co.
Harris, Patricia R.	May 31, 1924	Mattoon
Levi, Edward H.	June 26, 1911	Chicago
Lincoln, Robert T.	Aug. 1, 1843	Springfield
Rawlins, John A.	Feb. 13, 1831	Galena
Reagan, Ronald W.	Feb. 6, 1911	Tampico
Rumsfeld, Donald	July 9, 1932	Chicago
Skinner, Samuel K.	June 10, 1938	Chicago
Stettinius, Edward R., Jr.	Oct. 22, 1900	Chicago
Wallace, Henry C.	May 11, 1866	Rock Island
West, Roy O.	Oct. 27, 1868	Georgetown
Wirtz, William W.	Mar. 14, 1912	DeKalb

INDIANA

Name	Birthdate	City or County
Barr, Joseph W.	Jan. 17, 1918	Vincennes
Butz, Earl L.	July 3, 1909	Albion
Denby, Edwin	Feb. 18, 1870	Evansville
Foster, John W.	Mar. 2, 1836	Pike Co.
Gresham, Walter Q.	Mar. 7, 1832	Lanesville
Hardin, Clifford M.	Oct. 9, 1915	Knightstown

Hay, John M.	Oct. 8, 1838	Salem
Hays, William H.	Nov. 5, 1879	Sullivan
McCrary, George W.	Aug. 29, 1835	Evansville
Marshall, Thomas R.	Mar. 14, 1854	North Manchester
New, Harry S.	Dec. 31, 1858	Indianapolis
Quayle, Danforth	Feb. 4, 1947	Indianapolis
Tyner, James N.	Jan. 17, 1826	Brockville
Wickard, Claude R.	Feb. 28, 1893	Carroll Co.

IOWA

Name	Birthdate	City or County
Ballinger, Richard A.	July 9, 1858	Boonesboro
Good, James W.	Sept. 24, 1866	Cedar Rapids
Hoover, Herbert C.	Aug. 10, 1874	West Branch
Hopkins, Harry L.	Aug. 17, 1890	Sioux City
Meredith, Edwin T.	Dec. 23, 1876	Avoca
Wallace, Henry A.	Oct. 17, 1888	Orient
Wilbur, Curtis D.	May 10, 1867	Boonesboro
Wilbur, Ray L.	Apr. 13, 1875	Boonesboro

KANSAS

Name	Birthdate	City or County
Clifford, Clark McA.	Dec. 25, 1906	Scott
Curtis, Charles	Jan. 25, 1860	North Topeka
Hickel, Walter J.	Aug. 18, 1919	Ellinwood
Woodring, Henry H.	May 31, 1890	Elk City

KENTUCKY

Name	Birthdate	City or County
Barkley, Alben W.	Nov. 24, 1877	Lowes
Blair, Montgomery	May 10, 1813	Franklin Co.
Breckinridge, John C.	Jan. 21, 1821	"Cabell's Dale"
Bristow, Benjamin H.	June 20, 1832	Elkton
Browning, Orville H.	Feb. 10, 1806	Cynthiana
Carlisle, John G.	Sept. 5, 1835	Campbell (now Kenton) Co.
Corwin, Thomas	July 29, 1794	Bourbon Co.
Crittenden, John J.	Sept. 9, 1787	Versailles
Davis, Jefferson	June 3, 1808	Christian (now Todd) Co.
Fall, Albert B.	Nov. 26, 1861	Frankfort

Francis, David R.	Oct. 1, 1850	Richmond
Guthrie, James	Dec. 5, 1792	Bardstown
Holt, Joseph	Jan. 6, 1807	Breckenridge Co.
Johnson, Richard M.	Oct. 17, 1781	Beargrass Creek (now Louisville)
Kreps, Juanita M.	Jan. 11, 1921	Lynch
Lincoln, Abraham	Feb. 12, 1809	Hodgen's Mill
McReynolds, James C.	Feb. 3, 1862	Elkton
Morton, Rogers C. B.	Sept. 14, 1914	Louisville
Speed, James	Mar. 11, 1812	Farmington
Stevenson, Adlai E.	Oct. 23, 1835	Christian Co.
Vinson, Frederick M.	Jan. 22, 1890	Louisa
Wickliffe, Charles A.	June 8, 1788	Springfield

LOUISIANA

Name	Birthdate	City or County
Landrieu, Moon E.	July 23, 1930	New Orleans
Marshall, Freddie R.	Aug. 22, 1928	Oak Grove

MAINE

Name	Birthdate	City or County
Hamlin, Hannibal	Aug. 27, 1809	Paris Hill
Howe, Timothy O.	Feb. 24, 1816	Livermore
King, Horatio	June 21, 1811	Paris
Long, John D.	Oct. 27, 1838	Buckfield
McCulloch, Hugh	Dec. 7, 1808	Kennebunk
Morrill, Lot M.	May 3, 1812	Belgrade
Muskie, Edmund S.	Mar. 28, 1914	Rumford
Rockefeller, Nelson A.	July 8, 1908	Bar Harbor
Washburne, Elihu B.	Sept. 23, 1816	Livermore

MARYLAND

Name	Birthdate	City or County
Agnew, Spiro T.	Nov. 9, 1918	Baltimore
Bonaparte, Charles J.	June 9, 1851	Baltimore
Creswell, John A. J.	Nov. 18, 1828	Port Deposit
Hanson, John	Apr. 3, 1715	Mulberry Grove, Charles Co.
Johnson, Reverdy	May 21, 1796	Annapolis

Kennedy, John P.	Oct. 25, 1795	Baltimore
Kirkwood, Samuel J.	Dec. 20, 1813	Harford Co.
Nelson, John	June 1, 1794	Fredericktown
Pinkney, William	Mar. 17, 1764	Annapolis
Stoddert, Benjamin	1751	Charles Co.
Taney, Roger B.	Mar. 17, 1777	Calvert Co.
Thomas, Philip F.	Sept. 12, 1810	Easton
Wirt, William	Nov. 8, 1772	Bladensburg

MASSACHUSETTS

Name	Birthdate	City or County
Adams, Charles F.	Aug. 2, 1866	Quincy
Adams, John	Oct. 30, 1735	Quincy
Adams, John Q.	July 11, 1767	Quincy
Bacon, Robert	July 5, 1860	Jamaica Plain
Bancroft, George	Oct. 3, 1800	Worcester
Bliss, Cornelius N.	Jan. 26, 1833	Fall River
Boutwell, George S.	Jan. 28, 1818	Brookline
Bush, George H.	June 12, 1924	Milton
Crowninshield, Benjamin W.	Dec. 27, 1772	Boston
Cushing, Caleb	Jan. 17, 1800	Salisbury
Devens, Charles	Apr. 4, 1820	Charlestown
Dexter, Samuel	May 14, 1761	Boston
Endicott, William C.	Nov. 19, 1826	Salem
Eustis, William	June 10, 1753	Cambridge
Evarts, William M.	Feb. 6, 1818	Boston
Everett, Edward	Apr. 11, 1794	Dorchester
Folger, Charles J.	Apr. 16, 1818	Nantucket
Gerry, Elbridge	July 17, 1744	Marblehead
Gorham, Nathaniel	May 21, 1738	Charlestown
Hancock, John	Jan. 12, 1737	Quincy
Henshaw, David	Apr. 2, 1791	Leicester
Hoar, Ebenezer R.	Feb. 21, 1816	Concord
Kendall, Amos	Aug. 16, 1789	Dunstable
Kennedy, John F.	May 29, 1917	Brookline
Kennedy, Robert F.	Nov. 20, 1925	Brookline
Knox, Henry	July 25, 1750	Boston
Knox, W. Franklin	Jan. 1, 1874	Boston
Lincoln, Levi	May 15, 1749	Hingham
Marcy, William L.	Dec. 12, 1786	Southbridge
Maynard, Horace	Aug. 30, 1840	Westboro
Meyer, George von L.	June 24, 1858	Boston
Moody, William H.	Dec. 23, 1853	Newbury
O'Brien, Lawrence F.	July 7, 1917	Springfield

Olney, Richard	Sept. 15, 1835	Oxford
Osgood, Samuel	Feb. 3, 1748	Andover
Payne, Henry C.	Nov. 23, 1843	Ashfield
Perkins, Frances	Apr. 10, 1882	Boston
Pickering, Timothy	July 17, 1745	Salem
Regan, Donald T.	Dec. 21, 1918	Cambridge
Richardson, Elliot L.	July 20, 1920	Boston
Richardson, William A.	Nov 2., 1821	Tyngsborough
Smith, Caleb	Apr. 16, 1808	Boston
Tobin, Maurice J.	May 22, 1901	Boston
Volpe, John A.	Dec. 8, 1908	Wakefield
Weeks, Sinclair	June 15, 1893	West Newton
Whiting, William F.	July 20, 1864	Holyoke
Whitney, William C.	July 5, 1841	Conway

MICHIGAN

Name	Birthdate	City or County
Chapin, Roy D.	Feb. 23, 1880	Lansing
Humphrey, George M.	Mar. 8, 1890	Cheboygan
Lamont, Robert P.	Dec. 1, 1867	Detroit
Mitchell, John N.	Sept. 15, 1913	Detroit
Morton, Paul	May 22, 1857	Detroit
Mueller, Frederick H.	Nov. 22, 1893	Grand Rapids
Murphy, Frank	Apr. 13, 1890	Harbor Beach
Newberry, Truman H.	Nov. 5, 1864	Detroit
Summerfield, Arthur E.	Mar. 17, 1899	Pinconning

MINNESOTA

Name	Birthdate	City or County
Bergland, Robert S.	July 22, 1928	Roseau
Freeman, Orville L.	May 9, 1918	Minneapolis
Hodgson, James D.	Dec. 3, 1915	Dawson
Mitchell, William D.	Sept. 9, 1874	Winona
Mondale, Walter F.	Jan. 5, 1928	Ceylon
Stans, Maurice H.	Mar. 22, 1908	Shakopee

MISSISSIPPI

Name	Birthdate	City or County
Dickinson, Jacob McG.	Jan. 30, 1851	Columbus
Gregory, Thomas W.	Nov. 6, 1861	Crawfordsville

MISSOURI

Name	Birthdate	City or County
Colby, Bainbridge	Dec. 22, 1869	St. Louis
Davis, Dwight F.	July 5, 1879	St. Louis
Hannegan, Robert E.	June 30, 1903	St. Louis
Hyde, Arthur M.	July 12, 1877	Princeton
Klutznick, Philip M.	July 9, 1907	Kansas City
Truman, Harry S.	May 8, 1884	Lamar
Wood, Robert C.	Sept. 16, 1923	St. Louis

MONTANA

NEBRASKA

Name	Birthdate	City or County
Baldridge, Malcolm	Oct. 4, 1922	Omaha
Brownell, Herbert, Jr.	Feb. 20, 1904	Peru
Cheney, Richard B.	Jan. 30, 1941	Lincoln
Dern, George H.	Sept. 8, 1872	Hooper
Ford, Gerald R., Jr.	July 14, 1913	Omaha
Hathaway, Stanley K.	July 19, 1924	Osceola
Laird, Melvin R.	Sept. 1, 1922	Omaha
Peterson, Peter G.	June 5, 1926	Kearny
Yeutter, Clayton K.	Dec. 10, 1930	Eustis

NEVADA

NEW HAMPSHIRE

Name	Birthdate	City or County
Akerman, Amos T.	Feb. 23, 1821	Portsmouth
Cass, Lewis	Oct. 9, 1782	Exeter
Chandler, William E.	Dec. 28, 1835	Concord
Chandler, Zachariah	Dec. 10, 1813	Bedford
Chase, Salmon P.	Jan. 13, 1808	Cornish
Clifford, Nathan	Aug. 18, 1803	Rumney
Dearborn, Henry	Feb. 23, 1751	North Hampton
Dix, John A.	July 24, 1798	Boscawen
Fessenden, William P.	Oct. 16, 1806	Boscawen
Jewell, Marshall	Oct. 20, 1825	Winchester

Pierce, Franklin	Nov. 23, 1804	Hillsboro
Smith, William French	Aug. 26, 1917	Wilton
Stone, Harlan F.	Oct. 11, 1872	Chesterfield
Webster, Daniel	Jan. 18, 1782	Franklin
Weeks, John W.	Apr. 11, 1860	Lancaster
Wilson, Henry	Feb. 16, 1812	Farmington
Woodbury, Levi	Dec. 22, 1789	Francestown

NEW JERSEY

Name	Birthdate	City or County
Berrien, John M.	Aug. 23, 1781	Rocky Hill
Brewster, Benjamin H.	Oct. 13, 1816	Salem Co.
Burr, Aaron	Feb. 6, 1756	Newark
Cleveland, Grover	Mar. 18, 1837	Caldwell
Dent, Frederick B.	Aug. 17, 1922	Cape May
Dickerson, Mahlon	Apr. 17, 1770	Hanover Neck
Donovan, Raymond J.	Aug. 31, 1930	Bayonne
Edison, Charles	Aug. 3, 1890	Llewellyn Park
Frelinghuysen, Frederick T.	Aug. 4, 1817	Millstone
Garrison, Lindley M.	Nov. 28, 1864	Camden
Griggs, John W.	July 10, 1849	Newton
Hobart, Garret A.	June 3, 1844	Long Branch
Livingston, Edward	May 26, 1764	Clermont
McLaughlin, Ann D.	Nov. 16, 1941	Newark
McLean, John	Mar. 11, 1785	Morris Co.
Miller, William H. H.	Sept. 6, 1840	Augusta
Mitchell, James P.	Nov. 12, 1900	Elizabeth
Paulding, James K.	Aug. 22, 1778	Great Nine Partners
Randall, Alexander W.	Oct. 31, 1819	Ames
Robeson, George	Mar. 16, 1829	Oxford Furnace
Simon, William E.	Nov. 27, 1927	Paterson
Southard, Samuel L.	June 9, 1787	Basking Ridge
Trowbridge, Alexander B.	Dec. 12, 1929	Englewood

NEW MEXICO

Name	Birthdate	City or County
Lujan, Manuel, Jr.	May 12, 1928	San Ildefonso

NEW YORK

Name	Birthdate	City or County
Belknap, William W.	Sept. 22, 1829	Newburgh
Bennett, William J.	July 3, 1943	Brooklyn
Bissell, Wilson S.	Dec. 31, 1847	New London
Brady, Nicholas F.	Apr. 11, 1930	New York
Brennan, Peter J.	May 24, 1918	New York
Brown, Harold	Sept. 19, 1927	New York
Butler, Benjamin F.	Dec. 17, 1795	Stuyvesant
Califano, Joseph A., Jr.	May 15, 1931	Brooklyn
Civiletti, Benjamin R.	July 17, 1935	Peekskill
Clinton, George	July 26, 1739	Little Britain
Colfax, Schuyler	Mar. 23, 1823	New York
Collamer, Jacob	Jan. 8, 1791	Troy
Colman, Norman J.	May 16, 1827	Richfield Springs
Connor, John T.	Nov. 3, 1914	Syracuse
Cortelyou, George B.	July 26, 1862	New York
Dickinson, Donald McD.	Jan. 17, 1846	Port Ontario
Fairchild, Charles S.	Apr. 30, 1842	Cazenovia
Farley, James A.	May 30, 1888	Grassy Point
Fillmore, Millard	Jan. 7, 1800	Summerhill
Fish, Hamilton	Dec. 15, 1836	New York
Flemming, Arthur S.	June 12, 1905	Kingston
Forrestal, James V.	Feb. 15, 1892	Matteawan
Gage, Lyman J.	June 28, 1836	De Ruyter
Hall, Nathan K.	Mar. 28, 1810	Skaneateles
Harriman, W. Averill	Nov. 15, 1891	New York
Heckler, Margaret M.	June 21, 1931	Flushing
Hughes, Charles E.	Apr. 11, 1862	Glens Falls
James, Thomas L.	Mar. 29, 1831	Utica
Jay, John	Dec. 12, 1745	New York
Kellogg, Frank B.	Dec. 22, 1856	Potsdam
Lamont, Daniel S.	Feb. 9, 1851	McGrawville
Lansing, Robert	Oct. 17, 1864	Watertown
Manning, Daniel	Aug. 16, 1831	Albany
Metcalf, Victor H.	Oct. 10, 1853	Utica
Morgenthau, Henry	May 11, 1891	New York
Morton, Julius S.	Apr. 22, 1832	Adams
Mosbacher, Robert A.	Mar. 11, 1927	Mt. Vernon
Patterson, Robert P.	Feb. 12, 1891	Glens Falls
Pierce, Samuel R., Jr.	Sept. 8, 1922	Glen Cove
Redfield, William C.	June 18, 1858	Albany
Rogers, William P.	June 23, 1913	Norfolk
Roosevelt, Franklin D.	Jan. 30, 1882	Hyde Park
Roosevelt, Theodore	Oct. 27, 1858	New York

Root, Elihu	Feb. 15, 1845	Clinton
Schlesinger, James R.	Feb. 15, 1929	New York
Schofield, John McA.	Sept. 29, 1831	Gerry
Seward, William H.	May 6, 1801	Florida
Sherman, James S.	Oct. 24, 1855	Utica
Shultz, George P.	Dec. 13, 1920	New York
Spencer, John C.	Jan. 8, 1788	Hudson
Stanbery, Henry	Feb. 20, 1803	New York
Stimson, Henry L.	Sept. 21, 1867	New York
Teller, Henry M.	May 23, 1830	Granger
Thompson, Smith	Jan. 17, 1768	Dutchess Co.
Tompkins, Daniel D.	June 21, 1774	Scarsdale
Tracy, Benjamin F.	Apr. 26, 1830	Oswego
Usher, John P.	Jan. 9, 1816	Brookfield
Van Buren, Martin	Dec. 5, 1782	Kinderhook
Wheeler, William A.	June 30, 1819	Malone
Williams, George H.	Mar. 23, 1823	New Lebanon
Wynne, Robert J.	Nov. 18, 1851	New York

NORTH CAROLINA

Name	Birthdate	City or County
Badger, George E.	Apr. 17, 1795	New Bern
Branch, John	Nov. 4, 1782	Halifax
Burnley, James H., IV	July 30, 1948	High Point
Daniels, Josephus	May 18, 1862	Washington
Dobbin, James C.	Jan. 17, 1814	Fayetteville
Dole, Elizabeth H.	July 20, 1936	Salisbury
Eaton, John H.	June 18, 1790	Scotland Neck
Graham, William A.	Sept. 5, 1804	Vesuvius Furnace
Houston, David F.	Feb. 17, 1866	Monroe
Johnson, Andrew	Dec. 29, 1808	Raleigh
King, William R. deV.	Apr. 17, 1786	Sampson Co.
Polk, James K.	Nov. 4, 1795	Little Sugar Creek
Royall, Kenneth C.	July 24, 1894	Goldsboro
Smith, Hoke	Sept. 2, 1855	Newton
Thompson, Jacob	May 15, 1810	Leasburg

NORTH DAKOTA

Name	Birthdate	City or County
Kleppe, Thomas S.	July 1, 1919	Kintyre

OHIO

Name	Birthdate	City or County
Alexander, Joshua W.	Jan. 22, 1852	Cincinnati
Alger, Russell	Feb. 27, 1836	Lafayette
Brown, Walter F.	May 31, 1869	Massillon
Daugherty, Henry M.	Jan. 26, 1860	Washington
Dawes, Charles G.	Aug. 27, 1865	Marietta
Day, William R.	Apr. 17, 1849	Ravenna
Dennison, William	Nov. 23, 1815	Cincinnati
Elkins, Stephen B.	Sept. 26, 1841	New Lexington
Fairbanks, Charles W.	May 11, 1852	Unionville Center
Foster, Charles	Apr. 12, 1828	Fostoria
Garfield, James A.	Nov. 19, 1831	Orange
Garfield, James R.	Oct. 17, 1865	Hiram
Grant, Ulysses S.	Apr. 27, 1822	Point Pleasant
Harding, Warren G.	Nov. 2, 1865	Blooming Grove
Harmon, Judson	Feb. 3, 1846	Newton
Harrison, Benjamin	Aug. 20, 1833	North Bend
Hatton, Frank	Apr. 28, 1846	Cambridge
Hayes, Rutherford B.	Oct. 4, 1822	Delaware
Hendricks, Thomas A.	Sept. 7, 1819	Zanesville
Hitchcock, Frank H.	Oct. 5, 1867	Amherst
Lynn, James T.	Feb. 27, 1927	Cleveland
McAdoo, William G.	Oct. 31, 1863	Marietta
McElroy, Neil H.	Oct. 30, 1904	Berea
McKinley, William, Jr.	Jan. 29, 1843	Niles
Noble, John W.	Oct. 26, 1831	Lancaster
Rusk, Jeremiah McL.	June 17, 1830	Malts
Sawyer, Charles	Feb. 10, 1887	Cincinnati
Saxbe, William	June 24, 1916	Mechanicsburg
Sherman, John	May 10, 1823	Lancaster
Sherman, William T.	Feb. 8, 1820	Lancaster
Stanton, Edwin McM.	Dec. 19, 1814	Steubenville
Taft, William H.	Sept. 15, 1857	Cincinnati
Verity, C. William, Jr.	Jan. 26, 1917	Middletown
Wilson, Charles E.	July 18, 1890	Minerva
Windom, William	May 10, 1827	Belmont Co.

OKLAHOMA

Name	Birthdate	City or County
Hurley, Patrick J.	Jan. 8, 1883	Choctaw Indian Terr. (now Lehigh)
Knebel, John A.	Oct. 4, 1936	Tulsa
Miller, G. William	March 9, 1925	Sapulpa

OREGON

Name	Birthdate	City or County
Andrus, Cecil D.	Aug. 25, 1931	Hood River
Goldschmidt, Neil E.	June 16, 1940	Eugene
Hodel, Donald P.	May 23, 1935	Portland
McKay, Douglas J.	June 24, 1893	Portland

PENNSYLVANIA

Name	Birthdate	City or County
Armstrong, John	Nov. 25, 1758	Carlisle
Black, Jeremiah	Jan. 1, 1810	Glades
Blaine, James G.	Jan. 31, 1830	West Brownsville
Borie, Adolph	Nov. 25, 1809	Philadelphia
Boudinot, Elias	May 2, 1740	Philadelphia
Bradford, William	Sept. 14, 1755	Philadelphia
Buchanan, James	Apr. 23, 1791	Cove Gap
Cameron, James D.	Mar. 14, 1833	Middletown
Cameron, Simon	Mar. 8, 1799	Maytown
Campbell, James	Sept. 1, 1812	Southwark
Carlucci, Frank C., III	Oct. 18, 1930	Scranton
Coleman, William T., Jr.	July 7, 1920	Philadelphia
Dallas, George M.	July 10, 1792	Philadelphia
Gates, Thomas S., Jr.	Apr. 10, 1906	Philadelphia
Haig, Alexander M., Jr.	Dec. 2, 1924	Bala-Cynwyd
Ickes, Harold L.	Mar. 15, 1874	Frankstown Twnshp.
Ingham, Samuel D.	Sept. 16, 1779	Great Spring
Jackson, Robert H.	Feb. 13, 1892	Spring Creek
Jones, William	ca. 1760	Philadelphia
Katzenbach, Nicholas de B.	Jan. 17, 1922	Philadelphia
Knox, Philander C.	May 6, 1853	Brownsville
Lewis, Andrew	Nov. 3, 1931	Philadelphia
McClelland, Robert	Aug. 1, 1807	Greencastle
McGranery, James P.	July 8, 1895	Philadelphia
McKean, Thomas	Mar. 19, 1734	New London Twnshp.
McKenna, Joseph	Aug. 10, 1843	Philadelphia
MacVeagh, Franklin	Nov. 22, 1837	Phoenixville
MacVeagh, Wayne	Apr. 19, 1833	Phoenixville
Marshall, George C.	Dec. 31, 1880	Uniontown
Mellon, Andrew W.	Mar. 24, 1855	Pittsburgh
Meredith, William M.	June 8, 1799	Philadelphia
Mifflin, Thomas	Jan. 10, 1744	Philadelphia
Palmer, Alexander M.	May 4, 1872	Moosehead

Porter, James M.	Jan. 6, 1793	Selma
Ramsey, Alexander	Sept. 8, 1915	Harrisburg
Rush, Richard	Aug. 29, 1780	Philadelphia
Schweiker, Richard	June 1, 1926	Norristown
Smith, Robert	Nov. 3, 1757	Lancaster
Thornburgh, Richard L.	July 16, 1932	Rosslyn Farms
Walker, Frank C.	May 30, 1886	Plymouth
Walker, Robert J.	July 19, 1801	Northumberland
Wanamaker, John	July 11, 1838	Philadelphia
Wickersham, George	Sept. 19, 1858	Pittsburgh
Wilkins, William	Dec. 20, 1779	Carlisle
Woodin, William H.	May 27, 1868	Berwick
Work, Hubert	July 3, 1860	Marion Center

RHODE ISLAND

Name	Birthdate	City or County
McGrath, James H.	Nov. 28, 1903	Woonsocket
Mills, Ogden L.	Aug. 23, 1884	Newport

SOUTH CAROLINA

Name	Birthdate	City or County
Byrnes, James F.	May 2, 1879	Charleston
Calhoun, John C.	Mar. 18, 1782	Abbeville
Hamilton, Paul	Oct. 16, 1762	St. Paul's Parish
Herbert, Hilary A.	Mar. 12, 1834	Lawrenceville
Hunt, William H.	June 12, 1823	Charleston
Jackson, Andrew	Mar. 15, 1767	Waxhaw
Laurens, Henry	Mar. 6, 1724	Charleston
Legaré, Hugh S.	Jan. 2, 1797	Charleston
Middleton, Henry	1717	Charleston
Poinsett, Joel R.	Mar. 2, 1779	Charleston
Roper, Daniel C.	Apr. 1, 1867	Marlboro Co.

SOUTH DAKOTA

Name	Birthdate	City or County
Anderson, Clinton P.	Oct. 28, 1895	Centerville
Humphrey, Hubert H., Jr.	May 22, 1911	Wallace

TENNESSEE

Name	Birthdate	City or County
Bell, John	Feb. 15, 1797	Nashville
Brock, William E., III	Nov. 23, 1930	Chattanooga
Garland, Augustus H.	June 11, 1832	Covington
Hull, Cordell	Oct. 2, 1871	Olympus
Johnson, Cave	Jan. 11, 1793	Springfield
Jones, Jesse H.	Apr. 5, 1874	Robertson Co.
Key, David McK.	Jan. 27, 1824	Greenville
Wright, Luke E.	Aug. 29, 1846	Memphis

TEXAS

Name	Birthdate	City or County
Anderson, Robert B.	June 4, 1910	Burleson
Baker, James A., III	Apr. 28, 1930	Houston
Burleson, Albert S.	June 7, 1863	San Marcos
Cavazos, Lauro F.	Jan. 4, 1927	King Ranch
Clark, Tom C.	Sept. 23, 1899	Dallas
Clark, William R.	Dec. 18, 1927	Dallas
Connally, John B.	Feb. 27, 1917	Floresville
Duncan, Charles W., Jr.	Sept. 9, 1926	Houston
Eisenhower, Dwight D.	Oct. 14, 1890	Denison
Garner, John N.	Nov. 22, 1868	Detroit
Hobby, Oveta C.	Jan. 19, 1905	Killeen
Johnson, Lyndon B.	Aug. 27, 1908	Stonewall
Lovett, Robert A.	Sept. 14, 1895	Huntsville
Nagel, Charles	Aug. 9, 1849	Colorado Co.
Smith, Cyrus R.	Sept. 9, 1899	Minerva
Watson, William M., Jr.	June 6, 1924	Oakhurst

UTAH

Name	Birthdate	City or County
Kennedy, David M.	July 21, 1905	Randolph

VERMONT

Name	Birthdate	City or County
Arthur, Chester A.	Oct. 5, 1830	Fairfield
Coolidge, Calvin	July 4, 1872	Plymouth Notch

Delano, Columbus	June 5, 1809	Shoreham
Morton, Levi P.	May 16, 1824	Shoreham
Proctor, Redfield	July 1, 1831	Proctorsville
Sargent, John G.	Oct. 13, 1860	Ludlow
Shaw, Leslie M.	Nov. 2, 1848	Morristown
Taft, Alphonso	Nov. 5, 1810	Townshend
Vilas, William F.	July 9, 1840	Chelsea

VIRGINIA

Name	Birthdate	City or County
Barbour, James	June 10, 1775	Frascati
Barry, William T.	Feb. 5, 1785	Lunenburg
Bates, Edward	Sept. 4, 1793	Belmont
Bibb, George M.	Oct. 30, 1776	Prince Edward Co.
Breckinridge, John	Dec. 2, 1760	Staunton
Brown, Aaron V.	Aug. 15, 1795	Brunswick Co.
Chapman, Oscar L.	Oct. 22, 1896	Omega
Clay, Henry	Apr. 12, 1877	"The Slashes"
Conrad, Charles M.	Dec. 24, 1804	Winchester
Crawford, William H.	Feb. 24, 1772	Nelson Co.
Doak, William N.	Dec. 12, 1882	Rural Retreat
Ewing, Thomas	Dec. 28, 1789	West Liberty
Floyd, John B.	June 1, 1806	Smithfield
Forsyth, John	Oct. 22, 1780	Fredericksburg
Fowler, Henry H.	Sept. 5, 1908	Roanoke
Gilmer, Thomas W.	Apr. 6, 1802	Gilmerton
Glass, Carter	Jan. 4, 1858	Lynchburg
Goff, Nathan	Feb. 9, 1843	Clarksburg (now W. Va.)
Griffin, Cyrus	July 16, 1748	Farnam Parish, Richmond Co.
Grundy, Felix	Sept. 11, 1777	Berkeley Co.
Harrison, William H.	Feb. 9, 1773	Berkeley
Hodges, Luther H.	Mar. 9, 1898	Pittsylvania Co.
Jefferson, Thomas	Apr. 2, 1743	Shadwell
Johnson, Louis A.	Jan. 10, 1891	Roanoke
Lee, Charles	July 1758	Fauquier Co.
Lee, Richard H.	Jan. 20, 1732	"Stratford," Westmoreland Co.
Madison, James	Mar. 16, 1751	Port Conway
Marshall, James W.	Aug. 14, 1822	Clarke Co.
Marshall, John	Sept. 24, 1755	Germantown
Mason, John Y.	Apr. 18, 1799	Emporia
Monroe, James	Apr. 28, 1758	Westmoreland Co.
Payne, John B.	Jan. 26, 1855	Pruntytown

		(now. W. Va.)
Preston, William B.	Nov. 29, 1805	Smithfield
Randolph, Edmund J.	Aug. 10, 1753	Williamsburg
Randolph, Peyton	Sept. 1721	Williamsburg
Stuart, Alexander H. H.	Apr. 2, 1807	Staunton
Swanson, Claude	Mar. 31, 1862	Swansonville
Taylor, Zachary	Nov. 24, 1784	Montebello
Thompson, Richard W.	June 9, 1809	Culpeper Co.
Tyler, John	Mar. 29, 1790	Greenway
Upshur, Abel P.	June 17, 1790	Northampton Co.
Washington, George	Feb. 22, 1732	Wakefield
Wilson, William L.	May 3, 1843	Middleway
Wilson, Woodrow	Dec. 28, 1856	Staunton

WASHINGTON

WEST VIRGINIA

Name	Birthdate	City or County
Baker, Newton D.	Dec. 3, 1871	Martinsburg
Fisher, Walter L.	July 4, 1862	Wheeling
Gore, Howard M.	Oct. 12, 1877	Harrison Co.
Strauss, Lewis L.	Jan. 31, 1896	Charleston
Vance, Cyrus R.	Mar. 27, 1917	Clarksburg

WISCONSIN

Name	Birthdate	City or County
Cohen, Wilbur J.	June 10, 1913	Milwaukee
Gronouski, John. A.	Oct. 26, 1919	Dunbar
Krug, Julius A.	Nov. 23, 1907	Madison
Schwellenbach, Lewis B.	Sept. 20, 1894	Superior

WYOMING

Name	Birthdate	City or County
Watt, James G.	Jan. 31, 1938	Lusk

OTHER COUNTRIES

Name	Birthdate	City and Country
Biddle, Francis B.	May 9, 1886	Paris, France
Blumenthal, W. Michael	Jan. 3, 1926	Berlin, Germany
Campbell, George W.	Feb. 8, 1768	Tongue, Scotland
Celebrezze, Anthony J.	Sept. 4, 1910	Anzi, Italy
Cox, Jacob D., Jr.	Oct. 27, 1828	Montreal, Canada
Dallas, Alexander	June 21, 1759	Jamaica, West Indies
Davis, James J.	Oct. 27, 1873	Thedegar South Wales
Dillon, C. Douglas	Apr. 21, 1909	Geneva, Switzerland
Duane, William J.	May 9, 1780	Clonmel, Ireland
Gallatin, Albert	Jan. 29, 1761	Geneva, Switzerland
Gilpin, Henry D.	Apr. 14, 1801	Lancaster, England
Hamilton, Alexander	Jan. 11, 1757	Nevis, West Indies
Herter, Christian	Mar. 28, 1895	Paris, France
Kissinger, Henry A.	May 27, 1923	Furth, Germany
Lane, Franklin K.	July 15, 1864	Charlottetown, Canada
McHenry, James	Nov. 16, 1753	Ballymena, Ireland
Romney, George W.	July 8, 1907	Chihuahua, Mexico
St. Clair, Arthur	Mar. 23, 1734	Thurso, Caithness, Scotland
Schurz, Carl	Mar. 2, 1829	Liblar-am-Rhein, Germany
Straus, Oscar S.	Dec. 23, 1850	Otterberg, Germany
Wilson, James	Aug. 16, 1835	Ayshire, Scotland
Wilson, William B.	Apr. 2, 1862	Blantyre, Scotland

Marital Information

SINGLE

Name	Name
Berrien, John M.	Jones, William
Brinegar, Claude S.	King, William R. deV.
Buchanan, James	Legaré, Hugh S.
Crawford, George W.	McReynolds, James C.
Devens, Charles	Marshall, Freddie R.
Dickerson, Mahlon	Marshall, James W.
Grundy, Felix	Moody, William H.
Henshaw, David	Murphy, Frank
Hitchcock, Frank H.	Nelson, John
Hubbard, Samuel D.	Tyner, James N.
Johnson, Richard M.	

MARRIED

Name	Date	Spouse
Acheson, Dean G.	1917	Alice Stanley
Adams, Brockman	1952	Mary Elizabeth Scott
Adams, Charles F.	n.a.	Frances Lovering
Adams, John	1764	Abigail Smith
Adams, John Q.	1797	Louisa Catherine Johnson
Agnew, Spiro T.	1942	Elinor Isobel Judefind
Akerman, Amos T.	*ca.* 1850	Martha Rebecca Galloway
Alexander, Joshua W.	1876	Roe Ann Richardson

Alger, Russell A.	1861	Annette Henry
Anderson, Clinton P.	1921	Henrietta McCartney
Anderson, Robert B.	1935	Ollie Mae Rawlings
Andrus, Cecil D.	1949	Carol Mae May
Armstrong, John	1789	Alida Livingston
Arthur, Chester A.	1859	Ellen Lewis Herndon
Bacon, Robert	1883	Martha Waldron Cowdin
Badger, George E.	n.a.	Rebecca Turner
Badger, George E.	n.a.	Mary Polk
Badger, George E.	n.a.	Dilia (Haywood) Williams
Baker, James A., III	1953	Mary McHenry
Baker, James A., III	1973	Susan Winson
Baker, Newton D.	1902	Elizabeth Leopold
Baldridge, Malcolm	1951	Margaret Murray
Ballinger, Richard A.	1886	Julia A. Bradley
Bancroft, George	1827	Sarah H. Dwight
Bancroft, George	1838	Mrs. Elizabeth (Davis) Bliss
Barbour, James	1792	Lucy Johnson
Barkley, Alben W.	1903	Dorothy Brower
Barkley, Alben W.	1949	Mrs. Carlton S. Hadley
Barr, Joseph W.	1939	Beth Ann Williston
Barry, William T.	1824	Lucy Overton
Barry, William T.	n.a.	Catherine Mason
Bates, Edward	1823	Julia Davenport Coalter
Bayard, Thomas F.	1856	Louise Lee
Bayard, Thomas F.	1889	Mary W. Clymer
Belknap, William W.	n.a.	Cora LeRoy
Belknap, William W.	n.a.	Carrie Tomlinson
Belknap, William W.	n.a.	Mrs. John Bower
Bell, Griffin B.	1943	Mary Foy Powell
Bell, John	n.a.	Sally Dickinson
Bell, John	n.a.	Mrs. Jane (Ervin) Eatman
Bell, Terrel H.	1957	Alta Martin
Bennett, William J.	1982	Mary Elayne Glover
Benson, Ezra T.	1926	Flora Smith Amussen
Bergland, Bob S.	1950	Helen Elaine Gromm
Bibb, George M.	(married twice; dates and wives' names unavailable)	
Biddle, Francis V.	1918	Katherine Garrison Chapin
Bissell, Wilson S.	1889	Louisa Fowler
Black, Jeremiah	1836	Mary Forward
Blaine, James G.	1850	Harriet Stonwood
Blair, Montgomery	1838	Caroline Buckner
Blair, Montgomery	1847	Mary Elizabeth Woodbury
Bliss, Cornelius N.	1859	Elizabeth Mary Plummer
Block, John R.	1960	Susan Rathjo
Blount, Winton M.	1942	Mary Katherine Archibald

Blumenthal, W. Michael	1951	Margaret Eileen Polley
Bonaparte, Charles J.	1875	Ellen Channing Day
Borie, Adolph	1839	Elizabeth Dundas McKean
Boudinot, Elias	1762	Hannah Stockton
Boutwell, George S.	1841	Sarah Adelia Thayer
Boyd, Alan S.	1943	Flavil Juanita Townsend
Bradford, William	n.a.	Susan Vergereau Boudinot
Brady, Nicholas F.	1952	Katherine Douglas
Branch, John	n.a.	Elizabeth Foort
Branch, John	n.a.	Mrs. Eliza (Jordan) Bond
Brannan, Charles F.	1932	Eda V. Seltzer
Breckinridge, John	1785	Mary Hopkins Cabell
Breckinridge, John C.	1843	Mary Cyrene Burch
Brennan, Peter J.	n.a.	Josephine Brickley
Brewster, Benjamin H.	1857	Elizabeth von Meyerbach de Reinfeldts
Bristow, Benjamin H.	1854	Abbie S. Briscoe
Brock, William E., III	1957	Laura Handley
Brock, William E., III	1986	Saundra Mitchell
Brown, Aaron V.	n.a.	Sarah Burruss
Brown, Aaron V.	1845	Mrs. Cynthia (Pillow) Saunders
Brown, Harold	1953	Colene Dunning McDowell
Brown, Walter F.	1903	Katharin Hafer
Brownell, Herbert, Jr.	1934	Doris A. McCarter
Browning, Orville H.	1836	Eliza Caldwell
Bryan, William J.	1884	Mary Baird
Burleson, Albert S.	1889	Adele Steiner
Burnley, James H., IV	1969	Jane Nady
Burr, Aaron	1782	Mrs. Theodosia (Bartow) Prevost
Burr, Aaron	1833	Mrs. Eliza Jumel
Bush, George H.	1945	Barbara Pierce
Butler, Benjamin F.	1818	Harriet Allen
Butz, Earl L.	1937	Mary Emma Powell
Byrnes, James F.	1906	Maud (Busch) Perkins
Calhoun, John C.	1811	Floride Bouneau Calhoun
Califano, Joseph A., Jr.	1955	Gertrude Zawacki
Cameron, James D.	n.a.	Mary McCormick
Cameron, James D.	1878	Elizabeth Sherman
Cameron, Simon	n.a.	Margaret Brua
Campbell, George W.	1812	Harriet Stoddert
Campbell, James	1845	Emilie S. Chapron
Carlisle, John G.	1857	Mary Jane Goodson
Carlucci, Frank C., III	1976	Marcia Myers
Carter, James E., Jr.	1946	Rosalynn Smith
Cass, Lewis	1806	Elizabeth Spencer
Cavazos, Lauro F.	1954	Peggy Ann Murdock

Celebrezze, Anthony J.	1938	Anne Marco
Chandler, William E.	1859	Ann Caroline Gilmore
Chandler, Zachariah	1844	Letitia Grace Douglass
Chapin, Roy D.	1914	Inez Tiedeman
Chapman, Oscar L.	1920	Olga Pauline Edholm
Chapman, Oscar L.	1940	Ann Kendrick
Chase, Salmon P.	1834	Katherine Jane Garmiss
Chase, Salmon P.	1839	Eliza Ann Smith
Chase, Salmon P.	1846	Sarah Bella Dunlap Ludlow
Cheney, Richard B.	1964	Lynn Ann Vincent
Civiletti, Benjamin R.	1957	Gail Lundgren
Clark, Tom C.	1924	Mary Jane Ramsey
Clark, William R.	1949	Georgia Welch
Clay, Henry	1799	Lucretia Hart
Clayton, John M.	1822	Sarah Ann Fisher
Cleveland, Grover	1886	Frances Folsom
Clifford, Clark McA.	1931	Margery Pepperell Kimball
Clifford, Nathan	*ca.* 1827	Hannah Ayer
Clinton, George	1770	Cornelia Tappen
Cobb, Howell	1834	Mary Ann Lamar
Cohen, Wilbur J.	1938	Eloise Bittel
Colby, Bainbridge	1895	Nathalie Sedgwick
Colby, Bainbridge	1929	Anne (Ahlstrand) Ely
Coleman, William T., Jr.	1945	Lovida Hardin
Colfax, Schuyler	1844	Evelyn Clark
Colfax, Schuyler	1868	Ellen Wade
Collamer, Jacob	1817	Mary N. Stone
Colman, Norman Jay	1851	Clara Porter
Colman, Norman Jay	1866	Catherine Wright
Connally, John B.	1940	Ida Nell Brill
Connor, John T.	1940	Mary O'Boyle
Conrad, Charles M.	n.a.	M. W. Angela Lewis
Coolidge, Calvin	1905	Grace Anna Goodhue
Cortelyou, George B.	1888	Lily Morris Hinds
Corwin, Thomas	1822	Sarah Ross
Cox, Jacob D., Jr.	1849	Helen Finney
Crawford, William H.	1804	Susanna Girardin
Creswell, John A. J.	after 1850	Hannah J. Richardson
Crittenden, John J.	1811	Sally O. Lee
Crittenden, John J.	1826	Maria K. Todd
Crittenden, John J.	1853	Mrs. Elizabeth Ashley
Crowninshield, Benjamin W.	1804	Mary Boardman
Cummings, Homer S.	1929	Cecilia Waterbury
Curtis, Charles	1884	Anna E. Baird
Cushing, Caleb	1824	Caroline Wilde
Dallas, Alexander	1780	Arabella Maria Smith
Dallas, George M.	1816	Sophia Chew (or Nicklin)

Daniels, Josephus	1888	Addie Worth Bagley
Daugherty, Harry M.	1884	Lucy Matilda Walker
Davis, Dwight F.	1904	Helen Brooks
Davis, Dwight F.	1936	Pauline (Morton) Sabin
Davis, James J.	1914	Jean Rodenbaugh
Davis, Jefferson	1835	Sarah Knox Taylor
Davis, Jefferson	1845	Varina Howell
Dawes, Charles G.	1889	Caro D. Blymer
Day, James E.	1941	Mary Louise Burgess
Day, William R.	1875	Mary Elizabeth Schaefer
Dearborn, Henry	1771	Mary Bartlett
Dearborn, Henry	1780	Dorcas (Osgood) Marble
Delano, Columbus	1834	Elizabeth Leavenworth
Denby, Edwin	1911	Marion Thurber
Dennison, William	n.a.	(Miss) Neil
Dent, Frederick B.	1944	Mildred Carrington Harrison
Dern, George H.	1899	Lottie Brown
Derwinski, Edward J.	1946	Patricia Van Der Giessen
Dexter, Samuel	1786	Catherine Gordon
Dickinson, Donald McD.	1869	Frances Platt
Dickinson, Jacob McG.	1876	Martha Overton
Dillon, C. Douglas	1931	Phyllis Chess Ellsworth
Dix, John A.	1826	Catherine Morgan
Doak, William N.	1908	Emma Maria Cricher
Dobbin, James C.	n.a.	Louisa Holmes
Dole, Elizabeth Hanforth	1975	Robert Dole
Donaldson, Jesse M.	1911	Nell Graybill
Donovan, Raymond J.	1957	Catherine Sblendorio
Duane, William J.	n.a.	Deborah Bache
Dulles, John F.	1912	Janet Pomeroy Avery
Duncan, Charles W., Jr.	1957	Thetis Smith
Dunlop, John T.	1937	Dorothy Webb
Durkin, Martin P.	1921	Anna H. McNicholas
Eaton, John H.	before 1816	Myra Lewis
Eaton, John H.	1829	Margaret O'Neill
Edison, Charles	1918	Carolyn Hawkinson
Edwards, James	1951	Ann Norris Darlington
Eisenhower, Dwight D.	1916	Mary (Mamie) Geneva Doud
Elkins, Stephen B.	1866	Sarah Jacobs
Elkins, Stephen B.	1875	Hallie Davis
Endicott, William C.	1859	Ellen Peabody
Eustis, William	1810	Caroline Langdon
Evarts, William M.	1843	Helen Minerva Wardner
Everett, Edward	1822	Charlotte Gray Brooks
Ewing, Thomas	1820	Maria Willis Boyle
Fairbanks, Charles W.	1874	Cornelia Cole
Fairchild, Charles S.	1871	Helen Linklaen

Fall, Albert B.	1883	Emma Garland Morgan
Farley, James A.	1920	Elizabeth Finnegan
Fessenden, William P.	1832	Ellen Maria Deering
Fillmore, Millard	1826	Abigail Powers
Fillmore, Millard	1858	Mrs. Caroline (Carmichael) McIntosh
Finch, Robert H.	1946	Carol Crother
Fish, Hamilton	1836	Julia Kean
Fisher, Walter L.	1891	Mabel Taylor
Flemming, Arthur S.	1934	Bernice Virginia Moler
Floyd, John B.	1830	Shelly Buchanon Preston
Folger, Charles J.	1844	Susan Rebecca Worth
Folsom, Marion B.	1918	Mary Davenport
Ford, Gerald R., Jr.	1948	Elizabeth Bloomer
Forrestal, James V.	1926	Josephine Ogden
Forsyth, John	n.a.	Clara Meigs
Forward, Walter	1808	Henrietta Barclay
Foster, Charles	1853	Ann M. Olmstead
Foster, John W.	1859	Mary Parke McFerson
Fowler, Henry H.	1938	Trudye Pamela Hathcote
Francis, David R.	1876	Jane Perry
Freeman, Orville L.	1942	Jane Charlotte Shields
Frelinghuysen, Frederick T.	1842	Matilde E. Griswold
Gage, Lyman J.	1864	Sarah Etheridge
Gallatin, Albert	1789	Sophie Allegre
Gallatin, Albert	1793	Hannah Nicholson
Gardner, John W.	1934	Aida Marroquin
Garfield, James A.	1858	Lucretia Rudolph
Garfield, James R.	1890	Helen Newell
Garland, Augustus H.	1853	Virginia Sanders
Garner, John N.	1895	Ettie Rheiner
Garrison, Lindley M.	1900	Margaret Hildeburn
Gary, James A.	1856	Lavina W. Corrie
Gates, Thomas S., Jr.	1928	Millicent Ann Brengle
Gerry, Elbridge	1786	Ann Thompson
Gilmer, Thomas W.	1826	Anne Baker
Gilpin, Henry D.	1834	Eliza (Sibley) Johnston
Glass, Carter	1886	Aurelia McDearmon
Glass, Carter	1940	Mary (Scott) Meade
Goff, Nathan	1865	Laura Ellen Despard
Goldberg, Arthur J.	1931	Dorothy Kurgans
Good, James W.	1894	Lucy Deacon
Gore, Howard M.	1906	Royalene Corder
Gorham, Nathaniel	1763	Rebecca Call
Graham, William A.	1836	Susannah Sarah Washington
Granger, Francis	1816	Cornelia Rutson Van Rensselaer
Granger, Gideon	1790	Mindwell Pease

Grant, Ulysses S.	1848	Julia Boggs Dent
Gregory, Thomas W.	1893	Julia Nalle
Gresham, Walter Q.	1858	Matilda McGrain
Griffin, Cyrus	1770	Lady Christina Stuart
Griggs, John W.	1874	Carolyn Webster
Griggs, John W.	1893	Laura Elizabeth Price
Gronouski, John A.	1948	Mary Louise Metz
Guthrie, James	1821	Eliza C. Prather
Habersham, Joseph	1776	Isabella Rae
Haig, Alexander M., Jr.	1950	Patricia Fox
Hall, Nathan K.	1832	Emily Paine
Hamilton, Alexander	1780	Elizabeth Schuyler
Hamilton, Paul	1782	Mary Wilkinson
Hamlin, Hannibal	1833	Sarah Jane Emery
Hamlin, Hannibal	1856	Ellen Vesta Emery
Hancock, John	1775	Dorothy Quincy
Hannegan, Robert E.	1903	Irma Protzmann
Hanson, John	before 1749	Jane Contee
Hardin, Clifford M.	1939	Martha Love Wood
Harding, Warren G.	1891	Florence (Kling) De Wolfe
Harlan, James	1845	Ann Eliza Peck
Harmon, Judson	1846	Olivia Scobey
Harriman, William A.	1915	Kitty Lanier Lawrence
Harriman, William A.	1930	Mary (Norton) Whitney
Harris, Patricia R.	1955	William Beasley Harris
Harrison, Benjamin	1853	Caroline Lavinia Scott
Harrison, Benjamin	1896	Mary Scott Lord Dimmick
Harrison, William H.	1795	Anna Tuthill Symmes
Hathaway, Stanley K.	1948	Roberta Harley
Hatton, Frank	1867	Lizzie Snyder
Hay, John M.	1874	Clara L. Stone
Hayes, Rutherford B.	1852	Lucy Webb
Hays, William H.	1902	Helen Louise Thomas
Hays, William H.	1930	Jesse Herron Stutsman
Heckler, Margaret M.	1954	John Heckler
Hendricks, Thomas A.	1845	Eliza C. Morgan
Herbert, Hilary A.	1867	Ella B. Smith
Herrington, John	1961	Lois Haight
Herter, Christian A.	1917	Mary Carolina Pratt
Hickel, Walter J.	1941	Janice Cannon
Hickel, Walter J.	1945	Ermalee Strutz
Hills, Carla A.	1958	Roderick Maltman Hills
Hitchcock, Ethan A.	1869	Margaret D. Collier
Hoar, Ebenezer R.	1840	Caroline Downes Brooks
Hobart, Garret A.	1869	Jennie Tuttle
Hobby, Oveta C.	1931	William Pettus Hobby
Hodel, Donald P.	1956	Barbara Stockman
Hodges, Luther H.	1922	Martha Elizabeth Blakeney

Hodgson, James D.	1943	Maria Denand
Holt, Joseph	n.a.	Mary Harrison
Holt, Joseph	n.a.	Margaret Wickliffe
Hoover, Herbert C.	1899	Lou Henry
Hopkins, Harry L.	1913	Ethel Gross
Hopkins, Harry L.	1931	Barbara MacPherson Duncan
Hopkins, Harry L.	1942	Louise Hill (Macy) Brown
Houston, David F.	1895	Helen Beall
Howe, Timothy O.	1841	Linda Ann Haynes
Hufstedler, Shirley Mount	1949	Seth Hufstedler
Hughes, Charles E.	1888	Antoinette Carter
Hull, Cordell	1917	Rose Frances Whitney
Humphrey, George M.	1913	Pamela Stark
Humphrey, Hubert H., Jr.	1936	Muriel Fay Buck
Hunt, William H.	1848	Frances Ann Andrews
Hunt, William H.	1852	Elizabeth Augusta Ridgeby
Huntington, Samuel	1761	Martha Devotion
Hurley, Patrick J.	1919	Ruth Wilson
Hyde, Arthur M.	1904	Hortense Cullers
Ickes, Harold L.	1911	Anna Wilmarth Thompson
Ickes, Harold L.	1938	Jane Dahlman
Ingham, Samuel D.	1800	Rebecca Dodd
Ingham, Samuel D.	1822	Deborah Kay Hall
Jackson, Andrew	1791	Mrs. Rachel (Donelson) Robards
Jackson, Robert H.	1916	Irene Gerhardt
James, Thomas L.	1852	Emily I. Freedburn
James, Thomas L.	n.a.	Mrs. E. R. Bordon
James, Thomas L.	n.a.	Edith Colborne
James, Thomas L.	1911	Mrs. Florence (MacDonnell) Gaffney
Jardine, William M.	1905	Effie Nebeker
Jay, John	1774	Sarah Livingston
Jefferson, Thomas		Mrs. Martha (Wayles) Skelton
Jewell, Marshall	1852	Esther E. Dickinson
Johnson, Andrew	1827	Eliza McCardle
Johnson, Cave	1838	Elizabeth (Dortch) Brunson
Johnson, Louis A.	1920	Ruth Frances Maxwell
Johnson, Lyndon B.	1934	Claudia Alta (Lady Bird) Taylor
Johnson, Reverdy	1819	Mary Mackall Bowie
Jones, Jesse H.	1929	May Gibbs
Katzenbach, Nicholas de B.	1946	Lydia King Phelps Stokes
Kellogg, Frank B.	1886	Clara M. Cook
Kemp, Jack	1956	Joanne Main
Kendall, Amos	1818	Mary B. Woolfolk
Kendall, Amos	1826	Jane Kyle

Kennedy, David M.	1925	Lenora Bingham
Kennedy, John F.	1953	Jacqueline Lee Bouvier
Kennedy, John P.	1824	Mary Tennant
Kennedy, John P.	1829	Elizabeth Gray
Kennedy, Robert F.	1950	Ethel Skakel
Key, David McK.	1857	Elizabeth Lenoir
King, Horatio	1835	Ann Collins
King, Horatio	1875	Isabella G. Osborne
Kirkwood, Samuel J.	1843	Jane Clark
Kissinger, Henry A.	1949	Ann Fleischer
Kissinger, Henry A.	1974	Nancy Maginnes
Kleindienst, Richard G.	1948	Margaret Dunbar
Kleppe, Thomas S.	1958	Glendora Loew Gompf
Klutznick, Philip M.	1930	Ethel Ricks
Knebel, John A.	1959	Zenia Irene Marks
Knox, Henry	1774	Lucy Flucker
Knox, Philander C.	1880	Lillie Smith
Knox, W. Franklin	1898	Annie Reid
Kreps, Juanita M.	1944	Clifton H. Kreps, Jr.
Krug, Julius A.	1926	Margaret Catherine Dean
Laird, Melvin R.	1945	Barbara Masters
Lamar, Lucius Q. C.	1847	Virginia Longstreet
Lamar, Lucius Q. C.	1887	Henrietta (Dean) Holt
Lamont, Daniel S.	n.a.	Juliet Kinney
Lamont, Robert P.	1894	Helen Gertrude Trotter
Landrieu, Moon E.	1954	Vera Satterlee
Lane, Franklin K.	1893	Anne Claire Wintermute
Lansing, Robert	1890	Eleanor Foster
Laurens, Henry	1750	Eleanor Ball
Lee, Charles	1789	Anne Lee
Lee, Charles	n.a.	Margaret C. Scott Peyton
Lee, Richard H.	1757	Anne Aylett
Lee, Richard H.	1769	Anne (Gaskins) Pinckard
Levi, Edward H.	1946	Kate Sulzberger
Lewis, Andrew	1950	Marilyn Stoughton
Lincoln, Abraham	1842	Mary Todd
Lincoln, Levi	1781	Martha Waldo
Lincoln, Robert T.	1868	Mary Harlan
Livingston, Edward	1788	Mary McEvers
Livingston, Edward	1805	Louise Moreau de Lassy
Long, John D.	1870	Mary Woodward Glover
Long, John D.	1886	Agnes Pierce
Lovett, Robert A.	1919	Adele Quarterly Brown
Lujan, Manuel, Jr.	1951	Jean Couchman
Lyng, Richard E.	1944	Bethel Ball
Lynn, James T.	1954	Joan Miller
McAdoo, William G.	1885	Sarah Houston Fleming
McAdoo, William G.	1914	Eleanor Randolph Wilson

McClelland, Robert	1837	Sarah E. Sabine
McCrary, George W.	1857	Helen Galett
McCulloch, Hugh	1838	Susan Mann
McElroy, Neil H.	1929	Mary Camilla Fry
McGranery, James P.	1939	Regina T. Clark
McGrath, James H.	1929	Estelle A. Cadorette
McHenry, James	1784	Margaret Allison Caldwell
McKay, Douglas J.	1917	Mabel Christine Hill
McKean, Thomas	1763	Mary Borden
McKean, Thomas	1774	Sarah Armitage
McKenna, Joseph	1869	Amanda F. Borneman
McKennan, Thomas M. T.	1815	Matilda Lourie Bowman
McKinley, William, Jr.	1871	Ida Saxton
McLane, Louis	1812	Catherine Mary Milligan
McLaughlin, Ann	1963	William Dore
McLaughlin, Ann Dore	1975	John McLaughlin
McLean, John	1843	Sarah Bella (Ludlow) Garrard
McNamara, Robert S.	1940	Margaret Craig
MacVeagh, Franklin	1868	Emily Eames
MacVeagh, Wayne	1856	Letty M. Lewis
MacVeagh, Wayne	1866	Virginia Rolette Cameron
Madison, James	1794	Dorothea (Dolley) (Payne) Todd
Manning, Daniel	1853	Mary Little
Manning, Daniel	1884	Mary Margaret Fryer
Marcy, William L.	1812	Dolly Newell
Marcy, William L.	1825	Cornelia Knower
Marshall, George C.	1902	Elizabeth Carter Coles
Marshall, George C.	1930	Katherine Boyce (Tupper) Brown
Marshall, John	1783	Mary Willis Ambler
Marshall, Thomas R.	1895	Lois Irene Kimsey
Mason, John Y.	1821	Mary Anne Port
Matthews, Forrest D.	1960	Mary Chapman
Maynard, Horace	1840	Laura Ann Washburn
Meese, Edwin, III	1959	Ursula Herrick
Meigs, Return J., Jr.	1764	Sophia Wright
Mellon, Andrew W.	1900	Nora McMullen
Meredith, Edwin T.	1896	Edna C. Elliott
Meredith, William M.	1834	Catherine Keppele
Metcalf, Victor H.	1882	Emily Corinne Nicholsen
Meyer, George von L.	1885	Marion Alice Appleton
Middleton, Henry	1741	Mary Williams
Middleton, Henry	1762	Maria Henrietta Bull
Middleton, Henry	1776	Lady Mary Mackenzie
Mifflin, Thomas	1767	Sarah Morris
Miller, G. William	1946	Ariadna Rogojarsky

Miller, William H. H.	1863	Gertrude A. Bunce
Mills, Ogden L.	1911	Margaret Stuyvesant Rutherford
Mills, Ogden L.	1924	Mrs. Dorothy (Randolph) Fell
Mitchell, James P.	1923	Isabelle Nulton
Mitchell, John N.	(first wife's name and date of marriage not available)	
Mitchell, John N.	n.a.	Martha (Beall) Jennings
Mitchell, William DeW.	1901	Gertrude Bancroft
Mondale, Walter F.	1955	Joan Adams
Monroe, James	1785	Elizabeth Kortright
Morgenthau, Henry	1916	Elinor Fatman
Morgenthau, Henry	1951	Marcelle Puthon
Morrill, Lot M.	1845	Charlotte Holland Vance
Morton, Julius S.	1854	Caroline Joy French
Morton, Levi P.	1856	Lucy Young Kimball
Morton, Paul	1880	Charlotte Goodridge
Morton, Rogers C. B.	1939	Anne Jones
Mosbacher, Robert A.		first wife unknown
Mosbacher, Robert A.	1985	Georgette Paulson
Mueller, Frederick H.	1915	Mary Darrah
Muskie, Edmund S.	1948	Jane Gray
Nagel, Charles	1876	Fanny Brandeis
Nagel, Charles	1895	Anne Shepley
New, Harry S.	1888	Kathleen Virginia Mulligan
New, Harry S.	1891	Catherine McLaen
Newberry, Truman H.	1888	Harriet Josephine Bornes
Niles, John M.	1824	Sarah Robinson
Niles, John M.	1845	Jane Pratt
Nixon, Richard M.	1940	Thelma (Pat) Ryan
Noble, John W.	1864	Lisabeth Halstead
O'Brien, Lawrence F.	1944	Elva I. Brassard
Olney, Richard	1861	Agnes Thomas
Osgood, Samuel	1775	Martha Brandon
Osgood, Samuel	1786	Maria Bowne Franklin
Palmer, Alexander M.	1898	Roberta Bartlett Dixon
Palmer, Alexander M.	1923	Margaret Fallon Burrall
Paulding, James K.	1818	Gertrude Kemble
Payne, Henry C.	1869	Lydia Wood Van Dyke
Payne, John B.	1878	Kate Bunker
Payne, John B.	1913	Jennie Byrd Bryan
Patterson, Robert P.	1920	Margaret Tarleton Winchester
Perkins, Frances	1913	Paul Caldwell Wilson
Peterson, Peter G.	1953	Sally Hornbagen
Pickering, Timothy	1776	Rebecca White

Pierce, Franklin	1834	Jane Means Appleton
Pierce, Samuel R., Jr.	1948	Barbara Wright
Pierrepont, Edwards	1846	Margaretta Willoughby
Pinkney, William	1789	Maria Rodgers
Poinsett, Joel R.	1833	Mrs. Mary (Izard) Pringle
Polk, James K.	1824	Sarah Childress
Porter, James M.	1821	Eliza Michler
Porter, Peter B.	1818	Letitia Breckinridge
Preston, William B.	1839	Lucinda Staples Redd
Proctor, Redfield	1858	Emily J. Dutton
Quayle, Danforth	1972	Marilyn Tucker
Ramsey, Alexander	1845	Anna Earl Jenks
Randall, Alexander W.	1842	Mary C. Van Vechten
Randall, Alexander W.	1863	Helen M. Thomas
Randolph, Edmund J.	1776	Elizabeth Nicholas
Randolph, Peyton	1745	Elizabeth Harrison
Rawlins, John A.	1856	Emily Smith
Rawlins, John A.	1863	Mary E. Hurlburt
Reagan, Ronald W.	1940	Jane Wyman
Reagan, Ronald W.	1952	Nancy Davis
Redfield, William C.	1885	Elise Mercein Fuller
Regan, Donald T.	1942	Ann Buchanan
Ribicoff, Abraham A.	1931	Ruth Siegel
Richardson, Elliot L.	1952	Ann Francis Hazard
Richardson, William A.	1849	Anna Maria Marston
Robeson, George	1872	Mary Isabelle (Ogston) Aulick
Rockefeller, Nelson A.	1930	Mary Todhunter Clark
Rockefeller, Nelson A.	1963	Margaretta Fitler Murphy
Rodney, Caesar A.	n.a.	Susan Hunn
Rogers, William P.	1936	Adele Langston
Romney, George W.	1931	Lenore La Fount
Roosevelt, Franklin D.	1905	Anna Eleanor Roosevelt
Roosevelt, Theodore	1880	Alice Hathaway Lee
Roosevelt, Theodore	1886	Edith Kermit Carow
Root, Elihu	1878	Clara Wales
Roper, Daniel C.	1889	Lou McKenzie
Royall, Kenneth C.	1917	Margaret Best
Rumsfeld, Donald	1954	Joyce Pierson
Rush, Richard	1809	Catherine E. Murray
Rusk, D. Dean	1937	Virginia Foisie
Rusk, Jeremiah McL.	1849	Mary Martin
Rusk, Jeremiah McL.	1856	Elizabeth M. Johnson
St. Clair, Arthur	1760	Phoebe Bayard
Sargent, John G.	1887	Mary Lorraine Gordon
Sawyer, Charles	1918	Margaret Sterrett
Sawyer, Charles	1942	Elizabeth De Veyrac
Saxbe, William	1940	Ardath Louise Kleinhans

Schlesinger, James R.	1954	Rachel Mellinger
Schofield, John McA.	1857	Harriet Bartlett
Schofield, John McA.	1891	Georgia Kilbourne
Schurz, Carl	1852	Margarethe Meyer
Schweiker, Richard	1955	Claire Coleman
Schwellenbach, Lewis B.	1935	Anne Duffy
Seaton, Frederick A.	1931	Gladys Hope Dowd
Seward, William H.	1824	Frances Miller
Shaw, Leslie M.	1877	Alice Crenshaw
Sherman, James S.	1881	Carrie Babcock
Sherman, John	1848	Margaret Sarah Cecilia Stewart
Sherman, William T.	1850	Elinor Byle Ewing
Shultz, George P.	1946	Helena Maria O'Brien
Simon, William E.	1950	Carol Girard
Skinner, Samuel K.	1960	Susan Thomas
Smith, Caleb	1831	Elizabeth B. Walton
Smith, Charles E.	1907	Nettie Nichols
Smith, Cyrus R.	1934	Elizabeth L. Manget
Smith, Hoke	1924	Mazie Crawford
Smith, Robert	1790	Margaret Smith
Smith, William French	1939	Margaret Dawson
Smith, William French	1964	Jean Vaugan
Snyder, John W.	1920	Evlyn Cook
Southard, Samuel L.	1811	Rebecca Harrow
Speed, James	1841	Jane Cochran
Spencer, John C.	1809	Elizabeth Scott Smith
Stanbery, Henry	1829	Frances E. Beecher
Stanbery, Henry	1840	Cecelia Bond
Stans, Maurice H.	1933	Kathleen Carmody
Stanton, Edwin McM.	1834	Mary Ann Lamson
Stanton, Edwin McM.	1856	Ellen M. Hutchinson
Stettinius, Edward R., Jr.	1926	Virginia Gordon Wallace
Stevenson, Adlai E.	1866	Letitia Green
Stimson, Henry L.	1893	Mabel Wellington White
Stoddert, Benjamin	1781	Rebecca Lowndes
Stone, Harlan F.	1899	Agnes Harvey
Straus, Oscar S.	1882	Sarah Lavanburg
Strauss, Lewis L.	1923	Alice Hanauer
Stuart, Alexander H. H.	1833	Frances Cordelia Baldwin
Summerfield, Arthur E.	1918	Miriam W. Graim
Swanson, Claude	1894	Lizzie Deane Lyons
Swanson, Claude	1923	Lulie (Lyons) Hall
Taft, Alphonso	1841	Fanny Phelps
Taft, Alphonso	1853	Louisa Torrey
Taft, William H.	1886	Helen Herron
Taney, Roger B.	1806	Anne P. C. Key
Taylor, Zachary	1810	Margaret Mackall Smith

Teller, Henry M.	1862	Harriet M. Bruce
Thomas, Philip F.	1835	Sarah Maria Kerr
Thomas, Philip F.	1876	Mrs. Clintonia (Wright) May
Thompson, Jacob	n.a.	Catherine Jones
Thompson, Richard W.	1836	Harriet Eliza Gardiner
Thompson, Smith	1794	Sarah Livingston
Thornburgh, Richard L.	1955	Virginia Hooton
Thornburgh, Richard L.	1963	Virginia Judson
Tobin, Maurice J.	1932	Helen M. Noonan
Tompkins, Daniel D.	1797	Hannah Minthorne
Toucey, Isaac	1827	Catharine Nichols
Tracy, Benjamin F.	1851	Delinda E. Catlin
Trowbridge, Alexander B.	1955	Nancy Horst
Truman, Harry S.	1919	Elizabeth Virginia {Bess} Wallace
Tyler, John	1813	Letitia Christian
Tyler, John	1844	Julia Gardiner
Udall, Stewart L.	1947	Ermalee Webb
Upshur, Abel P.	1817	Elizabeth Dennis
Upshur, Abel P.	1824	Elizabeth Ann Brown
Usery, Willie J., Jr.	1942	Gussie Mae Smith
Usher, John P.	1844	Margaret Patterson
Van Buren, Martin	1807	Hannah Hoes
Vance, Cyrus R.	1947	Grace Elsie Sloane
Verity, C. William, Jr.	1941	Margaret Wymond
Vilas, William F.	1866	Anna M. Fox
Vinson, Frederick M.	1923	Roberta Dixon
Volpe, John A.	1934	Jennie Benedetto
Walker, Frank C.	1914	Hallie Victoria Boucher
Walker, Robert J.	1825	Mary Blechynder Bacle
Wallace, Henry A.	1914	Ilo Browne
Wallace, Henry C.	n.a.	Carrie May Broadhead
Wanamaker, John	1860	Mary Erringer
Washburne, Elihu B.	1845	Adele Gratiot
Washington, George	1759	Mrs. Martha (Dandridge) Custis
Watkins, James D.	1950	Sheila Jo McKinney
Watson, William M., Jr.	n.a.	Marion Baugh
Watt, James G.	1957	Leilani Bomgardner
Weaver, Robert C.	1935	Ella V. Hiath
Webster, Daniel	1808	Grace Fletcher
Weeks, John W.	1885	Martha A. Sinclair
Weeks, Sinclair	1915	Beatrice Dowse
Weinberger, Caspar W.	1942	Jane Calton
Welles, Gideon	1835	Mary Jane Hale
West, Roy O.	1898	Louisa Augustus
West, Roy O.	1904	Louise McWilliams
Wheeler, William A.	1845	Mary King

Whiting, William F.	1892	Anne Chapin
Whitney, William C.	1869	Flora Payne
Whitney, William C.	*ca.* 1895	Mrs. Edith Sibyl (May) Randolph
Wickard, Claude R.	1918	Louisa Eckert
Wickersham, George	1883	Mildred Wendell
Wickliffe, Charles A.	1813	Margaret Crepps
Wilbur, Curtis D.	1893	Ella T. Chilson
Wilbur, Curtis D.	1898	Olive Doolittle
Wilbur, Ray L.	1898	Marguerite May Blake
Wilkins, William	1815	Catherine Holmes
Wilkins, William	1818	Matilda Dallas
Williams, George H.	1850	Kate Van Antwerp
Williams, George H.	1867	Kate (Hughes) George
Wilson, Charles E.	1912	Jessie Ann Curtis
Wilson, Henry	1840	Harriet Malvina Howe
Wilson, James	1863	Esther Wilbur
Wilson, William B.	1883	Agnes Williamson
Wilson, William L.	1868	Nannine Huntington
Wilson, Woodrow	1885	Ellen Louise Axson
Wilson, Woodrow	1915	Edith (Boling) Galt
Windom, William	1856	Ellen P. Hatch
Wirt, William	1795	Mildred Gilmer
Wirt, William	1802	Elizabeth Washington
Wirtz, William W.	1936	Mary Jane Quisenberry
Wolcott, Oliver, Jr.	1785	Elizabeth Stoughton
Wood, Robert C.	1952	Margaret Byers
Woodbury, Levi	1819	Elizabeth Williams Clapp
Woodin, William H.	1899	Annie Jessup
Woodring, Henry H.	1933	Helen Coolidge
Work, Hubert	1887	Laura M. Arbuckle
Work, Hubert	1933	Ethel Reed Gano
Wright, Luke E.	1869	Kate Semmes
Wynne, Robert J.	1875	Mary McCabe
Yeutter, Clayton K.	1952	Jeanne Vierk

About the Editor

A Professor of History at New College of Hofstra University, Robert Sobel is the author of numerous books, including *The Age of Giant Corporations* (1972, 1984), *N.Y.S.E.: A History of the New York Stock Exchange* (1975), *IBM: Colossus in Transition* (1981) and *Trammell Crow: Master Builder* (1989). He also serves as the series editor of the Greenwood Press reprint program entitled: *The Money Markets*, and is editor for the Greenwood series, *Contributions in Economics and Economic History*.

About the Editor